NOTES

ON THE

NEW TESTAMENT

EXPLANATORY AND PRACTICAL

BY

ALBERT BARNES

ENLARGED TYPE EDITION

EDITED BY

ROBERT FREW D.D.

ROMANS

BAKER BOOK HOUSE
GRAND RAPIDS, MICHIGAN

Library of Congress Catalog Card Number: 50-7190

ISBN: 0-8010-0516-7

First Printing, April 1949
Second Printing, April 1950
Third Printing, July 1953
Fourth Printing, August 1956
Fifth Printing, April 1959
Sixth Printing, May 1961
Seventh Printing, May 1963
Eighth Printing, October 1965
Ninth Printing, December 1967
Tenth Printing, October 1970
Eleventh Printing, August 1972
Twelfth Printing, February 1974

PHOTOLITHOPRINTED BY CUSHING - MALLOY, INC.
ANN ARBOR, MICHIGAN, UNITED STATES OF AMERICA
1974

PUBLISHERS' PREFACE.

THE republication, in this country, of Barnes' Notes on the Romans, will sustain and extend the author's well-earned reputation. Those who have been delighted with the perspicuity and elegance of his Notes on the Evangelists and Acts of the Apostles, will admire the same excellencies in the present volume. Regarding the meaning of certain passages in the Epistle to the Romans, many, indeed, will differ from our author. Nor is this difference of opinion surprising. The Epistle is confessedly the most difficult in the New Testament, and has given occasion to much theological controversy.

The principal point, in which Barnes is supposed to differ from orthodox divines, in this country, is the doctrine of imputation; which occupies so conspicuous a place in the opening chapters of the Romans, and is argued at great length in the fifth chapter. In some other points also, of less moment, he may be accused of using inaccurate or unguarded language. To remedy these defects, supplementary Notes have been added in several places throughout the volume; these, however, are invariably printed in a smaller type, to distinguish them from those of the author.

But whatever may be said of the author's views on imputation and other points connected with it; the most ardent lovers of orthodoxy will be unable to challenge the accuracy of his Notes on predestination and election. In his illustration of chapters viii. and ix., he maintains unconditional election against the Arminian view, and establishes the Calvinistic doctrine of the saints' perseverance, ch. viii. 29; ix. 11–15, 20.

Moreover, the excellencies of the volume are sufficient, even in the eyes of those who differ from the author, to redeem its faults. It contains a mass of varied, striking, and often original illustration; and presents, in small compass, the results of extensive reading and profound thinking. With the humble profession of writing only for Sabbath Schools and Sabbath School Teachers, ALBERT BARNES has furnished a commentary on the Romans, from which the lecturer in the pulpit may draw some of his richest stores.

AUTHOR'S PREFACE.

THE Epistle to the Romans has been usually regarded as the most difficult portion of the New Testament. It is from this cause, probably, as well as from the supposition that its somewhat abstruse discussions could not be made interesting to the young, that so few efforts have been made to introduce it into Sunday Schools and Bible Classes. It will doubtless continue to be a fact, that Sunday School instruction will be confined chiefly to the *historical* parts of the Bible. In the Sacred Scriptures there is this happy adaptedness to the circumstances of the world, that so large a portion of the volume *can* thus be made interesting to the minds of children and youth; that so much of it is occupied with historical narrative; with parables; with interesting biographies of the holy men of other times, and with the life of our blessed Lord. But still, while this is true, there is a considerable portion of the youth, in various ways under the instruction of the Bible, who may be interested in the more abstruse statements and discussions of the *doctrinal* parts of the Holy Scriptures. For such; for Sunday School teachers; for Bible Classes; and for the higher classes in Sabbath Schools, these Notes have been prepared. The humble hope has been cherished that this epistle might be introduced to this portion of the youth of the churches; and thus tend to imbue their minds with correct views of the great *doctrines* of the Christian Revelation.

This object has been kept steadily in view. The design has not been to make a *learned* commentary; nor to enter into theological discussions; nor to introduce, at length, practical reflections; nor to enter minutely into critical investigations. All these can be found in books professedly on these subjects. The design has been to state, with as much brevity and simplicity as possible, the real meaning of the sacred writer; rather the *results* of critical inquiry, as far as the author has had ability and time to pursue it, than the *process* by which those results were reached. The design has been to state what appeared to the author to be the real *meaning* of the Epistle, without *any* regard to any existing theological system; and without any deference to the opinions of others, further than the respectful deference and candid examination, which are due to the opinions of the learned, the wise, and the good, who have made this epistle their particular study. At the same time that this object has been kept in view, and the reference to the Sabbath

School teacher, and the Bible Class, has given character to the work, still it is hoped that the expositions are of such a nature as not to be uninteresting to Christians of every age and of every class. He accomplishes a service of no little moment in the cause of the church of God, and of truth, who contributes in any degree to explain the profound argument, the thorough doctrinal discussion, the elevated views, and the vigorous, manly, and masterly reasonings of the Epistle to the Romans.

Of the defects of this work, even for the purpose contemplated, no one will probably be more deeply sensible than the author. Of the time and labour necessary to prepare even such brief Notes as these, few persons, probably, are aware. This work has been prepared amidst the cares and toils of a most responsible pastoral charge. My brethren in the ministry, so far as they may have occasion to consult these Notes, will know how to appreciate the cares and anxieties amidst which they have been prepared. They will be indulgent to the faults of the book; they will not censure harshly what is well-meant for the rising generation: they will be the patrons of every purpose, however, humble, to do good.

It remains only to add, that free use has been made of all the helps within the reach of the author. The language of other writers has not been adopted without particular acknowledgment, but their ideas have been freely used where they were thought to express the sense of the text. In particular, aid has been sought and obtained from the following works: the CRITICI SACRI, CALVIN'S COMMENTARY ON THE ROMANS, DODDRIDGE, MACKNIGHT, and ROSENMULLER; and the commentaries of THOLUCK and FLATT—so far as an imperfect knowledge of the German language could render their aid available. A considerable portion was written before Professor STUART'S Commentary appeared. In the remaining portion, important aid has been freely derived from that work. The aim of this work is substantially the same as that of the "Notes on the Gospels," and on the Acts of the Apostles; and the earnest wish and prayer of the author is, that it may be one among many means of establishing the truth, and of promoting its advancement and ultimate triumph in the world.

ADVERTISEMENT TO THE FIFTH EDITION.

Notwithstanding the difficulty of correcting a work which is stereotyped, the following Notes have undergone a careful revision, and several alterations have been made. The changes refer to a few phrases which did not accurately express my meaning, and to some entire paragraphs. My desire has been to make the work as little exceptionable as possible. Some expressions in the former editions have been misunderstood; some are now seen to have been ambiguous; a few that have given offence have been changed, because, without abandoning any principle of doctrine or interpretation, I could convey my ideas in language more acceptable, and less fitted to produce offence. The changes have been made with a wish to make the work more useful, and with a desire to do all that can be done, without abandoning *principle*, to promote peace and to silence the voice of alarm. On some of these passages, as is extensively known to the public, charges of inculcating dangerous doctrines have been alleged against me before the Presbytery of which I am a member. After a fair and full trial the Presbytery acquitted me; and I have taken the opportunity *after* the trial was passed and I had been acquitted, to make these changes for the sake of peace, and not to appear to have been *urged* to make them by the dread of a trial.

When the work was first published, it was not anticipated that more than two or three editions would be demanded. The fact that, within less than eight months, a *fourth* edition should be called for, is a source of gratitude, and an inducement to do all that can be done to make the work as complete as possible, that it may more perfectly accomplish the design for which it was written. Some of the alterations have been made by the suggestions of friends; some by the cry of alarm which has been raised; but, whether from the one or the other, I hold that an author should be grateful for *all* the suggestions which may go to improve his works, and should amend them accordingly.

ALBERT BARNES.

INTRODUCTION

TO THE

EPISTLE TO THE ROMANS.

THIS Epistle has been, with great uniformity, attributed to the apostle Paul, and received as a part of the sacred canon. It has *never* in the church been called in question as a genuine, an inspired book, except by three of the ancient sects deemed heretical—the Ebionites, the Encratites, and Cerinthians. But they did not deny that it was written by the apostle Paul. They rejected it because they could not make its *doctrines* harmonize with their views of other parts of the Scriptures. Their rejecting it, therefore, does not militate against its genuineness. That is a question to be settled *historically*, like the genuineness of any other ancient writing. On this point the testimony of antiquity is uniform. The proof on this subject may be seen at length in Lardner's works. The *internal* evidence that this was written by Paul is stated in a most ingenious and masterly manner by Dr. Paley in his *Horæ Paulinæ.*

It is agreed by all, that this epistle was written in *Greek*. Though addressed to a people whose language was the *Latin*, yet this epistle to them, like those to other churches, was in Greek. On this point also there is no debate. The reasons why this language was chosen were probably the following. (1.) The epistle was designed doubtless to be read by other churches as well as the Roman; comp. Col. iv. 16. Yet the Greek language, being generally known and spoken, was more adapted to this design than the Latin. (2.) The Greek language was then understood at Rome, and extensively spoken. It was a part of polite education to learn it. The Roman youth were taught it; and it was the fashion of the times to study it, even so much so as to make it matter of complaint that the Latin was neglected for it by the Roman youth. Thus Cicero (Pro Arch.) says, *The Greek language is spoken in almost all nations; the Latin is confined to our comparatively narrow borders.* Tacitus (Orator 29) says, *An infant born now is committed to a Greek nurse.* Juvenal (vi. 185) speaks of its being considered as an indispensable part of polite education, to be acquainted with the Greek. (3.) It is not impossible that the Jews at Rome, who constituted a separate colony, were better acquainted with the Greek than the Latin. They had a Greek, but no Latin translation of the Scriptures, and it is very possible that they used the language in which they were accustomed to read their Scriptures, and which was extensively spoken by their brethren throughout the world. (4.) The apostle was himself probably more familiar with the Greek than the Latin. He was a native of Cilicia, where the Greek was doubtless spoken, and he not unfrequently quotes the Greek poets in his addresses and epistles. Acts xxi. 37; xvii. 28; Titus i. 12; 1 Cor. xv. 33.

This epistle is placed *first* among Paul's epistles, not because it was the first written, but because of the length and importance of the epistle itself, and the importance of the church in the imperial city. It has uniformly had this place in the sacred canon, though there is reason to believe that the Epistle to the

Galatians, the first to the Corinthians, and perhaps the two to the Thessalonians, were written before this. Of the *time* when it was written, there can be little doubt. About the year 52 or 54 the Emperor Claudius banished all Jews from Rome. In Acts xviii. 2, we have an account of the *first* acquaintance of Paul with Aquila and Priscilla, who had departed from Rome in consequence of that decree. This acquaintance was formed in Corinth; and we are told that Paul abode with them, and worked at the same occupation; Acts xviii. 3. In Romans xvi. 3, 4, he directs the church to greet Priscilla and Aquila, who had for his life laid down their own necks. This service which they rendered him must have been therefore *after* the decree of Claudius; and of course the epistle must have been written *after* the year 52.

In Acts xviii. 19, we are told that he left Aquila and Priscilla at Ephesus. Paul made a journey through the neighbouring regions, and then returned to Ephesus; Acts xix. 1. Paul remained at Ephesus at least two years (Acts xix. 8, 9, 10), and while here probably wrote the first Epistle to the Corinthians. In that epistle (xvi. 19) he sends the salutation of Priscilla and Aquila, who were of course still at Ephesus. The Epistle to the Romans, therefore, in which he sends his salutation to Aquila and Priscilla, as being then at Rome, could not be written until they had left Ephesus and returned to Rome; that is, until three years at least after the decree of Claudius in 52 or 54.

Still further. When Paul wrote this epistle, he was about to depart for Jerusalem to convey a collection which had been made for the poor saints there, by the churches in Macedonia and Achaia; Rom. xv. 25, 26. When he had done this, he intended to go to Rome; Rom. xv. 28. Now, by looking at the Acts of the Apostles, we can determine when this occurred. At this time he sent Timotheus and Erastus before him into Macedonia, while he remained in Asia for a season; Acts xix. 22. After this (Acts xx. 1, 2), Paul himself went into Macedonia, passed through Greece, and remained about three months there. In this journey it is almost certain that he went to Corinth, the capital of Achaia, at which time it is supposed this epistle was written. From this place he set out for Jerusalem, where he was made a prisoner, and after remaining a prisoner two years (Acts xxiv. 27), he was sent to Rome about A.D. 60. Allowing for the time of his travelling and his imprisonment, it must have been about *three* years from the time that he purposed to go to Jerusalem; that is, from the time that he finished the epistle (Rom. xv. 25–29) to the time when he reached Rome, and thus the epistle must have been written about A.D. 57.

It is clear also, that the epistle was written from Corinth. In chap. xvi. 1, Phebe, a member of the church at Cenchrea, is commended to the Romans. She probably had charge of the epistle, or accompanied those who had it. Cenchrea was the port of the city of Corinth, about seven or eight miles from the city. In chap. xvi. 23, Gaius is spoken of as the *host* of Paul, or he of whose hospitality Paul partook, but Gaius was baptized by Paul at Corinth, and Corinth was manifestly his place of residence; 1 Cor. i. 14. Erastus is also mentioned as the chamberlain of the city where the epistle was written; but this Erastus is mentioned as having his abode at Corinth; 2 Tim. iv. 20. From all this it is manifest that the Epistle was written at Corinth, about the year 57.

Of the state of the church at Rome at that time it is not easy to form a precise opinion. From this epistle it is evident that it was composed of Jews and Gentiles; and that one design of writing to it was to reconcile their jarring opinions, particularly about the obligation of the Jewish law; the advantage of the Jew; and the way of justification. It is probable that the two parties in the church were endeavouring to defend each their peculiar opinions, and that the apostle took this opportunity and mode to state to his converted countrymen the great doctrines of Christianity, and the relation of the law of Moses to the Christian system. The epistle itself is full proof that the church to whom it was addressed was composed of Jews and Gentiles. No small part of it is an argument expressly with the Jews; chap. ii. iii. iv. ix. x. xi. And no small part of the epistle also is designed to state the true doctrine about the character of the Gentiles and the way in which they could be justified before God.

At this time there was a large number of Jews at Rome. When Pompey the Great overran Judea, he sent a large number of Jews prisoners to Rome, to be sold as slaves. But it was not easy to control them. They persevered resolutely and obstinately in adhering to the rites of their nation; in keeping the Sabbath, &c. So that the Romans chose at last to give them their freedom, and assigned them a place in the vicinity of the city across the Tiber. Here a town was built, which was principally inhabited by Jews. Josephus mentions that 4000 Jews were banished from Rome at one time to Sardinia, and that a still greater number were punished who were unwilling to become soldiers; Ant. xviii. chap. 3, § 5. Philo (Legat. ad Caium) says, that many of the Jews at Rome had obtained their freedom; for, says he, *being made captive in war, and brought into Italy, they were set at liberty by their masters, neither were they compelled to change the rites of their fathers;* see also Josephus, Ant. xvii. chap. ii. § 1; Suetonius' Life of Tiberius, 36, and Notes on Acts vi. 9. From that large number of Jews, together with those converted from the Gentiles, the church at Rome was collected, and it is easy to see that *in* that church there would be a great diversity of sentiment, and, no doubt, warm discussions about the authority of the Mosaic law.

At what time, or by whom, the gospel was first preached at Rome has been a matter of controversy. The Roman Catholic church have maintained that it was founded by Peter, and have thence drawn an argument for their high claims and infallibility. On this subject they make a confident appeal to some of the fathers. There is strong evidence to be derived from this epistle itself, and from the Acts, that *Paul* did not regard Peter as having any such *primacy* and *ascendency* in the Roman church as are claimed for him by the Papists. (1.) In this whole epistle there is no mention of Peter at all. It is not suggested that he had been, or was then at Rome. If he had been, and the church had been founded by him, it is incredible that Paul did not make mention of that fact. This is the more striking, as it was done in *other* cases where churches had been founded by other men; see 1 Cor. i. 12–15. Especially is *Peter*, or Cephas, mentioned repeatedly by the apostle Paul in his other epistles; 1 Cor. iii. 22; ix. 5; xv. 5; Gal. ii. 9; i. 18; ii. 7, 8, 14. In these places *Peter* is mentioned in connection with the churches at Corinth and Galatia, yet never there as appealing to his authority, but in regard to the latter, expressly calling it in question. Now, it is incredible that if Peter *had been* then at Rome, and had founded the church there, and was regarded as invested with any peculiar authority over it, that Paul should never once have even suggested his name. (2.) It is clear that Peter was *not* there when Paul wrote this epistle. If he had been, he could not have failed to have sent him a salutation, amid the numbers that he saluted in the xvith chapter. (3.) In the Acts of the Apostles there is no mention of Peter's having been at Rome, but the presumption from

that history is almost conclusive that he had not been.   In Acts xii. 3, 4, we
have an account of his having been imprisoned by Herod Agrippa near the close
of his reign (comp. v. 23).   This occurred about the third or fourth year of the
reign of Claudius, who began to reign A.D. 41.   It is altogether improbable that
he had been at Rome before this.   Claudius had not reigned more than three
years, and all the testimony that the fathers give is, that Peter came to Rome
in his reign.   (4.) Peter was at Jerusalem still in the *ninth* or *tenth* year of the
reign of Claudius; Acts xv. 6, &c.   Nor is there any mention made then of his
having been at Rome.   (5.) Paul went to Rome about A.D. 60.   There is no
mention made then of Peter's being with him or being there.   If he had been,
it could hardly have failed of being recorded.   Especially is this remarkable
when Paul's meeting with *the brethren* is expressly mentioned (Acts xxviii. 14,
15), and when it is recorded that he met the Jews, and abode with them, and
spent at Rome no less than two years.   If *Peter* had been there, such a fact
could not fail to have been recorded or alluded to, either in the Acts or the
Epistle to the Romans.   (6.) The Epistles to the Ephesians, Philippians, Colos-
sians, to Philemon, and the second Epistle to Timothy (Lardner, vi. 235) were
written from Rome during the residence of Paul as a prisoner; and the Epistle
to the Hebrews probably also while he was still in Italy.   In none of these
epistles is there any hint that Peter was then or had been at Rome; a fact that
cannot be accounted for if he was regarded as the founder of that church, and
especially if he was then in that city.   Yet in those epistles there are the salutations of a number to those churches.   In particular, Epaphras, Luke the beloved
physician (Col. iv. 12, 14), and the saints of the household of Cæsar are mentioned; Phil. iv. 22.   In 2 Tim. iv. 11, Paul expressly affirms that *Luke only
was with him*, a declaration utterly irreconcilable with the supposition that
Peter was then at Rome.   (7.) If Peter was ever at Rome, therefore, of which
indeed there is no reason to doubt, he must have come there after Paul; at
what time is unknown.   That he *was* there cannot be doubted without calling
in question the truth of all history.

When, or by whom, the gospel was preached first at Rome, it is not easy,
perhaps not possible, to determine.   In the account of the day of Pentecost
(Acts ii. 10), we find, among others, that there were present *strangers of Rome*,
and it is not improbable that *they* carried back the knowledge of Jesus Christ,
and became the founders of the Roman church.   One design and effect of that
miracle was doubtless to spread the knowledge of the Saviour among all nations;
see Notes on Acts ii.   In the list of persons who are mentioned in Rom. xvi. it
is not improbable that some of those early converts are included; and that Paul
thus intended to show honour to their early conversion and zeal in the cause of
Christianity.   Thus, xvi. 7, he designates Andronicus and Junia his kinsmen
and fellow-prisoners, who were *distinguished among the apostles*, and who had
been converted before himself, *i.e.* before A.D. 34, *at least* eight years before it
was ever pretended that Peter was at Rome.   Other persons are mentioned also
as distinguished, and it is not improbable that they were the early founders of
the church at Rome, chap. xvi. 12, 13, &c.

That the church at Rome was founded early is evident from the celebrity
which it had acquired.   At the time when Paul wrote this epistle (A.D. 57),
their faith was spoken of throughout the world, chap. i. 8.   The *character* of
the church at Rome cannot be clearly ascertained.   Yet it is clear that it was
not made up merely of the lower classes of the community.   In Phil. iv. 22, it

appears that the gospel had made its way to the family of Cæsar, and that a part of his household had been converted to the Christian faith. Some of the fathers affirm that *Nero* in the beginning of his reign was favourably impressed in regard to Christianity; and it is possible that this might have been through the instrumentality of his family. But little on this subject can be known. While it is probable that the great mass of believers in all the early churches was of obscure and plebeian origin, it is also certain that some who were rich, and noble, and learned, became members of the church of Christ; see 1 Tim. ii. 9; 1 Pet. iii. 3; 1 Tim. vi. 20; Col. ii. 8; 1 Cor. i. 26; Acts xvii. 34.

This epistle has been usually deemed the most difficult of interpretation of any part of the New Testament; and no small part of the controversies in the Christian church have grown out of discussions about its meaning. Early in the history of the church, even before the death of the apostles, we learn from 2 Pet. iii. 16, that the writings of Paul were some of them regarded as being hard to be understood; and that the unlearned and unstable wrested them to their own destruction. It is probable that Peter has reference here to the high and mysterious doctrines about justification and the sovereignty of God, and the doctrines of election and decrees. From the epistle of James, it would seem probable also, that already the apostle Paul's doctrine of justification by faith had been perverted and abused. It seems to have been inferred that good works were unnecessary; and here was the beginning of the cheerless and withering system of Antinomianism—than which a more destructive or pestilential heresy never found its way into the Christian church. Several reasons might be assigned for the controversies which have grown out of this epistle. (1.) The very structure of the argument, and the peculiarity of the apostle's manner of writing. He is rapid; mighty; profound; often involved; readily following a new thought; leaving the regular subject; and returning again after a considerable interval. Hence his writings abound with parentheses and with complicated paragraphs. (2.) Objections are often introduced, so that it requires close attention to determine their precise bearing. Though he employs no small part of the epistle in answering objections, yet an objector is never once formally introduced or mentioned. (3.) His *expressions* and *phrases* are many of them liable to be misunderstood, and capable of perversion. Of this class are such expressions as the righteousness of faith, the righteousness of God, &c. (4.) The doctrines themselves are high and mysterious. They are those subjects on which the profoundest minds have been in all ages exercised in vain. On them there has been, and always will be a difference of opinion. Even with the most honest intentions that men ever have, they find it difficult or impossible to approach the investigation of them without the bias of early education, or the prejudice of previous opinion. In this world it is not given to men fully to understand these great doctrines. And it is not wonderful that the discussion of them has given rise to endless controversies: and that they who have

> Reasoned high
> Of Providence, foreknowledge, will, and fate;
> Fixed fate, free will, foreknowledge absolute,
> Have found no end, in wandering mazes lost.

(5.) It cannot be denied that *one* reason why the epistles of Paul have been regarded as so difficult has been an unwillingness to admit the truth of the plain doctrines which he teaches. The heart is by nature opposed to them; and comes to believe them with great reluctance. This feeling will account for no small part of the difficulties felt in regard to this epistle. There is one great maxim in interpreting the scriptures that can never be departed from. It is, that men can never understand them aright, until they are *willing* to suffer them to speak out their fair and proper meaning. When men are determined *not* to find certain doctrines in the Bible, nothing is more natural than that they should find difficulties in it, and complain much of its great obscurity and mystery. I add, (6.) That one principal reason why so much difficulty has been felt here, has been an unwillingness to stop where the apostle does. Men have desired to advance farther, and penetrate the mysteries which the Spirit of inspiration has not disclosed. Where Paul states a simple *fact*, men often advance a *theory*. The *fact* may be clear and plain; their *theory* is obscure, involved, mysterious, or absurd. By degrees they learn to *unite* the fact and the theory:—they regard *their* explanation as the only possible one; and as the *fact* in question has the authority of divine revelation, so they insensibly come to regard their theory in the same light; and he that calls in question their speculation about the *cause*, or the *mode*, is set down as heretical, and as denying the doctrine of the apostle. A melancholy instance of this we have in the account which the apostle gives (chap. v.) about the effect of the sin of Adam. The simple *fact* is stated that that sin was followed by the sin and ruin of all his posterity. Yet he offers no explanation of the *fact*. He leaves it as indubitable; and as not demanding an explanation in his argument—perhaps as not admitting it. This is the whole of his doctrine on that subject. Yet men have not been satisfied with that. They have sought for a theory to account for it. And many suppose they have found it in the doctrine that the sin of Adam is *imputed*, or set over by an arbitrary arrangement to beings otherwise innocent, and that they are held to be responsible for a deed committed by a man thousands of years before they were born. This is the *theory;* and men insensibly forget that it *is mere theory*, and they blend that and the *fact* which the apostle states together; and deem the denial of the one, heresy as much as the denial of the other, *i.e.* they make it as impious to call in question *their philosophy*, as to doubt *the facts* stated on the authority of *the apostle Paul.* If men desire to *understand* the epistles of Paul, and avoid difficulties, they should be willing to leave it where *he* does; and this single rule would have made useless whole years and whole tomes of controversy.

Perhaps, on the whole, there is no book of the New Testament that more demands a humble, docile, and prayerful disposition in its interpretation than this epistle. Its profound doctrines; its abstruse inquiries; and the opposition of many of those doctrines to the views of the unrenewed and unsubdued heart of man, make a spirit of docility and prayer peculiarly needful in its investigation. No man ever yet understood the reasonings and views of the apostle Paul but under the influence of elevated piety. None ever found opposition to his doctrines recede, and difficulties vanish, who did not bring the mind in an humble frame to receive *all* that has been revealed; and that, in a spirit of humble prayer, did not purpose to lay aside all bias, and open the heart to the full influence of the elevated truths which he inculcates. Where there is a willingness that God should reign and do all his pleasure, this epistle may be in its general character easily understood. Where this is wanting, it will appear full of mystery and perplexity; the mind will be embarrassed, and the heart dissatisfied with its doctrines; and the unhumbled spirit will rise from its study only confused, irritated, perplexed, and dissatisfied.

ANALYSIS OF THE EPISTLE TO THE ROMANS.

SHOWING THE DESIGN AND ARGUMENT OF THE EPISTLE.

I. *Introduction to the Epistle:* ch. I. 1—15.

Salutation to the Romans: chapter I. 1—7.
The faith of the Roman Christians commended; and Paul's desire to see them, *and his readiness to serve them,* expressed: ch. I. 8—15.

II. *The subject, or main argument of the Epistle proposed:* ch. I. 16, 17.

The main subject and design of the Epistle proposed to set forth *the distinguishing traits of the Gospel,* and *its value.* The peculiarity of the Gospel consists in the doctrine of JUSTIFICATION BY FAITH, in contradistinction from the plan of salvation by works; and IN ITS BEING ADAPTED TO ALL NATIONS: ch. I. 16, 17.

III. *The argument for the doctrine of justification by faith derived from the fact, that all other plans have failed, and that all men are guilty:* ch. I. 18—32, ch. II. III. IV.

I. IN RELATION TO THE GENTILES · ch. I. 18—32.

(1.) God is just, and has revealed his intention to punish sinners; ch. I. 18.
(2.) The Gentiles have the means of knowing God and his will, from the works of creation, and therefore have no excuse: ch. I. 19—21.
(3.) They have failed to honour him; to obey his law; and are, *in fact, universally depraved;* and, therefore, *cannot* be justified by the works of the law. This account sustained by an appeal to fact. ch. I. 22—32. Compare the conclusion: ch. III. 20—26.

II. IN RELATION TO THE JEWS. They are equally guilty with the Gentiles. ch. II., III. 1—19.

(1.) Their national privileges cannot screen them from guilt and punishment: ch. II. 1—4.
(2.) They know that God is just, and impartial, and will judge all men according to their deeds: ch. II. 4—16.
(3.) The peculiar advantages which the Jew had for knowing the will of God over the Gentiles. His obligations, therefore, to practise righteousness: ch. II. 17—20.
(4.) His increased guilt if he fails of obedience: ch. II. 20—23.
(5.) The actual character of the Jews: ch. II. 24.
(6.) Their outward ceremonies avail nothing in freeing them from guilt, and are useless unless attended with purity of heart: ch. II. 25—29.
(7.) *Answer to the objections of the Jew to the proof of his guilt:* ch. III. 1—9.

  (a.) If as guilty as the Gentiles, what advantage has he? ch. III. 1. ANSWER. His advantage is great from having the Scriptures ch. III. 2.
  (b.) The unbelief of a part will not destroy the faithfulness of God: ch. III. 3. ANSWER. No such consequence follows as that God will be unfaithful and false. God is always true and right. *This is to be held as a great fixed principle:* ch. III. 4.
  (c.) If God's character is illustrated, and his faithfulness and truth confirmed by means of our unbelief, will it not be unjust for him to punish us: ch. III. 5. ANSWER. The admitted fact that God will judge the world, and condemn the guilty, shows that it will be *right* to inflict punishment: ch. III. 6.
  (d.) But if my lie promotes his truth, how *can* I be guilty? ch. III. 7. ANSWER. If this be a just principle, it should be carried out, and made universal, and then it will be that "we should do all the evil we can, that good may come·" ch. III. 8.

(8.) The Jews have no pre-eminence at all in regard to moral character. Proof of their depravity from their own Scriptures. ch. III. 9—19.

III. THE CONCLUSION IN REGARD TO BOTH JEWS AND GENTILES THAT ALL ARE SINNERS, AND THAT THE PLAN OF JUSTIFICATION BY THE LAW HAS FAILED: ch. III. 20—26.

IV. THE NEW, OR CHRISTIAN PLAN OF JUSTIFICATION STATED. IT IS BY GRACE THROUGH CHRIST TO THOSE WHO BELIEVE: ch. III. 24—31.

(1.) What it is. It is without the law. It is borne witness to by the law and the prophets. It is on all *who believe* without distinction: ch. III. 22—24.
(2.) It is freely by grace through the atonement. The design of the atonement: ch. III. 25, 26.
(3.) Its effect is to humble human pride: ch. III. 27, 28.
(4.) The Gentiles may be justified in this way as well as the Jews,—all are on a level: ch. III. 29, 30.
(5.) It in fact goes to establish and confirm the law: ch. III. 31

V. THE SAME DOCTRINE OF JUSTIFICATION BY FAITH TAUGHT IN THE OLD TEST. ch. IV.

Proved, (1.) By the case of Abraham, who was justified by faith *before* he was circumcised: ch. IV. 1—5; 9—22
Proved, (2.) By what David taught: ch. IV. 6—8.
Inference, (3.) If Abraham was justified by faith, others may be in the same way: ch. IV. 23—25

XII. *Practical conclusions and exhortations from the epistle;* ch. XII.—XVI.

1. EXHORTATION TO VARIOUS PERSONAL CHRISTIAN DUTIES: ch. XII.

(a.) To entire consecration to God: ch. XII. 1.
(b.) Against conformity to the world: ch. XII. 2.
(c.) Exhortation to humility. ch. XII. 3—5.
(d.) To fidelity in the discharge of our *official* duties: ch. XII. 6—9.
(e.) To fidelity in our *relative* duties as Christians—to brotherly love; mutual respect; diligence; hospitality; sympathy, &c.: ch. XII. 10—16.
(f.) To forgiveness of enemies, and kind treatment of those who injure us: ch. XII. 17—21.

2. EXHORTATION TO OBEY CIVIL MAGISTRATES; TO HOLY CONDUCT; AND TO PREPARATION FOR DEATH: ch. XIII.

(a.) Duty of *subjection* to those in authority, because it is the appointment of God: ch. XIII. 1—5.
(b.) On the same account we ought to pay tribute: ch. XIII. 6, 7.
(c.) On the same account we ought to meet *all* the claims which others have on us, and thus to fulfil the law of love. ch. XIII. 8—10.
(d.) These duties enforced from the fact that life is short; that Christians are near heaven; and that they should live as becomes such: ch. XIII. 11—14.

3. CAUTION AGAINST MAKING EXTERNAL OBSERVANCES THE OCCASION OF STRIFE AND DIVISION IN THE CHURCH: ch. XIV. XV. 1—13.

(a.) Our duty to receive and acknowledge our Christian brethren: ch. XIV. 1, 2.
(b.) Every one answerable for himself to God: ch. XIV. 3, 4.
(c.) Every man should be fully persuaded in his own mind; and though there may be a difference of opinion, yet each may desire to honour God: ch. XIV. 5—9.
(d.) We have no right to judge or despise others. Every one must answer for himself: ch. XIV. 10—12.
(e.) He ought not to put a stumbling-block in the way of a brother: ch. XIV. 13—17.
(f.) He who really *serves Christ* in these things is acceptable, and we should live with him in peace: ch. XIV. 18—23.
(g.) We ought to bear the infirmities of the weak, and thus imitate the example of Christ: ch. XV. 1—7.
(h.) The intention of God was to bring in the Gentiles according to the ancient promise, and therefore *all* Christians should live in peace: ch. XV. 8—13.

4. VARIOUS EXPRESSIONS OF PAUL'S FEELINGS TOWARDS THE ROMAN CHRISTIANS: ch. XV. 14—33.

(a.) His view of their kindness, and knowledge, and ability to regulate properly their own affairs: ch. XV. 14.
(b.) Reason why he had written this epistle, *his being a minister to the Gentiles.* Summary view of his labours and successes: ch. XV. 15—21.
(c.) His great desire to see the Roman Christians, and purpose to visit them: ch. XV. 22—29.
(d.) Their prayers asked in his behalf that he might be delivered from impending dangers, and permitted to go to Rome: ch. XV. 30—33.

5. CONCLUSION OF THE EPISTLE ch. XVI.

(a.) Various salutations: ch. XVI. 1—16.
(b.) Caution against divisions: ch. XVI. 17 -20.
(c.) Other salutations: ch. XVI. 21—24.
(d.) Closing ascription of praise to God: ch. XVI. 25—27

THE
EPISTLE TO THE ROMANS.

CHAPTER I.

PAUL, a ^aservant of Jesus Christ, ^bcalled *to be* an apos-

a Ac.27.23.   b Ac.9.15; 1 Co.1.1.

CHAPTER I.

1. *Paul.* The original name of the author of this epistle was *Saul,* Acts vi. 58; vii. 1; viii. 1, &c. This was changed to Paul (see Note, Acts xiii. 9), and by this name he is generally known in the New Testament. The reason why he assumed this name is not certainly known. It was, however, in accordance with the custom of the times; see Note, Acts xiii. 9. The name *Saul* was Hebrew; the name *Paul* was Roman. In addressing an epistle to the Romans, he would naturally make use of the name to which they were accustomed, and which would excite no prejudice among them. The ancient custom was to *begin* an epistle with the name of the writer, as Cicero to Varro, &c. *We* record the name at the end. It may be remarked, however, that the placing the *name* of the writer at the *beginning* of an epistle was always done, and is still, when the letter was one of authority, or when it conferred any peculiar privileges. Thus in the proclamation of Cyrus (Ezra i. 2), "Thus saith Cyrus, king of Persia," &c.; see also Ezra iv. 11; vii. 12, "Artaxerxes, king of kings, unto Ezra the priest," &c.; Dan. iv. 1. The commencement of a letter by an apostle to a Christian church in this manner was peculiarly proper as indicating *authority.* ¶ *A servant.* This name was that which the Lord Jesus himself directed his disciples to use, as their *general* appellation, Mat. x. 25; xx. 27; Mark x. 44. And it was the customary name which they assumed, Gal. i. 10; Col. iv. 12; 2 Pet. i. 1; Jude 1; Acts iv. 29; Tit. i. 1; Jam. i. 1. The *proper*

tle, ^cseparated unto the gospel of God,

2 (Which he had promised afore

c Ac.13.2; Ga.1.15.

meaning of this word servant, δοῦλος, is *slave,* one who is not free. It expresses the condition of one who has a master, or who is at the control of another. It is often, however, applied to *courtiers,* or the officers that serve under a king; because in an eastern monarchy the relation of an absolute king to his courtiers corresponded nearly to that of a master and a slave. Thus the word is expressive of *dignity* and *honour;* and the servants of a king denote officers of a high rank and station. It is applied to the prophets as those who were honoured by God, or peculiarly intrusted by him with office, Deut. xxxiv. 5; Josh. i. 2; Jer. xxv. 4. The name is also given to the Messiah, Isa. xlii. 1, "Behold my servant in whom my soul delighteth," &c.; liii. 11, "Shall my righteous servant justify many." The apostle uses it here evidently to denote *his* acknowledging Jesus Christ as his master; as indicating his dignity, as peculiarly appointed by him to his great work; and as showing that in this epistle he intended to assume no authority of his own, but simply to declare the will of his master and theirs. ¶ *Called* to be *an apostle.* This word *called* means here not merely to be *invited,* but has the sense of *appointed.* It indicates that he had not assumed the office himself, but that he was set apart to it by the authority of Christ himself. It was important for Paul to state this, (1) Because the other apostles had been called or chosen to this work (John xv. 16, 19; Mat. x. 1; Luke vi. 13); and (2) Because Paul was not one of those originally appointed. It was of consequence for him, therefore, to affirm that he had not taken this high office

89

by his prophets in the holy scriptures,)

to himself, but that he had been *called* to it by the authority of Jesus Christ. His appointment to this office he not unfrequently takes occasion to vindicate, 1 Cor. ix. 1, &c.; Gal. i. 12–24; 2 Cor. xii. 12; 1 Tim. ii. 7; 2 Tim. i. 11; Rom. xi. 13. ¶ *An apostle.* One *sent* to execute a commission. It is applied because the apostles were *sent out* by Jesus Christ to preach his gospel, and to establish his church; Note, Mat. x. 2; Luke vi. 13. ¶ *Separated.* The word translated *separated unto,* ἀφορίζω, means to designate, to mark out by fixed limits, to bound as a field, &c. It denotes those who are *separated,* or called out from the common mass, Acts xix. 9; 2 Cor. vi. 17. The meaning here does not materially differ from the expression, *called to be an apostle,* except that perhaps this includes the notion of the *purpose* or *designation* of God to this work. Thus Paul uses the same word respecting himself, Gal. i. 15, "God, who separated me from my mother's womb, and called me by his grace," *i.e.* God designated me; marked me out; or *designed* that I should be an apostle from my infancy. In the same way Jeremiah was designated to be a prophet, Jer. i. 5. ¶ *Unto the gospel of God.* Designated or designed by God that I should make it *my business* to preach the gospel. Set apart to this as the peculiar, great work of my life; as having no other object for which I should live. For the meaning of the word *gospel,* see Note, Mat. i. 1. It is called the gospel *of God* because it is *his* appointment; it has been originated by him, and has his authority. The office of an apostle was to preach the gospel. Paul regarded himself as *separated* to this work. It was not to live in splendour, wealth, and ease, but to devote himself to this great business of proclaiming good news, that God was reconciled to men in his Son. This is the sole business of all ministers of religion.

2. *Which he had promised afore.* Which gospel, or which doctrines, he had before announced. ¶ *By the*

3 Concerning his Son Jesus Christ our Lord, which was made

prophets. The word *prophets* here is used to include those who *wrote* as well as those who *spake.* It included the teachers of the ancient Jews generally. ¶ *In the holy scriptures.* In the *writings* of the Old Testament. They were called *holy* because they were inspired of the Holy Ghost, and were regarded as *separated* from all other writings, and worthy of all reverence. The apostle here declares that he was not about to advance anything *new.* His doctrines were in accordance with the acknowledged oracles of God. Though they might *appear* to be new, yet he regarded the *gospel* as entirely consistent with all that had been declared in the Jewish dispensation; and not only consistent, but as actually promised there. He affirms, therefore, (1) That all this was *promised,* and no small part of the epistle is employed to show this. (2) That it was confirmed by the authority of holy and inspired men. (3) That it depended on no vague and loose *tradition,* but was *recorded,* so that men might examine for themselves. The reason why the apostle was so anxious to show that his doctrine coincided with the Old Testament was because the church at Rome was made up in part of Jews. He wished to show them, and the remainder of his countrymen, that the Christian religion was built on the foundation of *their* prophets, and their acknowledged writings. So doing, he would disarm their prejudice, and furnish a proof of the truth of religion. It was a constant position with the apostle that he advanced nothing but what was maintained by the best and holiest men of the nation, Acts xxvi. 22, 23, "Saying none other things than those which the prophets and Moses did say should come," &c. There was a further reason here for his appealing so much to the Old Testament. He had never been at Rome. He was therefore personally a stranger, and it was proper for him then especially to show his regard for the doctrines of the prophets. Hence he appeals here so often to the Old Testament; and defends every point by the authority of the Bible. The particular *passages* of the Old Testament on which he relied will come before us in the course of the epistle. See particularly chap. iii. iv. ix. x. xi. We may see here, (1) The reverence which Paul showed for the Old Testament. He never undervalued it. He never regarded it as obsolete, or useless. He manifestly *studied* it; and never fell into the impious opinion that the Old Testament is of little value. (2) If these things were *promised—predicted* in the Old Testament, then Christianity is true. Every passage which he adduces is therefore proof that it is from God.

3. *Concerning his Son.* This is connected with the first verse, with the word *gospel.* The gospel of God concerning his Son. The design of the gospel was to make a communication relative to his Son Jesus Christ. This is the whole of it. There is no *good news* to man respecting salvation except that which comes by Jesus Christ. ¶ *Which was made.* The word translated *was made* means usually *to be,* or *to become.* It is used, however, in the sense of *being born.* Thus, Gal. iv. 4, "God sent forth his Son *made* of a woman," born of a woman; John viii. 58, "Before Abraham *was* [*born*], I am." In this sense it seems to be used here,—who was born, or descended from the seed of David. ¶ *Of the seed of David.* Of the *posterity* or lineage of David. He was a descendant of David. David was perhaps the most illustrious of the kings of Israel. The promise to him was that there should not fail a man to sit on this throne, 1 Kings ii. 4; viii. 25; ix. 5; 2 Chron. vi. 16. This ancient promise was understood as referring to the Messiah, and hence in the New Testament he is called the descendant of David, and so much pains is taken to show that he was of his line, Luke i. 27; Mat. ix. 27; xv. 22; xii. 23; xxi. 9, 15; xxii. 42, 45; John vii. 42; 2 Tim. ii. 8. As the Jews universally believed that the Messiah would be descended from David (John vii. 42), it was of great importance for the sacred writers to make it out clearly that Jesus of Nazareth was of that line and family. Hence it happened, that though our Saviour was humble, and poor, and obscure, yet he had that on which no small part of the world have been accustomed so much to pride themselves, an illustrious ancestry. To a Jew there could be scarcely any honour so high as to be descended from the best of their kings; and it shows how little the Lord Jesus esteemed the honours of this world, that he could always evince his deep humility in circumstances where men are usually proud; and that when he spoke of the honours of this world, and told how little they were worth, he was not denouncing that which was not within his reach. ¶ *According to the flesh.* The word *flesh*, σάρξ, is used in the Scriptures in a great variety of significations. (1) It denotes, as with us, the flesh literally of any living being, Luke xxiv. 39, "A spirit hath not flesh and bones," &c. (2) The animal system, the body, including flesh and bones, the *visible* part of man, in distinction from the *invisible*, or the soul," Acts ii. 31, "Neither did his *flesh*" (his body) "see corruption;" 1 Cor. v. 5; xv. 39. (3) The man, the whole animated system, body and soul, Rom. viii. 3, "In the likeness of sinful *flesh;*" 1 Cor. xv. 50; Mat. xvi. 17; Luke iii. 6. (4) *Human nature.* As a man. Thus, Acts ii. 30, "God hath sworn with an oath that of the fruit of his loins according to the flesh [*i.e.* in his human nature] he would raise up Christ to sit on his throne;" Rom. ix. 5, "Whose are the fathers, and of whom, as concerning the flesh, Christ came, who is over all, God blessed for ever." The same is its meaning here. He was a descendant of David in his human nature, or as a man. This implies, of course, that he had *another* nature besides his human, or that while he was a man he was also something else; that there was a nature in which he was *not* descended from David. That this is its meaning will still further appear by the following observations. (1) The apostle *expressly* makes a contrast between

of ^dthe seed of David according to the flesh;

his condition according to the flesh, and that according to the spirit of holiness. (2) The expression "according to the flesh" is applied to no other one in the New Testament but to Jesus Christ. Though the word *flesh* often occurs, and is often used to denote *man*, yet the peculiar expression *according to the flesh* occurs in no other connection. In all the Scriptures it is never said of any prophet or apostle, any lawgiver or king, or any man in any capacity, that he came in the flesh, or that he was descended from certain ancestors *according to the flesh*. Nor is such an expression ever used anywhere else. If it were applied to a mere man, we should instantly ask in what other way *could* he come than in the flesh? Has he a higher nature? Is he an angel, or a seraph? The expression would be unmeaning. And when, therefore, it is applied to Jesus Christ, it implies, if language has any meaning, that there *was* a sense in which Jesus was not descended from David. What that was, appears in the next verse.

4. *And declared.* In the margin, *determined.* Τοῦ ὁρισθέντος. The ancient Syriac has, "And he was *known* to be the Son of God by might and by the Holy Spirit, who rose from the house of the dead." The Latin Vulgate, "Who was *predestinated* the Son of God," &c. The Arabic, "The Son of God *destined* by power peculiar to the Holy Spirit," &c. The word translated "declared to be"–-means properly *to bound, to fix limits to*, as to a field, to determine its proper limits or boundaries, to define, &c., Acts xvii. 26, "And *hath determined the bounds* of their habitation." Hence it means to determine, constitute, ordain, decree; *i.e.* to fix or designate the proper boundaries of a truth, or a doctrine; to distinguish its lines and marks from error; or to show, or declare a thing to be so by any action, Luke xxii. 22, "The Son of man goeth as it was *determined*," as it was fixed,

4 And ¹declared *to be* ^ethe Son of God with power, according

purposed, defined, in the purpose of God, and declared in the prophets; Acts ii. 23, "Him being delivered by the *determinate counsel*," the definite, constituted will, or design, of God; xi. 29; Heb. iv. 7, "He *limiteth* a certain day," fixes it, defines it. In this sense it is clearly used in this place. The act of raising him from the dead *designated* him, or *constituted* him the Son of God. It was such an act *as in the circumstances of the case* showed that he was the Son of God in regard to a nature which was not "according to the flesh." The ordinary resurrection of a man, like that of Lazarus, would not show that he was the Son of God; but *in the circumstances of Jesus Christ* it did; for he had *claimed* to be so; he had taught it; and God now *attested* the truth of his teaching by raising him from the dead. ¶ *The Son of God.* The word *son* is used in a great variety of senses, denoting literally a son, then a descendant, posterity near or remote, a disciple or ward, an adopted son, or one that imitates or resembles another; see Note, Mat. i. 1. The expression *sons of God*, or son of God, is used in an almost equal latitude of signification. It is, (1) Applied to Adam, as being immediately created by God without an earthly father, Luke iii. 38. (2) It is applied to saints or Christians, as being *adopted* into his family, and sustaining to him the relation of children, John i. 12, 13; 1 John iii. 1, 2, &c. This name is given to them because they *resemble* him in their *moral* character, Mat. v. 45. (3) It is given to *strong* men as resembling God in *strength*, Gen. vi. 2, "The sons of God saw the daughters of men," &c. Here these men of violence and strength are called sons of God, just as the high hills are called *hills of God*, the lofty trees of Lebanon are called *cedars of God*, &c. (4) Kings are sometimes called his sons, as resembling him in dominion and power, Ps. lxxxii. 6. (5) The name is given to *angels* because they resemble God; because he is their Creator and Father, &c., Job i. 6; ii. 1; Dan. iii. 25.

But the name THE *Son of God* is in the New Testament given by way of eminence to the Lord Jesus Christ. This was the common and favourite name by which the apostles designated him. The expression *Son of God* is applied to him no less than twenty-seven times in the Gospels and the Acts of the Apostles, and fifteen times in the Epistles and the Revelation. The expression *my Son*, and *his Son, thy Son*, &c., is applied to him in his peculiar relation to God, times almost without number. The other most common appellation which is given to him is *Son of man*. By this name he commonly designated himself. There can be no doubt that *that* was assumed to denote that he was a man, that he sustained a peculiar relation to man, and that he chose to speak of himself *as* a man. The first, the most obvious, impression on the use of the name *Son of man* is that he was *truly a man*, and it was used doubtless to guard against the impression that one who manifested so many *other* qualities, and did so many things like a celestial being, was *not* truly a human being. The phrase *Son of God* stands in contrast with the title *Son of man*, and as the *natural* and *obvious* import of that is that he was *a man*, so the *natural* and *obvious* import of the title *Son of God* is that he was divine; *or that he sustained relations to God designated by the name* SON OF GOD, *corresponding to the relations which he sustained to man designated by the name* SON OF MAN. The natural idea of the term Son of God therefore is, that he sustained a relation to God in his nature which implied more than was human or angelic—which implied *equality* with God. Accordingly, this idea was naturally suggested to the Jews by his calling God his Father, John v. 18, "But said also that God was his Father, *making himself equal with God.*" This idea Jesus immediately proceeded to confirm; see Note, John v. 19–30. The same idea is also suggested in John x. 29–31, 33, 36,

"Say ye of him whom the Father hath sanctified, and sent into the world, Thou blasphemest; *because I said I am the Son of God?*" There is in these places the fullest proof that the title suggested *naturally* the idea of equality with God; or the idea of his sustaining a relation to God corresponding to the relation of equality to man suggested by the title Son of man. This view is still further sustained in the first chapter of the Epistle to the Hebrews, ver. 1, 2, "God hath spoken unto us BY HIS SON." He is *the brightness of his glory*, and the *express image of his person*, ver. 3. He is higher than the angels, and they are required to worship him, ver. 4–6. He is called *God*, and his throne is for ever and ever, ver. 8. He is *the Creator of the heavens and the earth*, and is IM-MUTABLY THE SAME, ver. 10–12. Thus the rank or title of *the Son of God* suggests the ideas and attributes of the Divinity. This idea is sustained throughout the New Testament. See John xiv. 9, "He that hath seen me hath seen the Father;" ver. 23, "That all men shall honour the Son even as they honour the Father;" Col. i. 19, "It hath pleased the Father that in him should all fulness dwell;" ii. 9, "For in him dwelleth all the fulness of the Godhead bodily;" Phil. ii. 2–11; Rev. v. 13, 14; ii. 23. It is not affirmed that this title was given to the second person of the Trinity *before* he became *incarnate;* or to suggest the idea of any *derivation* or *extraction* before he was made flesh. There is no instance in which the appellation is not conferred to express his relation *after* he assumed human flesh. Of any *derivation* from God, or emana-tion from him in eternity, the Scrip-tures are silent. The title is conferred on him, it is supposed, with reference to his condition in this world, as the Messiah. And it is conferred, it is believed, for the following reasons, or to denote the following things, viz. (1) To designate his peculiar relation to God, as equal with him (John i. 14, 18; Mat. xi. 27; Lu. x. 22; iii. 22; 2 Pet. i. 17), or as sustaining a most intimate and close connection with him, such as neither man nor angels could do, an acquaintance with his nature (Mat. xi. 27), plans, and counsels, such as no being but one who' was *equal* with God *could* possess. In this sense I regard it as conferred on him in the passage under consideration. (2) It designates him as the anointed king, or the Messiah. In this sense it accords with the use of the word in Ps. lxxxii. 6. See Mat. xvi. 16, "Thou art *the Christ, the Son of the living God;*" Mat. xxvi. 63, "I adjure thee by the living God, that thou tell us whether thou *be the Christ, the Son of God;*" Mark xiv. 61; Lu. xxii. 70; John i. 34; Ac. ix. 20, "He preached *Christ* in the synagogues, that *he is the Son of God.*" (3) It was conferred on him to denote his miraculous conception in the womb of the Virgin Mary, Lu. i. 35, "The Holy Ghost shall come upon thee, THEREFORE (διὸ) also that holy thing which shall be born of thee shall be called *the Son of God.*"

[It is readily admitted that on the subject of the *eternal Sonship* very much has been said of an unintelligible kind. Terms applicable only to the relation as it exists among men have been freely applied to this mystery. But whatever may be thought of such language as "the eternal generation," "the eternal procession," and "the subordination" of the Son, the doctrine itself, which this mode of speaking was invented to illustrate, and has perhaps served to obscure, is in no way affected. The question is not, Have the friends of the doctrine at all times employed judicious illustration? but, What is the *Scripture evidence* on the point? If the eternal Sonship is to be discarded on such grounds, we fear the doctrine of the Trinity must share a similar fate. Yet, those who maintain the divinity of Christ, and, notwithstanding, deny the eternal Sonship, seem generally to found their objections on these incomprehensible illustrations, and from thence leap to the conclusion that the doctrine itself is false.

That the title Son of God, when applied to Jesus, denotes a *natural* and not merely an *official* Sonship, a *real* and not a *figurative* relation; in other words, that it takes origin from the divine nature, is the view which the Catholic Church has all along maintained on this subject: no explanation which falls short of divinity will exhaust the meaning of the title. Christ is indeed called the Son of God on account of his miraculous conception; "That holy thing," said the angel to the Virgin, "which shall be born of thee, shall be called

the Son of the Highest." But the creation of Adam, by the immediate power of God, without father or mother, would constitute *him* the Son of God in a sense *equally* or even *more exalted* than that in which the title is applied to Jesus if the miraculous conception were allowed to exhaust its meaning. Nor will an appeal to the *resurrection of Christ* serve the purpose of those who deny the divine origin of the title, since *that* is assigned as the *evidence only* and not the *ground* of it. The Redeemer was not *constituted*, but "*declared*" or *evidenced to be* " the Son of God with power by the resurrection from the dead." In the search for a solution short of divine Sonship recourse is next had to the office of Christ as Mediator. Yet though the appellation in question be frequently given in connection with the official character of Jesus, a careful examination of some of these passages will lead to the conclusion, that *though the Son of God hold the office, yet the office does not furnish the reason or ground of the title.* The name is given to distinguish Jesus from all others who have held office, and *in such a way as to convince us that the office is rendered honourable by the exalted personage discharging its duties, and not that the person merits the designation in virtue of the office.* "When the fulness of the time was come, God sent forth *his Son*, made of a woman," &c. "God so loved the world that he gave *his only begotten Son*," &c. Now the glory of the mission in the first of these passages, and the greatness of the gift in the second, is founded on the *original dignity* of the person sent and given. But if the person derive his title from the office only, there would seem to be comparatively little grandeur in the mission and small favour in the gift. The passages quoted would more readily prove that God had bestowed favour on Jesus by giving *him* an office from which he derived so much personal dignity!

The following are some of the passages in which the appellation "Son of God" is found connected with the office of Christ. "These are written that ye might believe that Jesus is the Christ (an official term signifying anointed Saviour), the Son of God;" "He answered and said, I believe that Jesus Christ (the official designation) is the Son of God;" "Whom say ye that I am? And Simon Peter answered and said, Thou art the Christ, the Son of the living God." Now it is reasonable to suppose that these declarations and confessions concerning the person of Christ contain not only an acknowledgment of his official character, but also of his personal dignity. "Thou art Jesus the Christ" is the acknowledgment of his office, and "thou art the Son of God" is an acknowledgment of his natural dignity. The confession of the Ethiopian eunuch and of Peter would be incomplete on any other supposition. It should be borne in mind also that the question of Christ to Peter was not, What office do ye suppose I hold? but, "Whom say ye that *I am?*" (See Haldane on Rom. i. 4.)

If, then, the miraculous conception, the resurrection, and the office of Christ do not all of them together exhaust the meaning of the appellation, we must seek for its origin higher still—we must ascend to the divine nature. We may, indeed, take one step more upwards before we reach the divine nature, and suppose, with Professor Stuart and others, that the name denotes "the complex person of the Saviour," as God and man, or. in one word, Mediator (*Comment. on Heb. Exc.* 2). But this is just the old resolution of it into official character, and is therefore liable to all the objections stated above. For while it is admitted by those who hold this view that Christ is divine, it is distinctly implied that the title Son of God would not have been his *but for his office.*

In the end, therefore, we must resolve the name into the divine nature. That it implies *equality* with God is clearly proved in this commentary. So the Jews understood it, and the Saviour tacitly admitted that their construction was right. And as there is no equality with God without divinity, the title clearly points to such a *distinction* in the Godhead as is implied in the relative terms Father and Son. Indeed, it is not easy to understand how the doctrine of the Trinity can be maintained apart from that of the eternal Sonship. If there be in the Godhead a distinction of persons, does not that distinction belong to the *nature* of the Godhead, independent of any *official* relations? Or will it be maintained that the distinction of Father, Son, and Holy Ghost arises entirely from the scheme of redemption and did not exist from eternity? We may find fault with Dr. Owen and others who speak of a "hypostatical subordination of persons in the Godhead" (Prof. Stuart, *Com. Heb. Exc.* 1). Yet, *the distinction* itself, though we cannot explain it, *must* be allowed to exist.

The remaining evidence of the eternal Sonship may be thus stated.

1. Christ is called God's "own Son," his "beloved," and "well beloved," and "only begotten Son" So strong and peculiar adjuncts seem intended to prevent any *such* idea as that of *figurative* Sonship. If these do not express the *natural* relationship. it is beyond the power of language to do it. Moreover, correct criticism binds us to adopt the natural and ordinary signification of words, unless in such cases as plainly refuse it.

2. In a passage already quoted God is said "to have sent *forth His Son* to redeem us," &c. And there are many passages to the same effect in which is revealed not only the pre-existence of Christ, but the *capacity in which* he *originally moved* and the *rank* which he held in heaven. "God sent *forth* his Son" implies that he held that title *prior* to his mission. This, at least, is the most obvious sense of the passage, and the sense which an ordinary reader would doubtless affix to it. The following objection, however, has been supposed fatal to this argument: "The name Son of God is indeed used when speaking of him previous to his having assumed human nature, but so are the names of Jesus and the Christ, which yet we know properly to belong to him only as united to humanity" It is readily allowed that the *simple fact* of the name being given *prior* to the incarnation proves nothing of itself. But the case is altered when this fact is viewed in connection with the difficulty or impossibility of resolving the Sonship into an official relation. No such difficulty exists in regard to the terms "Jesus" and "Christ," for they are *plainly* official names, signifying "anointed Saviour."

3. Rom. i. 3, 4. If in this passage we understand the apostle to declare that Christ was *of the* seed of David *according to his human nature*, the rule of antithesis demands that we understand him next to assert what he was *according to his divine nature*, viz. the Son of God.

The views given in this Note are those adopted by the most eminent orthodox divines. The language of the Westminster divines is well known : "The only Redeemer of the covenant of grace is the Lord Jesus Christ, who *being the eternal Son of God*, of one substance," &c. (*Larger Catechism*). Mr. Scott " is decidedly of opinion that Christ is called the only Son of God *in respect of his divine nature*" (*Comment. Heb.* i. 3, 4). The late Principal Hill, in his *Theological System*, having exposed what he deemed erroneous views on this subject, adds, "There is a more ancient and a more exalted title to this name (Son of God) which is inseparable from the *nature* of Christ" (3d edit. vol. i. p. 363).].

¶ *With power* (ἐν δυνάμει). By some, this expression has been supposed to mean *in* power or authority, *after* his resurrection from the dead. It is said, that he was before a man of sorrows ; now he was clothed with power and authority. But I have seen no instance in which the expression *in power* denotes *office*, or authority. It denotes *physical* energy and might, and this was bestowed on Jesus *before* his resurrection as well as after, Acts x. 38, "God anointed Jesus of Nazareth with the Holy Ghost, and *with power;*" Rom. xv. 19; 1 Cor. xv. 43. With *such* power Jesus will come to judgment, Mat. xxiv. 30. If there is any passage in which the word *power* means authority, office, &c., it is Mat. xxviii. 18, "All power in heaven and earth is given unto me." But this is not a power which was given unto him *after* his resurrection, or which he did not possess before. The same authority to commission his disciples he had exercised *before* this on the same ground, Mat. x. 7, 8. I am inclined to believe, therefore, that the expression means *powerfully, efficiently;* he was with great power, or conclusiveness, shown to be the Son of God by his resurrection from the dead. Thus the phrase *in power* is used to qualify a verb in Col. i. 29, "which worketh in me *mightily* "— *Greek,* in power, *i.e.* operating in me effectually, or powerfully. The ancient versions seem to have understood it in the same way. *Syriac,* "He was known to be the Son of God by power, and by the Holy Ghost." *Æthiopic,* "Whom he declared to be the Son of God by his own power, and by his Holy Spirit," &c. *Arabic,* "Designated the Son of God by power appropriate to the Holy Spirit." ¶ *According to the spirit of holiness* (Κατὰ πνεῦμα ἁγιωσύνης). This expression has been variously understood. We may arrive at its meaning by the following considerations. (1) It is not the third person in the Trinity that is referred to here. The designation of that person is *always* in a different form. It is *the Holy Spirit,* the Holy Ghost, πνεῦμα ἅγιον, or τὸ πνεῦμα τὸ ἅγιον; never *the Spirit of holiness.* (2) It stands in contrast with *the flesh;* ver. 3, "According to the flesh, the seed of David: according to the spirit of holiness, the Son of God." As the former refers doubtless to his human nature, so this must refer to the nature designated by the title Son of God, that is, to his superior or divine nature. (3) The expression is altogether peculiar to the Lord Jesus Christ. Nowhere in the Scriptures,

or in any other writings, is there an affirmation like this. What would be meant by it if affirmed of a mere man? (4) It cannot mean that the Holy Spirit, the third person in the Trinity, showed that Jesus was the Son of God by raising him from the dead, because that act is nowhere attributed to him. It is uniformly ascribed either to God, *as God* (Acts ii. 24, 32; iii. 15, 26; iv. 10; v. 30; x. 40; xiii. 30, 33, 34; xvii. 31; Rom. x. 9; Eph. i. 20), or to the Father (Rom. vi. 4), or to Jesus himself (John x. 18). In no instance is this act ascribed to the Holy Ghost. (5) It indicates a state far more elevated than any human dignity, or honour. In regard to his earthly descent, he was of a royal race; in regard to the Spirit of holiness, much more than that, he was the Son of God. (6) The word *Spirit* is used often to designate God, the holy God, as distinguished from all the *material* forms of idol worship, John iv. 24. (7) The word Spirit is applied to the Messiah, in his more elevated or divine nature. 1 Cor. xv. 45, "The last Adam was made a quickening Spirit." 2 Cor. iii. 17, "Now the Lord (Jesus) is that Spirit." Heb. ix. 14, Christ is said to have offered himself "*through the eternal Spirit.*" 1 Pet. iii. 18, he is said to have been "put to death in the flesh, but quickened by the Spirit." 1 Tim. iii. 16, he is said to have been "justified in the Spirit." In most of these passages there is the same contrast noticed between *his flesh,* his human nature, and his other state, which occurs in Rom. i. 3, 4. In all these instances, the design is, doubtless, to speak of him *as a man,* and as something more than a man: he was one thing as a man; he was another thing in his other nature. In the one, he was of David; was put to death, &c. In the other, he was of God, he was manifested to be such, he was restored to the elevation which he had sustained before his incarnation and death, John xvii. 1–5; Phil. ii. 2–11. The expression, *according to the Spirit of holiness,* does not indeed of itself imply divinity. It denotes that *holy* and more *exalted nature* which he possessed as distinguished from the human. What that is, is to be learned from other declarations. *This expression implies simply that it was such as to make proper the appellation, the Son of God.* Other places, as we have seen, show that *that* designation naturally implied divinity. And that this was the true idea couched under the expression, *according to the Spirit of holiness*, appears from those numerous texts of Scripture which explicitly assert his divinity; see John i. 1, &c., and the Note on that place. ¶ *By the resurrection from the dead.* This has been also variously understood. Some have maintained that the word *by*, ἐξ, denotes AFTER. He was declared to be the Son of God *in* power *after* he rose from the dead; that is, he was solemnly invested with the dignity that became the Son of God after he had been so long in a state of voluntary humiliation. But to this view there are some insuperable objections. (1) It is not the natural and usual meaning of the word *by.* (2) It is not the object of the apostle to state the *time* when the thing was done, or the *order*, but evidently to declare the *fact*, and the evidence of the fact. If such had been his design, he would have said that *previous* to his death he was *shown* to be of the seed of David, but *afterwards* that he was invested with power. (3) Though it must be admitted that the preposition *by*, ἐξ, sometimes means AFTER (Mat. xix. 20; Luke viii. 27; xxiii. 8, &c.), yet its proper and usual meaning is to denote the efficient cause, or the agent, or origin of a thing, Mat. i. 3, 18; xxi. 25; John iii. 5; Rom. v. 16; xi. 36, "OF him are all things;" 1 Cor. viii. 6, "One God, the Father, OF whom are all things," &c. In this sense I suppose it is used here; and that the apostle means to affirm that he was *clearly* or *decisively* shown to be the Son of God *by* his resurrection from the dead. But here will it be asked, *how* did his *resurrection* show this? Was not Lazarus raised from the dead? And did not many saints rise also after Jesus? And were not

the dead raised by the apostles, by Elijah, by the bones of Elisha, and by Christ himself? And did *their* being raised prove that they were the sons of God? I answer that the mere fact of the *resurrection* of the body proves nothing *in itself* about the character and rank of the being that is raised. But *in the circumstances* in which Jesus was placed it might show it conclusively. When Lazarus was raised, it was not in attestation of anything which he had taught or done. It was a mere display of the power and benevolence of Christ. But in regard to the resurrection of Jesus, let the following circumstances be taken into the account. (1) He came as the Messiah. (2) He uniformly taught that he was the Son of God. (3) He maintained that God was his father in such a sense as to imply equality with him, John v. 17–30; x. 36. (4) He claimed authority to abolish the laws of the Jews, to change their customs, and to be himself absolved from the observance of those laws, even as his Father was, John v. 1–17; Mark ii. 28. (5) When God raised *him* up therefore, it was not an ordinary event. It was *a public attestation, in the face of the universe, of the truth of his claims to be the Son of God.* God would not sanction the doings and doctrines of an impostor. And when, therefore, he raised up Jesus, he, by this act, showed the truth of his claims, that he was the Son of God. Further, in the view of the apostles, the *resurrection* was intimately connected with the *ascension* and *exaltation* of Jesus. The one made the other certain. And it is not improbable that when they spoke of his resurrection, they meant to include, not merely that single act, but the entire series of doings of which that was the *first*, and which was the *pledge* of the elevation and majesty of the Son of God. Hence, when they had proved his *resurrection*, they *assumed* that all the others would follow. That involved and supposed all. And the *series*, of which that was the first, *proved* that he was the Son of God; see Acts xvii. 31, "He will judge the world in righteousness, by

to the *spirit of holiness, by the resurrection from the dead :

5 By whom we have received

f He.9.14.

grace and apostleship, [2]for *g*obedience to the faith among all nations, for his name:

2 or, *to the obedience of faith.*   *g* Ac.6.7; ch.16.26.

that man whom he hath ordained, whereof he hath given ASSURANCE to all men, *in that he hath raised him from the dead.*" The one involves the other; see Acts i. 6. Thus Peter (Acts ii. 22–32) having proved that Jesus was raised up, adds, ver. 33, "THEREFORE, being by the right hand exalted, he hath shed forth this," &c.; and ver. 36, "THEREFORE, let all the house of Israel KNOW ASSUREDLY that God hath made that same Jesus whom ye have crucified, BOTH LORD AND CHRIST."

This verse is a remarkable instance of the apostle Paul's manner of writing. Having mentioned a subject, his mind seems to catch fire; he presents it in new forms, and amplifies it, until he seems to forget for a time the subject on which he was writing. It is from this cause that his writings abound so with parentheses, and that there is so much difficulty in following and understanding him.

5. *By whom.* The apostle here returns to the subject of the salutation of the Romans, and states to them his authority to address them. That authority he had derived from the Lord Jesus, and not from man. On this fact, that he had received his apostolic commission, not from man, but by the direct authority of Jesus Christ, Paul not unfrequently insisted. Gal. i. 12, "For I neither received it of man, neither was I taught it, but by revelation of Jesus Christ;" 1 Cor. xv. 1–8; Eph. iii. 1–3. ¶ *We.* The plural here is probably put for the singular; see Col. iv. 3; comp. Eph. vi. 19, 20. It was usual for those who were clothed with authority to express themselves in this manner. Perhaps here, however, he refers to the general nature of the apostolic office, as being derived from Jesus Christ, and designs to assure the Romans that *he* had received the apostolic commission as the others had. ' *We,* the apostles, have received the appointment from Jesus Christ.'

¶ *Grace and apostleship.* Many suppose that this is a figure of speech, *hendiadys,* by which one thing is expressed by two words, meaning the grace or favour of the apostolic office. Such a figure of speech is often used. But it may mean, as it does probably here, the two things, *grace,* or the favour of God to his own soul, as a personal matter; and the apostolic office as a distinct thing. He often, however, speaks of the office of the apostleship as a matter of special favour, Rom. xv. 15, 16; Gal. ii. 9; Eph. iii. 7–9. ¶ *For obedience to the faith.* In order to produce, or promote obedience to the faith; that is, to induce them to render that obedience to God which *faith* produces. There are two things, therefore, implied. (1) That the design of the gospel and of the apostleship is to induce men to *obey* God. (2) That the tendency of *faith* is to produce obedience. There is no true faith which does not produce that. This is constantly affirmed in the New Testament, Rom. xv. 18; xvi. 19; 2 Cor. vii. 15 ; Jam. ii. ¶ *Among all nations.* This was the original commission which Jesus gave to his apostles, Mark xvi. 15, 16; Mat. xxviii. 18, 19. This was the special commission which Paul received when he was converted, Acts ix. 15. It was important to show that the commission extended thus far, as he was now addressing a distant church which he had not seen. ¶ *For his name.* This means probably *on his account,* that is, on account of Christ, John xiv. 13, 14; xvi. 23, 24. The design of the apostleship was to produce obedience to the gospel among all nations, that *thus* the name of Jesus might be honoured. Their work was not one in which they were seeking to honour themselves, but it was solely for the honour and glory of Jesus Christ. For him they toiled, they encountered perils, they laid down their lives, because by so doing they might bring

6 Among whom are ye also the called of Jesus Christ:

7 To all that be in Rome, beloved of God, *h*called *to be* saints:

h 1 Co.1.2; 1 Th.4.7.

*i*Grace to you, and peace, from God our Father, and the Lord Jesus Christ.

8 First, I thank my God through

i 1 Co.1.3,&c.; 2 Pe.1.2.

men to obey the gospel, and thus Jesus Christ might wear a brighter crown, and be attended by a longer and more splendid train of worshippers in the kingdom of his glory.

6. *Among whom.* That is, among the Gentiles who had become obedient to the Christian faith in accordance with the design of the gospel, ver. 8. This proves that the church at Rome was made up *partly* at least, if not mainly, of Gentiles or pagans. This is fully proved in chapter xvi. by the *names* of the persons whom Paul salutes. ¶ *The called of Jesus Christ.* Those whom Jesus Christ has called to be his followers. The word *called* (see ver. 1) denotes not merely an external invitation to a privilege, but it also denotes the *internal* or *effectual* call which secures conformity to the will of him who calls, and is thus synonymous with the name Christians, or believers. That true Christians are contemplated by this address, is clear from the whole scope of the epistle; see particularly chap. viii.; comp. Phil. iii. 14; Heb. iii. 1.

7. *To all that be in Rome.* That is, to all who bear the Christian name. Perhaps he here included not only *the church* at Rome, but all who might have been there from abroad. Rome was a place of vast concourse for foreigners; and Paul probably addressed all who happened to be there. ¶ *Beloved of God.* Whom God loves. This is the privilege of all Christians. And this proves that the persons whom Paul addressed were *not* those merely who had been invited to the external privileges of the gospel. The importance of this observation will appear in the progress of these Notes. ¶ *Called* to be *saints.* So called, or influenced by God who had called them, as to become saints. The word *saints*, ἅγιοι, means those who are holy, or those who are devoted or consecrated to God. The radical idea of the word is, that which is separ-

ated from a common to a sacred use, and answers to the Hebrew word קדוש, *kadosh.* It is applied to anything that is set apart to the service of God, to the temple, to the sacrifices, to the utensils about the temple, to the garments, &c., of the priests, and to the priests themselves. It was applied to the Jews as a people *separated* from other nations, and devoted or consecrated to God, while other nations were devoted to the service of idols. It is also applied to Christians, as being a people devoted or set apart to the service of God. The *radical* idea, then, as applied to Christians, is, that *they are separated from other men, and other objects and pursuits, and consecrated to the service of God.* This is the peculiar characteristic of the *saints.* And this characteristic the Roman Christians had shown. For the use of the word, as stated above, see the following passages of Scripture: Luke ii. 23; Ex. xiii. 2; Rom. xi. 16; Mat. vii. 6; 1 Pet. i. 16; Acts ix. 13; 1 Pet. ii. 5; Acts iii. 21; Eph. iii. 5; 1 Pet. ii. 9; Phil. ii. 15; 1 John iii. 1, 2. ¶ *Grace.* This word properly means *favour.* It is very often used in the New Testament, and is employed in the sense of benignity or benevolence; felicity, or a prosperous state of affairs; the Christian religion, as the highest expression of the benevolence or favour of God; the happiness which Christianity confers on its friends in this and the future life; the apostolic office; charity, or alms; thanksgiving; joy, or pleasure; and the benefits produced on the Christian's heart and life by religion—the grace of meekness, patience, charity, &c. (Schleusner). In this place, and in similar places in the beginning of the apostolic epistles, it seems to be a word including *all* those blessings that are applicable to Christians in common; denoting an ardent wish that *all* the mercies and favours of God for time

Jesus Christ for you all, that ^{k} your faith is spoken of throughout the whole world.

and eternity, *blended* under the general name *grace*, may be conferred on them. It is to be understood as connected with a word implying invocation. I *pray*, or I desire, that *grace*, &c., may be conferred on you. It is the customary form of salutation in nearly all the apostolic epistles, 1 Cor. i. 3; 2 Cor. i. 2; Gal. i. 3; Eph. i. 2; Phil. i. 2; Col. i. 2; 1 Thes. i. 1; 2 Thes. i. 2; Philem. 3. ¶ *And peace. Peace* is the state of freedom from war. As war conveys the idea of discord and numberless calamities and dangers, so peace is the opposite, and conveys the idea of concord, safety, and prosperity. Thus, to wish one *peace* was the same as to wish him all safety and prosperity. This form of salutation was common among the Hebrews, Gen. xliii. 23, "Peace to you! fear not," Judg. vi. 23; xix. 20; Luke xxiv. 36. But the word *peace* is also used in contrast with that state of agitation and conflict which a sinner has with his conscience, and with God. The sinner is like the troubled sea, which cannot rest, Isa. lvii. 20. The Christian is at peace with God through the Lord Jesus Christ, Rom. v. 1. By this word, denoting reconciliation with God, the blessings of the Christian religion are often described in the Scriptures, Rom. viii. 6; xiv. 17; xv. 13; Gal. v. 22; Phil. iv. 7. A prayer for peace, therefore, in the epistles, is not a mere formal salutation, but has a special reference to those *spiritual* blessings which result from reconciliation with God through the Lord Jesus Christ. ¶ *From God our Father.* The Father of all Christians. He is the Father of all his creatures, as they are his offspring, Acts xvii. 28, 29. He is especially the Father of all Christians, as they have been "begotten by him to a lively hope," have been adopted into his family, and are like him, Mat. v. 45; 1 Pet. i. 3; 1 John v. 1; iii. 1, 2. The expres-

9 For God is my witness, ^{l} whom I serve ^{3} with my spirit in the gospel of his Son, that without ceasing

sion here is equivalent to a *prayer* that God the Father *would* bestow grace and peace on the Romans. It implies that these blessings proceed from God, and are to be expected from him. ¶ *And the Lord Jesus Christ. From* him. The Lord Jesus Christ is especially regarded in the New Testament as the source of *peace*, and the procurer of it; see Luke ii. 14; xix. 38, 42; John xiv. 27; xvi. 33; Acts x. 36; Rom. v. 1; Eph. ii. 17. Each of these places will show with what propriety *peace* was invoked from the Lord Jesus. From thus connecting the Lord Jesus with the Father in this place, we may see, (1) That the apostle regarded *him* as the source of grace and peace as *really* as he did the Father. (2) He introduced them in the same connection, and with reference to the bestowment of the same blessings. (3) If the mention of the Father in this connection implies a *prayer* to him, or an act of worship, the mention of the Lord Jesus implies the same thing, and was an act of homage to him. (4) All this shows that *his* mind was *familiarized* to the idea that he was divine. No man would introduce his name in such connections if he did not believe that he was equal with God; comp. Phil. ii. 2–11. It is from this *incidental* and *unstudied* manner of expression, that we have one of the most striking proofs of the manner in which the sacred writers regarded the Lord Jesus Christ.

These seven verses are one sentence. They are a striking instance of the manner of Paul. The subject is simply a salutation to the Roman church. But at the mention of some single words, the mind of Paul seems to catch fire, and to burn and blaze with signal intensity. He leaves the immediate subject before him, and advances some vast thought that awes us, and fixes us in contemplation, and

I *m* make mention of you always in my prayers;

m 1 Th.3.10.

10 Making request if by any means now at length I might have

---

involves us in difficulty about his meaning, and then returns to his subject. This is the characteristic of his great mind; and it is this, among other things, that makes it so difficult to interpret his writings. 8. *First.* In the first place, not in point of importance, but before speaking of other things, or before proceeding to the main design of the epistle. ¶ *I thank my God.* The God whom I worship and serve. The expression of thanks to God for his mercy to them was fitted to conciliate their feelings, and to prepare them for the truths which he was about to communicate to them. It showed the deep interest which he had in their welfare; and the happiness it would give him to do them good. It is proper to give thanks to God for his mercies to others as well as to ourselves. We are members of one great family, and we should make it a subject of thanksgiving that he confers any blessings, and especially the blessing of salvation, on any mortals. ¶ *Through Jesus Christ.* The duty of presenting our thanks to God *through* Christ is often enjoined in the New Testament, Eph. v. 20; Heb. xiii. 15; comp. John xiv. 14. Christ is the *mediator* between God and men, or the *medium* by which we are to present our prayers and also our thanksgivings. We are not to approach God *directly*, but *through* a mediator at all times, depending on him to present our cause before the mercy-seat; to plead for us there; and to offer the desires of our souls to God. It is no less proper to present *thanks* in his name, or through him, than it is *prayer.* He has made the way to God accessible to us, whether it be by prayer or praise; and it is owing to *his* mercy and grace that *any* of our services are acceptable to God. ¶ *For you all.* On account of you all, *i.e.* of the entire Roman church. This is one evidence that that church then was remarkably

pure. How few churches have there been of whom a similar commendation could be expressed. ¶ *That your faith.* Faith is put here for the whole of religion, and means the same as your piety. Faith is one of the principal things of religion; one of its first requirements; and hence it signifies religion itself. The readiness with which the Romans had embraced the gospel, the firmness with which they adhered to it, was so remarkable, that it was known and celebrated everywhere. The same thing is affirmed of them in chap. xvi. 19, "For your obedience is come abroad unto all men." ¶ *Is spoken of.* Is celebrated, or known. They were in the capital of the Roman empire; in a city remarkable for its wickedness; and in a city whose influence extended everywhere. It was natural, therefore, that their remarkable conversion to God should be celebrated everywhere. The religious or irreligious influence of a great city will be felt far and wide, and this is one reason why the apostles preached the gospel so much in such places. ¶ *Throughout the whole world.* As we say, everywhere; or throughout the Roman empire. The term *world* is often thus limited in the Scriptures; and here it denotes those parts of the Roman empire where the Christian church was established. All the churches would hear of the work of God in the capital, and would rejoice in it; comp. Col. i. 6, 23; John xii. 19. It is not improper to *commend* Christians, and to remind them of their influence; and especially to call to their mind the great power which they may have on other churches and people. Nor is it improper that great displays of divine mercy should be celebrated everywhere, and excite in the churches praise to God. 9. *For God is my witness.* The reason of this strong appeal to God is to show to the Romans the deep interest which he felt in their welfare.

a prosperous journey *n*by the will of God to come unto you.

n Ja.4.15.

11 For *o*I long to see you, that *p*I may impart unto you some

o ch.15.23,32.   *p* ch.15.29.

This interest was manifested in his prayers, and in his earnest desires to see them. A deep interest shown in this way was well fitted to prepare them to receive what he had to say to them. ¶ *Whom I serve.* See ver. 1; comp. Acts xvii. 23. The expression denotes that he was devoted to God in this manner; that he obeyed him; and had given himself to do his will in making known his gospel. ¶ *With my spirit.* Greek, ἐν, *in* my spirit, *i.e.* with my *heart.* It is not an external service merely; it is internal, real, sincere. He was really and sincerely devoted to the service of God. ¶ *In the gospel of his Son.* In making known the gospel, or as a minister of the gospel. ¶ *That without ceasing* (ἀδιαλείπτως). This word means constantly, always, without intermission. It was not only *once,* but repeatedly. It had been the burden of his prayers. The same thing he also mentions in regard to other churches, 1 Thes. i. 3; ii. 13. ¶ *I make mention.* I call you to remembrance, and present your case before God. This evinced his remarkable interest in a church which he had never seen, and it shows that Paul was a man of prayer; praying not for his friends and kindred only, but for those whom he had never seen. If with the same intensity of prayer all Christians, and Christian ministers, would remember the churches, what a different aspect would the Christian church soon assume! ¶ *Always.* This word should be connected with the following verse, "Always making request," &c.

10. *Making request.* It was his earnest desire to see them, and he presented the subject before God. ¶ *If by any means.* This shows the earnest desire which he had to see them, and implies that he had designed it, and had been hindered; see ver. 13. ¶ *Now at length.* He had purposed it a long time, but had been hindered. He doubtless cherished this purpose

for years. The expressions in the Greek imply an earnest wish that this long-cherished purpose might be accomplished before long. ¶ *A prosperous journey.* A safe, pleasant journey. It is right to regard all success in travelling as depending on God, and to pray for success and safety from danger. Yet all such prayers are not answered according to the *letter* of the petition. The prayer of Paul that he might see the Romans was granted, but in a remarkable way. He was persecuted by the Jews, and arraigned before King Agrippa. He appealed to the Roman emperor, and was taken there in chains as a prisoner. Yet the journey *might* in this way have a more deep effect on the Romans, than if he had gone in any other way. In so mysterious a manner does God often hear the prayers of his people; and though their prayers *are* answered, yet it is in his own time and way; see the last chapters of the Acts. ¶ *By the will of God.* If God shall grant it; if God will by his mercy grant me the great favour of my coming to you. This is a proper model of a prayer; and is in accordance with the direction of the Bible; see Jam. iv. 14, 15.

11. *For I long to see you.* I earnestly desire to see you; comp. chap. xv. 23, 32. ¶ *That I may impart.* That I may *give,* or communicate to you. ¶ *Some spiritual gift.* Some have understood this as referring to *miraculous gifts,* which it was supposed the apostles had the power of conferring on others. But this interpretation is forced and unnatural. There is no instance where this expression denotes the power of working miracles. Besides, the apostle in the next verse explains his meaning, "That I may be comforted together *by the mutual faith,*" &c. From this it appears that he desired to be among them to exercise the office of the ministry, to establish them in the gospel,

spiritual gift, to the end you may be established :

12 That is, that I may be comforted together [4]with you [q]by the mutual faith both of you and me.

[4] or, *in.*   [q] 2 Pe.1.1.

13 Now I would not have you ignorant, brethren, that oftentimes I purposed to come unto you, (but was let hitherto,) that I might have some fruit [5]among

[5] or, *in.*

---

and to confirm their hopes. He expected that the preaching of the gospel would be the means of confirming them in the faith; and he desired to be the means of doing it. It was a wish of benevolence, and accords with what he says respecting his intended visit in chap. xv. 29, " And I am sure that when I come, I shall come in the fulness of the blessing of the gospel of Christ." To make known to them more fully the blessings of the gospel, and *thus* to impart spiritual gifts, was the design he had in view. ¶ *To the end,* &c. With the design, or purpose. ¶ *Ye may be established.* That is, that they might be *confirmed* in the truths of the gospel. This was one design of the ministry, that Christians may be established or strengthened, Eph. iv. 13. It is not to have dominion over their faith, but to be "helpers of their joy," 2 Cor. i. 24. Paul did not doubt that this part of his office might be fulfilled among the Romans, and he was desirous there also of making full proof of his ministry. His wish was to preach not simply where he *must,* but where he *might.* This is the nature of this work.

12. *That I may be comforted,* &c. It was not merely to confirm *them* that Paul wished to come. He sought the communion of saints; he expected to be *himself* edified and strengthened, and to be comforted by seeing their strength of faith, and their rapid growth in grace. We may remark here, (1) That one effect of religion is to produce the desire of the communion of saints. It is the nature of Christianity to seek the society of those who are the friends of Christ. (2) Nothing is better fitted to produce growth in grace than such communion. Every Christian should have one or more Christian friends to whom he may unbosom himself.

No small part of the difficulties which young Christians experience would vanish, if they should communicate their feelings and views to others. Feelings which *they* suppose no Christians ever had, which greatly distress them, they will find are common among those who are experienced in the Christian life. (3) There is nothing better fitted to excite the feelings, and confirm the hopes of Christian ministers, than the firm faith of young converts, of those just commencing the Christian life, 3 John 4. (4) The apostle did not disdain to be taught by the humblest Christians. He expected to be strengthened himself by the faith of those just beginning the Christian life. " There is none so poor in the church of Christ, that he cannot make some addition of importance to our stores " (Calvin).

13. *That oftentimes I purposed.* See ver. 10. How often he had purposed this we have no means of ascertaining. The fact, however, that he had done it, showed his strong desire to see them, and to witness the displays of the grace of God in the capital of the Roman world; comp. chap. xv. 23, 24. One *instance* of his having purposed to go to Rome is recorded in Acts xix. 21, " After these things were ended [viz. at Ephesus], Paul purposed in the spirit, when he had passed through Macedonia and Achaia, to go to Jerusalem, saying, After I have been there, I must also see Rome." This purpose expressed in this manner in the *epistle,* and the *Acts* of the Apostles, has been shown by Dr. Paley (*Horæ Paulinæ,* on Rom. i. 13) to be one of those *undesigned coincidences* which strongly show that both books are genuine ; comp. Rom. xv. 23, 24, with Acts xix. 21. A forger of these books would not have *thought* of such a contrivance as to

you also, even as among other Gentiles.

14 I am *debtor both to the

r 1 Co.9.16.

feign such a purpose to go to Rome at that time, and to have mentioned it in that manner. Such coincidences are among the best proofs that can be demanded, that the writers did not intend to impose on the world; see Paley. ¶ *But was let hitherto.* The word "let" means to *hinder*, or to *obstruct.* In what way this was done we do not know, but it is probable that he refers to the various openings for the preaching of the gospel where he had been, and to the obstructions of various kinds from the enemies of the gospel to the fulfilment of his purposes. ¶ *That I might have some fruit among you.* That I might be the means of the conversion of sinners and of the edification of the church in the capital of the Roman empire. It was not curiosity to see the splendid capital of the world that prompted this desire; it was not the love of travel, and of roaming from clime to clime; it was the specific purpose of doing good to the souls of men. To *have fruit* means to obtain success in bringing men to the knowledge of Christ. Thus the Saviour said (John xv. 16), "I have chosen you, and ordained you that you should bring forth fruit, and that your fruit should remain."

14, 15. *I am debtor.* This does not mean that *they* had conferred any favour on *him*, which bound him to make this return, but that he was under *obligation* to preach the gospel to all to whom it was possible. This *obligation* arose from the favour that God had shown him in appointing him to this work. He was specially chosen as a vessel to bear the gospel to the Gentiles (Acts ix. 15; Rom. xi. 13), and he did not feel that he had discharged the obligation until he had made the gospel known as far as possible among all the nations of the earth. ¶ *To the Greeks.* This term properly denotes those who dwelt in Greece. But as the Greeks were the most polished people of antiquity, the

Greeks and to the barbarians, both to the wise and to the unwise.

15 So, as much as in me is, I am

term came to be synonymous with the polished, the refined, the wise, as opposed to barbarians. In this place it doubtless means the same as "the wise," and includes the Romans also, as it cannot be supposed that Paul would designate the Romans as barbarians. Besides, the Romans claimed an origin from Greece, and Dionysius Halicarnassus (book i.) shows that the Italian and Roman people were of Greek descent. ¶ *Barbarians.* All who were not included under the general name of Greeks. Thus Ammonius says that "all who were not Greeks were barbarians." This term *barbarian*, Βάρβαρος, properly denotes one who speaks a foreign language, a foreigner, and the Greeks applied it to all who did not use their tongue; comp. 1 Cor. xiv. 11, "I shall be unto him that speaketh *a barbarian*," &c. *i.e.* I shall speak a language which he cannot understand. The word did not, therefore, of necessity denote any rusticity of manners, or any want of refinement. ¶ *To the wise.* To those who esteemed themselves to be wise, or who boasted of their wisdom. The term is synonymous with "the Greeks," who prided themselves much in their wisdom, 1 Cor. i. 22, "The Greeks seek after wisdom;" comp. 1 Cor. i. 19; iii. 18, 19; iv. 10; 2 Cor. xi. 19. ¶ *Unwise.* Those who were regarded as the ignorant and unpolished part of mankind. The expression is equivalent to ours, "to the learned and the unlearned." It was an evidence of the proper spirit to be willing to preach the gospel to either. The gospel claims to have power to instruct all mankind, and they who are called to preach it, should be *able* to instruct those who esteem themselves to be wise, and who are endowed with science, learning, and talent; and they should be *willing* to labour to enlighten the most obscure, ignorant, and degraded portions of the race. This is the true spirit of the Christian ministry.

ready to preach the gospel to you that are at Rome also.

---

15. *So, as much as in me is.* As far as opportunity may be offered, and according to my ability. ¶ *I am ready,* &c. I am prepared to preach among you, and to show the power of the gospel, even in the splendid metropolis of the world. He was not deterred by any fear; nor was he indifferent to their welfare; but he was under the direction of God, and as far as *he* gave him opportunity, he was ready to make known to them the gospel, as he had done at Antioch, Ephesus, Athens, and Corinth. This closes the *introduction* or *preface* to the epistle. Having shown his deep interest in their welfare, he proceeds in the next verse to state to them the great doctrines of that gospel which he was desirous of proclaiming to them.

16. *For I am not ashamed,* &c. The Jews had cast him off, and regarded him as an apostate; and by the *wise* among the Gentiles he had been persecuted, and despised, and driven from place to place, and regarded as the filth of the world, and the offscouring of all things (1 Cor. iv. 13), but still he was not ashamed of the gospel. He had so firm a conviction of its value and its truth; he had experienced so much of its consolations; and had seen so much of its efficacy; that he was so far from being ashamed of it that he gloried in it as the power of God unto salvation. Men should be ashamed of crime and folly. They are ashamed of their own offences, and of the follies of their conduct, when they come to reflect on it. But they are not ashamed of that which they feel to be right, and of that which they know will contribute to their welfare, and to the benefit of their fellow-men. Such were the views of Paul about the gospel; and it is one of his favourite doctrines that they who believe on Christ shall not be ashamed, Rom. x. 11; v. 5; 2 Cor. vii. 14; 2 Tim. i. 12; Phil. i. 20; Rom. ix. 33; 2 Tim. i. 8; comp. Mark viii. 38; 1 Pet. iv. 16; 1 John ii. 28.

16 For I am not *s* ashamed of the gospel of Christ: for it

s Mar.8.38; 2 Ti.1.8.

¶ *Of the gospel.* This word means the *good news,* or the glad intelligence; see Note, Mark i. 1. It is so called because it contains the glad annunciation that sin may be pardoned, and the soul saved. ¶ *Of Christ.* The good news respecting the Messiah; or which the Messiah has brought. The expression probably refers to the former, the good news which relates *to* the Messiah, to his character, advent, preaching, death, resurrection, and ascension. Though this was "to the Jews a stumbling-block, and to the Greeks foolishness," yet he regarded it as the only hope of salvation, and was ready to preach it even in the rich and splendid capital of the world. ¶ *The power of God.* This expression means that it is the way in which God exerts his power in the salvation of men. It is the efficacious or mighty plan, by which power goes forth to save, and by which all the obstacles of man's redemption are taken away. This expression implies, (1) That it is God's plan, or *his* appointment. It is not the device of man. (2) It is adapted to the end. It is fitted to overcome the obstacles in the way. It is not *merely* the instrument by which God exerts his power, but it has an inherent adaptedness to the end; it is *fitted* to accomplish salvation to man so that it may be denominated *power.* (3) It is mighty, hence it is called power, and the power of God. It is not a feeble and ineffectual instrumentality, but it is "mighty to the pulling down of strong holds," 2 Cor. x. 4, 5. It has shown its power as applicable to every degree of sin, to every combination of wickedness. It has gone against the sins of the world, and evinced its power to save sinners of all grades, and to overcome and subdue every mighty form of iniquity; comp. Jer. xxiii. 29, "Is not my word like as a fire? saith the Lord; and like a hammer *that* breaketh the rock in pieces?" 1 Cor. i. 18, "The preaching of the cross is to them that

is the *power of God unto salvation, "to every one that believeth; to *the Jew first, and also to the Greek.

t Je.23.29; 1 Co.1.18.　　u Mar.16.16.　　v Ac.3.26.

perish, foolishness, but unto us which are saved, it is the power of God." ¶ *Unto salvation.* This word means complete deliverance from sin and death, and all the foes and dangers that beset man. It cannot imply anything less than eternal life. If a man should believe and then fall away, he could in no correct sense be said *to be saved.* And hence when the apostle declares that it is the power of God unto salvation " to *every* one that believeth," it implies that *all* who become believers shall be "kept by the power of God through faith unto salvation" (see 1 Pet. i. 5), and that none shall ever fall away and be lost. The apostle thus *commences* his discussion with one of the important doctrines of the Christian religion, the final preservation of the saints. He is not defending the gospel for any *temporary* object, or with any temporary hope. He looks *through* the system, and sees in it a plan for the complete and eternal recovery of *all* those who believe in the Lord Jesus Christ. When he says it is the power of God *unto* salvation, he means that it is the power of God for the *attainment* of salvation. This is the *end,* or the design of this exertion of power. ¶ *To every one that believeth.* Comp. Mark xvi. 16, 17. This expresses the condition, or the terms, on which salvation is conferred through the gospel. It is not indiscriminately to *all* men, whatever may be their character. It is only to those who confide or trust in it; and it *is* conferred on all who receive it in this manner. If this qualification is possessed, it bestows its blessings freely and fully. All men know what *faith* is. It is exercised when we confide in a parent, a friend, a benefactor. It is such a reception of a promise, a truth, or a threatening, as to suffer it to make its *appropriate* impression on the mind, and such as to lead us to act under its influence, or to act as

17 For *therein is the righteousness of God revealed from faith to faith: as it is written, *The just shall live by faith.

w ch.3.21,25.　　x Hab.2.4.

we *should* on the supposition that it is true. Thus a sinner credits the threatenings of God, and fears. This is faith. He credits his promises and hopes. This is faith. He feels that he is lost, and relies on Jesus Christ for mercy. This is faith. And, in general, faith is such an impression on the mind made by truth as to lead us to feel and act as if it were *true;* to have the *appropriate* feelings, and views, and conduct under the commands, and promises, and threatenings of God; see Note, Mark xvi. 16. ¶ *To the Jew first.* First *in order of time.* Not that the gospel was any more adapted to Jews than to others; but to them had been committed the oracles of God; the Messiah had come through them; they had had the law, the temple, and the service of God, and it was natural that the gospel should be proclaimed to them before it was to the Gentiles. This was the order in which the gospel was *actually* preached to the world, first to the Jews, and then to the Gentiles. Comp. Acts ii. and x.; Mat. x. 6; Luke xxiv. 49; Acts xiii. 46, " It was necessary that the word of God should first have been spoken to you; but seeing ye put it from you, and judge yourselves unworthy of everlasting life, lo, we turn to the Gentiles." Comp. Mat. xxi. 43. ¶ *And also to the Greek.* To all who were not Jews, that is, to all the world. It was not confined in its intention or efficacy to any class or nation of men. It was *adapted* to all, and was designed to be extended to all.

17. *For.* This word implies that he is now about to give a *reason* for that which he had just said, a reason why he was not ashamed of the gospel of Christ. That reason is stated in this verse. It embodies the *substance* of all that is contained in the epistle. It is the *doctrine* which he seeks to establish; and there is not perhaps a

more important passage in the Bible than this verse; or one more difficult to be understood. ¶ *Therein.* In it, ἐν οὕτῳ, *i.e.* in the gospel. ¶ *Is the righteousness of God* (δικαιοσύνη Θεοῦ). There is not a more important expression to be found in the epistle than this. It is capable of only the following interpretations.

(1) Some have said that it means that the *attribute* of God which is denominated *righteousness* or *justice*, is here displayed. It has been supposed that this was the design of the gospel to make this known; or to evince his *justice* in his way of saving men. There is an important sense in which this is true (chap. iii. 26). But this does not seem to be the meaning in the passage before us. For, (*a*) The leading design of the gospel is not to evince the *justice* of God, or the attribute of *justice*, but the *love* of God; see John iii. 16; Eph. ii. 4; 2 Thes. ii. 16; 1 John iv. 8. (*b*) The attribute of *justice* is not that which is principally evinced in the gospel. It is rather mercy, *or mercy in a manner consistent with justice*, or that does not interfere with justice. (*c*) The passage, therefore, is not designed to teach simply that the righteousness of God, *as an attribute*, is brought forth in the gospel, or that the main idea is to reveal his justice.

(2) A second interpretation which has been affixed to it is, to make it the same as *goodness*, the *benevolence* of God is revealed, &c. But to this there are still stronger objections. For, (*a*) It does not comport with the design of the apostle's argument. (*b*) It is a departure from the established meaning of the word *justice*, and the phrase "the righteousness of God." (*c*) If this had been the design, it is remarkable that the usual words expressive of *goodness*, or mercy had not been used. Another meaning, therefore, is to be sought as expressing the sense of the phrase.

(3) The phrase *righteousness of God* is equivalent to *God's plan of justifying men; his scheme of declaring them just in the sight of the law; or of acquitting them from punishment, and admitting them to favour.* In this sense it stands opposed to *man's* plan of justification, *i.e.* by his own works. God's plan is by faith. The *way* in which that is done is revealed in the gospel. The object contemplated to be done is to treat men as if they were righteous. Man attempted to accomplish this by obedience to the law. The plan of God was to arrive at it by *faith.* Here the two schemes differ; and the great design of this epistle is to show that man cannot be justified on his own plan, to wit, by works; and that the plan of God is the only way, and a wise and glorious way, of making man just in the eye of the law. No small part of the perplexity usually attending this subject will be avoided if it is remembered that the discussion in this epistle pertains to the question, "How can mortal man be just with God?" The apostle shows that it *cannot* be by works; and that it *can be* by faith. This *latter* is what he calls the *righteousness of God* which is revealed in the gospel.

To see that this is the meaning, it is needful only to look at the connection; and at the usual meaning of the words. The word to *justify*, δικαιόω, means properly *to be just, to be innocent, to be righteous.* It then means to *declare*, or treat as righteous; as when a man is charged with an offence, and is acquitted. If the crime alleged is not *proved* against him, he is declared by the law *to be innocent.* It then means to *treat as if innocent*, to *regard as innocent;* that is, to pardon, to forgive, and consequently to treat *as if* the offence had not occurred. It does not mean that the man *did not* commit the offence; or that the law might not have held him *answerable* for it; but that the offence is forgiven; and it is consistent to receive the offender into favour, and treat him *as if* he had not committed it. *In what way* this may be done rests with him who has the pardoning power. And in regard to the salvation of man, it rests solely with God, and must be done in that way only which he appoints and approves. The design of Paul in this epistle is to show *how* this is done, or to show that it *is* done by faith. It may be remarked here that the expression before us does not imply any particular *manner* in which it is done; it does not touch the question whether it is by imputed righteousness or not; it does not say that it is on legal principles; it simply affirms *that the gospel contains God's plan of justifying men by faith.* The primary meaning of the word is, therefore, *to be innocent, pure,* &c., and hence the name means *righteousness* in general. For this use of the word, see Mat. iii. 15; v. 6, 10, 20; xxi. 32; Luke i. 75; Acts x. 35; xiii. 10; Rom. ii. 26; viii. 4, &c.

In the sense of pardoning sin, or of treating men as if they were innocent, on the condition of faith, it is used often, and especially in this epistle; see Rom. iii. 24, 26, 28, 30; iv. 5; v. 1; viii. 30; Gal. ii. 16; iii. 8, 24; Rom. iii. 21, 22, 25; iv. 3, 6, 13; ix. 30, &c.

It is called *God's* righteousness, because it is God's plan, in distinction from all the plans set up by men. It was originated by him; it differs from all others; and it claims him as its author, and tends to his glory. It is called his *righteousness,* as it is the way by which he receives and treats men *as* righteous. The same plan was foretold in various places where the word *righteousness* is nearly synonymous with *salvation:* Isa. lvi. 5, "My righteousness is near, my salvation is gone forth;" 6, "My salvation shall be for ever, and my righteousness shall not be abolished;" Isa. lvi. 1, "My salvation is near to come, and my righteousness to be revealed;" Dan. ix. 24, "To make reconciliation for iniquity, and to bring in everlasting righteousness."

[There is yet another sense lying on the very surface of the passage, and adopted by nearly all the evangelical expositors, according to which "the righteousness of God" is that righteousness which Christ wrought out in his active and passive obedience. This is a righteousness which GOD hath devised, procured, and accepted. It is therefore eminently HIS. It is imputed to believers, and *on account of it* they are held righteous in the sight of God. It is of the highest importance that the true meaning of this leading expression be preserved, for if it be explained away the doctrine of imputed righteousness is materially affected, as will appear in a subsequent Note.

That the phrase is to be understood of the righteousness which Christ has procured by his obedience and death appears from the general sense of the original term δικαιοσύνη. Mr. Haldane, in a long and elaborate comment on Rom. iii. 21, has satisfactorily shown that it signifies "righteousness in the abstract, and also conformity to law," and that "WHEREVER it refers to the subject of man's salvation, and is not merely a personal attribute of Deity, it signifies that righteousness which, in conformity with his justice, God has appointed and provided."

Besides, if the expression be understood of "God's plan of justifying men," we shall have great difficulty in explaining the parallel passages. They will not tend to any such principle of interpretation. In chap. v. 17 this righteousness is spoken of as a "gift" which we "receive," and in the 18th and 19th verses the "righteousness of one" and "the obedience of one" are used as convertible terms. Now it is easy to understand how the righteousness which Christ has procured by his obedience becomes "a gift," but "a plan of justification" is appropriately said to be declared or promulgated. It cannot be spoken of in the light of a *gift received.* The same observation applies with still greater force to the passage in 2 Cor. v. 21, "For he hath made him to be sin for us, who knew no sin; that we might be made *the righteousness of God* in him." How would this passage appear if "plan of justification" were substituted for righteousness of God?

In Phil. iii. 9 Paul desires to be found in Christ, "not having his own righteousness, which is of the law, but that which is through the faith of Christ, the righteousness which is of God by faith." Is not his own righteousness that which he could attain to by his works or obedience, and is not the righteousness of Christ that which Jesus had procured by *his* obedience?

Lastly, in Rom. x. 3, the righteousness of God is thus opposed to the righteousness of man, "they being ignorant of *God's righteousness,* and going about to establish *their own righteousness,* have not submitted themselves to the righteousness of God." Now what is that righteousness which natural men seek to establish, and which is peculiarly called "their own?" Doubtless it is a righteousness founded on *their own works,* and therefore that which is here properly opposed to it is a righteousness founded on the *work of God.* (See Haldane, Hodge, Scott, Guyse, &c.) This meaning of the term furnishes a key to unlock *all* the passages in which it is used in connection with the sinner's justification, whereas any other sense, however it may suit a few places, will be found generally inapplicable.]

In regard to this plan it may be observed, (1) That it is not to declare that men *are* innocent and pure. That would not be true. The truth is just the reverse; and God does not esteem men to be different from what they are. (2) It is not to *take part* with the sinner, and to mitigate his offences. It admits them to their full extent; and makes *him* feel them also. (3) It is not that we become partakers of the essential righteousness of God. That is impossible. (4) It is not that *his* righteousness becomes *ours*. This is not true; and there is no intelligible sense in which that can be understood.

[It is true, indeed, that the righteousness of Christ cannot be called *ours* in the sense of our having *actually* accomplished it *in our own persons*. This is a view of imputation easily held up to ridicule, yet *there is a sense* in which the righteousness of Christ may be *ours*. Though we have not achieved it, yet it may be so placed to our account that we shall be *held righteous, and treated as such*. I have said, first, we shall be *held* righteous, and then *treated* as such. for God treats none as righteous who in some sense or other are not really so. See the Note on chap. iv. 3.]

But it is God's plan for *pardoning* sin, and for *treating us* as if we had not committed it; that is, adopting us as his children, and admitting us to heaven on the ground of what the Lord Jesus has done in our stead. This is God's plan. Men seek to save themselves by their own works. God's plan is to save them by the merits of Jesus Christ. ¶ *Revealed.* Made known, and communicated. The gospel states the *fact* that God *has* such a plan of justification; and shows the *way* or *manner* in which it might be done. The *fact* seems to have been understood by Abraham, and the patriarchs (Heb. xi.), but the full mode or manner in which it was to be accomplished, was not revealed until it was done in the gospel of Christ. And *because* this great and glorious truth was thus made known, Paul was not ashamed of the gospel. Nor should *we* be. ¶ *From faith* (ἐκ πίστεως). This phrase I take to be connected with the expression, "the righteousness of God." Thus, the righteousness of God, or God's plan of justifying men *by faith*, is revealed in the gospel. Here the great truth of the gospel is brought out, that men are justified *by faith*, and not by the deeds of the law. The common interpretation of the passage has been, that the righteousness of God in this is revealed *from one degree of faith to another.* But to this interpretation there are many objections. (1) It is not true. The gospel was not *designed* for this. It did not *suppose* that men had a certain *degree* of faith by nature which needed only to be *strengthened* in order that they might be saved. (2) It does not make good sense. To say that the righteousness of God, meaning, as is commonly understood, his *essential justice*, is *revealed* from one degree of faith to another, is to use words without any meaning. (3) The connection of the passage does not admit of this interpretation. The design of the passage is evidently to set forth the doctrine of justification as the grand theme of remark, and it does not comport with that design to introduce here the advance from one degree of faith to another, as the main topic. (4) The epistle is intended clearly to establish the fact that men are justified *by faith.* This is the grand idea which is kept up; and to show *how* this may be done is the main purpose before the apostle; see chap. iii. 22, 30; ix. 30, 32; x. 6, &c. (5) The passage which he immediately quotes shows that he did not speak of different *degrees* of faith, but of the doctrine that men are to be justified *by* faith. ¶ *To faith.* Unto those who believe (comp. chap. iii. 22); or to every one that believeth, ver. 16. The abstract is here put for the concrete. It is designed to express the idea, *that God's plan of justifying men is revealed in the gospel, which plan is by faith, and the benefits of which plan shall be extended to all that have faith, or that believe.* ¶ *As it is written.* See Hab. ii. 4. ¶ *The just shall live by faith.* The LXX.

18 For the *y* wrath of God is | revealed from heaven against all

y Ep.5.6.

translate the passage in Habakkuk, "If any man shall draw back, my soul shall have no pleasure in him; but the just by my faith," or by faith in me, "shall live." The very words are used by them which are employed by the apostle, except they add the word "my, μου," *my* faith. The Syriac renders it in a similar manner. "The just by faith shall live." The meaning of the Hebrew in Habakkuk is the same. It does not refer originally to the doctrine of justification by faith; but its meaning is this, "The just man, or the righteous man, shall live by his confidence in God." The prophet is speaking of the woes attending the Babylonish captivity. The Chaldeans were to come upon the land and destroy it, and remove the nation, chap. i. 6–10. But this was not to be perpetual. It should have an end (chap. ii. 3), and they who had confidence in God should live (ver. 4); that is, should be restored to their country, should be blessed and made happy. Their *confidence in God* should sustain them, and preserve them. This did not refer primarily to the doctrine of justification by faith, nor did the apostle so quote it, but it expressed a *general principle* that those who had confidence in God should be happy, and be preserved and blessed. This would *express* the doctrine which Paul was defending. It was not by relying on his own *merit* that the Israelite would be delivered, but it was by confidence in God, by *his* strength and mercy. On the same *principle* would men be saved under the gospel. It was not by reliance on their own works or merit; it was by *confidence* in God, by *faith*, that they were to live. ¶ *Shall live.* In Habakkuk this means to be made happy, or blessed; shall find comfort, and support, and deliverance. So in the gospel the blessings of salvation are represented as *life*, eternal life. Sin is represented as death, and man by nature is represented as dead in trespasses and sins, Eph. ii. 1. The gospel restores to *life* and salvation, John iii. 36; v. 29, 40; vi. 33, 51, 53; xx.

31; Acts ii. 28; Rom. v. 18; viii. 6.— This expression, therefore, does not mean, as it is sometimes supposed, the *justified by faith shall live*; but it is expressive of a *general principle* in relation to men, that they shall be defended, preserved, made happy, not by their own merits, or strength, but by *confidence* in God. This *principle* is exactly applicable to the gospel plan of salvation. Those who rely on God the Saviour shall be justified, and saved.

18. *For.* This word denotes that the apostle is about to give a *reason* for what he had just said. This verse commences the argument of the epistle, an argument designed to establish the proposition advanced in verse 17. The proposition is, that God's plan of justification is revealed in the gospel. To show this, it was necessary to show that all other plans had failed; and that there was need of some *new* plan or scheme to save men. To this he devotes this and the two following chapters. The design of this argument is, to show that men were sinners. And in order to make this out, it was necessary to show that they were under law. This was clear in regard to the Jews. They had the Scriptures; and the apostle in *this* chapter shows that it was equally clear in regard to the Gentiles, and *then* proceeds to show that *both* had failed of obeying the law. To see this clearly it is necessary to add only, that there can be but *two* ways of justification conceived of; one by obedience to law, and the other by grace. The former was the one by which Jews and Gentiles had sought to be justified; and if it could be shown that in this they had failed, the way was clear to show that there was need of some other plan. ¶ *The wrath of God* (ὀργὴ Θεοῦ). The word rendered *wrath* properly denotes that earnest appetite or desire by which we seek anything, or an intense effort to obtain it. And it is particularly applied to the desire which a man has to take vengeance who is injured, and who is enraged.

It is thus synonymous with revenge, Eph. iv. 31, " Let all bitterness, and *wrath*," &c.; Col. iii. 8, " Anger, *wrath*, malice," &c.; 1 Tim. ii. 8; Jam. i. 19. But it is also often applied to God; and it is clear that when we think of the word as applicable to him, it must be divested of everything like human passion, and especially of the passion of *revenge*. As he cannot be *injured* by the sins of men (Job xxv. 6-8), he has no motive for vengeance properly so called, and it is one of the most obvious rules of interpretation that we are not to apply to God passions and feelings which, among us, have their origin in evil. In making a revelation, it was indispensable to use words which men used; but it does not follow that when applied to *God* they mean *precisely* what they do when applied to *man*. When the Saviour is said (Mark iii. 5), to have looked on his disciples with *anger* (Greek, *wrath*, the same word as here), it is not to be supposed that he had the feelings of an implacable *man* seeking vengeance. The nature of the feeling is to be judged of by the character of the person. So, in this place, the word denotes the *divine displeasure* or *indignation* against sin; the divine purpose to *inflict punishment*. *It is the opposition of the divine character against sin;* and the determination of the divine mind to *express* that opposition in a proper way, by excluding the offender from the favours which he bestows on the righteous. It is not an unamiable, or arbitrary principle of conduct. We all admire the character of a father who is *opposed* to disorder, and vice, and disobedience in his family, and who *expresses* his opposition in a proper way. We admire the character of a ruler who is *opposed* to all crime in the community, and who *expresses* those feelings in the laws. And the more he is *opposed* to vice and crime, the more we admire his character and his laws; and why shall we be not equally pleased with God, who is opposed to *all* crime in all parts of the universe, and who determines to *express* it in the proper way for the sake of preserving order and promot-

ing peace? The word divine *displeasure* or *indignation*, therefore, expresses the meaning of this phrase; see Mat. iii. 7; Luke iii. 7; xxi. 23; John iii. 36; Rom. ii. 5, 8; iii. 5; iv. 15; v. 9; ix. 22; xii. 19; xiii. 4, 5; Eph. ii. 3; v. 6; 1 Thes. i. 10; ii. 16, &c. The word occurs thirty-five times in the New Testament. ¶ *Is revealed.* That is, revealed to the Jews by their law; and to the Gentiles in their reason, and conscience, as the apostle proceeds to show. ¶ *From heaven.* This expression I take to mean simply that the divine displeasure against sin is made known by a divine appointment; by an arrangement of events, communications, and arguments, which evince that they have had their origin in heaven; or are divine. How this is, Paul proceeds to state, in the works of creation, and in the law which the Hebrews had. A variety of meanings have been given to this expression, but this seems the most satisfactory. It does not mean that the wrath *will be sent* from heaven; or that the heavens *declare* his wrath; or that the heavenly bodies are proofs of his wrath against sin; or that Christ, the executioner of wrath, will be manifest from heaven (Origen, Cyril, Beza, &c.); or that it is from God *who is in heaven;* but that it is by an arrangement which shows that it had its origin in heaven, or has proofs that it is divine. ¶ *Against all ungodliness.* This word properly means *impiety* towards God, or neglect of the worship and honour due to him—ἀσέβειαν. It refers to the fact that men had failed to honour the true God, and had paid to idols the homage which was due to him. Multitudes also in every age refuse to honour him, and neglect his worship, though they are not idolaters. Many men suppose that if they do not neglect their duty to their fellow-men, if they are honest and upright in their dealings, they are not guilty, even though they are not righteous, or do not do their duty to God; as though it were a less crime to dishonour God than man; and as though it were innocence to neglect and disobey our Maker and Redeemer. The apostle here shows that the wrath of God is as really revealed against the *neglect* of God as it is against positive iniquity; and that this is an offence of so much consequence as to be placed *first*, and as deserving the divine indignation more than the neglect of our duties towards men; comp. Rom. xi. 26; 2 Tim. ii. 16; Tit. ii. 12; Jude 15, 18. The word does not elsewhere occur in the New Testament. ¶ *Unrighteousness of men.* Unrighteousness, or iniquity *towards* men. All offences against our neighbour, our parents, our country, &c. The word *ungodliness* includes all crimes against God; this, all crimes against our fellow-men. The two words express that which comprehends the violation of all the commands of God, "Thou shalt love the Lord thy God, &c., and thy neighbour as thyself," Mat. xxii. 37-40. The wrath of God is thus revealed against *all* human wickedness. ¶ *Who hold the truth.* Who *keep back*, or *restrain* the truth. The word translated *hold* here, sometimes means *to maintain, to keep, to observe* (1 Cor. vii. 30; 2 Cor. vi. 12); but it also means *to hold back, to detain, to hinder.* Luke iv. 42, "The people sought him [Jesus], and came to him, and *stayed* him" (Greek, the same as here). Philemon 13, "Whom I would have *retained* with me," &c.; 2 Thes. ii. 6, "And now ye know what *withholdeth*," &c. In this place it means also that they *held back*, or *restrained* the truth by their wickedness. ¶ *The truth.* The truth of God, in whatever way made known, and particularly, as the apostle goes on to say, that which is made known by the light of nature. The truth pertaining to his perfections, his law, &c. They *hold it back*, or restrain its influence. ¶ *In unrighteousness.* Or rather, *by* their iniquity. Their *wickedness* is the cause why *the truth* had had so little progress among them, and had exerted so little influence. This was done by their yielding to corrupt passions and propensities, and by their being therefore unwilling to retain the knowledge of a pure and holy God, who is opposed to such deeds, and who will punish

them. As they were determined to *practise* iniquity, they chose to exclude the knowledge of a pure God, and to worship impure idols, by which they might give a sanction to their lusts. Their vice and tendency to iniquity was, therefore, the reason why they had so little knowledge of a holy God; and by the love of this, they *held back* the truth from making progress, and becoming diffused among them.

The same thing is substantially true now. Men hold back or resist the truth of the gospel by their sins in the following ways. (1) Men of influence and wealth employ both in directly opposing the gospel. (2) Men directly resist the *doctrines* of religion, since they know they could not hold to those doctrines without abandoning their sins. (3) Men who resolve to live in sin, of course, resist the gospel, and endeavour to prevent its influence. (4) Pride and vanity, and the love of the world also resist the gospel, and oppose its advances. (5) Unlawful business—business that begins in evil, and progresses, and ends in evil—has this tendency to hold back the gospel. Such is the effect of the traffic in ardent spirits, in the slave-trade, &c. They begin in the love of money, the root of all evil (1 Tim. vi. 10); they progress in the tears and sorrows of the widow, the orphan, the wife, the sister, or the child; and they end in the deep damnation of multitudes in the world to come. Perhaps there has been nothing that has so much *held back* the influence of truth, and of the gospel, as indulgence in the vice of intemperance, and traffic in liquid fire. (6) Indulgence in vice, or wickedness of *any kind*, holds back the truth of God. Men who are resolved to indulge their passions *will not* yield themselves to this truth. And hence all the wicked, the proud, and vain, and worldly are responsible, not only for their own sins directly, but for hindering, by their example and their crimes, the effect of religion on others. They are answerable for standing in the way of God and his truth; and for *opposing* him in the

ungodliness, and unrighteousness of men, who hold the truth in unrighteousness:

19 Because that which may be

benevolent design of doing good to all men. There is nothing that prevents the universal spread and influence of truth but sin. And men of wickedness are answerable for all the ignorance and woe which are spread over the community, and which have extended themselves over the world.

19. *Because.* The apostle proceeds to show *how* it was that the heathen hindered the truth by their iniquity. This he does by showing that the truth *might* be known by the works of creation; and that nothing but their iniquity prevented it. ¶ *That which may be known of God.* That which is *knowable* concerning God. The expression implies that there may be many things concerning God which cannot be known. But there are also many things which may be ascertained. Such are his existence, and many of his attributes, his power, and wisdom, and justice, &c. The object of the apostle was not to say that *everything* pertaining to God could be known by them, or that they could have as clear a view of him as if they had possessed a revelation. We must interpret the expression according to the object which he had in view. That was to show that so much might be known of God as to prove that they had *no excuse* for their crimes; or that God would be just in punishing them for their deeds. For this, it was needful only that his existence and his justice, or his determination to punish sin, should be known; and this, the apostle affirms, *was* known among them, and had been from the creation of the world. This expression, therefore, is not to be pressed as implying that they knew *all* that *could* be known about God, or that they knew as much as they who had a revelation; but that they knew enough to prove that they had no excuse for their sins. ¶ *Is manifest.* Is known; is understood. ¶ *In them.* *Among* them. So the preposition *in* is often

known of God is manifest [6]in them; for [z]God hath showed *it* unto them.

20 For the invisible things of

6 or, *to.*   z Jn.1.9.

used. It means that they *had* this knowledge; or it had been communicated to them. The great mass of the heathen world was indeed ignorant of the true God; but their leaders, or their philosophers, *had* this knowledge; see Note on ver. 21. But this was not true of the mass, or body of the people. Still it was true that this knowledge was in the possession of man, or was *among* the pagan world, and would have spread, had it not been for the love of sin. ¶ *God hath showed* it *unto them.* Comp. John i. 9. He had endowed them with reason and conscience (chap. ii. 14, 15); he had made them capable of seeing and investigating his works; he had spread before them the proofs of his wisdom, and goodness, and power, and had thus given them the *means* of learning his perfections and will.

20. *For the invisible things of him.* The expression "his invisible things" refers to those things which cannot be perceived by the senses. It does not imply that there *are* any things pertaining to the divine character which *may* be seen by the eye; but that there are things which may be known of him, though not discoverable by the eye. We judge of the objects around us by the senses, the sight, the touch, the ear, &c. Paul affirms, that though we cannot judge thus of God, yet there *is* a way by which we may come to the knowledge of him. What he means by the *invisible* things of God he specifies at the close of the verse, *his eternal power and Godhead.* The affirmation extends only to that; and the argument implies that that was enough to leave them without any excuse for their sins. ¶ *From the creation of the world.* The word *creation* may either mean the *act* of creating, or more commonly it means *the thing created,* the world, the universe. In this sense it is commonly used in the New Testament; comp.

him from the creation of the world are clearly seen, being understood by *a* the things that are made,

a Ps.19.1,&c.

even his eternal power and Godhead : [7] so that they are without excuse.

[7] or, *that they may be.*

Mark x. 6; xiii. 19; xvi. 5; Rom. i. 25; 2 Cor. v. 17; Gal. vi. 15; Col. i. 15, 23; Heb. iv. 13; ix. 11; 1 Pet. ii. 13; 2 Pet. iii. 4; Rev. iii. 14. The word "from" may mean *since,* or it may denote *by means of.* And the expression here may denote that, as an historical fact, God *has been* known *since* the act of creation; or it may denote that he is known *by means of* the material universe which he has formed. The latter is doubtless the true meaning. For, (1) This is the common meaning of the word *creation;* and, (2) This accords with the design of the argument. It is not to state an *historical fact,* but to show that they had the means of knowing their duty within their reach, and were without excuse. Those means were in the wisdom, power, and glory of the universe, by which they were surrounded. ¶ *Are clearly seen.* Are made manifest; or may be perceived. The word used here does not occur elsewhere in the New Testament. ¶ *Being understood.* His perfections may be investigated, and comprehended by means of his works. They are the *evidences* submitted to our intellects, by which we may arrive at the true knowledge of God. ¶ *Things that are made.* By his works; comp. Heb. xi. 3. This means, not by the original *act* of creation, but by the continual operations of God in his providence, by his *doings,* ποιήμασι, by what he is continually producing and accomplishing in the displays of his power and goodness in the heavens and the earth. What they were capable of understanding he immediately adds, and shows that he did not intend to affirm that *every* thing could be known of God by his works; but so much as to free them from excuse for their sins. ¶ *His eternal power.* Here are two things implied. (1) That the universe contains an exhibition of his *power,* or a display of that attribute which we

call *omnipotence;* and, (2) That this power has existed from eternity, and of course implies an eternal existence in God. It does not mean that this power has been exerted or put forth *from eternity,* for the very idea of *creation* supposes that it had not, but that there is proof, in the works of creation, of power which must have *existed* from eternity, or have belonged to an eternal being. The proof of this was clear, even to the heathen, with their imperfect views of creation and of astronomy; comp. Ps. xix. The majesty and grandeur of the heavens would strike their eye, and be full demonstration that they were the work of an infinitely great and glorious God. But to us, under the full blaze of modern science, with our knowledge of the magnitude, and distances, and revolutions of the heavenly bodies, the proof of this *power* is much more grand and impressive. *We* may apply the remark of the apostle to the present state of the science, and his language will cover all the ground, and the proof to human view is continually rising of the amazing power of God, by every new discovery in science, and especially in astronomy. Those who wish to see this object presented in a most impressive view, may find it done in Chalmers' *Astronomical Discourses,* and in Dick's *Christian Philosopher.* Equally clear is the proof that this power must have been *eternal.* If it had not *always* existed, it could in no way have been produced. But it is not to be supposed that it was *always exerted,* any more than it is that God *now* puts forth *all* the power that he *can,* or than that *we* constantly put forth all the power which we possess. God's power was *called forth* at the creation. He *showed* his omnipotence; and gave, by that one great act, eternal demonstration that he was almighty; and we may survey the *proof* of that, as clearly as if we had *seen* the operation of his hand

21 Because that, when they knew God, they glorified *him* not as God, neither were thankful, but became *b* vain in their imaginations,

b Je.2.5; Ep.4.17,18.

there. The proof is not weakened because we do not see the process of creation constantly going on. It is rather augmented by the fact that he *sustains* all things, and controls continually the vast masses of matter in the material worlds. ¶ *Godhead.* His deity; divinity; divine nature, or essence. The word is not elsewhere used in the New Testament. Its meaning cannot therefore be fixed by any parallel passages. It proves the truth that the *supremacy*, or supreme divinity of God, was exhibited in the works of creation, or that he was exalted above all creatures and things. It would not be proper, however, to *press* this word as implying that all that we know of God by revelation was known to the heathen; but that so much was known as to show his supremacy, his right to their homage, and of course the folly and wickedness of idolatry. This is all that the argument of the apostle demands, and, of course, on this principle the expression is to be interpreted. ¶ *So that they are without excuse.* God has given them so clear evidence of his existence and claims, that they have no excuse for their idolatry, and for hindering the truth by their iniquity. It is implied here that in order that men should be responsible, they should have the means of knowledge; and that he does not judge them when their ignorance is involuntary, and the means of knowing the truth have not been communicated. But where men *have* these means within their reach, and will not avail themselves of them, all excuse is taken away. This was the case with the Gentile world. They *had* the means of knowing *so much* of God, as to show the folly of worshipping dumb idols; comp. Isa. xliv. 8–20. They had also *traditions* respecting his perfections; and they could not plead for their crimes and folly that they had no means of knowing him. If this was true of the pagan world then, how much more is it true of the world now? And especially how true and fearful is this, respecting that great multitude in Christian lands who have the Bible, and who never read it; who are within the reach of the sanctuary, and never enter it; who are admonished by friends, and by the providences of God, and who regard it not; and who look upon the heavens, and *even yet* see no proof of the eternal power and Godhead of him who made them all! Nay, there are those who are apprised of the discoveries of modern astronomy, and who yet do not seem to reflect that all these glories are proof of the existence of an eternal God; and who live in ignorance of religion as really as the heathen, and in crimes as decided and malignant as disgraced the darkest ages of the world. For such there is no excuse, or shadow of excuse, to be offered in the day of doom. And there is no fact more melancholy in our history, and no one thing that more proves the stupidity of men, than this sad forgetfulness of Him that made the heavens, even amid all the wonders and glories that have come fresh from the hand of God, and that everywhere speak his praise.

21. *Because that.* The apostle here is showing that it was right to condemn men for their sins. To do this it was needful to show them that they *had* the knowledge of God, and the means of knowing what was right; and that the true source of their sins and idolatries was a corrupt and evil heart. ¶ *When they knew God.* Greek, *knowing God.* That is, they had an acquaintance with the existence and many of the perfections of one God. That many of the philosophers of Greece and Rome had a knowledge of one God, there can be no doubt. This was undoubtedly the case with Pythagoras, who had travelled extensively in Egypt, and even in Palestine; and also with Plato and his disciples. This point is clearly shown by Cudworth in his *Intellectual System,* and by Bishop Warburton in the *Divine Legation of Moses.* Yet the knowledge of this great truth was not

communicated to the people. It was confined to the philosophers; and not improbably one design of the *mysteries* celebrated throughout Greece was to keep up the knowledge of the one true God. Gibbon has remarked that "the philosophers regarded all the popular superstitions as equally false; the common people as equally true; and the politicians as equally useful." This was probably a correct account of the prevalent feelings among the ancients. A single extract from Cicero (*de Natura Deorum*, lib. ii. c. 6) will show that they *had* the knowledge of one God. "There is something in the nature of things, which the mind of man, which reason, which human power cannot effect; and certainly that which produces this must be better than man. What can this be called but *God?*" Again (c. 2), "What can be so plain and manifest, when we look at heaven, and contemplate heavenly things, as that there is some divinity of most excellent mind, by which these things are governed?" ¶ *They glorified* him *not as God.* They did not *honour* him as God. This was the true source of their abominations. To glorify him *as God* is to regard with proper reverence all his perfections and laws; to venerate his name, his power, his holiness, and presence, &c. As they were not *inclined* to do this, so they were given over to their own vain and wicked desires. Sinners are not willing to give honour to God, *as God.* They are not pleased with his perfections; and therefore the mind becomes fixed on other objects, and the heart gives free indulgence to its own sinful desires. A willingness to honour God as God—to reverence, love, and obey him, would effectually restrain men from sin. ¶ *Neither were thankful.* The obligation to be *thankful* to God for his mercies, for the goodness which we experience, is plain and obvious. Thus we judge of favours received of our fellow-men. The apostle here clearly regards this unwillingness to render *gratitude* to God for his mercies as one of the causes of their subsequent corruption and idolatry. The reasons of this are the following. (1) The effect of *ingratitude* is to render the heart hard and insensible. (2) Men seek to *forget* the Being to whom they are unwilling to exercise gratitude. (3) To do this, they fix their affections on other things; and hence the heathen expressed their gratitude not to God, but to the sun, and moon, and stars, &c., the *mediums* by which God bestows his favours on men. And we may here learn that an unwillingness to thank *God* for his mercies is one of the most certain causes of alienation and hardness of heart. ¶ *But became vain.* To *become vain,* with us, means to be elated, or to be self-conceited, or to seek praise from others. The meaning here seems to be, they became foolish, frivolous in their thoughts and reasonings. They acted foolishly; they employed themselves in useless and frivolous questions, the effect of which was to lead the mind farther and farther from the truth respecting God. ¶ *Imaginations.* This word means properly *thoughts,* then *reasonings,* and also *disputations.* Perhaps our word *speculations* would convey its meaning here. It implies that they were unwilling to honour God, and *being* unwilling to honour him, they commenced *those speculations* which resulted in all their vain and foolish opinions about idols, and the various rites of idolatrous worship. Many of the speculations and inquiries of the ancients were among the most vain and senseless which the mind can conceive. ¶ *And their foolish heart.* The word *heart* is not unfrequently used to denote the *mind,* or the *understanding.* We apply it to denote the *affections.* But such was not its common use among the Hebrews. We speak of the *head* when we refer to the understanding, but this was not the case with the Hebrews. They spoke of the *heart* in this manner, and in this sense it is clearly used in this place; see Eph. i. 18; Rom. ii. 15; 2 Cor. iv. 6; 2 Pet. i. 19. The word *foolish* means literally that which is without *understanding,* Mat. xv. 16. ¶ *Was darkened.* Was rendered

and their foolish heart was darkened:

22 Professing themselves to be wise, *c*they became fools,

23 And changed the glory of

c Je.8.8,9.

the uncorruptible God into *d*an image like to corruptible man, and to birds, and four-footed beasts, and creeping things.

24 Wherefore *e*God also gave

d Is.40.18,26; Eze.8.10.　　*e* Ps.81.12; 2 Th.2.11.

---

obscure, so that they did not perceive and comprehend the truth. The process which is stated in this verse is, (1) That men had the knowledge of God. (2) That they refused to *honour* him when they knew him, and were *opposed* to his character and government. (3) That they were ungrateful. (4) That they then began to doubt, to reason, to speculate, and wandered far into darkness. This is substantially the process by which men wander away from God now. They *have* the knowledge of God, but they do not love him; and being dissatisfied with his character and government, they begin to speculate, fall into error, and then "find no end in wandering mazes lost," and sink into the depths of heresy and of sin.

22. *Professing themselves to be wise.* This was the common boast of the *philosophers* of antiquity. The very word by which they chose to be called, *philosophers*, means literally *lovers of wisdom.* That it was their *boast* that they were wise, is well known; comp. chap. i. 14; 1 Cor. i. 19, 20–22; iii. 19; 2 Cor. xi. 19. ¶ *They became fools.* Comp. Jer. viii. 8, 9. They became really foolish in their opinions and conduct. There is something particularly pungent and cutting in this remark, and as true as it is pungent. In what way they *evinced* their folly, Paul proceeds immediately to state. Sinners of all kinds are frequently spoken of as fools in the Scriptures. In the sense in which it is thus used, the word is applied to them as void of understanding or moral sense; as idolaters, and as wicked, Ps. xiv. 1; Prov. xxvi. 4; i. 17, 22; xiv. 8, 9. The senses in which this word here is applied to the heathen are, (1) That their speculations and doctrines were senseless; and (2) That their conduct was corrupt.

23. *And changed.* This does not mean that they literally *transmuted* God himself; but that in their views they exchanged him; or they changed him *as an object of worship* for idols. They produced, of course, no *real* change in the glory of the infinite God, but the *change* was in themselves. They *forsook* him of whom they had knowledge (ver. 21), and offered the homage which was due to him, to idols. ¶ *The glory.* The majesty, the honour, &c. This word stands opposed here to the *degrading* nature of their worship. Instead of adoring a Being clothed with *majesty* and *honour*, they bowed down to reptiles, &c. They exchanged a *glorious* object of worship for that which was degrading and humiliating. The *glory* of God, in such places as this, means his essential *honour*, his *majesty*, the concentration and expression of his perfections, as the *glory of the sun* (1 Cor. xv. 41) means his shining, or his splendour; comp. Jer. ii. 11; Ps. cvi. 20. ¶ *The uncorruptible God.* The word *uncorruptible* is here applied to God in opposition to *man.* God is unchanging, indestructible, immortal. The word conveys also the idea that God is eternal. As he is incorruptible, he is the proper object of worship. In all the changes of life, man may come to him, assured that he is the same. When man decays by age or infirmities, he may come to God, assured that *he* undergoes no such change, but is the same yesterday, to-day, and for ever; comp. 1 Tim. i. 17. ¶ *Into an image.* An image is a representation or likeness of anything, whether made by painting, or from wood, stone, &c. Thus the word is applied to *idols*, as being *images* or *representations* of heavenly objects, 2 Chron. xxxiii. 7; Dan. iii. 1; Rev. xi. 4, &c. See instances of this among the

them up to uncleanness through the lusts of their own hearts, to

dishonour their own bodies between themselves:

Jews described in Isa. xl. 18–26, and Ezek. viii. 10. ¶ *To corruptible man.* This stands opposed to the *incorruptible* God. Many of the images or idols of the ancients were in the forms of men and women. Many of their gods were heroes and benefactors, who were *deified*, and to whom temples, altars, and statues were erected. Such were Jupiter, and Hercules, and Romulus, &c. The worship of these *heroes* thus constituted no small part of their idolatry, and their *images* would be, of course, representations of them in human form. It was proof of great degradation, that they thus adored *men* with like passions as themselves; and attempted to *displace* the true God from the throne, and to substitute in his place an idol in the likeness of men. ¶ *And to birds.* The *ibis* was adored with peculiar reverence among the Egyptians, on account of the great benefits resulting from its destroying the *serpents* which, but for this, would have overrun the country. The *hawk* was also adored in Egypt, and the *eagle* at Rome. As one great principle of pagan idolatry was to adore all objects from which important benefits were derived, it is probable that all *birds* would come in for a share of pagan worship, that rendered service in the destruction of noxious animals. ¶ *And four-footed beasts.* Thus the ox, under the name *Apis*, was adored in Egypt; and even the dog and the monkey. In imitation of the Egyptian ox, the children of Israel made their golden calf, Ex. xxii. 4. At this day, two of the most sacred objects of worship in Hindostan are the cow and the *monkey.* ¶ *And creeping things.* Reptiles. "Animals that have no feet, or such short ones that they seem to creep or crawl on the ground" (Calmet). Lizards, serpents, &c., come under this description. The *crocodile* in Egypt was an object of adoration, and even the serpent. So late as the second century of the Christian era, there was a sect in Egypt called

Ophites from their worshipping a serpent, and who even claimed to be Christians (Murdock's *Mosheim*, vol. i. p. 180, 181). There was scarcely an object, animal or vegetable, which the Egyptians did not adore. Thus the *leek*, the *onion*, &c., were objects of worship, and men bowed down and paid adoration to the sun and moon, to animals, to vegetables, and to reptiles. Egypt was the source of the views of religion that pervaded other nations, and hence their worship partook of the same wretched and degrading character. See Leland's *Advantage and Necessity of Revelation.*

24. *Wherefore.* That is, because they were unwilling to retain him in their knowledge, and chose to worship idols. Here is traced the practical tendency of heathenism; not as an *innocent* and *harmless* system, but as resulting in the most gross and shameless acts of depravity. ¶ *God gave them up.* He abandoned them, or he ceased to restrain them, and suffered them to *act out* their sentiments, and to manifest them in their life. This does not imply that he exerted any *positive* influence in inducing them to sin, any more than it would if we should seek, by argument and entreaty, to restrain a headstrong youth, and when neither would prevail, should *leave him to act out* his propensities, and to go as he chose to ruin. It is implied in this, (1) That the tendency of *man* was to these sins; (2) That the tendency of *idolatry* was to promote them; and (3) That all that was needful, in order that men should commit them, was for God to leave him to follow the devices and desires of his own heart; comp. Ps. lxxxi. 12; 2 Thes. ii. 10, 12. ¶ *To uncleanness.* To impurity, or moral defilement; particularly to those impurities which he proceeds to specify, ver. 26, &c. ¶ *Through the lusts of their own hearts.* Or, in consequence of their own evil and depraved passions and desires. He left them to act out, or manifest, their depraved affections and

25 Who *changed the truth of God into a lie, and worshipped and served the creature [8]more

f Am.2.4.

than the Creator, who is blessed for ever. Amen.

26 For this cause God gave

[8] or, *rather.*

---

inclinations. ¶ *To dishonour.* To disgrace, ver. 26, 27. ¶ *Between themselves.* Among themselves; or mutually. They did it by unlawful and impure connections with one another.

25. *Who changed the truth of God.* This is a repetition of the declaration in ver. 23, in another form. The phrase, "the truth of God" is a Hebrew phrase, meaning *the true God.* In such a case, where two nouns come together, one is employed as an adjective to qualify the other. Most commonly the latter of two nouns is used as the adjective, but sometimes it is the former, as in this case. God is called the *true God* in opposition to idols, which are called false gods. There is but one *real* or *true* God, and all others are false. ¶ *Into a lie.* Into *idols,* or false gods. Idols are not unfrequently called *falsehood* and *lies,* because they are not true representations of God, Jer. xiii. 25; Isa. xxviii. 15; Jer. x. 14; Ps. xl. 4. ¶ *The creature.* Created things, as the sun, moon, animals, &c. ¶ *Who is blessed for ever.* It was not uncommon to add a *doxology,* or ascription of praise to God, when his name was mentioned; see Rom. ix. 5; 2 Cor. xi. 31; Gal. i. 5. The Jews also usually did it. In this way they preserved veneration for the name of God, and accustomed themselves to speak of him with reverence. "The Mahometans also borrowed this custom from the Jews, and practise it to a great extent. Tholuck mentions an Arabic manuscript in the library at Berlin which contains an account of heresies in respect to Islamism, and as often as the writer has occasion to mention the name of a new heretical sect, he adds, 'God be exalted above all which they say'" (Stuart). ¶ *Amen.* This is a Hebrew word denoting strong affirmation. So let it be. It implies here the solemn assent of the writer to what was just

said; or his strong wish that what he had said might be—that the name of God might be esteemed and be blessed for ever. The mention of the degrading idolatry of the heathens was strongly calculated to impress on his mind the superior excellency and glory of the one living God. It is mentioned respecting the honourable Robert Boyle, that he never *mentioned* the name of God without a solemn pause, denoting his profound reverence. Such a practice would tend eminently to prevent an unholy familiarity and irreverence in regard to the sacred name of the Most High; comp. Exod. xx. 7.

26. *For this cause.* On account of what had just been specified; to wit, that they did not glorify him as God, that they were unthankful, that they became polytheists and idolaters. In the previous verses he had stated their *speculative belief.* He now proceeds to show its practical influences on their conduct. ¶ *Vile affections.* Disgraceful passions or desires. That is, to those which are immediately specified. The great object of the apostle here, it will be remembered, is to show the state of the heathen world, and to prove that they had need of some other way of justification than the law of nature. For this purpose, it was necessary for him to enter into a detail of their sins. The sins which he proceeds to specify are the most indelicate, vile, and degrading which can be charged on man. But this is not the fault of the apostle. If they *existed,* it was necessary for him to charge them on the pagan world. His argument would not be complete without it. The shame is not in *specifying* them, but in *their existence;* not in the apostle, but in those who practised them, and imposed on him the necessity of accusing them of these enormous offences. It may be further remarked, that the *mere fact* of his charging them with these sins is strong

them up unto *g*vile affections: for even their women did change the natural use into that which is against nature:

27 And likewise also the men,

g Ep.5.12; Jude 10.

leaving the natural use of the woman, burned in their lust one toward another; men with men working that which is unseemly, and receiving in themselves that

---

presumptive proof of their being practised. If they did *not* exist, it would be easy for them to *deny it*, and *put him to the proof of it*. No man would venture charges like these without evidence; and the presumption is, that these things were known and practised without shame. But this is not all. There is still abundant proof on record in the writings of the heathen themselves, that these crimes were known and extensively practised. ¶ *For even their women*, &c. Evidence of the shameful and disgraceful fact here charged on the women is abundant in the Greek and Roman writers. Proof may be seen, which it would not be proper to specify, in the lexicons, under the words τριϐὰς, ὄλισϐον, and ἑταιρίστης. See also Seneca, epis. 95; Martial, epis. i. 90. Tholuck on the State of the Heathen World, in the *Biblical Repository*, vol. ii. ; Lucian, *Dial. Meretric.* v.; and Tertullian *de Pallio*.

27. *And likewise the men*, &c. The sin which is here specified is that which was the shameful sin of Sodom, and which from that has been called *sodomy*. It would scarcely be credible that man had been guilty of a crime so base and so degrading, unless there was ample and full testimony to it. Perhaps there is no sin which so deeply shows the depravity of man as this; none which would so much induce one "to hang his head, and *blush* to think himself a man." And yet the evidence that the apostle did not bring a *railing accusation* against the heathen world, that he did not advance a charge which was unfounded, is too painfully clear. It has been indeed a matter of controversy whether *pœderasty*, or the love of boys, among the ancients was not a pure and harmless love, but the evidence is against it. (See this discussed in Dr. Leland's *Advantage and Necessity of Revela-*

tion, vol. i. 49–56.) The crime with which the apostle charges the Gentiles here was by no means confined to the *lower* classes of the people. It doubtless pervaded *all* classes, and we have distinct specifications of its existence in a great number of cases. Even Virgil speaks of the attachment of Corydon to Alexis, without seeming to feel the necessity of a blush for it. Maximus Tyrius (Diss. 10) says, that in the time of Socrates this vice was common among the Greeks, and is at pains to vindicate *Socrates* from it as almost a solitary exception. Cicero (*Tuscul. Ques.* iv. 34) says, that " Dicearchus had accused *Plato* of it, and probably not *unjustly*." He also says (*Tuscul. Q.* iv. 33), that the practice was common among the Greeks, and that their poets and great men, and even their learned men and philosophers, not only practised, but gloried in it. And he adds, that it was the custom, not of particular cities only, but of Greece in general (*Tuscul. Ques.* v. 20). Xenophon says, that " the unnatural love of boys is so common, that in many places it is established by the public laws." He particularly alludes to Sparta. (See Leland's *Advantage*, &c. i. 56.) Plato says that the *Cretans* practised this crime, and justified themselves by the example of Jupiter and Ganymede (*Book of Laws*, i.). And Aristotle says, that among the Cretans there was a law encouraging that sort of unnatural love (Arist. *Politic.* b. ii. chap. 10). Plutarch says, that this was practised at Thebes, and at Elis. He further says, that *Solon*, the great lawgiver of Athens, "was not proof against beautiful boys, and had not courage to resist the force of love " (*Life of Solon*). Diogenes Laertius says that this vice was practised by the Stoic Zeno. Among the Romans, to whom Paul was writing, this vice

recompense of their error which was meet.

28 And even as they did not

9 *or, to acknowledge.*

was no less common. Cicero introduces, without any mark of disapprobation, *Cotta*, a man of the first rank and genius, freely and familiarly owning to other Romans of the same quality, that this worse than beastly vice was practised by himself, and quoting the authority of ancient philosophers in vindication of it (*De Natura Deorum*, b. i. chap. 28). It appears from what Seneca says (epis. 95), that in his time it was practised openly at Rome, and without shame. He speaks of flocks and troops of boys, distinguished by their colours and nations; and says that great care was taken to train them up for this detestable employment. Those who may wish to see a further account of the *morality* in the pagan world may find it detailed in Tholuck's "Nature and Moral Influence of Heathenism," in the *Biblical Repository*, vol. ii., and in Leland's *Advantage and Necessity of the Christian Revelation.* There is not the least evidence that this abominable vice was *confined* to Greece and Rome. If so common there, if it had the sanction even of their philosophers, it may be presumed that it was practised elsewhere, and that the sin against nature was a common crime throughout the heathen world. Navaratte, in his account of the empire of China (book ii. chap. 6), says that it is extremely common among the Chinese. And there is every reason to believe that, both in the Old World and the New, this abominable crime is still practised. If such was the state of the pagan world, then surely the argument of the apostle is well sustained, that there was need of some other plan of salvation than was taught by the light of nature. ¶ *That which is unseemly.* That which is shameful, or disgraceful. ¶ *And receiving in themselves*, &c. The meaning of this doubtless is, that the effect of such base and unnatural passions was, to enfeeble the body, to produce prema-

like 9 to retain God in *their* knowledge, God gave them over to 1 a reprobate mind, to do

1 *or, a mind void of judgment.*

ture old age, disease, decay, and an early death. That this is the effect of the indulgence of licentious passions, is amply proved by the history of man. The despots who practise polygamy, and keep harems in the East, are commonly superannuated at forty years of age; and it is well known, even in Christian countries, that the effect of licentious indulgence is to break down and destroy the constitution. How much more might this be expected to follow the practice of the vice specified in the verse under examination! God has marked the indulgence of licentious passions with his frown. Since the time of the Romans and the Greeks, as if there had not been sufficient restraints before, he has originated a new disease, which is one of the most loathsome and distressing which has ever afflicted man, and which has swept off millions of victims. But the effect on the body was not all. It tended to debase the mind; to sink man below the level of the brute; to destroy the sensibility; and to "sear the conscience as with a hot iron." The last remnant of reason and conscience, it would seem, must be extinguished in those who would indulge in this unnatural and degrading vice. See Suetonius' *Life of Nero*, 28.

28. *And even as they did not like*, &c. This was the true source of their crimes. They did not *choose* to acknowledge God. It was not because they *could not*, but because they were *displeased* with God, and chose to forsake him, and follow their own passions and lusts. ¶ *To retain God*, &c. To think of him, or to serve and adore him. This was the *first step* in their sin. It was not that God *compelled* them; or that he did not give them knowledge; nor even is it said that he arbitrarily abandoned them as the first step; but they forsook *him*, and as a consequence he gave them up to a reprobate mind. ¶ *To a reprobate mind.* A mind destitute of judgment.

those things which are not convenient;

29 Being filled with all un-

In the Greek the same word is used here, which, in another form, occurs in the previous part of the verse, and which is translated "like." The apostle meant doubtless to retain a reference to that in this place. "As they did not *approve*, ἐδοκιμασαν, or choose to retain God, &c., he gave them up to a mind *disapproved, rejected*, reprobate," ἀδοκιμον; and he means that the state of their minds was such that God could not *approve* it. It does not mean that they were *reprobate* by any arbitrary decree; but that, *as a consequence* of their headstrong passions, their determination to *forget* him, he left them to a state of mind which was *evil*, and which he could not *approve*. ¶ *Which are not convenient*. Which are not fit or proper; which are disgraceful and shameful; to wit, those things which he proceeds to state in the remainder of the chapter.

29. *Being filled*. That is, the things which he specifies were *common* or *abounded* among them. This is a strong phrase, denoting that these things were so often practised as that it might be said they were *full of them*. We have a phrase like this still, when we say of one that he is *full of mischief*,&c. ¶ *Unrighteousness*(ἀδικια). This is a word denoting *injustice*, or iniquity in general. The particular specifications of the iniquity follow. ¶ *Fornication*. This was a common and almost universal sin among the ancients, as it is among the moderns. The word denotes *all illicit intercourse*. That this was a common crime among the ancient heathen, it would be easy to show, were it proper, even in relation to their wisest and most learned men. They who wish to see ample evidence of this charge may find it in Tholuck's "Nature and Moral Influence of Heathenism," in the *Biblical Repository*, vol. ii. p. 441–464. ¶ *Wickedness*. The word used here denotes *a desire of injuring others;* or, as we should express it, *malice*. It is that depravity and obli-

righteousness, fornication, wickedness, covetousness, maliciousness; full of envy, murder, de-

quity of mind which strives to produce injury on others (Calvin). ¶ *Covetousness*. Avarice, or the desire of obtaining that which belongs to others. This vice is common in the world; but it would be particularly so where the other vices enumerated here abounded, and men were desirous of luxury, and the gratification of their senses. Rome was particularly desirous of the wealth of other nations, and hence its extended wars, and the various evils of rapine and conquest. ¶ *Licentiousness* (κακια). This word denotes evil in general; rather the *act* of doing wrong than the *desire*, which was expressed before by the word *wickedness*. ¶ *Full of envy*. "Pain, uneasiness, mortification, or discontent, excited by another's prosperity, accompanied with some degree of hatred or malignity, and often with a desire or an effort to depreciate the person, and with pleasure in seeing him depressed" (Webster). This passion is so common still, that it is not necessary to attempt to prove that it was common among the ancients. It seems to be natural to the human heart. It is one of the most common manifestations of wickedness, and shows clearly the deep depravity of man. Benevolence rejoices at the happiness of others, and seeks to promote it. But envy exists almost everywhere, and in almost every human bosom:

"All human virtue, to its latest breath,
Finds *envy* never conquered but by death."
POPE.

¶ *Murder*. "The taking of human life with premeditated malice by a person of a sane mind." This is necessary to constitute murder now, but the word used here denotes all manslaughter, or taking human life, except that which occurs as the punishment of crime. It is scarcely necessary to show that this was common among the Gentiles. It has prevailed in all communities, but it was particularly prevalent in Rome. It is necessary only to refer the reader to the com-

bate, deceit, malignity; whisperers,
30 Backbiters, haters of God,

despiteful; proud, boasters, inventors of evil things, disobedient to parents,

mon events in the Roman history of assassinations, deaths by poison, and the destruction of slaves. But in a special manner the charge was properly alleged against them, on account of the inhuman contests of the gladiators in the amphitheatres. These were common at Rome, and constituted a favourite amusement with the people. Originally captives, slaves, and criminals were trained up for combat; but it afterwards became common for even Roman citizens to engage in these bloody combats, and Nero at one show exhibited no less than four hundred senators and six hundred knights as gladiators. The fondness for this bloody spectacle continued till the reign of Constantine the Great, *the first Christian emperor*, by whom they were abolished about six hundred years after the original institution. "Several hundred, perhaps several thousand, victims were annually slaughtered in the great cities of the empire" (Gibbon's *Decline and Fall*, chap. xxx. A.D. 404). As an instance of what *might* occur in this inhuman spectacle, we may refer to what took place on such an occasion in the reign of Probus (A.D. 281). During his triumph, near *seven hundred* gladiators were reserved to shed each other's blood for the amusement of the Roman people. But "disdaining to shed their blood for the amusement of the populace, they killed their keepers, broke from their place of confinement, and filled the streets of Rome with blood and confusion" (Gibbon's *Decline and Fall*, chap. xii.). With such views and with such spectacles before them, it is not wonderful that *murder* was regarded as a matter of little consequence, and hence *this* crime prevailed throughout the world. ¶ *Debate.* Our word *debate* does not commonly imply evil. It denotes commonly *discussion* for elucidating truth; or for maintaining a proposition, as the *debates* in Parliament, &c. But the word in the original meant also *contention, strife*, altercation, connected with anger and

heated zeal, Rom. xiii. 13; 1 Cor. i. 11; iii. 3; 2 Cor. xii. 20; Gal. v. 20; Phil. i. 15; 1 Tim. vi. 4; Tit. iii. 9. This contention and strife would, of course, follow from malice and covetousness, &c. ¶ *Deceit.* This denotes *fraud, falsehood*, &c. That this was common is also plain. The *Cretans* are testified by one of the Greek poets to have been always liars, Tit. i. 12. Juvenal charges the same thing on the Romans (*Sat.* iii. 41). "What," says he, "should I do at Rome? *I cannot lie.*" Intimating that if he were there, it would follow, of course, that he would be expected to be false. The same thing is still true. Writers on India tell us that the word of a Hindoo, even under oath, is not to be regarded; and the same thing occurs in most pagan countries. ¶ *Malignity.* This word signifies here, not malignity in general, but that particular species of it which consists in misinterpreting the words or actions of others, or putting the worst construction on their conduct. ¶ *Whisperers.* Those who secretly, and in a sly manner, by hints and innuendoes, detract from others, or excite suspicion of them. It does not mean those who *openly calumniate*, but that more dangerous class who give *hints* of evil in others, who affect great knowledge, and communicate the evil report under an injunction of secrecy, knowing that it will be divulged. This class of people abounds everywhere, and there is scarcely anyone more dangerous to the peace or happiness of society.

30. *Backbiters.* Those who calumniate, slander, or speak ill of those who are absent. Whisperers declare secretly, and with great reserve, the supposed faults of others. Backbiters proclaim them publicly and avowedly. ¶ *Haters of God.* There is no charge which can be brought against men more severe than this. It is the highest possible crime; yet it is a charge which the conduct of men will abundantly justify, and the truth of which all those experience who are brought

to see their true character. To an awakened sinner there is often nothing more plain and painful than that he is a hater of God. His heart rises up against Him, and his law, and his plan of saving men; and he deeply feels that nothing can subdue this but the mighty power of the Holy One. This is a charge which is not unfrequently brought against men in the Bible; see John vii. 7; xv. 18, 24, 25; iii. 19, 20. Surely, if this be the native character of man, then it is "far gone from original righteousness." No more striking proof of depravity could be given; and in no creed or confession of faith is there a more painful and humiliating representation given of human wickedness, than in this declaration of an inspired apostle, that men are by nature HATERS OF GOD. ¶ *Despiteful.* This word denotes those who abuse, or treat with unkindness or disdain, *those who are present. Whisperers* and *backbiters* are those who calumniate those who are *absent.* ¶ *Proud.* Pride is well understood. It is an inordinate self-esteem; an unreasonable conceit of one's superiority in talents, beauty, wealth, accomplishments, &c. (Webster). Of the existence of this everywhere, there is abundant proof. And it was particularly striking among the ancients. The sect of the *Stoics* was distinguished for it, and this was the general character of their philosophers. Men will be proud where they suppose none are superior; and it is only the religion that reveals a great and infinite God, and that teaches that *all* blessings are *his* gift, and that *he* has given us the station which we occupy, that will produce true humility. We may add, that the system of heathenism did not disclose the wickedness of the heart, and that this was a main reason why they were elevated in self-esteem. ¶ *Boasters.* Those who arrogate to themselves that which they do not possess, and glory in it. This is closely connected with *pride.* A man who has an inordinate self-conceit, will not be slow to proclaim his own merits to those around him. ¶ *Inventors of evil things.* This doubtless refers to their seeking to find out new arts or plans to prac-

tise evil; new devices to gratify their lusts and passions; new forms of luxury, and vice, &c. So intent were they on practising evil, so resolved to gratify their passions, that the mind was excited to discover new modes of gratification. In cities of luxury and vice, this has always been done. Vices change their form, men become satiated, and they are obliged to resort to some new form. The passions cease to be gratified with old forms of indulgence, and consequently men are obliged to resort to new devices to pamper their appetites, and to rekindle their dying passions to a flame. This was eminently true of ancient Rome; a place where all the arts of luxury, all the devices of passion, all the designs of splendid gratification, were called forth to excite and pamper the evil passions of men. Their splendid entertainments, their games, their theatres, their sports— cruel and bloody — were little else than new and ever-varying inventions of evil things to gratify the desires of lust and of pride. ¶ *Disobedient to parents.* This expresses the idea that they did not show to parents that honour, respect, and attention which was due. This has been a crime of paganism in every age; and though among the Romans the duty of honouring parents was enjoined by the laws, yet it is not improbable that the duty was often violated, and that parents were treated with great neglect and even contempt. "Disobedience to parents was punished by the Jewish law with death, and with the Hindoos it is attended with the loss of the child's inheritance. The ancient Greeks considered the neglect of it to be extremely impious, and attended with the most certain effects of divine vengeance. Solon ordered all persons who refused to make due provision for their parents to be punished with infamy, and the same penalty was incurred for personal violence towards them" (Kent's *Commentaries on American Law,* vol. ii. p. 207; comp. Virg. *Æneid,* ix. 283). The feelings of pride and haughtiness would lead to disregard of parents. It might also

31 Without understanding,
covenant-breakers, [2] without na-

[2] or, *unsociable*.

---

tural affection, implacable, unmerciful: '

---

be felt that to provide for them when
aged and infirm was a burden; and
hence there would arise disregard for
their wants, and probably open opposition to their wishes, as being the
demands of petulance and age. It
has been one characteristic of heathenism everywhere, that it leaves
children to treat their parents with neglect. Among the Sandwich Islanders
it was customary, when a parent was
old, infirm, and sick beyond the hope
of recovery, for his own children to
bury him alive; and it has been the
common custom in India for children
to leave their aged parents to perish
on the banks of the Ganges.

31. *Without understanding.* Inconsiderate, or foolish; see ver. 21,
22. ¶ *Covenant-breakers.* Perfidious;
false to their contracts. ¶ *Without
natural affection.* This expression denotes the want of affectionate regard
towards their children. The attachment of parents to children is one
of the strongest in nature, and nothing can overcome it but the most
confirmed and established wickedness.
And yet the apostle charges on the
heathen generally the want of this
affection. He doubtless refers here
to the practice so common among
heathens of *exposing* their children, or
putting them to death. This crime,
so abhorrent to all the feelings of
humanity, was common among the
heathen, and is still. The Canaanites,
we are told (Ps. cvi. 37, 38), "sacrificed their sons and their daughters
unto devils, and shed innocent blood,
even the blood of their sons and their
daughters, whom they sacrificed unto
the idols of Canaan." Manasseh
among the Jews imitated their example, and introduced the horrid custom of sacrificing children to Moloch,
and set the example by offering his
own, 2 Chron. xxxiii. 6. Among
the ancient Persians it was a common
custom to bury children alive. In
most of the Grecian states, infanticide was not merely permitted, but

actually enforced by law. The Spar-
tan lawgiver expressly ordained that
every child that was born should be
examined by the ancient men of the
tribe, and that if found weak or deformed, should be thrown into a deep
cavern at the foot of Mount Tay-
getus. Aristotle, in his work on government, enjoins the exposure of children that are naturally feeble and
deformed, in order to prevent an
excess of population. But among all
the nations of antiquity, the Romans
were the most unrelenting in their
treatment of infants. Romulus obliged the citizens to bring up *all*
their male children, and the *eldest* of
the females, proof that the others
were to be destroyed. The Roman
father had an absolute right over the
life of his child, and we have abundant proof that that right was often
exercised. Romulus expressly autho-
rized the destruction of all children
that were deformed, only requiring
the parents to exhibit them to their
five nearest neighbours, and to obtain
their consent to their death. The
law of the Twelve Tables, enacted in
the 301st year of Rome, sanctioned
the same barbarous practice. Minu-
cius Felix thus describes the barbarity of the Romans in this respect:
"I see you exposing your infants to
wild beasts and birds, or strangling
them after the most miserable manner" (chap. xxx.). Pliny the elder
defends the right of parents to destroy their children, upon the ground
of its being necessary in order to preserve the population within proper
bounds. Tertullian, in his *Apology*,
expresses himself boldly on this subject. "How many of you (addressing himself to the Roman people,
and to the governors of cities and
provinces) might I deservedly charge
with infant murder; and not only
so, but among the different kinds of
death, for choosing some of the cruel-
est for their own children, such as
drowning, or starving with cold or
hunger, or exposing to the mercy of

32 Who knowing the judgment of God, that they which commit such things are worthy of death, not only do the same, but ³have pleasure in them that do them.

³ or, *consent with them.*

dogs; dying by the sword being too sweet a death for children." Nor was this practice arrested in the Roman government until the time of Constantine, the first Christian prince. The Phœnicians and Carthaginians were in the habit of sacrificing infants to the gods. It may be added that the crime is no less common among modern pagan nations. No less than 9000 children are exposed in Pekin in China annually. Persons are employed by the police to go through the city with carts every morning to pick up all the children that may have been thrown out during the night. The bodies are carried to a common pit without the walls of the city, into which all, whether *dead or living,* are promiscuously thrown (Barrow's *Travels in China,* p. 113, Am. ed.). Among the Hindoos the practice is perhaps still more common. In the provinces of Cutch and Guzerat alone the number of infantile murders amounted, according to the lowest calculation in 1807, to 3000 annually; according to another calculation, to 30,000. Females are almost the only victims (Buchanan's *Researches in Asia,* Eng. ed. p. 49; Ward's *View of the Hindoos*). In Otaheite, previously to the conversion of the people to Christianity, it was estimated that at least *two-thirds* of the children were destroyed (Turnbull's *Voyage round the World in 1800,* 2, 3, and 4). The natives of New South Wales were in the habit of burying the child with its mother, if she should happen to die (Collins' *Account of the Colony of New South Wales,* p. 124, 125). Among the Hottentots, infanticide is a common crime. "The altars of the *Mexicans* were continually drenched in the blood of infants." In Peru, no less than two hundred infants were sacrificed on occasion of the coronation of the Inca. The authority for these melancholy statements may be seen in Beck's *Medical Jurisprudence,* vol. i. 184–197,

ed. 1823; see also Robertson's *History of America,* p. 221, ed. 1821. This is a *specimen* of the views and feelings of the heathen world; and the painful narrative might be continued to almost any length. After this statement, it cannot surely be deemed a groundless charge when the apostle accused them of being destitute *of natural affection.* ¶ *Implacable.* This word properly denotes those who will not be reconciled where there is a quarrel; or who pursue the offender with unyielding revenge. It denotes an unforgiving temper; and was doubtless common among the ancients, as it is among all heathen people. The aborigines of America have given the most striking manifestation of this that the world has known. It is well known that among them, neither time nor distance will obliterate the memory of an offence; and that the avenger will pursue the offender over hills and streams, and through heat or snow, happy if he may at last, though at the expiration of years, bury the tomahawk in the head of his victim, though it may be at the expense of his own life. See Robertson's *America,* book iv. § lxxiii.–lxxxi. ¶ *Unmerciful.* Destitute of compassion. As a proof of this, we may remark that no provisions for the poor or the infirm were made among the heathen. The sick and the infirm were cast out, and doomed to depend on the stinted charity of individuals. Pure religion, only, opens the heart to the appeals of want; and nothing but Christianity has yet expanded the hearts of men to make public provisions for the poor, the ignorant, and the afflicted.

32. *Who knowing.* That the Gentiles had a *moral sense,* or were capable of knowing the will of God in this case, is clear from chap. ii. 14, 15. The means which they had of arriving at the knowledge of God were, their own reason, their conscience, and an observation of the *effects*

of depravity. ¶ *The judgment of God.* The word *judgment* here denotes the declared *sentiment* of God that such things deserved death. It does not mean his *inflictions,* or his *statutes* or *precepts;* but it means that God *thought* or *judged* that they which did such things ought to die. As they were aware of this, it showed their guilt in still persevering in the face of his judgments, and his solemn purpose to inflict punishment. ¶ *Were worthy of death.* The word *death* in the Scriptures is often used to denote punishment. But it does not mean here that these deserved capital punishment from the civil magistrate, but that they knew they were *evil,* and offensive to God, and deserving of punishment from his hand; see John viii. 51; Rom. v. 12–19. ¶ *Have pleasure,* &c. They delight in those who commit sin; and hence encourage them in it, and excite them to it. This was a grievous aggravation of the offence. It greatly heightens guilt when we excite others to do it, and seduce them from the ways of innocence. That this was the case with the heathen there can be no doubt. Men do not commit sin often alone. They need the countenance of others. They "join hand in hand," and become confederate in iniquity. *All* social sins are of this class; and most of those which the apostle mentioned were sins of this character.

If this revolting and melancholy picture of the pagan world was a true representation, then it was clear that there was need of some other plan of religion. And that it was true has already in part been seen. In the conclusion of this chapter we may make a few additional observations.

1. The charges which the apostle makes here were evidently those which were well known. He does not even appeal to their writings, as he does on some other occasions, for proof; comp. Titus i. 12. So well known were they, that there was no need of proof. A writer would not advance charges in this manner unless he was *confident* that they were well-founded, and could not be denied.

2. They are abundantly sustained by the heathen writers themselves. This we have in part seen. In addition we may adduce the testimony of two Roman writers respecting the state of things at Rome in the time of the apostle. Livy says of the age of Augustus, in some respects the brightest period of the Roman history, "Rome has increased by her virtues until now, *when we can neither bear our vices nor their remedy*" (Preface to his *History*). Seneca, one of the purest moralists of Rome, who died A.D. 65, says of his own time, "All is full of criminality and vice; indeed much more of these is committed than can be remedied by force. A monstrous contest of abandoned wickedness is carried on. The lust of sin increases daily; and shame is daily more and more extinguished. Discarding respect for all that is good and sacred, lust rushes on wherever it will. Vice no longer hides itself. It stalks forth before all eyes. So public has abandoned wickedness become, and so openly does it flame up in the minds of all, that innocence is no longer *seldom,* but has wholly 'ceased to exist'" (Seneca *de Ira,* ii. 8). Further authorities of this kind could be easily given, but these will show that the apostle Paul did not speak at random when he charged them with these enormous crimes.

3. If this was the state of things then it was clear that there was need of another plan of saving men. It will be remembered that, in these charges, the apostle speaks of the most enlightened and refined nations of antiquity; and especially that he speaks of the Romans at the very height of their power, intelligence, and splendour. The experiment whether man could save himself by his own works, had been fairly made. After all that their greatest philosophers could do, this was the result, and it is clear that there was need of some better plan than this. More profound and laborious philosophers than had arisen, the pagan world could not hope to see; more refinement and civilization than then ex-

CHAPTER II.

THEREFORE thou art inexcusable, O man, whosoever thou art that judgest: ᵃ for

isted, the world could not expect to behold under heathenism. At this time, when the experiment had been made for four thousand years, and when the inefficacy of all human means, even under the most favourable circumstances, to reform mankind, had been tried, *the gospel* was preached to men. It disclosed *another* plan; and its effects were seen at once throughout the most abandoned states and cities of the ancient world.

4. If this was the state of things in the ancient heathen world, the same may be expected to be the state of heathenism still. And it is so. The account given here of ancient heathens would apply substantially still to the pagan world. The same things have been again and again witnessed in China, and Hindostan, and Africa, the Sandwich Islands, and in aboriginal America. It would be easy to multiply proofs almost without end of this; and to this day the heathen world is exhibiting substantially the same characteristics that it was in the time of Paul.

5. There was need of some better religion than the pagan. After all that infidels and deists have said of the sufficiency of natural religion, yet here is the sad result. This shows what man can do, and these facts will demonstrate for ever that there was need of some other religion than that furnished by the light of nature.

6. The account in this chapter shows the propriety of missionary exertions. So Paul judged; and so we should judge still. If *this* be the state of the world, and if Christianity, as all Christians believe, contains the remedy for all these evils, then it is wisdom and benevolence to send it to them. And it is not *wisdom* or *benevolence* to withhold it from them. Believing as they do, Christians are

wherein thou judgest another, thou condemnest thyself; for thou that judgest, doest the same things.

bound to send the gospel to the heathen world. It is on this principle that modern missions to the heathen are established; and if the toils of the apostles were demanded to spread the gospel, then are the labours of Christians now. If it was right, and wise, and proper for *them* to go to other lands to proclaim "the unsearchable riches of Christ," then it is equally proper and wise to do it now. If there was danger that the heathen world *then* would perish without the gospel, there is equal danger that the heathen world will perish now.

7. If it should be said that many of these things are practised now in nations which are called *Christian*, and that, therefore, the charge of the apostle that this was the effect of heathenism could not be well-founded, we may reply, (1) That this is true, too true. But this very fact shows the deep and dreadful depravity of human nature. If such things exist in lands that have a *revelation*, what must have been the state of those countries that had none of its restraints and influences? But, (2) These things do *not* exist where religion exerts its influence. They are *not* in the bosom of the Christian church. They are not practised by Christians. And the effect of the Christian religion, so far as it has influence, is to call off men from such vices, and to make them holy and pure in their life. Let religion exert its *full influence* on any nominally Christian nation, and these things would cease. Let it send its influence into other lands, and the world, the now polluted world, would become pure before God.

CHAPTER II.

1. *Therefore* (Διὸ). The force of this word here has been the subject of much discussion. The design of this and the following chapter is to show that the *Jews* were no less guilty than

the Gentiles, and that *they* needed the benefit of the same salvation. This the apostle does by showing that they had *greater light* than the Gentiles; and yet that they did the same things. Still they were in the habit of accusing and condemning the Gentiles as wicked and abandoned; while they *excused* themselves on the ground that they possessed the *law* and *oracles* of God, and were his favourite people. The apostle here affirms that they were *inexcusable* in their sins, that *they* must be condemned in the sight of God, on the *same ground* on which they condemned the Gentiles; to wit, that they had light and yet committed wickedness. If the *Gentiles* were without excuse (chap. i. 20) in *their* sins, much more would the Jew, who condemned them, be without excuse on the same ground. The word *therefore,* I suppose, refers not to any particular word in the previous chapter, or to any particular verse, but to the general considerations which were suggested by a view of the whole case. And its sense might be thus expressed: "Since you Jews condemn the Gentiles for their sins, on the ground that they *have* the means of knowing their duty, THEREFORE you, who are far more favoured than they, are entirely without an excuse for the same things." ¶ *Thou art inexcusable.* This does not mean that they were inexcusable for *judging others;* but that they had no excuse for their *sins* before God; or that they were under condemnation for their crimes, and needed the benefits of another plan of justification. As the *Gentiles* whom they judged were *condemned,* and were without excuse (i. 20), so were the *Jews* who condemned them without excuse on the same principle; and in a still greater degree. ¶ *O man.* This address is *general* to *any* man who should do this. But it is plain, from the connection, that he means especially the Jews. The use of this word is an instance of the apostle's skill in argument. If he had openly named the Jews here, it would have been likely to have excited opposition from them. He therefore approaches

the subject gradually, affirms it of man in general, and then makes a particular application to the Jews. This he does not do, however, until he has advanced so far in the *general principles* of his argument that it would be impossible for them to evade his conclusions; and then he does it in the most tender, and kind, as well as convincing manner, ver. 17, &c. ¶ *Whosoever thou art that judgest.* The word *judgest* (κρίνεις) here is used in the sense of *condemning.* It is not a word of equal strength with that which is rendered "*condemnest*" (κατακρίνεις). It implies, however, that they were accustomed to express themselves freely and severely of the character and doom of the Gentiles. And from the New Testament, as well as from their own writings, there can be no doubt that such was the fact; that they regarded the entire Gentile world with abhorrence, considered them as shut out from the favour of God, and applied to them terms expressive of the utmost contempt. Comp. Mat. xv. 27. ¶ *For wherein.* For in the *same thing.* This implies that substantially the same crimes which were committed among the heathen were also committed among the Jews. ¶ *Thou judgest another.* The meaning of this clearly is, "for the same thing for which you condemn *the heathen,* you condemn yourselves." ¶ *Thou that judgest.* You Jews who condemn other nations. ¶ *Doest the same things.* It is clearly implied here, that they were guilty of offences similar to those practised by the Gentiles. It would not be a just principle of interpretation *to press* this declaration as implying that *precisely* the same offences, and *to the same extent,* were chargeable on them. Thus they were not guilty, in the time of the apostle, of *idolatry;* but of the other crimes enumerated in the first chapter, the Jews might be guilty. The character of the nation, as given in the New Testament, is that they were " an evil and adulterous generation " (Mat. xii. 39; comp. John viii. 7; that they were a " generation of vipers " (Mat. iii. 7; xii. 34); that they were wicked (Mat.

2 But we are sure that the judgment of God is according to

xii. 45); that they were sinful (Mark viii. 38); that they were proud, haughty, hypocritical, &c. (Mat. xxiii.) If such was the character of the Jewish nation *in general,* there is no improbability in supposing that they practised most of the crimes specified in chap. i. On this verse we may remark, (1) That men are prone to be severe judges of others. (2) This is often, perhaps commonly, done when the accusers themselves are guilty of the same offences. It often happens, too, that men are remarkably zealous in opposing those offences which they themselves secretly practise. A remarkable instance of this occurs in John viii. 1, &c. Thus David readily condemned the supposed act of injustice mentioned by Nathan, 2 Sam. xii. 1–6. Thus also kings and emperors have enacted severe laws against the very crimes which they have constantly committed themselves. Nero executed the laws of the Roman empire against the very crimes which he was constantly committing; and it was a common practice for Roman *masters* to commit offences which they punished with death in their slaves. (See instances in Grotius on this place.) (3) Remarkable zeal against sin may be no proof of innocence; compare Mat. vii. 3. The zeal of persecutors, and often of pretended reformers, may be far from proof that *they* are free from the very offences which they are condemning in others. It may all be the work of the hypocrite to conceal some base design; or of the man who seeks to show his hostility to one kind of sin, in order to be a salvo to his conscience for committing some other. (4) The heart is deceitful. When we judge others we should make it a rule to examine ourselves *on that very point.* Such an examination might greatly *mitigate the severity of our judgment;* or might turn the whole of our indignation against ourselves.

2. *But we are sure.* Greek, "We know." That is, it is the common and admitted sentiment of mankind.

truth, against them which commit such things.

It is known and believed by men generally that God will punish such crimes. It is *implied* in this declaration that this was known to the Jews, and it was particularly to the purpose of the apostle so to express himself as to *include* the Jews. *They* knew it because it was everywhere taught in the Old Testament, and it was the acknowledged doctrine of the nation. The design of the apostle here, says Calvin, is to take away the subterfuges of the hypocrite, lest he should pride himself if he obtained the praise of men, for a far more important trial awaited him at the bar of God. Outwardly he might appear well to men; but *God* searched the heart, and saw the secret as well as the open deeds of men, and they who practised *secretly* what they condemned openly, could not expect to escape the righteous judgment of God. God, without respect of persons, would punish wickedness, whether it was *open,* as among the Gentiles, or whether it was concealed under the guise of great regard for religion, as among the Jews. ¶ *The judgment of God.* That God condemns it, and will punish it. He regards those who do these things as guilty, and will treat them accordingly. ¶ *According to truth.* This expression is capable of two meanings. The Hebrews sometimes use it to denote *truly* or *certainly.* God will *certainly* judge and punish such deeds. Another meaning, which is probably the correct one here, is that God will judge those who are guilty of such things, not according *to appearance,* but in *integrity,* and with *righteousness.* He will judge men according to the *real nature* of their conduct, and *not* as their conduct may appear unto men. The secret, as well as the open sinner, therefore; the hypocrite, as well as the abandoned profligate, must expect to be judged according to their true character. This meaning comports with the design of the apostle, which is to show that the *Jew,* who *secretly* and *hypocritically* did the very things which he condemned in

3 And thinkest thou this, O man, that judgest them which do such things, and doest the same, that thou shalt escape the judgment of God?

4 Or despisest thou *b* the riches

b ch.9.23.

the Gentile, could not escape the righteous judgment of God. ¶ *Against him.* That is, against *every man*, no matter of what age or nation. ¶ *Which commit such things.* The crimes enumerated in chap. i. The apostle is not to be understood as affirming that each and every individual among the Jews was guilty of the specific crimes charged on the heathen, but that they were *as a people* inclined to the same things. Even where they might be *externally* moral, they might be guilty of cherishing evil desires in their hearts, and thus be guilty of the offence, Mat. v. 28. When men *desire* to do evil, and are prevented by the providence of God, it is right to punish them for their evil intentions. The fact that *God* prevents them from carrying their evil purposes into execution, does not constitute a difference between their *real* character and the character of those who are suffered to *act out* their wicked designs.

3. *And thinkest thou*, &c. This is an appeal to their common sense, to their deep and instinctive conviction of what was *right.* If *they* condemned those who practised these things; if, imperfect and obscure as their sense of justice was; if, unholy as they were, they yet condemned those who were guilty of these offences, would not a holy and just God be far more likely to pronounce judgment? And could *they* escape who had themselves delivered a similar sentence? God is of "purer eyes than to behold evil, and cannot look upon iniquity," Hab. i. 13. And if *men* condemned their fellow-men, *how much more* would a pure and holy God condemn iniquity. This appeal is evidently directed against the *Jew.* It was doubtless a prevalent sentiment among them, that provided they adhered to the rites of their religion, and observed the ceremonial law, God would not judge them with the same severity as he would the abandoned and idolatrous Gentiles; compare Mat. iii. 9; John viii.

33. The apostle shows them *that crime is crime*, wherever committed; that sin does not lose its essential character by being committed in the midst of religious privileges; and that those who professed to be the *people of God* have no peculiar *license* to sin. Antinomians in all ages, like the Jews, have supposed that *they*, being the friends of God, have a right to do many things which would not be proper in others; that what *would be* sin in others, *they* may commit with impunity; and that God will not be strict to mark the offences of his people. Against all this Paul is directly opposed, and the Bible uniformly teaches that the most aggravated sins among men are those committed by the professed people of God; comp. Isa. i. 11–17; lxv. 2–5; Rev. iii. 16.

4. *Or despisest.* This word properly means to *contemn*, or to treat with neglect. It does not mean here that they *professedly* treated God's goodness with neglect or contempt; but that they *perverted* and *abused* it; they did not make a proper use of it; they did not regard it as fitted to lead them to repentance; but they derived a *practical impression*, that because God *had* not come forth in judgment and cut them off, but had continued to follow them with blessings, that *therefore* he did not regard them as *sinners*, or they inferred that they were innocent and safe. This argument the Jews were accustomed to use (comp. Luke xiii. 1–5; John ix. 2); and thus sinners still continue to abuse the goodness and mercy of God. ¶ *The riches of his goodness.* This is a Hebrew mode of speaking, for "his rich goodness," *i.e.* for his *abundant* or *great* goodness. *Riches* denote superfluity, or that which *abounds*, or which *exceeds* a man's present wants; and hence the word in the New Testament is used to denote *abundance;* or that which is very great and valuable; see Note, chap. ix. 23; compare chap. xi. 12, 33; 2 Cor. viii. 2;

of his *c*goodness and forbearance and *d*long-suffering, not knowing

c Is.63.7,&c.   d Jn.4.2.

Eph. i. 7, 18; iii. 8, 16; Col. i. 27; Eph. ii. 4. The word is used here to qualify *each* of the words which follow it, his *rich* goodness, and forbearance, and long-suffering. ¶ *Goodness.* Kindness, benignity. ¶ *Forbearance* (ἀνοχῆς). Literally, his *holding in* or *restraining* his indignation; or forbearing to manifest his displeasure against sin. ¶ *Long-suffering.* This word denotes his slowness to anger; or his suffering them to commit sins *long* without punishing them. It does not differ essentially from forbearance. This is shown by his not coming forth, at the moment that sin is committed, to punish it. He might do it justly, but he spares men from day to day, and year to year, to give them opportunity to repent, and be saved. The way in which men *despise* or *abuse* the goodness of God is to *infer* that He does not intend to punish sin; that they may do it safely; and instead of turning from it, to go on in committing it more constantly, as if they were safe. "Because sentence against an evil work is not executed speedily, therefore the heart of the sons of men is fully set in them to do evil," Eccl. viii. 11. The same thing was true in the time of Peter, 2 Pet. iii. 3, 4. And the same thing is true of wicked men in every age; nor is there a more decisive proof of the wickedness of the human heart, than this disposition to abuse the goodness of God, and because he shows kindness and forbearance, to take occasion to plunge deeper into sin, to forget his mercy, and to provoke him to anger. ¶ *Not knowing.* Not *considering.* The word used here, ἀγνοῶν, means not merely *to be ignorant of*, but it denotes such a degree of inattention as to result in ignorance; comp. Hos. ii. 8. In this sense it denotes a *voluntary*, and therefore a *criminal* ignorance. ¶ *Leadeth thee,* &c. Or the tendency, the design of the goodness of God is to induce men to repent of their sins, and not to lead them to deeper and more aggravated iniquity. The same sentiment is

that *e*the goodness of God leadeth thee to repentance?

e Is.30.18.

expressed in 2 Pet. iii. 9, "The Lord is long-suffering to us-ward, not willing that any should perish; but that all should come to repentance." See also Isa. xxx. 18, "And therefore will the Lord wait, that he may be gracious unto you," Hos. v. 15; Ezek. xviii. 23, 32. ¶ *Repentance.* Change of mind, and purpose, and life. The word here evidently means, not merely sorrow, but a forsaking of sin, and turning from it. The tendency of God's goodness and forbearance to lead men to repentance, is manifest in the following ways. (1) It shows the *evil* of transgression when it is seen to be committed against so kind and merciful a Being. (2) It is fitted to melt and soften the heart. Judgments often harden the sinner's heart, and make him obstinate. But if while *he* does evil God is as constantly doing him good; if the patience of God is seen from year to year, while the man is rebellious, it is adapted to melt and subdue the heart. (3) The *great* mercy of God in this often appears to men to be overwhelming; and so it would to all, if they saw it as it is. God bears with men from childhood to youth; from youth to manhood; from manhood to old age; often while *they* violate every law, contemn his mercy, profane his name, and disgrace their species; and still, notwithstanding all this, his anger is turned away, and the sinner lives, and "riots in the beneficence of God." If there is anything that can affect the heart of man, it is this; and when he is brought to see it, and contemplate it, it rushes over the soul and overwhelms it with bitter sorrow. (4) The mercy and forbearance of God are constant. The manifestations of his goodness come in every form; in the sun, and light, and air; in the rain, the stream, the dewdrop; in food, and raiment, and home; in friends, and liberty, and protection; in health, and peace; and in the gospel of Christ, and the offers of life; and in all these ways God is appealing to his creatures each moment,

5 But, after thy hardness and impenitent heart, *f* treasurest up unto thyself wrath, against the

f De.32.34.

and setting before them the evils of ingratitude, and beseeching them to turn and live.

And from this passage, we cannot but remark, (1) That the most effectual preaching is that which sets before men most of the goodness of God. (2) Every man is under obligation to forsake his sins, and turn to God. There is no man who has not seen repeated proofs of his mercy and love. (3) Sin is a stubborn and an amazing evil. Where it can resist all the appeals of God's mercy; where the sinner can make his way down to hell through *all* the proofs of God's goodness; where he can refuse to hear God speaking to him each day, and each hour, it shows an amazing extent of depravity to resist all this, and still remain a sinner. Yet there are thousands and millions who do it, and who can be won by no exhibition of love or mercy to forsake their sins and turn to God. Happy is the man who is melted into contrition by the goodness of God, and who sees and mourns over the evil of sinning against so good a Being as is the Creator and Parent of all.

5. *But after thy hardness.* The word "after" here (κατὰ) means *in respect to,* or you act according *to the direct tendency* of a hard heart in treasuring up wrath. The word *hardness* is used to denote *insensibility* of mind. It properly means that which is insensible to the *touch,* or on which no *impression* is made by contact, as a stone, &c. Hence it is applied to the *mind,* to denote a state where no motives make an impression; which is *insensible* to all the appeals made to it; see Mat. xxv. 24; xix. 8; Acts xix. 9. And here it expresses a state of mind where the *goodness* and *forbearance* of God have no effect. The man still remains *obdurate,* to use a word which has precisely the meaning of the Greek in this place. It is implied in this expression that the *direct tendency,* or the *inevitable*

day of wrath, and *g* revelation of the righteous judgment of God;

g Ec.12.14.

result, of that state of mind was to treasure up wrath, &c. ¶ *Impenitent heart.* A heart which is not affected with sorrow for sin, in view of the mercy and goodness of God. This is an *explanation* of what he meant by *hardness.* ¶ *Treasurest up.* To *treasure up,* or to *lay up treasure,* commonly denotes a laying by in a place of security of property that may be of use to us at some future period. In this place it is used, however, in a more general sense, to *accumulate,* to *increase.* It still has the idea of *hoarding up,* carries the thought beautifully and impressively *onward* to future times. *Wrath,* like wealth treasured up, is not exhausted at present, and hence the sinner becomes bolder in sin. But it exists, *for future use;* it is *kept in store* (comp. 2 Pet. iii. 7) against future times; and the man who commits sin is only *increasing* this by every act of transgression. The same sentiment is taught in a most solemn manner in Deut. xxxii. 34, 35. —It may be remarked here, that most men have an *immense treasure* of this kind in store, which eternal ages of pain will not exhaust or diminish! Stores of wrath are thus reserved for a guilty world, and in due time it "will come upon man *to the uttermost,*" 1 Thes. ii. 16. ¶ *Unto thyself.* For thyself, and not for another; to be exhausted on *thee,* and not on your fellow man. This is the case with every sinner, as really and as certainly as though he were the only solitary mortal in existence. ¶ *Wrath.* Note, chap. i. 18. ¶ *Day of wrath.* The day when God shall show or execute his wrath against sinners; comp. Rev. vi. 17; 1 Thes. i. 10; John iii. 36; Eph. v. 6. ¶ *And revelation.* On the day when the righteous judgment of God will be *revealed,* or made known. Here we learn, (1) That the punishment of the wicked will be *just.* It will not be a judgment of *caprice* or *tyranny,* but a *righteous* judgment, that is, such a judgment as it will be

6 Who[h] will render to every man according to his deeds;

h Pr.24.12; Mat.16.27; Re.20.12.

7 To them who, by patient continuance in well doing, seek

right to render, or as *ought* to be rendered, and THEREFORE such as God *will* render, for he will do right, 2 Thes. i. 6. (2) The punishment of the wicked is *future*. It is *not* exhausted in this life. It is *treasured* up for a future day, and that day is a day of wrath. How contrary to this text are the pretences of those who maintain that *all* punishment is executed in this life. (3) How foolish as well as wicked is it to lay up *such* a treasure for the future; to have the *only* inheritance in the eternal world, an inheritance of *wrath* and *woe!*

6. *Who will render.* That is, who will make *retribution* as a righteous Judge; or who will *give* to every man as he deserves. ¶ *To every man.* To each one. This is a general principle, and it is clear that in this respect God would deal with the Jew as he does with the Gentile. This *general principle* the apostle is establishing, that he may bring it to bear on the *Jew*, and to show that *he* cannot escape *simply because he is a Jew.* ¶ *According to his deeds.* That is, *as he deserves;* or God will be just, and will treat every man as he *ought* to be treated, or according to his character. The word *deeds* (ἔργα) is sometimes applied to the *external conduct.* But it is plain that this is not its meaning here. It denotes everything connected with conduct, including the *acts* of the mind, the motives, the principles, as well as the mere external act. Our word *character* more aply expresses it than any single word. It is not true that God will treat men according to their *external* conduct; but the whole language of the Bible implies that he will judge men according to the *whole* of their conduct, including their thoughts, and principles, and motives; *i.e.* as they deserve. The doctrine of this place is elsewhere abundantly taught in the Bible, Prov. xxiv. 12; Mat. xvi. 27; Rev. xx. 12; Jer. xxxii. 19. It is to be observed here that the apostle does

not say that men will be rewarded *for* their deeds (comp. Luke xvii. 10), but *according to* (κατὰ) their deeds. Christians will be saved *on account of* the merits of the Lord Jesus Christ (Tit. iii. 5), but still the rewards of heaven will be *according to* their works; that is, they who have laboured most, and been most faithful, shall receive the highest reward, or their fidelity in their Master's service shall be the measure or rule according to which the rewards of heaven shall be distributed, Mat. xxv. 14–29. Thus the ground or reason *why* they are saved shall be the merits of the Lord Jesus. The measure of their happiness shall be according to their *character and deeds.* On what principle God will distribute his rewards the apostle proceeds immediately to state.

7. *To them.* Whoever they may be. ¶ *Patient continuance.* Who by *perseverance* in well doing, or in a good work. It means they who so continue, or persevere, in good works as to evince that they are disposed to obey the law of God. It does not mean those who perform one *single act*, but those who so live as to show that this is their *character* to obey God. It is the uniform doctrine of the Bible that none will be saved but those who *persevere* in a life of holiness, Rev. ii. 10; Mat. x. 22; Heb. x. 38, 39. No other conduct gives evidence of piety but that which *continues* in the ways of righteousness. Nor has God ever promised eternal life to men unless they so *persevere* in a life of holiness as to show that this is their *character*, their settled and firm rule of action. The words *well doing* here denote such conduct as shall be conformed to the law of God; not merely *external* conduct, but that which proceeds from a heart attached to God and his cause. ¶ *Seek for.* This word properly denotes the act of endeavouring to find anything that is lost, Mat. xviii. 12; Luke ii. 48, 49. But it also denotes the act when one

for glory and honour and immortality, eternal life:

8 But unto them that are ᶜcontentious, and ᵏdo not obey the

earnestly strives, or desires to obtain anything; when he puts forth his efforts to accomplish it. Thus, Mat. vi. 33, "Seek ye first the kingdom of God," &c.; Acts xvi. 10; 1 Cor. x. 24; Luke xiii. 24. In this place it denotes an earnest and intense desire to obtain eternal life. It does not mean simply the desire of a sinner *to be happy*, or the efforts of those who are *not willing* to forsake their sins and yield to God, but the intense effort of those who are willing to forsake all their crimes, and submit to God and obey his laws. ¶ *Glory and honour and immortality.* The three words used here denote the happiness of the heavenly world. They vary somewhat in their meaning, and are *each* descriptive of *something* in heaven, that renders it an object of intense desire. The expressions are *cumulative*, or they are designed to express the happiness of heaven in the highest possible degree. The word *glory* (δόξαν) denotes properly *praise, celebrity,* or anything distinguished for beauty, ornament, majesty, splendour, as of the sun, &c.; and then it is used to denote the highest happiness or felicity, as expressing everything that shall be splendid, rich, and grand. It denotes that there will be an absence of everything *mean, grovelling, obscure.* The word *honour* (τιμὴν) implies rather the idea of *reward,* or just retribution—the honour and reward which shall be conferred in heaven on the friends of God. It stands opposed to contempt, poverty, and want among men. Here they are *despised* by men; there, they shall be *honoured* by God. ¶ *Immortality.* That which is not corruptible or subject to decay. It is applied to heaven as a state where there shall be no *decay* or *death,* in strong contrast with our present condition, where all things are corruptible, and soon vanish away. These expressions are undoubtedly descriptive of a state of things *beyond the grave.* They are never applied in the Scriptures to any condition of things *on the earth.* This

consideration proves, therefore, that the expressions in the next verse, *indignation,* &c., apply to the punishment of the wicked *beyond the grave.* ¶ *Eternal life.* That is, God will "*render*" eternal life to those who seek it in this manner. This is a great principle; and this shows that the apostle means by "*their deeds*" (ver. 6), not merely their *external conduct,* but their inward thoughts, and efforts *evinced by* their *seeking* for glory, &c. For the meaning of the expression "eternal life," see Note on John v. 24.

8. *Who are contentious.* This expression usually denotes those who are of a quarrelsome or litigious disposition; and generally has reference to controversies *among men.* But here it evidently denotes a disposition *towards God,* and is of the same signification as *rebellious,* or as *opposing God.* They who contend with the Almighty; who resist his claims, who rebel against his laws, and refuse to submit to his requirements, however made known. The LXX. use the verb to translate the Hebrew word מרה, *marah,* in Deut. xxi. 20. One striking characteristic of the sinner is, that he *contends* with God, *i.e.* that he opposes and resists his claims. This is the case with *all* sinners; and it was particularly so with the Jews, and hence the apostle used the expression here to characterize them particularly. His argument he intended to apply to the Jews, and hence he used such an expression as would *exactly* describe them. This character of being a *rebellious people* was one which was *often* charged on the Jewish nation, Deut. ix. 7, 24; xxxi. 27; Isa. i. 2; xxx. 9; lxv. 2; Jer. v. 23; Ezek. ii. 3, 5. ¶ *Do not obey the truth.* Comp. chap. i. 18. The *truth* here denotes the divine will, which is alone the light of truth (Calvin). It means true doctrine in opposition to false opinions; and to refuse to *obey it* is to regard it as false, and to resist its influence.

truth, but obey unrighteousness; indignation and wrath,

The *truth* here means all the correct representations which had been made of God, and his perfections, and law, and claims, whether by the light of nature or by revelation. The description thus included Gentiles and Jews, but particularly the *latter,* as they had been more signally favoured with the light of truth. It had been an eminent characteristic of the Jews that they had refused to obey the commands of the *true* God, Josh. v. 6; Judg. ii. 2; vi. 10; 2 Kings xviii. 12; Jer. iii. 13, 25; xlii. 21; xliii. 4, 7; ix. 13. ¶ *But obey unrighteousness.* The expression means that they yielded themselves to iniquity, and thus became *the servants of sin,* Rom. vi. 13, 16, 17, 19. Iniquity thus may be said to *reign* over men, as they follow the dictates of evil, make no resistance to it, and implicitly obey all its hard requirements. ¶ *Indignation and wrath.* That is, these *shall be rendered* to those who are contentious, &c. The difference between indignation and wrath, says Ammonius, is that the former is of *short duration,* but the latter is a long-continued remembrance of evil. The one is *temporary,* the other denotes *continued* expressions of hatred of evil. Eustathius says that the word *indignation* denotes the *internal* emotion, but *wrath* the *external* manifestation of indignation (Tholuck). Both words refer to the opposition which God will cherish and express against sin in the world of punishment.

9. *Tribulation.* This word commonly denotes *affliction,* or the situation of being *pressed down* by a burden, as of trials, calamities, &c.; and hence to be *pressed down* by punishment or pain inflicted for sins. As applied to future punishment, it denotes the pressure of the calamities that will come upon the soul as the just reward of sin. ¶ *And anguish* (στενοχωρία). This noun is used in but three other places in the New Testament: Rom. viii. 35; 2 Cor. vi. 4; xii. 10. The *verb* is used in 2 Cor. iv. 8; vi. 12. It means literally *narrowness of place, want of room,* and then the anxiety

9 Tribulation and anguish, upon every soul of man that doeth evil,

and distress of mind which a man experiences who is pressed *on every side* by afflictions, and trials, and want, or by punishment, and who does not know where he may turn himself to find relief (Schleusner). It is thus expressive of the punishment of the wicked. It means that they shall be *compressed* with the manifestations of God's displeasure, so as to be in deep distress, and so as not to know where to find relief. These words *affliction and anguish* are often connected, Rom. viii. 35. ¶ *Upon every soul of man.* Upon *all* men. In Hebrew the word *soul* often denotes the man himself. But still, the apostles, by the use of this word here, meant perhaps to signify that the punishment should not be *corporeal,* but afflicting the *soul.* It should be a *spiritual* punishment, a punishment of *mind* (Ambrose. See Tholuck). ¶ *Of the Jew first.* Having stated the *general principle* of the divine administration, he comes now to make the application. To the *principle* there could be no objection. And the apostle now shows that it was applicable to the Jew as well as the Greek, and to the Jew pre-eminently. It was applicable *first,* or in an *eminent degree,* to the Jew, because, (1) He had been peculiarly favoured with light and knowledge on all these subjects. (2) These principles were fully stated in his own law, and were in strict accordance with all the teaching of the prophets; see Note on ver. 6; also Ps. vii. 11; ix. 17; cxxxix. 19; Prov. xiv. 32. ¶ *Of the Gentile.* That is, of all who were not Jews. On what principles God will inflict punishment on them, he states in ver. 12–16. It is clear that this refers to the *future* punishment of the wicked, for, (1) It stands in contrast with the *eternal life* of those who seek for glory (ver. 7). If this description of the effect of sin refers to *this life,* then the effects spoken of in relation to the righteous refer to this life also. But in no place in the Scriptures is it said that men experience *all* the blessings of *eternal* life

of the Jew first, and also of the ¹Gentile:

10 But ¹glory, honour, and peace, to every man that worketh

¹ or, *Greek*.　　　*l* 1 Pe.1.7.

good, to the Jew first, and also to the ¹Gentile:

11 For*ᵐ* there is no respect of persons with God.

m De.10.17; 2 Ch.19.7; Ga.6.7,8; 1 Pe.1.17.

in this world; and the very supposition is absurd. (2) It is not *true* that there is a just and complete retribution to every man, according to his deeds, in this life. Many of the wicked are prospered in *life*, and "there are no bands in their death, but their strength is firm," Ps. lxxiii. 4. Many of the righteous pine in poverty and want and affliction, and die in the flames of persecution. Nothing is more clear than that there is *not* in this life a full and equitable distribution of rewards and punishments; and as the *proposition* of the apostle here is, that *God* WILL *render to every man* ACCORDING *to his deeds* (ver. 6), it follows that this must be accomplished in another world. (3) The Scriptures uniformly affirm, that for *the very things* specified here, God will consign men to eternal death, 2 Thes. i. 8, "In flaming fire, taking vengeance on them that know not God, and that OBEY NOT the gospel of our Lord Jesus Christ, who shall be punished with everlasting destruction," &c.; 1 Pet. iv. 17. We may remark also, that there could be no more alarming description of future suffering than is specified in this passage. It is *indignation*, it is *wrath*, it is *tribulation*, it is *anguish* which the sinner is to endure for ever. Truly men exposed to this awful doom should be alarmed, and should give diligence to escape from the woe which is to come.

11. *For.* This particle is used here to *confirm* what is said before, particularly that this punishment should be experienced by the *Jew* as well as the *Gentile.* For God would deal with both on the principles of justice. ¶ *Respect of persons.* The word thus rendered means *partiality*, in pronouncing judgment, in favouring one party or individual more than another, not because his cause is more just, but on account of something personal— on account of his wealth, or rank, or

VOL. IV.

office, or influence, or by personal friendship, or by the fear of him. It has special reference to a *judge* who pronounces judgment between parties at law. The exercise of such partiality was strictly and often forbidden to the Jewish magistrates, Lev. xix. 15; Deut. i. 17; Prov. xxiv. 23; Jam. ii. 1, 3, 9. In his capacity as a *Judge*, it is applied often to God. It means that he will not be influenced in awarding the retributions of eternity, in *actually* pronouncing and executing sentence, by any partiality, or by regard to the wealth, office, rank, or appearance of men. He will judge righteous judgment; he will judge men as they *ought* to be judged; according to their *character* and deserts; and not contrary to their character, or by partiality. The *connection* here demands that this affirmation should be limited *solely to his dealing with men* AS THEIR JUDGE. And in this sense, and this only, this is affirmed often of God in the Scriptures, Deut. x. 17; 2 Chron. xix. 7; Eph. vi. 9; Col. iii. 25; Gal. vi. 7, 8; 1 Pet. i. 17; Acts x. 34. It does not affirm that he *must* make all his creatures *equal* in talent, health, wealth, or privilege; it does not imply that, as a sovereign, he may not make a difference in their endowments, their beauty, strength, or graces; it does not imply that he may not bestow his favours where he pleases where *all* are undeserving, or that he may not make a difference in the *characters* of men by his providence, and by the agency of his Spirit. All these are *actually* done, done not out of any respect to their *persons*, to their rank, office, or wealth, but according to his own sovereign good pleasure, Eph. i. To deny that this *is* done, would be to deny the manifest arrangement of things everywhere on the earth. To deny that God had a *right* to do it, would be, (1) To maintain that sinners had a

12 For as many as have sinned without law, shall also perish

claim on his favours. (2) That he might not do what he willed with his own; or (3) To affirm that God was under obligation to make all men with just the same talents and privileges, *i.e.* that all creatures *must be*, in all respects, *just alike.* This passage, therefore, is very improperly brought to *disprove* the doctrine of decrees, or election, or sovereignty. It has respect to a different thing, to the *actual exercise* of the office of *the Judge of the world;* and whatever may be the truth about God's decrees, or his electing love, *this* passage teaches nothing in relation to either. It may be added that this passage contains a most alarming truth for guilty men. It is that God will not be influenced by *partiality*, but will treat them *just as they deserve.* He will not be won or awed by their rank or office; by their wealth or endowments; by their numbers, their power, or their robes of royalty and splendour. Every man should tremble at the prospect of falling into the hands of a *just God,* who will treat him just as he deserves, and should without delay seek a refuge in the Saviour and Advocate provided for the guilty, 1 John ii. 1, 2.

12. *For.* This is used to give a *reason* for what he had just said, or to show on what principles God would treat man, so as not to be a respecter of persons. ¶ *As many. Whosoever.* This includes *all* who have done it, and evidently has respect to the Gentile world. It is of the more importance to remark this, because he does not say that it is applicable to a *few* only, or to great and incorrigible instances of pagan wickedness, but it is a universal, sweeping declaration, obviously including *all.* ¶ *Have sinned.* Have been guilty of crimes of any kind toward God or man. Sin is the transgression of a rule of conduct, however made known to mankind. ¶ *Without law* (ἀνόμως). This expression evidently means without *revealed* or *written* law, as the apostle immediately says that they *had* a law of nature (ver. 14, 15). The word law, νόμος, is often used to denote the re-

vealed law of God, the Scriptures, or revelation in general, Mat. xii. 5; Luke ii. 23, 24; x. 26; John viii. 5, 17. ¶ *Shall also perish* (ἀπολοῦνται). The Greek word used here occurs frequently in the New Testament. It means to *destroy*, to *lose*, or to *corrupt*, and is applied to *life* (Mat. x. 39); to a *reward* of labour (Mat. x. 42); to *wisdom* (1 Cor. i. 19); to *bottles* (Mat. ix. 17). It is also used to denote future punishment, or the destruction of soul and body in hell (Mat. x. 28; xviii. 14; John iii. 15), where it is *opposed to eternal life*, and therefore denotes *eternal death*, Rom. xiv. 15; John xvii. 12. In this sense the word is evidently used in this verse. The connection demands that the reference should be to a future judgment to be passed on the heathen. It will be remarked here that the apostle does not say they shall *be saved* without law. He does not give even an intimation respecting their salvation. The strain of the argument, as well as this express declaration, shows that they who had *sinned* — and in the first chapter he had proved that *all* the heathen were sinners—would be punished. If any of the heathen are saved, it will be, therefore, an exception to the *general rule* in regard to them. The apostles evidently believed that the great mass of them would be destroyed. *On this ground* they evinced such zeal to save them; on this ground the Lord Jesus commanded the gospel to be preached to them; and on this ground Christians are now engaged in the effort to bring them to the knowledge of the Lord Jesus. It may be added here, that all modern investigations have gone to confirm the position that the heathen are as degraded now as they were in the days of Paul. ¶ *Without law.* That is, they shall not be judged by a law which they have not. They shall not be tried and condemned by the *revelation* which the Jews had. They shall be condemned only according to the knowledge and the law which they actually possess. This is the equit-

without law: and as many as have sinned in the law, shall be judged by the law;

13 (For[n] not the hearers of the law *are* just before God, but the doers of the law shall be justified.

n Ja.1.22-25.

able rule on which God will judge the world. According to this, it is not to be apprehended that they will suffer *as much* as those who have the revealed will of God; comp. Mat. x. 15; xi. 24; Luke x. 12. ¶ *Have sinned in the law.* Have sinned *having* the revealed will of God, or endowed with greater light and privileges than the heathen world. The apostle here has undoubted reference to the *Jews*, who had the law of God, and who prided themselves much on its possession. ¶ *Shall be judged by the law.* This is an equitable and just rule; and to this the Jews could make no objection. Yet the admission of this would have led directly to the point to which Paul was conducting his argument, to show that *they* also were under condemnation, and needed a Saviour. It will be observed here, that the apostle uses a different expression in regard to the Jews from what he does of the Gentiles. He says of the former, that they " *shall be judged;* " of the latter, that they " *shall perish.*" It is not certainly known why he varied this expression. But if conjecture may be allowed, it may have been for the following reasons. (1) If he had affirmed of the Jews that they should *perish*, it would at once have excited their prejudice, and have armed them against the conclusion to which he was about to come. Yet they could bear the word to be applied to *the heathen*, for it was in accordance with their own views and their own mode of speaking, and was strictly true. (2) The word "judged" is *apparently* more *mild*, and yet *really* more *severe*. It would arouse no prejudice to say that they would be judged by their law. It was indeed paying a sort of tribute or regard to that on which they prided themselves so much, the possession of the law of God. Still, it was a word *implying* all that he wished to say, and *involving* the idea that *they*

would be punished and destroyed. If it was admitted that the heathen would perish; and if God was to judge the Jews by an unerring rule, that is, according to their privileges and light; then it would follow that they would also be condemned, and *their own minds* would come at once to the conclusion. The change of words here may indicate, therefore, a nice *tact*, or delicate address in argument, urging home to the conscience an offensive truth rather by the deduction of the mind of the opponent *himself*, than by a harsh and severe charge of the writer. In instances of this, the Scriptures abound; and it was this especially that so eminently characterized the arguments of our Saviour.

13. *For not the hearers,* &c. The same sentiment is implied in James i. 22; Mat. vii. 21, 24; Luke vi. 47. The apostle here doubtless designed to meet an objection of the Jews; to wit, that they had the law, that they manifested great deference for it, that they heard it read with attention, and professed a willingness to yield themselves to it. To meet this, he states a very plain and obvious principle, that this was insufficient to justify them before God, unless they rendered actual obedience. ¶ *Are just.* Are justified before God, or are personally holy. Or, in other words, simply *hearing* the law is not meeting all its requirements, and making men holy. If they expected to be saved by the *law*, it required something more than merely to *hear* it. It demanded *perfect obedience.* ¶ *But the doers of the law.* They who comply entirely with its demands; or who yield to it perfect and perpetual obedience. This was the plain and obvious demand, not only of common sense, but of the Jewish law itself, Deut. iv. 1; Lev. xviii. 5; comp. Rom. x. 9. ¶ *Shall be justified.* This expression is evidently synonymous with that in Lev. xviii. 5, where it is said that "he shall live in

14 For when the Gentiles, which have not the law, do by nature the things contained in the law, these having not the law, are *o* a law unto themselves.

15 Which show the work of

o 1 Co.11.14.

them." The meaning is, that it is a *maxim* or *principle* of the law of God, that if a creature will keep it, and obey it entirely, he shall not be *condemned*, but shall be *approved* and *live for ever.* This does not affirm that anyone ever *has* thus lived in this world, but it is an affirmation of a great general principle of law, that if a creature is justified BY *the law*, the obedience must be entire and perpetual. If such *were* the case, as there would be no ground of condemnation, man would be saved by the law. If the Jews, therefore, expected to be saved by their law, it must be, not by *hearing* the law, nor by being called a Jew, but by perfect and unqualified obedience to all its requirements. This passage is designed, doubtless, to meet a very common and pernicious sentiment of the Jewish teachers, that *all* who became hearers and listeners to the law would be saved. The *inference* from the passage is, that no man can be saved by his *external* privileges, or by an *outward* respectful deference to the truths and ordinances of religion.

14. *For when.* The apostle, in ver. 13, had stated a general principle, that the *doers of the law* only can be justified, if justification is attempted by the law. In this verse and the next, he proceeds to show that the same *principle* is applicable to the heathen; that though they have not the *written* law of God, yet that they have sufficient knowledge of his will to take away every excuse for sin, and consequently that the course of reasoning by which he had come to the conclusion that they were guilty, is well founded. This verse is not to be understood as affirming, as an *historical fact*, that any of the heathen ever *did* perfectly obey the law which they had, any more than the previous verse affirms it of the Jews. The main point in the argument is, that if men are justified by the *law*, their obedience must be *entire* and *perfect* that this is not to

be external only, or to consist in *hearing* or in acknowledging the justice of the law; and that the Gentiles had an opportunity of illustrating this principle as well as the Jews, since they also had a law among themselves. The word *when* (ὅταν) does not imply that the thing *shall certainly* take place, but is one form of introducing a supposition, or of stating the connection of one thing with another, Mat. v. 11; vi. 2, 5, 6, 16; x. 19. It is, however, true that the main things contained in this verse, and the next, actually occurred, that the Gentiles did *many* things which the law of God required. ¶ *The Gentiles.* All who were not Jews. ¶ *Which have not the law.* Who have not a revelation, or the written word of God. In the Greek the article is omitted, "who have not law," *i.e.* any revealed law. ¶ *By nature.* By some, this phrase has been supposed to belong to the previous member of the sentence, "who have not the law *by nature.*" But our translation is the more natural and usual construction. The expression means clearly by the light of conscience and reason, and whatever other helps they may have *without* revelation. It denotes simply, *in that state which is without the revealed will of God.* In that condition they had many helps of tradition, conscience, reason, and the observation of the dealings of divine Providence, so that to a considerable extent they knew what was right and what was wrong. ¶ *Do the things.* Should they not merely *understand* and *approve*, but actually *perform* the things required in the law. ¶ *Contained in the law.* Literally the things *of* the law, *i.e.* the things which the law *requires.* Many of those things might be done by the heathen, as *e.g.* respect to parents, truth, justice, honesty, chastity. *So far* as they *did* any of those things, so far they showed that they *had* a law among themselves. And wherein they *failed* in these things they showed

the law written in their hearts,
[2]their conscience also bearing witness, and *their* thoughts [3]the mean

2 or, *the conscience witnessing with them.*

while accusing or else excusing one
another;)

16 In the day when God shall

3 or, *between themselves.*

---

that they were justly condemned.
¶ *Are a law unto themselves.* This
is explained in the following verse. It
means that their own reason and conscience constituted, *in these things*, a
law, or prescribed that for them which
the revealed law did to the Jews.

15. *Which show.* Who thus evince
or show. ¶ *The work of the law.*
The design, purpose, or object which
is contemplated by the revealed law;
that is, to make known to man his
duty, and to *enforce* the obligation to
perform it. This does not mean, by
any means, that they had *all* the
knowledge which the law would impart, for then there would have been
no need of a revelation, but that, *as far
as it went*, as far as they had a knowledge of right and wrong, they *coincided* with the revealed will of God.
In other words, the will of God, whether made known by reason or revelation, will be *the same* so far as reason
goes. The difference is that revelation
goes farther than reason; sheds light
on new duties and doctrines; as the
information given by the naked eye
and the telescope is the same, except
that the telescope carries the sight
forward, and reveals new worlds to
the sight of man. ¶ *Written in their
hearts.* The revealed law of God was
written on tables of stone, and then
recorded in the books of the Old Testament. This law the Gentiles did
not possess, but, to a certain extent,
the same requirements were written on
their hearts. Though not *revealed* to
them as to the Jews, yet they had
obtained the knowledge of them by the
light of nature. The word *hearts* here
denotes the *mind itself*, as it does also
frequently in the sacred Scriptures;
not the heart, as the seat of the affections. It does not mean that they
loved or even approved of the law, but
that they had knowledge of it; and
that that knowledge was deeply engraven on their minds. ¶ *Their conscience.* This word properly means

the judgment of the mind respecting
right and wrong; or the judgment
which the mind passes on the morality
or immorality of its own actions, when
it instantly approves or condemns
them. It has usually been termed
the *moral sense*, and is a very important principle in a moral government.
Its design is to answer the purposes
of an *ever attendant witness* of a man's
conduct; to compel him to pronounce
on his own doings, and thus to excite
him to virtuous deeds, to give comfort and peace when he does right, to
deter from evil actions by making him,
whether he will or no, *his own executioner;* see John viii. 9; Acts xxiii.
1; xxiv. 16; Rom. ix. 1; 1 Tim. i. 5.
By nature every man thus approves
or condemns his own acts; and there
is not a profounder principle of the
Divine administration, than thus compelling every man to pronounce on the
moral character of his own conduct.
Conscience may be enlightened or
unenlightened; and its use may be
greatly perverted by false opinions.
Its province is not to communicate
any *new truth*, it is simply to express
judgment, and to impart pleasure or
inflict pain for a man's own good or
evil conduct. The apostle's argument does not require him to say that
conscience *revealed* any truth, or any
knowledge of duty, to the Gentiles,
but that *its actual exercise* proved that
they *had* a knowledge of the law of
God. Thus it was a *witness* simply of
that fact. ¶ *Bearing witness.* To
bear witness is to furnish testimony,
or proof. And the exercise of the
conscience here showed or proved that
they *had* a knowledge of the law. The
expression does not mean that the
exercise of *their* conscience bore witness of anything to *them*, but that its
exercise may be alleged as a proof
that they were not without some knowledge of the law. ¶ *And their thoughts.*
The word thoughts (λογισμῶν) means
properly *reasonings*, or *opinions*, sen-

judge *p* the secrets of men, by Jesus | Christ, *q* according to my gospel.

p Lu.8.17.   *q* Ro.16.25.

timents, &c. Its meaning here may be expressed by the word *reflections.* Their reflections on their own conduct would be attended with pain or pleasure. It differs from *conscience,* inasmuch as the decisions of conscience are *instantaneous,* and without any process of reasoning. This supposes subsequent reflection, and it means that such reflections would only deepen and confirm the decisions of conscience. ¶ *The mean while.* Margin, "between themselves." The rendering in the margin is more in accordance with the Greek. The expression sometimes means, in the meantime, or at the same time; and sometimes *afterward,* or *subsequently.* The Syriac and Latin Vulgate render this *mutually.* They seem to have understood this as affirming that the heathen among themselves, by their writings, accused or acquitted one another. ¶ *Accusing.* If the actions were evil. ¶ *Excusing.* That is, if their actions were good. ¶ *One another.* The margin renders this expression in connection with the adverb, translated "in the mean while," "between themselves." This view is also taken by many commentators, and this is its probable meaning. If so, it denotes the fact that in their *reflections,* or their *reasonings,* or *discussions,* they accused each other of crime, or acquitted one another; they showed that they *had* a law; that they acted on the supposition that they had. To show this was the design of the apostle; and there was no further proof of it needed than that which he here adduced. (1) They had a *conscience,* pronouncing on their *own* acts; and, (2) Their *reasonings, based on the supposition of some such common and acknowledged standard* of accusing or acquitting, supposed the same thing. If, therefore, they condemned or acquitted *themselves;* if, in these reasonings and reflections, they proceeded on the principle that they *had* some rule of right and wrong, *then* the proposition of the apostle was made out, that it was right for God to judge

them, and to destroy them, ver. 8–12.

16. *In the day.* This verse is doubtless to be connected with verse 12, and the intermediate verses are a parenthesis, and it implies that the heathen world, as well as the Jews, will be arraigned at the bar of judgment. At that time God will judge all in righteousness, the Jew by the law which *he* had, and the heathen by the law which *he* had. ¶ *When God shall judge.* God is often represented as the Judge of mankind, Deut. xxxii. 36; Ps. l. 4; 1 Sam. ii. 10; Eccl. iii. 17; Rom. iii. 6; Heb. xiii. 4. But this does not militate against the fact that he will do it *by* Jesus Christ. God has appointed his Son to administer judgment; and it will be not by God *directly,* but by Jesus Christ that it will be administered. ¶ *The secrets of men.* See Luke viii. 17; Eccl. xii. 14, "For God shall bring every work into judgment, *with every secret thing,*" &c.; Mat. x. 26; 1 Cor. iv. 5. The expression denotes the hidden desires, lusts, passions, and motives of men; the thoughts of the heart, as well as the outward actions of the life. It will be a characteristic of the day of judgment, that all these will be brought out, and receive their appropriate reward. The propriety of this is apparent, for, (1) It is by these that the *character* is really determined. The *motives* and *principles* of a man constitute his character, and to judge him impartially, these must be known. (2) They are not judged or rewarded in this life. The external conduct only can be seen by men, and of course that only can be rewarded or punished here. (3) Men of pure motives and pure hearts are often here basely aspersed and calumniated. They are persecuted, traduced, and often overwhelmed with ignominy. It is proper that the *secret* motives of their conduct should be brought out and approved. On the other hand, men of base motives, men of unprincipled character, and who are corrupt at the heart, are often lauded, flattered, and exalted into pub-

17 Behold, *r* thou art called a Jew, and restest in the

r ver.28.

law, and makest thy boast of God,

---

lic estimation. It is proper that their secret principles should be detected, and that they should take their proper place in the government of God. In regard to this expression, we may further remark, (1) That the fact that *all* secret thoughts and purposes will be brought into judgment, invests the judgment with an awful character. Who should not tremble at the idea that the secret plans and desires of his soul, which he has so long and so studiously concealed, should be brought out into noon-day in the judgment? All his artifices of concealment shall be then at an end. He will be able to practise disguise no longer. He will be seen as he is; and he will receive the doom he deserves. There will be *one* place, at least, where the sinner shall be treated as he ought. (2) To execute this judgment implies the power of searching the heart; of knowing the thoughts; and of developing and unfolding all the purposes and plans of the soul. Yet this is intrusted to Jesus Christ, and the fact that *he* will exercise this, shows that he is divine. ¶ *Of men.* Of all men, whether Jew or Gentile, infidel or Christian. The day of judgment, therefore, may be regarded as a day of universal development of all the plans and purposes that have ever been entertained in this world. ¶ *By Jesus Christ.* The fact that Jesus Christ is appointed to judge the world is abundantly taught in the Bible, Acts xvii. 31; 2 Tim. iv. 1; 1 Pet. iv. 5; John v. 22, 27; 1 Thes. iv. 16–18; Mat. xxv. 31–46. ¶ *According to my gospel.* According to the gospel which *I preach;* comp. Acts xvii. 31; 2 Tim. iv. 8. This does not mean that the gospel which he preached would be the *rule* by which God would judge all mankind, for he had just said that the heathen world would be judged by a different rule, ver. 12. But it means that he was intrusted with the gospel to make it known; and that one of the great and prime articles of that gospel was, that God would judge the world by

Jesus Christ. To make *this* known he was appointed; and it could be called *his* gospel only as being a part of the important message with which he was intrusted.

17. *Behold.* Having thus stated the *general principles* on which God would judge the world; having shown how they condemned the Gentiles; and having removed all objections to them, he now proceeds to *another* part of his argument, to show how they applied to the *Jews.* By the use of the word *behold,* he calls their attention to it, as to an important subject; and with great skill and address, he states their privileges, before he shows them how those privileges might enhance their condemnation. He admits all their claims to pre-eminence in privileges, and then with great faithfulness proceeds to show how, if abused, these might deepen their final destruction. It should be observed, however, that the word rendered *behold* is in many MSS. written in two words, ἔι δὲ, instead of ἴδε. If this, as is probable, is the correct reading there, it should be rendered, "if now thou art," &c. Thus the Syriac, Latin, and Arabic read it. ¶ *Thou art called.* Thou art *named* Jew, implying that this name was one of very high honour. This is the *first* thing mentioned on which the Jew would be likely to pride himself. ¶ *A Jew.* This was the name by which the Hebrews were at that time generally known; and it is clear that they regarded it as a name of honour, and valued themselves much on it; see Gal. ii. 15; Rev. ii. 9. Its origin is not certainly known. They were called the children of Israel until the time of Rehoboam. When the *ten* tribes were carried into captivity, but two remained, the tribes of *Judah* and Benjamin. The name *Jews* was evidently given to denote those of the tribe of *Judah.* The reasons why the name of *Benjamin* was lost in that of *Judah,* were probably, (1) Because the tribe of Benjamin was small, and

18 And ^sknowest *his* will, and ⁴approvest^t the things that are

s Ps.147.19,20.
4 or, *triest the things that differ.* *t* Phi.1.10.

comparatively without influence or importance. (2) The *Messiah* was to be of the tribe of *Judah* (Gen. xlix. 10); and that tribe would therefore possess a consequence proportioned to their expectation of that event. The name of *Jews* would therefore be one that would suggest the facts that they were preserved from captivity, that they had received remarkably the protection of God, and that the Messiah was to be sent to that people. Hence it is not wonderful that they should regard it as a special favour to be a *Jew*, and particularly when they added to this the idea of *all* the other favours connected with their being the peculiar people of God. The name *Jew* came thus to denote all the peculiarities and special favours of their religion. ¶ *And restest in the law.* The word *rest* here is evidently used in the sense of *trusting to*, or *leaning upon.* The Jew *leaned on*, or *relied* on the law for acceptance or favour; on the fact that he *had* the law, and on his obedience to it. It does not mean that he relied on his own works, though that was true, but that he leaned on *the fact* that he had the law, and was thus distinguished above others. The *law* here means the entire Mosaic economy; or all the rules and regulations which Moses had given. Perhaps also it includes, as it sometimes does, the whole of the Old Testament. ¶ *Makest thy boast in God.* Thou dost boast, or glory, that thou hast the knowledge of the true God, while other nations are in darkness. On this account the Jew felt himself far elevated above all other people, and despised them. It was true that they only had the true knowledge of God, and that he had declared himself to be their God (Deut. iv. 7; Ps. cxlvii. 19, 20); but this was not a ground for *boasting*, but for *gratitude.* This passage shows us that it is much more common to *boast* of privileges than to be *thankful* for them, and that it is no

more excellent, being instructed out of the law;

evidence of piety for a man to *boast* of his knowledge of God. An humble, ardent thankfulness that we *have* that knowledge—a thankfulness which leads us not to *despise* others, but to desire that *they* may have the same privilege—*is* an evidence of piety.

18. *And knowest* his *will.* The will or commands of God. This knowledge they obtained from the Scriptures; and of course in this they were distinguished from other nations. ¶ *And approvest.* The word used here is capable of two interpretations. It may mean either to *distinguish*, or to *approve.* The word is properly and usually applied to the process of testing or trying metals by fire. Hence it comes to be used in a general sense to *try* or to *distinguish* anything; to ascertain its nature, quality, &c., Luke xii. 56. This is probably its meaning here, referring rather to the *intellectual* process of discriminating, than to the *moral* process of approving. It could not, perhaps, be said with propriety, at least the scope of the passage does not properly suppose this, that the Jew *approved* or *loved* the things of God; but the scope of the passage is, that the Jew valued himself on his *knowledge* of that which was conformable to the will of God; see Notes on chap. xiv. ¶ *The things that are more excellent.* The word here translated *more excellent* denotes properly the things that *differ* from others, and then also the things that *excel.* It has an ambiguity similar to the word translated "approved." If the interpretation of that word above given is correct, then this word here means those things that differ from others. The reference is to the rites and customs, to the distinctions of meats and days, &c., prescribed by the law of Moses. The Jew would pride himself on the fact that he had been taught by the law to make these distinctions, while all the heathen world had been left in ignorance of them. This was one of the advantages on

19 And art confident that thou thyself art a guide of the blind, a light of them which are in darkness,

20 An instructor of the foolish, a teacher of babes, which hast *the form of knowledge and of the truth in the law:

u 2 Ti.1.13; 3.5.

which he valued himself and his religion. ¶ *Being instructed*, &c. That is, in regard to the one God, his will, and the distinguishing rites of his worship.

19. *And art confident.* This expression denotes the full assurance of the Jew that he was superior in knowledge to all other people. It is a remarkable fact that the Jews put the fullest confidence in their religion. Though proud, wicked, and hypocritical, yet they were not speculative infidels. It was one of their characteristics, evinced through all their history, that they had the fullest assurance that God was the author of their institutions, and that their religion was his appointment. ¶ *A guide of the blind.* A guide of the blind is a figurative expression to denote an instructor of the ignorant. The *blind* here properly refers to the *Gentiles,* who were thus regarded by the Jews. The meaning is, that they esteemed themselves qualified to instruct the heathen world, Mat. xv. 14; xxiii. 15. ¶ *A light.* Another figurative expression to denote a *teacher;* comp. Isa. xlix. 6; John i. 4, 5, 8, 9. ¶ *In darkness.* A common expression to denote the *ignorance* of the Gentile world; see Note, Mat. iv. 16.

20. *Of the foolish.* The word *foolish* is used in the Scriptures in two significations: to denote those who are void of understanding, and to denote the wicked. Here it is clearly used in the former sense, signifying that the Jew esteemed himself qualified to instruct those without knowledge. ¶ *Of babes.* This is the *literal* meaning of the original word. The expression is figurative, and denotes those who were as *ignorant as children*—an expression which they would be likely to apply to all the Gentiles. It is evident that the character here given by Paul to the Jews is one which they claimed, and of which they were proud. They are often mentioned as arrogating this

prerogative to themselves, of being qualified to be guides and teachers of others, Mat. xv. 14; xxiii. 2, 16, 24. It will be remembered, also, that the Jews considered themselves to be qualified to teach all the world, and hence evinced great zeal to make proselytes. And it is not improbable (Tholuck) that their rabbies were accustomed to give the names "foolish" and "babes" to the ignorant proselytes which they had made from the heathen. ¶ *Which hast the form of knowledge.* The word here translated *form* properly denotes a *delineation* or *picturing* of a thing. It is commonly used to denote also the *appearance* of any object; that which we see, without reference to its internal character; the external figure. It sometimes denotes the external appearance *as distinguished* from that which is internal; or a hypocritical profession of religion without its reality, 2 Tim. iii. 5, "Having the form of godliness, but denying its power." It is sometimes used in a good and sometimes in a bad sense. Here it denotes that in their teaching they retained the *semblance,* *sketch* or *outline* of the true doctrines of the Old Testament. They had in the Scriptures a correct *delineation* of the truth. Truth is the representation of things as they are; and the doctrines which the Jews had in the Old Testament were a correct representation or delineation of the objects of knowledge; comp. 2 Tim. i. 13. ¶ *In the law.* In the Scriptures of the Old Testament. In these verses the apostle concedes to the Jews all that they would claim. Having made this concession of their superior knowledge, he is prepared with the more fidelity and force to convict them of their deep and dreadful depravity in sinning against the superior light and privileges which God had conferred on them.

21. *Thou therefore,* &c. He who

21 Thou [v] therefore which teachest another, teachest thou not thyself? thou that preachest a man should not steal, dost thou steal?

22 Thou that sayest a man should not commit adultery, dost

[v] Mat.23.3,&c.

thou commit adultery? thou that abhorrest idols, dost thou commit sacrilege?

23 Thou that makest thy boast of the law, through breaking the law dishonourest thou God?

24 For the name of God is

is a teacher of others may be expected to be learned himself. They *ought* to be found to be possessed of superior knowledge; and by this question the apostle *impliedly* reproves them for their ignorance. The form of a *question* is chosen because it conveys the truth with greater force. He puts the question as if it were undeniable that they were grossly ignorant; comp. Mat. xxiii. 3, "They say and do not," &c. ¶ *That preachest.* This word means to *proclaim* in any manner, whether in the synagogue, or in any place of public teaching. ¶ *Dost thou steal?* It cannot be proved, perhaps, that the Jews were extensively guilty of this crime. It is introduced partly, no doubt, to make the inconsistency of their conduct more apparent. We expect a man to set an example of what he means by his public instruction.

22. *Dost thou commit adultery?* There is no doubt that this was a crime very common among the Jews; see Notes, Mat. xii. 39; John viii. 1–11. The Jewish Talmud accuses some of the most celebrated of their rabbies, by name, of this vice (Grotius). Josephus also gives the same account of the nation. ¶ *Thou that abhorrest idols.* It was one of the doctrines of their religion to abhor idolatry. This they were everywhere taught in the Old Testament; and this they doubtless inculcated in their teaching. It was impossible that they could recommend idolatry. ¶ *Dost thou commit sacrilege?* Sacrilege is the crime of violating or profaning sacred things; or of appropriating to common purposes what has been devoted to the service of religion. In this question, the apostle shows remarkable tact and skill. He could not accuse them of *idolatry,* for the Jews, after the Baby-

lonish captivity, had never fallen into it. But then, though they had not the *form,* they might have the *spirit* of idolatry. That spirit consisted in withholding from the true God that which was his due, and bestowing the affections upon something else. This the Jews did by perverting from their proper use the offerings which were designed for his honour; by withholding that which he demanded of tithes and offerings; and by devoting to other uses that which was devoted to him, and which properly belonged to his service. That this was a common crime among them is apparent from Mal. i. 8, 12–14; iii. 8, 9. It is also evident from the New Testament that the temple was in many ways desecrated and profaned in the time of our Saviour; Notes, Mat. xxi. 12, 13.

23. *Makest thy boast,* &c. To boast in the law implied their conviction of its excellence and obligation, as a man does not boast of that which he esteems to be of no value. ¶ *Dishonourest thou God?* By boasting of the law, they proclaimed their conviction that it was from God. By breaking it, they denied it. And as actions are a true test of man's real opinions, their breaking the law did it more dishonour than their boasting of it did it honour. This is always the case. It matters little what a man's speculative opinions may be; his practice may do far more to disgrace religion than his profession does to honour it. It is the life and conduct, and not merely the profession of the lips, that does real honour to the true religion. Alas, with what pertinency and force may this question be put to many who call themselves Christians!

24. *The name of God.* The name and character of the true God. ¶ *Is blasphemed.* Note, Mat. ix. 3. That is, your conduct is such as to lead the

blasphemed among the Gentiles through you, *as it is written.

w Eze.36.20,23.

25 For circumcision verily profiteth, if thou keep the law : *but

x Ga.5.3.

heathen world to blaspheme and reproach both your religion and its Author. By your hypocrisy and crimes the pagan world is led to despise a religion which is observed to have no effect in purifying and restraining its professors; and of course the reproach will terminate on the Author of your religion—that is, the true God. A life of purity would tend to honour religion and its Author; a life of impurity does the reverse. There is no doubt that this was actually the effect of the deportment of the Jews. They were scattered everywhere; everywhere they were corrupt and wicked; and everywhere they and their religion were despised. ¶ *Among the Gentiles.* In the midst of whom many Jews lived. ¶ *Through you.* By means of you, or as the result of your conduct. It *may* mean, that you Jews do it, or profane the name of God; but the connection seems rather to require the former sense. ¶ *As it is written.* To what place the apostle has reference, cannot be certainly determined. There are two passages in the Old Testament which will bear on the case, and perhaps he had them both in his view, Isa. lii. 5; Ezek. xxxvi. 22, 23. The meaning is not that the passages in the Old Testament, referred to by the phrase, "as it is written," had any particular reference to the conduct of the Jews in the time of Paul, but that this had been the *character of the people*, and the effect of their conduct *as a nation*, instances of which had been before observed and recorded by the prophets. The same thing has occurred to a most melancholy extent in regard to professed Christian nations. For purposes of commerce, and science, and war, and traffic, men from nations nominally Christian have gone into almost every part of the heathen world. But they have not often been real Christians. They have been intent on gain; and have to a melancholy extent been profane, and unprincipled, and profligate men. Yet the heathen

have regarded them as *Christians;* as fair specimens of the effect of the religion of Christ. They have learned, therefore, to abuse the name of Christian, and the Author of the Christian religion, as encouraging and promoting profligacy of life. Hence *one* reason, among thousands, of the importance of Christian missions to the heathen. It is well to disabuse the pagan world of their erroneous opinions of the tendency of Christianity. It is well to teach them that we do not regard these men as Christians. As we have sent to them the *worst part* of our population, it is well to send them holy men, who shall exhibit to them the true nature of Christianity, and raise our character in their eyes as a Christian people. And were there no other result of Christian missions, it would be worth all the expense and toil attending them, *to raise the national character* in the view of the pagan world.

25. *For circumcision.* Note, John vii. 22; Acts vii. 8. This was the peculiar rite by which the relation to the covenant of Abraham was recognized; or by which the right to all the privileges of a member of the Jewish commonwealth was acknowledged. The Jews of course affixed a high importance to the rite. ¶ *Verily profiteth.* Is truly a benefit; or is an advantage. The meaning is, that their being recognized as members of the Jewish commonwealth, and introduced to the privileges of the Jew, was an advantage; see chap. iii. 1, 2. The apostle was not disposed to deny that they possessed this advantage, but he tells them *why* it was a benefit, and how it might fail of conferring any favour. ¶ *If thou keep the law.* The mere *sign* can be of no value. The mere fact of being a Jew is not what God requires. It may be a favour to *have* his law, but the mere possession of the law cannot entitle to the favour of God. So it is a privilege to be born in a Christian land; to have had pious

if thou be a breaker of the law, thy circumcision is made uncircumcision.

26 Therefore^y if the uncircumcision keep the righteousness of

y Ac.10.34,35.

the law, shall not his uncircumcision be counted for circumcision?

27 And shall not uncircumcision which is by nature, if it fulfil the law, ^zjudge thee, who by the

z Mat.12.41,42.

parents; to be amidst the ordinances of religion; to be trained in Sunday-schools; and to be devoted to God in baptism: for all these are favourable circumstances for salvation. But none of them entitle to the favour of God; and unless they are improved as they should be, they may be only the means of increasing our condemnation, 2 Cor. ii. 16. ¶ *Thy circumcision is made uncircumcision.* Thy circumcision, or thy being called a Jew, is of no value. It will not distinguish you from those who are *not* circumcised. You will be treated as a heathen. No external advantages, no name, or rite, or ceremony will save you. God requires the obedience of the heart and of the life. Where there is a disposition to render that, there *is* an advantage in possessing the external means of grace. Where that is wanting, no rite or profession can save. This applies with as much force to those who have been baptized in infancy, and to those who have made a profession of religion in a Christian church, as to the Jew.

26. *Therefore if the uncircumcision.* If those who are not circumcised, *i.e.* the heathen. ¶ *Keep the righteousness of the law.* Keep that which the law of Moses commands. It could not be supposed that a heathen would understand the requirements of the *ceremonial* law; but reference is had here to the *moral* law. The apostle does not expressly affirm that this was ever done; but he supposes the case, to show the true nature and value of the rites of the Jews. ¶ *Shall not his uncircumcision.* Or, shall the fact that he is uncircumcised stand in the way of the acceptance of his services? Or, shall he not as certainly and as readily be accepted by God as if he were a Jew? Or in other words, the apostle teaches the doctrine that acceptance with God does not depend

on a man's external privileges, but on the state of the heart and life. ¶ *Be counted for circumcision.* Shall he not be *treated* as if he were circumcised? Shall his being uncircumcised be any barrier in the way of his acceptance with God? The word rendered "be counted" is that which is commonly rendered *to reckon,* TO IMPUTE; and its use here shows that the Scripture use of the word is not to *transfer,* or to charge with that which is not deserved, or not true. It means simply that a man shall be treated as if it were so; that this want of circumcision shall be no bar to acceptance. There is nothing set over to his account; nothing transferred; nothing reckoned different from what it is. God judges things as they are; and as the man, though uncircumcised, who keeps the law, *ought* to be treated *as if* he had been circumcised, so he who believes in Christ agreeably to the divine promise, *and trusts to his merits alone for salvation,* ought to be treated *as if* he were himself righteous. God judges the thing as *it is,* and treats men as it is proper to treat them, *as being* pardoned and accepted through his Son.

27. *Which is by nature.* Which is the natural state of man; his condition before he is admitted to any of the peculiar rites of the Jewish religion. ¶ *If it fulfil the law.* If they who are uncircumcised keep the law. ¶ *Judge thee.* Condemn thee as guilty. As we say, the conduct of such a man condemns us. He acts so much more consistently and uprightly than we do, that we see our guilt. For a similar mode of expression, see Mat. xii. 41, 42. ¶ *Who by the letter,* &c. The translation here is certainly not happily expressed. It is difficult to ascertain its meaning. The evident meaning of the original is, "Shall not a heathen man who has none of your external

letter and circumcision dost transgress the law?

28 For*a* he is not a Jew which
is one outwardly; neither *is that*
circumcision which is outward in
the flesh:

a Mat.3.9; Jn.8.39; ch.9.6,7; Ga.6.15; Re.2.9.

29 But he *is* a Jew, which is
one inwardly; and *b*circumcision
is that of the heart, in the spirit,
and not in the letter; *c*whose
praise *is* not of men, but of
God.

b De.10.16; 30.6; Je.4.4; Phi.3.3; Col.2.11.
c 2 Co.10.18.

---

privileges, if he keeps the law, condemn
you who are Jews; who, *although* you
have the letter and circumcision, are
nevertheless transgressors of the law?"
¶ *The letter.* The word *letter* properly
means the mark or character from
which syllables and words are formed.
It is also used in the sense of *writing*
of any kind (Luke xvi. 6, 7; Acts
xxviii. 21; Gal. vi. 11), particularly
the writings of Moses, denoting, by
way of eminence, *the letter*, or *the
writing*, Rom. vii. 6; 2 Tim. iii. 15.
28. *For he is not a Jew*, &c. He
who is merely descended from Abraham, and is circumcised, and externally
conforms to the law only, does not
possess the true character, and manifest the true spirit, contemplated by
the separation of the Jewish people.
Their separation required much more.
¶ *Neither* is that *circumcision*, &c.
Neither does it meet the full design
of the rite of circumcision, that it is
externally performed. It contemplated
much more; see ver. 29.
29. *But he* is *a Jew.* He comes up
to the design of the Jewish institution;
he manifests truly what it is to be a
Jew. ¶ *Which is one inwardly.* Who
is *in heart* a Jew. Who has the true
spirit, and fulfils the design of their
being separated as a peculiar people.
This passage proves that the *design* of
separating them was not merely to
perform certain external rites, or to
conform to external observances, but
to be a people holy in heart and in life.
It cannot be denied that this design
was not generally understood in the
time of the apostles; but it was abundantly declared in the Old Testament:
Deut. vi. 5; x. 12, 13, 20; xxx. 14;
Isa. i. 11–20; Mic. vi. 8; Ps. li. 16,
17; l. 7–23. ¶ *And circumcision* is
that *of the heart.* That is, that circumcision which is acceptable to God,

and which meets the design of the
institution, is that which is attended
with holiness of heart; with the cutting
off of sins; and with a pure life. The
design of circumcision was to be a sign
of separation from the heathen world,
and of consecration to the holy God.
And this design implied the renunciation and forsaking of all sins; or the
cutting off of everything that was
offensive to God. This was a work
peculiarly of the heart. This design
was often stated and enforced in the
writings of the Old Testament, Deut.
x. 16, "Circumcise, therefore, the
foreskin of your heart, and be no more
stiff-necked;" Jer. iv. 4; Deut. xxx. 6.
¶ *In the spirit.* This is an expression
explaining further what he had just
said. It does not mean *by the Holy
Spirit*, but that the work was to take
place *in* the soul, and not in the body
only. It was to be an internal, spiritual
work, and not merely an external
service. ¶ And *not in the letter.* That
is, not only according to the literal,
external command. ¶ *Whose praise*,
&c. Whose object is not to secure
the praise of men. One of the main
characteristics of the Jews in the time
of Christ was, a desire to secure
honour among men, as being exactly
scrupulous in the performance of all
the duties of their religion. They
prided themselves on their descent
from Abraham, and on their regular
conformity to the precepts of the law
of Moses, Mat. iii. 9; vi. 2, 5; Luke
xviii. 10, 11, 12; Mat. xxiii. 23. ¶ *But
of God.* "Man looketh on the outward appearance, but the Lord looketh
on the heart," 1 Sam. xvi. 7. The
praise of God can be bestowed only
on those who conform *really*, and not
externally only, to his requirements.
The remarks which are made here
respecting the Jews, are also strictly

CHAPTER III.

WHAT advantage then hath the Jew? or what profit *is there* of circumcision?

2 Much every way: chiefly, because that *a* unto them were committed the oracles of God.

3 For what if *b* some did not

a De.4.7,8.   *b* ch.10.16; He.4.2.

applicable to professing Christians, and we may learn,

1. That the external rites of religion are of much less importance than the state of the heart.

2. That the only value of those rites is to promote holiness of heart and life.

3. That the mere fact that we are born of pious ancestors will not save us.

4. That the fact that we were dedicated to God in baptism will not save us.

5. That a mere profession of religion, however orthodox may be our creed, will not save us.

6. That the estimate which men may put on our piety is not the proper measure of our true character and standing.

7. It is an inexpressible privilege to be in possession of the word of God, and to know our duty. It may, if improved, conduce to our elevation in holiness and happiness here, and to our eternal felicity hereafter.

8. It is also a fearful thing to neglect the privileges which we enjoy. We shall be judged according to the light which we have; and it will be an awful event to go to eternity from a Christian land unprepared.

9. Whatever may be the destiny of the heathen, it is *our* duty to make preparation to meet God. The most wicked of the heathen may meet a far milder doom than many who are externally moral, or who profess religion in Christian lands. Instead, therefore, of speculating on what may be their destiny, it is the duty of every individual to be at peace himself with God, and to flee from the wrath to come.

CHAPTER III.

1. *What advantage*, &c. The design of the first part of this chapter is to answer some of the objections which might be offered by a Jew to the statements in the last chapter.

The *first* objection is stated in this verse. A Jew would naturally ask, if the view which the apostle had given were correct, what *peculiar* benefit could the Jew derive from his religion? The objection would arise particularly from the position advanced (chap. ii. 25, 26), that if a heathen should do the things required by the law, he would be treated *as if* he had been circumcised. Hence the question, "What profit is there of circumcision?"

2. *Much every way*. Or, in every respect. This is the answer of the apostle to the objection in ver. 1. ¶ *Chiefly*. That is, this is the *principal* advantage, and one including all others. The *main* benefit of being a Jew is, to possess the sacred Scriptures and their instructions. ¶ *Unto them were committed*. Or were intrusted, were *confided*. The word translated "were committed," is that which is commonly employed to express *faith* or *confidence*, and it implied *confidence* in them on the part of God in intrusting his oracles to them; a confidence which was not misplaced, for no people ever guarded a sacred trust or deposit with more fidelity, than the Jews did the sacred Scriptures. ¶ *The oracles*. The word *oracle* among the heathen meant properly the answer or response of a god, or of some priest supposed to be inspired, to an inquiry of importance, usually expressed in a brief sententious way, and often with great ambiguity. The *place* from which such a response was usually obtained was also called *an oracle, as the oracle at Delphi*, &c. These oracles were frequent among the heathen, and affairs of great importance were usually submitted to them. The word rendered *oracles* occurs in the New Testament but four times: Acts vii. 38; Heb. v. 12; 1 Pet. iv. 11; Rom. iii. 2. It is evidently here used to denote the Scriptures, as being that which was

believe? Shall their unbelief make
the faith of God without effect?

spoken by God, and particularly perhaps the divine promises. To possess
these was of course an eminent privilege, and including all others, as they
instructed them in their duty, and
were their guide in everything that
pertained to them in this life and the
life to come. They contained, besides,
many precious promises respecting
the future dignity of the nation in
reference to the Messiah. No higher
favour can be conferred on a people
than to be put in possession of the
sacred Scriptures. And this fact
should excite us to gratitude, and lead
us to endeavour to extend them also
to other nations; comp. Deut. iv. 7, 8;
Ps. cxlvii. 19, 20.

3. *For what if some did not believe?*
This is to be regarded as another
objection of a Jew. "What then? or
what follows? If it be admitted that
some of the nation did not believe,
does it not follow that the faithfulness
of God in his promises will fail?" The
points of the objection are these: (1)
The apostle had maintained that the
nation was sinful (chap. ii.); that is,
that they had not obeyed or believed
God. (2) This the objector for the
time admits or supposes in relation to
some of them. But, (3) He asks
whether this does not involve a consequence which is not admissible, that
God is unfaithful. Did not the fact
that God chose them as his people,
and entered into covenant with them,
imply that the Jews *should* be kept
from perdition? It was evidently their
belief that *all* Jews would be saved,
and this belief they grounded on his
covenant with their fathers. The
doctrine of the apostle (chap. ii.)
would seem to imply that in certain
respects they were on a level with the
Gentile nations; that if they sinned,
they would be treated just like the
heathen; and hence they asked of
what value was the promise of God?
Had it not become vain and nugatory?
¶ *Make the faith.* The word *faith*
here evidently means the *faithfulness*
or *fidelity of God to his promises.*
Comp. Mat. xiii. 23; 2 Tim. iii. 10;

4 God forbid: yea, let God be
true, but every man a liar; as it

Hos. ii. 20. ¶ *Of none effect.* Destroy
it; or prevent him from fulfilling his
promises. The meaning of the objection is, that the fact supposed, that
the Jews would become unfaithful and
be lost, would imply that God had
failed to keep his promises to the
nation; or that he had made promises
which the result showed he was not
able to perform.

4. *God forbid.* Greek, Let not
this be. The sense is, *let not this by
any means be supposed.* This is the
answer of the apostle, showing that
no such consequence followed from
his doctrines; and that *if* any such
consequence should follow, the doctrine should be at once abandoned,
and that every *man*, no matter who,
should be rather esteemed false than
God. *The veracity of God was a
great first principle,* which was to be
held, whatever might be the consequence. This implies that the apostle believed that the fidelity of God
could be maintained in strict consistency with the fact that any number
of the Jews might be found to be
unfaithful, and be cast off. The
apostle has not entered into an explanation of this, or shown how it
could be, but it is not difficult to
understand how it was. The promise
made to Abraham, and the fathers,
was not unconditional and absolute,
that *all* the Jews should be saved. It
was *implied* that they were to be
obedient; and that if they were not,
they would be cast off, Gen. xviii. 19.
Though the apostle has not stated it
here, yet he has considered it at
length in another part of this epistle,
and showed that it was not only *consistent* with the original promise that
a part of the Jews should be found
unfaithful, and be cast off, but that it
had *actually occurred* according to
the prophets, chap. x. 16–21; xi.
Thus the *fidelity* of God was preserved; at the same time that it was
a matter of fact that no small part
of the nation was rejected and lost.
¶ *Let God be true.* Let God be
esteemed true and faithful, whatever

is written, *That thou mightest be justified in thy sayings, and

c Ps.51.4.

mightest overcome when thou art judged.

consequence may follow. This was a first principle, and should be now, that God should be believed to be *a God of truth*, whatever consequence it might involve. How happy would it be, if *all* men would regard this as a fixed principle, a matter not to be questioned in their hearts, or debated about, that God is true to his word! How much doubt and anxiety would it save professing Christians; and how much error would it save among sinners! Amidst all the agitations of the world, all conflicts, debates, and trials, it would be a fixed position where every man might find rest, and which would do more than all other things to allay the tempests and smooth the agitated waves of human life. ¶ *But every man a liar.* Though every man and every other opinion should be found to be false. Of course this included the apostle and his reasoning; and the expression is one of those which show his magnanimity and greatness of soul. It implies that every opinion which he and all others held; every doctrine which had been defended; should be at once abandoned, if it implied that God was false. It was to be assumed as a *first principle* in all religion and all reasoning, that if a doctrine implied that God was not faithful, it was of course a false doctrine. This showed *his* firm conviction that the doctrine which he advanced was strictly in accordance with the veracity of the divine promise. What a noble principle is this! How strikingly illustrative of the humility of true piety, and of the confidence which true piety places in God above all the deductions of human reason! And if all men were willing to sacrifice their opinions when they appeared to impinge on the veracity of God; if they started back with instinctive shuddering at the very supposition of such a want of fidelity in him; how soon would it put an end to the boastings of error, to the pride of philosophy, to lofty dictation in reli-

gion! No man with this feeling could be for a moment a universalist; and none could be an infidel. ¶ *As it is written.* Ps. li. 4. To confirm the sentiment which he had just advanced, and to show that it accorded with the spirit of religion as expressed in the Jewish writings, the apostle appeals to the language of David, uttered in a state of deep penitence for past transgressions. Of all quotations ever made, this is one of the most beautiful and most happy. David was overwhelmed with grief; he saw his crime to be awful; he feared the displeasure of God, and trembled before him. Yet *he held it as a fixed, indisputable principle that* GOD WAS RIGHT. This he never once thought of calling in question. He had sinned against God, God only; and he did not once think of calling in question the fact that God was just altogether in reproving him for his sin, and in pronouncing against him the sentence of condemnation. ¶ *That thou mightest be justified.* That thou mightest *be regarded as just or right*, or, that it may appear that God is not unjust. This does not mean that David had sinned against God *for the purpose* of justifying him, but that he now clearly saw that his sin had been so *directly* against him, and so aggravated, that God was right in his sentence of condemnation. ¶ *In thy sayings.* In what thou hast spoken; that is, in thy sentence of condemnation; in thy words in relation to this offence. It may help us to understand this, to remember that the psalm was written immediately after Nathan, at the command of God, had gone to reprove David for his crime (see the title of the psalm). God, by the mouth of Nathan, had *expressly* condemned David for his crime. To this expression of condemnation David doubtless refers by the expression "in thy sayings;" see 2 Sam. xii. 7 –13. ¶ *And mightest overcome.* In the Hebrew, "*mightest be pure,*" or mightest be esteemed pure, or just.

5 But if our unrighteousness commend the righteousness of God, what shall we say? *Is* God unrighteous, who taketh vengeance? (I speak as a man)

The word which the LXX. and the apostle have used, "mightest *overcome*," is sometimes used with reference to litigations or trials in a court of justice. He that was accused and acquitted, or who was adjudged to be innocent, might be said to *overcome*, or to gain the cause. The expression is thus used here. As if there were a *trial* between David and God, God would overcome; that is, would be esteemed pure and righteous in his sentence condemning the crime of David. ¶ *When thou art judged.* The Hebrew is, *when thou judgest;* that is, in thy judgment pronounced on this crime. The Greek *may* also be in the middle voice as well as the passive, and may correspond, therefore, in meaning precisely with the Hebrew. So the Arabic renders it. The Syriac renders it, "*when they* [*i.e. men*] *shall judge thee.*" The meaning, as expressed by David, is, that God is to be esteemed right and just in condemning men for their sins, and that a true penitent, *i.e.* a man placed in the best circumstances to form a proper estimate of God, will see this, though it should condemn himself. The meaning of the expression, in the connection in which Paul uses it, is, that it is to be held as a fixed, unwavering principle, that God is right and true, whatever consequences it may involve, whatever doctrine it may overthrow, or whatever man it may prove to be a liar.

5. *But if our unrighteousness.* If our *sin.* The *particular* sin which had been specified (ver. 3) was *unbelief.* But the apostle here gives the objection a general form. This is to be regarded as an *objection* which a Jew might make. The force of it is this: (1) It had been conceded that some had not believed; that is, had sinned. (2) But God was true to his promises. Notwithstanding *their* sin, God's character was the same. Nay, (3) *In the very midst of sin*, and as one of the *results* of it, the character

of God, as a just Being, shone out illustriously. The question then was, (4) If his glory resulted from it; if the effect of all was to *show* that his character was pure; how could he *punish* that sin from which his own glory resulted? And this is a question which is often asked by sinners. ¶ *Commend.* Recommend; show forth; render illustrious. ¶ *The righteousness of God.* His just and holy character. This was the effect on David's mind, that he saw more clearly the justice of God in his threatenings against sin, in consequence of his own transgression. And if *this* effect followed, if honour was thus done to God, the question was, how he could consistently *punish* that which tended to promote his own glory? ¶ *What shall we say?* What follows? or, what is the inference? This is a mode of speech as if the objector *hesitated* about expressing an inference which would seem to follow, but which was horrible in its character. ¶ *Is God unrighteous?* The meaning of this would be better expressed thus: "Is *not* God unrighteous in punishing? Does it not follow that if God is honoured by sin, that it would be wrong for him to inflict punishment?" ¶ *Who taketh vengeance.* The meaning of this is simply, *who inflicts punishment.* The idea of *vengeance* is not necessarily in the original (ὀργήν). It is commonly rendered *wrath*, but it often means simply *punishment*, without any reference to the state of the mind of him who inflicts it, Mat. iii. 7; Luke iii. 7; xxi. 23; John iii. 36; Note, Rom. i. 18; iv. 15. ¶ *I speak as a man.* I speak after the manner of men. I speak as appears to be the case to human view; or as would strike the human mind. It does not mean that the language was such as *wicked men* were accustomed to use; but that the objector expressed a sentiment which to human view would seem to follow from what had been said. This I regard as the language

6 God forbid: for then *how shall God judge the world?

d Job 8.3.

7 For if the truth of God hath more abounded through my lie

of an objector. It implies a degree of reverence for the character of God, and a seeming unwillingness to *state* an objection which seemed to be dishonourable to God, but which nevertheless pressed itself so strong on the mind as to appear irresistible. No way of stating the objection could have been more artful or impressive.

6. *God forbid.* Note, ver. 4. ¶ *For then.* If it be admitted that it would be unjust for God to inflict punishment. ¶ *How shall God*, &c. How will it be *right* or consistent for him to judge the world. ¶ *Judge.* To *judge* implies the possibility and the correctness of *condemning* the guilty; for if it were not right to condemn them, judgment would be a farce. This does not mean that God would condemn all the world; but that the fact of *judging* men implied the possibility and propriety of condemning those who were guilty. It is remarkable that the apostle does not attempt to explain *how* it could be that God could take occasion from the sins of men to promote his glory; nor does he even admit the fact; but he meets *directly* the objection. To understand the force of his answer, it must be remembered that it was *an admitted fact*, a fact which *no one* among the Jews would call in question, that God would judge the world. This fact was fully taught in their own writings, Gen. xviii. 25; Eccl. xii. 14; xi. 9. It was besides an admitted point with them that God would *condemn the heathen world;* and perhaps the term "world" here refers particularly to them. But how could this be if it *were not right* for God to inflict punishment at all? The inference of the objector, therefore, *could not* be true; though the apostle does not tell us *how* it was consistent to inflict punishment for offences from which God took occasion to promote his glory. It may be remarked, however, that God will judge offences, not from what *he* may do in *overruling* them, but from the nature of the crime itself. The ques-

tion is not, what good God may bring out of it, but what does the crime itself deserve? what is the character of the offender? what was his intention? It is not what God may do to overrule the offence when it *is* committed. The just punishment of the murderer is to be determined by the law, and by his own desert; and not from any reputation for integrity and uprightness which the *judge* may manifest on his trial; or from any honour which may accrue to the police for detecting him; or any security which may result to the commonwealth from his execution; or from any honour which the *law* may gain as a just law by his condemnation. Nor should any of these facts and advantages which may result from his execution, be pleaded in bar of his condemnation. So it is with the sinner under the divine administration. It is indeed a truth (Ps. lxxvi. 10) that the wrath of man shall praise God, and that he will take *occasion* from men's wickedness to glorify himself as a just judge and moral governor; but this will be no ground of acquittal for the sinner.

7. *For if*, &c. This is an objection similar to the former. It is indeed but another form of the same. ¶ *The truth of God.* His truth or faithfulness in adhering to his threatenings. God threatened to punish the guilty. By their guilt he will take *occasion* to show his own truth; or their crime will furnish occasion for such an exhibition. ¶ *Hath more abounded.* Has been more striking, or more manifest. His *truth* will be shown by the fulfilment of all his promises to his people, and of all his predictions. But it will also be shown by fulfilling his threatenings on the guilty. It will, therefore, *more abound* by their condemnation; that is, their condemnation will furnish new and striking *instances* of his truth. Every lost sinner will be, therefore, an eternal monument of the truth of God. ¶ *Through my lie.* By means of my lie, or as one of the results of my falsehood. The word *lie* here

unto his glory, why yet am I also judged as a sinner?

means falsehood, deceitfulness, *unfaithfulness.* If by the unfaithfulness of the Jewish people to the covenant, occasion should be given to God to glorify himself, how could they be condemned for it? ¶ *Unto his glory.* To his praise, or so as to show his character in such a way as to excite the praise and admiration of his intelligent creation. ¶ *Why yet am I*, &c. How *can* that act be regarded as evil, which tends to promote the glory of God? The fault in the reasoning of the objector is this, that he takes for granted that the *direct* tendency of his conduct is to promote God's glory, whereas it is just the reverse; and it is by God's *reversing* that tendency, or overruling it, that he obtains his glory. The *tendency* of murder is not to honour the law, or to promote the security of society, but just the reverse. Still, his execution shall avert the *direct* tendency of his crime, and do honour to the law and the judge, and promote the peace and security of the community by restraining others.

8. *And not* rather. This is the answer of the apostle. He meets the objection by showing its tendency if *carried out*, and if it were made a principle of conduct. The meaning is, "If the glory of God is to be promoted by sin, and if a man is not therefore to be condemned, or held guilty for it; if this fact absolves man from crime, *why not carry the doctrine out, and make it a principle of conduct, and* DO ALL THE EVIL WE CAN, *in order to promote his glory.*" This was the fair consequence of the objection. And yet this was a result so shocking and monstrous, that all that was necessary in order to answer the objection was merely to state this consequence. Every man's moral feelings would revolt at the doctrine; every man would *know* that it could not be true; and every man, therefore, could see that the objection was not valid. ¶ *As we.* This refers, doubtless, to the apostles, and to Christians generally. It is unquestionable, that this accusation was often brought against them.

8 And not *rather,* (as we be slanderously reported, and as some

¶ *Slanderously reported.* Greek, as we are *blasphemed.* This is the legitimate and proper use of the word *blaspheme*, to speak of one in a reproachful and calumnious manner. ¶ *As some affirm*, &c. Doubtless Jews. Why they should affirm this, is not known. It was doubtless, however, some *perversion* of the doctrines that the apostles preached. The doctrines which were thus misrepresented and abused, were probably these: the apostles taught that the *sins* of men were the occasion of promoting God's glory in the plan of salvation. That "where sin abounded, grace did much more abound," chap. v. 20. That God, in the salvation of men, would be glorified just in proportion to the depth and pollution of the guilt which was forgiven. This was true; but how easy was it to misrepresent this as teaching that men *ought* to sin in order to promote God's glory! and instead of stating it as an *inference* which THEY drew from the doctrine, to state it as what the apostles *actually taught.* This is the common mode in which charges are brought against others. Men draw an *inference* themselves, or suppose that the doctrine *leads* to such an inference, and then *charge* it on others as what they actually *hold* and *teach.* There is one maxim which should never be departed from : *That a man is not to be held responsible for the inferences which* WE *may draw from his doctrine ; and that he is never to be represented as holding and teaching that which* WE *suppose follows from his doctrine.* He is answerable only for what he avows. ¶ *Let us do evil.* That is, since sin is to promote the glory of God, let us commit as much as possible. ¶ *That good may come.* That God may take occasion by it to promote his glory. ¶ *Whose damnation is just.* Whose *condemnation ;* see Note, chap. xiv. 23. This does not necessarily refer to future punishment, but it means that the conduct of those who thus slanderously perverted the doctrines of the Christian religion, and affirm that we say,) *Let us do evil, that good may come? whose damnation is just.

9 What then? are we better *than they?* No, in no wise: for

e ch.6.1,15.

we have before [1]proved both Jews and Gentiles, that they are all under sin :

10 As it is written, *There is none righteous, no, not one.

[1] *charged.*   *f* Ps.xiv.liii.

accused the apostles of teaching this doctrine, was deserving of condemnation or punishment. Thus he expressly disavows, in strong language, the doctrine charged on Christians. Thus he silences the objection. And thus he teaches, as a great fundamental law, *that evil is not to be done that good may come.* This is a universal rule. And this is *in no case* to be departed from. Whatever is evil is not to be done under any pretence. Any imaginable good which we may think will result from it; any advantage to ourselves or to our cause; or any glory which we may think may result to God, will not sanction or justify the deed. Strict, uncompromising integrity and honesty is to be the maxim of our lives; and in *such* a life only can we hope for success, or for the blessing of God.

9. *What then?* This is another remark supposed to be made by a Jewish objector. "What follows? or are we to infer that we are better than others?" ¶ *Are we better* than they? Are we Jews better than the Gentiles? Or rather, have we any *preference,* or advantage as to character and prospects, over the Gentiles? These questions refer only *to the great point in debate,* to wit, about justification before God. The apostle had admitted (ver. 2) that the Jews *had* important advantages *in some respects,* but he now affirms that those advantages did not make a difference between them and the Gentiles about justification. ¶ *No, in no wise.* Not at all. That is, the Jews have no preference or advantage over the Gentiles in regard to the subject of justification before God. They have failed to keep the law; they are sinners; and if they are justified, it must be in the same way as the rest of the world. ¶ *We have before proved,* &c. Chap. i. 21–32; chap. ii. ¶ *Under sin.* Sinners Under the power and dominion of sin.

10. *As it is written.* The apostle is reasoning with Jews; and he proceeds to show from their own Scriptures, that what he had affirmed was true. The point to be proved was, that the Jews, in the matter of justification, had no advantage or preference over the Gentiles; that the Jew had failed to keep the law which had been given *him,* as the Gentile had failed to keep the law which had been given *him;* and that both, therefore, were equally dependent on the mercy of God, incapable of being justified and saved by their works. To show this, the apostle adduces texts to show what was *the character of the Jewish people;* or to show that according to their own Scriptures, they were sinners no less than the Gentiles. The point, then, is to prove the depravity of *the Jews,* not that of *universal* depravity. The interpretation should be confined to the bearing of the passages on the Jews, and the quotations should not be adduced as *directly* proving the doctrine of universal depravity. In a certain sense, which will be stated soon, they may be adduced as bearing on that subject. But their direct reference is to the Jewish nation. The passages which follow, are taken from various parts of the Old Testament. The design of this is to show, that this characteristic of sin was not confined to any particular period of the Jewish history, but pertained to them *as a people;* that it had characterized them *throughout* their existence as a nation. Most of the passages are quoted in the language of the Septuagint. The quotation in ver. 10–12, is from Ps. xiv. 1–3; and from Ps. liii. 1–3. The 53d Psalm is the same as the 14th, with some slight variations.

[Yet if we consult Ps. xiv. and liii., from which the quotations in verses 10–12 are taken, we shall be constrained to admit that their original application is nothing short of universal. The Lord is represented as looking down from heaven (not upon the Jewish people only, but upon the "children of men" at large, "to see if there were *any* that did understand and seek God);" and declaring, as the result of his unerring scrutiny, "there is *none* that doeth good, no, not one."

That the apostle applies the passages to the case of the Jews is admitted, yet it is evident more is contained in them than the single proof of Jewish depravity. They go all the length of proving the depravity of mankind, and are cited expressly with this view. "We have before proved both Jews and Gentiles," says Paul in the 9th verse, "that they are all under sin." Immediately on this the quotations in question are introduced with the usual formula, "as it is written," &c. Now since the apostle adduces his Scripture proofs to establish the doctrine that "*both* Jews and Gentiles are *all* under sin," we cannot reasonably decide against him by confining their application to the Jews only.

In the 19th verse Paul brings his argument to bear *directly* on the Jews. That they might not elude his aim by interpreting the universal expressions he had introduced of all the heathen only, leaving themselves favourably excepted, he reminds them that "whatsoever things the law saith, it saith to them that were under it." Not contented with having placed them alongside of the Gentiles in the 9th verse, by this second application of the general doctrine of human depravity to their particular case he renders escape or evasion impossible. The scope of the whole passage then is, that all men are depraved, and that the Jews form no exception. This view is farther strengthened by the apostle's conclusion in the 20th verse: "Therefore, by the deeds of the law there shall no *flesh* be justified in his (God's) sight." "If the words," says President Edwards, " which the apostle uses do not most fully and determinately signify an universality, no words ever used in the Bible are sufficient to do it. I might challenge any man to produce any one paragraph in the Scriptures, from the beginning to the end, where there is such a repetition and accumulation of terms, so strongly, and emphatically, and carefully, to express the most perfect and absolute universality, or any place to be compared to it" (Edwards *on Original Sin;* Haldane's *Commentary*).]

¶ *There is none righteous.* The Hebrew (Ps. xiv. 1) is, There is none that doeth good. The Septuagint has the same. The apostle quotes according to the *sense* of the passage. The design of the apostle is to show that none could be *justified* by the law. He uses an expression, therefore, which is exactly conformable to his argument, and which accords in meaning with the Hebrew, *there is none just—δίκαιος.* ¶ *No, not one.* This is not in the Hebrew, but is in the Septuagint. It is a strong universal expression, denoting the state of almost universal corruption which existed in the time of the psalmist. The expression should not be interpreted to mean that there was not literally *one pious man* in the nation; but that the characteristic of the nation was, at that time, that it was exceedingly corrupt. Instead of being righteous, as the Jew claimed, *because* they were Jews, the testimony of their own Scriptures was, that they were universally wicked.

[The design of the apostle, however, is not to prove that there were few or none pious. He is treating of the impossibility of justification by works, and alleges in proof, that, according to the judgment of God in the 14th Psalm, there were none righteous, &c., in regard to their natural estate, or the condition in which man is previous to his being justified. In this condition all are deficient in righteousness, and have nothing to commend them to the Divine favour. What men may afterwards become by grace is another question, on which the apostle does not, in this place, enter. Whatever number of pious men, therefore, there might be in various places of the world, the argument of the apostle is not in the least affected. It will hold good even in the millennium!]

11. *There is none that understandeth.* In the Hebrew (Ps. xiv. 2), God is represented as looking down from heaven *to see,* that is, to make investigation, whether there were any that understood or sought after him. This circumstance gives not only high poetic beauty to the passage, but deep solemnity and awfulness. God, the searcher of hearts, is represented as making investigation *on this very point.* He looks down from heaven for this very purpose, to ascertain whether there were any righteous. In the Hebrew it is not asserted, though it it is clearly and strongly implied, that *none such were found.* That fact the apostle *states.* If, as the

11 There is none that understandeth, there is none that seeketh after God.

12 They are all gone out of the way, they are together become unprofitable; there is none that doeth good, no, not one.

13 Their*g* throat *is* an open

g Ps.5.9.

result of such an investigation, none were found; if God did not specify that there *were* any such; then it follows that there were none. For none could escape the notice of his eye; and if there *had* been any, the benevolence of his heart would have led him to record it. To *understand* is used in the sense of being wise; or of having such a state of moral feeling as to dispose them to serve and obey God. The word is often used in the Bible, not to denote a mere *intellectual* operation of the mind, but the state of the heart *inclining the mind* to obey and worship God, Ps. cvii. 43; cxix. 27, 100; Prov. v. 5; Isa. vi. 10, "Lest they should understand with their heart," &c. ¶ *That seeketh after God.* That endeavours to know and do his will, and to be acquainted with his character. A disposition *not* to seek after God—that is, to neglect and forget him—is one of the most decided proofs of depravity. A righteous man counts it his highest privilege and honour to know God, and to understand his will. A man can indulge in wickedness only by forgetting God. Hence a disposition *not* to seek God is full proof of depravity.

12. *They have all gone out of the way.* They have *declined* from the true path of piety and virtue. ¶ *They are together.* They have *at the same time,* or *they have equally,* become unprofitable. They are *as one;* they are joined, or *united* in this declension. The expression denotes *union,* or *similarity.* ¶ *Become unprofitable.* This word in Hebrew means to become *putrid* and *offensive,* like fruit that is spoiled. In Arabic, it is applied to *milk* that becomes sour. Applied to moral subjects, it means to become corrupt and useless. They are of *no value* in regard to works of righteousness. ¶ *There is none,* &c. This is taken literally from the Hebrew.

13. *Their throat,* &c. This expression is taken from Ps. v. 9, literally from the Septuagint. The design of the psalm is to reprove those who were false, traitorous, slanderous, &c. (Ps. v. 6). The psalmist has the sin of deceit, and falsehood, and slander particularly in his eye. The expressions here are to be interpreted in accordance with that. The sentiment here may be, As the grave is ever open to receive all into it, that is, into destruction, so the mouth or the throat of the slanderer is ever open to swallow up the peace and happiness of all. Or it may mean, As from an open sepulchre there proceeds an offensive and pestilential vapour, so from the mouths of slanderous persons there proceed noisome and ruinous words (Stuart). I think the connection demands the former interpretation. ¶ *With their tongues,* &c. In their conversation, their promises, &c., they have been false, treacherous, and unfaithful. ¶ *The poison of asps.* This is taken literally from the Septuagint of Ps. cxl. 3. The *asp,* or adder, is a species of serpent whose poison is of such active operation that it kills almost the instant that it penetrates, and that without remedy. It is small, and commonly lies concealed, often in the *sand* in a road, and strikes the traveller before he sees it. It is found chiefly in Egypt and Libya. It is said by ancient writers that the celebrated Cleopatra, rather than be carried a captive to Rome by Augustus, suffered an asp to bite her in the arm, by which she soon died. The precise species of serpent which is here meant by the psalmist, however, cannot be ascertained. All that is necessary to understand the passage is, that it refers to a serpent whose bite was deadly, and rapid in its execution. ¶ *Is under their lips.* The poison of the serpent is contained in a small bag which is concealed at the root of the tooth. When the tooth is struck into the flesh, the poison is

sepulchre; with their tongues they have used deceit; *h* the poison of asps *is* under their lips.

14 Whose *i* mouth *is* full of cursing and bitterness.

15 Their *k* feet *are* swift to shed blood:

h Ps.140.3.　　*i* Ps.10.7.　　*k* Is.59.7,8.

16 Destruction and misery *are* in their ways:

17 And the way of peace have they not known:

18 There *l* is no fear of God before their eyes.

19 Now we know, that what

l Ps.36.1.

pressed out, through a small hole in the tooth, into the wound. Whether the psalmist was acquainted with that fact, or referred to it, cannot be known; his words do not of necessity imply it. The sentiment is, that as the poison of the asp is rapid, certain, spreading quickly through the system, and producing death; so the words of the slanderer are deadly, pestiferous, quickly destroying the reputation and happiness of man. They are as subtle, as insinuating, and as deadly to the reputation, as the poison of the adder is to the body. Wicked men in the Bible are often compared to serpents, Mat. xxiii. 33; Gen. xlix. 17.

14. *Whose mouth.* Ps. x. 7. The apostle has not quoted this literally, but has given the sense. David in the psalm is describing his bitter enemies. ¶ *Cursing.* Reproachful and opprobrious language, such as Shimei used in relation to David, 2 Sam. xvi. 5, 7, 8. ¶ *Bitterness.* In the psalm, *deceits.* The word *bitterness* is used to denote severity, harshness, cruelty; reproachful and malicious words.

15. *Their feet,* &c. The quotation in this and the two following verses is abridged or condensed from Isa. lix. 7, 8. The expressions occur in the midst of a description of the character of the nation in the time of the prophet. The apostle has selected a few expressions out of many, rather making a reference to the entire passage, than a formal quotation. The expression, "their feet are swift," &c., denotes the eagerness of the nation to commit crime, particularly deeds of injustice and cruelty. They thirsted for the blood of innocence, and *hasted* to shed it, to gratify their malice, or to satisfy their vengeance.

16. *Destruction.* That is, they

cause the destruction or the ruin of the reputation, happiness, and peace of others. ¶ *Misery.* Calamity, ruin. ¶ *In their ways.* Wherever they go. This is a striking description not only of the wicked *then,* but of all times. The tendency of their conduct is to destroy the virtue, happiness, and peace of all with whom they come in contact.

17. *And the way of peace,* &c. What tends to promote their own happiness, or that of others, they do not regard. Intent on their plans of evil, they do not know or regard that which is fitted to promote the welfare of themselves or others. This is the case with all who are selfish, and who seek to gain their own purposes of crime and ambition.

18. *There is no fear of God.* Ps. xxxvi. 1. The word *fear* here denotes *reverence, awe, veneration.* There is no such regard or reverence for the character, authority, and honour of God as to restrain them from crime. Their conduct shows that they are not withheld from the commission of iniquity by any regard to the fear or favour of God. The only thing that will be effectual in restraining men from sin, will be a regard to the honour and law of God.

In regard to these quotations from the Old Testament, we may make the following remarks. (1) They fully establish the position of the apostle, that the nation, as such, was far from being righteous, or that they could be justified by their own works. By quotations from no less than six distinct places in their own writings, referring to different periods of their history, he shows what the character of the nation was. And as this was the characteristic of *those* times, it followed that a Jew could not hope to be saved simply

things soever the law saith, it saith to them who are under the law; that *m* every mouth may be

m Ps.107.42.

stopped, and all the world may become [2] guilty before God.

20 Therefore *n* by the deeds

2 or, *subject to the judgment of God.* *n* Ps.143.2.

---

because he was a Jew. He needed, as much as the Gentile, the benefit of some other plan of salvation. (2) These passages show us how to use the Old Testament, and the facts of ancient history. They are to be adduced not as showing *directly* what the character of man is, *now*, but to show what *human nature* is. They demonstrate what man is when under the most favourable circumstances, in different situations, and at different periods of the world. The concurrence of *past* facts shows what the race is. And as past facts are uniform; as man thus far, in the most favourable circumstances, has been sinful, it follows that this is the characteristic of man everywhere. It is settled by the *facts* of the world, just as any other characteristic of man is settled by the uniform occurrence of facts in all circumstances and times. Ancient facts, and quotations of Scripture, therefore, are to be adduced as proofs of *the tendency of human nature.* So Paul used them, and so it is lawful for us to use them. (3) It may be observed further, that the apostle has given a view of human depravity which is very striking. He does not confine it to one faculty of the mind, or to one set of actions; he *specifies* each member and each faculty as being perverse, and inclined to evil. The depravity extends to all the departments of action. The *tongue*, the *mouth*, the *feet*, the *lips*, are all involved in ·it; all are perverted, and all become the occasion of the commission of sin. The *entire man* is corrupt; and the painful description extends to every department of action. (4) If such was the character of the Jewish nation under all its advantages, what must have been the character of the heathen? We are prepared thus to credit all that is said in chap. i., and elsewhere, of the sad state of the pagan world. (5) What a melancholy view we have thus of

human nature! From whatever quarter we contemplate it, we come to the same conclusion. Whatever record we examine; whatever history we read; whatever time or period we contemplate; we find the same facts, and are forced to the same conclusion. All are involved in sin, and are polluted, and ruined, and helpless. Over these ruins we should sit down and weep, and lift our eyes with gratitude to the God of mercy, that he has pitied us in our low estate, and has devised a plan by which "these ruins may be built again," and lost, fallen man be raised up to forfeited "glory, honour, and immortality."

19. *Now we know.* We all admit. It is a conceded plain point. ¶ *What things soever.* Whether given as precepts, or recorded as historical facts. Whatever things are found *in* the law. ¶ *The law saith.* This means here evidently the Old Testament. From that the apostle had been drawing his arguments, and his train of thought requires us here to understand the whole of the Old Testament by this. The same principle applies, however, to all law, that it speaks only to those to whom it is expressly given. ¶ *It saith to them,* &c. It speaks to them for whom it was expressly intended; to them for whom the law was made. The apostle makes this remark in order to prevent the Jew from evading the force of his conclusion. He had brought proofs from their *own* acknowledged laws, from writings given expressly *for* them, and which recorded their own history, and which they admitted to be divinely inspired. These proofs, therefore, they could not evade. ¶ *That every mouth may be stopped.* This is, perhaps, a proverbial expression, Job v. 15; Ps. cvii. 42. It denotes that they would be thoroughly convinced; that the argument would be so conclusive as that they would have nothing to reply; that all objections would be silenced. Here it denotes that the

of the law there shall no flesh be justified in his sight : for | by the law *is* the knowledge of sin.

argument for the depravity of the Jews from the Old Testament was so clear and satisfactory, that nothing could be alleged in reply. This may be regarded as the *conclusion* of his whole argument, and the expressions may refer not to the Jews only, but to all the world. Its meaning may, perhaps, be thus expressed, "The Gentiles are proved guilty by their own deeds, and by a violation of the laws of nature. *They* sin against their own conscience; and have thus been shown to be guilty before God (chap. i.). The Jews have also been shown to be guilty; all their objections have been silenced by an independent train of remark ; by appeals to *their own law;* by arguments drawn from the authority which *they* admit. Thus the mouths of both are stopped. Thus the whole world becomes guilty before God." I regard, therefore, the word "*that*" here (ἵνα) as referring, not particularly to the argument from the *law* of the Jews, but to *the whole previous train of argument,* embracing both Jews and Gentiles. His conclusion is thus *general* or *universal,* drawn from arguments adapted to the two great divisions of mankind. ¶ *And all the world.* Both Jews and Gentiles, for so the strain of the argument shows. That is, all by nature; all who are out·of Christ; all who are not pardoned. All are guilty where there is not some scheme contemplating forgiveness, and which is not applied to purify them. The apostle in all this argument speaks of what man is, and ever would be, without some plan of justification appointed by God. ¶ *May become.* May *be.* They are not *made* guilty by the law ; but the argument *from* the law, and from fact, *proves* that they *are* guilty. ¶ *Guilty before God* (ὑπόδικος τῷ Θεῷ). Margin, *subject to the judgment of God.* The phrase is taken from courts of justice. It is applied to a man who has not vindicated or defended himself ; against whom, therefore, the charge or the indictment is found true ; and who is

in consequence subject to punishment. The idea is that of subjection to *punishment;* but *always* because the man personally *deserves* it, and because, being unable to vindicate himself, he *ought* to be punished. It is never used to denote simply an obligation to punishment, but with reference to the fact that the punishment is personally *deserved.* This word, rendered *guilty,* is not elsewhere used in the New Testament, nor is it found in the Septuagint. The *argument* of the apostle here shows, (1) That in order to guilt, there must be a *law,* either that of nature or by revelation (chap. i. ii. iii.) ; and, (2) That in order to *guilt,* there must be a violation of that law which may be charged on them as individuals, and for which they are to be held personally responsible.

20. *By the deeds of the law.* By works ; or by such deeds as the law requires. The word *law* has, in the Scriptures, a great variety of significations. Its strict and proper meaning is, a *rule* of conduct prescribed by superior authority. The course of reasoning in these chapters shows the sense in which the apostle uses it here. He intends evidently to apply it to those *rules* or laws by which the Jews and Gentiles pretended to frame their lives ; and to affirm that men could be justified by no conformity to those laws. He had shown (chap. i.) that *the heathen, the entire Gentile world,* had violated the laws of nature; the rules of virtue made known to them by reason, tradition, and conscience. He had shown the same (chap. ii. iii.) in respect to the Jews. They had equally failed in rendering obedience to *their* law. In both these cases the reference was, not to *ceremonial* or *ritual* laws, but to the moral law ; whether that law was made known by reason or by revelation. The apostle had not been discussing the question whether they had yielded obedience to their ceremonial law, but whether they had been found *holy, i.e.* whether they had obeyed

21 But now the righteousness of

the *moral* law. The conclusion was, that in all this they had failed, and that therefore they could not be justified by that law. That the apostle did not intend to speak of *external* works only is apparent; for he all along charges them with a want of conformity of the heart no less than with a want of conformity of the life; see chap. i. 26, 29–31; ii. 28, 29. The conclusion is therefore a general one, that by no law, made known either by reason, conscience, tradition, or revelation, could man be justified; that there was no form of *obedience* which could be rendered, that would justify men in the sight of a holy God. ¶ *There shall no flesh.* No man; no human being, either among the Jews or the Gentiles. It is a strong expression, denoting the absolute universality of his conclusion; see Note on chap. i. 3. ¶ *Be justified.* Be regarded and treated as righteous. None shall be esteemed as having *kept* the law, and as being entitled to the rewards of obedience; see Note, chap. i. 17. ¶ *In his sight.* Before him. God sits as a Judge to determine the characters of men, and he shall not adjudge any to have kept the law. ¶ *For by the law.* That is, by *all* law. The connection shows that this is the sense. Law is a rule of action. The effect of *applying* a rule to our conduct is to show us what sin is. The meaning of the apostle clearly is, that the application of a law to try our conduct, instead of being a ground of justification, will be merely to show us our own sinfulness and departures from duty. A man may esteem himself to be very right and correct, until he compares himself with a rule, or law; so whether the Gentiles compared their conduct with *their* laws of reason and conscience, or the Jew his with his *written* law, the effect would be to show them how far they had departed. The more closely and faithfully it should be applied, the more they would see it. So far from being justified by it, they would be more and more condemned; comp. Rom. vii.

God without the law is manifested,

7–10. The same is the case now. This is the way in which a sinner is converted; and the more closely and faithfully the law is preached, the more will it condemn him, and show him that he needs some other plan of salvation.

21. *But now.* The apostle, having shown the entire failure of all attempts to be justified by the *law*, whether among Jews or Gentiles, proceeds to state fully the plan of justification by Jesus Christ in the gospel. To do this, was the main design of the epistle, chap. i. 17. He makes, therefore, in the close of this chapter, an explicit statement of the nature of the doctrine; and in the following parts of the epistle he fully proves it, and illustrates its effects. ¶ *The righteousness of God.* God's plan of justifying men; see Note, chap. i. 17. ¶ *Without the law.* In a way different from personal obedience to the law. It does not mean that God *abandoned* his law; or that Jesus Christ did not *regard* the law, for he came to "magnify" it (Isa. xlii. 21); or that sinners *after* they are justified have no regard to the law; but it means simply what the apostle had been endeavouring to show, that justification could not be accomplished by *personal* obedience to any law of Jew or Gentile, and that it must be accomplished in some other way. ¶ *Being witnessed.* Being borne witness to. It was not a *new* doctrine; it was found in the Old Testament. The apostle makes this observation with special reference to the *Jews.* He does not declare any *new* thing, but that which was fully declared in their own sacred writings. ¶ *By the law.* This expression here evidently denotes, as it did commonly among the Jews, the five books of Moses. And the apostle means to say that this doctrine was found in *those books;* not that it was in the ten commandments, or in the *law,* strictly so called. It is not a part of *law* to declare justification except by strict and perfect obedience. That it was found *in* those books, the apostle

being witnessed ᵒby the law and the prophets;

o Ac.26.22.

22 Even the righteousness of God, *which is* ᵖby faith of Jesus

p ch.5.1,&c.

shows by the case of Abraham, chap. iv.; see also his reasoning on Lev. xviii. 5, Deut. xxx. 12–14, in Rom. x. 5–11; comp. Ex. xxxiv. 6, 7. ¶ *And the prophets.* Generally, the remainder of the Old Testament. The phrase "the law and the prophets" comprehended the whole of the Old Testament, Mat. v. 17; xi. 13; xxii. 40; Acts xiii. 15; xxviii. 23. That this doctrine was contained in *the prophets*, the apostle showed by the passage quoted from Hab. ii. 4, in chap. i. 17, "The just shall live by faith." The same thing he showed in chap. x. 11, from Isa. xxviii. 16, xlix. 23; chap. iv. 6–8, from Ps. xxxii. The same thing is fully taught in Isa. liii. 11; Dan. ix. 24. Indeed, the general tenor of the Old Testament, the appointment of sacrifices, &c., taught that man was a sinner, and that he could not be justified by obedience to the moral law.

22. *Even the righteousness of God.* The apostle, having stated that the design of the gospel was to reveal a new plan of becoming just in the sight of God, proceeds here more fully to explain it. The explanation which he offers, makes it plain that the phrase so often used by him, "righteousness of God," does not refer to an *attribute* of God, but to his plan of making men righteous. Here he says that it is by faith in Jesus Christ; but surely an *attribute* of God is not produced by faith in Jesus Christ. It means God's mode of regarding men as righteous through their belief in Jesus Christ.

[That the "righteousness of God" cannot be explained of the attribute of justice is obvious enough. It cannot be said of divine justice that *it* is "unto and upon all them that believe." But we are not reduced to the alternative of explaining the phrase either of God's justice or God's plan of justifying men. Why may we not understand it of that righteousness which Jehovah devised, Jesus executed, and the Spirit applies, and which is therefore justly denominated the righteousness of GOD? It consists in that

conformity to law which Jesus manifested in his atoning death and meritorious obedience. His death, by reason of his divine nature, was of infinite value. And when he *voluntarily* submitted to yield a life that was forfeited by no transgression of his own, the law, in its *penal* part, was more magnified than if every descendant of Adam had sunk under the weight of its vengeance. Nor was the *preceptive* part of the law less honoured in the spotless obedience of Christ. He abstained from every sin, fulfilled every duty, and exemplified every virtue. Neither God nor man could accuse him of failure in duty. To God he gave his piety, to man his glowing love, to friends his heart, to foes his pity and his pardon. And by the obedience of the Creator in human form the precept of the law was more honoured than if the highest angels had come down to do reverence to it in presence of men. Here then is a righteousness worthy of the name, divine, spotless, broad, lasting—beyond the power of language to characterize. It is that everlasting righteousness which Daniel predicted the Messiah should bring in. Adam's righteousness failed and passed away. That of once happy angels perished too, but this shall endure. "The heavens," says Jehovah, "shall vanish away like smoke, and the earth shall wax old like a garment, and they that dwell therein shall die in like manner: but *my salvation* shall be for ever, and *my righteousness* shall not be abolished." This righteousness is broad enough to cover every sinner and every sin. It is pure enough to meet the eye of God himself It is therefore the sinner's only shield. See Note, chap. i. 17, for the true meaning of the expression "righteousness of God."]

¶ *By faith of Jesus Christ.* That is, by faith *in* Jesus Christ. Thus the expression, Mark xi. 22, "Have the faith of God" (*margin*), means, have faith *in* God. So Acts iii. 16, the "faith of his name" (*Greek*), means, faith *in* his name. So Gal. ii. 20, the "faith of the Son of God" means, faith *in* the Son of God. This cannot mean that faith is the meritorious cause of salvation, but that it is the instrument or means by which we become justified. It is the *state of mind*, or *condition of the heart*, to which God has been pleased to promise justification. (On the nature of faith see Note, Mark xvi. 16.) God

Christ, unto all and upon all them that believe: for there is no difference:

23 For *q* all have sinned, and come short of the glory of God; 24 Being justified freely by his

q Ec.7.20.

has promised that they who believe in Christ shall be pardoned and saved. This is *his* plan, in distinction from the plan of those who seek to be justified by works. ¶ *Unto all and upon all.* It is evident that these expressions are designed to be emphatic, but why both are used is not very apparent. Many have supposed that there was no essential difference in the meaning. If there be a difference, it is probably this: the first expression, "unto all" (εἰς πάντας), may denote that this plan of justification has come (Luther) *unto* all men, to Jews and Gentiles; *i.e.* that it has been provided for them, and offered to them without distinction. The plan was ample for all, was fitted for all, was equally necessary for all, and was offered to all. The second phrase, "upon all" (ἐπὶ πάντας), may be designed to guard against the supposition that *all* therefore would be benefited by it, or be saved by the mere fact that the announcement had come to all. The apostle adds, therefore, that the benefits of this plan must actually come *upon* all, or must be *applied* to all, if they would be justified. They could not be justified merely by the fact that the plan was provided, and that the knowledge of it had come to all, but by their actually coming *under* this plan, and availing themselves of it. Perhaps there is reference in the last expression, "upon all," to a robe, or garment, that is placed upon one to hide his nakedness, or sin; comp. Isa. lxiv. 6, also Phil. iii. 9. ¶ *For there is no difference.* That is, there is no difference *in regard to the matter under discussion.* The apostle does not mean to say that there is no difference in regard to the talents, dispositions, education, and property of men; but there is no distinction in regard to the way in which they must be justified. All must be saved, if saved at all, in the same mode, whether Jews or Gentiles, bond or free, rich or poor,

learned or ignorant. None can be saved by works; and all are therefore dependent on the mercy of God in Jesus Christ.

23. *For all have sinned.* This was the point which he had fully established in the discussion in these chapters. ¶ *Have come short.* Greek, *are deficient in regard to;* are wanting, &c. Here it means, that they had *failed to obtain,* or were destitute of. ¶ *The glory of God.* The praise or approbation of God. They had sought to be justified, or *approved, by God;* but all had failed. Their works of the law had not secured his approbation; and they were therefore under condemnation. The word *glory* (δόξα) is often used in the sense of *praise,* or *approbation,* John v. 41, 44; vii. 18; viii. 50, 54; xii. 43.

24. *Being justified.* Being treated as if righteous; that is, being regarded and treated as if they had kept the law. The apostle has shown that they *could not* be so regarded and treated by any merit of their own, or by personal obedience to the law. He now affirms that if they were so treated, it must be by mere favour, and as a matter not of right, but of gift. This is the essence of the gospel. And to show this, and the way in which it is done, is the main design of this epistle. The expression here is to be understood as referring to *all* who are justified, ver. 22. The righteousness of God by faith in Jesus Christ, is "upon all who believe," who are all "justified freely by his grace." ¶ *Freely* (δωρεάν). This word stands opposed to that which is purchased, or which is obtained by labour, or which is a matter of claim. It is a free, undeserved gift, not merited by our obedience to the law, and not that to which we have any claim. The apostle uses the word here in reference to those who are justified. To *them* it is a mere undeserved gift. It does not mean that it has been obtained, however, without any price or merit from any-

grace through the redemption that is in Christ Jesus.

25 Whom God hath ³set forth *to be* a propitiation through faith

³ or, *fore-ordained.*

in his blood, to declare his righteousness for the ⁴remission of sins that are past, through the forbearance of God;

⁴ or, *passing over.*

one, for the Lord Jesus has purchased it with his own blood, and *to him* it becomes a matter of justice that those who were given to him should be justified, 1 Cor. vi. 20; vii. 23; 2 Pet. ii. 1; 1 Pet. ii. 9 (*Greek*); Acts xx. 28; Isa. liii. 11. *We* have no offering to bring, and no claim. To us, therefore, it is entirely a matter of gift. ¶ *By his grace.* By his favour; by his mere undeserved mercy; see Note, chap i. 7. ¶ *Through the redemption* (διὰ τῆς ἀπολυτρώσεως). The word used here occurs but ten times in the New Testament: Luke xxi. 28; Rom. iii. 24; viii. 23; 1 Cor. i. 30; Eph. i. 7, 14; iv. 30; Col. i. 14; Heb. ix. 15; xi. 35. Its root (λύτρον, *lutron*) properly denotes the price which is paid for a prisoner of war; the ransom, or stipulated purchase-money, which being paid, the captive is set free. The word here used is then employed to denote liberation from bondage, captivity, or evil of any kind, usually keeping up the idea of a *price,* or a *ransom paid,* in consequence of which the delivery is effected. It is sometimes used in a large sense, to denote simple deliverance *by any means,* without reference to a price paid, as in Luke xxi. 28; Rom. viii. 23; Eph. i. 14. That this is *not* the sense here, however, is apparent. For the apostle in the next verse proceeds to specify the *price* which has been paid, or the means by which this redemption has been effected. The word *here* denotes that *deliverance from sin, and from the evil consequences of sin,* which has been effected by the offering of Jesus Christ as a propitiation, ver. 25. ¶ *That is in Christ Jesus.* Or, that has been effected by Christ Jesus; that of which he is the author and procurer; comp. John iii. 16.

25. *Whom God hath set forth.* Margin, *fore-ordained* (προέθετο). The word properly means, *to place in public view;* to exhibit in a conspicuous situa-

ation, as goods are exhibited or exposed for sale, or as premiums or rewards of victory were exhibited to public view in the games of the Greeks. It *sometimes* has the meaning of decreeing, purposing, or constituting, as in the margin (comp. Rom. i. 13; Eph. i. 9); and many have supposed that this is its meaning here. But the connection seems to require the usual signification of the word; and it means that God has *publicly exhibited Jesus Christ* as a propitiatory sacrifice for the sins of men. This public exhibition was made by his being offered on the cross, in the face of angels and of men. It was not concealed; it was done openly. He was put to open shame; and *so* put to death as to attract towards the scene the eyes of angels, and of the inhabitants of all worlds. ¶ To be *a propitiation* (ἱλαστήριον). This word occurs but in one other place in the New Testament, Heb. ix. 5, "And over it [the ark] the cherubim of glory shadowing the *mercy-seat.*" It is used here to denote the lid or cover of the ark of the covenant. It was made of gold, and over it were the cherubim. In this sense it is often used by the LXX.: Ex. xxv. 17, "And thou shalt make a propitiatory (ἱλαστήριον) of gold," 18, 19, 20, 22; xxx. 6; xxxi. 7; xxxv. 11; xxxvii. 6–9; xl. 18; Lev. xvi. 2, 13. The Hebrew name for this was *capphoreth,* from the verb *caphar,* to cover, or conceal. It was from *this* place that God was represented as speaking to the children of Israel, Ex. xxv. 22, "And I will speak to thee from above the *hilasterion,*" the propitiatory, the mercy-seat; Lev. xvi. 2, "For I will appear in the cloud upon the mercy-seat." This seat, or cover, was covered with the smoke of the *incense,* when the high-priest entered the most holy place, Lev. xvi. 13. And the blood of the bullock offered on the great day of atonement, was to be sprinkled "upon the mercy-seat," and "before the mercy-seat," "seven times," Lev. xvi. 14, 15. This sprinkling or offering of blood was called making "an atonement for the holy place because of the uncleanness of the children of Israel," &c., Lev. xvi. 16. It was from this mercy-seat that God pronounced pardon, or expressed himself as *reconciled* to his people. The atonement was made, the blood was sprinkled, and the reconciliation thus effected. The *name* was thus given to that cover of the ark, because it .was the place from which God declared himself reconciled to his people. Still the inquiry is, Why is this name given to Jesus Christ? In what sense is *he* declared to be a propitiation? It is evident that it cannot be applied to him in any *literal* sense. Between the golden cover of the ark of the covenant and the Lord Jesus the analogy *must* be *very* slight, if *any* such analogy can be perceived. We may observe, however, (1) That the *main idea*, in regard to the cover of the ark called the mercy-seat, was that of God's being *reconciled* to his people; and that this is the main idea in regard to the Lord Jesus whom "God hath set forth." (2) This reconciliation was effected *then* by the sprinkling of blood on the mercy-seat, Lev. xvi. 15, 16. The same is true of the Lord Jesus — by blood. (3) In the former case it was by the blood of atonement, the offering of the bullock on the great day of atonement, that the reconciliation was effected, Lev. xvi. 17, 18. In the case of the Lord Jesus it was also by blood; by the blood of atonement. But it was by his *own* blood. This the apostle distinctly states in this verse. (4) In the former case there was a *sacrifice*, or *expiatory* offering; and so it is in reconciliation by the Lord Jesus. In the former, the mercy-seat was the visible, declared place where God would express his reconciliation with his people. So in the latter, the offering of the Lord Jesus is the manifest and open way by which God will be reconciled to men. (5) In the former, there was joined the idea of a *sacrifice* for sin, Lev. xvi. So in the latter. And hence the *main idea* of the apostle

here is to convey the idea of *a sacrifice for sin;* or to set forth the Lord Jesus as such a sacrifice. Hence the word "propitiation" in the original may express the idea of a *propitiatory sacrifice,* as well as the cover to the ark. The word is an *adjective,* and may be joined to the noun *sacrifice,* as well as to denote the mercy-seat of the ark. This meaning accords also with its classic meaning to denote *a propitiatory offering,* or an offering to produce reconciliation. Christ is thus represented, not *as a mercy - seat,* which would be unintelligible; but as the medium, the offering, the expiation, by which reconciliation is produced between God and man. ¶ *Through faith.* Or by means of faith. The offering will be of no avail without *faith.* The offering has been made; but it will not be applied, except where there is faith. He has made an offering which may be efficacious in putting away sin; but it produces no reconciliation, no pardon, except where it is accepted by faith. ¶ *In his blood.* Or in his death – his bloody death. Among the Jews, *the blood* was regarded as the seat of life, or vitality, Lev. xvii. 11, "The life of the flesh is in the blood." Hence they were commanded not to eat blood, Gen. ix. 4, "But flesh with the life thereof, which is the blood thereof, shall ye not eat;" Lev. xix. 26; Deut. xii. 23; 1 Sam. xiv. 34. This doctrine is contained uniformly in the sacred Scriptures. And it has been also the opinion of not a few celebrated physiologists, as well in modern as in ancient times. The same was the opinion of the ancient Parsees and Hindoos. Homer thus often speaks of *blood* as the seat of life, as in the expression πορφυρεος θανατος, or *purple death.* And Virgil speaks of *purple life,*

Purpuream vomit ille animam.
Æneid, ix. 349

Empedocles and Critias, among the Greek philosophers, also embraced this opinion. Among the moderns, Harvey, to whom we are indebted for a knowledge of the circulation of the blood, fully believed it. Hoffman and Huxham believed it. Dr. John Hunter has fully adopted the belief, and sustained it, as he supposed, by a great variety of considerations. See Good's *Book of Nature*, pp. 102, 108, ed. New York, 1828. This was undoubtedly the doctrine of the Hebrews; and hence with them to shed the blood was a phrase signifying to kill; hence the efficacy of their sacrifices was supposed to consist in the *blood*, that is, in *the life* of the victim. Hence it was unlawful to *eat* it, as it were the *life*, the seat of vitality; the more immediate and direct gift of God. When, therefore, *the blood of Christ* is spoken of in the New Testament, it means *the offering of his life as a sacrifice*, or his *death* as an expiation. *His* life was given to make atonement. See the word *blood* thus used in Rom. v. 9; Eph. i. 7; Col. i. 14; Heb. ix. 12, 14; xiii. 12; Rev. i. 5; 1 Pet. i. 19; 1 John i. 7. By faith in his death as a sacrifice for sin; by believing that he took *our* sins; that he died in *our* place; by thus, in some sense, making his offering ours; by *approving* it, loving it, embracing it, trusting it, our sins become pardoned, and our souls made pure. ¶ *To declare* (εἰς ἔνδειξιν). For *the purpose* of showing, or exhibiting; to present it to man. The meaning is, that the plan was adopted; the Saviour was given; he suffered and died: and the scheme is proposed to men, *for the purpose* of making a full manifestation of *his* plan, in contradistinction from all the plans of men. ¶ *His righteousness.* His plan of justification. The method or scheme which *he* has adopted, in distinction from that of man, and which he now exhibits, or proffers to sinners. There is great variety in the explanation of the word here rendered *righteousness.* Some explain it as meaning *veracity;* others as *holiness;* others as *goodness;* others as *essential justice.* Most interpreters, perhaps, have explained it as referring to an attribute of God. But the whole connection requires us to understand it here, as in chap. i. 17, not of an *attribute* of God, but of his *plan* of justifying sinners. He has adopted and proposed a plan by which men may become *just* by faith in Jesus Christ, and not by their own works. His acquitting men from sin; his re-

garding them and treating them as just, is set forth in the gospel by the offering of Jesus Christ as a sacrifice on the cross.* ¶ *For the remission of sins.* Margin, *passing over.* The word here used (πάρεσιν) occurs nowhere else in the New Testament, nor in the Septuagint. It means *passing by,* as not noticing, and hence forgiving. A similar idea occurs in 2 Sam. xxiv. 10, and Micah vii. 18, "Who is a God like unto thee, that passeth by the transgression of the remnant of his inheritance?" In Romans it means for the *pardoning,* or in order to pardon, past transgression. ¶ *That are past.* That have been committed; or that have existed before. This has been commonly understood to refer to past generations, as affirming that sins under all dispensations of the world are to be forgiven in this manner, through the sacrifice of Christ. And it has been supposed that all who have been justified, have received pardon by the merits of the sacrifice of Christ. This may be true; but there is no reason to think that this is the idea in *this* passage. For, (1) The scope of the passage does not require it. The argument is not to show how men *had* been justified, but how they *might* be. It is not to discuss an historical *fact,* but to state the way in which sin was to be forgiven under the gospel. (2) The language has no immediate or necessary reference to past generations. It evidently refers to the past lives of the *individuals* who are justified, and not to the sins of former times. All that the passage means, therefore, is, that the plan of pardon is such as completely to remove all the former sins of *the life,* not of all former generations. If it referred to the sins of former times, it would not be easy to avoid the doctrine of universal salvation.

[The design of the apostle is to show the alone ground of a sinner's justification. That ground is "the righteousness of God." To manifest this righteousness Christ had been set forth in the beginning of the gospel age as a propitiatory sacrifice. But though at this time *manifested* or declared, it had in reality

* For the true meaning of this phrase, see Supplementary Notes, chap. i. 17; iii. 22.

26 To declare, *I say*, at this time, his righteousness : *r* that he

r Ac.13.38,39.

been the ground of justification *all along.* Believers in every past dispensation, looking forward to the period of its revelation, had built their hopes on it, and been admitted into glory.

The idea of *manifestation* in gospel times seems most intimately connected with the fact that, in past ages, the ground of pardon had been *hidden*, or at best but dimly seen through type and ceremony. There seems little doubt that these two things were associated in the apostle's mind. Though the ground of God's procedure in remitting the sins of his people during the former economy had long been concealed, it was now gloriously displayed before the eyes of the universe. Paul has the very same idea in Heb. ix. 15, "And for this cause he is the mediator of the new testament, that by means of death, *for the redemption of the transgressions that were under the first testament*, they which are called might receive the promise of eternal inheritance." It may be noticed also that the expression in the 20th verse, "at this time," *i.e.* in the gospel age, requires us to understand the other clause, "sins that are past," as pointing to sin committed under former dispensations. Nor is there any fear of lending support to the doctrine of universal salvation if we espouse this view, the sins remitted in past ages being obviously those of *believers only.* The very same objection might be urged against the parallel passage in Heb. ix. 15.]

¶ *Through the forbearance of God.* Through his patience, his long-suffering. That is, he did not come forth in judgment *when* the sin was committed ; he spared us, though deserving of punishment ; and now he comes forth completely to *pardon* those sins concerning which he has so long and so graciously exercised forbearance. This expression obviously refers, not to the *remission* of sins, but to the fact that they were *committed* while he evinced such long-suffering ; comp. Acts xvii. 30. I do not know better how to show the practical value and bearing of this important passage of Scripture, than by transcribing a part of the affecting experience of the poet Cowper. It is well known that *before* his conversion he was oppressed by a long and dreadful melancholy ; that this was finally heightened to despair ;

might be just, and the justifier of him which believeth in Jesus.

and that he was then subjected to the kind treatment of Dr. Cotton in St. Alban's, as a melancholy case of derangement. His leading thought was that he was doomed to inevitable destruction, and that there was no hope. From this he was roused only by the kindness of his brother, and by the promises of the gospel (see Taylor's *Life of Cowper*). The account of his conversion I shall now give in his own words. "The happy period, which was to shake off my fetters, and afford me a clear discovery of the free mercy of God in Christ Jesus, was now arrived. I flung myself into a chair near the window, and seeing a Bible there, ventured once more to apply to it for comfort and instruction. The first verse I saw was the 25th of the 3d of Romans, *Whom God hath set forth*, &c. Immediately I received strength to believe, and the full beam of the Sun of Righteousness shone upon me. I saw the sufficiency of the atonement he had made for my pardon and justification. In a moment I believed, and received the peace of the gospel. Unless the Almighty arm had been under me, I think I should have been overwhelmed with gratitude and joy. My eyes filled with tears, and my voice choked with transport. I could only look up to heaven in silent fear, overwhelmed with love and wonder. How glad should I now have been to have spent every moment in prayer and thanksgiving. I lost no opportunity of repairing to a throne of grace ; but flew to it with an earnestness irresistible, and never to be satisfied."

26. *At this time.* The time now since the Saviour has come ; now is the time when he manifests it. ¶ *That he might be just.* This verse contains the substance of the gospel. The word "just" here does not mean benevolent, or merciful, though it *may* sometimes have that meaning ; see Note, Mat. i. 19, also John xvii. 25. But it refers to the fact that God had retained the integrity of his character as a moral

27 Where *is* boasting then? It is excluded. By what law? of works? Nay; but by the law of faith.

governor; that he had shown a due regard to his law, and to the penalty of the law, by his plan of salvation. Should he forgive sinners without an atonement, *justice* would be sacrificed and abandoned, the law would cease to have any terrors for the guilty, and its penalty would be a nullity. In the plan of salvation, therefore, he has shown a regard to the law by appointing his Son to be *a substitute* in the place of sinners; not to endure its precise penalty, for his sufferings were not eternal, nor were they attended with remorse of conscience, or by despair, which are the proper *penalty* of the law; but he endured so much as to accomplish the same ends as if those who shall be saved by him had been doomed to eternal death. That is, he showed that the law could not be violated without introducing suffering; and that it could not be broken with impunity. He showed that he had so great a regard for it, that he would not pardon *one sinner* without an atonement. And *thus* he secured the proper honour to his character as a lover of his law, a hater of sin, and a just God. He has shown that if sinners do not avail themselves of the offer of pardon by Jesus Christ, *they* must experience in their own souls for ever the pains which this substitute for sinners endured in behalf of men on the cross. Thus no principle of justice has been abandoned; no threatening has been modified; no claim of his law has been let down; no disposition has been evinced to do *injustice* to the universe by suffering the guilty to escape. He is, in all this great transaction, a just moral governor, as *just* to his law, to himself, to his Son, to the universe, when he *pardons*, as he is when he sends the incorrigible sinner down to hell. A full compensation, an equivalent, has been provided by the sufferings of the Saviour in the sinner's stead, and the sinner may be pardoned. ¶ *And the justifier of him,* &c. Greek, *even justifying him that believeth,* &c. This is the peculiarity and the wonder of

the gospel. *Even while* pardoning, and treating the ill-deserving *as if* they were innocent, he can retain his pure and holy character. His treating the guilty with favour does not show that he loves guilt and pollution, for he has expressed his abhorrence of it in the atonement. His admitting them to friendship and heaven does not show that he *approves* their past conduct and character, for he showed how much he hated even *their* sins by giving his Son to a shameful death *for* them. When an executive pardons offenders, there is an abandonment of the principles of justice and law. The sentence is *set aside;* the threatenings of the law are departed from; and it is done without compensation. It is declared that in certain cases the law *may be* violated, and its penalty *not* be inflicted. But not so with God. He shows no less regard to his law in pardoning than in punishing. This is the grand, glorious, peculiar feature of the gospel plan of salvation. ¶ *Him which believeth in Jesus.* Greek, *him who is of the faith of Jesus;* in contradistinction from him who is of the works of the law; that is, who depends on his own works for salvation.

27. *Where* is *boasting then?* Where is there ground or occasion of boasting or pride? Since all have sinned, and since all have failed of being able to justify themselves by obeying the law, and since all are alike dependent on the mere mercy of God in Christ, all ground of boasting is of course taken away. This refers particularly to the Jews, who were much addicted to *boasting* of their peculiar privileges; see Note, chap. iii. 1, &c. ¶ *By what law?* The word *law* here is used in the sense of *arrangement, rule,* or *economy.* By what arrangement, or by the operation of what *rule,* is boasting excluded? (Stuart). See Gal. iii. 21; Acts xxi. 20. ¶ *Of works.* The law which commands works, and on which the Jews relied. If this were complied with, and they were thereby justified, they would have had ground of self-confidence, or boasting, as

28 Therefore we conclude *that a man is justified by faith without the deeds of the law.

29 *Is he* the God of the Jews only? *is he* not also of the Gentiles? Yes, of the Gentiles also:

s ver.20–22; ch.8.3; Ga.2.16.

30 Seeing *it is* one God, *t* which shall justify the circumcision by faith, and uncircumcision through faith.

31 Do we then make void the law *u* through faith? God forbid: yea, we establish the law.

t Ga.3.8,28. *u* He.10.15,16.

being justified by their own merits. But a plan which led to this, which ended in boasting, and self-satisfaction, and pride, could not be true. ¶ *Nay.* No. ¶ *The law of faith.* The rule, or arrangement which proclaims that we have no merit; that we are lost sinners; and that we are to be justified *only* by faith.

28. *Therefore.* As the result of the previous train of argument. ¶ *That a man.* That *all* who are justified; that is, that there is no other way. ¶ *Is justified by faith.* Is regarded and treated as righteous, by believing in the Lord Jesus Christ. ¶ *Without the deeds of the law.* Without works as a meritorious ground of justification. The apostle, of course, does not mean that Christianity does not *produce* good works, or that they who are justified will not obey the law, and be holy; but that no righteousness of their own will be the ground of their justification. They are sinners; and as such can have no claim to be treated as righteous. God has devised a plan by which they may be pardoned and saved; and that is by faith alone. This is the grand peculiarity of the Christian religion. This was the peculiar point in the reformation from popery. Luther often called this doctrine of justification by faith, the article on which the church stood or fell— *articulus stantis, vel cadentis ecclesiæ* —and it is so. If this doctrine is held entire, all others will be held with it. If this is abandoned, all others will fall also. It may be remarked here, however, that this doctrine by no means interferes with the doctrine that good works are to be performed by Christians. Paul urges this as much as any other writer in the New Testament. His doctrine is, that they are not to be relied on as a *ground* of jus-

tification; but that he did not mean to teach that they are not to be performed by Christians is apparent from the connection, and from the following places in his epistles: Rom. ii. 7; 2 Cor. ix. 8; Eph. ii. 10; 1 Tim. ii. 10; v. 10, 25; vi. 18; 2 Tim. iii. 17; Tit. ii. 7, 14; iii. 8; Heb. x. 24. That we are not *justified* by our works is a doctrine which he has urged and repeated with great power and frequency. See Rom. iv. 2, 6; ix. 11, 32; xi. 6; Gal. ii. 16; iii. 2, 5, 10; Eph. ii. 9; 2 Tim. i. 9.

29, 30. Is he *the God,* &c. The Jews supposed that he was the God of their nation only, that *they* only were to be admitted to his favour. In these verses Paul showed that as all had alike sinned, Jews and Gentiles; and as the plan of salvation by faith was adapted to *sinners,* without any special reference to *Jews;* so God could show favours to all, and all might be admitted on the same terms to the benefits of the plan of salvation.

30. It is *one God.* The same God, there is but one, and his plan is equally fitted to Jews and Gentiles. ¶ *The circumcision.* Those who are circumcised—the *Jews.* ¶ *The uncircumcision.* Gentiles; all who were not Jews. ¶ *By faith...through faith.* There is no difference in the meaning of these expressions. Both denote that faith is the instrumental cause of justification, or acceptance with God.

31. *Do we then make void the law?* Do we render it vain and useless; do we destroy its moral obligation; and do we prevent obedience to it, by the doctrine of justification by faith? This was an *objection* which would naturally be made, and which has thousands of times been since made, that the doctrine of justification by faith tends to licentiousness. The

word *law* here, I understand as referring to the *moral law*, and not merely
to the Old Testament. This is evident from ver. 20, 21, where the apostle
shows that no man could be justified
by *deeds of law*, by conformity with
the moral law; see Note. ¶ *God forbid.* By no means; Note, ver. 4.
This is an explicit denial of any such
tendency. ¶ *Yea, we establish the law.*
That is, by the doctrine of justification by faith; by this scheme of treating men as righteous, the moral law is
confirmed, its obligation is enforced,
obedience to it is secured. This is
done in the following manner: (1) God
showed respect to it, in being unwilling to pardon sinners without an atonement. He showed that it could not
be violated with impunity; that he was
resolved to fulfil its threatenings. (2)
Jesus Christ came to magnify it, and
to make it honourable. He showed
respect to it in his life; and he died
to show that God was determined to
inflict its penalty. (3) The plan of
justification by faith leads to an observance of the law. The sinner sees
the evil of transgression. He sees
the respect which God has shown to
the law. He gives his heart to God,
and yields himself to obey his law.
All the sentiments that arise from the
conviction of sin; that flow from gratitude for mercies; that spring from
love to God; all his views of the
sacredness of the law, prompt him to
yield obedience to it. The fact that
Christ endured such sufferings to show
the evil of violating the law, is one of
the strongest motives prompting to
obedience. We do not easily and
readily repeat that which overwhelms
our best friends in calamity; and we
are brought to *hate* that which inflicted
such woes on the Saviour's soul. The
sentiment recorded by Watts is as
true as it is beautiful:—

" 'Twas for my sins my dearest Lord
   Hung on the cursed tree,
And groan'd away his dying life,
   For thee, my soul, for thee.

" O how I hate those lusts of mine
   That crucified my Lord;
Those sins that pierc'd and nail'd his flesh
   Fast to the fatal wood.

" Yes, my Redeemer, they shall die,
   My heart hath so decreed;

Nor will I spare the guilty things
   That made my Saviour bleed."

This is an advantage in moral influence which no cold abstract law ever
has over the human mind. And one
of the chief glories of the plan of
salvation is, that while it justifies the
sinner, it brings a new set of influences
from heaven, more tender and mighty
than can be drawn from any other
source, to produce obedience to the
law of God.

[This is indeed a beautiful and just view of
the moral influence of the gospel, and especially of the doctrine of justification by faith
alone. It may be questioned, however, whether
the apostle in this place refers chiefly, or even
at all, to the sanctifying tendency of his doctrine. *This* he does very fully in the 6th chap.;
and therefore, if another and consistent sense
can be found, we need not resort to the supposition that he now anticipates what he
intended, in a subsequent part of his epistle,
more fully to discuss. In what other way,
then, does the apostle's doctrine establish the
law? How does he vindicate himself from
the charge of making it void? In the preceding chapter he had pointed out the true ground
of pardon in the "righteousness of God." He
had explained that *none* could be justified but
they who had by faith received it. "Do we
THEN," he asks in conclusion, "make void the
law by maintaining thus, that no sinner can
be accepted who does not receive a righteousness commensurate with all its demands?"
"Yea, we establish the law," is the obvious
answer. Jesus has died to satisfy its claims,
and lives to honour its precepts. Thus he hath
brought in "righteousness," which, being
imputed to them that believe, forms such a
ground of pardon and acceptance, as the law
CANNOT CHALLENGE.

Calvin, in his commentary on the passage,
though he does not exclude the idea of sanctification, yet gives prominence to the view
now stated. "When," says he, "we come to
Christ, *the exact righteousness of the law is
FIRST* found in him, which also becomes ours
by imputation; in the next place sanctification is acquired," &c.]

CHAPTER IV.

The main object of this chapter is
to show that the doctrine of justification by faith, which the apostle was
defending, was found in the Old Testament. The argument is to be regarded
as addressed particularly to *a Jew*, to
show him that no *new* doctrine was
advanced. The argument is derived,

CHAPTER IV.

WHAT shall we say, then, that Abraham, *a* our father as pertaining to the flesh, hath found?

<small>a Mat.3.9.</small>

first, from the fact that Abraham was so justified, ver. 1–5; secondly, from the fact that the same thing is declared by David, ver. 6–8.

A question might still be asked, whether this justification was not in consequence of their being circumcised, and thus grew out of conformity to the law? To answer this, the apostle shows (ver. 9–12) that Abraham was justified by faith *before* he was circumcised, and that even his circumcision was *in consequence* of his being justified by faith, and a public seal or attestation of that fact.

Still further, the apostle shows that if men were to be justified by works, faith would be of no use; and the promises of God would have no effect. The law works wrath (ver. 13, 14), but the conferring of the favour by faith is demonstration of the highest favour of God, ver. 16. Abraham, moreover, had evinced a strong faith; he had shown what it was; he was an example to all who should follow. And he had thus shown that as *he* was justified *before* circumcision, and *before* the giving of the law, so the same thing might occur in regard to those who had never been circumcised. In chap. ii. and iii., the apostle had shown that all had failed of keeping the law, and that there was no other way of justification but by faith. To the salvation of the heathen, the Jew would have strong objections. He supposed that none could be saved but those who had been circumcised, and who were Jews. This objection the apostle meets in this chapter, by showing that Abraham was justified in the very way in which he maintained the heathen *might be;* that Abraham was justified by faith *without* being circumcised. If the father of the faithful, the ancestor on whom the Jews so much prided themselves, was thus justified, then Paul was advancing no new doctrine in maintaining that the same thing might occur now. He was

2 For if Abraham were justified by works, he hath *whereof* to glory: *b* but not before God.

3 For what saith the scripture?

<small>b ch.3.27.</small>

keeping strictly within the spirit of their religion in maintaining that the Gentile world might also be justified by faith. This is the outline of the reasoning in this chapter. The reasoning is such as a serious Jew must feel and acknowledge. And keeping in mind the main object which the apostle had in it, there will be found little difficulty in its interpretation.

1. *What shall we say then?* See chap. iii. 1. This is rather the objection of a Jew. "How does your doctrine of justification by faith agree with what the Scriptures say of Abraham? Was the law set aside in his case? Did he derive no advantage in justification from the rite of circumcision, and from the covenant which God made with him?" The object of the apostle now is to answer this inquiry. ¶ *That Abraham our father.* Our ancestor; the father and founder of the nation; see Note, Mat. iii. 9. The Jews valued themselves much on the fact that he was their father; and an argument drawn from his example or conduct, therefore, would be peculiarly forcible. ¶ *As pertaining to the flesh.* This expression is one that has been much controverted. In the original, it may refer either to Abraham as their father "according to the flesh," that is their natural father, or from whom they were descended; or it may be connected with "hath found." "What shall we say that Abraham our father hath found in respect to the flesh?"—κατὰ σάρκα. The latter is doubtless the proper connection. Some refer the word *flesh* to external privileges and advantages; others to his own strength or power (Calvin and Grotius); and others make it refer to circumcision. This latter I take to be the correct interpretation. It agrees best with the connection, and equally well with the usual meaning of the word. The idea is, "If men are justified by *faith;* if works are to have no place; if, therefore, all rites

and ceremonies, all legal observances, are useless in justification; what is the advantage of circumcision? What benefit did Abraham derive from it? Why was it appointed? And why is such an importance attached to it in the history of his life?" A similar question was asked in chap. iii. 1. ¶ *Hath found.* Hath obtained. What advantage has he derived from it?

2. *For if Abraham,* &c. This is the answer of the apostle. If Abraham was justified on the ground of his own merits, he would have reason to boast, or to claim praise. He might regard himself as the author of it, and take the praise to himself; see ver. 4. The inquiry, therefore, was, whether, in the account of the justification of Abraham, there was to be found any such statement of a reason for self-confidence and boasting. ¶ *But not before God.* In the sight of God. That is, in his recorded judgment, he had no ground of boasting on account of works. To show this, the apostle appeals at once to the Scriptures, to show that there was no such record as that Abraham could boast that he was justified by his works. As God judges right in all cases, so it follows that Abraham had no just ground of boasting, and of course that he was not justified by his own works. The sense of this verse is well expressed by Calvin. "If Abraham was justified by his works, he might boast of his own merits. But he has no ground of boasting before God. Therefore he was not justified by works."

3. *For what saith the scripture?* The inspired account of Abraham's justification. This account was final, and was to settle the question. This account is found in Gen. xv. 6. ¶ *Abraham believed God.* In the Hebrew, "Abraham believed *Jehovah.*" The sense is substantially the same, as the argument turns on the *art* of believing. The faith which Abraham exercised was, that his posterity should be like the stars of heaven in number. This promise was made to him when he had no child, and of course when he had no prospect of such a posterity. See the strength and nature of this faith further illustrated in ver. 16–21. The

reason why it was counted to him for righteousness was, that it was such a strong, direct, and unwavering act of confidence in the promise of God. ¶ *And it.* The word "it" here evidently refers to the *act* of believing. It does not refer to the righteousness of another—of God, or of the Messiah; but the discussion is solely of the *strong act* of Abraham's faith, which *in some sense* was counted to him for righteousness. In what sense this was, is explained directly after. All that is material to remark here is, that *the act* of Abraham, the strong confidence of his mind in the promises of God, his unwavering assurance that what God had promised he would perform, was reckoned for righteousness. The same thing is more fully expressed in ver. 18–22. When, therefore, it is said that the righteousness of Christ is accounted or imputed to us; when it is said that his merits are transferred and reckoned as ours; whatever may be the truth of the doctrine, it cannot be defended by *this* passage of Scripture.

[Dr. Doddridge in a note on the clause, "faith was reckoned to Abraham for righteousness," seems to give the true meaning of the apostle. "Nothing,"says he, "can be easier than to understand how this may be said, in full consistence with our being justified by the imputation of the righteousness of Christ, that is, our being treated by God as righteous for the sake of what he has done and suffered; for though this be the meritorious cause of our acceptance with God, yet faith may be said to be imputed to us εἰς δικαιοσυνην, *in order to our being justified*, or becoming righteous; that is, as we are charged as debtors in the book of God's account, what Christ has done in fulfilling all righteousness for us, is charged as the grand balance of the account; but that it may appear that we are, according to the tenor of the gospel, entitled to the benefit of this, it is also entered in the book of God's remembrance that we are believers, and this appearing, we are graciously discharged, yea, and rewarded, as if we ourselves had been perfectly innocent and obedient."

This view, it will be noticed, turns upon the force of the preposition εἰς before δικαιοσυνην. That it should be translated *unto*, and not *for*, is evident from the sense it bears in such passages as Rom. vi. 3; x. 1, 10, where εἰς τον θανατον, εἰς σωτηριαν, and εἰς δικαιοσυνην, clearly signify *unto* "death," *unto* "salvation " (Eng. Trans. *that* "they might be saved," *i. e.* Israel), and *unto* "righteousness." Faith, therefore, is not counted *as* righteousness, or accepted *in any way instead of it;* but is counted only *unto, i.e.* in order to the reception of righteousness. Instead of faith itself being the righteousness that justifies, the apostle repeatedly tells us, that it is "revealed *to* faith, received "*by*" and "*through* faith," that faith indeed is only the instrument of reception, and can therefore no more be confounded with the righteousness in question, than the beggar's hand with the money that relieves his indigence, or the robe that covers his nakedness, Rom. i. 17; iii. 22; Phil. iii. 8, 9.]

Faith is uniformly an act of the mind. It is not a created essence which is placed within the mind. It is not a substance created independently of the soul, and placed within it by almighty power. It is not a *principle*, for the expression *a principle of faith* is as unmeaning as a principle of joy, or a principle of sorrow, or a principle of remorse. God promises; the man believes; and this is the whole of it.

[A principle is the "element or original cause," out of which certain consequences arise, and to which they may be traced. And if faith be the *root* of all acceptable obedience, then certainly, in this sense, it *is* a principle. But whatever faith be, it is not here asserted that it is imputed *for*, or *instead of*, righteousness. See the Note above.]

While the word *faith* is sometimes used to denote *religious doctrine*, or the system that is to be believed (Acts vi. 7; xv. 9; Rom. i. 5; x. 8; xvi. 26; Eph. iii. 17; iv. 5; 1 Tim. ii. 7, &c.); yet, when it is used to denote that which is required of men, it *always* denotes *an acting of the mind* exercised in relation to some object, or some promise, or threatening, or declaration of some other being; see the Note, Mark xvi. 16. ¶ *Was counted* (ἐλογίσθη). The same word in ver. 22, is rendered "it was imputed." The word occurs frequently in the Scriptures. In the Old Testament, the verb בָשַׁח (*hashab*), which is translated by the word λογίζομαι, means literally, *to think, to intend,* or *purpose; to imagine, invent,* or *derive; to reckon,* or *account; to esteem; to impute, i.e.* to impute to a man what belongs to himself, or what *ought* to be imputed to him. It occurs only in the following places: 1 Sam. xviii.

25; Est. viii. 3; ix. 24, 25; Isa. xxxiii. 8; Jer. xlix. 20; l. 45; Lam. ii. 8; 2 Sam. xiv. 14; Jer. xlix. 30; Gen. l. 20; Job xxxv. 2; 2 Sam. xiv. 13; Ezek. xxxviii. 10; Jer. xviii. 8; Ps. xxi. 12; cxl. 3, 5; Jer. xi. 19; xlviii. 2; Amos vi. 5; Ps. x. 2; Isa. liii. 3, 4; Jer. xxvi. 3; Mic. ii. 3; Nah. i. 11; Jer. xviii. 11; Job xiii. 34; xli. 19, 24; Ps. xxxii. 2; xxxv. 5; Isa. x. 7; Job xix. 11; xxxiii. 10; Gen. xvi. 6; xxxviii. 15; 1 Sam. i. 13; Ps. lii. 4; Jer. xviii. 18; Zec. vii. 10; Job vi. 40; xix. 16; Isa. xiii. 17; 1 Kings x. 21; Num. xviii. 27, 30; Ps. lxxxviii. 4; Isa. xl. 17; Lam. iv. 2; Isa. xl. 15; Gen. xxxi. 16. I have examined *all* the passages, and as the result of my examination have come to the conclusion, that there is not *one* in which the word is used in the sense of *reckoning* or *imputing* to a man that which does not strictly *belong* to him; or of charging on him that which *ought* not to be charged on him as a matter of personal right. The word is never used to denote *imputing* in the sense of *transferring*, or of charging that on one which does not properly belong to him. The same is the case in the New Testament. The word occurs about forty times (see Schmidius' *Concord.*), and in a similar signification. No doctrine of *transferring*, or of setting over to a man what does not properly belong to him, be it sin or holiness, can be derived, therefore, from this word. Whatever is meant by it here, it evidently is declared that the act of believing is that which is intended, both by Moses and by Paul.

[The above list of passages in which the original word חָשַׁב occurs, cannot be reckoned altogether complete. Gesenius, in his *Hebrew Lexicon*, cites under the word two passages from Leviticus, viz. vii. 18; xvii. 4, in both of which it is employed, and in one of them, plainly with the sense of reckoning *that* to a man, which *did not, and could not personally or actually belong to him*, and yet neither of these passages have obtained a place in the author's catalogue. In the last mentioned passage it is declared, that whosoever bringeth not his victim "unto the door of the tabernacle of the congregation, to offer an offering unto the Lord, before the tabernacle of the Lord, דָּם יֵחָשֵׁב, *blood shall be imputed* unto that man; he hath shed blood, and that man shall be cut off from among his people." Now it is manifest that the transgression alluded to in the text involved no actual murder, and yet *that* crime is imputed to the individual. God declares that he shall hold him guilty of it, and visit him with consequent punishment.

Nor can it be proved that the Greek λογίζομαι, which corresponds to the Hebrew word חָשַׁב, is *always* used in the sense of imputing to a man that which does strictly or personally belong to him. Philem. ver. 18, 19, forms an exception, in which Paul begs that a wrong might be placed to his account, though he had no hand in committing it. He says to Philemon, in regard to his slave Onesimus, "if he hath wronged thee, or oweth thee ought, *put that on mine account*, τοῦτο ἐμοὶ ἐλλόγει. I Paul have written it with mine own hand, I will repay it." We are entitled also to assert, till the contrary be established, that the passages in this very chapter of the Epistle to the Romans, in which "*righteousness*" is said to be "*imputed without works*," are exceptions exactly to the point. Surely that righteousness which is "WITHOUT WORKS," is altogether different from the actual or personal righteousness of men, which cannot be but BY WORKS.

The doctrine of the imputation of Christ's righteousness has indeed been assailed by numerous objections. Generally, however, these originate in a misconception or misstatement of the doctrine itself. It is readily admitted that the righteousness of Christ cannot be made ours, *in the same sense that it is his*. It can never be ours in the sense of having actually accomplished it. Yet the doctrine, time after time, is represented as if it involved this absurd conclusion, and then gravely condemned. This is "to fight without an antagonist, and triumph without a victory." Nor does the doctrine involve any transference of moral character. "It never was the doctrine of the Reformation," says Professor Hodge, "or of the Lutheran and Calvinistic divines, that the imputation of righteousness affected the moral character of those concerned. It is true, whom God justifies he also sanctifies; but justification is not sanctification, and the imputation of righteousness is not the infusion of it." Here, then, is another false view of the subject, on which a second class of objections is seriously founded. Indeed, to these two sources may be traced *almost every objection* that at any time has been raised against this doctrine. It would, therefore, greatly simplify the subject, if it were once for all distinctly understood, that the friends of imputed righteousness fully admit all that their brethren on the opposite side of the question allege, in regard to the two points noticed above. *On these there is no dispute.* What then? That while we make these admissions, we yet hold the doctrine in its integrity, and cannot allow it to be explained away as intimating only "that God treats us as righteous." This is true. It is, however, a part of the truth only, and not the whole, for the judgment of God proceeds upon just principles, and he *can and will treat none as righteous*, whom he does not in some sense *esteem to be really such*. Nor is it less evasive to allege that only "the results or benefits of Christ's death" are imputed. "To *talk* of their imputation, I think, is an affront to sound sense, as I am sure to be *put off* with their imputation, would be a fatal disappointment of our hopes; all these benefits are not imputed, but imparted. They are not reckoned to us, but are really enjoyed by us. Ours they are, not barely in the divine estimation, but by proper and personal possession" (Hervey, *Ther. and Asp.* dial. x.).

We may quarrel with the term imputation, but will find it difficult to get quit of the thing that is intimated by it. When the righteousness of Christ is said to be imputed to us, the meaning is, that God so places it to our account, that in the eyes of law we are *held* righteous, and therefore *treated* accordingly. And what is there so unreasonable in all this? Were not our sins laid to the charge of Christ, when he who knew no sin *was made sin for us?* Is not Adam's sin imputed to his posterity? The fact that we do suffer on account of it, cannot be denied, even on the principles of those who deny imputed sin, and allow only the transmission of depravity. For the question recurs, Why have we been visited with this impurity of nature, this disorganization both of physical and mental powers? Why *this, antecedent* to all personal transgression? One answer only can be given. *It is the punishment of the first sin,* which, as it was not personally ours, must have been imputed to us, unless we adopt the other side of the alternative, and maintain that God can punish where there is no guilt. Many, moreover, who can be charged with no personal sin are subjected to the pain of dying; and the agonies of tender infants, who have scarce opened their eyes on the light, irresistibly prove the imputation of the first sin. But if we allow the imputation of our sins to Christ, and of Adam's guilt to his posterity, the imputation of the Redeemer's righteousness cannot consistently be denied. These doctrines stand or fall together. Christ is the representative of his people, as Adam is the representative of mankind; and the apostle in the next chapter runs a parallel between them, which concludes with these words: "Therefore, as by the *offence of one*, judgment came upon all men to condemnation, even so by *the righteousness of one*, the free gift came upon all men unto justification. For as by *one man's disobedience*, many were *made sinners*, so by the *obedience of one*, shall many be *made righteous*."]

Abraham[c] believed God, and it was counted unto him for righteousness.

      c Ge.15.6.

¶ *For righteousness.* In order to justification; or to regard and treat him in connection with this *as a* righteous man; as one who was admitted to the favour and friendship of God. In reference to this we may remark, (1) That it is evidently not intended that the act of believing, on the part of Abraham, was the *meritorious* ground of acceptance, for then it would have been a work. Faith was as much his own act, as any act of obedience to the law. (2) The design of the apostle was to show that by the *law*, or by *works*, man could not be justified, chap. iii. 28; iv. 2. (3) *Faith* was not that which the law required. It demanded complete and perfect obedience; and if a man was justified by *faith*, it was *in some other way* than by the law. (4) As the law did not demand this; and as faith was something different from the demand of the law; so if a man were justified by that, it was *on a principle* altogether different from justification by works. It was not by personal merit. It was not by complying with the law. It was in a mode entirely different. (5) In being justified by faith, it is meant, therefore, that we are treated as righteous; that we are forgiven; that we are admitted to the favour of God, and treated as his friends. (6) In this act, *faith* is a mere instrument, an antecedent, a *sine qua non*, that which God has been pleased to appoint as a condition on which men may be treated as righteous. It expresses a state of mind which is demonstrative of love to God, of affection for his cause and character; of reconciliation and friendship; and is therefore that state to which he has been graciously pleased to promise pardon and acceptance. (7) As this is not a matter of law; as the law could not be said to *demand* it; as it is on a different principle; and as the acceptance of faith, or of a believer, cannot be a matter of merit or claim, so justification is of grace, or mere favour. It is

4 Now to [d]him that worketh is the reward not reckoned of grace, but of debt.

      d ch.11.6.

in no sense a matter of merit on our part, and thus stands distinguished entirely from justification by works, or by conformity to the law. From beginning to end it is, so far as *we* are concerned, a matter of grace. The *merit* by which all this is obtained, is the work of the Lord Jesus Christ, through whom this plan is proposed, and by whose atonement alone God can consistently pardon and treat as righteous those who are in themselves ungodly; see ver. 5. In this place we have also evidence that *faith* is always substantially of the same character. In the case of Abraham it was confidence in God and his promises. All faith has the same nature, whether it be confidence in the Messiah, or in any of the divine promises or truths. As this *confidence* evinces the same state of mind, so it was as consistent to justify Abraham by it, as it is to justify him who believes in the Lord Jesus Christ under the gospel; see Heb. xi.

4. *Now to him that worketh,* &c. This passage is not to be understood as affirming that any actually *have* worked out their salvation by conformity to the law so as to be saved by their own merits; but it expresses a general truth in regard to works. *On that plan,* if a man were justified by his works, it would be a matter *due* to him. It is a general principle in regard to contracts and obligations, that where a man fulfils them he is entitled to the reward as that which is *due* to him, and which he can claim. This is well understood in all the transactions among men. Where a man has fulfilled the terms of a contract, to pay him is not a matter of *favour;* he has *earned* it; and we are *bound* to pay him. So says the apostle, it *would* be, if a man were justified by his works. He would have a *claim* on God. It would be wrong *not* to justify him. And this is an additional reason why the doctrine cannot be true; comp. Rom. xi. 6. ¶ *The reward.* The pay, or wages. The word

5 But to him that worketh not, but believeth on him that justifieth the ungodly, *his faith is counted for righteousness.

e Hab.2.4.

6 Even as David also describeth the blessedness of the man unto whom God imputeth righteousness without works.

is commonly applied to the pay of soldiers, day-labourers, &c., Mat. xx. 8; Luke x. 7; 1 Tim. v. 18; James v. 4. It has a similar meaning here. ¶ *Reckoned.* Greek, imputed. The same word which, in ver. 3, is rendered *counted*, and in ver. 22, *imputed.* It is here used in its strict and proper sense, to *reckon* that as belonging to a man which is his own, or which is due to him; see the Note on verse 3. ¶ *Of grace.* Of favour; as a gift. ¶ *Of debt.* As due; as a claim; as a fair compensation according to the contract.

5. *But to him that worketh not.* Who does not rely on his conformity to the law for his justification; who does not depend on his works; who seeks to be justified in some other way. The reference here is to the Christian plan of justification. ¶ *But believeth.* Note, chap. iii. 26. ¶ *On him.* On God. This the connection requires; for the discussion has immediate reference to Abraham, whose faith was in the promise of God. ¶ *That justifieth the ungodly.* This is a very important expression. It implies, (1) That men are sinners, or are ungodly. (2) That God regards them as such when they are justified. He does not justify them *because* he sees them to be, or regards them to be righteous; but knowing that they are *in fact* polluted. He does not *first* esteem them, contrary to fact, to be pure; but knowing that they *are* polluted, and that they deserve no favour, he resolves to forgive them, and to treat them as his friends. (3) In themselves they are equally undeserving, whether they are justified or not. Their souls have been defiled by sin; and that is known when they are pardoned. God judges things as they are; and sinners who are justified, he judges *not* as if they were pure, or as if they had a claim; but he regards them *as united by faith to the Lord Jesus; and* IN THIS RELATION *he judges that they* SHOULD *be treated*

as his friends, though they have been, are, and always will be, personally undeserving. It is not meant that the righteousness of Christ is *transferred* to them, so as to become personally theirs — for moral character cannot be transferred;—nor that it is *infused* into them, making them personally meritorious — for then they could not be spoken of as ungodly; but that Christ died in their stead, to atone for their sins, and is regarded and esteemed by God to have died; and that the results or benefits of his death are so reckoned or imputed to believers as to make it proper for God to regard and treat them as if they had themselves obeyed the law; that is, as righteous in his sight; see the Note on verse 3.

6. *Even as David.* The apostle having adduced the example of Abraham to show that the doctrine which he was defending was not new, and contrary to the Old Testament, proceeds to adduce the case of David also; and to show that he understood the same doctrine of justification without works. ¶ *Describeth.* Speaks of. ¶ *The blessedness.* The happiness; or the desirable state or condition. ¶ *Unto whom God imputeth righteousness.* Whom God treats as righteous, or as entitled to his favour in a way different from his conformity to the law. This is found in Ps. xxxii. And the whole scope and design of the psalm is to show the blessedness of the man who is *forgiven*, and whose sins are not charged on him, but who is freed from the punishment due to his sins. Being thus pardoned, he is treated as a righteous man. And it is evidently in this sense that the apostle uses the expression "imputeth righteousness," *i.e.* he does *not* impute, or charge on the man his sins; he reckons and treats him as a pardoned and righteous man, Ps. xxxii. 2. See Note on verse 3. He regards him as one who is forgiven

7 *Saying,* *f* Blessed *are* they whose iniquities are forgiven, and whose sins are covered.

8 Blessed *is* the man to whom the Lord will not impute sin.

9 *Cometh* this blessedness then

f Ps.32.1,2.

upon the circumcision *only,* or *g* upon the uncircumcision also? for we say that faith was reckoned to Abraham for righteousness.

10 How was it then reckoned? when he was in circumcision, or in

g Ac.10.45.

and admitted to his favour, and who is to be treated henceforward as though he had not sinned. That is, he partakes of the benefits of Christ's atonement, so as not henceforward to be treated as a sinner, but as a friend of God.

7. *Blessed.* Happy are they; they are highly favoured; see Note, Mat. v. 3. ¶ *Whose sins are covered.* Are concealed; or hidden from the view. On which God will no more look, and which he will no more remember. "By these words," says Calvin (*in loco*), "we are taught that justification with Paul is nothing else but pardon of sin." The word *cover* here has not reference to the atonement, but is expressive of *hiding,* or *concealing, i.e.* of forgiving sin.

8. *Will not impute sin.* On whom the Lord will not charge his sins; or who shall not be *reckoned* or regarded as guilty. This shows clearly what the apostle meant by imputing faith without works. It is to pardon sin, and to treat with favour; *not* to reckon or charge a man's sin to him; but to treat him, though personally undeserving and ungodly (ver. 5), as though the sin had not been committed. The word "impute" here is used in its natural and appropriate sense, as denoting to charge on man that which properly belongs to him. See the Note on verse 3.

9. *Cometh,* &c. The apostle has now prepared the way for an examination of the inquiry whether this came *in consequence* of obedience to the law? or whether it was *without* obedience to the law? Having shown that Abraham was justified by faith in accordance with the doctrine which he was defending, the only remaining inquiry was whether it was *after* he was circumcised or before; whether *in consequence* of his circumcision or

not. If it was *after* his circumcision, the Jew might still maintain that it was by complying with the works of the law; but if it was *before,* the point of the apostle would be established, that it was without the works of the law. Still further, if he was justified by faith *before* he was circumcised, then here was an instance of justification and acceptance without conformity to the Jewish law; and if the father of the Jewish nation was so justified, and reckoned as a friend of God, *without* being circumcised, *i.e.* in the condition in which the heathen world then was, then it would follow that the Gentiles might be justified in a similar way now. It would not be departing, therefore, from the spirit of the Old Testament itself, to maintain, as the apostle had done (chap. iii.), that the Gentiles who had not been circumcised might obtain the favour of God as well as the Jew; that is, that it was *independent* of circumcision, and might be extended to all. ¶ *This blessedness.* This happy state or condition. This state of being justified by God, and of being regarded as his friends. This is the sum of all blessedness; the only state that can be truly pronounced happy. ¶ *Upon the circumcision* only. The *Jews* alone, as *they* pretended. ¶ *Or upon the uncircumcision also.* The *Gentiles* who believed, as the *apostle* maintained. ¶ *For we say.* We all admit. It is a conceded point. It was the doctrine of the apostle, as well as of the Jews, and as much theirs as his. With this, then, as a conceded point, what is the fair inference to be drawn from it?

10. *How.* In what circumstances, or time? ¶ *When he was in circumcision,* &c. Before or after he was circumcised? This was the very point of the inquiry. For if he was justified

uncircumcision?   Not in circumcision, but in uncircumcision.

11 And[h] he received the sign of
circumcision ; a seal of the righteousness of the faith which *he had,*
yet being uncircumcised ; that he

h Ge.17.10,11.

might be *i* the father of all them that
believe, though they be not circumcised ; that righteousness might be
imputed unto them also :

12 And the father of circumcision
to them who are not of the circum-

i Lu.19.9.

by faith *after* he was circumcised, the
Jew might pretend that it was in virtue of his circumcision ; that even his
faith was acceptable, *because* he was
circumcised. But if it was *before* he
was circumcised, this plea could not
be set up ; and the argument of the
apostle was confirmed by the case of
Abraham, the great father and model
of the Jewish people, that circumcision and the deeds of the law did not
conduce to justification ; and that as
Abraham was justified *without* those
works, so might others be, and the
heathen, therefore, might be admitted
to similar privileges. ¶ *Not in circumcision.* Not *being* circumcised, or
after he was circumcised, but before.
This was the record in the case, Gen.
xv. 6; comp. Gen. xvii. 10.

11. *And he received the sign,* &c.
A *sign* is that by which anything is
shown, or *represented.* And circumcision thus *showed* that there was a *covenant* between Abraham and God, Gen.
xvii. 1–10. It became the public mark
or token of the relation which he sustained to God. ¶ *A seal.* See Note,
John iii. 33. A *seal* is that mark of
wax or other substance, which is
attached to an instrument of writing,
as a deed, &c., to confirm, ratify it, or
to make it binding. Sometimes instruments were sealed, or made authentic,
by *stamping* on them some word, letter,
or device, which had been engraved
on silver, or on precious stones. The
seal or *stamp* was often worn as an
ornament on the finger, Est. viii. 8;
Gen. xli. 42; xxxviii. 18 ; Ex. xxviii.
11, 36; xxix. 6. To *affix* the seal, whether of wax or otherwise, was to confirm a contract or an engagement. In
allusion to this, circumcision is called
a *seal* of the covenant which God had
made with Abraham. That is, he appointed this as a public attestation to
the fact that he had previously ap-

proved of Abraham, and had made
important promises to him. ¶ *Which*
he had, yet *being uncircumcised.* He
believed (Gen. xv. 5) ; was accepted,
or justified; was admitted to the favour
of God, and favoured with clear and
remarkable promises (Gen. xv. 18–
21 ; xvii. 1–9), *before* he was circumcised. Circumcision, therefore, could
have contributed neither to his justification, nor to the promises made to
him by God. ¶ *That he might be the
father,* &c. All this was done that
Abraham might be held up as an example, or a model, of the very doctrine
which the apostle was defending.
The word *father* here is used evidently
in a spiritual sense, as denoting that
he was the ancestor of all true believers ; that he was their model and
example. They are regarded as his
children because they are possessed of
his spirit, are justified in the same
way, and are imitators of his example;
see Note, Mat. i. 1. In this sense
the expression occurs in Luke xix. 9;
John viii. 33; Gal. iii. 7, 29. ¶ *Though
they be not circumcised.* This was
stated in opposition to the opinion of
the Jews that all *ought* to be circumcised. As the apostle had shown that
Abraham enjoyed the favour of God
previous to his being circumcised, *i.e.
without* circumcision ; so it followed
that others might on the same principle also. This instance settles the
point; and there is nothing which a
Jew can reply to this. ¶ *That righteousness,* &c. That is, in the same
way, by faith without works; that
they might be accepted, and treated
as righteous.

12. *And the father of circumcision.*
The father, *i.e.* the ancestor, exemplar, or model of those who are circumcised, and who possess the same
faith that he did. Not only the father
of all believers (ver. 11), but in a

cision only, but also walk in the steps of the faith of our father Abraham, which *he had*, being *yet* uncircumcised.

13 For the promise, *ᵏthat* he should be the heir of the world,

k Ge.17.4,&c.

was not to Abraham, or to his seed, through the law, but through the righteousness of faith.

14 For*ˡ* if they which are of the law *be* heirs, faith is made void, and the promise made of none effect;

l Ga.3.18.

---

special sense the father of the Jewish people. In this the apostle intimates that though *all* who believed would be saved as he was, yet the Jews had a special *proprietorship* in Abraham; they had special favours and privileges from the fact that he was their ancestor. ¶ *Not of the circumcision only.* Who are not merely circumcised, but who possess his spirit and his faith. Mere circumcision would not avail; but circumcision connected with faith like his, showed that they were peculiarly his descendants; see Note, chap. ii. 25. ¶ *Who walk in the steps,* &c. Who imitate his example; who imbibe his spirit; who have his faith. ¶ *Being* yet *uncircumcised.* Before he was circumcised. Comp. Gen. xv. 6, with Gen. xvii.

13. *For the promise,* &c. To show that the faith of Abraham, on which his justification depended, was not by the law, the apostle proceeds to show that the promise concerning which his faith was so remarkably evinced was *before* the law was given. If this was so, then it was an additional important consideration in opposition to the Jew, showing that acceptance with God depended on faith, and not on works. ¶ *That he should be heir of the world.* An *heir* is one who succeeds, or is to succeed, to an estate. In this passage *the world,* or the entire earth, is regarded as the *estate* to which reference is made, and the promise is that the posterity of Abraham should succeed to that, or should possess it as their inheritance. The precise expression here used, "heir of the world," is not found in the promises made to Abraham. Those promises were, that God would make of him a great nation (Gen. xii. 2); that in him all the families of the earth should be blessed (ver. 3); that his posterity should be as the stars for

multitude (Gen. xv. 5); and that he should be a father of many nations (Gen. xvii. 5). As this latter promise is one to which the apostle particularly refers (see ver. 17), it is probable that he had this in his eye. This promise had, at first, respect to his numerous natural descendants, and to their possessing the land of Canaan. But it is also regarded in the New Testament as extending to the Messiah (Gal. iii. 16) as his descendant, and to all his followers as the spiritual seed of the father of the faithful. When the apostle calls him "the heir of the world," he sums up in this comprehensive expression all the promises made to Abraham, intimating that his spiritual descendants, *i.e.* those who possess his faith, shall yet be so numerous as to possess all lands. ¶ *Or to his seed.* To his posterity, or descendants. ¶ *Through the law.* By the observance of the law; or made in consequence of observing the law; or depending on the condition that he should observe the law. The covenant was made *before* the law of circumcision was given, and long before the law of Moses (comp. Gal. iii. 16, 17, 18), and was independent of both. ¶ *But through,* &c. In consequence of or in connection with the strong confidence which he showed in the promises of God, Gen. xv. 6.

14. *For if they which are of the law.* Who seek for justification and acceptance by the law. ¶ *Faith is made void.* Faith would have no place in the scheme; and consequently the strong commendations bestowed on the faith of Abraham, would be bestowed without any just cause. If men are justified by the *law,* they cannot be by faith, and faith would be useless in this work. ¶ *And the promise,* &c. A *promise* looks to the future. Its design and tendency is to

15 Because ^mthe law worketh wrath: for ⁿwhere no law is, *there is* no transgression.

16 Therefore *it is* of faith, that

m ch.5.20.　　　*n* 1 Jn.3.4.

excite trust and confidence in him who makes it. All the promises of God have this design and tendency; and consequently, as God has given *many* promises, the object is to call forth the lively and constant *faith* of men, all going to show that in the divine estimation, *faith* is of inestimable value. But if men are justified by the *law;* if they are rendered acceptable by conformity to the institutions of Moses; then they cannot depend for acceptance on any *promise* made to Abraham, or his seed. They cut themselves off from that promise, and stand independent of it. That promise, like all other promises, was made to excite faith. If, therefore, the Jews depended on the *law* for justification, they were cut off from all the *promises* made to Abraham; and if they *could* be justified by the law, the promise was useless. This is as true now as it was then. If men seek to be justified by their morality or their forms of religion, they cannot depend on any *promise* of God; for he has *made* no promise to any such attempt. They stand independently of any promise, covenant, or compact, and are depending on a scheme of their *own*—a scheme which would render his plan vain and useless; which would render his promises, and the atonement of Christ, and the work of the Spirit of no value. It is clear, therefore, that *such* an attempt at salvation cannot be successful.

15. *Because the law.* All law. It is the tendency of law. ¶ *Worketh wrath.* Produces or causes wrath While man is fallen, and a sinner, its tendency, so far from *justifying* him, and producing peace,is just the reverse. It condemns, denounces wrath, and produces suffering. The word *wrath* here is to be taken in the sense of *punishment,* chap. ii. 8. And the meaning is, that the law of God, demanding perfect purity, and denounc-

it might be by grace; to the end the promise might be sure to all the seed; not to that only which is of the law, but to that also

ing every sin, condemns the sinner, and consigns him to punishment. As the apostle had proved (chap. i. ii. iii.) that *all* were sinners, so it followed that if any attempted to be justified by the *law,* they would be involved only in condemnation and wrath. ¶ *For where no law is,* &c. This is a general principle; a maxim of common justice and of common sense. Law is a *rule* of conduct. If no such rule is given and known, there can be no crime. Law expresses what may be done, and what may not be done. If there is no command to pursue a certain course, no injunction to forbid certain conduct, actions will be innocent. The connection in which this declaration is made here, seems to imply that as the Jews had a multitude of clear laws, and as the Gentiles had the laws of nature, there could be no hope of escape from the charge of their violation. Since human nature was depraved, and men were prone to sin, the more just and reasonable the laws, the less hope was there of being justified *by* the law, and the more certainty was there that the law would produce wrath and condemnation.

16. *Therefore.* In view of the course of reasoning which has been pursued. We have come to this conclusion. ¶ It is *of faith.* Justification is by faith; or the plan which God has devised of saving men is by faith, chap. iii. 26. ¶ *That* it might be *by grace.* As a matter of mere undeserved mercy. If men were justified by *law,* it would be by their own merits; now it is of mere unmerited favour. ¶ *To the end.* For the purpose, or design. ¶ *The promise,* &c. Ver. 13. ¶ *Might be sure.* Might be firm, or established. On any other ground, it could not be established. If it had depended on entire conformity to the *law,* the promise would never have been established, for none would have yielded such obedience. But

which is of the faith of Abraham, who is the father of us all,

17 (As it is written, [o] I have made thee a father of many nations,) [1] before him whom he believed, *even* God, [p] who quickeneth the dead, and calleth [q] those things which be not as though they were.

18 Who against hope believed in hope, that he might become the father of many nations, according to that which was spoken, [r] So shall thy seed be.

19 And being not weak in faith, he considered not his own body now dead, when he was about an

o Ge.17.5. 1 or, *like unto*. p Ep.2.1,5. q 1 Co.1.28; 1 Pe.2.10. r Ge.15.5.

now it may be secured to all the posterity of Abraham. ¶ *To all the seed.* Ver. 13. ¶ *Not to that only.* Not to that part of his descendants alone who were *Jews*, or who had the law. ¶ *But to that*, &c. To *all* who should possess the same faith as Abraham. ¶ *The father of us all.* Of all who believe, whether they be Jews or Gentiles.

17. *As it is written.* Gen. xvii. 5. ¶ *I have made thee.* The word here used in the Hebrew (Gen. xvii. 5) means literally, *to give, to grant;* and also, to set, or constitute. This is also the meaning of the Greek word used both by the LXX. and the apostle. The quotation is taken literally from the Septuagint. The argument of the apostle is founded in part on the fact that the *past* tense is used—I *have* made thee—and that God spoke of a thing as already *done*, which he had promised or purposed to do. The sense is, he had, *in his mind* or *purpose*, constituted him the father of many nations; and so certain was the fulfilment of the divine purposes, that he spoke of it as already accomplished. ¶ *Of many nations.* The apostle evidently understands this promise as referring, not to his *natural* descendants only, but to the great multitude who should believe as he did. ¶ *Before him.* In his view, or sight; *i.e.* God regarded him as such a father. ¶ *Whom he believed.* Whose *promise* he believed; or in whom he trusted. ¶ *Who quickeneth the dead.* Who gives *life* to the dead, Eph. ii. 1, 5. This expresses the power of God to give life. But why it is used here has been a subject of debate. I regard it as having reference to the strong natural improbability of the fulfilment of the prophecy when it was given, arising from the age of Abraham and Sarah, ver. 19. Abraham exercised power in the God who gives life, and who gives it as he pleases. It is one of his prerogatives to give life to the dead (νεκρους), to raise up those who are in their graves; and a power *similar* to that, or strongly *reminding* of that, was manifested in fulfilling the promise to Abraham. The giving of this promise, and its fulfilment, were such as strongly to remind us that God has power to give life to the dead. ¶ *And calleth*, &c. That is, those things which he foretells and promises are so certain, that he may speak of them as already in existence. Thus in relation to Abraham, God, instead of simply *promising* that he *would* make him the father of many nations, speaks of it as already done, "I *have* made thee," &c. In his own mind, or purpose, he had so constituted him, and it was so certain that it *would* take place, that he might speak of it as *already* done.

18. *Who against hope.* Who against all apparent or usual ground of hope. He refers here to the prospect of a posterity; see ver. 19–21. ¶ *Believed in hope.* Believed in that which was promised to excite his hope. Hope here is put for the object of his hope—that which was promised. ¶ *According to that which was spoken.* Gen. xv. 5. ¶ *So shall thy seed be.* That is, as the stars in heaven for multitude. Thy posterity shall be very numerous.

19. *And being not weak in faith.* That is, having strong faith. ¶ *He considered not.* He did not regard the fact that his body was now dead, as any obstacle to the fulfilment of the promise. He did not suffer that fact to influence him, or to produce any doubt about the fulfilment. Faith looks to the strength of God, not to second

hundred years old, neither yet *the deadness of Sarah's womb;

20 He staggered not at the promise of God through unbelief; but was strong in faith, giving glory to God;

21 And being fully persuaded that what he had promised, *the was able also to perform.

s He.11.11.　　*t* Ge.18.14; Lu.1.37,45; He.11.19.

22 And therefore it was imputed to him for righteousness.

23 Now *u* it was not written for his sake alone, that it was imputed to him;

24 But *v* for us also, to whom it shall be imputed, *w* if we believe on him that raised up Jesus our Lord from the dead;

u ch.15.4; 1 Co.10.11.　　*v* Ac.2.39.
w Mar.16.16; Jn.3.14-16.

causes, or to difficulties that may appear formidable to man. ¶ *Now dead.* Aged; dead as to the purpose under consideration; comp. Heb. xi. 12, "As good as dead." That is, he was now at an age when it was highly improbable that he would have any children; comp. Gen. xvii. 17. ¶ *Deadness,* &c. Heb. xi. 11, "When she was past age;" comp. Gen. xviii. 11.

20. *He staggered not.* He was not moved, or agitated; he steadily and firmly believed the promise. ¶ *Giving glory to God.* Giving honour to God by the firmness with which he believed his promises. His conduct was such as to honour God; that is, to show Abraham's conviction that he was worthy of implicit confidence and trust. In this way *all* who believe in the promises of God do honour to him. They bear testimony to him that he is worthy of confidence. They become so many witnesses in his favour; and furnish to their fellow-men evidence that God has a claim on the credence and trust of mankind.

21. *And being fully persuaded.* Thoroughly or entirely convinced, Lu. i. 1; Rom. xiv. 5; 2 Tim. iv. 5, 17. ¶ *He was able.* Comp. Gen. xviii. 14. This was not the *only* time in which Abraham evinced this confidence. His faith was equally implicit and strong when he was commanded to sacrifice his promised son, Heb. xi. 19.

22. *And therefore.* His faith was so implicit, and so unwavering, that it was a demonstration that he was the firm friend of God. He was tried, and he had such confidence in God that he showed that he was supremely attached to him, and would obey and serve him. This was reckoned as a

full proof of friendship; and he was recognized and treated as righteous; *i.e.* as the friend of God. See Note on ver. 3, 5.

[The true sense of faith being imputed for righteousness is given in a Supplementary Note at the beginning of the chapter.]

23. *Now it was not written.* The record of this extraordinary faith was not made on his account only; but it was made to show the way in which men may be regarded and treated as righteous by God. If Abraham was so regarded and treated, then, on the same principle, all others may be. God has but one mode of justifying men. ¶ *Imputed.* Reckoned; accounted. He was regarded and treated as the friend of God.

24. *But for us also.* For our use (comp. chap. xv. 4; 1 Cor. x. 11), that we might have an example of the way in which men may be accepted of God. It is recorded for our encouragement and imitation, to show that *we* may in a similar manner be accepted and saved. ¶ *If we believe on him,* &c. Abraham showed his faith in God by believing *just what God revealed to him.* This was *his* faith, and it might be as *strong* and *implicit* as could be exercised under the fullest revelation. Faith, now, is belief in God *just so far as he has revealed his will to us.* It is therefore the same *in principle,* though it may have reference to different objects. It is confidence in the same God, according to what we know of his will. Abraham showed *his* faith mainly in confiding in the promises of God respecting a numerous posterity. This was the leading truth made known to *him,* and this he believed.

25 Who[x] was delivered for our offences, and [y] was raised again for our justification.

[x] Is.53.5,6; 2 Co.5.21; He.9.28; 1 Pe.2.24; Re.1.5.
[y] 1 Co.15.17; 1 Pe.1.21.

[The promise made to Abraham was, "in thy seed shall all nations of the earth be blessed," on which we have the following inspired commentary: "And the scriptures foreseeing that God would justify the heathen through faith, preached before *the gospel* unto Abraham, saying, In thee shall all nations be blessed," Gal. iii. 8. It would seem, then, that this promise, like that made immediately after the fall, contained the very germ and principles of the gospel. So that after all there is not so great difference between the object of Abraham's faith, and that of ours. Indeed, the object in both cases is manifestly the same.]

The main or leading truths that God has made known to *us* are, that he has given his Son to die; that he has raised him up; and that through him he is ready to pardon. To put confidence in these truths is to believe now. Doing this, we believe in the same God that Abraham did; we evince the same spirit; and thus show that we are the friends of the same God, and may be treated in the same manner. This is *faith* under the gospel (comp. Notes, Mar. xvi. 16), and shows that the faith of Abraham and of all true believers is substantially the same, and is varied only by the difference of the truths made known.

25. *Who was delivered.* To death; comp. Notes, Acts ii. 23. ¶ *For our offences.* On account of our crimes. He was delivered up to death in order to make expiation for our sins. ¶ *And was raised again.* From the dead. ¶ *For our justification.* On account of our justification. In order that we may be justified. The word *justification* here seems to be used in a large sense, to denote acceptance with God; including not merely the formal act by which God pardons sins, and by which we become reconciled to him, but also the *completion* of the work—the treatment of us as righteous, and raising us up to a state of glory. By the *death* of Christ an atonement is made for sin. If it be asked how his *resurrection* contributes to our acceptance with God, we may answer, (1)

CHAPTER V.

THEREFORE[a] being justified by faith, we have peace with

[a] Is.32.17; Ep.2.14; Col.1.20.

It rendered *his* work complete. His *death* would have been unavailing, his work would have been imperfect, if he had not been raised up from the dead. He submitted to death as a sacrifice, and it was needful that he should rise, and thus conquer death and subdue our enemies, that the work which he had undertaken might be complete. (2) His resurrection was a proof that his work was *accepted* by the Father. What he had done, in order that sinners might be saved, was approved. Our justification, therefore, became sure, as it was *for* this that he had given himself up to death. (3) His resurrection is the mainspring of all our hopes, and of all our efforts to be saved. Life and immortality are thus brought to light, 2 Tim. i. 10. God " hath begotten us again to a lively hope [a living, active, real hope] by the resurrection of Jesus Christ from the dead," 1 Pet. i. 3. Thus the fact that *he* was raised becomes the ground of hope that *we* shall be raised and accepted of God. The fact that *he* was raised, and that all who love him shall be raised also, becomes one of the most efficient motives to *us* to seek to be justified and saved. There is no higher motive that can be presented to　duce man to seek salvation than the fact that he may be raised up from death and the grave, and made immortal. There is no satisfactory proof that man *can* be thus raised up, but the resurrection of Jesus Christ. In that resurrection we have a pledge that all his people will rise. "For if we believe that Jesus died and rose again, even so them also which sleep in Jesus will God bring with him," 1 Thes. iv. 14. "Because I live," said the Redeemer, "ye shall live also," John xiv. 19; comp. 1 Pet. i. 21.

CHAPTER V.

The design of this chapter, which has usually been considered as one of the most difficult portions of the New Testament, especially ver. 12–21, is evidently to show the *results* or *benefits* of the doctrine of justification by faith. That doctrine the apostle had now fully established. He had shown in the previous chapters, (1) That men were under condemnation for sin; (2) That this extended alike to the Jews and the Gentiles; (3) That there was no way of escape now but by the doctrine of pardon, not by personal merit, but by grace; (4) That this plan was fully made known by the gospel of Christ; and, (5) That this was no *new* doctrine, but was in fact substantially the same by which Abraham and David had been accepted before God.

Having thus stated and vindicated the doctrine, it was natural to follow up the demonstration, by stating its bearing and its practical influence. This he does by showing that its *immediate* effect is to produce *peace*, ver. 1. It gives us the privilege of access to the favour of God, ver. 2. But not only this. We are in a world of affliction. Christians, like others, are surrounded with trials; and a very important question was, whether this doctrine would have an influence in supporting the soul in those trials. This question the apostle discusses in ver. 3–11. He shows that *in fact* Christians glory in tribulation, and that the reasons why they do so are, (1) That the natural effect of tribulations under the gospel was to lead to *hope*, ver. 3, 4. (2) That the *cause* of this was, that the love of God was shed abroad in the heart by the Holy Ghost. This doctrine he further confirms by showing the consolation which would be furnished by the fact that Christ had died for them. This involved a security that they would be sustained in their trials, and that a victory would be given them. For, (1) It was the highest expression of love that he should die for enemies, ver. 6, 7, 8. (2) It followed that if he was given for them when *they* were enemies, it was much more probable, it was *certain*, that all needful grace would be furnished to them now that they were reconciled, ver. 9, 10, 11.

But there was another very material inquiry. Men were not only exposed to affliction, but they were in the midst of *a wreck of things—of a fallen world—of the proofs and memorials of sin everywhere.* The first man had sinned, and the *race* was subject to sin and death. The monuments of death and sin were everywhere. It was to be expected that a remedy from God would have reference to this universal state of sin and woe; and that it would tend to meet and repair these painful and widespread ruins. The apostle then proceeds to discuss the question, how the plan of salvation which involved justification by faith was adapted to meet these universal and distressing evils, ver. 12–21. The design of this part of the chapter is to show that the blessings procured by the redemption through Christ, and the plan of justification through him, greatly exceed all the evils which had come upon the world in consequence of the apostasy of Adam. And if this was the case, the scheme of justification by faith was complete. It was adapted to the condition of fallen and ruined man; and was worthy of his affection and confidence. A particular examination of this argument of the apostle will occur in the Notes on ver. 12–21.

1. *Therefore* (οὖν). Since we are thus justified, or as a consequence of being justified, we have peace. ¶ *Being justified by faith.* See Notes, chap. i. 17; iii. 24; iv. 5. ¶ *We.* That is, all who *are* justified. The apostle is evidently speaking of true Christians. ¶ *Have peace with God.* See Note, John xiv. 27. True religion is often represented as *peace* with God; see Acts x. 36; Rom. viii. 6; x. 15; xiv. 17; Gal. v. 22; see also Isa. xxxii. 17,

"And the work of righteousness shall be peace;
And the effect of righteousness,
Quietness and assurance for ever."

This is called *peace*, because, (1) The sinner is represented as the enemy of God, Rom. viii. 7; Eph. ii. 16; Jam. iv. 4; John xv. 18, 24; xvii. 14; Rom. i. 30. (2) The state of a sinner's mind is far from peace. He is often agitated, alarmed, trembling. He feels that he is alienated from God.

God through our Lord Jesus Christ;

2 By [b] whom also we have access

b Jn.14.6.

For

"The wicked are like the troubled sea,
For it never can be at rest;
Whose waters cast up mire and dirt."

Isa. lvii. 20.

The sinner in this state regards God as his enemy. He trembles when he thinks of his law; fears his judgments; is alarmed when he thinks of hell. His bosom is a stranger to peace. This has been felt in all lands, alike under the thunders of the law of Sinai among the Jews; in the pagan world; and in lands where the gospel is preached. It is the effect of an alarmed and troubled conscience. (3) The plan of salvation by Christ reveals God as willing to be reconciled. He is ready to pardon, and to be at peace. If the sinner repents, and believes, God can now consistently forgive him, and admit him to favour. It is therefore a plan by which the mind of God and of the sinner can become reconciled, or united in feeling and in purpose. The obstacles on the part of God to reconciliation, arising from his justice and law, have been removed, and he is now willing to be at peace. The obstacles on the part of man, arising from his sin, his rebellion, and his conscious guilt, may be taken away, and he can now regard God as his friend. (4) The *effect* of this plan, when the sinner embraces it, is to produce *peace* in his own mind. He *experiences* peace; a peace which the world gives not, and which the world cannot take away, Phil. iv. 7; 1 Pet. i. 8; John xvi. 22. Usually in the work of conversion to God, this *peace* is the first evidence that is felt of the change of heart. Before, the sinner was agitated and troubled. But often suddenly, a peace and calmness is felt which is before unknown. The alarm subsides; the heart is calm; the fears die away, like the waves of the ocean after a storm. A sweet tranquillity visits the heart—a pure shining light, like the sunbeams that break through the opening clouds after a tempest. The views, the feelings, the desires

by faith into this grace wherein we stand, [c] and rejoice in hope of the glory of God.

c He.3.6.

are changed; and the bosom that was just before filled with agitation and alarm, that regarded God as its enemy, is now at peace with him, and with all the world. ¶ *Through our Lord Jesus Christ.* By means of the atonement of the Lord Jesus. It is *his* mediation that has procured it.

2. *We have access.* See Note, John xiv. 6, "I am the way,"&c. Doddridge renders it, "by whom we have *been introduced,*" &c. It means, *by whom we have the privilege of obtaining the favour of God which we enjoy when we are justified.* The word rendered "access" occurs but in two other places in the New Testament, Eph. ii. 18; iii. 12. By Jesus Christ the way is opened for us to obtain the favour of God. ¶ *By faith.* By means of faith, chap. i. 17. ¶ *Into this grace.* Into this *favour* of reconciliation with God. ¶ *Wherein we stand.* In which we now are in consequence of being justified. ¶ *And rejoice.* Religion is often represented as producing joy, Isa. xii. 3; xxxv. 10; lii. 9; lxi. 3, 7; lxv. 14, 18; John xvi. 22, 24; Acts xiii. 52; Rom. xiv. 17; Gal. v. 22; 1 Pet. i. 8. The sources or *steps* of this joy are these: (1) We are justified, or regarded by God as righteous. (2) We are admitted into his favour, and abide there. (3) We have the prospect of still higher and richer blessings in the fulness of his glory when we are admitted to heaven. ¶ *In hope.* In the earnest desire and expectation of obtaining that glory. *Hope* is a complex emotion made up of a *desire* for an object, and an *expectation* of obtaining it. Where either of these is wanting, there is not *hope.* Where they are mingled in improper proportions, there is not peace. But where the *desire* of obtaining an object is attended with an *expectation* of obtaining it, in proportion to that desire, there exists that peaceful, happy state of mind which we denominate *hope.* And the apostle here implies that the

3 And not only *so*, but ^dwe glory in tribulations also: know-
 d Mat.5.11,12; Ja.1.2,12.

ing that tribulation worketh patience;

Christian *has* an earnest *desire* for that glory; and that he has a confident *expectation* of obtaining it. The result of that he immediately states to be, that we are by it sustained in our afflictions. ¶ *The glory of God.* The glory that God will bestow on us. The word *glory* usually means splendour, magnificence, honour; and the apostle here refers to that honour and dignity which will be conferred on the redeemed when they are raised up to the full honours of redemption; when they shall triumph in the completion of the work; and be freed from sin, and pain, and tears, and permitted to participate in the full splendours that shall encompass the throne of God in the heavens; see Note, Luke ii. 9; comp. Rev. xxi. 22–24; xxii. 5; Isa. lx. 19, 20.

3. *And not only so.* We not only rejoice in times of prosperity, and of health. Paul proceeds to show that this plan is not less adapted to produce support in trials. ¶ *But we glory.* The word used here is the same that is in ver. 2, translated "we rejoice" (καυχώμεθα). It should have been so rendered here. The meaning is, that we rejoice not only *in hope;* not only in the *direct* results of justification, in the immediate effect which religion itself produces; but we carry our joy and triumph even into the midst of trials. In accordance with this, our Saviour directed his followers to rejoice in persecutions, Mat. v. 11, 12; comp. Jam. i. 2, 12. ¶ *In tribulations.* In afflictions. The word used here refers to *all kinds* of trials which men are called to endure; though it is possible that Paul referred particularly to the various persecutions and trials which they were called to endure *as Christians.* ¶ *Knowing.* Being assured of this. Paul's assurance might have arisen from reasoning on the nature of religion, and its tendency to produce comfort; or it is more probable that he was speaking here the language of his own experience. He had found it to be so. This was writ-

ten near the close of his life, and it states the personal experience of a man who endured, perhaps, as much as anyone ever did, in attempting to spread the gospel; and *far more* than commonly falls to the lot of mankind. Yet he, like all other Christians, could leave his deliberate testimony to the fact that Christianity was sufficient to sustain the soul in its severest trials; see 2 Cor. i. 3–6; xi. 24–29; xii. 9, 10. ¶ *Worketh.* Produces; the effect of afflictions on the minds of Christians is to make them patient. Sinners are irritated and troubled by them; they murmur, and become more and more obstinate and rebellious. They have no sources of consolation; they deem God a hard master; and they become fretful and rebellious just in proportion to the depth and continuance of their trials. But in the mind of a Christian, who regards his Father's hand in it; who sees that he deserves no mercy; who has confidence in the wisdom and goodness of God; who feels that it is necessary for his own good to be afflicted; and who experiences its happy, subduing, and mild effect in restraining his sinful passions, and in weaning him from the world—the effect is to produce *patience.* Accordingly it will usually be found that those Christians who are longest and most severely afflicted are the most patient. Year after year of suffering produces increased peace and calmness of soul; and at the end of his course the Christian is more willing to be afflicted, and bears his afflictions more calmly, than at the beginning. He who on earth was most afflicted was the most patient of all sufferers; and not less patient when he was "led as a lamb to the slaughter," than when he experienced the first trial in his great work. ¶ *Patience.* "A calm temper, which suffers evils without murmuring or discontent" (Webster).

4. *And patience, experience.* Patient endurance of trial produces experience. The word rendered experience (δοκιμήν) means *trial, testing,*

4 And patience, experience; and experience, hope;

5 And *e* hope maketh not ashamed; because the love of God

e Phi.1.20.

or that thorough examination by which we ascertain the quality or nature of a thing, as when we test a metal by fire, or in any other way, to ascertain that it is genuine. It also means *approbation,* or the *result* of such a trial; the being approved, and accepted as the effect of a trying process. The meaning is, that long afflictions borne patiently show a Christian what he is; they test his religion, and prove that it is genuine. Afflictions are often sent for this purpose, and patience in the midst of them shows that the religion which can sustain them is from God. ¶ *And experience, hope.* The result of such long trial is to produce *hope.* They show that religion is genuine; that it is from God; and not only so, but they direct the mind *onward* to another world; and sustain the soul by the prospect of a glorious immortality there. The various steps and stages of the benefits of afflictions are thus beautifully delineated by the apostle in a manner which accords with the experience of all the children of God.

5. *And hope maketh not ashamed.* That is, this hope will not disappoint or deceive. When we hope for an object which we do not obtain, we are conscious of disappointment; perhaps sometimes of a feeling of shame. But the apostle says that the Christian hope is such that it will be fulfilled; it will not disappoint; what we hope for we shall certainly obtain; see Phil. i. 20. The expression used here is probably taken from Ps. xxii. 4, 5,

"Our fathers trusted in thee:
They trusted, and thou didst deliver them.
They cried unto thee,
And were delivered;
They trusted in thee,
And were not confounded [ashamed]."

¶ *Because the love of God.* Love toward God. There is produced an abundant, an overflowing love to God. ¶ *Is shed abroad.* Is diffused; is

is shed abroad in our hearts *f* by the Holy Ghost, which is given unto us.

6 For when we were yet with-

f Ep.1.13,14.

poured out; is abundantly produced (ἐκκέχυται). This word is properly applied to *water,* or to any other liquid that is poured out or diffused. It is used also to denote imparting, or communicating freely or abundantly, and is thus expressive of the influence of the Holy Spirit *poured down,* or abundantly imparted to men, Acts x. 45. Here it means that love towards God is copiously or abundantly given to a Christian; his heart is conscious of high and abundant love to God, and by this he is sustained in his afflictions. ¶ *By the Holy Ghost.* It is produced by the influence of the Holy Spirit. All Christian graces are traced to his influence, Gal. v. 22, "But the fruit of the Spirit is *love,* joy," &c. ¶ *Which is given unto us.* Which *Spirit* is given or imparted to us. The Holy Spirit is thus represented as dwelling in the hearts of believers, 1 Cor. vi. 19; iii. 16; 2 Cor. vi. 16. In all these places it is meant that Christians are under his sanctifying influence; that he produces in their hearts the Christian graces; and fills their minds with peace, and love, and joy.

6. *For when,* &c. This opens a new view of the subject, or it is a new argument to show that our hope will not make ashamed, or will not disappoint us. The first argument he had stated in the previous verse, that the Holy Ghost was given to us. The next, which he now states, is, that God had given the most ample proof that he would save us by giving his Son when we were sinners; and that he who had done so much for us when we were *enemies,* would not now fail us when we are his friends, ver. 6–10. He has performed the more *difficult* part of the work by reconciling us when we were enemies; and he will not now forsake us, but will carry forward and *complete* what he has begun. ¶ *We were yet without strength.* The word here used

out strength, [1]in *g*due time Christ died for the ungodly.

7 For scarcely for a righteous

(ασθενῶν) is usually applied to those who are sick and feeble, deprived of strength by disease, Mat. xxv. 38; Luke x. 9; Acts iv. 9; v. 15. But it is also used in a *moral* sense, to denote inability or feebleness with regard to any undertaking or duty. Here it means that we were without strength *in regard to the case which the apostle was considering;* that is, we had no power to devise a scheme of justification, to make an atonement, or to put away the wrath of God, &c. While all hope of man's being saved by any plan of his own was thus taken away; while he was thus lying exposed to divine justice, and dependent on the mere mercy of God, God provided a plan which met the case, and secured his salvation. The remark of the apostle here has reference *only* to the condition of the race *before* an atonement is made. It does not pertain to the question whether man has strength to repent and to believe after an atonement *is* made, which is a very different inquiry. ¶ *In due time.* Margin, *according to the time* (κατὰ καιρὸν). In a *timely* manner; at the proper time, Gal. iv. 4, "But when the fulness of time was come," &c. This may mean, (1) That it was a *fit* or *proper* time. All experiments which had failed to save men. For four thousand years the trial had been made under the law among the Jews; and by the aid of the most enlightened reason in Greece and Rome; and still it was in vain. No scheme had been devised to meet the maladies of the world, and to save men from death. It was then *time* that a better plan should be presented to men. (2) It was the time *fixed* and appointed by God for the Messiah to come; the time which had been designated by the prophets, Gen. xlix. 10; Dan. ix. 24-27; see John xiii. 1; xvii. 1. (3) It was a most *favourable* time for the spread of the gospel. The world was expecting such an event;

man will one die; yet peradventure for a good man some would even dare to die.

was at peace; and was subjected mainly to the Roman power; and furnished facilities never before experienced for introducing the gospel rapidly into every land; see Notes, Mat. ii. 1, 2. ¶ *For the ungodly.* Those who do not worship God. It here means *sinners* in general, and does not differ materially from what is meant by the word translated "without strength;" see Note, chap. iv. 5.

7. *For scarcely,* &c. The design of this verse and the following is, to illustrate the great love of God by comparing it with what *man* was willing to do. "It is an unusual occurrence, an event which is all that we can hope for from the highest human benevolence and the purest friendship, that one would be willing to die for *a good man.* There are none who would be willing to die for a man who was seeking to do us injury, to calumniate our character, to destroy our happiness or our property. But Christ was willing to die for bitter foes." ¶ *Scarcely.* With difficulty. It is an event which cannot be expected to occur often. There would scarcely be found an instance in which it would happen. ¶ *A righteous man.* A just man; a man distinguished simply for *integrity* of conduct; one who has no remarkable claims for amiableness of character, for benevolence, or for personal friendship. Much as we may *admire* such a man, and applaud him, yet he has not the characteristics which would appeal to our hearts to induce us to lay down our lives for him. Accordingly, it is not known that any instance has occurred where for *such* a man one would be willing to die. ¶ *For a righteous man.* That is, in his place, or in his stead. A man would scarcely lay down his own life to save that of a righteous man. ¶ *Will one die.* Would one be willing to die. ¶ *Yet peradventure.* Perhaps; implying that this was an event which

8 But God commendeth his
love towards us, in that, ʰ while
we were yet sinners, Christ died
for us.

9 Much more then, being now

ʰ Jn.15.13; 1 Pe.3.18; 1 Jn.3.16.

---

might be expected to occur. ¶ *For a
good man.* That is, not merely a man
who is coldly just; but a man whose
characteristic is that of kindness,
amiableness, tenderness. It is evident
that the case of such a man would
be much more likely to appeal to
our feelings, than that of one who
is merely a man of integrity. Such
a man is susceptible of tender friendship; and probably the apostle intended to refer to such a case—a case
where we would be willing to expose
life for a kind, tender, faithful friend.
¶ *Some would even dare to die.* Some
would have courage to give his life.
Instances of this kind, though not
many, have occurred. The affecting
case of Damon and Pythias is one.
Damon had been condemned to death
by the tyrant Dionysius of Sicily,
and obtained leave to go and settle
his domestic affairs on promise of
returning at a stated hour to the
place of execution. Pythias pledged
himself to undergo the punishment
if Damon should not return in time,
and deliver himself into the hands
of the tyrant. Damon returned at
the appointed moment, just as the
sentence was about to be executed
on Pythias; and Dionysius was so
struck with the fidelity of the two
friends, that he remitted their punishment, and entreated them to permit
him to share their friendship (Val.
Max. 4. 7). This case stands almost
alone. Our Saviour says that it is
the highest expression of love among
men: "Greater love hath no man
than this, that a man lay down his
life for his friends," John xv. 13.
The friendship of David and Jonathan seems also to have been of
this character, that one would have
been willing to lay down his life for
the other.

8. *But God commendeth,* &c. God
has exhibited or showed his love in
this unusual and remarkable manner.

ⁱ justified by his blood, we shall
be ᵏ saved from wrath through
him.

10 For if, when we were enemies, we were reconciled to God

ⁱ He.9.14,22.   ᵏ 1 Th.1.10.

¶ *His love.* His kind feeling; his
beneficence; his willingness to submit to sacrifice to do good to others.
¶ *While we were yet sinners.* And
of course his enemies. In this, his love
surpasses all that has ever been manifested among men. ¶ *Christ died for
us.* In our stead; to save us from
death. He took our place; and by
dying himself on the cross, saved us
from dying eternally in hell.

9. *Much more, then.* It is much
more reasonable to expect it. There
are fewer obstacles in the way. If,
when we were enemies, he overcame
all that was in the way of our salvation; much more have we reason to
expect that he will afford us protection now that we are his friends.
This is one ground of the hope expressed in ver. 5. ¶ *Being now justified.* Pardoned; accepted as his
friends. ¶ *By his blood.* By his
death; Note, chap. iii. 25. The fact
that we are purchased by his blood,
and sanctified by it, renders us *sacred*
in the eye of God; bestows a value
on us proportionate to the worth of
the price of our redemption; and is a
pledge that he will *keep* that which
has been so dearly bought. ¶ *Saved
from wrath.* From hell; from the
punishment due to sin; Note, chap.
ii. 8.

10. *For if.* The idea in this verse
is simply a repetition and enlarge-
ment of that in ver. 9. The apostle
dwells on the thought, and places it
in a new light, furnishing thus a
strong confirmation of his position.
¶ *When we were enemies.* The work
was undertaken while we were enemies. From being enemies we were
changed to friends by that work.
Thus it was commenced by God; its
foundation was laid while we were
still hostile to it; it evinced, therefore, a determined purpose on the
part of God to perform it; and he
has thus given a pledge that it shall

by the death of his Son, [l]much more, being reconciled, [m]we shall be saved by his life.

[l] ch.8.32.   [m] Jn.14.19.

be perfected. ¶ *We were reconciled.* Note, Mat. v. 24. We are brought to an *agreement; to a state of friendship and union.* We became his friends, laid aside our opposition, and embraced him as our friend and portion. To effect this is the great design of the plan of salvation, 2 Cor. v. 1–20; Col. i. 21; Eph. ii. 16. It means that there were *obstacles* existing on both sides to a reconciliation; and that these have been removed by the death of Christ; and that a union has thus been effected. This has been done in removing the obstacles on the part of God—by maintaining the honour of his law; showing his hatred of sin; upholding his justice, and maintaining his truth, at the same time that he pardons; Note, chap. iii. 26. And on the part of man, by removing his *unwillingness* to be reconciled; by subduing, changing, and sanctifying his heart; by overcoming his hatred of God, and of his law; and bringing him into submission to the government of God. So that the Christian is in fact reconciled to God; he is his friend; he is pleased with his law, his character, and his plan of salvation. And all this has been accomplished by the sacrifice of the Lord Jesus as an offering in our place. ¶ *Much more.* It is much more to be expected; there are still stronger and more striking considerations to show it. ¶ *By his life.* We were reconciled by his death. *Death* may include possibly his low, humble, and suffering condition. Death has the appearance of great feebleness; the death of Christ had the appearance of the *defeat* of his plans. His enemies triumphed and rejoiced over him on the cross, and in the tomb. Yet the effect of this feeble, low, and humiliating state was to reconcile us to God. If in *this* state, when humble, despised, dying, *dead,* he had power to accomplish so great a work as to reconcile us to God, how much more may we expect

11 And not only *so,* but we also [n]joy in God, through our Lord Jesus Christ, by whom we

[n] Hab.3.18.

that he will be able to keep us now that he is a living, exalted and triumphant Redeemer. If his fainting powers in *dying* were such as to reconcile us, how much more shall his full, vigorous powers as an exalted Redeemer be sufficient to keep and save us. This argument is but an expansion of what the Saviour himself said, John xiv. 19, "Because I live, ye shall live also."

11. *And not only* so. The apostle states *another* effect of justification. ¶ *We also joy in God.* In ver. 2, he had said that we rejoice in tribulations, and in hope of the glory of God. But he here adds that we rejoice *in God himself;* in his existence; his attributes; his justice, holiness, mercy, truth, love. The Christian rejoices that God is such a being as he is; and glories that the universe is under his administration. The sinner is opposed to him; he finds no pleasure in him; he fears or hates him; and deems him unqualified for universal empire. But it is one characteristic of true piety, one evidence that we are truly reconciled to God, that we rejoice in him *as he is;* and find pleasure in the contemplation of his perfections as they are revealed in the Scriptures. ¶ *Through our Lord,* &c. By the mediation of our Lord Jesus, who has revealed the true character of God, and by whom we have been reconciled to him. ¶ *The atonement.* Margin, or *reconciliation.* This is the only instance in which our translators have used the word *atonement* in the New Testament. The word frequently occurs in the Old, Ex. xxix. 33, 36, 37; xxx. 10, 15, 16, &c. As it is now used by us, it commonly means *the ransom,* or *the sacrifice* by means of which reconciliation is effected between God and man. But in this place it has a different sense. It means the *reconciliation itself* between God and man; not the *means* by which reconciliation is effected. It denotes, not that we have received a

ransom, or an offering by which reconciliation *might* be effected, but that *in fact we have become reconciled through him*. This was the ancient meaning of the English word *atonement*—AT ONE MENT—being *at one*, or reconciled.

> He seeks to make *atonement*
> Between the Duke of Glo'ster and your brothers.
>   SHAKSPEARE.

The Greek word which denotes the expiatory offering by which a reconciliation is effected, is different from the one here; see Note, chap. iii. 25. The word used here (καταλλαγή) is never used to denote such an offering, but denotes the *reconciliation itself*.

12–21. This passage has been usually regarded as the most difficult part of the New Testament. It is not the design of these Notes to enter into a minute criticism of contested points like this. They who wish to see a full discussion of the passage, may find it in the professedly critical commentaries; and especially in the commentaries of Tholuck and of Professor Stuart on the Romans. The meaning of the passage in its *general* bearing is not difficult; and probably the whole passage would have been found *far less* difficult if it had not been attached to a *philosophical theory* on the subject of man's sin, and if a strenuous and indefatigable effort had not been made to prove that it teaches what it was never designed to teach. The plain and obvious design of the passage is this, *to show one of the benefits of the doctrine of justification by faith.* The apostle had shown, (1) That that doctrine produced peace, ver. 1. (2) That it produces joy in the prospect of future glory, ver. 2. (3) That it sustained the soul in afflictions, (*a*) by the regular *tendency* of afflictions under the gospel, ver. 3, 4; and (*b*) by the fact that the Holy Ghost was imparted to the believer. (4) That this doctrine rendered it certain that we should be saved, because Christ had died for us, ver. 6; because this was the highest expression of love, ver. 7, 8; and because, if we had been *reconciled* when thus alienated, we should be saved now that we are the friends of God, ver.

9, 10. (5) That it led us to rejoice *in God himself;* produced joy in his presence, and in all his attributes. He now proceeds to show the bearing on that great mass of evil which had been introduced into the world by sin, and to prove that the benefits of the atonement were far greater than the evils which had been introduced by the acknowledged effects of the sin of Adam. "The design is to exalt our views of the work of Christ, and of the plan of justification through him, by comparing them with the evil consequences of the sin of our first father, and by showing that the blessings in question not only extend to the removal of these evils, but far beyond this, so that the grace of the gospel has not only abounded, but *superabounded* " (Prof. Stuart). In doing this, the apostle admits, as an undoubted and well-understood fact—

1. That sin came into the world by one man, and death as the consequence, ver. 12.

2. That death had passed on all; even on those who had not the light of revelation, and the express commands of God, ver. 13, 14.

3. That Adam was the figure, the type of him that was to come; that there was some sort of analogy or resemblance between the results of his act and the results of the work of Christ. That analogy consisted in the fact that the effects of his doings did not terminate on himself, but extended to numberless other persons, and that it was thus with the work of Christ, ver. 14. But he shows,

4. That there were very material and important differences in the two cases. There was not a perfect parallelism. The effects of the work of Christ were far more than simply to counteract the evil introduced by the sin of Adam. The *differences* between the effect of his act and the work of Christ are these: (1) The sin of Adam led to condemnation. The work of Christ has an opposite tendency, ver. 15. (2) The condemnation which came from the sin of Adam was the result of one offence. The work of Christ was to deliver from *many* offences, ver. 16. (3) The work of

have now received the [2]atone-
ment.

12 Wherefore, [o] as by one man sin

[2] or, *reconciliation.*　　[o] Ge.3.6,19.

entered into the world, and death
by sin; and so death passed upon
all men, [3] for that all have sinned:

[3] or, *in whom.*

Christ was far more abundant and
overflowing in its influence. It extended deeper and farther. It was
more than a compensation for the
evils of the fall, ver. 17.

5. As the act of Adam threw its
influence over all men to secure their
condemnation, so the work of Christ
was fitted to affect all men, Jews and
Gentiles, in bringing them into a state
by which they might be delivered from
the fall, and restored to the favour of
God. It was *in itself* adapted to produce far more and greater benefits
than the crime of Adam had done evil;
and was thus a glorious plan, just fitted
to meet the actual condition of a
world of sin; and to repair the evils
which apostasy had introduced. It
had thus the evidence that it originated in the benevolence of God, and
that it was adapted to the human
condition, ver. 18–21.

[The learned author denies the doctrine of
imputed sin, and labours to prove that it is not
contained in Rom. v. 12, 19. The following
introductory Note is intended to exhibit the
orthodox view of the subject, and meet the
objections which the reader will find in the
Commentary. The very first question that
demands our attention is, What character did
Adam sustain under the covenant of works—
that of a single and independent individual, or
that of the representative of the human kind?

This is one of the most important questions
in theology, and according to the answer we
may be prepared to give, in the affirmative or
negative, will be almost the entire complexion
of our religious views. If the question be resolved in the affirmative, then what Adam did
must be held *as* done by us, and the imputation of his guilt would seem to follow as a
necessary consequence.

1. That Adam sustained the character of
representative of the human race; in other
words that he was *the federal as well as natural
head* of his descendants, is obvious from the
circumstances of the history in the book of
Genesis. It has been said, indeed, that in the
record of the threatening no mention is made
of the posterity of Adam, and that on this
account all idea of federal headship or representation must be abandoned as a mere theological figment, having no foundation in Scrip-

ture. But if God regarded Adam only in his
individual capacity when he said unto him,
" In the day thou eatest thereof thou shalt
surely die," then the other addresses of God to
Adam, which form part of the same history.
must be construed in the same way. And was
it to Adam only, and not to the human kind
at large, viewed in him, that God said, " Be
fruitful, and multiply, and replenish the
earth?" Was it to Adam in his individual
capacity that God gave the grant of the earth,
with all its rich and varied productions? or
was it to mankind at large? Was it to Adam
alone that God said, " In the sweat of thy face
shalt thou eat bread, till thou return unto the
ground," &c.? The universal infliction of the
penalty shows that the threatening was addressed to Adam as the federal head of the
race. All toil, and sweat, and die. Indeed, the
entire history favours the conclusion that God
was dealing with Adam, not in his individual,
but representative capacity; nor can its consistency be preserved on any other principle.

2. Moreover, there are certain facts connected with the moral history of mankind
which present insuperable difficulties if we
deny the doctrines of representation and imputed sin. *How shall we on any other principle
account for the universality of death, or rather
of penal evil?* It can be traced back beyond
all *personal* guilt. Its origin is higher. *Antecedent* to all actual transgression, man is visited
with penal evil. He *comes into the world* under
a necessity of dying. His whole constitution is
disordered. His body and his mind bear on
them the marks of a blighting curse. It is
impossible on any theory to deny this. And
why is man thus visited? Can the righteous
God punish where there is no guilt? We *must*
take one side or other of the alternative, that
God inflicts punishment without guilt, or that
Adam's sin is imputed to his posterity. If
we take the latter branch of the alternative,
we are furnished with the ground of the divine
procedure, and freed from many difficulties
that press upon the opposite view.

It may be noticed in this place also, that the
death of infants is a striking proof of the infliction of penal evil *prior* to personal or actual
sin. Their tender bodies are assailed in a multitude of instances by acute and violent diseases, that call for our sympathy the more
that the sufferers cannot disclose or communicate the source of their agony. They labour
with death, and struggle hard in his hands,
till they resign the gift of life they had retained
for so short a while. It is said, indeed, that

the case of infants is not introduced in Scripture in connection with this subject, and our author tells us that they are not at all referred to in any part of this disputed passage, nor included in the clause, "death reigned, *even* over them that had not sinned after the similitude of Adam's transgression." On this some observations will be found in the proper place. Meanwhile there is *the fact itself*, and with it we are concerned now. *Why do infants die?* Perhaps it will be said that, though they have committed no actual sin, yet they have a depraved nature; but this cedes the whole question, for that depraved nature is just a part of the penal evil formerly noticed. Why are innocent infants visited with that which entails death on them? One answer only can be given, and no ingenuity can evade the conclusion—" In Adam all die." The wonder is that this doctrine should ever have been denied. On the human family at large, on man and woman, on infant child and hoary sire, on earth and sky, are traced the dismal effects of the first sin.

3. The parallelism between Adam and Christ is another branch of evidence on this subject. That they bear a striking resemblance to each other is allowed on all hands. Hence Christ is styled in the 15th of 1st Corinthians " the last Adam " and " the second man," and in this very passage Adam is expressly called a type or " figure of him that was to come." Now in what does this resemblance consist? Between these two persons there are very many points of dissimilarity or contrast. The first man is earthy; the second is the Lord from heaven. From the one come guilt, and condemnation, and death; and from the other righteousness, justification, and life. Where, then, is the similarity? " They are alike," says Beza, "in this, that each of them shares what he has with his." Both are covenant or representative heads, and communicate their respective influences to those whom they represent. Here, then, is one great leading point of similarity, nor is it possible in any other view to preserve the parallel. For suppose we disturb the parallel as now adjusted, and argue that Adam was not a federal head, that we are therefore neither held guilty of Adam's sin nor condemned and punished on account of it, where shall we find the counterpart of this in Christ? Must we also maintain that he does not represent his people; that they are neither esteemed righteous on account of his work, nor justified and saved by it? Such is the legitimate consequence of the opposite views. If we hold that from Adam we receive only a corrupt nature, in consequence of which we sin personally and *then* become guilty, and are in consequence condemned; we must also argue that we receive from Christ only a pure or renewed nature, in consequence of

which we become personally righteous, and are *then and therefore* justified and saved. But such a scheme would undermine the whole gospel. Though the derivation of holiness from Christ be a true and valuable doctrine, we are not justified on account of that derived holiness. On the contrary, we are justified on account of something *without* us—something that has no dependence whatever on our personal holiness, viz. the righteousness of Christ. Nay, according to the doctrine of Paul, justification in order *of* nature is before sanctification, and the cause of it.

It is but justice to state that the commentator maintains that a resemblance between Adam and Christ lies not at all *in the mode* in which sin and righteousness, life and death, have been respectively introduced by them, but is found in the *simple fact* that " the effect of their doings did not terminate on themselves, but extended to numberless other persons" (pp. 124, 134). Indeed, he repeatedly affirms that in regard to the introduction of sin by Adam nothing whatever is said in this passage in regard to *the mode* of it. The fact alone is announced. If this were true, it is allowed that the arguments we have now employed would be much weakened. But the assertion cannot be substantiated. If the analogy do not lie in *the mode*, but in the simple fact that the effects of their doings do not terminate on themselves, what greater resemblance is there between Adam and Christ than between any two persons that might be named? David and Ahab might be compared in the same way—the good deeds of the one and the evil deeds of the other not terminating with themselves. Besides, Paul certainly does state in the previous chapter *the mode* in which the righteousness of Christ becomes available for salvation. He states plainly that " God imputeth it without works." When, then, in the 5th chapter he looks back upon this subject, and introduces his parallel with " WHEREFORE AS by one man," &c., are we to believe that he intends no similarity in the mode? Shall we make the apostle explain *the manner* in which the righteousness becomes available, and say nothing of *the way* in which its opposite is introduced at the very time he is professedly comparing the two?

Such is a brief outline of the evidence on which the doctrine of imputed sin is based. The principal arguments are those derived from the universality of penal evil, and the parallel between Adam and Christ. And these are the very topics handled by the apostle in this much-vexed passage. Our author, indeed, in his opening remarks maintains that nothing is said by the apostle of original sin in this place. " The apostle here is not discussing the doctrine of original sin," and " his design is to show one of the benefits of the doctrine of justification." But the design of Paul is to *illustrate* the doctrine of justification, and not simply to show one of its benefits. For in the former part of this chapter (ver. 1–11) the apostle had fully enlarged on these benefits, and there is no evidence that ver. 12, 19 are a continuation of the same theme. On the contrary, there is obviously a break in the discourse at ver. 12, where the apostle, recalling the discussion, introduces a new illustration of his principal point, viz. justification through the righteousness of Christ. On this the apostle had discoursed largely in the 3d and 4th chapters. And, lest any should think it anomalous and irrational to justify men on account of a work they themselves had no hand in accomplishing, he now appeals to the "great analogous fact in the history of the world." This seems the most natural construction. "No wonder," says President Edwards, "when the apostle is treating so fully and largely of our restoration, righteousness, and life by Christ, that he is led by it to consider our fall, sin, death, and ruin by Adam" (*Orig. Sin*, p. 303). The following analysis will assist the reader in understanding the whole passage : "As the point to be illustrated is the justification of sinners on the ground of the righteousness of Christ, and the source of illustration is the fall of all men in Adam, the passage begins with a statement of this latter truth, ' As on account of one man death has passed on all men ; so on account of one,' &c., ver. 12. Before, however, carrying out the comparison, the apostle stops to establish his position that all men are regarded and treated as sinners on account of Adam. His proof is this. The infliction of a penalty implies the transgression of a law, since sin is not imputed where there is no law, ver. 13. All mankind are subject to death or penal evils, therefore all men are regarded as transgressors of a law, ver. 13. The law or covenant which brings death on all men is not the law of Moses, because multitudes died before that law passed, ver. 14. Nor is it the law of nature, since multitudes die who have never violated even that law, ver. 14. Therefore we must conclude that men are subject to death on account of Adam—that is, it is for the offence of one that many die, ver. 13, 14. Adam is therefore a type of Christ. Yet the cases are not completely parallel. There are certain points of dissimilarity, ver. 15, 17. Having thus limited and illustrated the analogy, the apostle resumes and carries the comparison fully out in ver. 18, 19, 'Therefore as on account of one man,' &c." (Prof. Hodge).]

12. *Wherefore* (διὰ τοῦτο). On this account. This is not an *inference* from what has gone before, but a *continuance* of the design of the apostle to show the advantages of the plan of justification by faith ; as if he had said, "The advantages of that plan have been seen in our comfort and peace, and in its sustaining power in afflictions. Further, the advantages of the plan are seen in regard to this, that it is applicable to the condition of man in a world where the sin of one man has produced so much woe and death. On this account also it is a matter of joy. It meets the ills of a fallen race; and it is therefore a plan adapted to man." Thus understood, the connection and design of the passage is easily explained. In respect to the state of things into which man is fallen, the benefits of this plan may be seen, as adapted to heal the maladies, and to be commensurate with the evils which the apostasy of one man brought upon the world. This explanation is not that which is usually given to this place, but it is that which seems to me to be demanded by the strain of the apostle's reasoning. The passage is *elliptical*, and there is a necessity of supplying something to make out the sense. ¶ *As* (ὥσπερ). This is the form of a *comparison*. But the other part of the comparison is deferred to ver. 18. The connection evidently requires us to understand the other part of the comparison of the work of Christ. In the rapid train of ideas in the mind of the apostle, this was deferred to make room for explanations (ver. 13–17). "As by one man sin entered into the world, &c., *so* by the work of Christ a remedy has been provided, commensurate with the evils. As the sin of one man had such an influence, *so* the work of the Redeemer has an influence to meet and to counteract those evils." The passage in ver. 13–17 is therefore to be regarded as a parenthesis thrown in for the purpose of making explanations, and to show how the cases of Adam and of Christ *differed* from each other. ¶ *By one man*, &c. By means of one man ; by the crime of one man. His act was the occasion of the introduction of all sin into all the world. The apostle here refers to the well-known his-

torical fact (Gen. iii. 6, 7), without any explanation of the *mode* or *cause* of this.   He adduced it as a fact that was well known; and evidently meant to speak of it not for the purpose of *explaining* the mode, or even of making this the leading or prominent topic in the discussion.   His *main* design is not to speak of the manner of the introduction of sin, but to show that the work of Christ meets and removes well-known and extensive evils.   His explanations, therefore, are chiefly confined to the work of Christ.   He speaks of the introduction, the spread, and the effects of sin, not as having any *theory* to defend on that subject, not as designing to enter into a minute description of the case, but as it was manifest *on the face of things*, as it stood on the historical record, and as it was understood and admitted by mankind. Great perplexity has been introduced by forgetting the *scope* of the apostle's argument here, and by supposing that he was defending a peculiar *theory* on the subject of the introduction of sin; whereas, nothing is more foreign to his design.   He is showing how the plan of justification *meets well understood and acknowledged universal evils.*   Those evils he refers to just as they were seen, and admitted to exist.   All men see them, and feel them, and practically understand them.   The truth is, that the doctrine of the fall of man, and the prevalence of sin and death, do not belong peculiarly to Christianity any more than the introduction and spread of disease does to the science of the *healing art.*   Christianity did not introduce sin; nor is it responsible for it.   The existence of sin and woe belongs to the *race;* appertains equally to all systems of religion, and is a part of the melancholy history of man, whether Christianity be true or false.   The existence and extent of sin and death are not affected if the infidel could show that Christianity was an imposition.   They would still remain.   The Christian religion is just *one mode of proposing a remedy for well-known and desolating evils;* just as the science of medicine pro-

poses a remedy for diseases which it did not introduce, and which could not be stayed in their desolations, or modified, if it could be shown that the whole science of healing was pretension and quackery.   Keeping this design of the apostle in view, therefore, and remembering that he is not defending or stating a theory about the introduction of sin, but that he is explaining the way in which the work of Christ delivers *from* a deep-felt universal evil, we shall find the explanation of this passage disencumbered of many of the difficulties with which it has been thought usually to be invested.   ¶ *By one man.*   By *Adam;* see ver. 14.   It is true that sin was literally introduced by *Eve,* who was first in the transgression, Gen. iii. 6; 1 Tim. ii. 14.   But the apostle evidently is not explaining the precise *mode* in which sin was introduced, or making this his *leading* point.   He therefore speaks of the introduction of sin in a *popular* sense, as it was generally understood.   The following reasons may be suggested why the *man* is mentioned rather than the woman as the cause of the introduction of sin: (1) It was the natural and usual way of expressing such an event.   We say that *man* sinned, that *man* is redeemed, *man* dies, &c.   We do not pause to indicate the sex in such expressions.   So in this, he undoubtedly meant to say that it was introduced by the *parentage* of the human race.   (2) The name *Adam* in Scripture was given to the *created pair,* the parents of the human family, a name designating their earthly origin, Gen. v. 1, 2, "In the day that God created man, in the likeness of God made he him; male and female created he them, and blessed them, and called THEIR *name Adam.*"   The name *Adam,* therefore, used in this connection (ver. 14), would suggest the *united parentage* of the human family.   (3) In transactions where man and woman are mutually concerned, it is usual to speak of the man first, on account of his being constituted superior in rank and authority.   (4) The comparison on the one side, in the apostle's argument, is of the *man* Christ Jesus; and to secure *the fitness, the congruity* (Stuart) of the comparison, he speaks of the *man* only in the previous transaction. (5) The sin of the woman was not complete in its effects without the concurrence of the man. It was their *uniting* in it which was the cause of the evil. Hence *the man* is especially mentioned as having *rendered the offence what it was;* as having completed it, and entailed its curses on the race. From these remarks it is clear that the apostle does not refer to the *man* here from any idea that there was any particular covenant transaction with *him,* but that he means to speak of it in the usual, popular sense; referring to him as being the fountain of all the woes that sin has introduced into the world.

["In the day thou eatest thereof thou shalt surely die," Gen. ii. 17. This is an account of the first great covenant transaction between God and man. It carries us back to the origin of mankind, and discloses the source of evil, about which so much has been written and spoken in vain. That God entered into covenant with Adam in innocence is a doctrine with which the Shorter Catechism has made us familiar from our infant years. Nor is it without higher authority. It would be improper, indeed, to apply to this transaction everything that may be supposed essential to a human compact or bargain. Whenever divine things are represented by things analogous among men care must be taken to exclude every idea that is inconsistent with the dignity of the subject. If the analogy be pressed beyond due bounds the subject is not illustrated but degraded. For example, in the present case, we must not suppose that because in human covenants the consent of parties is essential, and both are at full liberty to receive or reject the proposed terms as they shall see fit, the same thing holds true in the case of Adam. He indeed freely gave his consent to the terms of the covenant, as a holy being could not fail to do, but he was not at liberty to withhold that consent. He was a creature entirely at the divine disposal, whose duty from the moment of his being was implicit obedience. He had no power either to dictate or reject terms. The relation of parties in this covenant renders the idea of power to withhold consent inadmissible.

But because the analogy cannot be pressed beyond certain limits must we therefore entirely abandon it? Proceeding on this principle we should speedily find it impossible to retain any term or figure that had ever been employed about religious subjects. *The leading essentials of a covenant are found in this great transaction,* and no more is necessary to justify the appellation which orthodox divines have applied to it. " A covenant is a contract or agreement between two or more parties on certain terms." It is commonly supposed to imply the existence of parties, a promise, and a condition. All these constituent parts of a covenant meet in the case under review. The parties are God and man, God and the first parent of the human race ; the promise is life, which, though not expressly stated, is yet distinctly implied in the penalty; and the condition is obedience to the supreme will of God. In human covenants no greater penalty is incurred than the forfeiture of the promised blessing, and therefore the idea of penalty is not supposed essential to a covenant. In every case of forfeited promise, however, there is the infliction of penalty to the exact amount of the value of the blessing lost. We cannot think of Adam losing life without the corresponding idea of suffering death. So that, in fact, the loss of the promise and the infliction of the penalty are nearly the same thing.

It is no valid objection to this view that "the word covenant," as our author tells us (p. 143), "is not applied in the transaction in the Bible," for there are many terms the accuracy of which is never disputed that are no more to be found in the Scriptures than this. Where do we find such terms as "the fall," and "the Trinity," and many others that might be mentioned ? The mere name, indeed, is not a matter of very great importance, and if we allow that in the transaction itself there were parties, and a promise, and a condition (which cannot easily be denied), it is of less moment whether we call it a covenant, or, with our author and others, "a divine constitution." It is obvious to remark, however, that this latter title is just as little to be found " applied in the transaction in the Bible " as the former, and besides, is more "liable to be misunderstood," being vague and indefinite, intimating only that Adam was under a divine law or constitution, whereas the word covenant distinctly expresses *the kind or form of law,* and gives definite character to the whole transaction.

But although the doctrine of the covenant of works is independent of the occurrence of the name in the Scriptures, even this narrow ground of objection is not so easily maintained as some imagine. In Hos. vi. 7 it is said (according to the marginal reading, which is in strict accordance with the original Hebrew), " they, *like Adam,* כְּאָדָם, have transgressed the covenant." And in that celebrated passage in the epistle to the Galatians, ch. iv. 24, when Paul speaks of "the two covenants," he alludes, in the opinion of some of the highest authorities, to the covenant of works and the covenant of grace. This opinion is espoused and defended with great ability by the late Mr. Bell of Glasgow, one of the most distinguished theologians of his times, in a learned dissertation on the subject, *Bell on the Covenants*, p. 85. Scripture authority, then, would seem not to be entirely awanting, *even* for the name.

This doctrine of the covenant is intimately connected with that of imputed sin, for if there were no covenant there could be no covenant or representative head, and if there were no covenant head there could be no imputation of sin. Hence the dislike to the name.]

¶ *Sin entered into the world.* He was the first sinner of the race. The word *sin* here evidently means the violation of the law of God. He was the first sinner among men, and in consequence all others became sinners. The apostle does not here refer to Satan, the tempter, though he was the *suggester* of evil; for his *design* was to discuss the effect of the plan of salvation in meeting the sins and calamities of *our race.* This design, therefore, did not require him to introduce the sin of *another order* of beings. He says, therefore, that Adam was the first sinner of the race, and that death was the consequence. ¶ *Into the world.* Among mankind, John i. 10; iii. 16, 17. The term *world* is often thus used to denote human beings, the race, the human family. The apostle here evidently is not discussing the doctrine of *original* sin, but he is stating a simple fact, intelligible to all: "The first man violated the law of God, and in this way sin was introduced among men." In this fact—this general, simple declaration—there is no mystery. ¶ *And death by sin.* Death was the consequence of sin; or was introduced *because* man sinned. This is a simple statement of an obvious and well-known fact. It is repeating simply what is said in Gen. iii. 19, "In the sweat of thy face shalt thou eat bread, till thou return into the ground; for out of it wast thou taken; for dust thou art, and unto dust shalt thou return." The threatening was (Gen. ii. 17), "Of the tree of the knowledge of good and evil, thou shalt

not eat of it; for in the day that thou eatest thereof thou shalt surely die." If an inquiry be made here, how *Adam* would understand this; I reply, that we have no reason to think he would understand it as referring to anything more than the loss of life as an expression of the displeasure of God. Moses does not intimate that he was learned in the nature of laws and penalties; and his narrative would lead us to suppose that this was *all* that would occur to Adam. And, indeed, there is the highest evidence that the case admits of that this *was* his understanding of it. For in the account of the *infliction* of the penalty *after* the law was violated; in God's own interpretation of it, in Gen. iii. 19, there is still *no* reference to anything further. "Dust thou art, and unto dust shalt thou return." Now it is incredible that Adam should have understood this as referring to what has been called "spiritual death," and to "eternal death," when neither in the threatening, nor in the account of the infliction of the sentence, is there the slightest recorded reference to it. Men have done great injury in the cause of correct interpretation by carrying *their* notions of doctrinal subjects to the explanation of words and phrases in the Old Testament. They have usually described Adam as endowed with all the refinement, and possessed of all the knowledge, and adorned with all the metaphysical acumen and subtility of a modern theologian. They have deemed him qualified, in the very infancy of the world, to understand and discuss questions which, under all the light of the Christian revelation, still perplex and embarrass the human mind. After these accounts of the endowments of Adam, which occupy so large a space in books of theology, one is surprised, on opening the Bible, to find how unlike all this is the simple statement in Genesis. And the wonder cannot be suppressed that men should describe the obvious *infancy* of the race as superior to its highest advancement; or that the *first* man, just looking upon a world of wonders, imperfectly acquainted with law, and moral relations, and the effects of transgression, should be represented as endowed with knowledge which four thousand years afterwards it required the advent of the Son of God to communicate!

[Yet it may be fairly questioned whether this singular account of the endowments of Adam is itself very consistent with "the simple statement in Genesis." It certainly appears as like "a philosophical theory" as a Scripture doctrine. Adam was created *in the image of God*, Gen. i. 27. On this we have an inspired commentary in Col. iii. 10 and Eph. iv. 24, where the divine image is made to consist in KNOWLEDGE, righteousness, and true holiness. Now, as none will deny that the *holiness* of Adam in innocence was of a perfect kind, what authority have we for depreciating his knowledge? The capacity of knowing, like the other powers of the soul, must have been perfect from the hands of God. No dark shades of sin could then obscure the intellectual vision. There is no authority in Scripture for speaking of Adam in innocence as if he possessed *less* "knowledge and refinement than modern theologians," and "were imperfectly acquainted with law and moral relations!" And though the question *how* Adam would understand the threatening does not determine its meaning, yet it would seem strange indeed that God should threaten Adam with a penalty which it was impossible for him to understand except in so limited a way as leaves more than half its meaning undisclosed.]

The account in Moses is simple. Created man was told not to violate a simple law, on pain of death. He did it; and God announced to him that the sentence would be inflicted, and that he should return to the dust whence he was taken. What else this *might* involve, what *other* consequences sin might introduce, might be the subject of future developments and revelations. It is absurd to suppose that *all* the consequences of the violation of a law can be foreseen, or must *necessarily* be foreseen, in order to make the law and the penalty just. It is sufficient that the law be known; that its violation be forbidden; and what the consequences of that violation will be, must be left in great part to future developments. Even we, yet, know not *half* the results of violating the law of God. The murderer knows not the results fully of taking a man's life. He breaks a just law,

and exposes himself to the numberless unseen woes which may flow from it.

We may ask, therefore, what light subsequent revelations have cast on the character and result of the first sin? and whether the apostle here meant to state that the consequences of sin were *in fact* as limited as they must have appeared to the mind of Adam? or had subsequent developments and revelations, through four thousand years, greatly extended the right understanding of the penalty of the law? This can be answered only by inquiring in what sense the apostle Paul here uses the word *death*. The passage before us shows in what sense he intended here to use the word. In his argument it stands opposed to "the grace of God, and the gift by grace" (ver. 15); to "justification," by the forgiveness of "many offences" (ver. 16); to the reign of the redeemed in eternal life (ver. 17); and to "justification of life" (ver. 18). To all these, the words "death" (ver. 12, 17) and "judgment" (ver. 16, 18) stand opposed. These are the benefits which result from the work of Christ; and these *benefits* stand opposed to the *evils* which sin has introduced; and as it cannot be supposed that these benefits relate to *temporal life*, or solely to the resurrection of the body, so it cannot be that the evils involved in the words "death, "judgment," &c., relate simply to temporal death. The evident meaning is, that the word "death," as here used by the apostle, refers to the *train of evils* which have been introduced by sin. It does not mean simply temporal death; but that group and collection of woes, including temporal death, condemnation, and exposure to eternal death, which is the consequence of transgression. The apostle often uses the word *death*, and *to die*, in this wide sense, Rom. i. 32; vi. 16, 31; vii. 5, 10, 13, 24; viii. 2, 6, 13; 2 Cor. ii. 16; vii. 10; Heb. ii. 14. In the same sense the word is often used elsewhere, John viii. 51; xi. 26; 1 John v. 16, 17; Rev. ii. 11; xx. 6, &c. &c. In contrasting with this the results of the work of Christ, he describes not the resurrection merely, nor deliverance from temporal death, but *eternal* life in heaven; and it therefore follows that he here intends by death that gloomy and sad train of woes which sin has introduced into the world. The consequences of sin are, besides, elsewhere specified to be far more than temporal death, Ezek. xviii. 4; Rom. ii. 8, 9, 12. Though, therefore, Adam might not have foreseen all the evils which were to come upon the race as the consequence of his sin, yet these evils might nevertheless follow. And the apostle, four thousand years after the reign of sin had commenced, and under the guidance of inspiration, had full opportunity to see and describe that *train of woes* which he comprehends under the name of death. That train included evidently temporal death, condemnation for sin, remorse of conscience, and exposure to eternal death, as the penalty of transgression. ¶ *And so.* Thus. In this way it is to be accounted for that death has passed upon all men, *to wit,* because all men have sinned. As death followed sin in the first transgression, so it has in all; for all have sinned. There is a connection between death and sin which existed in the case of Adam, and which subsists in regard to all who sin. And as all have sinned, so death has passed on all men. ¶ *Death passed upon* (διῆλθεν). Passed through; pervaded; spread over the whole race, as pestilence passes through, or pervades a nation. Thus death, with its train of woes, with its withering and blighting influence, has passed through the world, laying prostrate all before it. ¶ *Upon all men.* Upon the race; all die. ¶ *For that* (ἐφ' ᾧ). This expression has been greatly controverted; and has been very variously translated. Elsner renders it, " on account of whom." Doddridge, "unto which all have sinned." The Latin Vulgate renders it, "in whom [Adam] all have sinned." The same rendering has been given by Augustine, Beza, &c. But it has never yet been shown that our translators have rendered the expression improperly. The old Syriac and the Arabic agree with the English translation in this interpretation.

With this agree Calvin, Vatablus, Erasmus, &c. And this rendering is sustained also by many other considerations. (1) If ᾧ be a relative pronoun here, it would refer naturally to *death,* as its antecedent, and not to *man.* But this would not make sense. (2) If this had been its meaning, the preposition ἐν would have been used; see Note of Erasmus on the place. (3) It comports with the apostle's argument to state a cause *why* all died, and not to state that men sinned *in* Adam. He was inquiring into the cause *why* death was in the world; and it would not account *for that* to say that all sinned *in* Adam. It would require an *additional* statement to see how *that* could be a cause. (4) As his posterity had not then an existence, they could not commit actual transgression. Sin is the transgression of the law by a moral agent; and as the interpretation "*because* all have sinned" meets the argument of the apostle, and as the Greek favours that certainly *as much* as it does the other, it is to be preferred. ¶ *All have sinned.* To sin is to transgress the law of God; to do wrong. The apostle in this expression does not *say* that all have sinned in Adam, or that their nature has become corrupt, which is true, but which is not affirmed here; nor that the sin of Adam is imputed to them; but simply affirms that all men have sinned. He speaks evidently of the great universal fact that all men are sinners. He is not settling a metaphysical difficulty; nor does he speak of the condition of man as he comes into the world. He speaks as other men would; he addresses himself to the common sense of the world; and is discoursing of universal, well-known facts. *Here is the fact—that all men experience calamity, condemnation, death.* How is this to be accounted for? The answer is, "All have sinned." This is a sufficient answer; it meets the case. And as his design cannot be shown to be to discuss a metaphysical question about the *nature* of man, or about the character of infants, the passage should be interpreted according to his design, and should not be pressed to bear on that of which he says nothing, and to which the passage evidently has no reference. I understand it, therefore, as referring to the fact that men sin *in their own persons, sin themselves* — as, indeed, how *can* they *sin* in any other way?— and that *therefore* they die. If men maintain that it refers to any metaphysical properties of the nature of man, or to infants, they should not *infer* or *suppose* this, but should show distinctly that it is in the text. Where is there evidence of any such reference?

[The following Note on ver. 12, is intended to exhibit its just connection and force. It is the first member of a comparison between Adam and Christ, which is completed in ver. 18, 19. "*As* by one man," &c. The first point which demands our attention, is the meaning of the words, "By one man *sin entered* into the world." Our author has rendered them, "He was the first sinner;" and in this he follows Prof. Stuart and Dr. Taylor; the former of whom gives this explanation of the clause: that Adam "began transgression;" and the latter interprets it by the word "commence." It is, however, no great discovery, that sin commenced with one man, or that Adam was the first sinner. If sin commenced at all, it must have commenced with some one. And if Adam sinned at all, while yet he stood alone in the world, he must have been the first sinner of the race! President Edwards, in his reply to Dr. Taylor of Norwich, has the following animadversions on this view: "That the world was full of sin, and full of death, were too great and notorious, deeply affecting the interests of mankind; and they seemed very wonderful facts, drawing the attention of the more thinking part of mankind everywhere, who often asked this question, 'whence comes this evil,' moral and natural evil? (the latter chiefly visible in death.) It is manifest the apostle here means to tell us how these came into the world, and prevail in it as they do. But all that is meant, according to Dr. Taylor's interpretation, is, 'he began transgression,' as if all the apostle meant, was to tell us who happened to sin first, not how such a malady came upon the world, or how anyone in the world, besides Adam himself, came by such a distemper" (*Orig. Sin*, p. 270).

The next thing that calls for remark in this verse, is the force of the connecting words "and so" (*και ούτως*). They are justly rendered "in this way," "in this manner," "in consequence of which." And therefore, the meaning of the first three clauses of the first verse is, that by one man sin entered into the world, and death by sin, in consequence of

Vol. IV.

which sin of this one man death passed upon all men.

It will not do to render "and so" by "in *like* manner," as Prof. Stuart does, and then explain with our author, "there is a connection between death and sin, which existed in the case of Adam, and which subsists in regard to all who sin." This is quite contrary to the acknowledged force of *και ούτως*, and besides, entirely destroys the connection which the apostle wishes to establish between the sin of the one man, and the penal evil, or death, that is in the world. It, in effect, says there is no connection whatever between those things, although the language may seem to imply it, and so large a portion of Christian readers in every age have understood it in this way. Adam sinned and he died, other men have sinned and they died! And yet this verse is allowed to be the first member of a comparison between Adam and Christ! Shall we supply, then, the other branch of the comparison, thus: Christ was righteous and lived, other men are righteous and they live? If we destroy the connection in the one case, how do we maintain it in the other? See the Supplementary Note at page 121.

The last clause "for that all have sinned," is to be regarded as explanatory of the sentiment, that death passed on all, in consequence of the sin of the one man. Some have translated *εφ' ώ*, in whom; and this, indeed, would assign the only just reason why all are visited with penal evil on account of Adam's sin. All die through him, because in him all have sinned. But the translation is objectionable on account of the distance of the antecedent. However, the common rendering gives precisely the same sense, "for that," or "because that" all have sinned, *i e.* according to an explanation in Bloomfield's Greek Testament, "are considered guilty in the sight of God on account of Adam's fall. Thus, the expression may be considered equivalent to *άμαρτωλοί κατεστάθησαν* at ver. 19." There can be no doubt that *ήμαρτον does* bear this sense, Gen. xliv. 32; xliii. 9. Moreover, the other rendering "because all have sinned personally," is inconsistent with fact. Infants have not sinned in this way; therefore, according to this view, their death is left unaccounted for, and so is all that evil comprehended in the term "death," that comes upon us *antecedent* to actual sin. See the Supplementary Note at page 121.

Lastly, this interpretation would render the reasoning of the apostle inconclusive. "If," observes Witsius, "we must understand this of some personal sin of each, the reasoning would not have been just, or worthy of the apostle. For his argument would be thus: that by the one sin of one, all were become guilty of death, because each in particular had

13 (For until the law, sin was in the world : but sin is

p not imputed when there is no law.

p ch.4.15; 1 Jn.3.4.

besides this one and first sin, his own personal sin—which is inconsequential." That men are punished for personal or actual transgression is true. But it is not the particular truth Paul seeks here to establish, any more than he seeks to prove, in the previous part of his epistle, that men are justified on account of *personal* holiness, which is clearly no part of his design.]

13. *For until the law*, &c. This verse, with the following verses to the 17th, is usually regarded as a parenthesis. The *law* here evidently means the law given by Moses. "Until the commencement of that administration, or state of things under the law." To see the reason why he referred to this period *between* Adam and the law, we should recall the design of the apostle, which is, to show the exceeding grace of God in the gospel, abounding, and superabounding, as a complete remedy for all the evils introduced by sin. For this purpose he introduces *three* leading conditions, or states, where men sinned, and where the effects of sin were seen; in regard to *each* and *all* of which the grace of the gospel superabounded. The *first* was that of Adam, with its attendant train of ills (ver. 12), which ills were all met by the death of Christ, ver. 15-18. The *second* period or condition was that long interval in which men had only the light of nature, that period occurring *between* Adam and Moses. This was a fair representation of the condition of the world without revelation, and without law, ver. 13, 14. Sin *then* reigned — reigned everywhere where there was no law. But the grace of the gospel abounded over the evils of *this* state of man. The *third* was *under* the law, ver. 20. The law entered, and sin was increased, and its evils abounded. But the gospel of Christ abounded even over this, and grace triumphantly reigned. So that the plan of justification met *all* the evils of sin, and was adapted to remove them—sin and its consequences as flowing from Adam; sin and its consequences when there was no written revelation; and sin and its consequences under the light and terrors of

the law. ¶ *Sin was in the world.* Men sinned. They did that which was evil. ¶ *But sin is not imputed.* Is not charged on men, or they are not held guilty of it where there is no law. This is a self-evident proposition, for sin is a violation of law; and if there is no law, there can be no wrong. Assuming this as a self-evident proposition, the connection is, that there must have been a law of some kind; a "law written on their hearts," since sin was in the world, and men could not be charged with sin, or treated as sinners, unless there was *some* law. The passage here states a great and important principle, that men will not be held to be guilty unless there is a law which binds them of which they are apprised, and which they voluntarily transgress; see Note, chap. iv. 15. This verse, therefore, meets an objection that might be started from what had been said in chap. iv. 15. The apostle had affirmed that "where no law is there is no transgression." He here stated that all were sinners. It might be objected, that as during this long period of time they had no law, they could not be sinners. To meet this, he says that men were then *in fact* sinners, and were treated as such, which showed that there must have been a law.

14. *Nevertheless.* Notwithstanding that sin is not imputed where there is no law, yet death reigned. ¶ *Death reigned.* Men died; they were under the dominion of death in its various melancholy influences. The expression "death reigned" is one that is very striking. It is a representation of death as a monarch, having dominion over all that period, and over all those generations. Under his dark and withering reign men sank down to the grave. We have a similar expression when we represent death as "the king of terrors." It is a striking and affecting personification; for, (1) His reign is absolute. He strikes down whom he pleases, and when he pleases. (2) There is no escape.

14 Nevertheless *q*death reigned from Adam to Moses, even over them that had not sinned after the

q He.9.27.

similitude of Adam's transgression, who is *r*the figure of him that was to come.

r 1 Co.15.22,45.

All must bow to his sceptre, and be humbled beneath his hand. (3) It is universal. Old and young alike are the subjects of his gloomy empire. (4) It would be an eternal reign if it were not for the gospel. It would shed unmitigated woes upon the earth ; and the ‧silent tread of this terrific king would produce only desolation and tears for ever. ¶ *From Adam to Moses.* From the time when God gave one revealed law to Adam, to the time when another revealed law was given to Moses. This was a period of 2500 years—no inconsiderable portion of the history of the world. Whether men were regarded and treated as sinners then, was a very material inquiry in the argument of the apostle. The fact that they *died* is alleged by him as‧ full proof that they were sinners ; and that sin had therefore scattered extensive and appalling woes among men. ¶ *Even over them.* Over all those generations. The *point* or *emphasis* of the remark here is, that it reigned over those that had sinned under a different economy from that of Adam. This was that which rendered it so remarkable ; and which showed that the withering curse of sin had been felt in all dispensations, and in all times. ¶ *After the similitude,* &c. In the same way ; in like manner. The expression "after the similitude" is an Hebraism, denoting in like manner, or *as.* The difference between their case and that of Adam was plainly that Adam had a revealed and positive law. They had not. They had only the law of nature, or of tradition. The giving of a law to Adam, and again to the world by Moses, were two great *epochs* between which no such event had occurred. The race wandered without revelation. The difference contemplated is not that Adam was an *actual* sinner, and that *they* had sinned only by *imputation.* For, (1) The expression "to sin by imputation" is unintelligible, and conveys no idea. (2) The apostle

makes no such distinction, and conveys no such idea. (3) His very object is different. It is to show that they *were actual sinners;* that they transgressed law; and the proof of this is that they died. (4) It is utterly absurd to suppose that men from the time of Adam to Moses were sinners *only by imputation.* All history is against it ; nor is there the slightest ground of plausibility in such a supposition. ¶ *Of Adam's transgression.* When he broke a plain, positive revealed law. This transgression was the open violation of a positive precept ; theirs the violation of the laws communicated in a different way—by tradition, reason, conscience, &c. Many commentators have supposed that *infants* are particularly referred to here. Augustine first suggested this, and he has been followed by many others. But probably, in the whole compass of the expositions of the Bible, there is not to be found a more unnatural and forced construction than this. For, (1) The apostle makes no mention of infants. He does not in the remotest form allude to them by name, or give any intimation that he had reference to them. (2) The scope of his argument is against it. Did infants only die? Were they the only persons that lived in this long period? His argument is complete without supposing that he referred to them. The question in regard to this long interval was, whether men were sinners? Yes, says the apostle. *They died.* Death reigned ; and this proves that they were sinners. If it should be said that the death of *infants* would prove that *they* were sinners also, I answer, (*a*) That this was an inference which the *apostle* does not draw, and for which he is not responsible. It is not affirmed by him. (*b*) If it did refer to infants, what would it prove? Not that the sin of Adam was imputed, but that they were *personally* guilty, and transgressors. For this is the only point to which the argument tends.

The apostle here says not *one word* about imputation. He does not even refer to infants by name; nor does he here introduce at all the doctrine of imputation. All this is mere philosophy introduced to explain difficulties; but whether true or false, whether the theory explains or embarrasses the subject, it is not needful here to inquire. (3) *The very expression* here is against the supposition that infants are intended. One form of the doctrine of imputation as held by Edwards, Stapfer, &c., has been that there was a constituted oneness or personal identity between Adam and his posterity; and that his sin was regarded as truly and properly theirs; and they as personally blameworthy or ill-deserving for it, in the same manner as a man at 40 is answerable for his crime committed at 20. If this doctrine be true, then it is certain that they not only *had* "sinned after the similitude of Adam's transgression," but had *committed the very identical sin*, and that they were answerable for it as their own. But this doctrine is now abandoned by all or nearly all who profess to be Calvinists; and as the apostle expressly says that they had *not* sinned after the similitude of Adam's transgression, it cannot be intended here. (4) The same explanation of the passage is given by interpreters who nevertheless held to the doctrine of imputation. Thus CALVIN says on this passage, "Although this passage is understood commonly of infants, who, being guilty of no actual sin, perish by original depravity, yet I prefer that it should be interpreted generally of those who have not the law. For this sentiment is connected with the preceding words, where it is said that sin is not imputed where there is no law. For they had not sinned according to the similitude of Adam's transgression, because they had not as he had the will of God revealed. For the Lord forbid Adam to touch the fruit [of the tree] of the knowledge of good and evil; but to them he gave no command but the testimony of conscience." Calvin, however, supposes that infants are included in the "universal catalogue"

here referred to. Turretine also remarks that the discussion here pertains to all the *adults* between Adam and Moses. Indeed, it is perfectly manifest that the apostle here has no particular reference to infants; nor would it have ever been supposed, but for the purpose of giving support to the mere *philosophy* of a theological system.

[According to our author the disputed clause in ver. 14, "even over them,"&c., is to be understood of those who had not sinned against "a revealed or positive law." Many eminent critics have explained the phrase in the same way and yet arrived at a very different conclusion from that stated in the commentary, viz. that men die simply on account of actual or personal sin (Bloomfield, *Crit. Dig.* vol. v. p. 520). There are, however, very strong objections against this interpretation. 1. It is not consistent with the scope of the passage. The apostle had asserted in ver. 12 that all die in consequence of the sin of the one man (see Supplem. Note), and in the 13th and 14th verses proceeds to prove his position thus:—Men universally die; they must, therefore, have transgressed some law—not the law of Moses, for men died before *that* was in being. Death absolutely reigned between Adam and Moses, even over them who had not broken a revealed law. THEREFORE men have died in consequence of the sin of the one man. But in this chain of reasoning there is a link awanting. The conclusion does not follow, for though the persons in question had not broken a positive law, they had yet broken the law of nature, written on the heart, and might, therefore, have been condemned on account of a breach of it, Rom. ii. 12. But if we explain the clause under discussion of infants who have not *personally* sinned *like* Adam against any law whatever, we ascend at once to the conclusion that all die on account of Adam's sin.

2. The particle "even" (και) seems to intimate that a new class different from that before mentioned, or, at all events, a subdivision of it, is now to be introduced. None of all the multitudes that lived between Adam and Moses had sinned against a positive or revealed law. To avoid an unmeaning tautology, therefore, some other sense must be attached to the clause. It is vain to affirm that the particle "even" simply lays "emphasis" on the fact that they die who had not sinned against a positive law, since, were we to admit this forced construction, we should still ask to what purpose is the emphasis? The fact to which it is supposed to draw attention, as has been noticed already, falls short of proving the apostle's point.

3. Moreover, since the "similitude," &c., is quite a general expression containing no particular intimation in itself as to that in which the likeness consists, we are just as much at liberty to find the resemblance in *personal* transgression as others in transgression against revealed laws. To sin personally *is* to sin *like* Adam. Nay, the resemblance in this case is complete; in the other view it is imperfect, scarcely deserving to be called a resemblance at all. For *they who have no revealed law may yet be said to sin like Adam in some very important respects.* They sin wilfully and presumptuously against the law written in their hearts, in spite of the remonstrances of conscience, &c. The only difference, in fact, lies in the *mode* or *manner* of revelation. But if we suppose the likeness to lie in *personal* sin, we can find a class who have not sinned like Adam *in any way whatever.* And why this class should be supposed omitted in an argument to prove that all men die in consequence of Adam's sin it is difficult to conceive.

What though infants are not "alluded to by name?" No one has ever asserted it. Had this been the case there could have been no dispute on the point. To say, however, that the apostle "does not give any intimation that he had reference to infants" is just a begging of the question, a taking for granted what requires to be proved. Perhaps, as Edwards suggests, "such might be the state of language among Jews and Christians at that day, that the apostle might have no phrase more aptly to express this meaning. The manner in which the epithets personal and actual are used and applied now in this case is probably of later date and more modern use" (p. 312, *Orig. Sin*).

The learned author of this commentary objects farther to the opinion that infants who have not sinned personally are embraced in the clause under discussion, that "to sin by imputation is unintelligible and conveys no idea." It is his own language, and he alone is responsible for it. He tells us also that "it is utterly absurd to suppose that men, from the time of Adam to Moses, were sinners *only by imputation.*" No one ever supposed so, nor does the view to which he objects at all involve any such consequence. Again he affirms "that the scope of the apostle's argument is against the application of the clause to infants," and asks, for what purpose we cannot divine, "Did infants only die?" The answer is obvious. No! Death reigned over all who lived from Adam to Moses, *even* over that class who had not sinned personally. As to the true scope of the passage and the view that is most consonant to it enough has been said already.]

¶ *Who is the figure* (τύπος). *Type.* This word occurs sixteen times in the New Testament: John xx. 25 (twice); Acts vii. 43, 44; xxiii. 25; Rom. v. 14; vi. 17; 1 Cor. x. 6, 11; Phil. iii. 17; 1 Thes. i. 7; 2 Thes. iii. 9; 1 Tim. iv. 12; Tit. ii. 7; Heb. viii. 5; 1 Pet. v. 3. It properly means, (1) Any *impression, note,* or *mark,* which is made by percussion, or in any way, John xx. 25, "the print (*type*) of the nails." (2) An effigy or image which is made or formed by any rule; a *model,* pattern, Acts vii. 43, 'Ye took up the tabernacle of Moloch, and the star of your god Remphan, figures (*types*) which ye had made;" 44, "That he should make it [the tabernacle] according to the fashion (*type*) which he had seen;" Heb. viii. 5. (3) A brief argument, or summary, Acts xxiii. 25. (4) A rule of doctrine, or a law or *form* of doctrine, Rom. vi. 17. (5) An *example* or model to be imitated; an example of what we ought to be (Phil. iii. 17; 1 Thes. i. 7; 2 Thes. iii. 9; 1 Tim. iv. 12; Tit. ii. 7; 1 Pet. v. 3); or an example which is to be *avoided,* an example to *warn us,* 1 Cor. x. 6, 11. In this place it is evidently applied to the Messiah. The expression "he who was to come" is often used to denote the Messiah. As applied to him, it means that there was in some respects a *similarity* between the results of the conduct of Adam and the effects of the work of Christ. It does not mean that Adam was constituted or appointed *a type* of Christ, which would convey no intelligible idea; but that a *resemblance* may be traced between the *effects* of Adam's conduct and the work of Christ. It does not mean that *the person* of Adam was typical of Christ; but that between the results of his conduct and the work of Christ, *there may be instituted a comparison,* there may be traced some resemblance. What that is, is stated in the following verses. It is mainly by way of *contrast* that the comparison is instituted, and may be stated as consisting in the following points of resemblance or contrast. (1) *Contrast.* (*a*) By the crime of one, many are dead; by the work of the other, grace will *much more* abound, ver. 15. (*b*) In regard to the *acts* of the two. In the case of

15 But not as the offence, so also *is* the free gift. For if through the offence of one many be dead; *much

s Ep.2.8.

more the grace of God, and the gift by grace, *which is* by one man, Jesus Christ, *t* hath abounded unto many.

t Is.53.11; Mat.20.28; 26.28; 1 Jn.2.2

Adam, one offence led on the train of woes; in the case of Christ, his work led to the remission of *many offences*, ver. 16. (*c*) In regard to the effects. *Death* reigned by the one; but life *much more* over the other. (2) *Resemblance*. By the disobedience of one, many were made sinners; by the obedience of the other, many shall be made righteous, ver. 18, 19. It is clear, therefore, that the comparison which is instituted is rather by way of *antithesis* or *contrast*, than by direct resemblance. *The main design is to show that greater benefits have resulted from the work of Christ, than evils from the fall of Adam.* A comparison is also instituted between Adam and Christ in 1 Cor. xv. 22, 45. The reason is, that Adam was the first of the race; he was the fountain, the head, the father; and the consequences of that first act could be seen everywhere. By a divine constitution the race was so connected with him, that it was made certain that, if he fell, all would come into the world with a nature depraved, and subject to calamity and death, and would be treated as if fallen, and his sin would thus spread crime, and woe, and death everywhere. The evil effects of the apostasy were everywhere seen; and the object of the apostle was to show that the plan of salvation was adapted to meet and more than countervail the evil effects of the fall. He argued on great and acknowledged facts— that Adam was the first sinner, and that from him, as a fountain, sin and death had flowed through the world. Since the consequences of that sin had been so disastrous and widespread, his design is to show that from the Messiah effects had flowed more beneficent than the former were ruinous.

"In him the tribes of Adam boast
More blessings than their father lost."—WATTS.

15. *But not as the offence.* This is the first point of *contrast* between the effect of the sin of Adam and of

the work of Christ. The word *offence* means properly *a fall*, where we *stumble* over anything lying in our way. It then means *sin* in general, or crime, Mat. vi. 14, 15; xviii. 35. Here it means the fall, or first sin of Adam. We use the word *fall* as applied to Adam, to denote his first offence, as being that act by which he *fell* from an elevated state of obedience and happiness into one of sin and condemnation. ¶ *So also.* The gift is *not* in its nature and effects like the offence. ¶ *The free gift.* The favour, benefit, or good bestowed gratuitously on us. It refers to the favours bestowed in the gospel by Christ. These are *free, i.e.* without merit on our part, and bestowed on the undeserving. ¶ *For if*, &c. The apostle does not labour *to prove* that this *is* so. This is not the point of his *argument*. He assumes that as what was seen and known everywhere. His *main point* is to show that greater benefits have resulted from the work of the Messiah than evils from the fall of Adam. ¶ *Through the offence of one.* By the fall of one. This simply *concedes the fact* that it is so. The apostle does not attempt an explanation of the *mode* or *manner* in which it happened. He neither says that it is by *imputation*, nor by *inherent depravity*, nor by *imitation*. Whichever of these modes may be the proper one of accounting for the fact, it is certain that the apostle *states* neither. His object was, not to *explain* the manner in which it was done, but to argue from the acknowledged existence of the fact. All that is certainly established from this passage is, that, as a certain fact resulting from the transgression of Adam, "many" were "dead." This simple fact is all that can be proved from this passage. Whether it is to be explained by the doctrine of imputation, is to be a subject of inquiry independent of this passage. Nor have we a right to *assume* that this teaches the doctrine of the imputation of the sin of Adam to his posterity. For, (1) The apostle says nothing of it. (2) That doctrine is nothing but an effort to explain the *manner* of an event which the apostle Paul did not think it proper to attempt to explain. (3) That doctrine is in fact no explanation. It is introducing an additional difficulty. For to say that I am blameworthy, or ill-deserving for a sin in which I had no agency, is no *explanation*, but is involving me in an additional difficulty still more perplexing, to ascertain how such a doctrine can possibly be just. The way of wisdom would be, doubtless, to rest satisfied with the simple statement of a fact which the apostle has assumed, without attempting to explain it by a philosophical theory. Calvin accords with the above interpretation. " For we do not so perish by his [Adam's] crime, as if we were ourselves innocent; but Paul ascribes our ruin to him *because his sin is* THE CAUSE *of our sin.*"

[This is not a fair quotation from Calvin. It leaves us to infer that the reformer affirmed that Adam's sin is the cause of *actual* sin in us, on account of which last *only* we are condemned. Now under the 12th verse Calvin says, " The inference is plain, that the apostle *does not treat of actual sin, for if every person was the cause of his own guilt,* why should Paul compare Adam with Christ?" If our author had not stopped short in his quotation he would have found immediately subjoined, as an explanation, " I call that our sin which is inbred, and with which we are born." Our being born with this sin is a proof of our guilt in Adam. But whatever opinion may be formed of Calvin's general views on this subject, nothing is more certain than that he did not suppose the apostle treated of actual sin in these passages.

Notwithstanding of the efforts that are made to exclude the doctrine of imputation from this chapter, *the full and varied manner* in which the apostle expresses it cannot be evaded: " Through the offence of one many be dead " — " The judgment was by one to condemnation " — ' By one man's offence death reigned by one " — " By the offence of one, judgment came upon all men to condemnation " — " By one man's disobedience, many were made sinners," &c.

It is vain to tell us, as our author does under each of these clauses respectively, that the apostle simply *states the fact* that the sin of Adam has involved the race in condemnation without adverting to the *manner*, for Paul does more than state the fact; he intimates that we are involved in condemnation in a way that bears a certain analogy to the *manner in which we become righteous.* And on this last he is, without doubt, sufficiently explicit. See a former Supplementary Note at p. 121.

In the 18th and 19th verses the apostle seems plainly to affirm the *manner* of the fact, " As by the offence of one," &c., " EVEN so," &c. ; " As by one man's disobedience," &c., " so," &c. There is a resemblance in the manner of the two things compared. If we wish to know *how* guilt and condemnation come by Adam, we have only to inquire how righteousness and justification come by Christ. " *So,*" *i.e.* in *this* way, not in *like* manner. It is not in a manner that has merely some likeness, but it is in the very same manner ; for although there is a contrast in the things, the one being disobedience and the other obedience, yet there is a perfect identity in the manner (Haldane).

It is somewhat remarkable that, while our author so frequently affirms that the apostle states the *fact* only, he himself should throughout assume the *manner.* He will not allow the apostle to explain the manner, nor anyone who has a different view of it from himself. Yet he tells us it is *not* by imputation that we become involved in Adam's guilt ; that men " sin in their own persons, and that *therefore* they die." This he affirms to be the apostle's meaning. And is this not an explanation of the manner? Are we not left to conclude that from Adam we simply derive a corrupt nature, in consequence of which we sin personally, and therefore die?]

¶ *Many.* Greek, *the many.* Evidently meaning *all;* the whole race ; Jews and Gentiles. That it means *all* here is proved in ver. 18. If the inquiry be, why the apostle used the word "*many*" rather than *all*, we may reply, that the design was to express an *antithesis* or contrast to the cause —one offence. *One* stands opposed to *many*, rather than to *all*. ¶ *Be dead.* See Note on the word *death*, ver. 12. The race is under the dark and gloomy reign of death. This is a simple fact which the apostle assumes, and which no man can deny. ¶ *Much more.* The reason of this "much more" is to be found in the abounding mercy and goodness of God. If a wise, merciful, and good Being has suffered such a train of woes to be introduced by the offence of one, have we not much more reason to expect that his grace will superabound? ¶ *The grace of God.*

The favour or kindness of God. We have reason to expect under the administration of God more extensive benefits, than we have ills, flowing from a constitution of things which is the result of his appointment. ¶ *And the gift by grace.* The gracious gift; the benefits flowing from that grace. This refers to the blessings of salvation. ¶ Which is *by one man.* Standing in contrast with Adam. His appointment was the result of grace; and as he was constituted to bestow favours, we have reason to expect that they will superabound. ¶ *Hath abounded.* Has been abundant, or ample; will be more than a counterbalance for the ills which have been introduced by the sin of Adam. ¶ *Unto many.* Greek, unto the many. The obvious interpretation of this is, that it is as unlimited as "the many" who are dead. Some have supposed that Adam represented *the whole* of the human race, and Christ a part, and that "the many" in the two members of the verse refer to the *whole* of those who were thus represented. But this is to do violence, to the passage; and to introduce a theological doctrine to meet a supposed difficulty in the text. The obvious meaning is—one from which we cannot depart without doing violence to the proper laws of interpretation—that "the many" in the two cases are co-extensive; and that as the sin of Adam has involved the race — the many—in death; so the grace of Christ has abounded *in reference to* the many, to the race. If asked how this can be possible, since all have not been, and will not be savingly benefited by the work of Christ, we may reply, (1) That it *cannot* mean that the benefits of the work of Christ should be *literally* coextensive with the results of Adam's sin, since it is a fact that men *have* suffered, and *do* suffer, from the effects of that fall. In order that the Universalist may draw an argument from this, he must show that it was the design of Christ to destroy ALL the effects of the sin of Adam. But this has *not* been in fact. Though the favours of that work have abounded, yet men have suffered and died. And though it may still

abound to *the many*, yet some may suffer here, and suffer on the same principle for ever. (2) Though men are indubitably affected by the sin of Adam, as *e.g.* by being born with a corrupt disposition, with loss of righteousness, with subjection to pain and woe, and with exposure to eternal death; yet there is reason to believe that all those who die in infancy are, through the merits of the Lord Jesus, and by an influence which we cannot explain, changed and prepared for heaven. As nearly half the race die in infancy, therefore, there is reason to think that, in regard to this large portion of the human family, the work of Christ has more than repaired the evils of the fall, and introduced them into heaven, and that his grace has *thus* abounded unto many. In regard to those who live to the period of moral agency, a scheme has been introduced by which the offers of salvation may be made to them, and by which they may be renewed, and pardoned and saved. The work of Christ, therefore, may have introduced advantages adapted to meet the evils of the fall as man comes into the world; and the original applicability of the one be as extensive as the other. In this way the work of Christ was *in its nature* fitted to abound unto the many. (3) The intervention of the plan of atonement by the Messiah prevented the immediate execution of the penalty of the law, and produced *all* the benefits to *all* the race resulting from the sparing mercy of God. In this respect it was coextensive with the fall. (4) He died for all the race, Heb. ii. 9 ; 2 Cor. v. 14, 15 ; 1 John ii. 2. Thus his death, in its adaptation to a great and glorious result, was as extensive as the ruins of the fall. (5) The *offer* of salvation is made to all, Rev. xxii. 17; John vii. 37; Mat. xi. 28, 29; Mark xvi. 15. Thus his grace has extended unto the many— to all the race. Provision has been made to meet the evils of the fall—a provision as extensive in its applicability as was the ruin. (6) More *will* probably be actually saved by the work of Christ than will be finally ruined by the fall of Adam. The number of those who shall be saved from all the human race, it is to be believed, will yet be many more than those who shall be lost. The gospel is to spread throughout the world. It is to be evangelized. The millennial glory is to rise upon the earth, and the Saviour is to reign with undivided empire. Taking the race as a whole, there is no reason to think that the number of those who shall be lost, compared with the immense multitudes that shall be saved by the work of Christ, will be more than are the *prisoners* in a community now, compared with the number of peaceful and virtuous citizens. A medicine may be discovered that shall be said to *triumph* over disease, though it may have been the fact that thousands *have* died since its discovery, and thousands yet *will not* avail themselves of it; yet the medicine shall have the properties of universal triumph; it is adapted to the many; it might be applied by the many; where it *is* applied, it completely answers the end. Vaccination is adapted to meet the evils of the small-pox everywhere, and *when* applied saves men from the ravages of this terrible disease, though thousands may die to whom it is not applied. It is a *triumphant* remedy. So of the plan of salvation. Thus, though all shall not be saved, yet the sin of Adam shall be counteracted; and grace abounds unto the many. All this fulness of grace the apostle says we have reason to expect from the abounding mercy of God.

[The "many" in the latter clause of this verse cannot be regarded as coextensive with the "many" that are said to be dead through the offence of Adam. Very much is affirmed of the "many to whom grace abounds," that cannot, "without doing violence to the whole passage," be applied to *all* mankind. They are said to "*receive* the gift of righteousness" and to "reign in life." They are actually "constituted righteous" (ver. 19), and these things cannot be said of all men *in any sense whatever.* The only way of explaining the passage, therefore, is to adopt that view which our author has introduced only to condemn, viz. "that Adam represented the whole of the human race, and Christ a part, and that 'the many' in the two members of

the verse refers to the whole of those who were thus represented."

The same principle of interpretation must be adopted in the parallel passage, "As in Adam all die, so in Christ shall all be made alive." It would be preposterous to affirm that the "all" in the latter clause is coextensive with the "all" in the former. The sense plainly is, that all whom Christ represented should be made alive in him, even as all mankind, or all represented by Adam, had died in him.

It is true, indeed, that all mankind are in some sense benefited on account of the atonement of Christ; and our author has enlarged on several things of this nature, which yet fall short of "saving benefit." But will it be maintained that the apostle in reality affirms no more than that the many to whom grace abounds participate in certain benefits short of salvation? If so, what becomes of the comparison between Adam and Christ? If "the many" in the one branch of the comparison are only benefited by Christ in a way that falls short of saving benefit, then "the many" in the other branch must be affected by the fall of Adam only in the same limited way, whereas the apostle affirms that in consequence of it they are *really* "dead."

"The principal thing," says Mr. Scott, "which renders the expositions generally given of these verses perplexed and unsatisfactory, arises from an evident misconception of the apostle's reasoning, in supposing that Adam and Christ represented exactly the same company; whereas Adam was the surety of the whole human species as his posterity, Christ only of that chosen remnant which has been or shall be one with him by faith, who alone 'are counted to him for a generation.' If we exclusively consider the benefits which believers derive from Christ, as compared with the loss sustained in Adam by the human race, we shall then see the passage most perspicuously and gloriously to our view" (*Commentary*, ch. v. 15, 19).

But our author does not interpret this passage upon any consistent principle, for "the many" in the 15th verse, to whom "grace abounded," are obviously the same with those in the 17th verse, who are said to receive abundance of grace, &c., and yet he interprets the one of all mankind, and the other of believers only. What is asserted in the 17th verse he says "is particularly true of the redeemed, of whom the apostle in this verse is speaking."]

16. *And not*, &c. This is the *second* point in which the effects of the work of Christ differ from the sin of Adam. The *first* part (ver. 15) was, that the

16 And not as *it was* by one that sinned, *so is* the gift: for the judgment *was* by one to condemnation; but the free gift *is*

evil consequences flowed from the sin of *one* MAN, Adam; and that the benefits flowed from the work of *one* MAN, Jesus Christ. The point in this verse is, that the evil consequences flowed from *one* CRIME, one act of guilt; but that the favours had respect to MANY ACTS of guilt. The effects of Adam's sin, whatever they were, pertained to the *one sin;* the effects of the work of Christ, to *many sins.* ¶ *By one that sinned* (δι' ἑνὸς ἁμαρτήσαντος). By means of *one* [*man*] *sinning;* evidently meaning by *one offence*, or by one act of sin. So the Vulgate, and many MSS. And the connection shows that this is the sense. ¶ *The gift.* The benefits resulting from the work of Christ. ¶ *The judgment.* The sentence; the declared penalty. The word expresses properly the *sentence* which is passed by a judge. Here it means the *sentence* which God passed, as a judge, on Adam for the one offence, involving himself and his posterity in ruin, Gen. ii. 17; iii. 17–19. ¶ Was *by one.* By one offence; or one act of sin. ¶ *To condemnation.* Producing condemnation; or involving in condemnation. It is proved by this, that the effect of the sin of Adam was to involve the race in condemnation, or to secure this as a result, that all mankind would be under the condemning sentence of the law, and be transgressors. But *in what way* it would have this effect, the apostle does not state. He does not intimate that his sin would be imputed to them; or that they would be held to be personally guilty for it. He speaks of a broad, everywhere perceptible fact, that the effect of that sin had been somehow to whelm the race in condemnation. In what *mode* this was done is a fair subject of inquiry; but the apostle does not attempt to explain it. ¶ *The free gift.* The unmerited favour, by the work of Christ. ¶ Is *of many offences.* In *relation* to many sins. It differs thus

of *"many offences unto justification.*

17 For if *[4] by one man's offence* death reigned by one; much more

u Is.1.18.   [4] or, *by one offence.*

from the condemnation. That had respect to one offence; this has respect to many crimes. Grace therefore abounds. ¶ *Unto justification.* Note, chap. iii. 24. The work of Christ is designed to have reference to many offences, so as to produce pardon or justification in regard to them all. But the apostle here does not intimate *how* this is done. He simply states the fact, without attempting in this place to explain it; and as we know that that work does not produce its effect to *justify* without some act on the part of the individual, are we not hence led to conclude the same respecting the condemnation for the sin of Adam? As the work of Christ does not benefit the race unless it is embraced, so does not the reasoning of the apostle imply, that the deed of Adam does not involve in criminality and ill-desert unless there be some voluntary act on the part of each individual? However this may be, it is certain that the apostle has in neither case here explained the *mode* in which it is done. He has simply stated the *fact*, a fact which he did not seem to consider himself called on to explain. Neither has he affirmed that in the two cases the *mode* is the same. On the contrary, it is strongly implied that it is *not* the same, for the leading object here is to present, not an entire *resemblance*, but a strong contrast between the effects of the sin of Adam and the work of Christ.

17. *For if.* This verse contains the same idea as before presented, but in a varied form. It is *condensing* the whole subject, and presenting it in a single view. ¶ *By one man's offence.* Or, by one offence (margin). The reading of the text is the more correct. "If, under the administration of a just and merciful Being, it has occurred that, by the offence of one, death hath exerted so wide a dominion; we have reason much more to expect,

they which *v*receive abundance of grace, and of *w*the gift of righteousness shall reign in life by one, Jesus Christ.)

v Jn.10.10.   *w* ch.6.23.

18 Therefore, as [5]by the offence of one *judgment came* upon all men to condemnation; even so [6]by the righteousness of one *the*

5 or, *by one offence.*   6 or, *by one righteousness.*

---

under that administration, that they who are brought under his plan of saving mercy shall be brought under a dispensation of life." ¶ *Death reigned.* Note, ver. 14. ¶ *By one.* By means of one man. ¶ *Much more.* We have much more reason to expect it. It evidently accords much more with the administration of a Being of infinite goodness. ¶ *They which receive abundance of grace.* The *abundant favour;* the mercy that shall counterbalance and surpass the evils introduced by the sin of Adam. That favour shall be more than sufficient to counterbalance all those evils. This is particularly true of the redeemed, of whom the apostle in this verse is speaking. The evils which *they* suffer in consequence of the sin of Adam bear no comparison with the mercies of eternal life that shall flow to them from the work of the Saviour. ¶ *The gift of righteousness.* This stands opposed to the evils introduced by Adam. As the effect of his sin was to produce condemnation, so here the gift of righteousness refers to the opposite, to pardon, to justification, to acceptance with God. To show that men were thus justified by the gospel, was the leading design of the apostle; and the argument here is, that if by one man's sin, death reigned over those who were under condemnation in consequence of it, we have much more reason to suppose that they who are delivered from sin by the death of Christ, and accepted of God, shall reign with him in life. ¶ *Shall reign.* The word *reign* is often applied to the condition of saints in heaven, 2 Tim. ii. 12, "If we suffer, we shall also reign with him;" Rev. v. 10; xx. 6; xxii. 5. It means that they shall be exalted to a glorious state of happiness in heaven; that they shall be triumphant over all their enemies; shall gain an ultimate victory; and shall partake with the Captain of their

salvation in the splendours of his dominion above, Rev. iii. 21; Luke xxii. 30. ¶ *In life.* This stands opposed to the *death* that reigned as the consequence of the sin of Adam. It denotes complete freedom from condemnation; from temporal death; from sickness, pain, and sin. It is the usual expression to denote the complete bliss of the saints in glory; Note, John iii. 36. ¶ *By one, Jesus Christ.* As the consequence of his work. The apostle here does not state the *mode* or manner in which this was done; nor does he say that it was perfectly parallel in the mode with the effects of the sin of Adam. He is comparing the *results* or *consequences* of the sin of the one and of the work of the other. There is a similarity in the consequences. The way in which the work of Christ had contributed to this he had stated in chap. iii. 24, 28.

18. *Therefore.* Wherefore ("Aρα οὖν). This is properly a *summing up,* a recapitulation of what had been stated in the previous verses. The apostle resumes the statement or proposition made in ver. 12, and after the intermediate explanation in the parenthesis (ver. 13–17), in this verse and the following sums up the whole subject. The explanation, therefore, of the previous verses is designed to convey the real meaning of ver. 18, 19. ¶ *As by the offence of one.* Admitting this as an undisputed and everywhere apparent fact, a fact which no one can call in question. ¶ Judgment came. This is not in the Greek, but it is evidently implied, and is stated in ver. 16. The meaning is, that all have been brought under the reign of death by one man. ¶ *Upon all men.* The whole race. This explains what is meant by "the many" in ver. 15. ¶ *To condemnation,* ver. 16. ¶ *Even so.* In the manner explained in the previous

free gift ˣ*came* upon all men unto justification of life.

19 For as by one man's diso-

x Jn.12.32.

verses. With the same certainty, and to the same extent. The apostle does not explain the *mode* in which it was done, but simply states the *fact*. ¶ *By the righteousness of one.* This stands opposed to the *one offence* of Adam, and must mean, therefore, the holiness, obedience, purity of the Redeemer. The *sin* of one man involved men in ruin; the *obedience unto death* of the other (Phil. ii. 8) restored them to the favour of God. ¶ Came *upon all men* (εἰς πάντας ἀνθρώπους). Was with reference to all men; had a bearing upon all men; was *originally adapted* to the race. As the sin of Adam was of such a nature in the relation in which he stood as to affect all the race, so the work of Christ in the relation in which he stood was adapted also to all the race. As the tendency of the one was to involve the race in condemnation, so the tendency of the other was to restore them to acceptance with God. There was an *original applicability* in the work of Christ to all men — a richness, a fulness of the atonement fitted to meet the sins of the entire world, and restore the race to favour. ¶ *Unto justification of life.* With reference to that justification which is connected with eternal life. That is, his work is *adapted* to produce acceptance with God, to the same extent as the crime of Adam has affected the race by involving them in sin and misery. The apostle does not affirm that in fact as many *will be* affected by the one as by the other; but that it is fitted to meet all the consequences of the fall; to be as wide-spread in its effects; and to be as salutary as that had been ruinous. This is all that the argument requires. Perhaps there could not be found a more striking declaration anywhere, that the work of Christ had *an original applicability* to all men; or that it is in its own nature fitted to save all. The course of argument here leads inevitably to this; nor is it pos-

bedience many were made sinners, so by the obedience of one shall many be made righteous.

sible to avoid it without doing violence to the obvious and fair course of the discussion. It does not prove that all will in fact be saved, but that the plan is *fitted* to meet all the evils of the fall. A certain kind of medicine may have an original applicability to heal all persons under the same disease; and may be abundant and certain, and yet *in fact* be applied to few. The sun is fitted to give light to all, yet many may be blind, or may voluntarily close their eyes. Water is adapted to the wants of all men, and the supply may be ample for the human family, yet *in fact,* from various causes, many may be deprived of it. So of the provisions of the plan of redemption. They are adapted to all; they are ample; and yet *in fact,* from causes which this is not the place to explain, the benefits, like those of medicine, water, science, &c., may never be enjoyed by all the race. Calvin concurs in this interpretation, and thus shows that it is one which commends itself even to the most strenuous advocates of the system which is called by his name. He says, "He [the apostle] makes the grace common to all, because it is offered to all, not because it is in fact applied to all. *For although Christ suffered for the sins* OF THE WHOLE WORLD (nam etsi passus est Christus pro peccatis totius mundi), and it is offered to all without distinction (indifferenter), yet all do not embrace it." See Cal. *Comm.* on this place.*

19. *For,* &c. This verse is not a *mere* repetition of the former, but it is an explanation. By the former statements it might perhaps be inferred that men were condemned without any guilt or blame of theirs. The apostle in this verse guards against this, and affirms that they are *in fact sinners.* He affirms that those who are sinners are condemned, and that the sufferings brought in on

* See the opposite view stated in a Supplementary Note at page 137.

account of the sin of Adam, are introduced because many were made *sinners*. Calvin says, "Lest anyone should arrogate to himself innocence, [the apostle] adds, that *each one is condemned because he is a sinner*."

[The same objection which was stated against a previous quotation from Calvin, applies here. The reformer does not mean that each is condemned because he is *actually* a sinner. He affirms that the *ground* of condemnation lies in something with which we are born, which belongs to us *antecedent* to actual transgression.]

¶ *By one man's disobedience.* By means of the sin of Adam. This affirms simply the fact that such a result followed from the sin of Adam. The word *by* (διά) is used in the Scriptures as it is in all books and in all languages. It may denote the efficient cause; the instrumental cause; the principal cause; the meritorious cause; or the chief occasion by which a thing occurred. (See Schleusner.) It does not express one mode, and one only, in which a thing is done; but that one thing is the result of another. When we say that a young man is ruined in his character *by* another, we do not express the *mode*, but the *fact*. When we say that thousands have been made infidels *by* the writings of Paine and Voltaire, we make no affirmation about the mode, but about the fact. In each of these, and in all other cases, we should deem it most inconclusive reasoning to attempt to determine the mode by the preposition *by;* and still more absurd if it were argued from the use of that preposition that the sins of the seducer were *imputed* to the young man; or the opinions of Paine and Voltaire *imputed* to infidels.

[What is here said of the various significations of διά is true. Yet it will not be denied, that in a multitude of instances it points to the *real* cause or ground of a thing. The sense is to be determined by the connection. "We have in this single passage no less than three cases, ver. 12, 18, 19, in which this preposition with the genitive indicates the *ground or reason* on account of which something is given or performed. All this is surely sufficient to prove that it may, in the case before us, express the ground why the sen-

tence of condemnation has passed upon all men." To draw an illustration from the injury inflicted by Voltaire and Paine, will not serve the author's purpose, till he can prove that *they* stand in a relation to those whom they have injured similar to that which Adam bears to the human family. When we say that thousands have been ruined by Voltaire, it is true we can have no idea of imputation; yet we *may* fairly entertain such an idea when it is said, "all mankind have been ruined *by* Adam."]

¶ *Many.* Greek, *the many*, ver. 15.
¶ *Were made* (κατεστάθησαν). The verb here used occurs in the New Testament in the following places: Mat. xxiv. 45, 47; xxv. 21, 23; Luke xii. 14, 42, 44; Acts vi. 3; vii. 10, 27, 35; xvii. 15; Rom. v. 19; Tit. i. 5; Heb. ii. 7; v. 1; vii. 28; viii. 3; Jam. iii. 6; iv. 4; 2 Pet. i. 8. It usually means to constitute, set, or appoint. In the New Testament it has *two* leading significations. (1) To appoint to an office, to set over others (Mat. xxiv. 45, 47; Luke xii. 42, &c.); and, (2) It means to *become*, to be in fact, &c., Jam. iii. 6, "So *is* the tongue among our members," &c.—that is, it *becomes* such; Jam. iv. 4, "The friendship of the world *is* enmity with God"— it becomes such; it is *in fact* thus, and is thus to be regarded. The word is *in no instance* used to express the idea of *imputing that to one which belongs to another*. It here either means that this was *by a constitution of divine appointment* that they in fact became *sinners*, or simply declares that they *were* so in fact. There is not the slightest intimation that it was by imputation. The whole scope of the argument is, moreover, against this; for the object of the apostle is not to show that they were charged with the sin of another, but that they were in fact *sinners* themselves. If it means that they were condemned for *his* act, without any concurrence of their own will, then the correspondent part will be true, that all are constituted righteous in the same way; and thus the doctrine of universal salvation will be inevitable. But as none are constituted righteous who do not voluntarily avail themselves of the provisions of mercy, so it follows that those

who are condemned, are not condemned for the sin of another without their own concurrence, nor unless they personally deserve it.

[Does not the word *κατεσταθησαν*, in the last clause of this verse, intimate that we are *really and directly* made righteous, by the obedience of Christ, *without the intervention of any obedience of our own?* Why then may not the same word, in the first clause, intimate that we are made sinners by the disobedience of Adam, without the intervention of any disobedience of our own? It is impossible otherwise to explain the analogy between Adam and Christ.

That we are involved in Adam's guilt "without (rather before) any concurrence of our own will" is true, and capable of proof from the author's own admission, that we *come into the world* with a depraved nature. But that our will is not concerned in the reception of righteousness, does not follow. To this, except in the case of infants, *faith* is essential, chap. i. 17; iii. 22. It is not a little surprising that the commentator should, in one place, deny that there is any resemblance between the *manner* in which sin and righteousness are respectively communicated, and, in another, gravely argue upon the analogy, and that, too, after having stretched it beyond its legitimate bounds!

"This whole reasoning of the apostle," says Principal Hill in his concluding observation on these verses, "favours the notion of an imputation of Adam's sin. The phrase, indeed, does not occur, but the thing meant by the phrase appears to be the natural meaning of the passage; and I know no better way in which you can satisfy yourselves that it is the true meaning, than by comparing the interpretation now given, with the forced paraphrases to which those are obliged to have recourse who wish to show that the fourth opinion (of imputation) does not receive any countenance from the authority of Paul" (Hill's *Lectures*, vol. ii. p. 28, 3d. edit.).]

¶ *Sinners.* Transgressors; those who deserve to be punished. It does not mean those who are condemned for the sin of another; but those who are violators of the law of God. All who are condemned are *sinners.* They are not *innocent* persons condemned for the crime of another. Men may be involved in the *consequences* of the sins of others without being to blame. The consequences of the crimes of a murderer, a drunkard, a pirate, may pass over from them, and affect thousands, and whelm them

in ruin. But this does not prove that they are blameworthy. In the divine administration none are *regarded* as guilty who are not guilty; none are condemned who do not *deserve* to be condemned. All who sink to hell are *sinners.* ¶ *By the obedience of one.* Of Christ. This stands opposed to the *disobedience* of Adam, and evidently includes the entire work of the Redeemer which has a bearing on the salvation of men, Phil. ii. 8, "He . . . became *obedient* unto death." ¶ *Shall many.* Greek, *the many;* corresponding to the term in the former part of the verse, and evidently commensurate with it; for there is no reason for limiting it to *a part* in this member, any more than there is in the former. ¶ *Be made.* The same Greek word as before—be appointed, or *become.* The apostle has explained the mode in which this is done, chap. i. 17; iii. 24-26; iv. 1-5. That explanation is to limit the meaning here. No more are considered righteous than become so *in that way.* And as *all* do *not* become righteous thus, the passage cannot be adduced to prove the doctrine of universal salvation.

The following remarks may express the doctrines which are established by this much-contested and difficult passage. (1) Adam was created holy; capable of obeying law; yet free to fall. (2) A law was given him, adapted to his condition—simple, plain, easy to be obeyed, and fitted to give human nature a trial in circumstances as favourable as possible. (3) Its violation exposed him to the threatened penalty as he had understood it, and to all the collateral woes which it might carry in its train—involving, as subsequent developments showed, the loss of God's favour; his displeasure evinced in man's toil, and sweat, and sickness, and death; in hereditary depravity, and the curse, and the pains of hell for ever. (4) Adam was the head of the race; he was the fountain of being; and human nature was so far tried in him, that it may be said he was on trial not for himself alone, but for his posterity, inasmuch as his fall would involve them in ruin. Many have chosen to call this a covenant, and to speak of him as a federal head; and if the above account is the idea involved in these terms, the explanation is not exceptionable. As the word covenant, however, is not applied in the transaction in the Bible, and as it is liable to be misunderstood, others prefer to speak of it as a *law* given to Adam, and as *a divine constitution,* under which he was placed. (5) *His posterity are, in consequence of his sin, subjected to the same train of ills as if they had been personally the transgressors.* Not that they are regarded as personally ill-deserving, or criminal for his sin;* God reckons things as they are, and not falsely (see Note, chap. iv. 3), and his imputations are all according to truth. He regarded Adam as standing at the head of the race; and regards and treats all his posterity as coming into the world subject to pain, and death, and depravity, as a consequence of his sin; see Note, p. 134. This is the Scripture idea of imputation; and this is what has been commonly meant when it has been said that "the GUILT of his first sin"—*not the sin itself*—"is imputed to his posterity." (6) There is *something* antecedent to the moral action of his posterity, and growing out of the relation which they sustain to him, which makes it certain that they will sin as soon as they begin to act as moral agents. What this is, we may not be able to say; but we may be certain that it is not physical depravity, or any created essence of the soul, or anything which prevents the first act of sin from being voluntary. This hereditary tendency to sin has been usually called "original sin;" and this the apostle evidently teaches. (7) As an infant comes into the world with a certainty that he will sin as soon as he becomes a moral agent here, there is the same certainty that, if he were removed to eternity, he would sin there also, unless he were changed. There is, therefore, need of the blood of the atonement, and of the agency of the Holy Ghost, that an infant may be saved. (8) The

facts here stated accord with all the analogy in the moral government of God. The drunkard secures as a result commonly, that his family will be reduced to beggary, want, and woe. A pirate, or a traitor, will whelm not himself only, but his family in ruin. Such is the great law or constitution on which society is now organized; and we are not to be surprised that the same *principle* occurred in the *primary organization* of human affairs. (9) As this is the *fact* everywhere, the analogy disarms all objections which have been made against the scriptural statements of the effects of the sin of Adam. If just *now,* it was just *then.* If it exists *now,* it existed *then.* (10) The doctrine should be left, therefore, simply as it is in the Scriptures. It is there the simple statement of *a fact,* without any attempt at explanation. That fact accords with all that we see and feel. It is a great principle in the constitution of things, that the conduct of one man may pass over in its effects on others, and have an influence on their happiness. The simple fact in regard to Adam is, that he sinned; and that such is the organization of the great society of which he was the head and father, that his sin has secured as a certain result that all the race will be sinners also. *How* this is, the Bible has not explained. It is a part of a great system of things. That it is *unjust* no man can prove, for none can show that any sinner suffers more than he deserves. That it is *wise* is apparent, for it is attended with numberless blessings. It is connected with all the advantages that grow out of the social organization. The race *might* have been composed of *independent individuals,* where the conduct of an individual, good or evil, might have affected no one but himself. But then *society* would have been impossible. All the benefits of organization into families, and communities, and nations would have been unknown. Man would have lived alone, wept alone, rejoiced alone, died alone. There would have been no sympathy, no compassion, no mutual aid. God has therefore *grouped* the race into sepa-

* See the foregoing Supplementary Notes.

20 Moreover,*y* the law entered, that the offence might abound.

y Jn.15.22; ch.7.8-13; Ga.3.19.

rate communities. He has organized society. He has constituted families, tribes, clans, nations; and though on the general principle the conduct of one *may* whelm another in misery, yet the union, the grouping, the constitution, is the source of most of the blessings which man enjoys in this life, and may be of numberless mercies in regard to that which is to come. If it was the organization on which the race might be plunged into sin, it is also the organization on which it may be raised to life eternal. If, on the one hand, it may be abused to produce misery, it may, on the other, be improved to the advancement of peace, sympathy, friendship, prosperity, salvation. At all events, such *is* the organization in common life and in religion, and it becomes man not to murmur, but to *act* on it, and to endeavour, by the tender mercy of God, to turn it to his welfare here and hereafter. As by this organization, through Adam, he has been plunged into sin, so by the same organization he shall, through "the second Adam," rise to life and ascend to the skies.

20. *Moreover*. But. What is said in this verse and the following seems designed to meet the Jew, who might pretend that the law of Moses was intended to meet the evils of sin introduced by Adam, and therefore that the scheme defended by the apostle was unnecessary. He therefore shows them that the *effect* of the law of Moses was to *increase* rather than to *diminish* the sins which had been introduced into the world. And if *such* was the fact, it could not be pled that it was adapted to overcome the acknowledged evils of the apostasy. ¶ *The law.* The Mosaic laws and institutions. The word seems to be used here to denote *all* the laws which were given in the Old Testament. ¶ *Entered.* This word usually means *to enter secretly* or *surreptitiously.* But it appears to be used here simply in the sense that the law came in, or was given. It came in addition to, or it supervened the state before Moses,

when men were living without a revelation. ¶ *That sin,* &c. The word "that" (*ἵνα*), in this place, does not mean that it was the *design* of giving the law that sin might abound or be increased, but that such was *in fact* the effect. It had this tendency, not to restrain or subdue sin, but to excite and increase it. That the word has this sense may be seen in the lexicons. The way in which the law produces this effect is stated more fully by the apostle in chap. vii. 7–11. The law expresses the duty of man; it is spiritual and holy; it is opposed to the guilty passions and pleasures of the world; and it thus excites opposition, provokes to anger, and is the occasion by which sin is called into exercise, and shows itself in the heart. All law, where there is a *disposition* to do wrong, has this tendency. A command given to a child that is *disposed* to indulge his passions, only tends to excite anger and opposition. If the heart was holy, and there was a disposition to do right, law would have no such tendency. See this subject further illustrated in the Notes on chap. vii. 7–11. ¶ *The offence.* The offence which had been introduced by Adam, *i.e.* sin. Compare ver. 15. ¶ *Might abound.* Might increase ; that is, would be more apparent, more violent, more extensive. The introduction of the Mosaic law, instead of diminishing the sins of men, only increases them. ¶ *But where sin abounded.* Alike in all dispensations—before the law, and under the law. In all conditions of the human family, before the gospel, it was the characteristic that sin was prevalent. ¶ *Grace.* Favour; mercy. ¶ *Did much more abound.* Superabounded. The word is used nowhere else in the New Testament, except in 2 Cor. vii. 4. It means that the pardoning mercy of the gospel greatly triumphed over sin, even over the sins of the Jews, though those sins were greatly aggravated by the light which they enjoyed under the advantages of divine revelation.

21. *That as sin hath reigned.* Note,

But where sin abounded, *grace did much more abound;

21 That as sin hath reigned unto

z Jn.10.10; 1 Ti.1.14.

death, even so might *a*grace reign through righteousness, unto eternal life, by Jesus Christ our Lord.

a Jn.1.17.

ver. 14. ¶ *Unto death.* Producing or causing death. ¶ *Even so.* In like manner, also. The provisions of redemption are in themselves ample to meet all the ruins of the fall. ¶ *Might grace reign.* Might mercy be triumphant; see John i. 17, "Grace and truth came by Jesus Christ." ¶ *Through righteousness.* Through, or by means of, God's plan of justification; Note, chap. i. 17. ¶ *Unto eternal life.* This stands opposed to "death" in the former part of the verse, and shows that there the apostle had reference to *eternal* death. The result of God's plan of justification shall be to produce *eternal life.* The triumphs of the gospel here celebrated cannot refer to the *number* of the subjects, for it has not actually freed all men from the dominion of sin. But the apostle refers to the fact that the gospel is able to overcome sin of the most malignant form, of the most aggravated character, of the longest duration. Sin in all dispensations and states of things can be thus overcome; and the gospel is more than sufficient to meet all the evils of the apostasy, and to raise up the race to heaven.

This chapter is a most precious portion of divine revelation. It brings into view the amazing evils which have resulted from the apostasy. The apostle does not attempt to deny or palliate those evils; he admits them fully; admits them in their deepest, widest, most melancholy extent; just as the physician *admits* the extent and ravages of the disease which he hopes to cure. At the same time Christianity is not responsible for those evils. It did not introduce them. It finds them in existence, as a matter of sober and melancholy fact, pertaining to all the race. Christianity is no more answerable for the introduction and extent of sin, than the science of medicine is responsible for the introduction and extent of disease. Like that science, it *finds* a state of wide-spread evils *in* existence; and like that science,

it is strictly a *remedial* system. And whether true or false, still the evils of sin exist, just as the evils of disease exist, whether the science of medicine be well-founded or not. Nor does it make any difference in the existence of these evils whether Christianity be true or false. If the Bible could be proved to be an imposition, it would not prove that men are not sinners. If the whole work of Christ could be shown to be imposture, still it would annihilate no sin, nor would it prove that man has not fallen. The fact would still remain—a fact certainly quite as universal, and quite as melancholy, as it is under the admitted truth of the Christian revelation—and a fact which the infidel is just as much concerned to account for as is the Christian. Christianity proposes a remedy; and it is permitted to the Christian to rejoice that that remedy is ample to meet all the evils; that it is just fitted to recover our alienated world; and that it is destined yet to raise the race up to life, and peace, and heaven. In the provisions of that scheme we may and should triumph; and on the same principle as we may rejoice in the triumph of medicine over disease, so may we triumph in the ascendency of the Christian plan over all the evils of the fall. And while Christians thus rejoice, the infidel, the deist, the pagan, and the scoffer shall contend with these evils which their systems cannot alleviate or remove, and sink under the chilly reign of sin and death; just as men pant, and struggle, and expire under the visitations of disease, because they *will* not apply the proper remedies of medicine, but choose rather to leave themselves to its unchecked ravages, or to use all the nostrums of quackery in a vain attempt to arrest evils which are coming upon them.

CHAPTER VI.

The argument commenced in this chapter is continued through the two following. The general design is the

CHAPTER VI.

WHAT shall we say then? ^aShall we continue in sin, that grace may abound?

_{a ch.3.8.}

same—*to show that the scheme of justification which God had adopted does not lead men to sin, but on the contrary to holiness.* This is introduced by answering an objection, chap. vi. 1. The apostle pursues this subject by various arguments and illustrations, all tending to show that the design and bearing of the scheme of justification was to produce the hatred of sin, and the love and practice of holiness. In this chapter, the argument is mainly drawn from the following sources: (1) From the *baptism* of Christians, by which they have professed to be dead to sin, and to be bound to live to God, ver. 2–13. (2) From the fact that they were now the *servants* of God, and under obligation, by the laws of servitude, to obey him, ver. 15–20. (3) From their former *experience* of the evil of sin, from its tendency to produce misery and death, and from the fact that by the gospel they had been made ashamed of those things, and had now given themselves to the pure service of God. By these various considerations he repels the charge, that the tendency of the doctrine was to produce licentiousness, but affirms that it was a system of purity and peace. The argument is continued in the two following chapters, showing still farther the purifying tendency of the gospel.

1. *What shall we say then?* This is a mode of presenting an objection. The objection refers to what the apostle had said in chap. v. 20. What shall we say to such a sentiment as, that where sin abounded grace did much more abound? ¶ *Shall we continue in sin?* &c. If sin has been the occasion of grace and favour, ought we not to continue in it, and commit as much as possible, in order that grace might abound? This objection the apostle proceeds to answer. He shows that the consequence does not follow; and proves that the doctrine of justification does not lead to it.

2 God forbid. How shall we that are ^bdead to sin, live any longer therein?

3 Know ye not, that so many of us

_{b ver.6-11; Col.3.3; 1 Pe.2.24.}

2. *God forbid.* By no means. Greek, It may not be; Note, chap. iii. 4. The expression is a strong *denial* of what is implied in the objection in ver. 1. ¶ *How shall we?* &c. This contains a *reason* of the implied statement of the apostle, that we should not continue in sin. The reason is drawn from the fact that we are dead in fact to sin. It is impossible for those who are *dead* to act as if they were alive. It is just as absurd to suppose that a Christian should desire to live in sin as that a dead man should put forth the actions of life. ¶ *That are dead to sin.* That is, all Christians. To be *dead* to a thing is a strong expression denoting that it has no influence over us. A man that is dead is uninfluenced and unaffected by the affairs of this life. He is insensible to sounds, and tastes, and pleasures; to the hum of business, to the voice of friendship, and to all the scenes of commerce, gaiety, and ambition. When it is said, therefore, that a Christian is *dead to sin*, the sense is, that it has lost its influence over him; he is not subject to it; he is, in regard to that, as the man in the grave is to the busy scenes and cares of this life. The expression is not infrequent in the New Testament: Gal. ii. 19, "For I...am dead to the law;" Col. iii. 3, "For ye are dead, and your life is hid with Christ in God;" 1 Pet. ii. 24, "Who...bare our sins...that we, being dead to sin," &c. The apostle does not here attempt to prove that Christians are thus dead, nor to state in what way they become so. He assumes the fact without argument. All Christians are thus in fact dead to sin. They do not live *to* sin; nor has sin dominion over them. The expression used here by the apostle is common in all languages. We familiarly speak of a man's being dead to sensual pleasures, to ambition, &c., to denote that they have lost their influence over him. ¶ *Live any longer*

as [1] were baptized into Jesus Christ | were [c] baptized into his death?

1 or, *are.*

c 1 Co.15.29.

therein. How shall we, who have become sensible of the evil of sin, and who have renounced it by solemn profession, continue to practise it? It is therefore abhorrent to the very nature of the Christian profession. It is remarkable that the apostle did not attempt to argue the question on metaphysical principles. He did not attempt to show by abstruse argument that this consequence did not follow; but he appeals at once to Christian *feeling,* and shows that the supposition is abhorrent to that. To convince the great mass of men, such an appeal is far better than laboured metaphysical argumentation. All Christians can understand that; but few would comprehend an abstruse speculation. The best way to silence objections is, sometimes, to show that they violate the feelings of all Christians, and that therefore the objection must be wrong.

[Considerable difficulty exists in regard to the meaning of the expression "dead to sin." Certainly the most obvious interpretation is that given above in the Commentary, viz. that Christians are insensible to sin, as dead persons to the charms and pleasures of life. It has, however, been objected to this view, that it is inconsistent with fact, since Christians, so far from being insensible to sin, are represented in the next chapter as carrying on a perpetual struggle with it. The corrupt nature, though weakened, is not eradicated, and too frequently occasions such mournful falls as leave little doubt concerning its existence and power. Mr. Scott seems to have felt this difficulty, for, having explained the phrase of "separation from iniquity, as a dead man ceases from the actions of life," he immediately adds, "not only *ought* this to be the believer's character, but in a measure it actually is so." It is not probable, however, that the apostle meant by the strong expression under discussion, that believers were not *altogether* "dead to sin," but only *in a measure.*

Perhaps we shall arrive at a more satisfactory meaning of the words by looking at the analogous expression in the context, used in reference to Christ himself. He also, in the 10th verse, is said to have "died unto sin," and the believer, in virtue of union with Christ, is regarded as "dead *with* him," ver. 8; and, in consequence of this death with Christ,

is moreover freed, or rather justified ($\delta\epsilon\delta\iota$-$\kappa\alpha\iota\omega\tau\alpha\iota$), from sin, ver. 7. Now it cannot be said of Christ that he died unto sin, in the sense of *becoming* dead to its charms, for it was never otherwise with him. The believer, therefore, cannot be dead *with* Christ in this way; nor *on this ground,* can he be *justified* from sin, since justification proceeds upon something very different from our insensibility to sinful pleasures. What, then, is the meaning of the language when applied to Christ? Sin is here supposed to be possessed of certain power. That power or strength, the apostle elsewhere tells us, is derived from the law. "The strength of sin is the law," which demands satisfaction to its injured honour, and insists on the infliction of its penalty. Though, then, Jesus had no sin of his own, yet when he voluntarily stood in the room of sinners, sin, or its strength, viz. the law, had power over him, *until* he died, and thus paid the penalty. His death cancelled every obligation. Henceforth sin had no more power to exact anything at his hands.

Now Christians are *one* with Christ. When he died unto sin, they are regarded as having died unto it also, and are therefore, equally with their covenant head, justified from it. Sin, or its strength, the law, has from the moment of the saint's union with Christ, no more power to condemn him, than human laws have to condemn one over again who had *already* died to answer the demands of justice. "The law has dominion over a man so long only as he liveth." On the whole, then, the expression "dead to sin" is to be regarded as entirely parallel with that other expression in the seventh chapter, "dead to the law," that is, *completely* delivered from its authority as a covenant of works, and more especially from its power to condemn.

This view exercises a decided influence on the believer's sanctification. "How shall we that are dead to sin, live any longer therein?" The two things are incompatible. If, in virtue of union with Christ, we are dead with him, and freed from the penalty of sin, shall not the same union secure our deliverance from its dominion? "If we be dead *with* Christ, we believe that we shall also live *with* him." The whole argument, from the 1st to the 11th verse, proceeds upon the fact of the saint's union with Christ.]

3. *Know ye not.* This is a farther appeal to the Christian profession, and the principles involved in it, in answer to the objection. The simple argument in this verse and the two

4 Therefore we are *d* buried with him by baptism into death; that *e* like as Christ was raised

d Col.2.12; 1 Pe.3.21.   e ch.8.11; 2 Co.13.4.

following is, that by our very profession, made in baptism, we have renounced sin, and have pledged ourselves to live to God. ¶ *So many of us*, &c. All who were baptized; *i.e.* all professed Christians. As this renunciation of sin had been thus made by all who professed religion, so the objection could not have reference to Christianity in any manner. ¶ *Were baptized.* The act of baptism denotes dedication to the service of him in whose name we are baptized. One of its designs is to dedicate or consecrate us to the service of Christ. Thus (1 Cor. x. 2) the Israelites are said to have been "baptized unto Moses in the cloud and in the sea;" *i.e.* they became consecrated, or dedicated, or bound *to* him as their leader and lawgiver. In the place before us, the argument of the apostle is evidently drawn from the supposition that we have been solemnly consecrated by baptism to the service of Christ; and that to sin is therefore a violation of the very nature of our Christian profession. ¶ *Into* (εἰς). This is the word which is used in Mat. xxviii. 19, "Teach all nations, baptizing them *into* (εἰς) the name of the Father," &c. It means, being baptized *unto* his service; receiving him as the Saviour and guide, devoting all *unto* him and his cause. ¶ *Were baptized unto his death.* We were baptized with special reference to his death. Our baptism had a strong resemblance to his death. By that he became insensible to the things of the world; by baptism we in like manner become dead to sin. Farther, we are baptized with particular reference to the *design* of his death, the great leading feature and purpose of his work. That was, to expiate sin; to free men from its power; to make them pure. We have professed our devotion to the same cause; and have solemnly consecrated ourselves to the same design—to put a period to the dominion of iniquity.

up from the dead *f* by the glory of the Father, even so we also should *g* walk in newness of life.

f Mat.28.2,3.   g Ga.6.15; Ep.4.22-24; 1 Jn.2.6.

4. *Therefore we are buried*, &c. It is altogether probable that the apostle in this place had allusion to the custom of baptizing by immersion. This cannot, indeed, be *proved*, so as to be liable to no objection; but I presume that this is the idea which would strike the great mass of unprejudiced readers. But while this is admitted, it is also certain that his main scope and intention was not to describe the *mode* of baptism; nor to affirm that that mode was to be universal. The design was very different. It was to show *that by the solemn profession made at our baptism, we had become dead to sin, as Christ was dead to the living world around him when he was buried;* and that as he was raised up to life, so *we* should also rise to a new life. A similar expression occurs in Col. ii. 12, "Buried with him in baptism," &c. ¶ *Into death* (εἰς). Unto death; *i.e.* with a solemn purpose *to be dead* to sin and to the world. Grotius and Doddridge, however, understand this as referring to the death of Christ—in order to represent the death of Christ; or to bring us into a kind of fellowship with his death. ¶ *That like as.* In a similar manner. Christ rose from death in the sepulchre; and so we are bound by our vows at baptism to rise to a holy life. ¶ *By the glory of the Father.* Perhaps this means, amidst the glory, the majesty and wonders evinced by the Father when he raised him up, Mat. xxviii. 2, 3. Or possibly the word *glory* is here used to denote simply his *power*, as the resurrection was a signal and glorious display of his *omnipotence.* ¶ *Even so.* As he rose to new life, so should we. As he rose from *death*, so we, being made *dead* to sin and the world by that religion whose profession is expressed by baptism, should rise to a new life, a life of holiness. ¶ *Should walk.* Should live, or conduct. The word *walk* is often used to express the course of a man's life, or the tenor of his conduct; Note, chap.

5 For[h] if we have been planted together in the likeness of his death,

we shall be also *in the likeness* of *his* resurrection :

h Phi. 3. 10.

---

iv. 12; viii. 1; 1 Cor. v. 7; x. 3; Eph. ii. 10; iv. 1, &c. ¶ *In newness of life.* This is a Hebraism to denote *new life.* We should rise with Christ to a new life; and having been made dead to sin, as he was dead in the grave, so should we rise to a holy life, as he rose from the grave. The argument in this verse is, therefore, drawn from the nature of the Christian profession. By our very baptism, by our very profession, we have become dead to sin, as Christ became dead; and being devoted to him by that baptism, we are bound to rise, as he did, to a new life.

While it is admitted that the allusion here was probably to the custom of immersion in baptism, yet the passage cannot be adduced as an argument that that is the only mode, or that it is binding on all Christians in all places and ages, for the following reasons : (1) The scope or design of the apostle is not to discuss the mode of baptism, or to state any doctrine on the subject. It is an incidental allusion in the course of an argument, without stating or implying that this was the universal mode even then, still less that it was the only possible mode. His *main design* was to state the obligation of Christians to be holy, from the nature of their profession at baptism—an obligation just as impressive, and as forcible, from the application of water in any other mode as by immersion. It arises from the *fact* of baptism, not from the mode. It is just as true that they who are baptized by affusion, or by sprinkling, are baptized into his death; become professedly dead to sin and the world, and under obligations to live to God, as those who are immersed. It results from the *nature* of the ordinance, not from the *mode.* (2) If this was the mode commonly, it does not follow that it was the *only* mode, nor that it was to be universally observed. *There is no command that this should be the only mode.* And the simple fact that

it was usually practised in a warm climate, where ablutions were common, does not prove that it is to be observed amidst polar snows and ice, and in infancy, and age, and feebleness, and sickness; see Note on Acts viii. 38, 39. (3) If this is to be pressed *literally* as a matter of obligation, why should not also the following expression, "If we have been *planted together,*" &c., be pressed literally, and it be demanded that Christians should somehow be "planted" as well as "buried?" Such an interpretation only shows the absurdity of insisting on a *literal* interpretation of the Scriptures in cases of simple allusion, or where the main scope is illustration by figurative language.

5. *For if we have been planted together.* The word here used (σύμφυτος) does not elsewhere occur in the New Testament. It properly means sown or planted at the same time; that which sprouts or springs up together; and is applied to plants and trees that are planted at the same time, and that sprout and grow together. Thus the name would be given to a field of grain that was sown at the same time, and where the grain sprung up and grew *simultaneously.* Hence it means *intimately connected,* or *joined together.* And here it denotes that Christians and the Saviour have been united intimately in regard to death; as he died and was laid in the grave, so have they by profession died to sin. And it is therefore natural to expect that, like grain sown at the same time, they should grow up in a similar manner, and resemble each other. ¶ *We shall be also.* We shall be also *fellow-plants; i.e.* we shall resemble him in regard to the resurrection. As he rose from the grave, so shall we rise from sin. As he lived a *new life,* being raised up, so shall we *live* a new life. The propriety of this figure is drawn from the doctrine, often referred to in the New Testament, of a union between Christ and his people. See this

6 Knowing this, that our old man is crucified with *him*, [i] that the

[i] Col.2.11.

body of sin might be destroyed, that henceforth we should not serve sin.

---

explained in the Notes on John xv. 1–10. The sentiment here inferred is but an illustration of what was said by the Saviour (John xiv. 19), "Because I live, ye shall live also." There is perhaps not to be found a more beautiful illustration than that employed here by the apostle—of seed sown together in the earth, sprouting together, growing together, and ripening together for the harvest. Thus the Saviour and his people are united together in his death, start up to life together in his resurrection, and are preparing together for the same harvest of glory in the heavens. ¶ In the likeness *of* his *resurrection*. This does not mean that we shall resemble him when we are raised up at the last day—which may be, however, true—but that our rising from sin will resemble his resurrection from the grave. As he rose from the tomb and lived, so shall we rise from sin and live a new life.

6. *Knowing this.* We all knowing this. All Christians are supposed to know this. This is a new illustration drawn from the fact that by his crucifixion our corrupt nature has been crucified also, or put to death; and that thus we should be free from the servitude of sin. ¶ *Our old man.* This expression occurs also in Eph. iv. 22, "That ye put off . . . . the old man, which is corrupt according to the deceitful lusts;" Col. iii. 9, "Lie not to one another, seeing that ye have put off the old man with his deeds." From these passages it is evident that Paul uses the expression to denote our sinful and corrupt nature; the passions and evil propensities that exist before the heart is renewed. It refers to the love of sin, the indulgence of sinful propensities, in opposition to the new disposition which exists after the soul is converted, and which is called "the new man." ¶ *Is crucified.* Is put to death, as if on a cross. In this expression there is a *personification* of the corrupt propensities of our nature, represented as "our old man," our

native disposition, &c. The figure is here carried out, and this old man, this corrupt nature, is represented as having been put to death in an agonizing and torturing manner. The pains of crucifixion were perhaps the most torturing of any that the human frame could bear. Death in this manner was most lingering and distressing. And the apostle here, by the expression "is crucified," doubtless refers to the painful and protracted struggle which every one goes through when his evil propensities are subdued; when his corrupt nature is slain; and when, a converted sinner, he gives himself up to God. Sin *dies* within him, and he becomes *dead* to the world, and to sin; "for as by the cross death is most lingering and severe, so that corrupt nature is not subdued but by anguish" (Grotius). All who have been born again can enter into this description. They remember "the wormwood and the gall." They remember the anguish of conviction; the struggle of corrupt passion for the ascendency; the dying convulsions of sin in the heart; the long and lingering conflict before it was subdued, and the soul became submissive to God. Nothing will better express this than the lingering agony of crucifixion: and the argument of the apostle is, that as sin has produced *such* an effect, and as the Christian is now free from its embrace and its power, he will live to God. ¶ *With him.* The word "with" (συν) here is joined to the verb "is crucified" and means "is crucified *as* he was." ¶ *That the body of sin.* This expression doubtless means the same as that which he had just used, "our old man." But why the term *body* is used, has been a subject in which interpreters have not been agreed. Some say that it is a Hebraism, denoting mere *intensity* or *emphasis*. Some that it means the same as *flesh, i.e.,* denoting our sinful propensities and lusts. Grotius thinks that the term "body" is elegantly attributed to *sin,*

7 For[k] he that is dead is [2]freed from sin.

8 Now if we be dead with Christ,

    k 1 Pe.4.1.   [2] *justified.*

we believe that we shall also live with him :

9 Knowing that Christ, [l]being

    l Re.1.18.

---

because the body of man is made up of many members joined together *compactly,* and sin also consists of numerous vices and evil propensities joined compactly, as it were, in one *body.* But the expression is evidently merely another form of conveying the idea contained in the phrase "our old man" —a personification of sin as if it had a living form, and as if it had been put to death on a cross. It refers to the *moral* destruction of the power of sin in the heart by the gospel, and not to any *physical* change in the nature or faculties of the soul; comp. Col. ii. 11. ¶ *Might be destroyed.* Might be put to death; might become inoperative and powerless. Sin becomes *enervated, weakened,* and finally annihilated, by the work of the cross. ¶ *We should not serve.* Should not *be the slave* of sin (δουλεύειν). That we should not be subject to its control. The sense is, that before this we were *slaves* of sin (comp. ver. 17), but that now we are made free from this bondage, because the *moral death* of sin has freed us from it. ¶ *Sin.* Sin is here personified as a *master* that had dominion over us, but is now dead.

7. *For he that is dead.* This is evidently an expression having a proverbial aspect, designed to illustrate the sentiment just expressed. The rabbins had an expression similar to this, "When one is dead he is free from commands" (Grotius). So, says Paul, when a man dies he is exempt from the power and dominion of his master, of him who reigned over him. The Christian *had* been subject to sin before his conversion. But he has now become *dead* to it. And as, when a servant dies, he ceases to be subject to the control of his master, so the Christian being now dead to sin, on the same principle is released from the control of his former master, sin. The idea is connected with ver. 6, where it is said that we should not be the *slaves* of sin any more. The

reason of this is assigned here, where it is said that we are freed from it as a slave is freed when he dies. Of course, the apostle here is saying nothing of the *future world.* His whole argument has respect to the state of the Christian here; to his being freed from the bondage of sin. It is evident that he who is not freed from this bondage here, will not be in the future world. But the argument of the apostle has no bearing on that point. ¶ *Is freed.* Greek, *is justified.* The word here is used clearly in the sense of *setting at liberty,* or *destroying the power or dominion.* The word is often used in this sense; comp. Acts xiii. 38, 39 ; comp. a similar expression in 1 Pet. iv. 1, "He that hath suffered in the flesh hath ceased from sin." The design of the apostle is not to say that the Christian is *perfect,* but that sin has ceased to have *dominion* over him, as a master ceases to have power over a slave when he is dead. That dominion may be broken, so that the Christian may not be a *slave* to sin, and yet he may be conscious of many failings and of much imperfection; see chap. vii.

8-11. This passage is a confirmation and illustration of what the apostle had said before, ver. 5-7. The argument is, that as Christ was once dead but now lives to God, and will no more die, so we, being dead to sin, but living unto God, should not obey sin, but should live only to God.

8. *Now if we be dead with Christ.* If we be dead in a manner similar to what he was; if we are made dead to sin by his work, as he was dead in the grave; see Note, ver. 4. ¶ *We believe.* All Christians. It is *an article of our faith.* This does not refer to the future world so much as to the present. It becomes an article of our belief that we are to live with Christ. ¶ *That we shall also live with him.* This does not refer primarily to the resurrection, and to the future

raised from the dead, dieth no more; death hath no more dominion over him.

10 For in that he died, [m] he died unto sin once : but in that he liveth, he liveth unto God.

11 Likewise reckon ye also your-

m He.9.28.

state, but to the present. *We hold it as an article of our faith, that we shall be alive with Christ.* As he was raised up from death, so we shall be raised from the death of sin. As he *lives,* so we shall live in holiness. We *are* in fact raised up here, and, as it were, made *alive* to him. This is not *confined,* however, to the present life, but as Christ lives for ever, so the apostle goes on to show that *we* shall. 9. *Knowing.* As we all know. This is assumed as an undoubted article of belief. ¶ *Dieth no more.* Will never die again. He will have occasion to make no other atonement for sin; for that which he has made is sufficient for all. He is beyond the dominion of death, and will live for ever, Rev. i. 18, "I am he that liveth and was dead, and behold I am alive for evermore." This is not only a *consolation* to the Christian, but it is an *argument* why he should be holy. ¶ *No more dominion.* No rule; no lordship; no power. He is free from its influence; and the king of terrors cannot reach his throne; comp. Heb. ix. 25–28; x. 12. 10. *For in that he died.* For in respect to the design of his death. ¶ *He died unto sin.* His death had *respect to sin.* The design of his death was to destroy sin; to make an atonement for it, and thus to put it away. As his death was designed to effect this, so it follows that Christians, being baptized into his death, and having it as their object to destroy sin, should not indulge in it. The whole force of the motive, therefore, drawn from the death of Christ, is to induce Christians to forsake sin ; comp. 2 Cor. v. 15, " And that he died for all, that they which live should not henceforth live unto themselves, but unto him which died for them and rose again."

selves to be [n] dead indeed unto sin, but [o] alive unto God through Christ Jesus our Lord.

12 Let [p] not sin therefore reign in your mortal body, that ye should obey it in the lusts thereof.

n ver.2.   o Ga.2.19.   p Ps.19.13; 119.133.

¶ *Once* ($\dot{\epsilon}\phi\acute{a}\pi a\xi$). Once only; once for all. This is an adverb denying a repetition (Schleusner), and implies that it will not be done again; comp. Heb. vii. 27; ix. 12; x. 10. The argument of the apostle rests much on this, that his death was once for all; that it would not be repeated. ¶ *In that he liveth.* The object, the design of his living. He aims with his living power to promote the glory of God. ¶ *Unto God.* He seeks to promote his glory. The argument of Paul is this : Christians by their profession are united to him. They are bound to imitate him. As *he* now lives only to advance the glory of God ; as all his mighty power, now that he is raised from the dead, and elevated to his throne in heaven, is exerted to promote *his* glory ; so should *their* powers, being raised from the death of sin, be exerted to promote the glory of God. 11. *Likewise.* In like manner. This is an exhortation drawn from the argument in the previous verses. It shows the design and tendency of the Christian scheme. ¶ *Reckon ye yourselves.* Judge, or esteem yourselves. ¶ *To be dead indeed unto sin.* So that sin shall have no influence or control over you, any more than the objects of this world have over the dead in their graves; see Note, ver. 2. ¶ *But alive unto God.* Bound to live to promote his glory ; to make this the great and sole object of your living. ¶ *Through Jesus Christ.* By means of the death, and resurrection, and example of Jesus Christ. The apostle regards all our disposition to live to God as resulting from the work of the Lord Jesus Christ. 12. *Let not sin therefore.* This is a conclusion drawn from the previous train of reasoning. The result of all

13 Neither yield ye *q* your members *as* [3] instruments of unrighteousness unto sin : but *r* yield yourselves unto God, as those that are alive from the dead, and your mem-

bers *as* instruments of righteousness unto God.

14 For *s* sin shall not have dominion over you: for ye are not under the law, but under grace.

q Col.3.5.   [3] *arms;* or, *weapons.*   *r* ch.12.1.   *s* Mi.7.19.

---

these considerations is, that sin should *not* be suffered to reign in us. ¶ *Reign.* Have dominion; obtain the ascendency, or rule. ¶ *In your mortal body.* In you. The apostle uses the word "mortal" here, perhaps, for these reasons, (1) To remind them of the tendency of the flesh to sin and corruption, as equivalent to "fleshly," since the *flesh* is often used to denote evil passions and desires (comp. chap. vii. 5, 23; viii. 3, 6); and, (2) To remind them of their *weakness*, as the body was mortal, was soon to decay, and was therefore liable to be overcome by temptation. Perhaps, also, he had his eye on the *folly* of suffering the "*mortal* body" to overcome the immortal mind, and to bring it into subjection to sin and corruption. ¶ *That ye should obey it.* That sin should get such an ascendency as to rule entirely over you, and make you the slave. ¶ *In the lusts thereof.* In its *desires*, or propensities.

13. *Neither yield ye your members.* Do not give up, or devote, or employ your members, &c. The word *members* here refers to the *members of the body*—the hands, feet, tongue, &c. It is a specification of what, in ver. 12, is included under the general term "body;" see chap. vii. 5, 23; 1 Cor. vi. 15; xii. 12, 18, 20. ¶ *As instruments.* This word (ὅπλα) properly signifies *arms*, or implements of war; but it also denotes an instrument of any kind which we use for defence or aid. Here it means that we should not devote our members—our hands, tongue, &c., as if under the direction of sinful passions and corrupt desires, to accomplish purposes of iniquity. We should not make the members of our bodies the slaves of sin reigning within us. ¶ *Unto sin.* In the service of sin; to work iniquity. ¶ *But yield yourselves*, &c. Give or devote yourselves to God. ¶ *That are alive,*

ver. 11. ¶ *And your members,* &c. Christians should devote every member of the body to God and to his service. Their *tongue* should be consecrated to his praise, and to the office of truth, and kindness, and benevolence; their *hands* should be employed in useful labour for him and his cause; their *feet* should be swift in his service, and should not go in the paths of iniquity; their *eyes* should contemplate his works to excite thanksgiving and praise; their *ears* should not be employed to listen to words of deceit, or songs of dangerous and licentious tendency, or to persuasion that would lead astray, but should be open to catch the voice of God as he utters his will in the Book of truth, or as he speaks in the gale, the zephyr, the rolling thunder, the ocean, or in the great events of his providence. He speaks to us every day, and we should hear him; he spreads his glories before us, and we should survey them to praise him; he commands, and our hands, and heart, and feet should obey.

14. *For sin,* &c. The propensity or inclination to sin. ¶ *Shall not have dominion.* Shall not reign, chap. v. 12; vi. 6. This implies that sin *ought* not to have this dominion; and it also expresses the conviction of the apostle that it *would* not have this rule over Christians. ¶ *For we are not under law.* We who are Christians are not subject to that law where sin is excited, and where it rages unsubdued. But it may be asked here, What is meant by this declaration? Does it mean that Christians are absolved from all the obligations of the law? I answer, (1) The apostle does not affirm that Christians are not bound to *obey the moral law.* The whole scope of his reasoning shows that he maintains that they are. The whole structure of Chris-

15 What then? shall we sin, because we are not under the law, but under grace? God forbid.

16 Know ye not, that to whom *ye yield yourselves servants to obey, his servants ye are to whom

t Jn.8.34; 2 Pe.2.19.

tianity supposes the same thing; comp. Mat. v. 17–19. (2) The apostle means to say that Christians are not under the law as *legalists*, or as attempting to be justified by it. They seek a different plan of justification altogether; and they do not attempt to be justified by their own obedience. The Jews did; they do not. (3) It is *implied* here that the effect of an attempt to be justified *by the law* was, not to *subdue* sins, but to excite them, and to lead to indulgence in them. Justification by works would destroy no sin, would check no evil propensity, but would leave a man to all the ravages and riotings of unsubdued passion. If, therefore, the apostle had maintained that men were justified by *works*, he could not have consistently exhorted them to abandon their sins. He would have had no powerful motives by which to urge it; for the scheme would not lead to it. But he here says that the Christian was seeking justification on a plan which *contemplated* and which *accomplished* the destruction of sin; and he therefore infers that sin should not have dominion over them. ¶ *But under grace.* Under a scheme of mercy, the design and tendency of which is to subdue sin, and destroy it. In what way the system of grace removes and destroys sin, the apostle states in the following verses.

15. *What then? shall we sin,* &c. The apostle proceeds to notice an objection which might be suggested. "If Christians are not under the law, which *forbids* all sin, but are under grace, which *pardons* sin, will it not follow that they will feel themselves released from obligation to be holy? Will they not commit sin freely, since the system of grace is one which contemplates pardon, and which will lead them to believe that they may be forgiven to any extent?" This consequence has been drawn by many professing Christians; and it was well, therefore, for the apostle to guard

against it. ¶ *God forbid.* Note, chap. iii. 4.

16. *Know ye not,* &c. The objection noticed in ver. 15, the apostle answers by a reference to the known laws of servitude or slavery (ver. 16–20), and by showing that Christians, who had been the slaves of sin, have now become the servants of righteousness, and were therefore bound by the proper laws of servitude to obey their new master: as if he had said, "I assume that you know: you are acquainted with the laws of servitude; you know what is required in such cases." This would be known to all who had been either masters or slaves, or who had observed the usual laws and obligations of servitude. ¶ *To whom ye yield yourselves.* To whom ye give up yourselves for servitude or obedience. The apostle here refers to voluntary servitude; but where this existed, the power of the master over the time and services of the servant was absolute. The argument of the apostle is, that Christians had become the *voluntary servants* of God, and were therefore bound to obey him entirely. Servitude among the ancients, whether voluntary or involuntary, was rigid, and gave the master an absolute right over his slave, Luke xvii. 9; John viii. 34; xv. 15. ¶ *To obey.* To be obedient; or for the purpose of obeying his commands. ¶ *To whom ye obey.* To whom ye come under subjection. That is, you are bound to obey his requirements. ¶ *Whether of sin.* The general law of servitude the apostle now applies to the case before him. If men became the servants of sin, if they gave themselves to its indulgence, they would obey it, let the consequences be what they might. Even with death, and ruin, and condemnation before them, they would obey sin. They give indulgence to their evil passions and desires, and follow them as obedient servants, even if they lead them down to hell. Whatever be the consequences of sin,

ye obey; whether of sin unto death, or of obedience unto righteousness?

17 But God be thanked, that ye

---

were the servants of sin; but ye have obeyed from the heart that [u] form of doctrine [4] which was delivered you.

u 2 Ti.1.13.   4 whereto ye were delivered.

---

yet he who yields to it must abide by them, even if it leads him down to death and eternal woe. ¶ *Or of obedience*, &c. The same law exists in regard to holiness or obedience. The man who becomes the servant of holiness will feel himself bound by the law of servitude to obey, and to pursue it to its regular consequences. ¶ *Unto righteousness*. Unto justification; that is, unto eternal life. The expression stands contrasted with "death," and doubtless means that he who thus becomes the voluntary servant of holiness, will feel himself bound to obey it, unto complete and eternal justification and life; comp. ver. 21, 22. The argument is drawn from what the Christian would *feel* of the nature of obligation. He *would* obey him to whom he had devoted himself.

[This would seem to imply that justification is the effect of obedience. Δικαιοσυνη, however, does not signify justification, but righteousness, *i.e.* in this case, personal holiness. The sense is, that while the service of sin leads to death, that of obedience issues in holiness or righteousness. It is no objection to this view that it does not preserve the antithesis, since "justification" is not the opposite of "death," any more than holiness. "There is no need," says Mr. Haldane, "that there should be such an exact correspondence in the parts of the antithesis, as is supposed. And there is a most obvious reason why it could not be so. Death is the wages of sin, but life is not the wages of obedience."]

17. *But God be thanked.* The argument in this verse is drawn from a direct appeal to the feelings of the Roman Christians themselves. From *their experience* Paul was able to draw a demonstration to his purpose, and this was with him a ground of gratitude to God. ¶ *That ye were*, &c. The *sense* of this passage is plain. The *ground* of the thanksgiving was not that they had been the slaves of sin; but it is, that notwithstanding this, or although they had been thus, yet that they were now obedient. To give

thanks to God that men were sinners, would contradict the whole spirit of this argument, and of the Bible. But to give thanks that *although* men had been sinners, yet that now they had become obedient; that is, *that great sinners had become converted*, is in entire accordance with the spirit of the Bible, and with propriety. The word *although* or *whereas*, understood here, expresses the sense — "But thanks unto God, that *whereas* ye were the servants of sin," &c. Christians should thank God that they themselves, though once great sinners, have become converted; and when others who are great sinners are converted, they should praise him. ¶ *The servants of sin*. This is a strong expression implying that they had been in *bondage* to sin; that they had been completely its slaves. ¶ *From the heart*. Not in external form only; but as a cordial, sincere, and entire service. No other obedience is genuine. ¶ *That form of doctrine*. Greek, *type;* see Note, chap. v. 14. The form or type of doctrine means that shape or model of instruction which was communicated. It does not differ materially from *the doctrine itself*— "you have obeyed that doctrine," &c. You have yielded obedience to the instructions, the rules, the tenor of the Christian revelation. The word *doctrine* does not refer to an abstract dogma, but means *instruction, that which is taught*. And the meaning of the whole expression is simply, that they had yielded a cheerful and hearty obedience to that which had been communicated to them by the teachers of the Christian religion; comp. chap. i. 8. ¶ *Which was delivered you*. Marg., "whereto ye were delivered." This is a literal translation of the Greek; and the sense is simply, in which you have been instructed.

18. *Being then made free from sin.* That is, as a *master*. You are not

18 Being then ᵛmade free from sin, ye became the servants of righteousness.

19 I speak after the manner of men, because of the infirmity of your flesh: for as ye have yielded your members servants to unclean-

v Jn.8.32.

ness, and to iniquity unto iniquity; even so now yield your members servants to righteousness, unto holiness.

20 For when ye were the ʷser vants of sin, ye were free ⁵from righteousness.

w ver.16.   ⁵ *to.*

under its dominion; you are no longer its slaves. They were made free, as a servant is who is set at liberty, and who is, therefore, no longer under obligation to obey. ¶ *Ye became the servants,* &c. You became voluntarily under the dominion of righteousness; you yielded yourselves to it, and are therefore bound to be holy; comp. Note, John viii. 32.

19. *I speak after the manner of men.* I speak as men usually speak; or I draw an illustration from common life, in order to make myself better understood. ¶ *Because of the infirmity of your flesh.* The word *infirmity* means weakness, feebleness; and is opposed to vigour and strength. The word *flesh* is used often to denote the corrupt passions of men; but it may refer here to their intellect, or understanding; "because of your imperfection of spiritual knowledge; or incapacity to discern arguments and illustrations that would be more strictly *spiritual* in their character." This dimness or feebleness had been caused by long indulgence in sinful passions, and by the blinding influence which such passions have on the mind. The sense here is, "I use an illustration drawn from common affairs, from the well-known relations of master and slave, because you will better see the force of such an illustration with which you have been familiar, than you would one that would be more abstract, and more strictly spiritual." It is a kind of apology for drawing an illustration from the relation of master and slave. ¶ *For as ye have yielded.* Note, ver. 13. ¶ *Servants to uncleanness.* Have been in bondage to impurity. The word *uncleanness* here refers to impurity of life in any form; to the degraded passions that were common among the heathen; see chap. i.

¶ *And to iniquity.* Transgression of law. ¶ *Unto iniquity.* For the purpose of committing iniquity. It implies that they had done it in an excessive degree. It is well for Christians to be reminded of their former lives, to awaken repentance, to excite gratitude, to produce humility and a firmer purpose to live to the honour of God. This is the use which the apostle here makes of it. ¶ *Unto holiness.* In order to practise holiness. Let the surrender of your members to holiness be as sincere and as unqualified as the surrender was to sin. This is all that is required of Christians. Before conversion they were *wholly* given to sin; after conversion they should be *wholly* given to God. If all Christians would employ the same energies in advancing the kingdom of God that they have in promoting the kingdom of Satan, the church would rise with dignity and grandeur, and every continent and island would soon feel the movement. No requirement is more reasonable than this; and it should be a source of lamentation and mourning with Christians that it is not so; that they have employed so mighty energies in the cause of Satan, and do so little in the service of God. This argument for *energy* in the divine life, the apostle proceeds further to illustrate by comparing the *rewards* obtained in the two kinds of servitude, that of the world, and of God.

20. *Ye were free from righteousness.* That is, in your former state, you were not at all under the influence of righteousness. You were entirely devoted to sin—a strong expression of total depravity. It settles the question, and proves that they had no native goodness. The argument which is *implied* here rather than expressed

21 What[x] fruit had ye then in those things whereof ye are now ashamed? [y] for the end of those things is death.

22 But now being made free from sin, and become servants to

x ch.7.5.   y ch.1.32; Ja.1.15.

God, ye have your fruit unto holiness; and the end, everlasting life.

23 For [z] the wages of sin is death; but [a] the gift of God is [b] eternal life, through Jesus Christ our Lord.

z Ge.2.17.   a ch.5.17,21.   b 1 Pe.1.4.

is, that now they *ought* to be equally free from sin, since they had become released from their former bondage, and had become the servants of another master. 21. *What fruit, then,* &c. What reward, or what advantage. This is an argument drawn from the experience of Christians respecting the indulgence of sinful passions. The question discussed throughout this chapter is, whether the gospel plan of justification by faith leads to indulgence in sin? The argument here is drawn from the past experience which Christians have had in the ways of transgression. They have tried it; they know its effects; they have tasted its bitterness; they have reaped its fruits. It is *implied* here that, having once experienced these effects, and *knowing* the tendency of sin, they will not indulge in it now; comp. chap. vii. 5. ¶ *Whereof ye are now ashamed.* Having seen their nature and tendency, you are now ashamed of them; comp. chap. i.; Eph. v. 12, "For it is a shame to speak of those things which are done of them in secret;" 2 Cor. iv. 2; Jude 13; Phil. iii. 19. ¶ *For the end.* The tendency; the result. Those things lead to death. ¶ *Is death.* Note, ver. 22.

22. *But now.* Under the Christian plan of justification. ¶ *Being made free from sin.* Being delivered from its dominion, and from bondage; in the same manner as before conversion they were free from righteousness, ver. 20. ¶ *Ye have your fruit unto holiness.* The fruit or result is holiness. *This* service produces holiness, as the other did sin. It is *implied* here, though not expressly affirmed, that in this service which leads to holiness they received important benefits, as in the service of sin they had experienced many evils. ¶ *And the end.*

The final result—the ultimate consequence will be. *At present* this service produces holiness; hereafter it will terminate in everlasting life. By this consideration the apostle states the tendency of the plan of justification, and urges on them the duty of striving after holiness. ¶ *Everlasting life.* Note, John iii. 36. This stands in contrast with the word *death* in ver. 21, and shows its meaning. *One is just as long in duration as the other;* and if the one is limited, the other is. If those who *obey* shall be blessed with life for ever, those who disobey will be cursed with death for ever. Never was there an antithesis more manifest and more clear. And there could not be a stronger proof that the word *death* in ver. 21 refers, not to temporal death, but to eternal punishment. For what force would there be in the argument on the supposition that temporal death only is meant? The argument would stand thus: "The end of those sins is to produce *temporal death;* the end of holiness is to produce *eternal life!*" Will not temporal death be inflicted, it would be immediately asked, at any rate? Are Christians exempt from it? And do not men suffer this, whether they become Christians or not? How then could this be an argument bearing on the tenor of the apostle's reasoning? But admit the fair and obvious construction of the passage to be the true one, and it becomes plain. They were pursuing a course tending to everlasting ruin; they are now in a path that shall terminate in eternal life. By this weighty consideration, therefore, they are urged to be holy.

23. *For the wages of sin.* The word here translated *wages* (ὀχώνια) properly denotes what is purchased to be eaten with bread, as fish, flesh, vegetables, &c. (Schleusner); and thence it means

CHAPTER VII.

KNOW ye not, brethren, (for I speak to them that know the law,) how that the law hath dominion over a man as long as he liveth.

the pay of the Roman soldier, because formerly it was the custom to pay the soldier in these things. It means hence that which a man earns or deserves; that which is his proper pay, or what he merits. As applied to sin, it means that death is what sin deserves; that which will be its proper reward. Death is thus called the wages of sin, not because it is an arbitrary, undeserved appointment, but (1) Because it is its proper *desert*. Not a pain will be inflicted on the sinner which he does not deserve. Not a sinner will die who ought not to do. *Sinners even in hell will be treated just as they deserve to be treated;* and there is not to man a more fearful and terrible consideration than this. No man can conceive a more dreadful doom than for himself to be treated for ever just as he deserves to be. But, (2) This is the wages of sin, because, like the pay of the soldier, it is just what was threatened, Ezek. xviii. 4, "The soul that sinneth, it shall die." God will not inflict anything more than was threatened, and therefore it is just. ¶ Is *death.* This stands opposed here to eternal life, and proves that one is just as enduring as the other. ¶ *But the gift of God.* Not the wages of man; not that which is due to him; but the mere gift and mercy of God. The apostle is careful to distinguish, and to specify that this is not what man deserves, but that which is gratuitously conferred on him; Note, ver. 15. ¶ *Eternal life.* The same words which in ver. 22 are rendered "everlasting life." The phrase is opposed to death; and proves incontestably that that means eternal death. We may remark, therefore, (1) That the one will be as long as the other. (2) As there is no doubt about the duration of *life,* so there can be none about the duration of death. The one will be rich, blessed, everlasting; the other sad, gloomy, lingering, awful, eternal. (3) If the sinner is lost, he will deserve to die. He will have his

reward. He will suffer only what shall be the *just due* of sin. He will not be a *martyr* in the cause of injured innocence. He will not have the compassion of the universe in his favour. He will have no one to take his part against God. He will suffer just as much, and just as long, as he *ought* to suffer. He will suffer as the culprit pines in the dungeon, or as the murderer dies on the gibbet, because this is *the proper reward of sin.* (4) They who are saved will be raised to heaven, not because they merit it, but by the rich and sovereign grace of God. All their salvation will be ascribed to him; and they will celebrate his mercy and grace for ever. (5) It becomes us, therefore, to flee from the wrath to come. No man is so foolish and so wicked as he who is willing to reap the proper wages of sin. None so blessed as he who has part in the mercy of God, and who lays hold on eternal life.

CHAPTER VII.

Few chapters in the Bible have been the subject of more decidedly different interpretations than this. And after all that has been written on it by the learned, it is still made a matter of discussion, whether the apostle has reference in the main scope of the chapter to his own experience *before* he became a Christian; or to the conflicts in the mind of a man who is renewed. Which of these opinions is the correct one I shall endeavour to state in the Notes on the particular verses in the chapter. The main design of the chapter is not very difficult to understand. It is, evidently, to show the insufficiency of the law to produce peace of mind to a troubled sinner. In the previous chapters he had shown that it was incapable of producing *justification*, chap. i.–iii. He had shown the way in which men were justified by faith, chap. iii. 21–31; iv. He had shown how that plan produced peace, and met the

2 For[a] the woman which hath an husband is bound by the law to

a 1 Co.7.39.

evils introduced by the fall of Adam, chap. v. He had shown that Christians were freed from the law as a matter of obligation, and yet that this freedom did not lead to a licentious life, chap. vi. And he now proceeds *still further* to illustrate the tendency of the law on a man both in a state of nature and of grace; to show that *its uniform effect* in the present condition of man, whether impenitent and under conviction, or in a state of grace under the gospel, so far from promoting peace, as the Jew maintained, was to excite the mind to conflict, and anxiety, and distress. Nearly all the peculiar opinions of the Jews the apostle had overthrown in the previous argument. He here gives the finishing stroke, and shows that the tendency of the law, as a practical matter, was everywhere the same. It was not *in fact* to produce peace, but agitation, conflict, distress. Yet this was not the fault of the *law*, which was in itself good, but of sin, ver. 7–24. I regard this chapter as not referring *exclusively* to Paul in a state of nature, or of grace. The discussion is conducted without particular reference to that point. It is rather designed to group together the actions of a man's life, whether in a state of conviction for sin, or in a state of grace, and to show that the effect of the law is everywhere the same. *It equally fails everywhere in producing peace and sanctification.* The argument of the Jew respecting the efficacy of the law, and its sufficiency for the condition of man, is thus overthrown by a succession of proofs relating to justification, to pardon, to peace, to the evils of sin, and to the agitated and conflicting moral elements in man's bosom. The effect is everywhere the same. The deficiency is apparent in regard to ALL the great interests of man. And having shown this, the apostle and the reader are prepared for the language of triumph and gratitude, that deliverance from all these evils is to be traced

her husband, so long as he liveth; but if the husband be dead, she

to the gospel of Jesus Christ the Lord, chap. vii. 25; viii.

1. *Know ye not.* This is an appeal to their own observation respecting the relation between husband and wife. The illustration (ver. 2, 3) is designed simply to show that as when a man dies, and the connection between him and his wife is dissolved, his law ceases to be binding on her, so also a separation has taken place between Christians and the law, in which *they* have become dead *to it*, and they are not now to attempt to draw their life and peace from it, but from that *new* source with which they are connected by the gospel, ver. 4. ¶ *For I speak to them*, &c. Probably the apostle refers here more particularly to the Jewish members of the Roman church, who were qualified particularly to understand the nature of the law, and to appreciate the argument. That there were many Jews in the church at Rome has been shown (see Introduction); but the illustration has no exclusive reference to them. The law to which he appeals is sufficiently general to make the illustration intelligible to all men. ¶ *That the law.* The immediate reference here is probably to the Mosaic law. But what is here affirmed is equally true of all laws. ¶ *Hath dominion.* Greek, rules; exercises lordship. The law is here personified, and represented as setting up a lordship over a man, and exacting obedience. ¶ *Over a man.* Over the man who is under it. ¶ *As long as he liveth.* The Greek here may mean either "as HE liveth," or "as IT liveth," *i.e.* the law. But our translation has evidently expressed the sense. The sense is, that death releases a man from the laws by which he was bound in life. It is a general principle, relating to the laws of the land, the law of a parent, the law of a contract, &c. This general principle the apostle proceeds to apply in regard to the law of God.

2. *For the woman.* This verse is a *specific* illustration of the general principle in ver. 1, that death dissolves

is loosed from the law of *her* husband.

3 So then, if, *b* while *her* husband liveth, she be married to another man, she shall be called an adulteress: but if her husband be dead, she is free from that

b Mat.5.32.

law; so that she is no adulteress, though she be married to another man.

4 Wherefore, my brethren, ye also are become *c* dead to the law by the body of Christ; that ye should be married to another, *even*

c Ga.5.18.

those connections and relations which make law binding in life. It is a simple illustration; and if this had been kept in mind, it would have saved much of the perplexity which has been felt by many commentators, and much of their wild vagaries in endeavouring to show that "men are the wife, the law the former husband, and Christ the new one;" or that "the old man is the wife, sinful desires the husband, sins the children" (Beza). (See Stuart.) Such expositions are sufficient to humble us, and to make us mourn over the puerile and fanciful interpretations which even wise and good men often give to the Bible. ¶ *Is bound by the law,* &c. See the same sentiment in 1 Cor. vii. 39. ¶ *To her husband.* She is united to him, and is under his authority as the head of the household. To *him* is particularly committed the headship of the family, and the wife is subject to his law, in the Lord, Eph. v. 23, 33. ¶ *She is loosed,* &c. The husband has no more authority. The connection from which obligation resulted is dissolved. 3. *So then if,* &c. Comp. Mat. v. 32. ¶ *She shall be called.* She will be. The word used here (χρηματίσει) is often used to denote being called by an oracle or by divine revelation. But it is here employed in the simple sense of being commonly called, or of being so regarded. 4. *Wherefore.* This verse contains an application of the illustration in the two preceding. The idea there is, that *death dissolves a connection from which obligation resulted.* This is the single point of the illustration, and consequently there is no need of inquiring whether by the wife the apostle meant to denote the old man, or the Christian, &c. The meaning

is, as death dissolves the connection between a wife and her husband, and of course the obligation of the law resulting from that connection, so the death of the Christian to the law dissolves *that* connection, so far as the scope of the argument here is concerned, and prepares the way for another union, a union with Christ, from which a new and more efficient obligation results. The design is to show that the *new* connection would accomplish more important effects than the old. ¶ *Ye also are become dead to the law.* Notes, chap. vi. 3, 4, 8. The connection between us and the law is dissolved, so far as the scope of the apostle's argument is concerned. He does not say that we are dead to it, or released from it as a rule of duty, or as a matter of obligation to obey it, for there neither is, nor can be, any such release; but we are dead to it as a way of justification and sanctification. In the great matter of acceptance with God, we have ceased to rely on the law, having become dead to it, and having embraced another plan. ¶ *By the body of Christ.* That is, by his body crucified; or in other words, by his death; comp. Eph. ii. 15, "Having abolished *in his flesh* the enmity," &c., *i.e.* by his death; Col. i. 22, "In the body of his flesh through death," &c.; ii. 14; 1 Pet. ii. 24, "Who bare our sins in his own body on the tree." The sense is, therefore, that by the death of Christ as an atoning sacrifice, by his suffering for us that which would be sufficient to meet the demands of the law, by his taking our place, he has released us from the law as a way of justification, freed us from its penalty, and saved us from its curse. Thus released, we are at liberty to be united to the law of him who has thus bought

to him who is raised from the dead, that we should *a*bring forth fruit unto God.

5 For when we were *e*in the flesh, the [1]motions of sins, which

d Ga.5.22. 　　 *e* ch.8.8,9. 　　 1 *passions.*

were by the law, did work in our members, *f*to bring forth fruit unto death.

6 But now we are delivered from the law, [2]that being dead

f ch.6.21. 　　 2 *or, being dead to that.*

us with his blood. ¶ *That ye should be married to another.* That you might be united to another, and come under his law. This is the completion of the illustration in ver. 2, 3. As the woman that is freed from the law of her husband by his death, when married again comes under the authority of another, so we who are made free from the law and its curse by the death of Christ, are brought under the new law of fidelity and obedience to him with whom we are thus united. The union of Christ and his people is not unfrequently illustrated by the most tender of all earthly connections, that of a husband and wife, Eph. v. 23–30; Rev. xxi. 9, "I will show thee the bride, the Lamb's wife;" xix. 7. ¶ *Even to him who is raised,* &c. See the force of this explained, chap. vi. 8. ¶ *That we should bring forth fruit unto God.* That we should live a holy life. This is the point and scope of all this illustration. The new connection is such as will make us holy. It is also implied that the tendency of the law was only to bring forth fruit unto death (ver. 5), and that the tendency of the gospel is to make man holy and pure; comp. Gal. v. 22, 23.

5. *For when,* &c. The illustration in this verse and the following is designed to show more at length the effect of the law, whenever and wherever applied, whether in a state of nature or of grace. It was *always* the same. It was the occasion of agitation and conflict in a man's own mind. This was true when a sinner was under conviction; and it was true when a man was a Christian. In all circumstances where the law was applied to the corrupt mind of man, it produced this agitation and conflict. Even in the Christian's mind it produced this agitation (ver. 14–24), as it had done and would do in the mind

VOL. IV.

of a sinner under conviction (ver. 7–12), and consequently there was *no* hope of release but in the delivering and sanctifying power of the gospel, ver. 25; chap. viii. 1–3. ¶ *In the flesh.* Unconverted; subject to the controlling passions and propensities of a corrupt nature; comp. chap. viii. 8, 9. The connection shows that this must be the meaning here, and the design of this illustration is to show the effect of the law *before* a man is converted (ver. 5 – 12). This is the obvious meaning, and all the laws of interpretation require us so to understand it. ¶ *The motions of sins* (τὰ παθήματα). This translation is unhappy. The expression "motions of sins" conveys no idea. The original means simply *the passions, the evil affections, the corrupt desires;* see the margin. The expression *passions of sins,* is a Hebraism meaning *sinful passions,* and refers here to the corrupt propensities and inclinations of the unrenewed heart. ¶ *Which were by the law.* Not that they were originated or created by the law; for a law does not *originate* evil propensities, and a holy law would not cause sinful passions; but they were *excited,* called up, inflamed by the law, which forbids their indulgence. ¶ *Did work in our members.* In our body; that is, in us. Those sinful propensities made use of our members as instruments, to secure gratification; Note, chap. vi. 12, 13; comp. ver. 23. ¶ *To bring forth fruit unto death.* To produce crime, agitation, conflict, distress, and to lead to death. We were brought under the dominion of death; and the consequence of the indulgence of those passions would be fatal; comp. Note, chap. vi. 21.

6. *But now.* Under the gospel. This verse states the consequences of the gospel, in distinction from the effects of the law. The way in which

wherein we were held; that we should serve in newness of spirit, and not *in* the oldness of the letter.

this is accomplished the apostle illustrates more at length in chap. viii., with which this verse is properly connected. The remainder of chap. vii. is occupied in illustrating the statement in ver. 5, of the effects of *the law;* and after having shown that its effects *always* were to increase crime and distress, he is prepared in chap. viii. to take up the proposition in this verse, and to show the superiority of the gospel in producing peace. ¶ *We are delivered.* We who are Christians. Delivered from it as a means of justification, as a source of sanctification, as a bondage to which we were subjected, and which tended to produce pain and death. It does not mean that Christians are freed from it as a rule of duty.

[Believers "are delivered from the law" as a covenant of works. In the language of the Confession they are "not under it to be thereby justified or condemned." This seems to be the *whole* import of the apostle's language. To say that Christians are delivered from the law "as a source of sanctification" is to affirm that *once* they were under it in this sense, otherwise there could be no deliverance in the case. But when or to whom was the law ever proposed as the source of sanctification? The *rule* of sanctification it always has been, the *source* never. This explanation is similar to that of Prof. Stuart, who renders, "no longer placing our reliance on it as a means of subduing and sanctifying our sinful natures;" on which Mr. Haldane justly remarks, that "to cease to rely on the law for such a purpose was not in any sense to be delivered from it. The law never proposed such a thing, and therefore to cease to look for such an effect is not a deliverance from the law."]

¶ *That being dead.* Margin, "being dead to that." There is a variation here in the MSS. Some read it, as in the text, as if the *law* was dead; others, as in the margin, as if we were dead. The majority is in favour of the reading as in the margin; and the connection requires us to understand it in this sense. So the Syriac, the Arabic, the Vulgate, Æthiopic. The sentiment here, that we are dead to the law, is that which

is expressed in ver. 4. ¶ *Wherein we were held.* That is, as captives, or as slaves. We were held in bondage to it, ver. 1. ¶ *That we should serve.* That we may now serve or obey *God.* ¶ *In newness of spirit.* In a new spirit; or in a new and spiritual manner. This is a form of expression implying, (1) That their service under the gospel was to be of a *new* kind, differing from that under the former dispensation. (2) That it was to be of a *spiritual* nature, as distinguished from that practised by the Jews; comp. 2 Cor. iii. 6; Note, Rom. ii. 28, 29. The worship required under the gospel is uniformly described as that of the spirit and the heart, rather than that of form and ceremony, John iv. 23, "The true worshippers shall worship the Father in spirit and in truth;" Phil. iii. 3. ¶ *And not in the oldness of the letter.* Not in the old letter. It is implied here in this, (1) That the form of worship here described pertained to an *old* dispensation that had now passed away; and, (2) That that was a worship that was in the *letter.* To understand this, it is necessary to remember that the *law* which prescribed the forms of worship among the Jews, was regarded by the apostle as destitute of that efficacy and power in renewing the heart which he attributed to the gospel. It was a service consisting in external forms and ceremonies: in the offering of sacrifices and of incense, according to the literal requirements of the law, rather than the sincere offering of the heart, 2 Cor. iii. 6, "The letter killeth; the spirit giveth life;" John vi. 63; Heb. x. 1-4; ix. 9, 10. It is not to be denied that there were many holy persons under the law. and that there were many spiritual offerings presented, but it is at the same time true that the great mass of the people rested in the mere form; and that the service offered was the mere service of the letter, and not of the heart. The main idea is, that the services under the gospel are purely

7 What shall we say then? *Is* the law sin? God forbid. Nay, I had not *g* known sin, but by the

g ch.3.20.

and entirely spiritual, the offering of the *heart*, and not the service rendered by external forms and rites.

[But the contrast here is not between services required under the legal and gospel dispensations respectively, but between services yielded in the opposite states of nature and grace. In the former state we are "under the law" though we live in gospel times, and in the latter we are "delivered from the law" as a covenant of works or of life, just as pious Jews might be though they lived under the dispensation of Moses. The design of God in delivering us from the law is that we might "serve him in newness of spirit, and not in the oldness of the letter," *i.e.* in such a spiritual way as the new state requires, and from such spiritual motives and aids as it furnishes, and not in the manner we were wont to do under our old condition of subjection to the law, in which we could yield only an external and forced obedience. "It is evident," says Prof. Hodge, "that the clause 'in the oldness of the letter' is substituted by the apostle for 'under the law' and 'in the flesh,' all which he uses to describe the legal and corrupt condition of men prior to the believing reception of the gospel."]

7. *What shall we say then?* The objection which is here urged is one that would very naturally rise, and which we may suppose would be urged with no slight indignation. The Jew would ask, "Are we then to suppose that the holy law of God is not only insufficient to sanctify us, but that it is the mere occasion of increased sin? Is its tendency to produce sinful passions, and to make men worse than they were before?" To this objection the apostle replies with great wisdom, by showing that the evil was not in *the law*, but *in man;* that though these effects often followed, yet that the law itself was good and pure. ¶ *Is the law sin?* Is it sinful? Is it evil? For if, as it is said in ver. 5, the sinful passions were "*by* the law," it might naturally be asked whether the law itself was not an evil thing? ¶ *God forbid.* Note, chap. iii. 4. ¶ *Nay, I had not known sin.* The word translated *nay* (ἀλλὰ) means more properly *but;* and this

law: for I had not known [3]lust, except the law had said, *h* Thou shalt not covet.

[3] or. *concupiscence.*   *h* Ex.20.17.

would have more correctly expressed the sense, "I deny that the law is sin. My doctrine does not lead to that; nor do I affirm that it is evil. I strongly repel the charge; BUT, notwithstanding this, I still maintain that it *had* an effect in exciting sins, yet so as that *I* perceived that the law itself was good," ver. 8–12. At the same time, therefore, that the law must be admitted to be the occasion of exciting sinful feelings, by crossing the inclinations of the mind, yet the fault was not to be traced to the law. The apostle in these verses refers, doubtless, to the state of his mind *before* he found that peace which the gospel furnishes by the pardon of sins. ¶ *But by the law.* Chap. iii. 20. By the *law* here, the apostle has evidently in his eye *every* law of God, however made known. He means to say that the effect which he describes attends *all* law, and this effect he illustrates by a single instance drawn from the tenth commandment. When he says that he should not have known sin, he evidently means to affirm, that he had not understood that certain things were sinful, unless they had been forbidden; and having stated this, he proceeds to *another* thing, to show the *effect* of their being thus forbidden on his mind. He was not merely acquainted abstractly with the nature and existence of sin, with what constituted crime because it was forbidden, but he was conscious of a certain effect on his mind resulting from this knowledge, and from the effect of strong, raging desires when thus restrained, ver. 8, 9. ¶ *For I had not known lust.* I should not have been acquainted with the nature of the sin of *covetousness.* The desire might have existed, but he would not have known it to be sinful, and he would not have experienced that raging, impetuous, and ungoverned propensity which he did when he found it to be forbidden. Man without law might have the strong feelings of desire,

8 But sin, taking occasion by the commandment, wrought in me

He might covet that which others possessed. He might take property, or be disobedient to parents; but he would not *know* it to be evil. The *law* fixes bounds to his desires, and teaches him what is right and what is wrong. It teaches him where lawful indulgence ends, and where sin begins. The word "lust" here is not limited as it is with us. It refers to *all* covetous desires; to all wishes for that which is forbidden us. ¶ *Except the law had said.* In the tenth commandment, Exod. xx. 17. ¶ *Thou shalt not covet.* This is the beginning of the command, and all the rest is implied. The apostle knew that it would be understood without repeating the whole. This particular commandment he selected because it was more pertinent than the others to his purpose. The others referred particularly to external actions. But his object was to show the effect of sin on the mind and conscience. He therefore chose one that referred particularly to the desires of the heart.

8. *But sin.* To illustrate the *effect* of the law on the mind, the apostle in this verse depicts its influence in exciting to evil desires and purposes. Perhaps nowhere has he evinced more consummate knowledge of the human heart than here. He brings an illustration that might have escaped most persons, but which goes directly to establish his position, that the law is insufficient to promote the salvation of man. *Sin* here is personified. It means not a real *entity;* not a physical subsistence; not something independent of the mind, having a separate existence, and lodged *in* the soul; but it means the corrupt passions, inclinations, and desires *of the mind itself.* Thus we say that lust burns, and ambition rages, and envy corrodes the mind, without meaning that lust, ambition, or envy are any independent physical subsistences, but meaning that the *mind* that is ambitious, or envious, is thus excited. ¶ *Taking occasion.* The word *occasion* (ἀφορμὴν)

all manner of concupiscence. For without the law, sin *was* dead.

properly denotes any material, or preparation for accomplishing anything; then any opportunity, occasion, &c., of doing it. Here it means that *the law* was the exciting cause of sin; or was that which called the sinful principle of the heart into exercise. *But for this,* the effect here described would not have existed. Thus we say that a tempting object of desire presented is the exciting cause of covetousness. Thus an object of ambition is the exciting cause of the principle of ambition. Thus the presentation of wealth, or of advantages possessed by others which we have not, may excite covetousness or envy. Thus the fruit presented to Eve was the exciting cause of sin; the wedge of gold to Achan excited his covetousness. Had not these objects been presented, the evil principles of the heart might have slumbered, and never have been called forth. And hence no men understand the full force of their native propensities until some object is presented that calls them forth into decided action. The *occasion* which called these forth in the mind of Paul was the law *crossing his path,* and irritating and exciting the native strong inclinations of the mind. ¶ *By the commandment.* By all law appointed to restrain and control the mind. ¶ *Wrought in me.* Produced or worked in me. The word used here means often to operate in a powerful and efficacious manner (Doddridge). ¶ *All manner of.* Greek, "all desire." Every species of unlawful desire. It was not confined to one single desire, but extended to everything which the law declared to be wrong. ¶ *Concupiscence.* Unlawful or irregular desire. Inclination for unlawful enjoyments. The word is the same which in ver. 7 is rendered lust. If it be asked in what way the law led to this, we may reply, that the main idea here is, that opposition by law to the desires and passions of wicked men only tends to inflame and exasperate them. This is the case with regard to sin in every form. An attempt to restrain it by

9 For I was alive without the law once: but when the com-

mandment came, sin revived, and I died.

force; to denounce it by laws and penalties; to cross the path of wickedness; only tends to irritate, and to excite into living energy, that which otherwise would be dormant in the bosom. This it does, because, (1) It crosses the path of the sinner, and opposes his intention, and the current of his feelings and his life. (2) The law acts the part of a *detector*, and lays open to view that which was in the bosom, but was concealed. (3) Such is the depth and obstinacy of sin in man, that the very *attempt* to restrain often only serves to exasperate, and to urge to greater deeds of wickedness. Restraint by law rouses the mad passions; urges to greater deeds of depravity; makes the sinner stubborn, obstinate, and more desperate. The very attempt to set up authority over him throws him into a posture of resistance, and makes him a party, and excites all the feelings of party rage. Anyone may have witnessed this effect often on the mind of a wicked and obstinate child. (4) This is particularly true in regard to a sinner. He is calm often, and apparently tranquil. But let the law of God be brought home to his conscience, and he becomes maddened and enraged. He spurns its authority, yet his conscience tells him it is right; he attempts to throw it off, yet trembles at its power; and to show his independence, or his purpose to sin, he plunges into iniquity, and becomes a more dreadful and obstinate sinner. It becomes a struggle for victory; and in the controversy with God he resolves *not* to be overcome. It accordingly happens that many a man is more profane, blasphemous, and desperate when under conviction for sin than at other times. In revivals of religion it often happens that men evince violence, and rage, and cursing, which they do not in a state of spiritual death in the church; and it is often a very certain indication that a man is under conviction for sin when he becomes particularly violent, and abusive, and outrageous in his opposition to

God. (5) The effect here noticed by the apostle is one that has been observed at all times, and by all classes of writers. Thus Cato says (Livy, xxxiv. 4), "Do not think, Romans, that it will be hereafter as it was before the law was enacted. It is more safe that a bad man should not be accused, than that he should be absolved; and luxury not excited would be more tolerable than it will be now, by the very chains irritated and excited as a wild beast." Thus Seneca says (*de Clementia*, i. 23), "Parricides began with the law." Thus Horace (*Odes*, i. 3), "The human race, bold to endure all things, rushes through forbidden crime." Thus Ovid (*Amor*. iii. 4), "We always endeavour to obtain that which is forbidden, and desire that which is denied." (These passages are quoted from Tholuck.) See also Prov. ix. 17, "Stolen waters are sweet, and bread eaten in secret is pleasant." If such be the effect of the law, then the inference of the apostle is unavoidable, that it is not adapted to save and sanctify man. ¶ *For without the law.* Before it was given; or where it was not applied to the mind. ¶ *Sin* was *dead.* It was inoperative, inactive, unexcited. This is evidently in a comparative sense. The connection requires us to understand it only so far as it was excited by the law. Men's passions would exist; but without law they would not be known to be evil, and they would not be excited into wild and tumultuous raging.

9. *For I.* There seems to be no doubt that the apostle here refers to his own past experience. Yet in this he speaks the sentiment of all who are unconverted, and who are depending on their own righteousness. ¶ *Was alive.* This is opposed to what he immediately adds respecting *another* state, in which he was when he *died.* It must mean, therefore, that he had a certain kind of peace; he deemed himself secure; he was free from the convictions of conscience and the agitations of alarm. The state to which

10 And the commandment, which
i Eze.20.11,&c.

was ⁱordained to life, I found *to be* unto death.

he refers here must be doubtless that to which he himself elsewhere alludes, when he deemed himself to be righteous, depending on his own works, and esteeming himself to be blameless, Phil. iii. 4–6; Acts xxiii. 1; xxvi. 4, 5. It means that he was then free from those agitations and alarms which he afterwards experienced when he was brought under conviction for sin. At that time, though he had the law, and was attempting to obey it, yet he was unacquainted with its spiritual and holy nature. He aimed at *external* conformity. Its claims on the heart were unfelt. This is the condition of every self-confident sinner, and of every one who is unawakened. ¶ *Without the law.* Not that Paul was ever really without the law, that is, without the law of Moses; but he means before the law was applied to his heart in its spiritual meaning, and with power. ¶ *But when the commandment came.* When it was applied to the heart and conscience. This is the only intelligible sense of the expression; for it *cannot* refer to the time when the law was given. *When* this was, the apostle does not say. But the expression denotes *whenever* it was so applied; when it was urged with power and efficacy on his conscience, to control, restrain, and threaten him, it produced this effect. We are unacquainted with the early operations of his mind, and with his struggles against conscience and duty. We know enough of him before conversion, however, to be assured that he was proud, impetuous, and unwilling to be restrained; see Acts viii. ix. In the state of his self-confident righteousness and impetuosity of feeling, we may easily suppose that the holy law of God, which is designed to restrain the passions, to humble the heart, and to rebuke pride, would produce only irritation, and impatience of restraint, and revolt. ¶ *Sin revived.* Lived again. This means that it was before dormant (ver. 8), but was now quickened into new life. The word is usually applied to a renewal of life

(Rom. xiv. 19; Luke xv. 24, 32), but here it means substantially the same as the expression in ver. 8, "Sin . . . wrought in me all manner of concupiscence." The power of sin, which was before dormant, became quickened and active. ¶ *I died.* That is, I was by it involved in additional guilt and misery. It stands opposed to "I was alive," and must mean the opposite of that; and evidently denotes that the effect of the commandment was to bring him under what he calls *death* (comp. chap. v. 12, 14, 15); that is, sin reigned, and raged, and produced its withering and condemning effects; it led to aggravated guilt and misery. It may also include this idea,—that before, he was self-confident and secure, but that by the commandment he was stricken down and humbled, his self-confidence was blasted, and his hopes were prostrated in the dust. Perhaps no words would better express the humble, subdued, melancholy, and helpless state of a converted sinner than the expressive phrase "*I died.*" The essential idea here is, that the law did not answer the purpose which the Jew would claim for it, to sanctify the soul and to give comfort, but that *all* its influence on the heart was to produce aggravated, unpardoned guilt and woe.

10. *And the commandment.* The law to which he had referred before. ¶ *Which* was ordained *to life.* Which was intended to produce life, or happiness. *Life* here stands opposed to *death,* and means felicity, peace, eternal bliss; Note. John iii. 36. When the apostle says that it was ordained to life, he probably has reference to the numerous passages in the Old Testament which speak of the law in this manner, Lev. xviii. 5, "Ye shall keep my statutes and my judgments; which if a man do, he shall live in them;" Ezek. xx. 11, 13, 21; xviii. 9, 21. The meaning of these passages, in connection with this declaration of Paul, may be thus expressed: (1) The law is good; it has no evil, and is itself fitted to produce no evil. (2)

11 For sin, taking occasion by the commandment, deceived me, and by it slew *me*.

12 Wherefore *k* the law *is* holy;

k Ps.19.7-9.

and the commandment holy, and just, and good.

13 Was then that which is good made death unto me? God forbid.

If man was pure, and it was obeyed perfectly, it would produce life and happiness only. On those who have obeyed it in heaven. it has produced only happiness. (3) For this it was ordained; it is adapted to it; and when perfectly obeyed, it produces no other effect. But, (4) Man is a sinner; he has *not* obeyed it; and in such a case the law threatens woe. It crosses the inclination of man, and instead of producing peace and life, as it would on a being perfectly holy, it produces only woe and crime. The law of a parent may be good, and may be appointed to promote the happiness of his children ; it may be admirably fitted to it if all were obedient; yet *in* the family there may be one obstinate, self-willed, and stubborn child, resolved to indulge his evil passions, and the results to him would be woe and despair. The commandment, which was ordained for the good of the family, and which would be adapted to promote their welfare, *he* alone, of all the number, would find to be unto death. ¶ *I found*. It was to me. It produced this effect. ¶ *Unto death*. Producing aggravated guilt and condemnation, ver. 9.

11. *For sin*. This verse is a repetition, with a little variation of the sentiment in ver. 8. ¶ *Deceived me*. The word here used properly means to lead or seduce from the right way; and then to deceive, solicit to sin, cause to err from the way of virtue, Rom. xvi. 18; 1 Cor. iii. 18; 2 Cor. xi. 3, "The serpent *beguiled* Eve through his subtilty;" 2 Thes. ii. 3. The meaning here seems to be, that his corrupt and rebellious propensities, excited by the law, led him astray; caused him more and more to sin; practised a species of deception on him by urging him on headlong, and without deliberation, into aggravated transgression. In this sense, all sinners are deceived. Their passions urge them on, deluding them, and

leading them farther and farther from happiness, and involving them, before they are aware, in crime and death. No being in the universe is more deluded than a sinner in the indulgence of evil passions. The description of Solomon in a particular case will apply to all, Prov. vii. 21–23,

"With much fair speech she caused him to yield,
With the flattering of her lips she forced him.
He goeth after her straigntway,
As an ox goeth to the slaughter,
Or as a fool to the correction of the stocks;
Till a dart strike through his liver,
As a bird hasteth to the snare."

¶ *By it*. By the law, ver. 8. ¶ *Slew me*. Meaning the same as "I died," ver. 8.

12. *Wherefore*. So that. The conclusion to which we come is, that the law is not to be blamed, though these are its effects under existing circumstances. The source of all this is not the law, but the corrupt nature of man. The law is good; and yet the position of the apostle is true, that it is not adapted to purify the heart of fallen man. Its tendency is to excite increased guilt, conflict, alarm, and despair. This verse contains an answer to the question in ver. 7, "Is the law sin?" ¶ *Is holy*. Is not sin; comp. ver. 7. It is pure in its nature. ¶ *And the commandment*. The word commandment is here synonymous with the law. It properly means that which is enjoined. ¶ *Holy*. Pure. ¶ *Just*. Righteous in its claims and penalties. It is not unequal in its exactions. ¶ *Good*. In itself good; and in its own nature tending to produce happiness. The sin and condemnation of the guilty is not the fault of the law. If obeyed, it would produce happiness everywhere. See a most beautiful description of the law of God in Ps. xix. 7–11.

13. *Was then that which is good*, &c. This is another objection which the apostle proceeds to answer. The objection is this, "Can it be possible that that which is admitted to be good

But sin, that it might appear sin, worketh death in me by that which is good; that sin by the command-

ment might become exceeding sinful.

14 For we know that the law

and pure, should be changed into evil? Can that which tends to life, be made death to a man?" In answer to this, the apostle repeats that the fault was not in the *law*, but was in himself, and in his sinful propensities. ¶ *Made death.* Ver. 8, 10. ¶ *God forbid.* Note, chap. iii. 4. ¶ *But sin.* This is a personification of sin as in ver. 8. ¶ *That it might appear sin.* That it might develop its true nature, and no longer be dormant in the mind. The law of God is often applied to a man's conscience, that he may see how deep and desperate is his depravity. No man knows his own heart until the law thus crosses his path, and shows him what he is. ¶ *By the commandment.* Note, ver. 8. ¶ *Might become exceeding sinful.* In the original this is a very strong expression, and is one of those used by Paul to express strong emphasis, or intensity (καθ᾽ ὑπερβολὴν) by hyperboles. In an excessive degree; to the utmost possible extent, 1 Cor. xii. 31; 2 Cor. i. 8; iv. 7; xii. 7; Gal. i. 13. The phrase occurs in each of these places. The sense here is, that by the giving of the command, and its application to the mind, sin was completely developed; it was excited, inflamed, aggravated, and showed to be excessively malignant and deadly. It was not a dormant, slumbering principle; but it was awfully opposed to God and his law. Calvin has well expressed the sense: "It was proper that the enormity of sin should be revealed by the law; because unless sin should break forth by some dreadful and enormous excess (as they say), it would not be known to be sin. This excess exhibits itself the more violently, while it turns life into death." The sentiment of the whole is, that the tendency of the law is to excite the dormant sin of the bosom into active existence, and to reveal its true nature. It is desirable that that should be done, and as that is all that the law accomplishes, it is not adapted to sanctify the soul. To show

that this was the design of the apostle, it is *desirable* that sin should be thus seen in its true nature; because, (1) Man should be acquainted with his true character. He should not deceive himself. (2) Because it is one part of God's plan to develop the secret feelings of the heart, and to show to all creatures what they are. (3) Because only by knowing this, will the sinner be induced to take a remedy, and strive to be saved. God often thus *suffers* men to plunge into sin; to act out their nature, that they may see themselves, and be alarmed at the consequences of their own crimes.

14. The remainder of this chapter has been the subject of no small degree of controversy. The question has been whether it describes the state of Paul before his conversion, or afterwards. It is not the purpose of these Notes to enter into controversy, or into extended discussion. But after all the attention which I have been able to give to this passage, I regard it as describing the state of a man under the gospel, as descriptive of the operations of the mind of Paul subsequent to his conversion. This interpretation is adopted for the following reasons: (1) Because it seems to me to be the most obvious. It is that which will strike plain men as being the natural meaning—men who have not a theory to support, and who understand language in its usual sense. (2) Because it agrees with the design of the apostle, which is to show that the law is not adapted to produce sanctification and peace. This he had done in regard to a man *before* he was converted. If this relates to the same period, then it is a useless discussion of a point already discussed. If it relates to that period also, then there is a large field of action, including the whole period after a man's conversion to Christianity, in which the question might still be unsettled, whether the law *there* might not be adapted to

sanctify. The apostle therefore makes thorough work with the argument, and shows that the operation of the law is everywhere the same. (3) Because the expressions which occur are such as cannot be understood of an impenitent sinner; see Notes on ver. 15, 32. (4) Because it accords with parallel expressions in regard to the state of the conflict in a Christian's mind. (5) Because there is a change made here from the past tense to the present. In ver. 7, &c., he had used the past tense, evidently describing some former state. In ver. 14 there is a change to the present, a change inexplicable, except on the supposition that he meant to describe some state different from that before described. That could be no other than to carry his illustration forward in showing the inefficacy of the law on a man in his renewed state; or to show that such was the remaining depravity of the man, that it produced substantially the same effects as in the former condition. (6) Because it accords with the experience of Christians, and not with sinners. It is just such language as plain Christians, who are acquainted with their own hearts, use to express their feelings. I admit that this last consideration is not by itself conclusive; but if the language did *not* accord with the experience of the Christian world, it would be a strong circumstance *against* any proposed interpretation. The view which is here expressed of this chapter, as supposing that the previous part (ver. 7–13) refers to a man in his unregenerate state, and that the remainder describes the effect of the law on the mind of a renewed man, was adopted by studying the chapter itself, without aid from any writer. I am happy, however, to find that the views thus expressed are in accordance with those of the late Rev. Dr. J. P. Wilson, than whom, perhaps, no man was ever better qualified to interpret the Scriptures. He says, "In the fourth verse, he (Paul) changes to the first person plural, because he intended to speak of the former experience of Christians, who had been Jews. In the seventh verse, he uses the first person singular, but

speaks in the past tense, because he describes his own experience when he was an unconverted Pharisee. In the fourteenth verse, and unto the end of the chapter, he uses the first person singular, and the present tense, because he exhibits his own experience since he became a Christian and an apostle." ¶ *We know.* We admit. It is a conceded, well understood point. ¶ *That the law is spiritual.* This does not mean that the law is designed to control the spirit, in contradistinction from the body, but it is a declaration showing that the evils of which he was speaking were not the fault of the law. That was not, in its nature, sensual, corrupt, earthly, carnal; but was pure and spiritual. The *effect* described was not the fault of the law, but of the man, who was sold under sin. The word spiritual is often thus used to denote that which is pure and holy, in opposition to that which is fleshly or carnal, chap. viii. 5, 6; Gal. v. 16–23. The *flesh* is described as the source of evil passions and desires; the *spirit* as the source of purity, or as that which is agreeable to the proper influences of the Holy Spirit. ¶ *But I am.* The present tense shows that he is describing himself as he was at the time of writing. This is the natural and obvious construction, and if this be not the meaning, it is impossible to account for his having changed the past tense (ver. 7) to the present. ¶ *Carnal.* Fleshly; sensual; opposed to spiritual. This word is used because in the Scriptures the *flesh* is spoken of as the source of sensual passions and propensities, Gal. v. 19–21. The sense is, that these corrupt passions still retained a strong and withering and distressing influence over the mind. The renewed man is exposed to temptations from his strong native appetites; and the power of these passions, strengthened by long habit before he was converted, has travelled over into religion, and they continue still to influence and distress him. It does not mean that he is *wholly* under their influence; but that the tendency of his natural inclinations is to indulgence. ¶ *Sold under sin.* This expression is often adduced

is spiritual, but I am carnal, *sold under sin.

15 For that which I do, I ⁴allow

l 2 Ki.17.17.   ⁴ *know.*

not: for what I would, that do I not; but what I hate, that do I.

---

to show that it cannot be of a renewed man that the apostle is speaking. The argument is, that it cannot be affirmed of a Christian that he is sold under sin. A sufficient answer to this might be, that IN FACT, this is the very language which Christians often now adopt to express the strength of that native depravity against which they struggle, and that no language would *better* express it. It does not mean that they choose or prefer sins. It strongly implies that the *prevailing bent* of their mind is against it, but that such is its strength that it brings them into slavery to it. The expression here used, "*sold* under sin," is "borrowed from the practice of selling captives taken in war, as slaves" (Stuart). It hence means to deliver into the power of anyone, so that he shall be dependent on his will and control (Schleusner). The emphasis is not on the word *sold*, as if any *act* of selling had taken place, but the *effect* was as if he had been sold; *i.e.* he was subject to it, and under its control; and it means that sin, contrary to the prevailing inclination of his mind (ver. 15-17), had such an influence over him as to lead him to commit it, and thus to produce a state of conflict and grief, ver. 19-24. The verses which follow this are an explanation of the sense, and of the manner in which he was "sold under sin."

15. *For that which I do.* That is, the evil which I do, the sin of which I am conscious, and which troubles me. ¶ *I allow not.* I do not approve; I do not wish it; the prevailing bent of my inclinations and purposes is against it. Greek, "I *know* not;" see the margin. The word *know*, however, is sometimes used in the sense of approving, Rev. ii. 24, "Which have not *known* [approved] the depths of Satan;" compare Ps. ci. 4, "I will not *know* a wicked person;" Jer. i. 5. ¶ *For what I would.* That which I approve; and which is my prevailing

and established desire. What I would wish *always* to do. ¶ *But what I hate.* What I disapprove of; what is contrary to my judgment, my prevailing inclination, my established principles of conduct. ¶ *That do I.* Under the influence of sinful propensities, and carnal inclinations and desires. This represents the strong native propensity to sin; and even the power of corrupt propensity under the restraining influence of the gospel. On this remarkable and important passage we may observe, (1) That the prevailing propensity, the habitual fixed inclination of the mind of the Christian, is to do right. The evil course is hated, the right course is loved. This is the characteristic of a pious mind. It distinguishes a holy man from a sinner. (2) The evil which is done is disapproved; is a source of grief; and the habitual desire of the mind is to avoid it, and be pure. This also distinguishes the Christian from the sinner. (3) There is no need of being embarrassed here with any metaphysical difficulties or inquiries *how* this can be; for, (*a*) It is *in fact* the experience of all Christians. The habitual, fixed inclination and desire of their minds is to serve God. They have a fixed abhorrence of sin; and yet they are conscious of imperfection, and error, and sin, that is the source of uneasiness and trouble. The strength of natural passion may in an unguarded moment overcome them. The power of long habits, of previous thoughts, may annoy them. A man who was an infidel before his conversion, and whose mind was filled with scepticism, and cavils, and blasphemy, will find the effect of his former habits of thinking lingering in his mind, and annoying his peace for years. These thoughts will start up with the rapidity of lightning. Thus it is with every vice and every opinion. It is one of the effects of *habit*. "The very passage of an impure thought through the mind leaves pollution behind it;"

16 If then I do that which I would not, I consent unto the law, that *it is* good.

17 Now then it is no more I that do it, but sin that dwelleth in me.

---

and where sin has been long indulged, it leaves its withering, desolating effect on the soul long after conversion, and produces that state of conflict with which every Christian is familiar. (*b*) An effect *somewhat* similar is felt by all men. All are conscious of doing that, under the excitement of passion and prejudice, which their conscience and better judgment disapprove. A conflict thus exists, which is attended with as much metaphysical difficulty as the struggle in the Christian's mind referred to here. (*c*) The same thing was observed and described in the writings of the heathen. Thus Xenophon (*Cyrop.* vi. 1): Araspes, the Persian, says, in order to excuse his treasonable designs, "Certainly I must have two souls; for plainly it is not one and the same which is both evil and good, and at the same time wishes to do a thing and not to do it. Plainly, then, there are two souls; and when the good one prevails, then it does good; and when the evil one predominates, then it does evil." So also Epictetus (*Enchixid.* ii. 26) says, "He that sins does not do what he would; but what he would not, that he does." With this passage it would almost seem that Paul was familiar, and had his eye on it when he wrote. So also the well-known passage from Ovid, *Meta.* vii. 9:

Aliudque Cupido.
Mens aliud suadet. Video meliora, proboque,
Deteriora sequor.

"Desire prompts to one thing, but the mind persuades to another. I see the good, and approve it, and yet pursue the wrong." See other passages of similar import quoted in Grotius and Tholuck.

16. *I consent unto the law.* The very struggle with evil shows that it is not loved, or approved, but that the law which condemns it is really loved. Christians may here find a test of their piety. The fact of struggling against evil — the desire to be free from it, and to overcome it, the anxiety and

grief which it causes—is an evidence that we do not love it, and that therefore we are the friends of God. Perhaps nothing can be a more decisive test of piety than a long-continued and painful struggle against evil passions and desires in every form, and a panting of the soul to be delivered from the power and dominion of sin.

17. *It is no more I that do it.* This is evidently figurative language, for it is really the man that sins when evil is committed. But the apostle makes a distinction between *sin* and that which he intends by the pronoun *I*. By the former he evidently means his corrupt nature. By the latter he refers to his renewed nature, his Christian principles. He means to say that he does not approve or love it in his present state, but that it is the result of his native propensities and passions. In his heart, and conscience, and habitual feeling, he did not choose to commit sin, but abhorred it. Thus every Christian can say that *he* does not choose to do evil, but would wish to be perfect; that he hates sin, and yet that his corrupt passions lead him astray. ¶ *But sin.* My corrupt passions and native propensities. ¶ *That dwelleth in me.* Dwelling in me as its home. This is a strong expression, denoting that sin had taken up its habitation in the mind, and abode there. It had not been yet wholly dislodged. This expression stands in contrast with another that occurs, where it is said that "the Spirit of God dwells" in the Christian, Rom. viii. 9; 1 Cor. iii. 16. The sense is, that he is strongly *influenced* by sin on the one hand, and by the Spirit on the other. From this expression has arisen the phrase so common among Christians, *indwelling sin.*

18. *For I know.* This is designed as an illustration of what he had just said, that sin dwelt in him. ¶ *That is, in my flesh.* In my unrenewed nature; in my propensities and inclinations before conversion. Does not

18 For I know that in me (that is, in my flesh) *m* dwelleth no good thing: for to will is present with me; but *how* to perform that which is good I find not.

m Ge.6.5.

19 For *n* the good that I would, I do not: but the evil which I would not, that I do.

20 Now if I do that I would not, it is no more I that do it, but sin that dwelleth in me.

n Ga.5.17.

this qualifying expression show that in this discussion he was speaking of himself as a renewed man? Hence he is careful to imply that there was at that time in him something that was right or acceptable with God, but that that did not pertain to him by nature. ¶ *Dwelleth.* His soul was wholly *occupied* by that which was evil. It had taken entire possession. ¶ *No good thing.* There could not be possibly a stronger expression of belief of the doctrine of *total depravity.* It is Paul's own representation of himself. It proves that his heart was wholly evil. And if this was true of him, it is true of all others. It is a good way to examine ourselves, to inquire whether *we* have such a view of our own native character as to say that we *know* that in our flesh there dwelleth no good thing. The sense here is, that so far as the flesh was concerned—that is, in regard to his natural inclinations and desires—there was nothing good; all was evil. This was true in his entire conduct before conversion, where the desires of the flesh reigned and rioted without control; and it was true *after* conversion, so far as the natural inclinations and propensities of the flesh were concerned. All those operations in every state were evil, and not the less evil because they are experienced under the light and amidst the influences of the gospel. ¶ *To will.* To purpose or intend to do good. ¶ *Is present with me.* I can do that. It is possible; it is in my power. The expression may also imply that it was *near* to him (παράκειται), that is, it was constantly before him; it was now his habitual inclination and purpose of mind. It is the uniform, regular, habitual purpose of the Christian's mind to do *right.* ¶ *But how.* The sense would have been better retained here if the translators had not introduced the word

how. The difficulty was not in the *mode* of performing it, but to do the *thing itself.* ¶ *I find not.* I do not find it in my power; or I find strong constant obstacles, so that I fail of doing it. The obstacles are not natural, but such as arise from long indulgence in sin; the strong native propensity to evil.

19. *For the good,* &c. This is substantially a repetition of what is said in ver. 15. The repetition shows how full the mind of the apostle was of the subject; and how much inclined he was to dwell upon it, and to place it in every variety of form. It is not uncommon for Paul thus to express his intense interest in a subject, by placing it in a great variety of aspects, even at the hazard of much repetition.

20. *Now if I do,* &c. This verse is also a repetition of what was said in ver. 16, 17.

21. *I find then a law.* There is a law whose operation I experience whenever I attempt to do good. There have been various opinions about the meaning of the word *law* in this place. It is evident that it is used here in a sense somewhat unusual. But it retains the notion which commonly attaches to it of that which *binds,* or *controls.* And though this to which he refers differs from a *law,* inasmuch as it is not imposed by a superior, which is the usual idea of a law, yet it has so far the sense of law that it binds, controls, influences, or is that to which he was subject. There can be no doubt that he refers here to his carnal and corrupt nature; to the evil propensities and dispositions which were leading him astray. His representing this as a *law* is in accordance with all that he says of it, that it is *servitude,* that he is in bondage to it, and that it impedes his efforts to be holy and pure. The meaning is this,

21 I find then a law, that when I would do good, *o* evil is present with me.

o Ps.65.3; Ga.5.17; Ep.6.12; Col.3.5,9; Is.1.6; 64.6.

22 For I *p* delight in the law of God after *q* the inward man.

23 But I see another law *r* in

p Ps.1.2.　*q* 2 Co.4.16; 1 Pe.3.4.　*r* ch.6.13,19.

" I find a habit, a propensity, an influence of corrupt passions and desires, which, when I would do right, impedes my progress, and prevents my accomplishing what I would." Comp. Gal. v. 17. Every Christian is as much acquainted with this as was the apostle Paul. ¶ *Do good.* Do right. Be perfect. ¶ *Evil.* Some corrupt desire, or improper feeling, or evil propensity. ¶ *Is present with me.* Is near; is at hand; it starts up unbidden, and undesired. It is in the path, and never leaves us, but is always ready to impede our going, and to turn us from our good designs; comp. Ps. lxv. 3, "Iniquities *prevail* against me." The sense is, that to do evil is agreeable to our strong natural inclinations and passions.

22. *For I delight.* The word used here (Συνήδομαι) occurs nowhere else in the New Testament. It properly means to rejoice with anyone; and expresses not only *approbation* of the understanding, as the expression, " I *consent* unto the law," in ver. 16, but more than that it denotes sensible pleasure in the heart. It indicates not only *intellectual* assent, but *emotion,* an emotion of pleasure in the contemplation of the law. And this shows that the apostle is not speaking of an unrenewed man. Of such a man it might be said that his conscience approved the law; that his understanding was convinced that the law was good; but never yet did it occur that an impenitent sinner found emotions of pleasure in the contemplation of the pure and spiritual law of God. If this expression can be applied to an unrenewed man, there is, perhaps, not a single mark of a pious mind which may not with equal propriety be so applied. It is the natural, obvious, and usual mode of denoting the feelings of piety, an assent to the divine law followed with emotions of sensible delight in the contemplation. Comp. Ps. cxix. 97, "O how love I

thy law! it is my meditation all the day;" Ps. i. 2, "But his delight is in the law of the Lord;" Ps. xix. 7–11; Job xxiii. 12. ¶ *In the law of God.* The word *law* here is used in a large sense, to denote all the communications which God had made to control man. The sense is, that the apostle was pleased with the whole. One mark of genuine piety is to be pleased with the whole of the divine requirements. ¶ *After the inward man.* In respect to the inward man. The expression "the inward man" is used sometimes to denote the rational part of man as opposed to the sensual; sometimes the mind as opposed to the body (comp. 2 Cor. iv. 16; 1 Pet. iii. 4). It is thus used by the Greek classic writers. Here it is used evidently in opposition to a carnal and corrupt nature; to the evil passions and desires of the soul in an unrenewed state; to what is called elsewhere "the old man which is corrupt according to the deceitful lusts," Eph. iv. 22. The "inward man" is elsewhere called "the *new* man" (Eph. iv. 24); and denotes not the mere intellect, or conscience, but is a personification of the principles of action by which a Christian is governed; the new nature; the holy disposition; the inclination of the heart that is renewed.

23. *But I see another law.* Note, ver. 21. ¶ *In my members.* In my body; in my flesh; in my corrupt and sinful propensities; Note, chap. vi. 13; comp. 1 Cor. vi. 15; Col. iii. 5. The body is composed of many members; and as the flesh is regarded as the source of sin (ver. 18), the law of sin is said to be in the members, *i.e.* in the body itself. ¶ *Warring against.* Fighting against; or resisting. ¶ *The law of my mind.* This stands opposed to the prevailing inclinations of a corrupt nature. It means the same as was expressed by the phrase "the inward man," and denotes the desires and purposes of a renewed

my members, warring against the law of my mind, *and bringing me into captivity to the law of sin which is in my members.

s Ps.142.7.   *t* Ps.38.2,10; 77.3-9.

24 O*t* wretched man that I am! who shall deliver me from [5]the *u*body of this death?

25 I*v* thank God, through Jesus Christ our Lord. So then, with

5 or, *this body of death.* *u* Ps.88.5. *v* 1 Co.15.57.

heart. ¶ *And bringing me into captivity.* Making me a prisoner, or a captive. This is the completion of the figure respecting the warfare. A captive taken in war was at the disposal of the victor. So the apostle represents himself as engaged in a warfare; and as being overcome, and made an unwilling captive to the evil inclinations of the heart. The expression is strong; and denotes strong corrupt propensities. But though strong, it is believed it is language which all sincere Christians can adopt of themselves, as expressive of that painful and often disastrous conflict in their bosoms when they contend against the native propensities of their hearts.

24. *O wretched man that I am!* The feeling implied by this lamentation is the result of this painful conflict, and this frequent subjection to sinful propensities. The effect of this conflict is, (1) To produce pain and distress. It is often an agonizing struggle between good and evil; a struggle which annoys the peace, and renders life wretched. (2) It tends to produce humility. It is humbling to man to be thus under the influence of evil passions. It is degrading to his nature; a stain on his glory; and it tends to bring him into the dust, that he is under the control of *such* propensities, and so often gives indulgence to them. In such circumstances, the mind is overwhelmed with wretchedness, and instinctively sighs for relief. Can the law aid? Can man aid? Can any native strength of conscience or of reason aid? In vain all these are tried, and the Christian then calmly and thankfully acquiesces in the consolations of the apostle, that aid can be obtained only through Jesus Christ. ¶ *Who shall deliver me.* Who shall rescue me: the condition of a mind in deep distress, and conscious of its

own weakness, and looking for aid. ¶ *The body of this death.* Marg., *this body of death.* The word *body* here is probably used as equivalent to *flesh,* denoting the corrupt and evil propensities of the soul; Note, ver. 18. It is thus used to denote the law of sin in the members, as being that with which the apostle was struggling, and from which he desired to be delivered. The expression "body of this death" is a Hebraism; denoting a body deadly in its tendency; and the whole expression may mean the corrupt principles of man; the carnal, evil affections that lead to death or to condemnation. The expression is one of vast strength, and strongly characteristic of the apostle Paul. It indicates, (1) That it was near him, attending him, and was distressing in its nature. (2) An earnest wish to be delivered from it. Some have supposed that he refers to a custom practised by ancient tyrants, of binding a dead body to a captive as a punishment, and compelling him to drag the cumbersome and offensive burden with him wherever he went. I do not see any evidence that the apostle had this in view. But such a fact may be used as a striking and perhaps not improper illustration of the meaning of the apostle here. No strength of words could express deeper feeling; none more feelingly indicate the necessity of the grace of God to accomplish that to which the unaided human powers are incompetent.

25. *I thank God.* That is, I thank God for effecting a deliverance to which I am myself incompetent. There *is* a way of rescue, and I trace it altogether to his mercy in the Lord Jesus Christ. What conscience could not do, what the law could not do, what unaided human strength could not do, has been accomplished by the plan of the gospel; and complete deliverance can be expected there, and there alone.

the mind I myself serve the law of God, but with the flesh the law of sin.

This is the point to which all his reasoning had tended; and having thus shown that the law was insufficient to effect this deliverance, he is now prepared to utter the language of Christian thankfulness that it can be effected by the gospel. The superiority of the gospel to the law in overcoming all the evils under which man labours, is thus triumphantly established; comp. 1 Cor. xv. 57. ¶ *So then.* As the result of the whole inquiry we have come to this conclusion. ¶ *With the mind.* With the understanding, the conscience, the purposes, or intentions of the soul. This is a characteristic of the renewed nature. Of no impenitent sinner could it be ever affirmed that with his mind he served the law of God. ¶ *I myself.* It is still the same person, though acting in this apparently contradictory manner. ¶ *Serve the law of God.* Do honour to it as a just and holy law (ver. 12, 16), and am inclined to obey it, ver. 22, 24. ¶ *But with the flesh.* The corrupt propensities and lusts, ver. 18. ¶ *The law of sin.* That is, in the members. The flesh throughout, in all its native propensities and passions, leads to sin; it has no tendency to holiness; and its corruptions can be overcome only by the grace of God. We have thus, (1) A view of the sad and painful conflict between sin and God. They are opposed in all things. (2) We see the raging, withering effect of sin on the soul. In all circumstances it tends to death and woe. (3) We see the feebleness of the law and of conscience to overcome this. The tendency of both is to produce conflict and woe. And, (4) We see that the gospel only can overcome sin. To us it should be a subject of ever-increasing thankfulness, that what could not be accomplished by the law, can be thus effected by the gospel; and that God has devised a plan that thus effects complete deliverance, and which gives to the captive in sin an everlasting triumph.

CHAPTER VIII.

THERE is, therefore, now [a]no condemnation to them which

a Jn.3.18.

CHAPTER VIII.

This chapter is one of the most interesting and precious portions of the sacred Scriptures. Some parts of it are attended with great difficulties; but its main scope and design is apparent to all. It is a continuation of the subject discussed in the previous chapter, and is intended mainly to show that the gospel could effect what the law was incapable of doing. In that chapter the apostle had shown that the law was incapable of producing sanctification or peace of mind. He had traced its influence on the mind in different conditions, and shown that, equally before regeneration and afterwards, it was incapable of producing peace and holiness. Such was man, such were his propensities, that the application of *law* only tended to excite, to irritate, to produce conflict. The conscience, indeed, testified to the law that it was good; but still it had shown that it was not adapted to produce holiness of heart and peace, but agitation, conflict, and a state of excited sin. In opposition to this, he proceeds to show in this chapter the power of the gospel to produce that which the law could not. In doing this, he illustrates the subject by several considerations. (1) The gospel does what the law could not do in giving life, and delivering from condemnation, ver. 1–13. (2) It produces a spirit of *adoption*, and all the blessings which result from the filial confidence with which we can address God as our Father, in opposition to the law, which produced only terror and alarm, ver. 14–17. (3) It sustains the soul amidst its captivity to sin, and its trials, with the hope of a future deliverance—a complete and final redemption, of the body from all the evils of this life, ver. 18–25. (4) It furnishes the aid of the Holy Spirit to sustain us in our trials and infirmities, ver. 26, 27. (5) It gives the assurance that all things shall work

are in Christ Jesus, [b] who walk not after the flesh, but after the Spirit.

2 For the law of [c] the Spirit of life

b Ga.5.16.　　　　　　*c* 2 Co.3.6.

together for good, since all things are connected with the purpose of God, and all that can occur to a Christian comes in as a part of the *plan* of him who has resolved to save him, ver. 28–30. (6) It ministers consolation, from the fact that everything that can affect the happiness of man is *on the side* of the Christian, and will co-operate in his favour; as *e.g.* (*a*) *God*, in giving his Son, and in justifying the believer, ver. 31–33. (*b*) *Christ*, in dying, and rising, and interceding for Christians, ver. 34. (*c*) The love of a Christian to the Saviour is in itself so strong, that nothing can separate him from it, ver. 35–39. By all these considerations the superiority of the gospel to the law is shown, and assurance is given to the believer of his final salvation. By this interesting and conclusive train of reasoning, the apostle is prepared for the triumphant language of exultation with which he closes this most precious portion of the word of God.

1. There is, *therefore, now.* This is connected with the closing verses of chap. vii. The apostle had there shown that the law could not effect deliverance from sin, but that such deliverance was to be traced to the gospel alone, chap. vii. 23–25. It is implied here that there *was* condemnation under the law, and would be still, but for the intervention of the gospel. ¶ *No condemnation.* This does not mean that sin in believers is not to be condemned as much as anywhere, for the contrary is everywhere taught in the Scriptures; but it means, (1) That the gospel does not pronounce condemnation like the law. Its office is to pardon; the office of the law, to condemn. The one never affords deliverance, but always condemns; the object of the other is to free from condemnation, and to set the soul at liberty. (2) There is no *final* condemnation under the gospel. The office, design, and tendency of the gospel is to free from the condemning sen-

in Christ Jesus [a] hath made me free from the law of sin and death.

3 For what the law [e] could not

d Ga.2.19; 5.1.　　　*e* Ac.13.39; He.7.18,19.

tence of law. This is its first and its glorious announcement, that it frees lost and ruined men from a most fearful and terrible condemnation.

[The first verse of this chapter seems to be an inference from the whole preceding discussion. The apostle having established the doctrine of justification, and answered the objections commonly urged against it, now asserts his triumphant conclusion, "There is, therefore," &c.; that is to say, it follows from all that has been said concerning the believer's justification by the righteousness of Christ, and his complete deliverance from the law as a covenant, that to him there can be no condemnation. The design of Paul is not so much to assert the different offices of the law and the gospel, as simply to state the fact in regard to the condition of a certain class, viz., those who are in Christ. To them there is *no* condemnation whatever; not only no *final* condemnation, but no condemnation *now*, from the moment of their union to Christ, and deliverance from the curse of the law. The reason is this: that Christ hath endured the penalty, and obeyed the precept of the law in their stead.

"Here," says Mr. Haldane on the passage, "it is often remarked that the apostle does not say, that there is in them (believers) neither matter of accusation, nor cause of condemnation; and yet this is all included in what he does say. And afterwards, in express terms, he denies that they can be either accused or condemned, which they might be, were there any ground for either. All that was condemnable in them, which was sin, has been condemned in their Surety, as is shown in the third verse."]

¶ *Which are in Christ Jesus.* Who are united to Christ. To be *in* him is an expression not seldom used in the New Testament, denoting close and intimate union, Phil. i. 1; iii. 9; 2 Cor. v. 17; Rom. xvi. 7–11. The *union* between Christ and his people is compared to that between the vine and its branches (John xv. 1–6), and hence believers are said to be *in* him in a similar sense, as deriving their support from him, and as united in feeling, in purpose, and destiny.[*] ¶ *Who walk.*

* See the Supplementary Note on ver. 10.

do in that it was weak through the flesh, God, sending ƒhis own Son in

ƒ Ga.3.13.

Who conduct, or live; Note, chap. iv. 12. ¶ *Not after the flesh*. Who do not live to gratify the corrupt desires and passions of the flesh; Note, chap. vii. 18. This is a characteristic of a Christian. What it is to walk after the flesh may be seen in Gal. v. 19–21. It follows that a man whose purpose of life is to gratify his corrupt desires, cannot be a Christian. Unless he lives not to gratify his flesh, he can have no evidence of piety. This is a test which is easily applied; and if every professor of religion were honest, there could be no danger of mistake, and there need be no doubts about his true character. ¶ *But after the Spirit*. As the Holy Spirit would lead or prompt. What the Spirit produces may be seen in Gal. v. 22, 23. If a man has these fruits of the Spirit, he is a Christian; if not, he is a stranger to religion, whatever else he may possess. And *this* test also is easily applied.

2. *For the law*. The word *law* here means that *rule*, *command*, or *influence* which "the Spirit of life" produces. That exerts a *control* which is here called *a law*, for a law often means anything by which we are ruled or governed; see Notes, chap. vii. 21, 23. ¶ *Of the Spirit*. I see no reason to doubt here that this refers to the Holy Spirit. Evidently, at the close of ver. 1, the word has this reference. The phrase "the Spirit of life" then means the Holy Spirit producing or giving life; *i.e.* giving peace, joy, activity, salvation; in opposition to the law spoken of in chap. vii. that produced death and condemnation. ¶ *In Christ Jesus*. Under the Christian religion; or sent by Christ to apply his work to men, John xvi. 7–14. The Spirit is sent by Christ; his influence is a part of the Christian scheme; and his power accomplishes that which the law could not do. ¶ *Hath made me free*. That is, has delivered me from the predominating influence and control of sin. He cannot mean that he was perfect, for the whole tenor of his reasoning is

the likeness of sinful flesh, and [1]for sin, condemned sin in the flesh.

1 or, *by a sacrifice for sin*.

opposed to that. But the design, the tendency, and the spirit of the gospel was to produce this freedom from what the law could not deliver; and he was now brought under the general power of this scheme. In the former state he was under a most bitter and galling bondage, chap. vii. 7–11. Now, he was brought under the influence of a scheme which contemplated freedom, and which produced it. ¶ *The law of sin and death*. The controlling influence of sin, leading to death and condemnation, chap. vii. 5–11.

[The law of sin and death may be explained of the moral law, which, though good in itself, has, ever since the fall, been the *occasion* both of sin and death. On the other hand, the law of the Spirit of life in Christ Jesus, may be explained of the gospel, which is ministered by the life-giving Spirit of Christ. He reveals and applies it. Now the gospel covenant sets free from the law of sin and death, and, therefore, this sense gives a good reason why there is no condemnation to them that are in Christ Jesus. But if we understand the apostle in the second verse to speak of the opposite principles of grace and corruption, and to affirm, that the law, or influence of the former, hath made him free from the influence of the latter, we make him assert what is not consistent with the experience of the people of God, and assign as a reason of the assertion in the first verse what is not a reason, since the *sanctification* of believers cannot be regarded as the ground of their deliverance from condemnation. The apostle must not be made to say, "there is no condemnation," &c., for we are sanctified, or freed from the law of corruption; but there is no condemnation, for the gospel hath delivered us from the condemning sentence of the law. This view likewise accords best with the continuation of the subject in the third verse, which assigns the reason of the assertion in verse second.]

3. *For what the law could not do*. The law of God; the moral law. It could not free from sin and condemnation. This the apostle had fully shown in chap. vii. ¶ *In that*. Because. ¶ *It was weak*. It was feeble and inefficacious. It could not accomplish it. ¶ *Through the flesh*. In consequence of the strength of sin, and of

4 That the righteousness of the law might be fulfilled in us, *g*who

g ver.1.

the evil and corrupt desires of the unrenewed heart. The fault was not in the law which was good (chap. vii. 12), but it was owing to the strength of the natural passions and the sinfulness of the unrenewed heart; see chap. vii. 7-11, where this influence is fully explained. ¶ *God, sending his own Son.* That is, God *did,* or *accomplished,* that, by sending his Son, which the law could not do. The word *did,* or *accomplished,* it is necessary to understand here, in order to complete the sense. ¶ *In the likeness of sinful flesh.* That is, he so far resembled sinful flesh that he partook of flesh, or the nature of man, but without any of its sinful propensities or desires. It was not human nature; not, as the Docetæ taught, human nature in appearance only; but it was human nature without any of its corruptions. ¶ *And for sin.* Margin, "by a sacrifice for sin." The expression evidently means, by an offering for sin, or that he was given as a sacrifice on account of sin. His being given had respect to sin. ¶ *Condemned sin in the flesh.* The *flesh* is regarded as the source of sin; Note, chap. vii. 18. The flesh being the seat and origin of transgression, the atoning sacrifice was made in the likeness of sinful flesh, that thus he might meet sin, as it were, on its own ground, and destroy it. He may be said to have *condemned* sin in this manner, (1) Because the fact that he was given for it, and died on its account, was a condemnation of it. If sin had been approved by God he would not have made an atonement to secure its destruction. The depth and intensity of the woes of Christ on its account show the degree of abhorrence with which it is regarded by God. (2) The word *condemn* may be used in the sense of *destroying, overcoming,* or *subduing,* 2 Pet. ii. 6, "And turning the cities of Sodom and Gomorrah into ashes, *condemned* them with an overthrow." In this sense the sacrifice of Christ has not only *condemned* sin as being evil, but has weakened its

walk not after the flesh, but after the Spirit.

power and destroyed its influence, and will finally annihilate its existence in all who are saved by that death.

[By the sacrifice of Christ, God indeed showed his abhorrence of sin, and secured its final overthrow. It is not, however, of the *sanctifying influence* of this sacrifice that the apostle seems here to speak, but of its *justifying power.* The sense, therefore, is that God passed a judicial sentence on sin, in the person of Christ, on account of which, *that* has been effected which the law could not effect (justification namely). Sin being condemned in the human nature of Christ, cannot be condemned and punished in the persons of those represented by him. They *must* be justified. This view gives consistency to the whole passage, from the first verse to the fourth inclusive. The apostle clearly *begins* with the subject of justification, when, in the first verse, he affirms, that to them who are in Christ Jesus there is no condemnation. If the question be put, Why is this? the second verse gives for answer, that believers are delivered from the law as a covenant of works. (See the foregoing Supplementary Note.) If the question again be put, Whence this deliverance? the third verse points to the sacrifice of Christ, which, the fourth verse assures us, was offered with the very design "that the righteousness of the law might be fulfilled in us." This clause, according to the principle of interpretation laid down above, does not relate to the believer's obedience to the righteous requirements of the law. The apostle has in view a more immediate design of the sacrifice of Christ. The right or demand of the law ($\delta\iota\varkappa\alpha\iota\omega\mu\alpha$) was satisfaction to its injured honour. Its penalty must be borne, as well as its precept obeyed. The sacrifice of Christ answered every claim. And as believers are *one* with him, the righteousness of the law has been "fulfilled in them."

The whole passage is thus consistently explained of justification.]

4. *That the righteousness of the law.* That we might be conformed to the law, or be obedient to its requirements, and no longer under the influence of the flesh and its corrupt desires. ¶ *Might be fulfilled.* That we might be obedient, or comply with its demands. ¶ *Who walk.* Note, ver. 1.

5. *For they that are after the flesh.* They that are under the influence of the corrupt and sinful desires of the

5 For *h*they that are after the flesh, do mind the *t*hings of the flesh; but they that are after the Spirit, *i*the things of the Spirit.

h Jn.3.6; 1 Co.15.48.　　　*i* 1 Co.2.14.

flesh, Gal. v. 19–21. Those who are unrenewed. ¶ *Do mind the things of the flesh.* They are supremely devoted to the gratification of their corrupt desires. ¶ *But they*|*that are after the Spirit.* Who are under its influence; who are led by the Spirit. ¶ *The things of the Spirit.* Those things which the Spirit produces, or which he effects in the mind, Gal. v. 21–23. This verse is for the purpose of illustration, and is designed to show that the tendency of religion is to produce as entire a devotedness to the service of God as men had before rendered to sin; that is, that they would be fully engaged in that to which they had devoted themselves. As the Christian, therefore, had devoted himself to the service of the Spirit, and had been brought under his influence, it was to be expected that he would make it his great and only object to cherish and cultivate the graces which that Spirit would produce.

6. *For to be carnally minded.* Margin, "the minding of the flesh." The sense is, that to follow the inclinations of the flesh, or the corrupt propensities of our nature, leads us to condemnation and death. The expression is one of great energy, and shows that it not only *leads* to death, or leads to misery, but that it is death itself; there is woe and condemnation in the *very act and purpose* of being supremely devoted to the corrupt passions. Its only tendency is condemnation and despair. ¶ *Is death.* The penalty of transgression; condemnation and eternal ruin; Note, chap. v. 12. ¶ *But to be spiritually minded.* Margin, "the minding of the Spirit." That is, making it the object of the mind, the end and aim of the actions, to cultivate the graces of the Spirit, and to submit to his influence. To be spiritually minded is to seek those feelings and views which the Holy Spirit produces, and to follow his leadings. ¶ *Is life.* This is opposed to *death*

6 For ²to be carnally minded *k*is death; but ³to be spiritually minded *is* life and peace:

7 Because the carnal mind is

² the minding of the flesh.　　*k* Ga.6.8.
³ the minding of the Spirit.

in ver. 5. It tends to life, and is in fact real life. For to possess and cultivate the graces of the Spirit, to be led where he would guide us, is the design of our existence, and is the only path of happiness. ¶ *And peace.* Note, chap. vi.

7. *Because.* This is given as a reason for what is said in ver. 6. In that verse the apostle had affirmed that to be carnally minded *was* death, but he had not stated *why* it was. He now explains it by saying that it is enmity against God, and thus involves a sinner in conflict with him, and exposes to his condemnation. ¶ *The carnal mind.* This is the same expression as occurs in ver. 6 (τὸ φρόνημα τῆς σαρκὸς). It does not mean the mind itself, the intellect, or the will; it does not suppose that the mind or soul is *physically* depraved, or opposed to God; but it means that *the minding of the things of the flesh,* giving to them supreme attention, is hostility against God, and involves the sinner in a controversy with him, and hence leads to death and woe. This passage should not be alleged in proof that the *soul is physically depraved,* but merely that where there is a supreme regard to the flesh there is hostility to God. It does not directly prove the doctrine of universal depravity; but it proves only that where such attention exists to the corrupt desires of the soul, *there* is hostility to God. It is indeed *implied* that that supreme regard to the flesh exists everywhere by nature, but this is not expressly affirmed. For the object of the apostle here is not to teach the doctrine of depravity, but to show that where such depravity in fact exists, it involves the sinner in a fearful controversy with God. ¶ *Is enmity.* Hostility; hatred. It means that such a regard to the flesh is in fact hostility to God, because it is opposed to his law, and to his plan for purifying the soul; comp. Jam. iv. 4; 1 John ii. 15. The minding of

enmity against God; for it is not subject to the law of God, neither indeed can be.

the things of the flesh also leads to the hatred of *God himself*, because he is opposed to it, and has expressed his abhorrence of it. ¶ *Against God.* Towards God; or in regard to him. It supposes hostility to him. ¶ *For it.* The word "*it*" here refers to the minding of the things of the flesh. It does not mean that the *soul itself* is not subject to his law, but that the *minding* of those things is hostile to his law. The apostle does not express any opinion about the metaphysical ability of man, or discuss that question at all. The amount of his affirmation is simply, that the *minding of the flesh*, the supreme attention to its dictates and desires, is not and cannot be subject to the law of God. They are wholly contradictory and irreconcilable, just as much as the love of falsehood is inconsistent with the laws of truth; as intemperance is inconsistent with the law of temperance; and as adultery is a violation of the seventh commandment. But whether the *man himself* might not obey the law,— whether *he* has, or has not, ability to do it,—is a question which the apostle does not touch, and on which this passage should not be adduced. For whether the law of a particular sin is utterly irreconcilable with an opposite virtue, and whether the sinner is able to abandon that sin and pursue a different path, are very different inquiries. ¶ *Is not subject.* It is not in *subjection* to the command of God. The minding of the flesh is opposed to that law, and thus shows that it is hostile to God. ¶ *Neither indeed can be.* This is absolute and certain. It is impossible that it should be. There is the utmost inability in regard to it. The things are utterly irreconcilable. But the affirmation does not mean that the *heart* of the sinner might not be subject to God; or that his *soul* is so physically depraved that he cannot obey, or that *he* might not obey the law. On that, the apostle here expresses no opinion. That is not the subject of the discussion. It is simply

8 So then they that are in the flesh cannot please God.

9 But ye are not in the flesh, but

that the supreme regard to the flesh, the minding of that, is *utterly irreconcilable* with the law of God. They are different things, and *can never* be made to harmonize; just as adultery *cannot* be chastity; falsehood *cannot* be truth; dishonesty *cannot* be honesty; hatred *cannot* be love. This passage, therefore, should not be adduced to prove the doctrine of man's inability to love God, for it does not refer to that, but it proves merely that a supreme regard to the things of the flesh is utterly inconsistent with the law of God; can never be reconciled with it; and involves the sinner in hostility with his Creator.

[Calvinists have been loudly accused of "taking an unfair advantage of this language, for the support of their favourite doctrine of the utter impotency of the unregenerate man in appreciating, much less conforming to the divine injunctions." It is alleged that φρονημα της σαρκος refers to the disposition of the mind, and is properly translated, "the minding of the flesh." Therefore, it is this *disposition or affection*, and not the *mind itself*, that is enmity against God. But the meaning of the passage is not affected by this change in the translation. For the apostle affirms that this minding of the flesh is the uniform and prevailing disposition of unregenerate men. "They that are after the flesh," *i.e.* unregenerate men, "*do mind* the things of the flesh." This is their character without exception. Now, if the natural mind be uniformly under the influence of this depraved disposition, is IT not enmity to God. Thus, in point of fact, there is no difference between the received and the amended translation. To affirm that the mind itself is not hostile to God, and that its disposition alone is so, is little better than metaphysical trifling, and deserves no more regard than the plea which any wicked man might easily establish, by declaring that his disposition only, and not himself, was hostile to the laws of religion and morals. On the whole, it is not easy to conceive how the apostle could more forcibly have affirmed the enmity of the natural mind against God. He first describes unrenewed men by their character or bent, and then asserts that this bent is the very essence of enmity against God—enmity in the abstract.

To anyone ignorant of the subtleties of theological controversy, the doctrine of *moral*

in the Spirit, if so be that the *inability* would seem a plain consequence from this view of the natural mind. "It is," says Mr. Scott on the passage, "*morally* unable to do anything but revolt against the divine law, and refuse obedience to it." We are told, however, that the passage under consideration affirms only, that unregenerate men, *while they continue in that state*, cannot please God, or yield obedience to his law, and leaves untouched the other question, concerning the power of the carnal mind to throw off the disposition of enmity, and return to subjection. But if it be not expressly affirmed by the apostle here, that *the carnal mind has not this power*, it would seem at least to be a plain enough *inference* from his doctrine. For if the disposition of the unregenerate man be enmity against God, whence is the motive to arise that shall make him dislike that dis position, and throw it aside, and assume a better in its stead? From *within* it cannot come, because, according to the supposition, *there* is enmity only; and love cannot arise out of hatred. If it come from without, from the aids and influences of the Spirit, the question is ceded, and the dispute at an end.

A very common way of casting discredit on the view which Calvinists entertain of the doctrine of man's inability, is to represent it as involving some *natural* or *physical* disqualification. Nothing can be more unfair. There is a wide difference between natural and moral inability. The one arises from "some defect or obstacle *extrinsic to the will*, either in the understanding, constitution of the body, or external objects:" the other from "the want of inclination, or the strength of a contrary inclination." Now the Scriptures nowhere assert, nor have rational Calvinists ever maintained, that there is any physical incapacity of this kind, apart from the corrupt bias and inclination of the will, on account of which the natural man cannot be subject to the law of God. But, on the other hand, the Scriptures are full of evidence on the subject of moral inability. Even were we to abandon this passage, the *general* doctrine of revelation is, that unregenerate men are *dead* in trespasses and in sins; and the entire change that takes place in regeneration and sanctification, is uniformly ascribed not to the "man himself," but to the power of the Spirit of God. Not only is the change carried on and perfected, but *begun* by him.]

8. **So then.** It follows; it leads to this conclusion. ¶ *They that are in the flesh.* They who are unrenewed sinners; who are following supremely the desires of the flesh, chap. vii. 18. Those are meant here who follow

Spirit of God *[i]* dwell in you. Now

l 1 Co.6.19; Ga.4.6.

fleshly appetites and desires, and who are not led by the Spirit of God. ¶ *Cannot please God.* That is, while they are thus in the flesh; while they thus pursue the desires of their corrupt nature, they cannot please God. But this affirms nothing respecting their ability to turn from this course, and to pursue a different mode of life. That is a different question. A child may be obstinate, proud, and disobedient; and *while in this state*, it may be affirmed of him that he cannot please his parent. But whether he might not *cease* to be obstinate, and become obedient, is a very different inquiry; and the two subjects should never be confounded. It follows from this, (1) That those who are unrenewed are *totally* depraved, since in this state they cannot please God. (2) That none of their actions while in this state can be acceptable to him, since he is pleased only with those who are spiritually minded. (3) That those who are in this state should turn from it without delay; as it is desirable that every man *should* please God. (4) That if the sinner does not turn from his course, he will be ruined. With his present character he can never please him; neither in health nor sickness; neither in life nor death; neither on earth nor in hell. He is engaged in hostility against God; and if he does not himself forsake it, it will be endless, and involve his soul in all the evils of a personal, and direct, and eternal warfare with the Lord Almighty.

9. *But ye.* You who are Christians. This is the opposite character to that which he had been describing, and shows the power of the gospel. ¶ *Not in the flesh.* Not under the full influence of corrupt desires and passions. ¶ *But in the Spirit.* That is, you are spiritually minded; you are under the direction and influence of the Holy Spirit. ¶ *The Spirit of God.* The Holy Ghost. ¶ *Dwell in you.* The Holy Spirit is often represented as dwelling in the hearts of Christians (comp. 1 Cor. ii. 16, 17; vi. 19; 2 Cor. vi. 16; Eph. ii. 21, 22; Gal. iv. 6);

if any man have not the Spirit of Christ, he is none of his.

10 And if Christ *be* in you, the

body *is* dead because of sin; but the spirit *is* life because of righteousness.

---

and the meaning is not that there.is a *personal* or *physical* indwelling of the Holy Ghost, but that he influences, directs, and guides Christians, producing meekness, love, joy, peace, long-suffering, gentleness, goodness, &c., Gal. v. 22, 23. The expression *to dwell in* one, denotes intimacy of connection, and means that those things which are the fruits of the Spirit are produced in the heart.* ¶ *Have not the Spirit of Christ.* The word *Spirit* is used in a great variety of significations in the Scriptures. It most commonly in the New Testament refers to the third person of the Trinity, the Holy Ghost. But the expression "the Spirit *of Christ*" is not, I believe, anywhere applied to him, except it may be 1 Pet. i. 11. He is called often the Spirit of God (Mat. iii. 16; xii. 28; 1 Cor. ii. 11, 14; iii. 16; vi. 11; Eph. iv. 30), but not the Spirit of the Father. The word *spirit* is often used to denote the temper, disposition; thus we say, a man of a generous *spirit*, or of a revengeful *spirit*, &c. It may possibly have this meaning here, and denotes that he who has not the temper or disposition of Christ is not his, or has no evidence of piety. But the connection seems to demand that it should be understood in a sense similar to the expression "the Spirit of God," and "the Spirit of him that raised up Jesus" (ver. 11); and if so, it means the Spirit which Christ imparts, or sends to accomplish his work (John xiv. 26), the Holy Spirit, sent to make us like Christ, and to sanctify our hearts. And in this sense it evidently denotes the Spirit which Christ would send to produce in us the views and feelings which he came to establish, and which shall assimilate us to himself. If this refers to the Holy Spirit, then we see the manner in which the apostle spoke of the Saviour. He regarded "the Spirit" as equally the Spirit of God and of Christ, as proceeding from both; and thus evi-

* See the Supplementary Note on ver. 10.

dently believed that there is a union of nature between the Father and the Son. Such language could never be used except on the supposition that the Father and Son are one; that is, that Christ is divine. ¶ *Is none of his.* Is not a Christian. This is a test of piety that is easily applied; and this settles the question. If a man is not influenced by the meek, pure, and holy spirit of the Lord Jesus, if he is not conformed to his image, if his life does not resemble that of the Saviour, he is a stranger to religion. No test could be more easily applied, and none is more decisive. It matters not what else he may have. He may be loud in his professions, amiable in his temper, bold in his zeal, or active in promoting the interests of his own party or denomination in the church; but if he has not the temper of the Saviour, and does not manifest his spirit, it is as sounding brass or a tinkling cymbal. May all who read this honestly examine themselves; and may they have that which is the source of the purest felicity, the spirit and temper of the Lord Jesus.

10. *And if Christ* be *in you.* This is evidently a figurative expression, where the word "Christ" is used to denote his spirit, his principles; that is, he influences the man. Literally, he cannot be *in* a Christian; but the close connection between him and Christians, and the fact that they are entirely under his influence, is expressed by this strong figurative language. It is language which is not unfrequently used; comp. Gal. ii. 20; Col. i. 27.

[The union between Christ and his people is sometimes explained of a merely *relative* in opposition to a *real* union. The union which subsists between a substitute, or surety, and the persons in whose room he has placed himself, is frequently offered in explanation of the Scripture language on the subject. In this view, Christ is regarded as *legally* one with his people, inasmuch as what he has done or obtained is held *as* done and obtained by them. Another relative union, employed to illustrate that which subsists between Christ and believers, is the union of a chief and his followers, which is simply a union of design, interest, sentiment, affection, destiny, &c. Now these representations are true *so far as they go*, and furnish much interesting and profitable illustration. They fall short, however, of the full sense of Scripture on the point. That there is a *real* or vital union between Christ and his people, appears from the *language* of the inspired writers in regard to it. The peculiar phraseology which they employ cannot well be explained of any relative union. At all events, it is as strong as they could have employed, on the supposition that they had wished to convey the idea of the *most intimate possible connection.* Christ is said to be "*in them,*" and they are represented as "*in him.*" He "*abides* in them, and they in him." They "*dwell*" in each other, John xiv. 20; xv. 4; 1 John iii. 24; iv. 12. Moreover, the Scripture *illustrations* of the subject furnish evidence to the same effect. The mystical union, as it has been called, is compared to the union of stones in a building, branches in a vine, members in a human body, and even to that which subsists between the Father and the Son, 1 Pet. ii. 4; Eph. ii. 20, 22; John xv. 1–8; 1 Cor. xii. 12–31; John xvii. 20–23. Now if all these are *real* unions, is not this union *real* also? If not, where is the propriety or justice of the comparisons? Instead of leading us to form accurate notions on the subject, they would seem calculated to mislead.

This real and vital union is formed by the one Spirit of Christ, the Holy Ghost pervading the Head and the members of the mystical body, 1 Cor. vi. 17; xii. 13; 1 John iii. 24; iv. 13. It is true, indeed, that the *essential* presence of Christ's Spirit is everywhere, but he is present in Christ's members, in a peculiar way, as the fountain of spiritual influence. This spiritual presence, which is the bond of union, is manifested immediately upon a man's reception of Christ by faith. From that hour he is one with Christ, because the same Spirit lives in both. Indeed this union is the *foundation* of all the relative unions which have been employed to illustrate the subject; without it, we could have no saving relation to Christ whatever. That it is mysterious cannot be denied. The apostle himself affirms as much, Eph. v. 32; Col. i. 27. Although we know the *fact*, we cannot explain the *manner* of it, but must not on this account reject it, any more than we would the doctrine of the Spirit's essential presence, because we do not understand *it*.]

¶ *The body* is *dead*. This passage has been interpreted in very different ways. Some understand it to mean that the body is dead *in respect to sin;* that is, that sin has no more power

to excite evil passions and desires; others, that the body must die on account of sin, but that the spiritual part shall live, and even the body shall live also in the resurrection. Thus Calvin, Beza, and Augustine. Doddridge understands it thus :— Though the body is to die on account of the first sin that entered into the world, yet the spirit is life, and shall continue to live on for ever, through that righteousness which the second Adam has introduced." To each of these interpretations there are serious objections, which it is not necessary to urge. I understand the passage in the following manner :—The *body* refers to that of which the apostle had said so much in the previous chapters—the flesh, the man before conversion. It is subject to corrupt passions and desires, and may be said thus to be *dead*, as it has none of the elements of spiritual life. It is under the reign of sin and death. The word *μὲν, indeed,* or *truly,* has been omitted in our translation, and the omission has obscured the sense. The expression is an *admission* of the apostle, or a summary statement of what had before been shown. "It is to be admitted, indeed, or it is true, that the unrenewed nature, the man before conversion, under the influence of the flesh, is spiritually dead. Sin has its seat in the fleshly appetites; and the whole body may be admitted thus to be dead or corrupt." ¶ *Because of sin. Through* sin (δι' ἁμαρτίαν); by means of sinful passions and appetites. ¶ *But the spirit.* This stands opposed to the body; and it means that the soul, the immortal part, the renovated man, was alive, or was under the influence of living principles. It was imbued with the life which the gospel imparts, and had become active in the service of God. The word "spirit" here does not refer to the Holy Ghost, but to the spirit of man, the immortal part, recovered, renewed, and imbued with life under the gospel. ¶ *Because of righteousness.* Through righteousness (διὰ δικαιοσύνην). This is commonly interpreted to mean, with reference to righteousness, or that it may become righteous. But I understand the ex-

11 But if the Spirit of him that raised up Jesus from the dead dwell in you, *m* he that raised up Christ from the dead shall also quicken your mortal bodies

m 2 Co.4.14.

⁴by his Spirit that dwelleth in you.

12 Therefore, brethren, we are debtors, *n* not to the flesh, to live after the flesh.

4 or, *because of.*   *n* Ps.116.16.

pression to be used in the sense in which the word is so frequently used in this epistle, as denoting *God's plan of justification;* see Note, chap. ⁖. 17. "The spirit of man has been recovered and made alive through his plan of justification. It communicates life, and recovers man from his death in sin to life."

[The "body" in this passage has generally been understood in the literal sense, which, doubtless, ought not to be rejected without some valid reason. There is nothing in the connection that demands the figurative sense. The apostle admits that, notwithstanding of the indwelling of the Spirit, the body *must* die. "It *indeed* (*μὲν*) is dead because of sin." The believer is not delivered from temporal death. Yet there are two things which may well reconcile him to the idea of laying aside for a while the clay tabernacle. The "mortal body," though it now die, is not destined to remain for ever under the dominion of death, but shall be raised again incorruptible and glorious, by the power of the same Spirit that raised up Jesus from the dead. Meanwhile, "the spirit, or soul, is life, because of righteousness." In consequence of that immaculate righteousness, of which Paul had said so much in the previous part of this epistle, the souls of believers, even now, enjoy spiritual life, which shall issue in eternal life and glory.

Those who understand *σῶμα* figuratively in the 10th verse, insist, indeed, that the resurrection in the 11th is figurative also. But "the best commentators," says Bloomfield, "both ancient and modern, with reason prefer the literal view, especially on account of the phrase *θνητὰ σώματα,* which seems to confine it to this sense."]

11. *But if the Spirit of him,* &c. The Holy Spirit, ver. 9. ¶ *He that raised up Christ,* &c. He that had *power* to restore him to life, has power to give life to you. He that did, *in fact,* restore him to life, will also restore you. The argument here seems to be founded, first, on the power of God; and, secondly, on the connection between Christ and his people; comp.

John xiv. 19, "Because I live, ye shall live also." ¶ *Shall also quicken.* Shall make alive. ¶ *Your mortal bodies.* That this does not refer to the resurrection of the dead seems to be apparent, because that is not attributed to the Holy Spirit. I understand it as referring to the body, subject to carnal desires and propensities; by nature under the reign of death, and therefore mortal; *i.e.* subject to death. The sense is, that under the gospel, by the influence of the Spirit, the entire man will be made alive in the service of God. Even the corrupt, carnal, and mortal body, so long under the dominion of sin, shall be made alive and recovered to the service of God. This will be done by the Spirit that dwells in us, because that Spirit has restored life to our souls, abides with us with his purifying influence, and because the design and tendency of his indwelling is to purify the entire man, and restore all to God. Christians thus in their bodies and their spirits become sacred. For even their body, the seat of evil passions and desires, shall become alive in the service of God.

12. *We are debtors.* We owe it as a matter of solemn obligation. This obligation arises, (1) From the fact that the Spirit dwells in us; (2) Because the design of his indwelling is to purify us; (3) Because we are thus recovered from the death of sin to the life of religion; and he who has imparted life, has a right to require that it be spent in his service. ¶ *To the flesh.* To the corrupt propensities and passions. We are not bound to indulge them, because the end of such indulgence is death and ruin, chap. vii. 21, 22. But we are bound to live to God, and to follow the leadings of his Spirit, for the end is life and peace, chap. vii. 22, 23. The reason for this is stated in the following verse.

13 For if ye live after the flesh, ye shall die: but if ye through the Spirit do °mortify the deeds of the body, ye shall live.

o Col.3.5.

14 For as many as are ᵖled by the Spirit of God, they are the sons of God.

15 For ye have not received the

p Ga.5.18.

13. *For if ye live*, &c. If you live to indulge your carnal propensities, you will sink to eternal death, chap. vii. 23. ¶ *Through the Spirit.* By the aid of the Spirit; by cherishing and cultivating his influences. What is here required can be accomplished only by the aid of the Holy Ghost. ¶ *Do mortify.* Do put to death; do destroy. Sin is mortified when its power is destroyed, and it ceases to be active. ¶ *The deeds of the body.* The corrupt inclinations and passions, called deeds of *the body*, because they are supposed to have their origin in the fleshly appetites. ¶ *Ye shall live.* You shall be happy and saved. Either your sins must die, or you must. If they are suffered to live, you will die. If they are put to death, you will be saved. No man can be saved in his sins. This closes the argument of the apostle for the superiority of the gospel to the law in promoting the purity of man. By this train of reasoning, he has shown that the gospel has accomplished what the law could not do—the sanctification of the soul, the destruction of the corrupt passions of our nature, and the recovery of man to God.

14. *For as many.* Whosoever; all who are thus led. This introduces a new topic, illustrating the benefits of the gospel, to wit, that it produces a spirit of *adoption*, ver. 14-17. ¶ *As are led.* As submit to his influence and control. The Spirit is represented as influencing, suggesting, and controlling. One evidence of piety is, a willingness to *yield* to that influence, and submit to him. One decided evidence of the want of piety is, where there is an unwillingness to submit to that influence, but where the Holy Spirit is grieved and resisted. All Christians submit to his influence; all sinners decidedly reject it and oppose it. The influence of the Spirit, if followed, would lead every man to

heaven. But when neglected, rejected, or despised, man goes down to hell. The glory belongs to the conducting Spirit when man is saved; the fault is man's when he is lost. The apostle here does not agitate the question *how* it is that the people of God are led by the Spirit, or why they yield to it when others resist it. His design is simply to state the fact, that they who *are* thus led are the sons of God, or have evidence of piety. ¶ *Are the sons of God.* Are adopted into his family, and are his children. This is a name of endearment, meaning that they sustain to him this relation; that they are his friends, disciples, and imitators; that they are parts of the great family of the redeemed, of whom he is the Father and Protector. It is often applied to Christians in the Bible, Job i. 6; John i. 12; Phil. ii. 15; 1 John iii. 1, 2; Mat. v. 9, 45; Luke vi. 35. This is a test of piety which is easily applied. (1) Are we conscious that an influence from above has been drawing us away from the corrupting passions and vanities of this world? This is the work of the Spirit. (2) Are we conscious of a desire to *yield* to that influence, and to be conducted in the path of purity and life? This is an evidence that we are the sons of God. (3) Do we offer no resistance; do we follow cheerfully, and obey this pure influence, leading us to mortify pride, subdue passion, destroy lust, humble ambition, and annihilate the love of wealth and of the world? If so, we are his children. God will not lead us astray; and our peace and happiness consists only in *yielding* ourselves to this influence entirely, and in being willing to be conducted by this unseen hand "beside the still waters of salvation."

15. *The spirit of bondage.* The spirit that binds you; or the spirit of a slave, that produces only fear. The slave is under constant fear and alarm.

spirit*q* of bondage again to fear; but*r* ye have received *s*the Spirit of adoption, whereby we cry, Abba, Father.

16 The Spirit itself *t* beareth

q 2 Ti.1.7.   *r* 1 Co.2.12.   *s* Je.3.19; Ga.4.5,6.
          t 2 Co.1.22; 1 Jn.4.13.

But the spirit of religion is that of freedom and of confidence; the spirit of children, and not of slaves; compare Note, John viii. 32–36. ¶ *Again to fear.* That you should again be afraid, or be subjected to servile fear. This implies that in their former state under the law they were in a state of servitude, and that the tendency of it was merely to produce alarm. Every sinner is subject to such fear. He has everything of which to be alarmed. God is angry with him; his conscience will trouble him; and he has everything to apprehend in death and in eternity. But it is not so with the Christian; comp. 2 Tim. i. 7. ¶ *The spirit of adoption.* The feeling of affection, love, and confidence which pertains to children; not the servile, trembling spirit of slaves, but the temper and affectionate regard of sons. Adoption is the taking and treating a stranger as one's own child. It is applied to Christians because God treats them as his children; he receives them into this relation, though they were by nature strangers and enemies. It implies, (1) That we by nature had no claim on him; (2) That, therefore, the act is one of mere kindness—of pure, sovereign love; (3) That we are now under his protection and care; and, (4) That we are bound to manifest towards him the spirit of children, and yield to him obedience. See Note, John i. 12; comp. Gal. iv. 5; Eph. i. 5. It is for this that Christians are so often called the sons of God. ¶ *Whereby we cry.* As children who need protection and help. This evinces the habitual spirit of a child of God; a disposition, (1) To express towards him the feelings due to a father; (2) To call upon him; to address him in the language of affection and endearing confidence; (3) To seek his protection and aid. ¶ *Abba.* This word is Chaldee (אבא), and means *father.* Why the apostle

witness with our spirit, that we are the children of God:

17 And if children, *u*then heirs; heirs of God, and *v*joint-heirs with Christ; if so be that we suffer with

u Ac.26.18; 1 Pe.1.4.   *v* 2 Ti.2.11,12.

repeats the word in a different language is not known. The Syriac reads it, "By which we call the Father our Father." It is probable that the repetition here denotes merely *intensity*, and is designed to denote the *interest* with which a Christian dwells on the name, in the spirit of an affectionate, tender child. It is not unusual to repeat such terms of affection; comp. Mat. vii. 22; Ps. viii. 1. This is an evidence of piety that is easily applied. He that can in sincerity and with ardent affection apply this term to God, addressing him with a filial spirit as his Father, has the spirit of a Christian. Every child of God has this spirit; and he that has it not is a stranger to piety.

16. *The Spirit.* The Holy Spirit. That the Holy Spirit here is intended, is evident, (1) Because this is the natural meaning of the expression; (2) Because it is of the Holy Spirit that the apostle is mainly treating here; (3) Because it would be an unnatural and forced construction to say of the *temper of adoption* that *it* bore witness. ¶ *Beareth witness.* Testifies, gives evidence. ¶ *With our spirit.* To our minds. This pertains to the adoption; and it means that the Holy Spirit furnishes evidence to our minds that we are adopted into the family of God. This effect is not unfrequently attributed to the Holy Spirit, 2 Cor. i. 22; 1 John v. 10, 11; 1 Cor. ii. 12. If it be asked *how* this is done, I answer, it is not by any revelation of new truth; it is not by inspiration; it is not always by assurance; it is not by a mere persuasion that we are elected to eternal life; but it is by *producing in us the appropriate effects of his influence.* It is his to renew the heart; to sanctify the soul; to produce "love, joy, peace, long-suffering, gentleness, goodness, faith, meekness, temperance," Gal. v. 22, 23. If a man

him, that we may be also glorified together.

18 For I reckon that *w* the sufferings of this present time *are*

w 2 Co.4.17.

has *these,* he has evidence of the witnessing of the Spirit with *his* spirit. If not, he has no such evidence. And the way, therefore, to ascertain whether we have this witnessing of the Spirit, is by an honest and prayerful inquiry whether these *fruits* of the Spirit actually exist in our minds. If they do, the evidence is clear. If not, all vain confidence of good estate; all visions, and raptures, and fancied revelations, will be mere delusions. It may be added, that the *effect* of these fruits of the Spirit on the mind is to produce a calm and heavenly frame; and in that frame, when attended with the appropriate fruits of the Spirit in a holy life, we may rejoice as an evidence of piety. ¶ *That we are the children of God.* That we are adopted into his family.

17. *And if children.* If adopted into his family. ¶ *Then heirs.* That is, he will treat us as sons. An *heir* is one who succeeds to an estate. The meaning here is, that if we sustain the relation of sons to God, that we shall be treated as such, and admitted to share his favours. An adopted son comes in for a part of the inheritance, Num. xxvii. ¶ *Heirs of God.* This expression means that we shall be partakers of that inheritance which God confers on his people. That inheritance is his favour here, and eternal life hereafter. This is an honour infinitely higher than to be heir to the most princely earthly inheritance; or than to be the adopted son of the most magnificent earthly monarch. ¶ *And joint-heirs with Christ.* Christ is by eminence THE *Son of God.* As such, he is heir to the full honours and glory of heaven. Christians are united to him; they are his friends; and they are thus represented as destined to partake with him of his glory. They are the sons of God in a different sense from what he is; *he* by his nature and high relation, *they* by adoption; but still the idea of *sonship* exists in both; and hence both will partake in the glories of the eternal inheritance; compare

Phil. ii. 8, 9; Heb. ii. 9, 10. The connection between Christ and Christians is often referred to in the New Testament. The fact that they are united here is often alleged as a reason why they will be in glory, John xiv. 19, "Because I live, ye shall live also;" 2 Tim. ii. 11, 12, "For if we be dead with him, we shall also live with him; if we suffer, we shall also reign with him;" Rev. iii. 21, "To him that overcometh will I grant to sit with me in my throne," &c.; John xvii. 22–24. ¶ *If so be.* If this condition exist. We shall not be treated as co-heirs with him, unless we here give evidence that we are united to him. ¶ *That we suffer with* him. Greek, "if we suffer together, that we may also be glorified together." If we suffer in his cause; bear afflictions as he did; are persecuted and tried for the same thing; and thus show that we are united to him. It does not mean that we suffer to the same *extent* that he did; but we may *imitate* him in the kind of our sufferings, and in the spirit with which they are borne, and thus show that *we are* united to him. ¶ *That we may be also glorified together.* If united in the same kind of sufferings, there is propriety in being united in destiny beyond the scenes of all suffering, the kingdom of blessedness and love.

18. *For I reckon.* I think; I judge. This verse commences a new division of the subject, which is continued to ver. 25. Its design is to show the power of the gospel in sustaining the soul in trials—a very important and material part of the scheme. This had been partially noticed before (chap. v. 3–5), but its full power to support the soul in the prospect of a glorious immortality had not been fully discussed. This topic seems here to have been suggested by what is said of *adoption.* The mind of the apostle instantly adverted to the effects or benefits of that adoption; and one of the most material of those benefits was the sustaining grace which the gospel im-

not worthy *to be compared* with the glory which shall be revealed in us.

19 For the earnest expectation of the creature waiteth for the manifestation of the sons of God.

parted in the midst of afflictions. It should be borne in mind that the early Christians were comparatively few and feeble, and exposed to many trials, and that *this* topic would be often, therefore, introduced into the discussions about their privileges and condition. ¶ *The sufferings.* The afflictions; the persecutions, sicknesses, &c. The expression evidently includes not only the *peculiar* trials of Christians at that time, but all that believers are ever called to endure. ¶ *Of this present time.* Probably the apostle had *particular* reference to the various calamities *then* endured. But the expression is equally applicable to afflictions of all times and in all places. ¶ Are *not worthy* to be compared. Are nothing in comparison; the one is far more than an equivalent, in compensation for the other. ¶ *With the glory.* The happiness; the honour in heaven. ¶ *Which shall be revealed in us.* That shall be disclosed to us; or of which we shall be the partakers in heaven. The usual representation of heaven is that of glory, splendour, magnificence, or light; comp. Rev. xxi. 10, 23, 24; xxii. 5. By this, therefore, Christians may be sustained. Their sufferings may seem great; but they should remember that they are nothing in comparison with future glory. They are nothing *in degree.* For these are light compared with that "eternal weight of glory" which they shall "work out," 2 Cor. iv. 17. They are nothing *in duration.* For these sufferings are but for a moment; but the glory shall be eternal. These will soon pass away; but that glory shall never become dim or diminished; it will increase and expand for ever and ever. ¶ *In us.* Unto us (εἰς ἡμᾶς).

19. *For the earnest expectation* (ἀποκαραδοκία). This word occurs only here and in Phil. i. 20, "According to my *earnest expectation* and my hope," &c. It properly denotes a state of earnest desire to see any object when the head is thrust forward; an intense anxiety; an ardent wish; and is thus

well employed to denote the intense interest with which a Christian looks to his future inheritance. ¶ *Of the creature* (τῆς κτίσεως). Perhaps there is not a passage in the New Testament that has been deemed more difficult of interpretation than this (ver. 19–23); and after all the labours bestowed on it by critics, still there is no explanation proposed which is perfectly satisfactory, or in which commentators concur. The object here will be to give what appears to the writer the true meaning, without attempting to controvert the opinions of critics. The *main design* of the passage is, to *show the sustaining power of the gospel in the midst of trials, by the prospect of the future deliverance and inheritance of the sons of God.* This scope of the passage is to guide us in the interpretation. The following are, I suppose, the leading points in the illustration. (1) The word *creature* refers to the renewed nature of the Christian, or to the Christian as renewed. (2) He is waiting for his future glory; *i.e.* desirous of obtaining the full development of the honours that await him as the child of God, ver. 19. (3) He is subjected to a state of trial and vanity, affording comparatively little comfort and much disquietude. (4) This is not in accordance with the desire of his heart, "not willingly," but is the wise appointment of God, ver. 20. (5) In this state there is the hope of deliverance into glorious liberty, ver. 21. (6) This condition of things does not exist merely in regard to the Christian, but is the common condition of the world. It all groans, and is in trial, as much as the Christian. He therefore should not deem his condition as peculiarly trying. It is the common lot of all things here, ver. 22. But, (7) Christians only have the prospect of deliverance. To them is held out the hope of final rescue, and of an eternal inheritance beyond all these sufferings. They wait, therefore, for the full benefits of the adoption;

the complete recovery even of the body from the effects of sin, and the toils and trials of this life; and thus they are sustained by hope, which is the argument which the apostle has in view, ver. 23, 24. With this view of the general scope of the passage, we may examine the particular phrases.

[The opinion which is perhaps most generally adopted of this difficult passage, is that which explains κτίσις of the whole irrational creation. According to this view, the apostle, having adverted to the glory that awaited the Christian, as a ground of joy and comfort under present sufferings, exalts our idea of it still higher by representing the external world as participating in, and waiting for it. "This interpretation is suitable to the design of the apostle. Paul's object is not to confirm the certainty of a future state, but to produce a strong impression of its glorious character. Nothing could be better adapted to this object, than the grand and beautiful figure of the whole creation waiting and longing for the glorious revelation of the Son of God, and the consummation of his kingdom" (Hodge). In the original it is the same word that is rendered alternately "creature" and "creation." And the meaning of the passage depends, in great measure, on the sense of this single word. Generally speaking, it signifies anything created. The particular kind of creation is determined by the context alone. Of course, whatever sense we may attach to, it, must be continued throughout the whole passage, as we cannot suppose the apostle uses the same word in two different senses, in one place, without any intimation of the change. To what, then, does κτίσις refer? It is maintained by those who adopt the view noticed above, that it cannot refer to angels, either elect or fallen, since the former have never been subject to the bondage of corruption, and the latter are not waiting for the manifestation of the sons of God; that it cannot allude to wicked men, for neither do they anxiously look out for this manifestation; that it can no more refer to saints or renewed men, since these are expressly distinguished as a separate class in the 23d verse; and that, therefore, it must be understood of the whole inanimate and irrational creation. It is further argued, that every part of the context may be explained consistently with this view. The passage is supposed to present a very bold and beautiful instance of the figure called prosopopœia, by which things inanimate are invested with life and feeling, a figure which is indeed very common in Scripture, and which we need not be surprised to find in this place, amid so much that is grand and elevating, Joel i. 10, 20; Jer. xii. 4; Is. xxiv. 4, 7. According to this interpretation of κτίσις, then, the general sense of the apostle may be thus given. The whole irrational creation is interested in the future glory of the sons of God, and is anxiously waiting for it. For then the curse will be removed from the very ground, and the lower animals relieved from oppression and cruelty. The very creation, on account of the sin of man, has been subjected to the curse, and has become "vain" or useless in regard to the original design of it, having been made subservient to the evil purposes and passions of man. This state of subjection to vanity is not willing, but by restraint. Violence is imposed, as it were, on external nature. But this shall not continue. There is hope in the heart of the subject world, that (ὅτι) it shall be delivered from this bondage, and participate in the liberty of the children of God. This representation may seem strange and unusual, but "we know" certainly, adds the apostle, that it is so; that "the whole creation" (πᾶσα ἡ κτίσις) groaneth and travaileth in pain throughout every part. Even we, who are saints of God, and have been favoured with the earnests of future bliss, feel the general oppression, and groan within ourselves, while we wait for the period of deliverance, in which the very body shall be ransomed from the grave and fashioned like unto Christ's glorious body.]

¶ Of the creature. The word here rendered creature (κτίσις), occurs in the New Testament nineteen times, and is used in the following senses: (1) Creation; the act of creating, Rom. i. 20. (2) The creature; that which is created or formed; the universe, Mark x. 6; xiii. 19; 2 Pet. iii. 4; Rom. i. 25; viii. 39. (3) The rational creation; man as a rational being; the world of mankind, Mark xvi. 15; Col. i. 23; 1 Pet. ii. 13. (4) Perhaps the church, the new creation of God taken collectively, Col. i. 15; Rev. iii. 14. (5) The *Christian*, the new creation, regarded individually; the work of the Holy Spirit on the renewed heart; the new man. After all the attention which I can give to this passage, I regard this to be the meaning here, for the following reasons, viz. (1) Because this alone seems to me to suit the connection, and to make sense in the argument. If the word refers, as has been supposed by different interpreters,

20 For the creature was made subject to vanity, not willingly,

either to angels, or to the bodies of men, or to the material creation, or to the rational creation—to men, or mankind, it is difficult to see what connection either would have with the argument. The apostle is discoursing of the benefits of the gospel to *Christians* in time of trial; and the bearing of the argument requires us to understand this illustration of them, unless we are compelled *not* to understand it thus by the proper laws of interpreting words. (2) The word *creature* is used in a similar sense by the same apostle. Thus 2 Cor. v. 17, "If any man be in Christ, he is a *new creature*" (καινὴ κτίσις); Gal. vi. 15, "For in Christ Jesus neither circumcision availeth any thing, nor uncircumcision, but a *new creature.*" (3) The verb *create* is thus used. Thus Eph. ii. 10, "For we are his workmanship, *created* in Christ Jesus unto good works;" ver. 15, "Having abolished in his flesh the enmity . . . for to make in himself of twain one new man;" Greek, "that he might *create* (κτίσῃ) the two into one new man;" iv. 24, "The new man, which *is created* in righteousness," &c. (4) Nothing was more natural than for the sacred writers thus to speak of a Christian as a new creation, a new creature. The great power of God involved in his conversion, and the strong resemblance between the creation and imparting spiritual life, led naturally to this use of the language. (5) Language similar to this occurs in the Old Testament, and it was natural to transfer it to the New. The Jewish people were represented as *made* or created by God for his service, and the phrase, therefore, might come to designate those who were thus formed by him to his service, Deut. xxxii. 6, "Hath he not *made thee*, and established thee?" Isaiah xliii. 7, ". . . Every one that is called by my name; for I have *created* him for my glory, I have formed him; yea, I have made him;" 21, "This people have I *formed* for myself." From all which reasons, it seems to me that the expression here is used to denote Christians, renewed men. Its mean-

ing, however, is varied in ver. 22. ¶ *Waiteth for.* Expects; is not in a state of possession, but is looking for it with interest. ¶ *The manifestation of the sons of God.* The full development of the benefits of the sons of God; the time when they shall be acknowledged, and received into the full privileges of sons. Here Christians have *some* evidence of their adoption. But they are in a world of sin; they are exposed to trials; they are subject to many calamities; and though they have evidence *here* that they are the sons of God, yet they wait for that period when they shall be fully delivered from all these trials, and be admitted to the enjoyment of all the privileges of the children of the Most High. The time when this shall take place will be at the day of judgment, when they shall be fully acknowledged in the presence of an assembled universe as his children. All Christians are represented as in this posture of *waiting* for the full possession of their privileges as the children of God, 1 Cor. i. 7, "Waiting for the coming of our Lord Jesus Christ;" 2 Thes. iii. 5; Gal. v. 5, "For we through the Spirit wait for the hope of righteousness by faith;" 1 Thes. i. 10.

20. *For the creature.* The renewed creature; the Christian mind. This is given as a reason for its *aspiring* to the full privileges of adoption, that the present state is not one of choice, or one which is preferred, but one to which it has been subjected for wise reasons by God. ¶ *Subject to vanity.* The word "subject to" means placed in such a state; subjected to it by the appointment of another, as a soldier has his rank and place assigned him in an army. The word *vanity* here (ματαιότης) is descriptive of the present condition of the Christian, as frail and dying; as exposed to trials, temptations, and cares; as in the midst of conflicts, and of a world which may be emphatically pronounced *vanity.* More or less, the Christian is brought under this influence; his joys are marred; his peace is discomposed; his affections wander; his life is a life of

but by reason of him who hath subjected *the same* in hope;

vanity and vexation. ¶ *Not willingly.* Not voluntarily. It is not a matter of choice. It is not that which is congenial to his renewed nature. That would aspire to perfect holiness and peace. But this subjection is one that is contrary to it, and from which he desires to be delivered. This describes substantially the same condition as chap. vii. 15–24. ¶ *But by reason. By* him (διὰ). It is the appointment of God, who has chosen to place his people in this condition, and who for wise purposes retains them in it. ¶ *Who hath subjected* the same. Who has appointed his people to this condition. It is his wise arrangement. Here we may observe, (1) That the instinctive feelings of Christians lead them to desire a purer and a happier world, Phil. i. 23. (2) That it is not what they desire, to be subjected to the toils of this life, and to the temptations and vanities of this world. They sigh for deliverance. (3) Their lot in life, their being subjected to this state of vanity, is the arrangement of God. *Why* it is, he has not seen fit to inform us fully. He *might* have taken his people at once to heaven as soon as they are converted. But though we know not *all* the reasons why they are continued here in this state of *vanity*, we can see some of them : (*a*) Christians are subjected to this state *to do good* to their fellow-sinners. They remain on earth for this purpose; and this should be their leading aim. (*b*) By their remaining here the power of the gospel is shown in overcoming their sin; in meeting their temptations; in sustaining them in trial, and in thus furnishing living evidence to the world of the power and excellency of that gospel. This could not be attained if they were removed at once to heaven. (*c*) It furnishes occasion for some interesting exhibitions of character—for hope, and faith, and love, and for increasing and progressive excellence. (*d*) It is a proper *training* for heaven. It brings out the Christian character, and *fits it* for the

21 Because[x] the creature itself also shall be delivered from the

x 2 Pe.3.13.

skies. There may be inestimable advantages, all of which we may not see, in subjecting the Christian to a process of *training* in overcoming his sins, and in producing confidence in God, before he is admitted to his state of final rest. (*e*) It is fit and proper that he should engage here in the service of Him who has redeemed him. He has been ransomed by the blood of Christ, and God has the highest claim on him in all the conflicts and toils, in all the labours and services to which he may be subjected in this life. ¶ *In hope.* See Note, chap. v. 4. Hope has reference to the future, and in this state of the Christian he sighs for deliverance, and expects it.

21. *Because.* This is the ground of his hope, and this sustains him now. It is the purpose of God that deliverance shall be granted, and this supports the Christian amidst the trials to which he is subjected here. The hope is, that this same renewed man shall be delivered from all the toils, and cares, and sins of this state. ¶ *The creature itself.* The very soul that is renewed; the ransomed man without essential change. It will be the same being, though purified; the same man, possessed of the same body and soul, though freed from all the corruptions of humanity, and elevated above all the degradations of the present condition. The idea is everywhere presented, that the identical person shall be admitted to heaven without essential change, 1 Cor. xv. 35–38, 42–44. That this is the hope of all Christians, see 2 Pet. iii. 13. ¶ *From the bondage of corruption.* This does not differ materially from " vanity," ver. 20. It implies that this state is not a *willing* state, or not a condition of choice, but is one of *bondage* or *servitude* (see chap. vii. 15–24); and that it is a *corrupt*, imperfect, perishing condition. It is one that leads to sin, and temptation, and conflict and anxiety. It is a condition often which destroys the peace, mars the happiness, dims the hope, enfeebles the faith, and

bondage of corruption into the glorious liberty of the children of God.

22 For we know that [5] the whole creation groaneth and travaileth in pain together until now.

[5] or, *every creature.*

weakens the love of Christians, and this is called the *bondage* of corruption. It is also one in which temporal death has dominion, and in the bondage of which, believers as well as unbelievers shall be held. Yet from *all* this bondage the children of God shall be delivered. ¶ *The glorious liberty.* Greek, the freedom of the glory of the children of God. This is, (1) *Liberty.* It is freedom from the bondage under which the Christian groans. It will be freedom from sin, from corruption, from evil desires, from calamity, from death. The highest *freedom* in the universe is that which is enjoyed in heaven, where the redeemed are under the sovereignty and government of their King, but where they do that, and that only, which they desire. All is slavery but the service of God; all is bondage but that law which accords with the supreme wish of the soul, and where commands accord with the perfect desires of the heart. (2) This is *glorious* liberty. It is encompassed with majesty, attended with honour, crowned with splendour. The heavenly world is often described as a state of glory; Note, chap. ii. 10. ¶ *Of the children of God.* That the children of God shall enjoy.

22. *For we know.* The sentiment of this verse is designed as an illustration of what had just been said. ¶ *That the whole creation.* Margin, "*every creature.*" This expression has been commonly understood as meaning the same as "the creature" in ver. 20, 21. But I understand it as having a different signification, and as being used in the natural and usual signification of the word creature, or creation. It refers, as I suppose, to the whole animate creation; to all living beings; to the state of all created things here, as in a condition of pain and disorder, and groaning and death. Everything which we see, every creature which lives, is thus subjected to a state of servitude, pain,

vanity, and death. The reasons for supposing that this is the true interpretation are, (1) That the apostle expressly speaks of "the *whole* creation," of every creature, qualifying the phrase by the expression "we know," as if he was drawing an illustration from a well-understood, universal fact. (2) This interpretation makes consistent sense, and makes the verse have a direct bearing on the argument. *It is just an argument from analogy.* He had (ver. 20, 21) said that the condition of a Christian was one of bondage and servitude. It was an imperfect, humiliating state; one attended with pain, sorrow, and death. This might be regarded as a melancholy description, and the question might arise, Why was not the Christian at once delivered from this? The answer is in this verse. *It is just the condition of everything.* It is the manifest principle on which God governs the world. *The whole creation is in just this condition;* and we are not to be surprised, therefore, if it is the condition of the believer. It is a part of the universal system of things; it accords with everything we see; and we are not to be surprised that the church exists on the same principle of administration; in a state of bondage, imperfection, sorrow, and sighing for deliverance. ¶ *Groaneth.* Greek, groans together. All is united in a condition of sorrow. The expression denotes mutual and universal grief. It is one wide and loud lamentation, in which a dying world unites, and in which it has united "until now." ¶ *And travaileth in pain together.* This expression properly denotes the extreme pain of parturition. It also denotes any intense agony, or extreme suffering; and it means here that the condition of all things has been that of intense, united, and continued suffering; in other words, that we are in a world of misery and death. This has been *united*—all have partaken of it;

23 And not only *they*, but ourselves also, which have *y*the firstfruits of the Spirit, even we ourselves *z*groan within ourselves, waiting for the adoption, *to wit*, *a*the redemption of our body.

y Ep.1.14.   *z* 2 Co.5.2,4.   *a* Lu.21.28.

---

it has been *intense*—all endure much; it has been *unremitted*—every age has experienced the repetition of the same thing. ¶ *Until now.* Till the time when the apostle wrote. It is equally true of the time since he wrote. It has been the characteristic of every age. It is remarkable that the apostle does not here say of "the whole creation," that it had any hope of deliverance; an additional consideration that shows that the interpretation above suggested is correct, ver. 20, 21, 23. Of the sighing and suffering universe, he says nothing with respect to its future state. He does not say that the suffering brutal creation shall be compensated, or shall be restored or raised up. He simply adverts to the fact that it suffers, as an illustration that the condition of the Christian is not singular and peculiar. The Scriptures say nothing of the future condition of the brutal creation.

23. *And not only* they. Not only the creation in general. ¶ *But ourselves also.* Christians. ¶ *Which have the first-fruits of the Spirit.* The word used (ἀπαρχή) denotes properly the first-fruits of the harvest, the portion that was first collected and consecrated to God as an offering of gratitude, Deut. xxvi. 2; Ex. xxiii. 19; Num. xviii. 13. Hence the word means that which is *first in order of time.* Here it means, as I suppose, that the Christians of whom Paul was speaking had partaken of the *first* influences of the Spirit, or had been among the first partakers of his influences in converting sinners. The Spirit had been sent down to attend the preaching of the gospel, and they were among the first who had partaken of those influences. Some, however, have understood the word to mean a pledge, or earnest, or foretaste of joys to come. This idea has been attached to the word because the first-fruits of the harvest were a pledge of the harvest, an evidence that it was ripe, &c. But the word does not seem to be used

in this sense in the New Testament. The only places where it occurs are the following: Rom. viii. 23; xi. 16; xvi. 5; 1 Cor. xv. 20, 23; xvi. 15; Jam. i. 18; Rev. xiv. 4. ¶ *Groan within ourselves.* We sigh for deliverance. The expression denotes strong internal desire; the deep anguish of spirit when the heart is oppressed with anguish, and earnestly wishes for succour. ¶ *Waiting for the adoption.* Waiting for the full blessings of the adoption. Christians are adopted when they are converted (ver. 15), but they have not been yet admitted to the full privileges of their adoption into the family of God. Their adoption when they are converted is secret, and may at the time be unknown to the world. The fulness of the adoption, their complete admission to the privileges of the sons of God, shall be in the day of judgment, in the presence of the universe, and amidst the glories of the final consummation of all things. This adoption is not different from the first, but is the *completion* of the act of grace when a sinner is received into the family of God. ¶ *The redemption of the body.* The complete recovery of the body from death and corruption. The particular and striking act of the adoption in the day of judgment will be the raising up of the body from the grave, and rendering it immortal and eternally blessed. The particular effects of the adoption in this world are on *the soul.* The completion of it on the last day will be seen particularly in *the body;* and thus *the entire man* shall be admitted into the favour of God, and restored from all his sins and all the evil consequences of the fall. The apostle here speaks the language of every Christian. The Christian has joys which the world does not know; but he has also sorrows; he sighs over his corruption; he is in the midst of calamity; he is going to the grave; and he looks forward to that complete deliverance, and to that

24 For we are saved by hope: but hope that is seen, is not hope; for what a man seeth, why doth he yet *b* hope for?

b 2 Co.5.7.

25 But if we hope for that we see not, *then* do we with patience wait for *it*.

26 Likewise the Spirit also help-

elevated state, when, in the presence of an assembled universe, he shall be acknowledged as a child of God. This elevated privilege gives to Christianity its high value; and the hope of being acknowledged in the presence of the universe as the child of God—the hope of the poorest and the humblest believer—is of infinitely more value than the prospect of the most princely inheritance, or of the brightest crown that a monarch ever wore.

24. *For we are saved by hope.* It cannot be said that *hope* is the instrument or condition of salvation. Most commentators have understood this as meaning that we have as yet attained salvation only *in* hope; that we have arrived only to a condition in which we hope for *future* glory; and that we are in an attitude of waiting for the future state of adoption. But perhaps the word *saved* may mean here simply, we are *kept, preserved, sustained* in our trials, by hope. Our trials are so great that nothing but the prospect of future deliverance would uphold us; and the prospect is sufficient to enable us to bear them with patience. This is the proper meaning of the word *save;* and it is often thus used in the New Testament; see Mat. viii. 25; xvi. 25; Mark iii. 4; viii. 35. The Syriac renders this, "For by hope we live." The Arabic, "We are preserved by hope." Hope thus sustains the soul in the midst of trials, and enables it to bear them without a murmur. ¶ *But hope that is seen.* Hope is a complex emotion, made up of an earnest desire, and an expectation of obtaining an object. It has reference, therefore, to that which is at present unseen. But when the object is seen, and is in our possession, it cannot be said to be an object of hope. The word *hope* here means the *object* of hope, the thing hoped for. ¶ *What a man seeth.* The word *seeth* is used here in the sense of possessing, or enjoying. What a man

already possesses, he cannot be said to hope for. ¶ *Why.* How. What a man actually possesses, *how* can he look forward to it with anticipation?

25. *But if we hope,* &c. The effect here stated is one which exists everywhere. Where there is a *strong desire* for an object, and a *corresponding expectation* of obtaining it—which constitutes true hope—then we can wait for it with patience. Where there is a strong desire without a corresponding expectation of obtaining it, there is *impatience.* As the Christian has a strong desire of future glory, and as he has an expectation of obtaining it just in proportion to that desire, it follows that he may bear trials and persecutions patiently in the hope of his future deliverance. Compared with our future glory, our present sufferings are light, and but for a moment, 2 Cor. iv. 17. In the hope of that blessed eternity which is before him, the Christian can endure the severest trial, and bear the intensest pain without a murmur.

26. *Likewise the Spirit.* This introduces a new source of consolation and support, that which is derived from the Spirit. It is a continuation of the argument of the apostle, to show the sustaining power of the Christian religion. The "Spirit" here undoubtedly refers to the Holy Spirit, who dwells in us, and who strengthens us. ¶ *Helpeth.* This word properly means, to sustain *with* us; to aid us in supporting. It is applied usually to those who *unite* in supporting or carrying a burden. The meaning may be thus expressed: "He greatly assists or aids us." ¶ *Our infirmities.* Assists us in our infirmities, or aids us to bear them. The word *infirmities* refers to the weaknesses to which we are subject, and to our various trials in this life. The Spirit helps us in this, (1) By giving us strength to bear them; (2) By exciting us to make efforts to sustain them; (3) By ministering to us consolations, and truths, and views of our

eth our infirmities: for we know not what we should pray for as we ought; *c*but the Spirit itself maketh intercession for us with groanings which cannot be uttered.

c Zec.12.10.

27 And *d*he that searcheth the hearts knoweth what *is* the mind of the Spirit, because [6]he maketh intercession for the saints *e*according to *the will of* God.

d Je.17.10; Re.2.23.　6 or, *that.*　e 1 Jn.5.14.

Christian privileges, that enable us to endure our trials. ¶ *For we know not,* &c. This is a *specification* of the aid which the Holy Spirit renders us. The reasons why Christians do not know what to pray for may be, (1) That they do not know what would be really best for them. (2) They do not know what God might be willing to grant them. (3) They are to a great extent ignorant of the character of God, the reason of his dealings, the principles of his government, and their own real wants. (4) They are often in real, deep, perplexity. They are encompassed with trials, exposed to temptations, feeble by disease, and subject to calamities. In these circumstances, if left alone, they would neither be able to bear their trials, nor know what to ask at the hand of God. ¶ *But the Spirit itself.* The Holy Spirit, ver. 9–11. ¶ *Maketh intercession.* The word here used (ὑπερεντυγχάνει) occurs nowhere else in the New Testament. The word ἐντυγχάνω, however, is used several times. It means properly to be present with anyone for the purpose of aiding, as an advocate does in a court of justice; hence to intercede for anyone, or to aid or assist in any manner. In this place it simply means that the Holy Spirit *greatly assists* or *aids* us; not by praying for us, but in our prayers and infirmities. ¶ *With groanings.* With *sighs,* or that deep feeling and intense anxiety which exists in the oppressed and burdened heart of the Christian. ¶ *Which cannot be uttered.* Or rather, perhaps, which is *not* uttered; those emotions which are too deep for utterance, or for expression in articulate language. This does not mean that the Spirit *produces* these groanings; but that *in* these deep-felt emotions, when the soul is oppressed and overwhelmed, he lends us his assistance and sustains us. The phrase may be thus translated:

"The Spirit greatly aids or supports us in those deep emotions, those intense feelings, those inward sighs which cannot be expressed in language, but which he enables us to bear, and which are understood by Him that searcheth the hearts."

27. *And he that searcheth the hearts.* God. To search the heart is one of his attributes which cannot be communicated to a creature, Jer. xvii. 10. ¶ *Knoweth what is the mind of the Spirit.* Knows the desires which the Holy Spirit excites and produces in the heart. He does not need that those deep emotions should be expressed in words: he does not need the eloquence of language to induce him to hear; but he sees the anxious feelings of the soul, and is ready to aid and to bless. ¶ *Maketh intercession for the saints.* Aids and directs Christians. ¶ *According to* the will of *God.* Greek, "according to God." It is according to his will in the following respects: (1) The Spirit is given according to his will. It is his gracious purpose to grant his aid to all who truly love him. (2) The desires which he excites in the heart of the Christian are those which are according to his will; they are such as God wishes to exist—the contrite, humble, and penitent pleading of sinners for mercy. (3) He superintends and guards Christians in their prayers. It is not meant that they are infallible, or that they *never* make an improper petition, or have an improper desire; but that he has a *general* superintendence over their minds, and that so far as they will yield themselves to his direction, they shall not be led into error. That man is most safe who yields himself most entirely to the influence of the Holy Spirit. And the doctrine here stated is one that is full of consolation to the Christian. We are poor, and needy, and ignorant,

28 And / we know that all things work together for good to them that

f Ps.46.1,2; He.12.6-12.

and blind; we are the creatures of a day, and are crushed before the moth. But in the midst of our feebleness we may look to God for the aid of his Spirit, and rejoice in his presence, and in his power to sustain us in our sighings, and to guide us in our wanderings.

28. *And we know.* This verse introduces another source of consolation and support, drawn from the fact that all things are under the direction of an infinitely wise Being, who has purposed the salvation of the Christian, and who has so appointed all things that they shall contribute to it. ¶ *All things.* All our afflictions and trials; all the persecutions and calamities to which we are exposed. Though they are numerous and long-continued, yet they are among the means that are appointed for our welfare. ¶ *Work together for good.* They shall co-operate; they shall mutually contribute to our good. They take off our affections from this world; they teach us the truth about our frail, transitory, and dying condition; they lead us to look to God for support, and to heaven for a final home; and they produce a subdued spirit, a humble temper, a patient, tender, and kind disposition. This has been the experience of all saints; and at the end of life they have been able to say it was good for them to be afflicted, Ps. cxix. 67, 71; Jer. xxxi. 18, 19; Heb. xii. 11. ¶ *For good.* For our real welfare; for the promotion of true piety, peace, and happiness in our hearts. ¶ *To them that love God.* This is a characteristic of true piety. To them, afflictions are a blessing; to others, they often prove otherwise. On others they are sent as chastisements; and they produce murmuring, instead of peace; rebellion, instead of submission; and anger, impatience, and hatred, instead of calmness, patience, and love. The Christian is made a better man by receiving afflictions as they should be received, and by desiring that they should accomplish the purpose for which they are sent; the

love God, to them who are the called according to *his* purpose.

sinner is made more hardened by resisting them, and refusing to submit to their obvious intention and design. ¶ *To them who are the called.* Christians are often represented as *called* of God. The word (κλητὸς) is sometimes used to denote an external invitation, offer, or calling, Mat. xx. 16; xxii. 14. But excepting in these places, it is used in the New Testament to denote those who had *accepted* the call, and were true Christians, Rom. i. 6, 7; 1 Cor. i. 2, 24; Rev. xvii. 14. It is evidently used in this sense here—to denote those who were true Christians. The connection as well as the usual meaning of the word requires us thus to understand it. Christians are said to be *called* because God has invited them to be saved, and has sent into their heart such an influence as to make the call effectual to their salvation. In this way their salvation is to be traced entirely to God. ¶ *According to* his *purpose.* The word here rendered *purpose* (πρόθεσις) means properly a *proposition*, or a laying down anything in view of others; and is thus applied to the *bread* that was laid on the table of *show-bread*, Mat. xii. 4; Mark ii. 26; Luke vi. 4. Hence it means, when applied to the mind, a *plan* or *purpose* of mind. It implies that God had a plan, purpose, or intention, in regard to all who became Christians. They are not saved by chance or hap-hazard. God does not convert men without design; and his designs are not new, but are eternal. What he does, he always meant to do. What it is *right* for him to do, it was right always to *intend* to do. What God always meant to do, is his purpose or plan. That he *has* such a purpose in regard to the salvation of his people, is often affirmed, Rom. ix. 11; Eph. i. 11; iii. 11; 2 Tim. i. 9; Jer. li. 29. This *purpose* of saving his people is, (1) One over which a creature can have no control; it is according to the counsel of his own will, Eph. i. 11. (2) It is without any merit on the part of the sinner—a purpose to save him

29 For whom he did ^gforeknow, he also did predestinate *to be* conformed to the image of his Son,

g 1 Pe.1.2.

that he might be the first-born among many brethren.

30 Moreover whom he did pre-

---

by grace, 2 Tim. i. 9. (3) It is eternal, Eph. iii. 11. (4) It is such as should excite lively gratitude in all who have been inclined by the grace of God to accept the offers of eternal life. They owe it to the mere mercy of God, and they should acknowledge *him* as the fountain and source of all their hopes of heaven.

29. *For whom he did foreknow.* The word used here (προέγνω) has been the subject of almost endless disputes in regard to its meaning in this place. The *literal* meaning of the word cannot be a matter of dispute. It denotes properly to *know beforehand;* to be acquainted with future events. But whether it means here simply to know that certain persons *would* become Christians; or to ordain, and constitute them to be Christians, and to be saved, has been a subject of almost endless discussion. Without entering at large into an investigation of the word, perhaps the following remarks may throw light on it. (1) It does not here have reference to *all* the human family; for all are not, and have not, been conformed to the image of his Son. It has reference, therefore, only to those who would become Christians, and be saved. (2) It implies *certain knowledge.* It was certainly foreseen, in some way, that they would believe, and be saved. There is nothing, therefore, in regard to them that is *contingent*, or subject to doubt in the divine Mind, since it was certainly foreknown. (3) The event which was thus foreknown must have been, for some cause, *certain* and *fixed;* since an uncertain event could not be possibly foreknown. To talk of a foreknowing a contingent event, that is, of foreknowing an event as certain which may or may not exist, is an absurdity. (4) In what way such an event became certain is not determined by the use of this word. But it must have been somehow in connection with a divine appointment or arrangement,

since in no other way can it be conceived to be certain. While the *word* used here, therefore, does not of necessity mean to decree, yet its use supposes that there *was* a purpose or plan; and the phrase is an explanation of what the apostle had just said, that it was *according to the purpose* of God that they were called. This passage does not affirm *why*, or *how*, or, *on what grounds* God foreknew that some of the human family would be saved. It simply affirms the fact; and the mode in which those who will believe were designated, must be determined from other sources. This passage simply teaches that he knew them; that his eye was fixed on them; that he regarded them as to be conformed to his Son; and that, thus knowing them, he designated them to eternal life. The Syriac renders it in accordance with this interpretation : "And from the beginning he knew them, and sealed them with the image of his Son," &c. As, however, none *would* believe but by the influences of his Spirit, it follows that they were not foreknown on account of any faith which they would themselves exercise, or any good works which they would themselves perform, but according to the purpose or plan of God himself. ¶ *He also did predestinate.* See the meaning of the original of this word explained in Notes on chap. i. 4; see also Note on Acts iv. 28; and 1 Cor. ii. 7. In these places the word evidently means to determine, purpose, or decree beforehand; and it *must* have this meaning here. No other idea could be consistent with the proper meaning of the word, or be intelligible. It is clear, also, that it does not refer to *external* privileges, but to real conversion and piety; since that to which they were predestinated was not the external privilege of the gospel, but conformity to his Son, and salvation; see ver. 30. No passage could possibly teach in stronger language that it was God's purpose to save those who will be saved.

destinate, them he also ^h called:
and whom he called, them he ^i also
justified: and whom he justified,
them he also ^k glorified.

h He.9.15.   *i* 1 Co.6.11.   *k* Jn.17.22.

31 What shall we then say to
these things? If ^l God *be* for us,
who *can be* against us?

32 He ^m that spared not his own

l Ps.118.6.   *m* ch.5.6–10.

Eph. i. 5, "Having predestinated us
unto the adoption of children by Jesus
Christ unto himself;" ver. 11, "Being
predestinated according to the purpose
of Him who worketh all things after
the counsel of his own will." ¶ To
be *conformed to the image of his Son.*
To resemble his Son; to be of like
form with the image of his Son. We
may learn here, (1) That God does
not determine to save men, whatever
their character may be. The decree
is not to save them in their sins, or
whether they be sinful or holy. But
it has primary respect to their character. It is that they *should be* holy;
and, as a *consequence* of this, that they
should be saved. (2) The only evidence which we can have that we are
the subjects of his gracious purpose is,
that we are *in fact* conformed to the
Lord Jesus Christ. For this was the
design of the decree. This is the only
satisfactory proof of piety; and by this
alone can we determine that we are
interested in his gracious plan of saving men. ¶ *That he might be the first-
born.* The *first-born* among the Hebrews had many peculiar privileges.
The idea here is, (1) That Christ
might be pre-eminent as the model
and exemplar; that he might be clothed with peculiar honours, and be so
regarded in his church; and yet, (2)
That he might still sustain a fraternal
relation to them; that he might be
one in the same great family of God
where *all* are sons; comp. Heb. ii. 12
–14. ¶ *Many brethren.* Not a few.
The purpose of God is that *many* of
the human family shall be saved.

30. *Moreover, &c.* In this verse,
in order to show to Christians the true
consolation to be derived from the fact
that they are predestinated, the apostle states the connection between that
predestination and their certain salvation. The one implied the other.
¶ *Whom he did predestinate.* All
whom he did predestinate. ¶ *Them*

he also called. Called by his Spirit
to become Christians. He called, not
merely by an *external* invitation, but
in such a way as that they *in fact* were
justified. This cannot refer simply to
an *external* call of the gospel, since
those who are here said to be called are
said also to be justified and glorified.
The meaning is, that there is a certain
connection between the predestination
and the call, which will be manifested
in due time. The connection is so certain that the one infallibly secures the
other. ¶ *He justified.* See Note, chap.
iii. 24. Not that he justified them
from eternity, for this was not true;
and *if* it were, it would also follow that
he *glorified* them from eternity, which
would be an absurdity. It means that
there is a regular *sequence* of events
—the predestination precedes and
secures the calling; and the calling
precedes and secures the justification.
The one is connected in the purpose of
God with the other; and the one, *in
fact,* does not take place without the
other. The purpose was *in eternity.*
The calling and justifying *in time.*
¶ *Them he also glorified.* This refers
probably to heaven. It means that
there is a connection between justification and glory. The one does not
exist without the other in its own proper time; as the calling does not subsist without the act of justification.
This *proves,* therefore, the doctrine of
the perseverance of the saints. There
is a connection infallible and ever existing between the predestination and
the final salvation. They who are
subjects of the one are partakers of
the other. That this is the sense is
clear, (1) Because it is the natural
and obvious meaning of the passage.
(2) Because this only would meet the
design of the argument of the apostle.
For how would it be a source of consolation to say to them that whom God
foreknew he predestinated, and whom
he predestinated he called, and whom

Son, but delivered him up for us all, how shall he not with him also freely give us all things?

he called he justified, and whom he justified *might fall away and be lost for ever?* 31. *What shall we then say*, &c. What fairly follows from the facts stated? or what conclusion shall we draw in regard to the power of the Christian religion to support us in our trials from the considerations which have been stated? What the influence *is* he proceeds to state. ¶ *If God be for us.* Be on our side, or is our friend, as he has shown himself to be by adopting us (ver. 15), by granting to us his Spirit (ver. 16, 17, 26, 27), and by his gracious purpose to save us, ver. 29, 30. ¶ *Who* can be *against us?* Who can injure or destroy us? Sinners may be against us, and so may the great enemy of our souls, but their power to destroy us is taken away. God is more mighty than all our foes, and he can defend and save us; see Ps. cxviii. 6, "The Lord is on my side; I will not fear what man can do unto me." The proposition advanced in this verse Paul proceeds to illustrate by various specifications, which continue to the end of the chapter.

32. *He that spared not.* Who did not retain, or keep from suffering and death. ¶ *His own Son.* Who thus gave the *highest* proof of love that a father could give, and the highest demonstration of his willingness to do good to those for whom he gave him. ¶ *But delivered him up.* Gave him into the hands of men, and to a cruel death; Note, Acts ii. 23. ¶ *For us all.* For all Christians. The connection requires that this expression should be understood here with this limitation. The argument for the security of *all* Christians is here derived from the fact, that God had shown them equal love in giving his Son for them. It was not merely for the apostles; not only for the rich and the great, but for the most humble and obscure of the flock of Christ. For them he endured as severe pangs, and expressed as much love, as for the rich and the great that shall be redeemed. The most humble

33 Who[n] shall lay anything to the charge of God's elect? It[o] *is* God that justifieth.

n Is.50.8,9.   *o* Re.12.10,11.

and obscure believer may derive consolation from the fact that Christ died for *him*, and that God has expressed the highest love for him which we can conceive to be possible. ¶ *How shall he not.* His giving his Son is a proof that he *will* give to us all things that we need. The argument is from the greater to the less. He that has given the greater gift will not withhold the less. ¶ *All things.* All things that may be needful for our welfare. These things he will give *freely;* without money and without price. His first great gift, that of his Son, was a free gift; and all others that we may need will be given in a similar manner. It is not by money, nor by our merit, but it is by the mere mercy of God; so that from the beginning to the end of the work it is all of grace. We see here, (1) The privilege of being a Christian. He has the friendship of God; has been favoured with the highest proofs of divine love; and has assurance that he shall receive all that he needs. (2) He has evidence that God will continue to be his friend. He that has give. *his Son* to die for his people will not withdraw the lesser mercies that may be necessary to secure their salvation. The argument of the apostle here, therefore, is one that strongly shows that God will not forsake his children, but will keep them to eternal life.

33. *Who shall lay any thing to the charge.* This expression is taken from courts of law, and means, who shall accuse, or condemn, or so charge with crime before the tribunal of God as to cause their condemnation? ¶ *God's elect.* His chosen people. Those who have been chosen according to his eternal purpose; Note, ver. 28. As they are the chosen of God, they are dear to him; and as he purposed to save them, he will do it in such a way as that none can bring against them a charge that would condemn them. ¶ *It is God that justifieth.* That is, who has pardoned them, and admitted

34 Who *is* he that condemneth?
It is Christ that died, yea rather,
that is risen again, who is even at

the right hand of God, who also
maketh intercession for us.

35 Who shall separate us from

them to his favour, and pronounced
them *just* in his sight; Note, chap. i.
17; iii. 24. It would be absurd to
suppose that *he* would again condemn
them. The fact that he has justified
them is, therefore, a strong proof that
they will be saved. This may be read
with more force as a question, "Who
shall lay any thing to the charge of
God's elect? Shall God who justifieth?" The Greek will bear either
mode of rendering. The passage implies that there would be a high degree of absurdity in supposing that
the same Being would both justify and
condemn the same individual. The
Christian, therefore, is secure.

34. *Who* is *he that condemneth?* Who
shall pass sentence of condemnation,
and consign to perdition? The office
of passing sentence of condemnation
on men shall pertain to Christ, the
judge of quick and dead, and the apostle proceeds to say that it was certain
that *he* would not condemn the elect
of God. They were therefore secure.
¶ It is *Christ that died.* Or, as it may
be rendered, "Shall Christ, who has
died, condemn them?" The argument
here is, that as Christ died *to save*
them, and not to destroy them, he will
not condemn them. His death *for*
them is a security that he will not
condemn them. As he died to save
them, and as they have actually *embraced* his salvation, there is the highest security that *he* will not condemn
them. This is the *first* argument for
their security from the death of Christ.
¶ *Yea rather, that is risen again.*
This is a *second* consideration for their
security from his work. He rose for
their justification (Note, chap. iv. 25);
and as this was the object which he
had in view, it follows that he will not
condemn them. ¶ *Who is even at the
right hand of God.* Invested with
power, and dignity, and authority in
heaven. This is a *third* consideration
to show that Christ will not condemn
us, and that Christians are secure. He
is clothed with power; he is exalted

to honour; he is placed at the head of
all things. And this solemn enthrone-
ment and investiture with power over
the universe is with express reference
to the salvation of his church and people, Mat. xxviii. 18, 19; John xvii. 2;
Eph. i. 20–23. The Christian is, therefore, under the *protection* of Christ,
and is secure from being condemned
by him. ¶ *Who also maketh intercession for us.* Note, ver. 26. Who pleads
our cause; who aids and assists us;
who presents our interests before the
mercy-seat in the heavens. For this
purpose he ascended to heaven, Heb.
vii. 25. This is the *fourth* consideration which the apostle urges for the
security of Christians drawn from the
work of Christ. By all these he argues
their complete security from being
subject to condemnation by him who
shall pronounce the doom of all mankind, and therefore their complete
safety in the day of judgment. Having the Judge of all for our friend, we
are safe.

35. *Who shall separate us.* That is,
finally or entirely separate us. This is
a new argument of the apostle, showing his strong confidence in the safety
of the Christian. ¶ *From the love of
Christ.* This expression is ambiguous, and may mean either our love *to*
Christ or *his* love to us. I understand
it in the former sense, and suppose it
means, "Who shall cause us to cease
to love the Saviour?" In other words,
the love which Christians have for
their Redeemer is so strong, that it
will surmount and survive all opposition and all trials. The reason for so
understanding the expression is, that it
is not conceivable how afflictions, &c.,
should have any tendency to alienate
Christ's love *from us;* but their supposed tendency to alienate *our* love
from him might be very strong. They
are endured in his cause. They are
caused, in a good degree, by professed
attachment to him. The persecutions
and trials to which Christians are exposed on account of their professed

the love of Christ? *Shall* tribulation, or distress, or persecution, or famine, or nakedness, or peril, or sword?

36 As it is written, *p* For thy sake we are killed all the day long;

p Ps.44.22; 1 Co.15.30,31.

attachment to him, might be supposed to make them weary of a service that involved so many trials. But no, says the apostle. Our love for him is so strong that we are willing to bear all; and nothing that these foes of our peace can do, can alienate us from him and from his cause. The argument, therefore, is drawn from the strong love of a Christian to his Saviour; and from the assurance that nothing would be able to separate him from that love.

[On the other hand, it is alleged that "the object of the apostle is to assure us, not so immediately of our love to God, as of his love to us, by directing our attention to his predestinating, calling, justifying, and glorifying us, and not sparing his own Son, but delivering him up for us; that, in addition to this, it contributes more to our consolation to have our minds fixed upon God's love to us, than upon our love to him, which is subject to so many failings and infirmities" (Haldane).

Indeed the whole of this passage proceeds, in its triumphing strain, on the ground of what God and Christ have done *for us*, and not on the ground of anything belonging to *us*. It is, therefore, improbable that the apostle, in the midst of such a strain, should introduce the love of the creature to God, as a just reason for such unparalleled confidence. It is more natural to the Christian to triumph in the love of Christ to him, than in any return he can make. He can glory in the strength of the former, while he mourns over the weakness of the latter. As to the objection that afflictions can have no tendency to alienate Christ's love, these are the *very things* that alienate men from us. There are persons who are called "summer friends" because they desert us in the winter of adversity. But the love of Christ is greatly exalted by the fact, that none of all possible adverse circumstances, of which the apostle enumerates not a few, shall ever change his love.]

¶ Shall *tribulation* (Θλίψις). Note, chap. ii. 9. The word properly refers to *pressure* from without; affliction arising from external causes. It means, however, not unfrequently, trial of any

we are accounted as sheep for the slaughter.

37 Nay, *q* in all these things we are more than conquerors, through *r* him that loved us.

38 For I am persuaded, *s* that

q 1 Co.15.57.　*r* Jude 24.　*s* Jn.10.28.

kind. ¶ *Or distress* (στενοχωρία). This word properly means *narrowness of place;* and then, great anxiety and distress of mind, such as arises when a man does not know where to turn himself or what to do for relief. It refers, therefore, to distress or anxiety *of mind*, such as the early Christians were often subject to from their trials and persecutions, 2 Cor. vii. 5, "Without were fightings, *within were fears;*" see Note, Rom. ii. 9. ¶ *Or persecutions*. Note, Mat. v. 11. To these the early Christians were constantly exposed. ¶ *Or famine*. To this they were also exposed as the natural result of being driven from home, and of being often compelled to wander amidst strangers, and in deserts and desolate places. ¶ *Or peril*. Danger of any kind. ¶ *Or sword*. The sword of persecution; the danger of their lives to which they were constantly exposed. As all these things happened to them in consequence of their professed attachment to Christ, it might be supposed that they would tend to alienate their minds from him. But the apostle was assured that they had not this power, but that their love to the Saviour was so strong as to overcome all, and to bind them unalterably to his cause in the midst of the deepest trials. The *fact* is, that the more painful the trials to which they are exposed on his account, the more strong and unwavering is their love to him, and their confidence in his ability to save.

36. *As it is written*. Ps. xliv. 22. This passage the apostle quotes not as having originally reference to Christians, but as *aptly descriptive* of their condition. The condition of saints in the time of the psalmist was similar to that of Christians in the time of Paul. The same language would express both. ¶ *For thy sake*. In thy

neither death, nor life, nor angels, nor principalities, nor powers, nor

things present, nor things to come,

---

cause; or on account of attachment to thee. ¶ *We are killed*. We are subject to, or exposed to death. We endure sufferings equivalent to dying; comp. 1 Cor. iv. 9, "God hath set forth us the apostles last, *as it were appointed to death*." ¶ *All the day long*. Continually; constantly. There is no intermission to our danger, and to our exposure to death. ¶ *We are accounted*. We are reckoned; we are regarded, or dealt with. That is, our enemies judge that we ought to die, and deem us the appropriate subjects of slaughter, with as little concern or remorse as the lives of sheep are taken. 37. *Nay*. But. Notwithstanding our severe pressures and trials. ¶ *In all these things*. In the very midst of them, while we are enduring them, we are able to triumph; comp. 1 Cor. xv. 57. ¶ *We are more than conquerors*. We gain the victory. That is, they have not power to subdue us; to alienate our love and confidence; to produce apostasy. *We* are the victors, not *they*. Our faith is not destroyed; our love is not diminished; our hope is not blasted. But it is not simple victory; it is not *mere* life, and continuance of what we had before; it is *more* than simple triumph; it augments our faith, increases our strength, expands our love to Christ. The word used here is a strong, emphatic expression, such as the apostle Paul often employs (comp. 2 Cor. iv. 17), and which is used with great force and appropriateness here. ¶ *Through him*, &c. Not by their own strength or power. It was by the might of the Saviour, and by his power pledged to them, and confirmed by the love evinced when he gave himself for them; comp. Phil. iv. 13, "I can do all things through Christ who strengtheneth me." 38. *For I am persuaded*. I have a strong and unwavering confidence. Latin Vulgate, "*I am certain*." The expression here implies unwavering certainty. ¶ *Neither death*. Neither the fear of death, nor all the pains and tortures of the dying scene, even in

the most painful trials of persecution; death in no form. ¶ *Nor life*. Nor the hope of life; the love of life; the offer of life made to us by our persecutors, on condition of abjuring our Christian faith. The words evidently refer to times of persecution; and it was not uncommon for persecutors to offer life to Christians, on condition of their renouncing attachment to the Saviour, and offering sacrifice to idols. All that was demanded in the times of persecution under the Roman emperors was, that they should throw a few grains of incense on the altar of a heathen god, as expressive of homage to the idol. But even this they would not do. The hope of life on so very easy terms would not, could not alienate them from the love of Christ. ¶ *Nor angels*. It seems to be apparent that *good angels* cannot be intended here. The apostle was saying that nothing would separate Christians from the love of Christ. Of course, it would be implied that the things which he specifies might be supposed to have some power or tendency to do it. But it is not conceivable that good angels, who are "sent forth to minister for them who shall be heirs of salvation" (Heb. i. 14), should seek to alienate the minds of Christians from the Saviour, or that their influence should have any such tendency. It seems to be clear, therefore, that he refers to the designs and temptations of evil spirits. The word *angels* is applied to evil spirits in Mat. xxv. 41; 1 Cor. vi. 3. ¶ *Nor principalities* (ἀρχαί). This word usually refers to magistrates and civil rulers. But it is also applied to evil angels, as having dominion over men, Eph. vi. 12, "For we wrestle against...*principalities;*" Col. ii. 15, "And having spoiled principalities;" 1 Cor. xv. 24, "When he shall have put down all *rule*"—Greek, ἀρχήν. Some have supposed that it refers here to magistrates and those in authority who persecuted Christians; but the connection of the word with *angels* seems to require us to understand it of evil

39 Nor height, nor depth, nor any other creature, shall be able to separate us from the love of God, which is in Christ Jesus our Lord.

spirits. ¶ *Nor powers*. This word (δυνάμεις) is often applied to magistrates; but it is also applied to evil spirits that have dominion over men, 1 Cor. xv. 24. The ancient rabbins also give the name *powers* to evil angels (Schleusner). There can be no doubt that the Jews were accustomed to divide the angels of heaven into various ranks and orders, traces of which custom we find often in the Scriptures. And there is also reason to suppose that they made such a division with reference to evil angels, regarding Satan as their leader, and other evil spirits, divided into various ranks, as subordinate to him; see Mat. xxv. 41; Eph. vi. 12; Col. ii. 15. To such a division there is probably reference here; and the meaning is, that no order of evil angels, however powerful, artful, or numerous, would be able to alienate the hearts of Christians from their Redeemer. ¶ *Nor things present*. Calamities and persecutions to which we are now subject. ¶ *Nor things to come*. Trials to which we may be yet exposed. It evinced strong confidence to say that no possible trials should be sufficient to destroy their love for Christ.

39. *Nor height*. This has been variously understood. Some have regarded it as referring to evil spirits in the air; others, to high and lofty speculation in doctrine; others, to heaven—to all that is in heaven. I regard it here as synonymous with prosperity, honour, elevation in this life. The meaning is, that *no possible circumstances* in which Christians could be placed, though surrounded with wealth, honour, splendour, and though elevated to rank and office, could alienate them from the love of Christ. The tendency of these things to alienate the mind, to engross the affections, and to occupy the time, all know; but the apostle says that even these would not be sufficient to withdraw their strong love from the Lord Jesus Christ. ¶ *Nor depth*. Nor the lowest circumstances of depression, poverty, contempt, and want; the very lowest rank of life. ¶ *Nor any other creature*. Nor any other created thing; any other thing in the universe; anything that can occur. This expresses the most unwavering confidence that all who were Christians would certainly continue to love the Lord Jesus, and be saved. ¶ *Shall be able*. Shall have *power* to do it. The love to Christ is stronger than any influence which they *can* exert on the mind. ¶ *The love of God*. The love which we have to God. ¶ *Which is in Christ Jesus*. Which is produced and secured by his work. Of which he is the bond, the connecting link. It was caused by his mediation; it is secured by his influence; it is *in* and through him, and him alone, that men love God. There is no true love of God which is not produced by the work of Christ. There is no man who truly loves the Father, who does not do it in and by the Son.

Perhaps there is no chapter in the Bible on the whole so interesting and consoling to the Christian as this; and there certainly is not to be found anywhere a specimen of more elevated, animated, and lofty eloquence and argumentation. We may remark in view of it, (1) That it is the highest honour that can be conferred on mortal man to be a Christian. (2) Our trials in this life are scarcely worth regarding in comparison with our future glory. (3) Calamities should be borne without a murmur; nay, without a sigh. (4) The Christian has every possible security for his safety. The purposes of God, the work of Christ, the aid of the Holy Ghost, and the tendency of all events under the direction of his Father and Friend, conspire to secure his welfare and salvation. (5) With what thankfulness, then, should we approach the God of mercy. In the gospel, we have a blessed and cheering hope which nothing else can produce, and which nothing can destroy. Safe in the hands of God our Redeemer, we may commit our way to him, whether it lead through persecutions, or trials, or sickness, or a martyr's grave; and

CHAPTER IX.

I SAY the truth in Christ,
I lie not, my conscience also

triumphantly we may wait until the day of our complete adoption, the entire redemption of soul and body, shall fully come.

CHAPTER IX.

This chapter opens in some degree a new train of thought and argumentation. Its main design probably was to meet objections which would be alleged against the positions advanced and defended in the previous parts of the epistle. In the previous chapters, Paul had defended the position that the barrier between the Jews and Gentiles had been removed; that the Jews could not be saved by any external advantages which they possessed; that all were alike guilty before God; and that there was but one way for Jews and Gentiles of salvation—by faith in Jesus Christ, chap. i. ii. iii. He had stated the benefits of this plan (chap. v.), and showed its bearing in accomplishing what the law of Moses could not effect in overcoming sin, chap. vi. vii. In chap. viii. he had stated also on what principles this was done; that it was according to the purpose of God—the principle of electing mercy applied indiscriminately to the *mass* of guilty Jews and Gentiles. To this statement two objections might arise: first, that it was unjust; and second, that the whole argument involved a departure from the promises made to the Jewish nation. It might further be supposed that the apostle had ceased to feel an interest in his countrymen, and had become the exclusive advocate of the Gentiles. To meet these objections and feelings, seems to have been the design of this chapter. He shows them, (1) His unabated love for his countrymen, and regard for their welfare, ver. 1–5. (2) He shows them from their own writings that the principle of *election* had existed in former times—in the case of Isaac (ver. 7–13); in the writings of Moses (ver. 15); in the case of Pharaoh (ver. 17); and in the prophecies of Hosea and Isaiah, ver.

bearing me witness in the Holy Ghost,

2 That I have great heaviness

25–29. (3) He takes occasion throughout the chapter to vindicate this principle of the divine administration; to answer objections; and to show that, on the acknowledged principles of the Old Testament, *a part* of the Jewish nation might be rejected; and that it was the purpose of God to call others to the privileges of the people of God, ver. 16, 19–23, 25, 26, 29–33. The chapter, therefore, has not reference to national election, or to choice to external privileges, but has direct reference to the doctrine of the election to salvation which had been stated in chap. viii. To suppose that it refers merely to *external* privileges and *national* distinctions, makes the whole discussion unconnected, unmeaning, and unnecessary.

1. *I say the truth.* In what I am about to affirm respecting my attachment to the nation and people. ¶ *In Christ.* Most interpreters regard this as a form of an oath, as equivalent to calling Christ to witness. It is certainly to be regarded, in its obvious sense, as an appeal *to* Christ as the searcher of the heart, and as the judge of falsehood. Thus the word translated "in" (ἐν) is used in the form of an oath in Mat. v. 34–36; Rev. x. 6, *Greek.* We are to remember that the apostle was addressing those who had been Jews; and the expression has all the force of an oath *by the Messiah.* This shows that it is *right* on great and solemn occasions, and in a solemn manner, AND THUS ONLY, to appeal to Christ for the sincerity of our motives, and for the truth of what we say. And it shows further, that it is *right* to regard the Lord Jesus Christ as present with us, as searching the heart, as capable of detecting insincerity, hypocrisy, and perjury, and as therefore divine. ¶ *My conscience.* Conscience is that act or judgment of the mind by which we decide on the lawfulness or unlawfulness of our actions, and by which we instantly approve or condemn them. It exists

and continual sorrow in my heart.

3 For I *a*could wish that myself

a Ex.32.32.

were [1]accursed from Christ for my brethren my kinsmen according to the flesh :

[1] or, *separated.*

in every man, and is a strong witness to our integrity or to our guilt. ¶ *Bearing me witness.* Testifying to the truth of what I say. ¶ *In the Holy Ghost.* He does not say that he speaks the truth by or in the Holy Ghost, as he had said of Christ; but that the conscience pronounced its concurring testimony *by* the Holy Ghost; that is, conscience as enlightened and influenced by the Holy Ghost. It was not simply natural conscience, but it was conscience under the full influence of the Enlightener of the mind and Sanctifier of the heart. The reasons of this solemn asseveration are probably the following: (1) His conduct and his doctrines had led some to believe that he was an apostate, and had lost his love for his countrymen. He had forsaken their institutions, and devoted himself to the salvation of the Gentiles. He here shows them that it was from no want of love to them. (2) The doctrines which he was about to state and defend were of a similar character; he was about to maintain that no small part of his own countrymen, notwithstanding their privileges, would be rejected and lost. In this solemn manner, therefore, he assures them that this doctrine had not been embraced because he did not love them, but because it was solemn, though most painful truth. He proceeds to enumerate their privileges as a people, and to show to them the strength and tenderness of his love.

2. *Great heaviness.* Great grief. ¶ *Continual sorrow.* The word rendered *continual* here must be taken in a popular sense. Not that he was literally all the time pressed down with this sorrow, but that, whenever he thought on this subject, he had great grief ; as we say of a painful subject, it is a source of constant pain. The cause of this grief, Paul does not *expressly* mention, though it is implied in what he immediately says. It was the fact that so large a part of the nation would be rejected, and cast off,

3. *For I could wish,* &c. This passage has been greatly controverted. Some have proposed to translate it, " I *did* wish," as referring to a former state, when he renounced Christ, and sought to advance the interests of the nation by opposing and defying him. But to this interpretation there are insuperable objections. (1) The object of the apostle is not to state his *former* feelings, but his *present* attachment to his countrymen, and willingness to suffer for them. (2) The proper grammatical construction of the word used here is not I *did* wish, but I *could* desire; that is, if the thing were possible. It is not I *do* wish, or *did* wish, but I *could* desire (Ηὐχόμην), implying that he was willing now to endure it; that his present love for them was so strong, that he would, if practicable, save them from the threatened ruin and apostasy. (3) It is not *true* that Paul ever *did* wish before his conversion to be accursed by Christ, *i.e.* by the Messiah. He opposed Jesus of Nazareth; but he did not believe that he was the Messiah. At no time would he have wished to be devoted to destruction *by the Messiah* or *by Christ.* Nothing would have been more terrible to a Jew; and Saul of Tarsus never doubted that he was the friend of the promised Messiah, and was advancing the true interests of his cause, and defending the hopes of his nation against an impostor. The word, therefore, expresses a feeling which the apostle had, when writing this epistle, in regard to the condition and prospects of the nation. ¶ *Were accursed from Christ.* Might be anathema by Christ (ἀναθεμα εἶναι ἀπὸ τοῦ Χριστοῦ). This passage has been much controverted. The word rendered *accursed* (anathema) properly means, (1) Anything that was *set up,* or set apart, or consecrated to the gods in the temples, as spoils of war, images, statues, &c. This is its classical Greek meaning. It has a similar meaning among the

4 Who are Israelites; to whom
pertaineth [b] the adoption, and [c] the
glory, and [d] the [2] covenants, and

b De.7.6.　　　*c* Ps.90.16; Is.60.19.
d Ge.17.2; De.29.14; Je.31.33.　　[2] or, *testaments.*

[e] the giving of the law, and the service *of God,* and [g] the promises;
5 Whose [h] *are* the fathers, and

e Ps.147.19; ch.3.2.　　*f* Ex.12.25.　　*g* Ep.2.12.
　　　　　h ch.11.28.

Hebrews. It denoted that which was
set apart or consecrated to the service
of God, as sacrifices or offerings of any
kind. In this respect it is used to
express the sense of the Hebrew word
חרם, *anything devoted to Jehovah
without the possibility of redemption,*
Lev. xxvii. 21; xxviii. 29; Num. xviii.
14; Deut. vii. 26; Josh. vi. 17, 18;
vii. 1; 1 Sam. xv. 21; Ezek. xliv. 29.
(2) As that which was thus dedicated
to Jehovah was alienated from the use
of him who devoted it, and was either
burnt or slain and devoted to destruction as an offering, the word came to
signify a devotion of anything to
destruction, or to complete ruin. And
as whatever is devoted to destruction
may be said to be subject to a *curse,*
or to be *accursed,* the word comes to
have this signification, 1 Kings xx.
42; Isa. xxxiv. 5. But in none of
these cases does it denote eternal
death. The idea, therefore, in these
places is simply, "I could be willing
to be destroyed, or devoted to death,
for the sake of my countrymen." And
the apostle evidently means to say
that he would be willing to suffer the
bitterest evils, to forego all pleasure,
to endure any privation and toil, nay,
to offer his *life,* so that he might be
wholly devoted to sufferings, as an
offering, if he might be the means of
benefiting and saving the nation. For
a similar case, see Ex. xxxii. 32. This
does *not* mean that Paul would be willing to be damned for ever. For, (1)
The words do not imply that, and will
not bear it. (2) *Such* a destruction
could in no conceivable way benefit
the Jews. (3) Such a willingness is
not and cannot be required. And,
(4) It would be impious and absurd.
No man has a right to be willing to be
the *eternal enemy* of God; and no
man ever yet was, or could be willing to endure everlasting torments.
¶ *From Christ.* By Christ. Grotius
thinks it means from the church of
Christ. Others think it means "after

the example of Christ;" and others,
from Christ for ever. But it evidently
means that he was willing to be devoted
by Christ; *i.e.* to be regarded *by* him,
and appointed *by* him, to suffering and
death, if by that means he could save
his countrymen. It was thus the highest expression of true patriotism and
benevolence. It was an example for
all Christians and Christian ministers.
They should be willing to be devoted
to pain, privation, toil, and death, if
by that they could save others from
ruin. ¶ *My kinsmen,* &c. My countrymen; all of whom he regarded as
his kinsmen, or relations, as descended
from the same ancestors. ¶ *According to the flesh.* By birth. They were
of the same blood and parentage, though
not now of the same religious belief.
4. *Who are Israelites.* Descended
from Israel or Jacob; honoured by
having such an ancestor, and by bearing a name so distinguished as that of
his descendants. It was formerly the
honourable appellation of the people of
God. ¶ *To whom* pertaineth. To
whom it belongs. It was their elevated external privilege. ¶ *The adoption.* Of the nation into the family
of God, or to be regarded as his peculiar people, Deut. vii. 6. ¶ *And the
glory.* The symbol of the divine presence that attended them from Egypt,
and that finally rested over the ark in
the first temple—*the Shechinah,* Ex.
xiii. 21, 22; xxv. 22. ¶ *And the covenants.* The various compacts or promises which had been made from time
to time with Abraham, Isaac, and
Jacob, and with the nation; the
pledges of the divine protection. ¶ *The
giving of the law.* On Mount Sinai,
Ex. xx.; comp. Ps. cxlvii. 19. ¶ *And
the service* of God. The temple service; regarded by them as the pride
and ornament of their nation. ¶ *And
the promises.* Of the Messiah; and
of the spread of the true religion from
them as a nation.
5. *Whose* are *the fathers.* Who

of ᶦwhom, as concerning the flesh, Christ *came*, ᵏwho is over all, God blessed for ever.   Amen.

6 Not as though the word of God hath ᶦtaken none effect. Forᵐ they *are* not all Israel which are of Israel.

i Lu.3.23,&c.   *k* Jn.1.1.   *l* Is.55.11.   *m* ch.2.28,29.

7 Neither, because they are the seed of Abraham, *are they* all children: but, ⁿIn Isaac shall thy seed be called.

8 That is, they which are the children of the flesh, these *are* not the children of God: but the chil-

n Ge.21.12.

---

have been honoured with so illustrious an ancestry.   Who are descended from Abraham, Isaac, &c.   On this they highly valued themselves, and in a certain sense not unjustly; comp. Mat. iii. 9.   ¶ *Of whom*.   Of whose nation.   This is placed as the crowning and most exalted privilege, that their nation had given birth to the long-expected Messiah, the hope of the world.   ¶ *As concerning the flesh*. So far as his human nature was concerned.   The use of this language supposes that there was a *higher* nature in respect to which he was *not* of their nation; see Note, chap. i. 3.   ¶ *Christ came*.   He had already *come;* and it was their high honour that he was one of their nation.   ¶ *Who is over all*. This is an appellation that belongs only to the true God.   It implies supreme divinity; and is full proof that the Messiah is divine.   Much effort has been made to show that this is not the true rendering, but without success.   There are no various readings in the Greek MSS. of any consequence; and the connection here evidently requires us to understand this of a nature that is not "according to the flesh," *i.e.*, as the apostle here shows, of the divine nature.   ¶ *God blessed for ever*.   This is evidently applied to the Lord Jesus; and it *proves* that he is divine.   If the translation is fairly made—and it has never been proved to be erroneous—it demonstrates that he is God as well as man.   The doxology "blessed for ever" was usually added by the Jewish writers after the mention of the name God, as an expression of reverence.   (See the various interpretations that have been proposed on this passage examined in Prof. Stuart's Notes on this verse.)

6. *Not as though*, &c.   Not as though

the promise of God had entirely failed. Though I grieve thus (ver. 2, 3), though I am deeply apprehensive for the nation, yet I do not affirm that *all* the nation is to be destroyed.   The promise of God will not entirely fail.   ¶ *Not all Israel*.   Not all the descendants of Jacob have the true spirit of Israelites, or are Jews in the scriptural sense of the term; see Note, chap. ii. 28, 29.

7. Are they *all children*.   Adopted into the true family of God.   Many of the descendants of Abraham were rejected.   ¶ *But in Isaac*.   This was the promise, Gen. xxi. 12.   ¶ *Shall thy seed*, &c.   Thy true people.   This implied a selection, or choice; and therefore the doctrine of *election* was illustrated in the very commencement of the history of the nation; and as God had *then* made such a distinction, he might still do it.   As he had then rejected a part of the natural descendants of Abraham, so he might still do it.   This is the argument which the apostle is pursuing.

8. *They which are the children of the flesh*.   The natural descendants. ¶ *These* are *not the children of God*. Are not of necessity the adopted children of God; or are not so in virtue of their descent merely.   This was in opposition to one of the most settled and deeply cherished opinions of the Jews.   They supposed that the mere fact of being a Jew entitled a man to the blessings of the covenant, and to be regarded as a child of God.   But the apostle shows them that it was not by their natural descent that these spiritual privileges were granted; that they were not conferred on men simply from the fact that they were Jews; and that consequently those who were not Jews might become interested in those spiritual blessings.   ¶ *But the children of the promise*.   The descend-

dren °of the promise are counted for the seed.

9 For this *is* the word of promise, °At this time will I come, and Sarah shall have a son.

o Ga.4.28.   *p* Ge.18.10,14.

10 And not only *this;* but when °Rebecca also had conceived by one, *even* by our father Isaac;

11 (For *the children* being not yet born, neither having done any good

q Ge.25.21,23.

ants of Abraham on whom the promised blessings would be bestowed. The sense is, that God at first contemplated a distinction among the descendants of Abraham, and intended to confine his blessings to such as he chose; that is, to those to whom the promise particularly appertained, to the descendants of Isaac. The argument of the apostle is, that *the principle* was thus established that a distinction might be made among those who were Jews; and as that distinction had been made in former times, so it might be under the Messiah. ¶ *Are counted.* Are regarded, or reckoned. God reckons things as they are; and therefore designed that they should be his true children. ¶ *As the seed.* The spiritual children of God; the partakers of his mercy and salvation. This refers, doubtless, to spiritual privileges and to salvation; and therefore has relation not to nations as such, but to individuals.

9. *For this* is *the word of promise.* This is the promise made to Abraham. The design of the apostle in introducing this, is doubtless to show to whom the promise appertained; and by specifying this, he shows that it had not reference to Ishmael, but to Isaac. ¶ *At this time.* Greek, according to this time; see Gen. xviii. 10, 14. Probably it means at the exact time promised; I will fulfil the prediction at the very time; comp. 2 Kings iv. 16.

10. *And not only* this. Not only is the *principle* of making a distinction among the natural descendants of Abraham thus settled by the promise, but it is still further seen and illustrated in the birth of the two sons of Isaac. He had shown that the principle of thus making a distinction among the posterity of Abraham was recognized in the original promise, thus proving that *all* the descendants of Abraham were not of course to be

saved; and he now proceeds to show that the principle was recognized in the case of his posterity in the family of Isaac. And he shows that it is not according to any natural principles that the selection was made; that he not only made a distinction between Jacob and Esau, but that he did it according to his good pleasure, choosing the younger to be the object of his favour, and rejecting the older, who, according to the custom of the times, was supposed to be entitled to peculiar honour and rights. And in order to prove that this was done according to his own pleasure, he shows that the distinction was made before they were born; before they had formed any character; and, consequently, in such a way that it could not be pretended that it was in consequence of any works which they had performed. ¶ *But when Rebecca.* The wife of Isaac; see Gen. xxv. 21, 23.

11. *For* the children *being not yet born.* It was not, therefore, by any works of theirs. It was not because they had formed a character and manifested qualities which made this distinction proper. It was laid *back* of any such character, and therefore had its foundation in the purpose or plan of God. ¶ *Neither having done any good or evil.* That is, when the declaration (ver. 12) was made to Rebecca. This is a very important passage in regard to the question about the purposes of God. (1) They had *done* nothing good or bad; and when that is the case, there can be, properly speaking, no moral character, for "a *character* is not formed when the person has not acquired stable and distinctive qualities" (Webster). (2) That the period of moral agency had not yet commenced; comp. Gen. xxv. 22, 23. *When* that agency commences, we do not know; but here is a case of which it is affirmed that it had not commenced.

or evil, that the purpose of God, according to election, might stand, not of works, but of him that calleth;)

---

(3) The purpose of God is antecedent to the formation of character, or the performance of any actions, good or bad. (4) It is not a purpose formed *because* he sees anything in the individuals as a ground for his choice, but for some reason which he has not explained, and which in the Scripture is simply called *purpose* and *good pleasure*, Eph. i. 5. (5) If it existed in this case, it does in others. If it was right then, it is now. And if God then dispensed his favours on this principle, he will now. But, (6) This affirmation respecting Jacob and Esau does not prove that they had not a nature inclined to evil, or a corrupt and sensual propensity, or that they would not sin as soon as they became moral agents. It proves merely that they had not yet committed *actual* sin. That they, as well as all others, *would* certainly sin as soon as they committed moral acts at all, is proved everywhere in the sacred Scriptures. ¶ *The purpose of God.* Note, chap. viii. 28. ¶ *According to election.* To dispense his favours according to his sovereign will and pleasure. Those favours were not conferred in consequence of the *merits* of the individuals, but according to a wise plan *lying back* of the formation of their characters, and before they had done good or evil. The favours were thus conferred according to his choice or election. ¶ *Might stand.* Might be confirmed, or might be proved to be true. The case shows that God dispenses his favours as a sovereign. The purpose of God was thus proved to have been formed without respect to the merits of either. ¶ *Not of works.* Not by anything which they had done either to merit his favour or to forfeit it. It was formed on other principles than a reference to their works. So it is in relation to all who shall be saved. God has good reasons for saving those who shall be saved. What the reasons are for choosing some to life, he has

12 It was said unto her, The ³elder shall serve the ⁴younger.

13 As it is written, ʳ Jacob

---

³ or, *greater.*　⁴ or, *lesser.*　ʳ Mal.1.2,3.

---

not revealed; but he *has* revealed to us that it is *not* on account of their works, either performed or foreseen. ¶ *But of him that calleth.* According to the will and purpose of him that chooses to dispense those favours in this manner. It is not by the merit of man, but it is by a purpose having its origin with God, and formed and executed according to his good pleasure. It is also implied here that it is formed in such a way as to secure *his* glory as the primary consideration.

12. *It was said unto her.* By Jehovah; see Gen. xxv. 23. ¶ *The elder.* The eldest son, which was Esau. By the law of primogeniture among the Hebrews, he would have been entitled to peculiar honours and privileges. But it was said that in his case this custom should be reversed, and that he should take the rank of the younger. ¶ *Should serve.* Shall be subject to; shall not have the authority and priority, but should be inferior to. The passage in Genesis (xxv. 23) shows that this had reference particularly to the posterity of Esau, and not to him as an individual. The sense is, that the descendants of Esau, who were Edomites, should be inferior to, and subject to the descendants of Jacob. Jacob was to have the priority; the promised land: the promises; and the honour of being regarded as the chosen of God. There was reference here, therefore, to the whole train of temporal and spiritual blessings which were to be connected with the two races of people. If it be asked how this bears on the argument of the apostle, we may reply, (1) That it settles *the principle* that God might make a distinction among men, in the same nation, and the same family, without reference to their works or character. (2) That he might confer his blessings on such as he pleased. (3)·If this is done in regard to nations, it may be in regard to individuals.

have I loved, but Esau have I hated.

14 What shall we say then? *Is*

s De.32.4.

The principle is the same, and the justice the same. If it be supposed to be unjust in God to make such a distinction in regard to individuals, it is surely not less so to make a distinction in nations. The fact that numbers are thus favoured, does not make it the more proper, or remove any difficulty. (4) If this distinction may be made in regard to *temporal* things, why not in regard to *spiritual* things? The *principle* must still be the same. If unjust in one case, it would be in the other. The fact that it is done in one case proves also that it will be in the other; for the same great principle will run through all the dealings of the divine government. And as men do not and cannot complain that God makes a distinction among them in regard to talents, health, beauty, prosperity, and rank, neither can they complain if he acts also as a sovereign in the distribution of his spiritual favours. They, therefore, who regard this as referring only to temporal and national privileges, gain no relief in respect to the real difficulty in the case, for the unanswerable question would still be asked, Why has not God made all men equal in everything? Why has he made any distinction among men? The *only* reply to all such inquiries is, "Even so, Father, for so it seemeth good in thy sight," Mat. xi. 26.

13. *As it is written.* Mal. i. 2, 3. That is, the distribution of favours is on the principle advanced by the prophet, and is in accordance with the declaration that God had in fact loved the one and hated the other. ¶ *Jacob.* This refers, doubtless, to the posterity of Jacob. ¶ *Have I loved.* I have shown affection for that people; I have bestowed on them great privileges and blessings, as proofs of attachment. I have preferred Jacob to Esau. ¶ *Esau.* The descendants of Esau, the Edomites; see Mal. i. 4. ¶ *Have I hated.* This does not mean any *positive* hatred, but that he had

there unrighteousness with God? God forbid.

15 For he saith to Moses, *I will

t Ex.33.19.

preferred Jacob, and had *withheld* from Esau those privileges and blessings which he had conferred on the posterity of Jacob. This is explained in Mal. i. 3, "And I hated Esau, and laid his mountains and heritage waste for the dragons of the wilderness;" comp. Jer. xlix. 17, 18; Ezek. xxxv. 6. It was common among the Hebrews to use the terms *love* and *hatred* in this comparative sense, where the former implied strong *positive* attachment, and the latter, not positive hatred, but merely a less love, or the withholding of the expressions of affection; comp. Gen. xxix. 30, 31; Prov. xiii. 24, "He that spareth his rod *hateth* his son; but he that *loveth* him chasteneth him betimes;" Mat. vi. 24, "No man can serve two masters, for either he will *hate* the one and *love* the other," &c.; Luke xiv. 26, "If any man come to me, and *hate* not his father and mother," &c.

14. *What shall we say then?* What conclusion shall we draw from these acknowledged facts, and from these positive declarations of Scripture? ¶ Is there *unrighteousness with God?* Does God do injustice or wrong? This charge has often been brought against the doctrine here advanced. But this charge the apostle strongly repels. He meets it by further showing that it is the doctrine explicitly taught in the Old Testament (ver. 15, 17), and that it is founded on the principles of equity, and on just views of the sovereignty of God, ver. 19–23. ¶ *God forbid.* Note, chap. iii. 4.

15. *For he saith to Moses.* Ex. xxxiii. 19. ¶ *I will have mercy.* This is said by God when he declared expressly that he would make all his *goodness* pass before Moses (Ex. xxxiii. 19), and when, therefore, it was regarded, not as a proof of stern and inexorable justice, but as *the very proof of his benevolence,* and the highest which he thought proper to exhibit. When men, therefore, under the influence of an unrenewed and hostile

have mercy on whom I will have mercy, and I will have compassion on whom I will have compassion.

16 So then *it is* not of him that willeth, nor of him that runneth, but of God that showeth mercy.

heart, charge this as an unjust and arbitrary proceeding, they are resisting and perverting that which God regards as the very demonstration of his benevolence. The sense of the passage clearly is, that he would choose the objects of his favour, and bestow his mercies as he chose. None of the human race deserved his favour; and he had a right to pardon whom he pleased, and to save men on his own terms, and according to his sovereign will and pleasure. ¶ *On whom I will have mercy.* On whom I *choose* to bestow mercy. The *mode* he does not explain. But there could not be a more positive declaration of these truths, (1) That he does it as a sovereign, without giving an account of the reason of his choice to any. (2) That he does it without regard to any claim on the part of man; or that man is regarded as destitute of merit, and as having no right to his mercy. (3) That he will do it to any extent which he pleases, and in whatever time and manner may best accord with his own good pleasure. (4) That he has regard to a definite number; and that on that number he intends to bestow eternal life; and, (5) That no one has a right to complain. It is proof of his benevolence that *any* are saved; and where none have a claim, where all are justly condemned, he has a right to pardon whom he pleases. The executive of a country may select any number of criminals whom he may see fit to pardon, or who may be forgiven in consistency with the supremacy of the laws and the welfare of the community, and none has a right to murmur, but every good citizen should rejoice that *any* may be pardoned with safety. So in the moral world, and under the administration of its holy Sovereign, it should be a matter of joy that *any* can be pardoned and saved; and not a subject of murmuring and complaint that those who shall finally deserve to die shall be consigned to woe.

16. *So then.* It follows as a consequence from this statement of God to Moses. Or it is a doctrine established by that statement.. ¶ *Not of him that willeth.* This does not mean that he that becomes a Christian, and is saved, does not *choose* eternal life; or is not made willing; or that he is *compelled* to enter heaven against his own choice. It is true that men by nature have no desire of holiness, and do not choose eternal life. But the effect of the influences of God's Spirit on the heart is to make it "willing in the day of his power," Ps. cx. 3. The meaning here is evidently, that eternal life is not bestowed because man had any original willingness or disposition to be saved; it is not because *he* commences the work, and is himself disposed to it; but it is because God inclines him to it, and disposes him to seek for mercy, and then confers it in his own way. The word *willeth* here denotes *wish* or *desire.* ¶ *Nor of him that runneth.* This denotes *strenuous, intense effort,* as when a man is anxious to obtain an object, or hastens from danger. The meaning is not that the sinner does not make an effort to be saved; nor that all who become Christians do not *in fact* strive to enter into the kingdom, or earnestly desire salvation, for the Scriptures teach the contrary, Luke xvi. 16; xiii. 24. There is no effort more intense and persevering, no struggle more arduous or agonizing, than when a sinner seeks eternal life. Nor does it mean that they who strive in a proper way, and with proper effort, shall not obtain eternal life, Mat. vii. 7. But the sense is, (1) That the sinner would not put forth any effort himself. If left to his own course, he would never seek to be saved. (2) That he is pardoned, not *on account* of his effort; not *because* he makes an exertion; but because God chooses to pardon him. There is no merit in his anxiety, and prayers, and agony, on account of

17 For the scripture saith unto Pharaoh, "Even for this same purpose have I raised thee up, that I

which God would forgive him; but he is still dependent on the mere mercy of God to save or destroy him at his will. The sinner, however anxious he may be, and however much or long he may strive, does not bring God under an obligation to pardon him, any more than the condemned criminal, trembling with the fear of execution, and the consciousness of crime, lays the judge or the jury under an obligation to acquit him. This fact it is of great importance for an awakened sinner to know. Deeply anxious he should be, but there is no *merit* in his distress. Pray he should, but there is no merit in his prayers. Weep and strive he may, but in this there is no ground of claim on God for pardon; and, after all, he is dependent on his mere sovereign mercy, as a lost, ruined, and helpless sinner, to be saved or lost at his will. ¶ *But of God that showeth mercy.* Salvation in its beginning, its progress, and its close, is of him. He has a right, therefore, to bestow it when and where he pleases. All our mercies flow from his mere love and compassion, and not from our deserts. The essential idea here is, that *God* is the original fountain of all the blessings of salvation.

17. *For the scripture saith.* Ex. ix. 16. That is, God saith to Pharaoh *in* the Scriptures, Gal. iii. 8, 22. This passage is designed to illustrate the doctrine that God shows mercy according to his sovereign pleasure by a reference to one of the most extraordinary cases of hardness of heart which has ever occurred. The design is to show that God has a right to pass by those to whom he does not choose to show mercy; and to place them in circumstances where they shall develop their true character, and where, in fact, they shall become more hardened and be destroyed, ver. 18. ¶ *Unto Pharaoh.* The haughty and oppressive king of Egypt; thus showing that the most mighty and wicked monarchs are at his control;

might show my power in thee, and that my name might be declared throughout all the earth.

comp. Isa. x. 5–7. ¶ *For this same purpose.* For the design, or with the intent that is immediately specified. This was the leading purpose or design of his sustaining him. ¶ *Have I raised thee up.* Margin in Ex. ix. 16, "made thee stand," *i.e.* sustained thee. The Greek word used by the apostle (ἐξήγειρα) means properly, *I have excited, roused,* or *stirred* thee up. But it may also have the meaning, "I have sustained or supported thee." That is, I have kept thee from death; I have preserved thee from ruin; I have ministered strength to thee, so that thy full character has been developed. It does not mean that God had infused into his mind any positive evil, or that by any direct influence he had excited any evil feelings, but that he had kept him in circumstances which were fitted to develop his true character. The meaning of the word and the truth of the case may be expressed in the following particulars: (1) God meant to accomplish some great purposes by his existence and conduct. (2) He kept him, or sustained him, with reference to that. (3) He had control over the haughty and wicked monarch. He could take his life, or he could continue him on earth. As he had control over all things that could affect the pride, the feelings, and the happiness of the monarch, so he had control over the monarch himself. (4) *He placed him in circumstances just fitted to develop his character.* He kept him amidst those circumstances until his character was fully developed. (5) He did not exert a positive evil influence on the mind of Pharaoh; for, (6) In all this the monarch acted freely. He did that which he chose to do. He pursued his own course. He was voluntary in his schemes of oppressing the Israelites. He was voluntary in his opposition to God. He was voluntary when he pursued the Israelites to the Red Sea. In all his doings he acted as he *chose* to do, and with a determined *choice of evil,* from which neither

18 Therefore hath he mercy on whom he will *have mercy*, and whom he will he hardeneth.

warning nor judgment would turn him away. Thus he is said to have hardened his own heart, Ex. viii. 15. (7) Neither Pharaoh nor any sinner can justly blame God for placing them in circumstances where they shall develop their own character, and show what they are. It is not the fault of God, but their own fault. The sinner is not compelled to sin; nor is God under obligation to save him contrary to the prevalent desires and wishes of the sinner himself. ¶ *My power in thee.* Or by means of thee. By the judgments exerted in delivering an entire oppressed people from thy grasp. God's most signal acts of *power* were thus shown in consequence of his disobedience and rebellion. ¶ *My name.* The name of Jehovah, as the only true God, and the deliverer of his people. ¶ *Throughout all the earth.* Or throughout all the land of Egypt; Note, Luke ii. 1. We may learn here, (1) That a leading design of God in the government of the world is to make his power, and name, and character known. (2) That this is often accomplished in a most signal manner by the destruction of the wicked. (3) That wicked men should be alarmed, since *their* arm cannot contend with God, and since his enemies shall be destroyed. (4) It is right that the incorrigibly wicked should be cut off. When a man's character is fully developed; when he is fairly tried; when, in all circumstances, he has shown that he *will* not obey God, neither justice nor mercy hinders the Almighty from cutting him down and consigning him to death.

18. *Therefore hath he mercy*, &c. This is a conclusion stated by the apostle as the result of all the argument. ¶ *Whom he will he hardeneth.* This is not stated in what the Scripture said to Pharaoh, but is a conclusion to which the apostle had arrived, in view of the case of Pharaoh. The word *hardeneth* means only to harden in the manner specified in the case of Pharaoh. It does not mean to exert

19 Thou wilt say then unto me, Why doth he yet find fault? for *v*who hath resisted his will?

v 2 Ch.20.6; Da.4.35.

a positive influence, but to leave a sinner to his own course, and to place him in circumstances where the character will be more and more developed; see Note, John xii. 40. It implies, however, an act of sovereignty on the part of God in thus *leaving* him to his chosen course, and in not putting forth that influence by which he could be saved from death. *Why* this is, the apostle does not state. We should, however, not dispute a fact everywhere prevalent; and should have sufficient confidence in God to believe that it is in accordance with infinite wisdom and rectitude.

19. *Thou wilt say then unto me.* The apostle here refers to an objection that might be made to his argument. If the position which he had been endeavouring to establish were true; if God had a purpose in all his dealings with men; if all the revolutions among men happened according to his decree, so that he was not disappointed, or his plan frustrated; and if his own glory was secured in all this, why could he blame men? ¶ *Why doth he yet find fault?* Why does he *blame* men, since their conduct is in accordance with his purpose, and since he bestows mercy according to his sovereign will? This objection has been made by sinners in all ages. It is the standing objection against the doctrines of grace. The objection is founded, (1) On the difficulty of reconciling the purposes of God with the free agency of man. (2) It *assumes*, what cannot be proved, that a plan or purpose of God *must* destroy the freedom of man. (3) It is said that if the *plan* of God is accomplished, then that which is best to be done is done, and, of course, man cannot be blamed. These objections are met by the apostle in the following argument. ¶ *Who hath resisted his will?* That is, who has *successfully opposed* his will, or frustrated his plan? The word translated *resist* is commonly used to denote the resistance offered

20 Nay but, O man, who art thou that ⁵repliest against God? Shall*ᵂ* the thing formed say to

5 or, *answerest again;* or, *disputest with God.*

him that formed *it,* Why hast thou made me thus?

21 Hath not *ˣ*the potter power

w Is.29.16.　　z Is.64.8.

by soldiers or armed men. Thus, Eph. vi. 13, "Take unto you the whole armour of God, that ye may be able to *withstand* (*resist* or successfully oppose) in the evil day;" see Luke xxi. 15, "I will give you a mouth and wisdom which all your adversaries shall not be able to gainsay or *resist;*" see also Acts vii. 10; xiii. 8, "But Elymas...*withstood* them," &c. The same Greek word, Rom. xiii. 2; Gal. ii. 11. This does not mean that no one has offered resistance or opposition to God, but that no one has done it successfully. God has accomplished his purposes *in spite of* their opposition. This was an established point in the sacred writings, and one of the admitted doctrines of the Jews. To establish it had even been a part of the apostle's design; and the difficulty now was to see how, *this* being admitted, men could be held chargeable with crime. That it was the doctrine of the Scriptures, see 2 Chron. xx. 6, "In thine hand *is there not* power and might, so that none is able to withstand thee?" Dan. iv. 35, "He doeth according to his will in the army of heaven, and *among* the inhabitants of the earth, and none can stay his hand, or say unto him, What doest thou?" See also the case of Joseph and his brethren, Gen. l. 20, "As for you, ye thought evil against me, *but* God meant it unto good."

20. *Nay but, O man,* &c. To this objection the apostle replies in *two* ways; first, by asserting the sovereignty of God, and affirming that he had a *right* to do it (ver. 20, 21); and secondly, by showing that he did it according to the principles of justice and mercy, or that it was *involved* of necessity in his dispensing *justice* and *mercy* to mankind, ver. 22, 23, 24. ¶ *Who art thou,* &c. Paul here strongly reproves the impiety and wickedness of arraigning God. This impiety appears, (1) Because man is a *creature* of God, and it is improper that he should arraign his Maker.

(2) He is *unqualified* to understand the subject. "Who art thou?" What qualifications has a creature of a day, —a being just in the *infancy* of his existence; of so limited faculties; so perverse, blinded, and interested as man,—to sit in judgment on the doings of the Infinite Mind? Who gave him the authority, or invested him with the prerogatives of a *judge* over his Maker's doings? (3) Even if man *were* qualified to investigate those subjects, what right has he to *reply* against God, to arraign him, or to follow out a train of argument tending to involve his Creator in shame and disgrace? Nowhere is there to be found a more cutting or humbling reply to the pride of man than this. And on no subject was it more needed. The experience of every age has shown that this has been a prominent topic of objection against the government of God; and that there has been no point in the Christian theology to which the human heart has been so ready to make objections as to the doctrine of the sovereignty of God. ¶ *Repliest against God.* Margin, "answerest again; or, disputest with God." The passage conveys the idea of *answering* again; or of arguing to the dishonour of God. It implies that when God declares his will, man should be still. God has his own plans of infinite wisdom, and it is not ours to reply against him, or to arraign him of injustice, when we cannot see the reason of his doings. ¶ *Shall the thing formed,* &c. This sentiment is found in Isa. xxix. 16; see also Isa. xlv. 9. It was peculiarly proper to adduce this to a *Jew.* The objection is one which is supposed to be made by a Jew, and it was proper to reply to him by a quotation from his own Scriptures. Any being has a right to fashion his work according to his own views of what is best; and as this right is not denied to *men,* we ought not to blame the infinitely wise God for acting in a similar way. They who have

over the clay, of the same lump to make one vessel unto honour, and another unto dishonour? 22 *What*y if God, willing to

y Pr.16.4.

received every blessing they enjoy from him, ought not to blame him for not making them different.

21. *Hath not the potter*, &c. This same sovereign right of God the apostle proceeds to urge from another illustration, and another passage from the Old Testament, Isa. lxiv. 8, "But now, O Lord, thou art our Father; we are the clay, and thou our potter; and we all are the work of thy hand." This passage is preceded in Isaiah by one declaring *the depravity of man*, Isa. lxiv. 6, "We are all as an unclean thing, and all our righteousnesses are as filthy rags; and we all do fade as a leaf; and our iniquities, like the wind, have taken us away." As they were polluted with sin, as they had transgressed the law of God, and had *no claim* and *no merit*, God might bestow his favours as he pleased, and mould them as the potter did the clay. He would do no injury to those who were left, and *who had no claim to his mercy*, if he bestowed favours on others, any more than the potter would do injustice to one part of the mass, if he put it to an ignoble use, and moulded another part into a vessel of honour. This is still the condition of sinful men. God does no injustice to a man if he leaves him to take his own course to ruin, and makes another, equally undeserving, the recipient of his mercy. He violated none of my rights by not conferring on me the talents of Newton or of Bacon; or by not placing me in circumstances like those of Peter and Paul. Where *all* are undeserving, the utmost that can be demanded is that he should not treat them with *injustice*. And this is secured even in the case of the lost. No man will suffer more than he deserves; nor will any man go to perdition feeling that he has *a claim* to better treatment than he receives. The same sentiment is found in Jer. xviii. 6, "O house of Israel, cannot I do with you as this potter? saith

show *his* wrath, and to make his power known, endured with much long-suffering z the vessels of wrath 6 fitted to destruction;

z 2 Ti.2.20.   6 or, *made up*.

the Lord. Behold, as the clay is in the potter's hand, so are ye in my hand, O house of Israel. At what instant I shall speak concerning a nation," &c. The passage in Isaiah proves that God has the right of a sovereign over guilty *individuals;* that in Jeremiah, that he has the same right over *nations;* thus meeting the whole case as it was in the mind of the apostle. These passages, however, assert only the *right* of God to do it, without affirming anything about the *manner* in which it is done. In fact, God bestows his favours in a *mode* very different from that in which a potter moulds his clay. God does not create holiness by a mere act of power, but he produces it in a manner consistent with the moral agency of men; and bestows his favours not to *compel* men, but to incline them to be *willing* to receive them, Ps. cx. 3, "Thy people shall be willing in the day of thy power." It should be further remarked, that the argument of the apostle here does not refer to *the original creation* of men, as if God had then made them one for honour and another for dishonour. He refers to man *as* fallen and lost. His argument is this: "Man is in ruins; he is fallen; he has no claim on God; all deserve to die; on this *mass*, where none have any claim, he may bestow life on whom he pleases, without injury to others; he may exercise the right of a sovereign to pardon whom he pleases; or of a potter to mould any part of the useless mass to purposes of utility and beauty." ¶ *Potter.* One whose occupation it is to make earthen vessels. ¶ *Power.* This word denotes here not merely *physical power*, but authority, right; see Mat. vii. 29, translated "authority;" xxi. 23; 2 Thes. iii. 9; Mark ii. 10; Luke v. 24, "The Son of man hath *power* on earth to forgive sins," &c. ¶ *Lump.* Mass. It denotes anything that is reduced to a fine consistency, and mixed, and made soft by water; either clay, as in this place, or the *mass* produced of grain pounded and mixed with water, Rom. xi. 16, "If the first-fruit be holy, the *lump* is also holy;" 1 Cor. v. 6, "Know ye not that a little leaven leaveneth the whole *lump?*" ¶ *One vessel.* A cup, or other utensil, made of clay. ¶ *Unto honour.* Fitted to an honourable use, or designed for a more useful and refined purpose. ¶ *Unto dishonour.* To a meaner service, or more common use. This is a common mode of expression among the Hebrews. The *lump* here denotes the mass of men, sinners, having no claim on God. The potter illustrates God's right over that mass, to dispose of it as seems good in his sight. The doctrine of the passage is, that men have no right to complain if God bestows his blessings where and when he chooses.

22, 23. What *if God,* &c. If God does what the apostle supposes, what then? Is it not right? This is the second point in the answer to the objection in ver. 19. The answer has respect to the *two classes* of men which actually exist on the earth—the righteous and the wicked. And the question is, whether *in regard to these two classes God does* IN FACT *do wrong?* If he does not, then the doctrine of the apostle is established, and the objection is not valid. It is assumed here, as it must be, that the world is *in fact* divided into two classes—saints and sinners. The apostle considers the case of sinners in ver. 22. ¶ *Willing.* Being disposed; having an inclination to. It denotes an inclination of mind towards the thing proposed. If the thing itself was right; if it was *proper to* "*show*" his wrath," then it was proper to be WILLING to do it. If it is right *to do* a thing, it is right to *purpose* or *intend* to do it. ¶ *His wrath* (τὴν ὀργὴν). This word occurs *thirty-five* times in the New Testament. Its meaning is derived from the idea of earnestly desiring or reaching for an object, and properly denotes, in its general sense, a vehement desire of attaining anything. Hence it comes

to denote an earnest desire of revenge, or of inflicting suffering on those who have injured us, Eph. iv. 31, "Let all bitterness and wrath," &c.; Col. iii. 8; 1 Tim. ii. 8. Hence it denotes *indignation* in general, which is *not* joined with a desire of revenge, Mark iii. 5, "He looked round about on them with *anger.*" It also denotes punishment for sin; the anger or displeasure of God against transgression; Note, Rom. i. 18; Luke iii. 7; xxi. 23, &c. In this place it is evidently used to denote *severe displeasure against sin.* As sin is an evil of so great magnitude, *it is right* for God to be *willing* to evince his displeasure against it; and just in proportion to the extent of the evil. This displeasure, or wrath, it is proper that God should *always* be willing to show; nay, it would not be right for him *not* to show it, for that would be the same thing as to be *indifferent* to it, or to *approve* it. In this place, however, it is *not* affirmed, (1) That God has any pleasure in sin, or its punishment; nor, (2) That he exerted any agency to *compel* man to sin. It affirms only that God is willing to show his hatred of incorrigible and long-continued wickedness when it *actually* exists. ¶ *To make his power known.* This *language* is the same as that which was used in relation to Pharaoh, ver. 17; Ex. ix. 16. But it is not probable that the apostle intended to confine it to the Egyptians only. In the following verse he speaks of "the vessels of mercy prepared *unto glory;*" which cannot be supposed to be language adapted to the *temporal* deliverance of the Jews. The case of Pharaoh was *one instance,* or *illustration* of the general principle on which God would deal with men. His government is conducted on great and uniform principles; and the case of Pharaoh was a development of the great laws on which he governs the universe. ¶ *Endured.* Bore with; was patient, or forbearing, Rev. ii. 3, "And hast borne, and hast patience," &c.; 1 Cor. xiii. 7, "Charity, [love] beareth all things;" Luke xviii. 7, "Will not God avenge his elect, though he *bear long* with them?" ¶ *With much long-suffering.* With much patience. He suffered them to live while they deserved to die. God bears with all sinners with much patience; he spares them amid all their provocations, to give them opportunity of repentance; and though they are fitted for destruction, yet he prolongs their lives, and offers them pardon, and loads them with benefits. This fact is a complete vindication of the government of God from the aspersions of all his enemies. ¶ *Vessels of wrath.* The word *vessel* means a cup, &c., made of earth. As the human body is frail, easily broken and destroyed, it comes to signify also the body, 2 Cor. iv. 7, "We have this treasure in earthen vessels;" 1 Thes. iv. 4, "That every one of you should know how to possess his *vessel* in sanctification and honour"—that everyone should keep *his body* from the indulgence of unlawful passions; comp. ver. 3. Hence also it means *the man himself,* Acts ix. 15, "He is a chosen *vessel* unto me," &c.; comp. Isa. xiii. 5. In this place there is, doubtless, allusion to what he had just said of clay in the hands of the potter. The phrase "vessels of wrath," denotes wicked men against whom it is *fit* or proper that wrath should be shown; as Judas is called "the son of perdition;" see Note on John xvii. 12. This does not mean that men by their very *creation,* or their physical nature, are thus denominated; but men who, from long continuance in iniquity, *deserve* to experience wrath; as Judas was not called "son of perdition" by any arbitrary appointment, or as an *original* designation, but because, in consequence of his avarice and treason, this was the name which *in fact* actually described him, or fitted his case. ¶ *Fitted* (κατηρτισμένα). This word properly means *to restore; to place in order; to render complete; to supply a defect; to fit to, or adapt to, or prepare for;* see Mat. iv. 21, "Were *mending* their nets;" Gal. vi. 1, "*Restore* such an one," &c. In this place it is a *participle,* and means those who *are* fitted for or *adapted to* destruction; those whose characters are such as to *deserve* destruction, or as to make destruction proper. See the

same use of the word in Heb. xi. 3, "Through faith we understand that the worlds were *framed*"—beautifully fitted up in proper proportions, one part adapted to another—"by the word of God;" Heb. x. 5, "A body hast thou *prepared* for me"—fitted, or adapted to me; comp. Ps. lxviii. 10; lxxiv. 16. In this place there is not the semblance of a declaration that GOD *had* PREPARED *them, or* FITTED *them for destruction.* It is a simple declaration that they were IN FACT fitted for it, without making an affirmation about the manner in which they became so. A reader of the English Bible may, perhaps, sometimes draw the impression that God had fitted them for this. But this is not affirmed; and there is an evident design in *not* affirming it, and a distinction made between them and the vessels of mercy which ought to be regarded. In relation to the latter it is expressly *affirmed* that *God* fitted or *prepared* them for glory; see ver. 23, "Which HE had afore prepared unto glory." The same distinction is remarkably striking in the account of the last judgment in Mat. xxv. 34, 41. To the righteous, Christ will say, "Come, ye blessed of my Father, inherit the kingdom prepared FOR YOU," &c. To the wicked, "Depart from me, ye cursed, into everlasting fire, prepared FOR THE DEVIL AND HIS ANGELS;" not said to have been originally prepared *for them.* It is clear, therefore, that God intends to keep the great truth in view, that *he* prepares his people *by direct agency* for heaven; but that he exerts *no such agency* in preparing the wicked for destruction. ¶ *For destruction* (εἰς ἀπώλειαν). This word occurs in the New Testament no less than twenty times: Mat. vii. 13, "Which leadeth to destruction;" John xvii. 12, "Son of perdition;" Acts viii. 20, "Thy money perish with thee"—Greek, be for destruction with thee; xxv. 16; Phil. i. 28, "Token of perdition;" iii. 19, "Whose end is destruction;" 2 Thes. ii. 3, "The son of perdition;" 1 Tim. vi. 9, "Which drown men in destruction and perdition;" Heb. x. 39, "Which draw back unto perdition;

23 And that he might make known *the riches of his glory on

a Ep.1.18.

see also 2 Pet. ii. 1, 3; iii. 7, 16; &c. In these places it is clear that the reference is to the future punishment of wicked men, and in *no instance* to national calamities. No such use of the word is to be found in the New Testament; and this is further clear from the contrast with the word "glory" in the next verse. We may remark here, that if men are *fitted* or prepared for destruction; if future torment is adapted to them, and they to it; if it is fit that they should be subjected to it; then God will do what is *fit* or *right* to be done, and, unless they repent, they must perish. Nor would it be right for God to take them to heaven as they are— to a place for which they are not *fitted*, and which is not adapted to their feelings, their character, or their conduct.

23. *And that he might make known.* That he might manifest or display. The apostle had shown (in ver. 22) that the dealings of God towards the wicked were not liable to the objection made in ver. 19. In this verse he proceeds to show that the objection could not lie against his dealings with the *other* class of men—the righteous. If his dealings towards *neither* were liable to the objection, then he has *met the whole case,* and the divine government is vindicated. This he proves by showing that for God to show the riches of his glory towards those whom he has prepared for it, cannot be regarded as unjust. ¶ *The riches of his glory.* This is a form of expression common among the Hebrews, meaning the same as *his rich* or *his abundant glory.* The same expression occurs in Eph. i. 18. ¶ *On the vessels of mercy.* Men towards whom his mercy was to be displayed (see ver. 22); that is, on those towards whom he has purposed to display his mercy. ¶ *Mercy.* Favour, or pity shown to the *miserable.* Grace is favour to the *undeserving;* mercy, favour to those in distress. This distinction is not, however, always strictly observed

the vessels of mercy, *b* which he had afore prepared unto glory.

b 1 Th.5.9.

by the sacred writers. ¶ *Which he had afore prepared.* We are here brought to a remarkable difference between God's mode of dealing with them and with the wicked. Here it is expressly affirmed that God himself had prepared them for glory. In regard to the wicked, it is simply affirmed that they *were fitted* for destruction, without affirming anything of the *agency* by which it was done. That *God* prepares his people for glory—commences and continues the work of their redemption — is abundantly taught in the Scriptures, 1 Thes. v. 9, "God hath appointed us to obtain salvation by our Lord Jesus Christ;" 2 Tim. i. 9, "Who hath saved us and called us with an holy calling, not according to our works, but according to his own purpose and grace, which was given us in Christ Jesus before the world began." See also Eph. i. 4, 5, 11; Rom. viii. 28, 29, 30; Acts xiii. 48; John i. 13. As the renewing of the heart and the sanctifying of the soul is an act of goodness, it is worthy of God, and of course no objection could lie against it. No man could complain of a course of dealings designed to make men *better;* and as this is the sole design of the electing love of God, his dealings with *this* class of men are easily vindicated. No Christian can complain that God has chosen him, renewed him, and made him pure and happy. And as this was an important part of the plan of God, it is easily defended from the objection in ver. 19. ¶ *Unto glory.* To happiness; and especially to the happiness of heaven, Heb. ii. 10, "It became him, in bringing many sons unto glory," &c.; Rom. v. 2, "We rejoice in hope of the glory of God; 2 Cor. iv. 17, "Our light affliction . . . worketh for us a far more exceeding and eternal weight of glory;" 2 Thes. ii. 14; 2 Tim. ii. 10; 1 Pet. v. 4. This eternal state is called "glory," because it blends together everything that constitutes honour, dignity, purity, love, and

24 Even us, whom he hath called, not of the Jews only, but also of the Gentiles?

25 As he saith also in Osee,

c I will call them my people, which were not my people; and her beloved, which was not beloved.

26 And*d* it shall come to pass,

c Ho.2.23.   d Ho.1.10.

happiness. All these significations are in various places attached to this word, and all mingle in the eternal state of the righteous. We may remark here, (1) That this word "glory" is not used in the Scriptures to denote any *external national privileges*, or to describe any external call of the gospel. No such instance is to be found. Of course the apostle here by vessels of mercy meant *individuals* destined to eternal life, and not *nations* externally called to the gospel. No instance can be found where God speaks of nations called to external privileges and speaks of them as "prepared unto glory." (2) As this word refers to the future state of individuals, it shows what is meant by the word "destruction" in ver. 22. That term stands contrasted with glory, and describes, therefore, the future condition of individual wicked men. This is also its uniform meaning in the New Testament. On this vindication of the apostle we may observe, (1) That all men will be treated as they *ought* to be treated. Men will be dealt with according to their characters at the end of life. (2) If men will suffer no injustice, then this is the same as saying that they will be treated justly. But what is this? That the wicked shall be treated as they deserve. What they *deserve* God has told us in the Scriptures. "These shall go away into everlasting punishment." (3) God has a right to bestow his blessings as he chooses. Where *all* are undeserving, where none have any claim, he may confer his favours on whom he pleases. (4) He actually *does* deal with men in this way. The apostle takes this for granted. He does not deny it. He most evidently believes it, and labours to show that it is *right* to do so. If *he* did not believe it, and meant to teach it, he would have said so. It would have met the objection at once, and saved all argument. He reasons as if he *did* believe

it; and this settles the question that the doctrine is true.

24. *Even us*, &c. See chap. i. 16; ii. 10; iii. 29, 30. To prove that the *Gentiles* might be called as well as the Jews, was a leading design of the epistle. ¶ *Us*. Christians, selected from both Jews and Gentiles. This proves that he did not refer to *nations* primarily, but to *individuals* chosen *out of* nations. Two things are established here. (1) That the grace of God was not confined to the Jewish people, as they supposed, so that it could be conferred on no others. (2) That God was not bound to confer grace on *all* the descendants of Abraham, as he bestowed it on those selected *from* the mass, according to his own will, and not of necessity *on the mass* itself.

25. *As he saith also*. The doctrine which he had established he proceeds now to confirm by quotations from the writings of *Jews*, that he might remove *every* objection. The doctrine was, (1) That God intended to call his people from the Gentiles as well as the Jews. (2) That he was bound by no promise and no principle of obligation to bestow salvation on *all* the Jews. (3) That, therefore, it was right for him to reject any or all of the Jews, if he chose, and cut them off from their privileges as a people and from salvation. ¶ *In Osee*. This is the Greek form of writing the Hebrew word *Hosea*. It means in the book of Hosea, as *in David* means in the book of David, or by David, Heb. iv. 7. The passage is found in Hosea ii. 23. This quotation is not made according to the *letter*, but the *sense* of the prophet is preserved. The meaning is the same in Hosea and in this place, that God would bring those into a covenant relation to himself, who were before deemed outcasts and strangers. Thus he supports his main position, that God would choose his people from among the Gentiles as well as the Jews, or

that in the place where it was said unto them, Ye *are* not my people; there shall they be called the children of the living God.

27 Esaias also crieth concerning Israel, *e*Though the number of the children of Israel be as the sand of the sea, a remnant shall be saved.

e Is.10.22,23.

---

would exercise towards both his right as a sovereign, bestowing or withholding his blessings as he pleases.

26. *And it shall come to pass.* It shall happen, or take place. This is a continuation of the quotation from the prophet Hosea (chap. i. 10), designed to confirm the doctrine which he was establishing. Both these quotations have the same design, and are introduced for the same end. In Hosea they did not refer to the calling of the Gentiles, but to the recalling the rejected Jews. God says, after the Jews had been rejected and scattered for their idolatry, after they had forfeited his favour, and been cast off as if they were not his people, he would *recall* them, and bestow on them again the appellation of sons. The apostle does not quote this as having original reference to the Gentiles, but for the following purposes :—(1) If God formerly purposed to recall to himself a people whom he had rejected, if he bestowed favours on his own people *after* they had forfeited his favour, and ceased to be entitled to the name of "his people;" then the same thing was not to be regarded as absurd if he dealt in a similar manner with the Gentiles—also a part of his original great family, the family of man, but long since rejected and deemed strangers. (2) The dealings of God towards the Jews in the time of Hosea settled *a general principle of government.* His treatment of them in this manner was a *part* of his great plan of governing the world. On the same plan he now admitted the Gentiles to favour. And as this *general principle* was established, as the history of the Jews themselves was a *precedent* in the case, it ought not to be objected in the time of Paul that the *same principle* should be carried out to meet the case also of the Gentiles. ¶ *In the place.* The place where they may be scattered, or where they may dwell. Or rather, perhaps, in those nations which were

not regarded as the people of God, *there* shall be a people to whom this shall apply. ¶ *Where it was said unto them.* Where the proper appellation of the people was, that they were not the people of God; where they were idolatrous, sinful, aliens, strangers; so that they had none of the marks of the children of God. ¶ *Ye are not my people.* People in covenant with God; under his protection, as *their* Sovereign, and keeping his laws. ¶ *There shall they be called.* That is, there they *shall be.* The verb *to call* in the Hebrew writings means often the same as *to be.* It denotes that this shall be the appellation which properly expresses their character. It is a figure perhaps almost peculiar to the Hebrews; and it gives additional interest to the case. Instead of saying coldly and abstractedly, "they *are* such," it introduces also the idea that such is the *favourable judgment* of God in the case; see Mat. v. 9, "Peace-makers . . . shall be called the children of God;" see the Note on that place; also ver. 19; Mat. xxi. 13, "My house shall *be called* the house of prayer;" Mark xi. 17; Luke i. 32, 35, 76; Isa. lvi. 7. ¶ *The children of,* &c. Greek, *sons;* see Note, Mat. i. 1. ¶ *Living God.* Called *living* God in opposition to dead idols; see Note, Mat. xvi. 16; also xxvi. 63; John vi. 69; Acts xiv. 15; 1 Thes. i. 9, "Turn from idols to serve the *living* and true God;" Jer. x. 10. This is a most honourable and distinguished appellation. No higher favour can be conferred on mortals than *to be* the sons of the living God; members of his family; entitled to his protection; and secure of his watch and care. This was an object of the highest desire with the saints of old; see Ps. xlii. 2; lxxxiv. 2, "My soul thirsteth for God, the *living* God;" "My heart and my flesh cry out for the *living* God."

27, 28. *Esaias.* The Greek way of writing the word *Isaiah.* ¶ *Crieth.*

28 For he will finish [7] the work, and cut *it* short in righteousness:

[7] or, *the account.*

Isa. x. 22, 23. Exclaims, or speaks aloud or openly; compare John i. 15. Isaiah brings forth the doctrine fully, and without any concealment or disguise. This doctrine related to the rejection of the Jews—a far more difficult point to establish than was that of the calling of the Gentiles. It was needful, therefore, to fortify it by some explicit passage of the Scriptures. ¶ *Concerning Israel.* Concerning *the Jews.* It is probable that Isaiah had reference primarily to the Jews of his own time; to that wicked generation that God was about to punish, by sending them captive into other lands. The case was one, however, which settled a *general principle of the Jewish government;* and, therefore, it was applicable to the case before the apostle. If the thing for which he was contending—that the Jews might be rejected—existed in the time of Isaiah, and was settled then us a precedent, it might exist also in his time, and under the gospel. ¶ *As the sand of the sea.* This expression is used to denote an indefinite or an innumerable multitude. It often occurs in the sacred writings. In the infancy of society, before the art of numbering was carried to a great extent, men were obliged to express themselves very much in this manner, Gen. xxii. 17, " I will multiply thy seed . . . as the sand which is upon the sea-shore; " xxxii. 12. Isaiah doubtless had reference to this promise; " Though all that was promised to Abraham shall be fulfilled, and his seed shall be as numerous as God declared, yet a remnant only," &c. The apostle thus shows that his doctrine does not conflict at all with the *utmost* expectation of the Jews drawn from the promises of God; see a similar use of the term *sand* in Judg. vii. 12; 1 Sam. xiii. 5; 2 Sam. xvii. 11, &c. In the same manner great numbers were denoted by the *stars of heaven,* Gen. xxii. 17; xv. 5. ¶ *A remnant shall be saved.* Meaning a remnant *only.* This implies that great multitudes of them would be *cast off,* and *be not saved.* If only

a *remnant* was to be saved, many must be lost; and this was just the point which the apostle was endeavouring to establish. The word *remnant* means *that which is left,* particularly what may remain after a battle or a great calamity, 2 Ki. xix. 31; x. 11; Judg. v. 11; Isa. xiv. 22. In this place, however, it means a small part or portion. Out of the great multitude there shall be so few left as to make it proper to say that it was a mere remnant. This implies, of course, that the great mass should be cast away or rejected. And this was the use which the apostle intended to make of it; compare the Wisdom of Sirach, xliv. 17, " Noah . . . was left unto the earth as *a remnant* when the flood came." ¶ *Shall be saved.* Shall be preserved or kept from destruction. As Isaiah had reference to the captivity of Babylon, this means that only a remnant should return to their native land. The great mass should be rejected and cast off. This was the case with the ten tribes, and also with many others who chose to remain in the land of their captivity. The use which the apostle makes of it is this : In the history of the Jews, by the testimony of Isaiah, a large part of the Jews of that time were rejected, and cast off from being the peculiar people of God. It is clear, therefore, that God has brought himself under no obligation to save *all* the descendants of Abraham. This case settles the principle. If God did it *then,* it was equally consistent for him to do it in the time of Paul, under the gospel. The conclusion, therefore, to which the apostle came, that it was the intention of God to reject and cast off the Jews as a people, was in strict accordance with their own history and the prophecies. It was still true that a remnant was to be saved, while the great mass of the people was rejected. The apostle is not to be understood here as affirming that the passage in Isaiah had reference to the gospel, but only that *it settled one great principle of the divine administration in regard to the Jews, and that their*

because ᶠa short work will the Lord make upon the earth.

ᶠ Is. 28. 22.

rejection under the gospel was strictly in accordance with that principle.

28. *He will finish the work.* This is taken from the Septuagint translation of Isa. x. 23. The Hebrew is, "The Lord God of hosts shall make a consumption, even determined, in the midst of all the land." Or, as it may be rendered, "Destruction is decreed which shall make justice overflow; yea, destruction is verily determined on; the Lord Jehovah will execute it in the midst of all the land" (Stuart). The Septuagint and the apostle adhere to *the sense* of the passage, but do not follow the *words.* The phrase, *will finish the work,* means *he will bring the thing to an end,* or will accomplish it. It is an expression applicable to a firm purpose to accomplish an object. It refers here to his *threat* of cutting off the people; and means that he will fulfil it. ¶ *Cut it short.* This word here means to *execute it speedily.* The destruction shall not be delayed. ¶ *In righteousness.* So as to manifest his own *justice.* The work, though apparently severe, yet shall be a *just* expression of God's abhorrence of the sins of the people. ¶ *Because a short work.* The word here rendered "short" means properly that which is *determined on* or *decreed.* This is the sense of the Hebrew; and the phrase here denotes *the purpose which was determined on* in relation to the Jews. ¶ *Upon the earth.* Upon the *land* of Israel; see Notes on Mat. v. 4; iv. 8. The design for which the apostle introduces this passage is, to show that God of old destroyed many of the Jews for their sin; and that, therefore, the doctrine of the apostle was no new thing, that *the Jews* might be excluded from the peculiar privileges of the children of God.

29. *And as Esaias said.* Isa. i. 9. ¶ *Before.* The apostle had just cited one prediction from the tenth chapter of Isaiah. He now says that Isaiah had affirmed the same thing in a previous part of his prophecy.

29 And as Esaias said before, ᵍExcept the Lord of Sabaoth had

ᵍ Is. 1. 9; La. 3. 22.

¶ *Except the Lord of Sabaoth.* In Isaiah, the Lord of Hosts. The word *Sabaoth* is the Hebrew word rendered *hosts.* It properly denotes *armies* or military hosts organized for war. Hence it denotes *the hosts of heaven,* and means, (1) The *angels,* who are represented as *marshalled* or arranged into military orders, Eph. i. 21; iii. 10; vi. 12; Col. i. 16; ii. 15; Jude 6; 1 Kings xxii. 19, "I saw the Lord sitting on his throne, and all the host of heaven standing by him;" Psalm ciii. 21; cxlviii. 2. (2) The stars, Jer. xxxiii. 22, "As the host of heaven cannot be numbered," &c.; Isa. xl. 26; Deut. iv. 19, &c. God is called the Lord of hosts, as being at the head of all these armies; their King and their Commander. It is a phrase properly expressive of his majesty and power, and is appropriately introduced here, as the act of saving "the seed" was a signal *act of power* in the midst of great surrounding wickedness. ¶ *Had left.* Had *preserved,* or kept from destruction. Here their preservation is ascribed to God, and it is affirmed that if God had not interposed *the whole nation* would have been cut off. This fully establishes the doctrine of the apostle, that God *might* cast off the Jews, and extend the blessings to the Gentiles. ¶ *A seed.* The Hebrew in Isaiah means *one surviving* or *escaping,* corresponding with the word *remnant.* The word *seed* commonly means in the Scriptures *descendants, posterity.* In this place it means *a part, a small portion; a remnant,* like the small portion of the harvest which is reserved for sowing. ¶ *We had been as Sodoma.* The nation was so wicked, that unless God had preserved a small number who were pious from the general corruption of the people, they would have been swept off by judgment, like Sodom and Gomorrah. We are told that ten righteous men would have saved Sodom, Gen. xviii. 32. Among the Israelites, in a time of great general depravity, a small number of holy men were found

left us a seed, *h* we had been as Sodoma, and been made like unto Gomorrha.

30 What shall we say then?

h Ge.19.24,25; Is.13.19.

i That the Gentiles, which followed not after righteousness, have attained to righteousness, even *k* the righteousness which is of faith.

i ch.10.20.   *k* ch.1.17; Phi.3.9.

who preserved the nation. The design of the apostle here was the same as in the previous verses—to show that it was settled in the Jewish history that God *might* cast off the people, and reject them from enjoying the peculiar privileges of his friends. It is true that in Isaiah he has reference to the *temporal* punishments of the Jews. But it settles *a great principle*, for which Paul was contending, that God *might* cast off the nation consistently with his promises and his plans.—We may learn here, (1) That the existence of religion among a people is owing to the love of God. "Except the Lord *had left us*," &c. (2) It is owing to his mercy that *any men* are kept from sin and any nation from destruction. (3) We see the value of religion and of pious men in a nation. Ten such would have saved Sodom; and a few such saved Judea; comp. Mat. v. 13, 14. (4) God has a right to withdraw his mercies from any other people, however exalted their privileges, and leave them to ruin; and we should not be high-minded, but fear, Rom. x. 20.

30. *What shall we say then?* What conclusion shall we draw from the previous train of remarks? To what results have we come by the passages adduced from the Old Testament? This question is asked preparatory to his summing up the argument; and he had so stated the argument that the conclusion which he was about to draw was inevitable. ¶ *The Gentiles.* That *many* of the Gentiles; or that the way was open for them, and many of them *had actually* embraced the righteousness of faith. This epistle was written as late as the year 57 (see Introduction), and at that time multitudes of heathens *had* embraced the Christian religion. ¶ *Which followed not after righteousness:* The apostle does not mean that none of the pagans had any solicitude about right and wrong, or that there were no anxious inquiries

among them; but he intends particularly to place them in contrast with the Jew. They had not made it their main object to justify themselves; they were not filled with prejudice and pride as the Jews were, who supposed that they *had* complied with the law, and who felt no need of any other justification; they were sinners, and they felt it, and had no such mighty obstacle in a system of self-righteousness to overcome as the Jew had. Still it was true that they were excessively wicked, and that the prevailing characteristic among them was that they did not follow after righteousness; see chap. i. The word "followed" here often denotes to pursue with intense energy, as a hunter pursues his game or a man pursues a flying enemy. The Jews had sought righteousness in that way; the Gentiles had not. The word *righteousness* here means the same as *justification*. The Gentiles, which sought not justification, have obtained justification. ¶ *Have attained to righteousness.* Have become justified. This was a matter of fact; and this was what the prophet had predicted. The apostle does not say that the sins of the Gentiles or their indifference to the subject was any *reason* why God justified them, or that men would be as safe in sin as in attempting to seek for salvation. He establishes the doctrine, indeed, that God is a sovereign; but still it is implied that the gospel had not the *peculiar* obstacle to contend with among the Gentiles that it had among the Jews. There was less pride, obstinacy, self-confidence; and men were more easily brought *to see* that they were sinners and to feel their need of a Saviour. Though God dispenses his favours as a sovereign, and though *all* are opposed by nature to the gospel, yet it is always true that the gospel finds *more* obstacles among some men than among others. This

31 But Israel, *which followed after the law of righteousness, hath not attained to the law of righteousness.

l ch.10.2; 11.7.

was a most cutting and humbling doctrine to the pride of a Jew; and it is no wonder, therefore, that the apostle guarded it as he did. ¶ *Which is of faith.* Justification by faith in Christ; see Note, chap. i. 17.

31. *But Israel.* The Jews. The apostle does not mean to affirm that *none* of the Jews had obtained mercy, but that *as a people,* or acting according to the prevalent principles of the nation to work out their own righteousness, they had not obtained it. ¶ *Which followed after the law of righteousness.* The phrase "the law of righteousness" means the law of justice, or *the just law.* That law demands perfect purity; and even its external observance demanded holiness. The Jews supposed that they rendered such *obedience* to that law as to constitute a *meritorious* ground of justification. This they had *followed after,* that is, pursued zealously and unremittingly. The reason why they did not obtain justification in that way is fully stated in chap. i.–iii., where it is shown that the law demands perfect compliance with its precepts, and that Jews as well as Gentiles had altogether failed in rendering such compliance. ¶ *Hath not attained to the law of righteousness.* They have not come to yield *true* obedience to the law, even though imperfect; not such obedience as to give *evidence* that they have been justified. We may remark here, (1) That no conclusion could have been more humbling to a Jew than this. It constituted the whole of the prevalent religion, and was the object of their incessant toils. (2) As they made the experiment fully, and failed; as they had the best advantages for it, and did not succeed, but reared only a miserable and delusive system of self-righteousness (Phil. iii. 4–9); it follows that all similar experiments must fail, and that none now can be justified

32 Wherefore? Because *they sought it* not by faith, but as it were by the works of the law : for they stumbled at that stumbling-stone ;

by the law. (3) Thousands fail in the same attempt. They seek to justify themselves before God. They attempt to weave a righteousness of their own. The moral man does this. The immoral man attempts it as much as the moral man, and is as confident in his own righteousness. The troubled sinner does this; and this it is which keeps him so long from the cross of Christ. All this must be renounced; and man must come as a poor, lost, ruined sinner, and throw himself upon the mere mercy of God in Christ for justification and life.

32. *Wherefore?* Why? The apostle proceeds to state the reason why so uniform and remarkable a result happened. ¶ They sought it *not by faith,* &c. They depended on their own righteousness, and not on the mercy of God to be obtained by faith. ¶ *By the works of the law.* By complying with *all* the demands of the law, so that they might *merit* salvation. Their attempted obedience included their prayers, fastings, sacrifices, &c., as well as compliance with the demands of the moral law. It may be asked here, perhaps, how the Jews could know any better than this? how should *they* know anything about justification by faith? To this I answer, (1) That the doctrine was stated in the Old Testament; see Hab. ii. 4, comp. Rom. i. 17; Ps. xxxii. cxxx. xiv., comp. Rom. iii., Job ix. 2. (2) The sacrifices had reference to a future state of things, and were doubtless so understood; see the Epistle to the Hebrews. (3) The *principle* of justification and of living by faith had been *fully* brought out in the lives and experience of the saints of old; see Rom. iv. and Heb. xi. ¶ *They stumbled.* They fell; or failed; or *this was the cause* why they did not obtain it. ¶ *At that stumbling-stone.* To wit, at that which he specifies in the following verse. A *stumbling-stone* is a stone or impediment in the path over

33 As it is written, *m* Behold, I lay in Sion a stumbling-stone and rock

m Ps.118.22; Is.8.14.

which men may fall. Here it means *that obstacle which prevented their attaining the righteousness of faith; and which was the occasion of their fall, rejection, and ruin.* That was the rejection and the crucifixion of their own Messiah; their unwillingness to be saved by him; their contempt of him and his message. For this God withheld from them the blessings of justification, and was about to cast them off as a people. This also, the apostle proceeds to prove, was foretold by the prophets.

33. *As it is written.* See Isa. viii. 14; xxviii. 16. The quotation here is made up of both these passages, and contains the substance of both; comp. also Ps. cxviii. 22, 1 Pet. ii. 6. ¶ *Behold I lay in Sion.* Mount Sion was the hill or eminence in Jerusalem, over against Mount Moriah, on which the temple was built. On this was the palace of David, and this was the residence of the court, 1 Chron. xi. 5–8. Hence the whole city was often called by that name, Ps. xlviii. 12; lxix. 35; lxxxvii. 2. Hence also it came to signify the capital, the glory of the people of God, the place of solemnities; and hence also the church itself, Ps. ii. 6; li. 18; cii. 13; cxxxvii. 3; Isa. i. 27; lii. 1; lix. 20, &c. In this place it means the church. God will place or establish in the midst of that church. ¶ *A stumbling-stone and rock of offence.* Something over which men shall fall; see Note, Mat. v. 29. This is by Paul referred to the Messiah. He is called *rock of stumbling,* not because it was the *design* of sending him that men *should* fall, but because such would be the result. The application of the term *rock* to the Messiah is derived from the custom of *building,* as he is the *corner-stone* or the *immovable foundation* on which the church is to be built. It is not on human merits, but by the righteousness of the Saviour, that the church is to be reared; see 1 Pet. ii. 6, " I lay in Sion a *chief corner-stone;* " Ps. cxviii. 22, "The stone which the

of offence; and whosoever believeth on him shall not be [8] ashamed.

[8] or, *confounded.*

builders rejected, is become the head stone of the corner;" Eph. ii. 20, " Jesus Christ himself being the chief corner-stone." This rock, *designed* as a corner-stone to the church, became, by the wickedness of the Jews, the block over which they fall into ruin, 1 Pet. ii. 8. ¶ *Shall not be ashamed.* This is taken substantially from the Septuagint translation of Isa. xxviii. 16, though with some variation. The Hebrew is, "shall not make haste," as it is in our English version. This is the literal meaning of the Hebrew word; but it means also *to be afraid,* as one who makes haste often is; to be agitated with fear or fright; and hence it has a signification nearly similar to that of shame. It expresses the substance of the same thing, viz. *failure of obtaining expected success and happiness.* The meaning here is, that the man who believes shall not be agitated, or thrown into commotion by fear or want of success; shall not be disappointed in his hopes; and, of course, he shall never be ashamed that he became a Christian. They who do *not* believe in Christ shall be agitated, fall, and sink into eternal shame and contempt, Dan. xii. 2. They who *do* believe shall be confident; shall not be deceived, but shall obtain the object of their desires. It is clear that Paul regarded the passage in Isaiah as referring to the Messiah. The same also is the case with the other sacred writers who have quoted it, 1 Pet. ii. 5–8; see also Mat. xxi. 42; Luke xx. 17, 18; ii. 34. The ancient Targum of Jonathan translates the passage, Isa. xxviii. 16, " Lo, I will place in Sion a king, a king strong, mighty, and terrible " —referring doubtless to the Messiah. Other Jewish writings also show that this interpretation was formerly given by the Jews to the passage in Isaiah.

In view of this argument of the apostle, we may remark, (1) That God is a sovereign, and has a right to dispose of men as he pleases. (2) The doctrine of election was manifest

CHAPTER X.

BRETHREN, my heart's desire and prayer to God for Israel is, that they might be saved.

in the case of the Jews as an established principle of the divine government, and is therefore true. (3) It argues great want of proper feeling to be opposed to this doctrine. It is saying, in other words, that we have not confidence in God; or that we do not believe that he is qualified to direct the affairs of his own universe as well as we. (4) The doctrine of election is a doctrine which is not *arbitrary;* but which will yet be seen to be wise, just, and good. It is the source of all the blessings that any mortals enjoy; and in the case before us, it can be *seen* to be benevolent as well as just. It is *better* that God should cast off a part of the small nation of the Jews, and extend these blessings to the Gentiles, than that they should always have been confined to Jews. The world is better for it, and more good has come out of it. (5) The fact that the gospel has been extended to all nations, is proof that it is from heaven. To a Jew there was no motive to attempt to break down all the existing institutions of his nation, and make the blessings of religion common to all nations, unless he knew that the gospel system was true. Yet the apostles were Jews; educated with all the prejudices of the Jewish people. (6) The interests of Christians are safe. They shall not be ashamed or disappointed. God will keep them, and bring them to his kingdom. (7) Men still are offended at the cross of Christ. They contemn and despise him. He is to them as a root out of dry ground, and they reject him, and fall into ruin. This is the cause why sinners perish; and this only. Thus, as the ancient Jews brought ruin on themselves and their country, so do sinners bring condemnation and woe on their souls. And as the ancient despisers and crucifiers of the Lord Jesus perished, so will all those who work iniquity and despise him now.

2 For I bear them record, that ^athey have a zeal of God, but not according to knowledge.

3 For they ^bbeing ignorant of

CHAPTER X.

1. *Brethren.* This expression seems intended particularly for the Jews, his ancient friends, fellow-worshippers, and kinsmen, but who had embraced the Christian faith. It is an expression of tenderness and affection, denoting his deep interest in their welfare. ¶ *My heart's desire.* The word " desire " (εὐδοκία) means benevolence, and the expression, *my heart's desire,* means my earnest and sincere wish. ¶ *Prayer to God.* He not only cherished this feeling, but he expressed it in a desire to God. He had no desire that his kinsmen should be destroyed; no pleasure in the appalling doctrine which he had been defending. He still wished their welfare; and could still pray for them that they might return to God. Ministers have no pleasure in proclaiming the truth that men must be lost. Even when they declare the truths of the Bible that some *will* be lost; when they are constrained by the unbelief and wickedness of men to proclaim it of *them,* they still can sincerely say that they seek their salvation. ¶ *For Israel.* For the Jewish nation. ¶ *That they might be saved.* This clearly refers to salvation from the sin of unbelief; and the consequences of sin in hell. It does not refer to the temporal calamities which were coming upon them, but to preservation from the eternal anger of God; comp. chap. xi. 26; 1 Tim. ii. 4. The reasons why the apostle commences this chapter in this tender manner are the following. (1) Because he had stated and defended one of the most offensive doctrines that could be preached to a Jew; and he was desirous to show them that it was not from any want of affection for them, but that he was urged to it by the pressure of truth. (2) He was regarded by them as an apostate. He had abandoned them when bearing their commission, and while on his way

to execute their favourite purposes, and had preached the doctrine which they had sent him to destroy; comp. Acts ix. He had opposed them everywhere; had proclaimed their pride, self-righteousness, and crime in crucifying their Messiah; had forsaken all that they valued; their pomp of worship, their city, and their temple; and had gone to other lands to bear the message of mercy to the nations that they despised. He was willing to show them that this proceeded from no want of affection for them, but that he still retained towards them the feelings of a Jew, and could give them credit for much that they valued themselves on, ver. 2. (3) He was aware of the deep and dreadful condemnation that was coming on them. In view of that he expressed his tender regard for their welfare, and his earnest prayer to God for their salvation. And we see here the proper feelings of a minister of the gospel when declaring the most terrible of the truths of the Bible. Paul was tender, affectionate, kind; convincing by cool argument, and not harshly denouncing; stating the appalling truth, and then pouring out his earnest desires to God that he would avert the impending doom. So should the awful doctrines of religion be preached by all the ambassadors of God.

2. *For I bear them record.* To bear record means to be a witness; to give evidence. This Paul was well qualified to do. He had been a Jew of the strictest order (Acts xxvi. 5; Phil. iii. 5), and he well knew the extraordinary exertions which they put forth to obey the commands of the law. ¶ *A zeal of God.* A zeal *for* God. Thus John ii. 17, "The zeal of thine house hath eaten me up"—an earnest desire *for* the honour of the sanctuary has wholly absorbed my attention; comp. Ps. lxix. 9; Acts xxi. 20, "Thou seest, brother, how many thousands of Jews there are which believe, and they are all zealous of the law; xxii. 3, "And was zealous toward God, as ye all are this day." Zeal for God here means passionate ardour in the things pertaining to God or in the things of religion.

In this they were, doubtless, many of them sincere; but sincerity does not of itself constitute true piety, John xvi. 2, "The time cometh that whosoever killeth you will think that he doeth God service." This would be an instance of extraordinary zeal, and in this they would be sincere; but persecution to death of apostles cannot be true religion; see also Mat. xxiii. 15; Acts xxvi. 9, "I thought that *I ought* to do," &c. So many persons suppose that, provided they are *sincere* and *zealous*, they must of course be accepted of God. But the zeal which is acceptable is that which aims at the glory of God, and which is founded on true benevolence to the universe, and which does not aim primarily to establish a system of self-righteousness, as did the Jew, or to build up *our own sect*, as many others do. We may remark here, that Paul was not insensible to what the Jews did, and was not unwilling to give them credit for it. A minister of the gospel should not be blind to the amiable qualities of men or to their zeal; and should be willing to speak of it tenderly, even when he is proclaiming the doctrine of depravity or denouncing the just judgments of God. ¶ *Not according to knowledge.* Not an enlightened, discerning, and intelligent zeal. Not that which was founded on correct views of God and of religious truth. Such zeal is enthusiasm, and often becomes persecuting. Knowledge without zeal becomes cold, abstract, calculating, formal, and may be possessed by devils as well as men. It is the union of the two—the action of the man called forth to intense effort by just *views* of truth and by right *feeling*—that constitutes true religion. This was the zeal of the Saviour and of the apostles.

3. *For they being ignorant.* The ignorance of the Jews was voluntary, and therefore criminal. The apostle does not affirm that they could not have known what the plan of God was, for he says (ver. 18-21) that they had full opportunity of knowing. An attentive study of their own Scriptures would have led them to the true knowledge of the Messiah and his righteous-

God's righteousness, and going about to establish their own righteousness, have not submitted themselves unto the righteousness of God.

ness; see John v. 39; comp. Isa. liii., &c. Yet the fact that they were ignorant, though not an excuse, is introduced here, doubtless, as a mild and mitigating circumstance that should take off the severity of what he might appear to them to be saying, 1 Tim. i. 13, "But I obtained mercy because I did it ignorantly, in unbelief;" Luke xxiii. 34, "Then said Jesus, Father, forgive them, for they know not what they do;" Acts vii. 60. Involuntary ignorance excuses from guilt; but ignorance produced by our sin or our indolence is no excuse for crime. ¶ *Of God's righteousness.* Not of the personal holiness of God, but *of God's plan of justifying men or of declaring them righteous by faith in his Son;* see Note, chap. i. 17. Here God's plan stands opposed to their efforts to make themselves righteous by their own works. ¶ *And seeking to establish,* &c. Endeavouring to *confirm* or *make valid* their own righteousness; to render it such as to constitute a ground of justification before God; or to make good their own claims to eternal life by their merits. This stands opposed to the justification by grace, or to God's plan. And they must *ever* be opposed. This was the constant effort of the Jews; and in this they supposed they had succeeded; see Paul's experience in Phil. iii. 4–6; Acts xxvi. 5. Instances of their belief on this subject occur in all the gospels, where our Saviour combats their notions of their own righteousness. See particularly their views and evasions exposed in Mat. xxiii.; comp. Mat. v. 20, &c.; vi. 2–5. It was this which mainly opposed the Lord Jesus and his apostles; and it is this confidence in their own righteousness which still stands in the way of the progress of the gospel among men. ¶ *Have not submitted themselves.* Confident in their own righteousness, they have not yielded their hearts to a plan which requires them to come

4 For Christ *is* ᶜthe end of the law for righteousness to every one that believeth.

5 For ᵈMoses describeth the right-

ᶜ He.10.14. ᵈ Le.18.5.

confessing that they have *no* merit, and to be saved by the merit of another. No obstacle to salvation by grace is so great as the self-righteousness of the sinner. ¶ *Righteousness of God.* His plan or scheme of justifying men. 4. *For Christ.* This expression implies *faith* in Christ. This is the design of the discussion, to show that justification cannot be obtained by our own righteousness, but by faith in Christ. As no direct benefit results to men from Christ unless they believe on him, faith in him is implied where the word occurs in this connection. ¶ *Is the end of the law.* The word translated "end" means that which *completes* a thing or renders it perfect; also the boundary, issue, or termination of anything, as the end of life, the result of a prophecy, &c., John xiii. 1; Luke xxii. 37. It also means the *design* or *object* which is had in view; the principal purpose for which it was undertaken, 1 Tim. i. 5, "The *end* of the commandment is charity"—the main design or purpose of the command is to produce love; 1 Pet. i. 9, "The end of your faith, the salvation of your souls"— the main design or purpose of faith is to secure salvation; Rom. xiv. 9, "To this end Christ both died," &c.—for this design or purpose. This is doubtless its meaning here. *The main design or object which the perfect obedience of the law would accomplish is accomplished by faith in Christ.* That is, perfect obedience to the law would accomplish justification before God, secure his favour and eternal life. The same end is now accomplished by faith in Christ. The great design of both is the same; and the same great end is finally gained. This was the subject of discussion between the apostle and the Jews; and this is all that is necessary to understand in the case. Some have supposed that the word *end* refers to the ceremonial law;

eousness which is of the law, That the man which doeth those things shall live by them.

that Christ fulfilled it and brought it to an end. Others, that he perfectly fulfilled the moral law. And others, that the law *in the end* leads us to Christ, or that its design is to point us to him. All this is true, but not the truth taught in this passage. That is simple and plain, that by faith in Christ the same end is accomplished in regard to our justification, that would be by perfect obedience to the moral law. ¶ *For righteousness.* Unto justification with God. ¶ *To every,* &c. See Note, chap. i. 17.

5. *For Moses describeth,* &c. This is found in Lev. xviii. 5, "Ye shall therefore keep my statutes and my judgments, which if a man do he shall live in them." This appeal is made to Moses, both in regard to the righteousness of the law and that of faith, in accordance with the usual manner of Paul to sustain all his positions by the Old Testament, and to show that he was introducing no new doctrine. He was only affirming that which had been long before taught in the writings of the Jews themselves. The word *describeth* is literally *writes* (γράφει), a word often used in this sense. ¶ *The righteousness,* &c. The righteousness which a perfect obedience to the law of God would produce. That consisted in perfectly *doing* all that the law required. ¶ *The man which doeth these things.* The man who shall perform or obey what was declared in the previous statutes. Moses here had reference to all the commandments which God had given, moral and ceremonial. And the doctrine of Moses is that which pertains to all laws, that he who shall render *perfect* and continued compliance with *all* the statutes made known, shall receive the reward which the law promises. This is a first principle of *all* law; for all law holds a man to be innocent, and, of course, entitled to whatever immunities and rewards it has to confer, until he is *proved* to be guilty. In this case, however, Moses did not affirm that *in fact*

6 But the righteousness which is of faith speaketh on this wise, *e* Say not in thine heart, Who

e De. 30. 12-14.

anyone either had yielded or would yield perfect obedience to the law of God. The Scriptures elsewhere abundantly teach that it never *has* been done. ¶ *Doeth.* Obeys, or yields obedience. So also Mat. v. 19, "Shall *do* and teach them;" vii. 24, 26, "Whosoever heareth these sayings . . . and *doeth* them;" xxiii. 3; Mark iii. 35; vi. 20; Luke vi. 46, 47, 49. ¶ *Shall live.* Shall obtain felicity. Obedience shall render him happy, and entitled to the rewards of the obedient. Moses doubtless referred here to *all* the results which would follow obedience. The *effect* would be to produce happiness in this life and in the life to come. The *principle* on which happiness would be conferred would be the same, whether in this world or the next. The tendency and result of obedience would be to promote order, health, purity, benevolence; to advance the welfare of man, and the honour of God, and thus *must* confer happiness. The idea of happiness is often in the Scriptures represented by the word *life;* see Note, John v. 24. It is evident, moreover, that the Jews understood Moses here as referring to more than temporal blessings. The ancient Targum of Onkelos renders the passage in Leviticus thus: "The man who does these things shall live in them to eternal life." So the Arabic version is, "The retribution of him who works these things is, that he shall live an eternal life." ¶ *By them* (ἐν αὐτοῖς). In them. *In* their observance he shall find happiness. Not simply as a *result,* or *reward,* but the *very act of obeying* shall carry its own reward. This is the case with all true religion. This declaration of Moses is still true. If perfect obedience were rendered, it would, from the nature of the case, confer happiness and life as long as the obedience was rendered. God would not punish the innocent. But in this world it never has been rendered, except in the case of the Lord Jesus; and the consequence is,

shall ascend into heaven? (that is, to bring Christ down *from above:*)

7 Or, Who shall descend into the deep? (that is, to bring up Christ again from the dead.)

---

that the course of man has been attended with pain, sorrow, and death.

6. *But the righteousness which is of faith.* It is observable here that Paul does not affirm that *Moses* describes anywhere the righteousness by faith, or the effect of the scheme of justification by faith. His object was different, to give the law, and state its demands and rewards. Yet though he had not *formally* described the plan of justification by faith, yet he had used language which would *fitly express* that plan. The scheme of justification by faith is here *personified*, as if it were living and describing its own effects and nature. One describing it would say, or the plan itself speaks in this manner. The words here quoted are taken from Deut. xxx. 11–14. The original meaning of the passage is this: Moses, near the end of his life, having given his commandments to the Israelites, exhorts them to obedience. To do this, he assures them that his commands are reasonable, plain, intelligible, and accessible. They did not require deep research, long journeys, or painful toil. There was no need of crossing seas, and going to other lands, of looking into the profound mysteries of the high heavens, or the deep abyss; but they were near them, had been plainly set before them, and were easily understood. To see the excellency of this characteristic of the divine law, it may be observed, that among the ancients, it was not uncommon for legislators and philosophers to travel to distant countries in pursuit of knowledge. They left their country, encountered dangers on the sea and land, to go to distant regions that had the reputation of wisdom. Egypt was peculiarly a land of such celebrity; and in subsequent times Pythagoras, and the principal philosophers of Greece, travelled into that country to converse with their priests, and to bear the fruits of their wisdom to benefit their native land. And it is not improbable that this had been done to some extent even in or before the

time of Moses. Moses says that *his* precepts were to be obtained by no such painful and dangerous journeys. They were near them, plain, and intelligible. This is the general meaning of this passage. Moses dwells on the thought, and places it in a variety of forms by the questions, "Who shall go up to heaven for us," &c.; and Paul regards this as *appropriately* describing the language of Christian faith; but without affirming that Moses himself had any reference in the passage to the faith of the gospel. ¶ *On this wise.* In this manner. ¶ *Say not in thine heart.* The expression *to say in the heart* is the same as *to think.* Do not *think*, or suppose, that the doctrine is so difficult to be understood, that one must ascend to heaven in order to understand it. ¶ *Who shall ascend into heaven?* This expression was used among the Jews to denote any difficult undertaking. To say that it was high as heaven, or that it was necessary to ascend to heaven to understand it, was to express the highest difficulty. Thus Job xi. 7, "Canst thou by searching find out God? . . . It is high as heaven, what canst thou do?" &c. Moses says it was not so with his doctrine. It was not impossible to be understood, but was plain and intelligible. ¶ *That is, to bring Christ, &c.* Paul does not here affirm that it was the original design of *Moses* to affirm this of Christ. His words related to his own doctrine. Paul makes this use of the words because, (1) They appropriately *expressed* the language of faith. (2) If this might be affirmed of the doctrines of Moses, much more might it of the Christian religion. Religion had no such difficult work to do as to ascend to heaven to bring down a Messiah. That work was already accomplished when God gave his Son to become a man, and to die. To save man it was indeed indispensable that Christ should have come down from heaven. But the language of faith was that this *had* already been done. Probably the word *Christ* here

8 But what saith it? The word is nigh thee, *even* in thy mouth,

includes all the *benefits* mentioned in ver. 4 as resulting from the work of Christ.

7. *Or, Who shall descend into the deep?* These words are also a part of the address of Moses, Deut. xxx. 13. But it is not literally quoted. The Hebrew is, "Neither is it beyond the sea, that thou shouldest say, Who shall go over the sea for us," &c. The *words* of the quotation are changed, but not the sense; and it is to be remembered that Paul is not professing to quote the *words* of Moses, but to *express the language of faith;* and this he does mainly by words which Moses had used, which also expressed *his* meaning. The words as used by Moses refer to that which is *remote,* and therefore difficult to be obtained. To cross the sea in the early times of navigation involved the highest difficulty, danger, and toil. The *sea* which was in view was doubtless the Mediterranean; but the crossing of that was an enterprise of the greatest difficulty, and the regions *beyond* that were regarded as being at a vast distance. Hence it is spoken of as being the *widest* object with which they were acquainted, and the fairest illustration of infinity, Job xi. 9. In the same sense Paul uses the word deep, ἄβυσσον —*the abyss.* This word is applied to anything the depth or bottom of which is not known. It is applied to the ocean (in the Septuagint), Job xli. 31, "He maketh the deep to boil as a pot;" Isa. xliv. 27, "That saith to the deep, Be dry," &c.; Gen. vii. 11; viii. 2; to a broad place, Job xxxvi. 16; and to the *abyss* before the world was formed, Gen. i. 2. In the New Testament it is not applied to *the ocean,* unless in the passage Luke viii. 31 (see Note on that place), but to the abode of departed spirits; and particularly to the dark, deep, and bottomless pit, where the wicked are to dwell for ever, Rev. ix. 1, 2, "And to him was given the key of the bottomless pit. And he opened the bottomless pit" (Greek, *the pit of the abyss*); Rev. xi. 7; xvii. 8; xx. 1, 3. In these

and in thy heart: that is, the word of faith, which we preach;

places the word means the deep, awful regions of the nether world. The word stands opposed to heaven; as deep as that is high; as dark as that is light; while the one is as vast as the other. In the place before us it is opposed to heaven; and to descend there to bring up one, is supposed to be as impossible as to ascend to heaven to bring one down. Paul does not affirm that Christ descended to those regions; but he says that there is no such difficulty in religion *as if one were required* to descend into those profound regions to call back a departed spirit. That which was *in fact* done, when Jesus was recalled from the dead, and now the work of salvation is easy. The word *abyss* here, therefore, answers to *hades,* or the dark regions of departed spirits. ¶ *That is, to bring up Christ,* &c. Justification by faith had no such difficult and impossible work to perform as would be an attempt for man to raise the dead. That would be impossible; but the work of religion is easy. *Christ, the ground of hope, is not by* OUR EFFORTS *to be brought down from heaven to save us, for that is done; nor* BY OUR EFFORTS *to be raised from the dead, for that is done; and what remains for us, that is* TO BELIEVE, *is easy, and is near us.* This is the meaning of the whole passage.

8. *But what saith it?* That is, what is the language of the doctrine of justification by faith? Or what is *to be done* according to that doctrine? ¶ *The word is nigh thee.* This is still a use of the language of Moses, Deut. xxx. 14. The meaning is, the doctrine is not difficult to be understood and embraced. What is *nigh us* may be easily obtained; what is remote, with difficulty. The doctrine of Moses and of the gospel was *nigh;* that is, it was easily obtained, embraced, and understood. ¶ *In thy mouth.* This is taken from the Septuagint, Deut. xxx. 14. The meaning is, that the doctrine was already so familiar, and so well understood, that it was actually in their mouth, that is, their

9 That *if thou shalt confess
with thy mouth the Lord Jesus,

f 1 Jn.4.2.

language, their common conversation.
Moses had so often inculcated it, that
it was understood and talked about by
the people, so that there was no need
to search in distant climes to obtain
it. The same was true of the gospel.
The facts were so well known by the
preaching of the apostles, that they
might be said to be *in every man's
mouth.* ¶ *In thy heart.* The word
heart is very variously used in the
sacred Scriptures. As used by Moses
in this place, it evidently means that
his doctrines were in their *mind*, or
were a subject of meditation and
reflection. They already possessed
them, and talked and thought about
them, so that there was no need of
going to distant places to learn them.
The same was true of the doctrine
requiring faith in Christ. It was
already among them by the preaching
of the apostles, and was a subject of
conversation and of thought. ¶ *That
is.* This is the use which the apostle
makes of it; not that Moses referred
to the gospel. His *language* conveys
the main idea which Paul wished to
do, that the doctrine was plain and
intelligible. ¶ *The word of faith.*
The doctrine which requires faith, *i.e.*
the gospel; comp. 1 Tim. iv. 6. The
gospel is called the *word* of faith, the
word of God, as being that which was
spoken, or communicated by God to
man, ver. 17; Heb. vi. 5; xi. 3.
¶ *Which we preach.* Which is proclaimed by the apostles, and made
known to Jews and Gentiles. As
this was now made known to all, as
the apostles preached it everywhere,
it could be said to be nigh them;
there was no need of searching other
lands for it, or regarding it as a
hidden mystery, for it was plain and
manifest to all. Its simplicity and
plainness he proceeds immediately to
state.

9. *That if thou shalt confess.* The
word here rendered *confess* (ὁμολογέω)
is often rendered *profess,* Mat. vii.
23, "Then will I profess to them, I
never knew you;" Tit. i. 16; iii. 14;

and shalt *g*believe in thine heart
that God hath raised him from the
dead, thou shalt be saved.

g Ac.8.37.

Rom. i. 22; 1 Tim. ii. 10; vi. 12, 13,
21; Heb. iii. 1, &c. It properly
means *to speak that which agrees with
something which others speak or maintain.* Thus confession or profession
expresses our *agreement or concord
with what* GOD *holds to be true, and
what he declares to be true.* It denotes a public declaration or assent to
that, here expressed by the words
" with thy mouth." A profession of
religion then denotes a public declaration of our agreement with what God
has declared, and extends to *all* his
declarations about our lost estate,
our sin, and need of a Saviour; to his
doctrines about his own nature, holiness, and law; about the Saviour and
the Holy Spirit; about the necessity
of a change of heart and holiness of
life; and about the grave and the
judgment; about heaven and hell.
As the doctrine respecting a Redeemer
is the main and leading doctrine, it is
put here by way of eminence, as *in
fact* involving all others; and publicly
to express our assent to this, is to
declare our agreement with God on
all kindred truths. ¶ *With thy mouth.*
To profess a thing *with the mouth* is
to speak of it; to declare it; to do it
openly and publicly. ¶ *The Lord
Jesus.* Shalt openly acknowledge
attachment to Jesus Christ. The
meaning of it may be expressed by
regarding the phrase "the Lord" as
the *predicate;* or the thing to be con-
fessed is, that *he is Lord;* comp.
Acts ii. 36; Phil. ii. 11, "And that
every tongue should confess that
Jesus Christ is Lord." Here it
means to acknowledge him as Lord,
i.e. as having a right to rule over the
soul. ¶ *Shalt believe in thy heart.*
Shalt *sincerely* and *truly* believe this,
so that the external profession shall
correspond with the real, internal
feelings. Where this is *not* the case,
it would be hypocrisy; where this *is*
the case, there would be the highest
sincerity, and this religion requires.
¶ *That God hath raised him.* This

10 For with the heart man believeth unto righteousness; and with the mouth confession is made unto salvation.

11 For the scripture saith, [h] Whosoever believeth on him shall not be ashamed.

[h] Is. 28. 16; 49. 23.

fact, or article of Christian belief, is mentioned here because of its great importance, and its bearing on the Christian system. If this be true, then *all* is true. Then it is true that he came forth from God; that he died for sin; and that God approved and accepted his work. Then it is true that he ascended to heaven, and is exalted to dominion over the universe, and that he will return to judge the quick and the dead. For all this was professed and taught; and all this was regarded as depending on the truth of his having been raised from the dead; see Phil. ii. 8–11; Eph. i. 21; Acts ii. 24, 32, 33; xvii. 31; 2 Cor. iv. 14; 1 Cor. xv. 13–20. To profess this doctrine was, therefore, virtually to profess *all* the truths of the Christian religion. No man could believe this who did not also believe *all* the truths dependent on it. Hence the apostles regarded this doctrine as so important, and made it so prominent in their preaching; see Note on Acts i. 3. ¶ *Thou shalt be saved.* From sin and hell. This is the doctrine of the gospel throughout; and all this shows that salvation by the gospel was easy.

10. *For with the heart.* Not with the understanding merely, but with such a faith as shall be sincere, and shall influence the life. There *can be* no other genuine faith than that which influences the *whole mind.* ¶ *Believeth unto righteousness.* Believes so that justification is obtained * (Stuart). In God's plan of justifying men, this is the way by which we may be declared just or righteous in his sight. The moment a sinner believes, therefore, he is justified; his sins are pardoned, and he is introduced into the favour of God. No man can be justified without this; for this is God's plan, and he will not depart from it. ¶ *With the mouth confession is made,* &c. That is, confession or profession

* See Supplementary Notes, chap. i. 17; iii. 22.

is so made as to obtain salvation. He who in all appropriate ways professes his attachment to Christ shall be saved. This profession is to be made in all the proper ways of religious duty; by an avowal of our sentiments; by declaring on all proper occasions our belief of the truth; and by an unwavering adherence to them in all persecutions, oppositions, and trials. He who *declares* his belief makes a profession. He who associates with Christian people does it. He who acts with them in the prayer-meeting, in the sanctuary, and in deeds of benevolence, does it. He who is baptized, and commemorates the death of the Lord Jesus, does it. And he who leads an humble, prayerful, spiritual life, does it. He shows his regard to the precepts and example of Christ Jesus; his regard for them more than for the pride, and pomp, and allurements of the world. All these are included in a profession of religion. In whatever way we can manifest attachment to it, it must be done. The reason why this is made so important is, that there *can be* no true attachment to Christ which will not manifest itself in the life. A city that is set on a hill cannot be hid. It is impossible that there should be true belief in the heart of man, unless it should show itself in the life and conversation. This is the only test of its existence and its power; and hence it is made so important in the business of religion. And we may here learn, (1) That *a profession* of religion is, by Paul, made *as really* indispensable to salvation *as believing.* According to him it is connected with salvation as really as faith is with justification; and this accords with all the declarations of the Lord Jesus, Mat. x. 32; xxv. 34–46; Luke xii. 8. (2) There can be no religion where there is not a willingness to confess the Lord Jesus. There is no true repentance where we are not willing to *confess* our faults. There is no true attach-

12 For[i] there is no difference between the Jew and the Greek:

i Ac.15.9; Ga.3.28.

[k]for the same Lord over all is rich unto all that call upon him.

k 1 Ti.2.5.

ment to a father or mother or friend, unless we are willing on all proper occasions to avow it. And so there can be no true religion where there is too much pride or vanity, or love of the world, or fear of shame to confess it. (3) Those who never profess any religion have none; and they are not safe. To deny God the Saviour before men is not safe. They who do not profess religion, profess the opposite. The *real* feelings of the heart will be expressed in the life. And they who profess by their lives that they have no regard for God and Christ, for heaven and glory, must expect to be met in the last day as those who deny the Lord that bought them, and who bring upon themselves quick destruction, 2 Pet. i. 2.

11. *For the scripture saith,* &c. Isa. xxviii. 16. This was the uniform doctrine of the Scripture, that he who holds an opinion on the subject of religion *will not* be ashamed to avow it. This is the nature of religion, and without this there can be none; see this passage explained in Rom. ix. 33.

12. *For there is no difference.* In the previous verse Paul had quoted a passage from Isa. xxviii. 16, which says that *every one* (Greek, πᾶς) that believeth shall not be ashamed; that is, every one of every nation and kindred. This implies that it was not to be confined to the *Jews.* This thought he now *further* illustrates and confirms by expressly declaring that there is no difference between the Jew and the Greek. This doctrine it was one main design of the epistle to establish, and it is fully proved in the course of the argument in chap. i.– iv. See particularly chap. iii. 26– 30. When the apostle says there is *no difference* between them, he means in regard to the subject under discussion. In many respects there might be a difference, but not in *the way of justification before God.* There *all* had sinned; all had failed of obeying the law; and all must be justified in the same way, by faith in the Lord

Jesus Christ. The word *difference* (διαστολή) means *distinction, diversity.* It also means *eminence, excellence, advantage.* There is no eminence or *advantage* which the Jew has over the Greek in regard to justification before God. ¶ *The Jew.* That portion of mankind which professed to yield obedience to the law of Moses. ¶ *The Greek.* Literally, those who dwelt in Greece, or those who spoke the Greek language. As the Jews, however, were acquainted chiefly with the Greeks, and knew little of other nations, the name *Greek* among them came to denote all who were not Jews; that is, the same as the Gentiles. The terms "Jew and Greek," therefore, include all mankind. There is no difference among men about the terms of salvation; they are the same to all. This truth is frequently taught. It was a most important doctrine, especially in a scheme of religion that was to be preached to all men. It was very offensive to the Jews, who had always regarded themselves as a peculiarly favoured people. Against this all their prejudices were roused, as it completely overthrew all their own views of national eminence and pride, and admitted despised Gentiles to the same privileges with the long favoured and chosen people of God. The apostles, therefore, were at great pains fully to establish it; see Acts x. 9; Gal. iii. 28. ¶ *For the same Lord over all,* &c. For there is the same Lord of all; that is, the Jews and Gentiles have one common Lord; comp. Rom. iii. 29, 30. The same God had formed them, and ruled them; and God now opened the same path to life. See this fully presented in Paul's address to the people of Athens, in Acts xvii. 26–30; see also 1 Tim. ii. 5. As there was but *one* God; as all, Jews and Gentiles, were his creatures; as one law was applicable to all; as all had sinned; and as all were exposed to wrath; so it was reasonable that there should be *the same way* of return — through the

13 For *l* whosoever shall *m* call upon the name of the Lord shall be saved.

l Joel 2.32.   *m* 1 Co.1.2.

14 How then shall they call on him in whom they have not believed? and how shall they believe

---

mere mercy of God. Against this the Jew ought not to object; and in this he and the Greek should rejoice. ¶ *Is rich unto all* (πλουτῶν εἰς παντάς). The word *rich* means to *have abundance*, to have in store much more than is needful for present or personal use. It is commonly applied to wealth. But applied to God, it means that he *abounds* in mercy, or goodness towards others. Thus Eph. ii. 4, "God, who is *rich in mercy*," &c.; 1 Tim. vi. 17, 18, "Charge them that are rich in this world . . . that they *be rich in good works;*" Jam. ii. 5, "God hath chosen the poor . . . *rich in faith*," *i.e. abounding* in faith and good works, &c. Thus God is said to be *rich* towards all, as he abounds in mercy and goodness towards them in the plan of salvation. ¶ *That call upon him.* This expression means properly *to supplicate, to invoke,* as in prayer. As prayer constitutes no small part of religion, and as it is a *distinguishing characteristic* of those who are true Christians (Acts ix. 11, "Behold, he prayeth"), to call on the name of the Lord is put for religion itself, and is descriptive of acts of devotion towards God, 1 Pet. i. 17, "And if ye call on the Father," &c.; Acts ii. 21; ix. 14, "He hath authority . . . to bind all *that call on thy name;*" Acts vii. 59; xxii. 16; Gen. iv. 26, "Then began men to call on the name of the Lord."

13. *For whosoever shall call,* &c. This sentiment is found substantially in Joel ii. 32, "And it shall come to pass, that whosoever shall call on the name of the Lord shall be delivered." This is expressly applied to the times of the gospel, by Peter, in Acts ii. 21; see Note on that place. To call on *the name* of the Lord is the same as to call on the Lord himself. The word *name* is often used in this manner, "The *name* of the Lord is a strong tower," &c., Prov. xviii. 10; "The name of the God of Jacob defend thee," Ps. xx. 1. That is, *God himself* is a strong tower, &c.

It is clear from what follows that the apostle applies this to Jesus Christ; and this is one of the numerous instances in which the writers of the New Testament apply to him expressions which in the Old Testament are applicable to God; see 1 Cor. i. 2. ¶ *Shall be saved.* This is the uniform promise; see Acts ii. 21; xxii. 16, "Arise, and be baptized, and wash away thy sins, *calling on the name of the Lord.*" This is proper and indispensable, because, (1) We have sinned against God, and it is right that we should confess it. (2) Because he only can pardon us, and it is fit that, if we obtain pardon, we should ask it of God. (3) To call upon him is to acknowledge him as our Sovereign, our Father, and our Friend; and it is right that we render him our homage. It is *implied* in this, that we call upon him with right feelings; that is, with a humble sense of our sinfulness and our need of pardon, and with a willingness to receive eternal life as it is offered us in the gospel. And if this be done, this passage teaches us that *all* may be saved who will do it. He will cast none away who come in this manner. The invitation and the assurance extend to all nations and to men of all times.

14. *How then shall they call,* &c. The apostle here adverts to an objection which might be urged to his argument. His doctrine was, that faith in Christ was essential to justification and salvation; and that this was needful for all; and that without this man must perish. The objection was, that they could not call on him in whom they had not believed; that they could not believe in him of whom they had not heard; and that this was *arranged by God himself,* so that a large part of the world was destitute of the gospel, and *in fact* did not believe, ver. 16, 17. The objection had *particular* reference to the Jews; and the ground of injustice which a Jew would complain of would be, that

in him of whom they have not heard? and how shall they hear without a preacher?

the plan made salvation dependent on *faith*, when a large part of the nation had not heard the gospel, and had had no opportunity to know it. This objection the apostle meets, so far as it was of importance to his argument, in ver. 18–21. The first part of the objection is, that they could "not call on him in whom they had not believed." That is, how could they call on one in whose existence, ability, and willingness to help, they did not believe? The objection is, that in order to our calling on one for help, we must be satisfied that there *is* such a being, and that he is able to aid us. This remark is just, and every man feels it. But the point of the objection is, that *sufficient evidence of the divine mission and claims of Jesus Christ had not been given to authorize the doctrine that eternal salvation depended on belief in him, or that it would be right to suspend the eternal happiness of Jew and Gentile on this.* ¶ *How shall they believe in him,* &c. This position is equally undeniable, that men could not believe in a being of whom they had not heard. And the implied objection was, that men could not be expected to believe in one of whose existence they knew nothing, and, of course, that they could not be blamed for not doing it. It was not right, therefore, to make eternal life depend, both among Jews and Gentiles, on faith in Christ. ¶ *And how shall they hear,* &c. How *can* men hear, unless some one *proclaim* to them, or preach to them that which is to be heard and believed? This is also true. The *objection* thence derived is, that it is not right to condemn men for not believing what has never been proclaimed to them; and, of course, that the doctrine that eternal life is suspended on faith cannot be just and right.

15. *And how shall they preach.* In what way shall there *be preachers,* unless they are commissioned by God? The word "*how*" does not refer to

15 And how shall they preach, except they be sent? as it is written, [n]How beautiful are the

n Is.52.7; Na.1.15.

the *manner* of preaching, but to the fact that there would be no preachers *at all* unless they were sent forth. To *preach* means to proclaim in a public manner, as a *crier* does. In the Scriptures it means to *proclaim* the gospel to men. ¶ *Except they be sent.* That is, except they are divinely commissioned, and sent forth by God. This was an admitted doctrine among the Jews, that a proclamation of a divine message must be made by one who was commissioned by God for that purpose, Jer. xxiii. 21; i. 7; xiv. 14, 15; vii. 25. He who sends a message to men can alone designate the proper persons to bear it. The point of the objection, therefore, was this : Men could not believe unless the message was sent to them; yet God had *not* actually sent it to all men: it could not, therefore, be *just* to make eternal life depend on so impracticable a thing as *faith*, since men had not the means of believing. ¶ *As it is written.* In Isa. lii. 7. ¶ *How beautiful,* &c. The reason why this passage is introduced here is, that it confirms what had just been advanced in the objection—the *importance* and *necessity* of there being messengers of salvation. That importance is seen in the high encomium which is passed on them in the sacred Scriptures. They are regarded as objects peculiarly attractive; their necessity is fully recognized; and a distinguished rank is given to them in the oracles of God. *How beautiful.* How attractive, how lovely. This is taken from the Hebrew, with a slight variation. In the Hebrew, the words "upon the mountains" occur, which makes the passage more picturesque, though the sense is retained by Paul. The image in Isaiah is that of a herald seen at first leaping or running on a distant hill, when he first comes in sight, with tidings of joy from a field of battle, or from a distant land. Thus, the appearance of such a man to those who were in captivity, would be an image full of

feet of them that preach the gospel of peace, and bring glad tidings of good things!

16 But *o* they have not all obeyed

o Ac.28.24; He.4.2.

the gospel.   For Esaias saith, *p* Lord, who hath believed [1] our [2] report.

17 So then faith *cometh* by

p Is.53.1; Jn.12.38.   [1] *the hearing of us.*
[2] *or, preaching.*

---

gladness and joy. ¶ *Are the feet.* Many have supposed that the meaning of this expression is this : The *feet* of a herald, naked and dusty from travelling, would be *naturally* objects of disgust. But that which would be naturally disagreeable is thus made pleasant by the joy of the message. But this explanation is far-fetched, and wants parallel instances. Besides, it is a violation of the image which the apostle had used. That was a *distant* object—a herald running on the distant hills; and it supposes a picture too remote to observe distinctly the *feet,* whether attractive or not. The meaning of it is clearly this : "How beautiful is the *coming* or the *running* of such a herald." The feet are emblematic of his coming. Their rapid motion would be seen; and their rapidity would be beautiful from the desire to hear the message which he brought. The whole meaning of the passage, then, as applied to ministers of the gospel, is, that their *coming* is an attractive object, regarded with deep interest, and productive of joy— an honoured and a delightful employment. ¶ *That preach,* &c. Literally, "that evangelize peace." That proclaim *the good news* of peace; or bring the glad message of peace. ¶ *And bring glad tidings,* &c. Literally, "and evangelize good things;" or that bring the glad message of good things. *Peace* here is put for good of any kind; and, as the apostle uses it, for the news of reconciliation with God by the gospel. *Peace,* at the end of the conflicts, distresses, and woes of war, is an image of all blessings. Thus it is put to denote the blessings when a sinner ceases to be the enemy of God, obtains pardon, and is admitted to the joys of those who are his children and friends. The coming of those messengers who proclaim it is joyful to the world. It fills the bosom of the anxious sinner

with peace; and they and their message will be regarded with deep interest, as sent by God, and producing joy in an agitated bosom, and peace to the world. This is an illustration of the proper feeling with which we should regard the ministers of religion. This passage in Isaiah is referred by the Jews themselves to the times of the gospel (Rosenmüller).

16. *But they have not all obeyed the gospel.* It is not easy to see the connection of this; and it has been made a question whether this is to be regarded as a *continuation* of the objection of the Jew, or as a part of the answer of the apostle. After all the attention which I have been able to give it, I am inclined to regard it as an *admission* of the apostle; as if he had said, "It must be *admitted* that all have not obeyed the gospel. So far as the objection of the Jew arises from *that fact,* and so far as that fact can bear on the case, it is to be conceded that *all* have not yielded obedience to the gospel. For this was clearly declared even by the prophet;" comp. Acts xxviii. 24; Heb. iv. 2. ¶ *For Esaias saith.* Isa. liii. 1. ¶ *Who hath believed our report?* That is, Isaiah complains that his declarations respecting the Messiah had been rejected by his countrymen. The form of expression, "Who hath believed?" is a mode of saying *emphatically* that few or none had done it. The great mass of his countrymen had rejected it. This was an example to the purpose of the apostle. In the time of Isaiah this fact existed; and it was not a new thing that it existed in the time of the gospel. *Our report.* Our message; or that which is delivered to be heard and believed. It originally means the doctrine which Isaiah delivered about the Messiah; and implies that the same thing would occur when the Messiah should actu-

hearing, and hearing by the word of God.

18 But I say, Have they not heard? Yes, verily, qtheir sound

q Ps.19.4; Mat.28.19; Col.1.6,23.

ally come. Hence in the fifty-third chapter he proceeds to give the reasons why the report would not be credited, and why the Messiah would be rejected. It would be because he was a root out of a dry ground; because he was a man of sorrows, &c. And this actually took place. Because he did not come with splendour and pomp, as a temporal prince, he was rejected, and put to death. On substantially the same grounds he is even yet rejected by thousands. The force of this verse, perhaps, may be best seen by including it in a parenthesis, "How beautiful are the feet," &c. How important is the gospel ministry —(although it must be admitted that all have not obeyed, for this was predicted also by Isaiah, &c.).

17. *So then faith* cometh, &c. This I take to be clearly the language of the objector. As if he had said, By the very quotation which you have made from Isaiah, it appears that *a report* was necessary. He did not condemn men for not believing what they had not *heard;* but he complains of those who did not believe a message actually delivered to them. Even by this passage, therefore, it seems that a message was necessary, that faith comes by *hearing,* and hearing by the divine message. It could not be right, therefore, to condemn those who had not *obeyed* the gospel because they had not *heard* it; and hence not right to make salvation dependent on a condition which was, by the arrangement of God, put beyond their power. The very quotation from Isaiah, therefore, goes to confirm the objection in the 14th and 15th verses. ¶ *By hearing.* Our translation has varied the expression here, which is the same in two places in the Greek: "Isaiah said, Who hath believed our report (τῇ ἀκοῇ)? So then, you must admit that faith comes *by that report* (ἐξ ἀκοῆς), and therefore this *report* or message is necessary." When it is said that faith cometh *by hearing,* it is not meant that all who hear actually believe, for that is not

true; but that faith does not exist unless there is a message, or report, to be heard or believed. It cannot come otherwise than *by* such a message; in other words, unless there is something *made known to be believed.* And this shows us at once the importance of the message, and the fact that men are converted by the instrumentality of truth, and of truth only. ¶ *And hearing.* And the *report,* or the message (ἡ ἀκοὴ), is by the word of God; that is, the message is sent by the *command* of God. It is *his* word, sent by his direction, and therefore if withheld *by* him, those who did not believe could not be blamed. The argument of the objector is, that God could not justly condemn men for not believing the gospel.

18. *But I say.* But to this objection I, the apostle, reply. The objection had been carried through the previous verses. The apostle comes now to reply to it. In doing this, he does not deny the *principle* contained in it, that the gospel should be *preached* in order that men might be justly condemned for not believing it; not that the messengers must be sent by God, not that faith comes by hearing. All this he fully admits. But he proceeds to show, by an ample quotation from the Old Testament, that this *had been actually furnished* to the Jews and to the Gentiles, and that they *were actually* in possession of the message, and could not plead that they had never heard it. This is the substance of his answer. ¶ *Have they not heard?* A question is often, as it is here, an emphatic way of affirming a thing. The apostle means to *affirm* strongly that they *had* heard. The word "they," in this place, I take to refer to the *Gentiles.* What was the fact in regard to *Israel,* or the Jew, he shows in the next verses. One main design was to show that the *same* scheme of salvation extended to both Jews and Gentiles. The objection was, that it had not been made known to either, and that therefore it could not be maintained to be

went into all the earth, and their words unto the ends of the world.

just to condemn those who rejected it. To this the apostle replies, that *then* it was extensively known to *both;* and *if so,* then the objection in ver. 14, 15 was not well founded, for *in fact* the thing existed which the objector maintained to be necessary, to wit, that they *had* heard, and that preachers *had* been sent to them. ¶ *Yes, verily.* In the original, a single word, μενοῦνγε, compounded of μεν and ουν and γε. An *intense* expression, denoting strong affirmation. ¶ *Their sound went,* &c. These *words* are taken in substance from Psalm xix. 4. The psalmist employs them to show that the *works* of God, the heavens and the earth, proclaim his existence everywhere. By using them here, the apostle does not affirm that David had reference to the gospel in them, but *he uses them to express his own meaning;* he makes an affirmation about the gospel in language used by David on another occasion, but without intimating or implying that David had such a reference. In this way we often quote the language of others as expressing in a happy way our own thoughts, but without supposing that the author had any such reference. The meaning here is, that that may be affirmed *in fact* of the gospel which David affirmed of the works of God, that their sound had gone into all the earth. ¶ *Their sound.* Literally, the sound or tone which is made by a stringed instrument (φθόγγος). Also a *voice,* a report. It means here they *have spoken,* or declared truth. As applied to the heavens, it would mean that they speak, or proclaim, the wisdom or power of God. As used by Paul, it means that the message of the gospel had been *spoken,* or proclaimed, far and wide. The Hebrew is, "their *line,*" &c. The Septuagint translation is the same as that of the apostle —their voice (ὁ φθόγγος αὐτῶν). The Hebrew word may denote the *string* of an instrument, of a harp, &c., and then the *tone* or sound produced by it; and thus was understood by the Septuagint. The apostle, however,

19 But I say, Did not Israel know? First Moses saith, *r* I
r De.32.21.

does not affirm that this was the *meaning* of the Hebrew; but he conveyed *his* doctrine in language which aptly expressed it. ¶ *Into all the earth.* In the psalm, this is to be taken in its utmost signification. The works of God *literally* proclaim his wisdom to *all* lands and to all people. As applied to the gospel, it means that it was spread far and wide, that it had been extensively preached in all lands. ¶ *Their words.* In the psalm, the heavens are represented as *speaking,* and teaching men the knowledge of the true God. But the meaning of the apostle is, that the message of the gospel *had* sounded forth; and he referred doubtless to the labours of the apostles in proclaiming it to the heathen nations. This epistle was written about the year 57. During the time which had elapsed after the ascension of Christ, the gospel had been preached extensively in all the known nations; so that it might be said that it was proclaimed in those regions designated in the Scripture as the uttermost parts of the earth. Thus it had been proclaimed in Jerusalem, Syria, Asia Minor, Greece, Rome, Arabia, and in the islands of the Mediterranean. Paul, reasoning before Agrippa, says, that *he* could not be ignorant of those things, for they had not been done in a corner, Acts xxvi. 26. In Col. i. 23, Paul says that the gospel had been preached to every creature which is under heaven; see Col. i. 6. Thus the great facts and doctrines of the gospel had *in fact* been made known; and the objection of the Jew was met. It would be *sufficiently* met by the declaration of the psalmist, that the true God was made known by his works, and that therefore they were without excuse (comp. Rom. i. 20); but *in fact* the *gospel* had been preached, and its great doctrines and duties had been proclaimed to all nations far and near.

19. *But I say,* &c. Still further to meet the objection, he shows that the doctrine which he was maintaining

will provoke you to jealousy by *them that are* no people, *and* by was *actually* taught in the Old Testament. ¶ *Did not Israel know?* Did not the *Jews* understand? Is it not recorded in their books, &c., that they had full opportunity to be acquainted with this truth? This *question* is an emphatic way of affirming that they *did* know. But Paul does not here state *what* it was that they knew. That is to be gathered from what he proceeds to say. From that it appears that he referred to the fact that the gospel was to be preached to the *Gentiles*, and that the *Jews* were to be cast off. This doctrine followed from what he had already maintained in ver. 12, 13, that there was no difference in regard to the terms of salvation, and that the Jew had no particular privileges. If so, then the barrier was broken down; and if the Jews did not believe in Jesus Christ, they must be rejected. Against this was the objection in ver. 14, 15, that they could not believe; that they had not heard; and that a preacher had not been sent to them. If, now, the apostle could show that it was an *ancient* doctrine of the Jewish prophets that the Gentiles *should* believe, and that the Jews *would not* believe, the whole force of the objection would vanish. Accordingly he proceeds to show that this doctrine was distinctly taught in the Old Testament. ¶ *First.* First in order; as we say, *in the first place.* ¶ *I will provoke you.* These words are taken from Deut. xxxii. 21. In that place the declaration refers to the idolatrous and wicked conduct of the Jews. God says that they had *provoked* him, or excited his indignation, by worshipping that which was not God, that is, by *idols;* and *he,* in turn, would excite *their* envy and indignation by showing favours to those who were not regarded as a people; that is, to the Gentiles. *They* had shown *favour,* or affection, for that which was not God, and by so doing had provoked him to anger; and *he* also would show favour to those whom *they* regarded as no people, and would thus excite *their* anger. Thus he would

a *foolish nation I will anger you.

s Tit. 3. 3.

illustrate the great principle of his government in 2 Sam. xxii. 26, 27, "With the merciful thou wilt show thyself merciful; with the pure, thou wilt show thyself pure; and with the froward thou wilt show thyself unsavoury," *i.e.* froward, Ps. xviii. 26. In this passage the great doctrine which Paul was defending is abundantly established—that the Gentiles were to be brought into the favour of God; and the *cause* also is suggested to be the obstinacy and rebellion of the Jews. It is not clear that Moses had particularly in view the times of the gospel; but he affirms *a great principle* which is applicable to those times—that if the Jews should be rebellious, and prove themselves unworthy of his favour, that favour would be withdrawn, and conferred on other nations. The effect of this would be, of course, to excite their indignation. This *principle* the apostle applies to his own times; and affirms that it ought to have been understood by the Jews themselves. ¶ That are *no people.* That is, those whom you regard as unworthy the name of a people. Those who have no government, laws, or regular organization; who wander in tribes and clans, and who are under no settled form of society. This was the case with most barbarians; and the Jews evidently regarded all ancient nations in this light, *as unworthy the name of a people.* ¶ *A foolish nation.* The word *fool* means one void of understanding. But it also means one who is *wicked,* or *idolatrous;* one who contemns God, Ps. xiv. 1, "The *fool* hath said in his heart, there is no God;" Prov. i. 7, "Fools despise wisdom and instruction." Here it means a nation who had *no understanding* of the true God (ἀσυνέτῳ). ¶ *I will anger.* My bestowing favours on them will excite your anger. We may remark here, (1) That God is a sovereign, and has a right to bestow his favours on whom he pleases. (2) That when men abuse his mercies, become proud, or

20 But Esaias is very bold, and saith, *I was found of them that sought me not; I was made manifest unto them that asked not after me.

t Is.65.1,2.

21 But to Israel he saith, All day long I have stretched forth my hands unto a disobedient and gainsaying people.

cold, or dead in his service, he often takes away their privileges, and bestows them on others. (3) That the *effect* of his sovereignty is to excite men to anger. Proud and wicked men are always enraged that he bestows his favours on others; and the effect of his sovereign dealings is, to provoke to anger the very men who by their sins have rejected his mercy. Hence there is no doctrine that proud man hates so cordially as he does the doctrine of divine sovereignty; and none that will so much *test* the character of the wicked.

20. *But Esaias.* Isaiah lxv. 1, 2. ¶ *Is very bold.* Expresses the doctrine openly, boldly, without any reserve. The word ἀποτολμάω means *to dare*, to be venturesome, to be bold. It means here that, however unpopular the doctrine might be, or however dangerous it was to avow that the Jews were extremely wicked, and that God for their wickedness would cast them off, yet that Isaiah had long since done it. This was the point which Paul was establishing; and against this the objection was urged, and all the Jewish prejudices excited. This is the reason why he so much insists on it, and is so anxious to defend every part by the writings of acknowledged authority among the Jews—the Old Testament. The quotation is made from the Septuagint, with only a slight change in the *order* of the phrases. The meaning is, that God was found, or the true knowledge of him was obtained, by those who had not sought after him; that is, by the Gentiles, who had worshipped idols, and who had not sought for the true God. This does not mean that *we* are to expect to find God if we do not seek for him; or that *in fact* any become Christians who do not *seek* for it, and make an effort. The contrary is abundantly taught in the Scriptures, Heb. xi. 6; 1 Chron. xxviii. 8, 9; Mat. vi. 33; vii. 7; Luke xi. 9. But

it means that the *Gentiles*, whose characteristic was *not* that they sought God, would have the gospel sent to them, and would embrace it. The phrase, "I *was* found," in the *past* tense here, is in the *present* in the Hebrew, intimating that the time would come when God would say this of himself; that is, that the time would come when the Gentiles would be brought to the knowledge of the true God. This doctrine was one which Isaiah had constantly in his eye, and which he did not fear to bring openly before the Jews.

21. *But to Israel he saith.* The preceding quotation established the doctrine that the Gentiles were to be called. But there was still an important part of his argument remaining— that the Jews were to be rejected. This he proceeds to establish; and he here, in the language of Isaiah (lxv. 2), says that while the *Gentiles* would be obedient, the character of the Jews was, that they were a disobedient and rebellious people. ¶ *All day long.* Continually, without intermission; implying that their acts of rebellion were not momentary; but that this was the *established* character of the people. ¶ *I have stretched forth my hands.* This denotes an attitude of entreaty; a willingness and earnest desire to receive them to favour; to invite and entreat, Prov. i. 24. ¶ *A disobedient.* In the Hebrew, *rebellious, contumacious.* The Greek answers substantially to that; *disbelieving*, not confiding or obeying. ¶ *Gainsaying. Speaking against;* resisting, opposing. This is not in the Hebrew, but the substance of it was implied. The prophet Isaiah proceeds to *specify* in what this rebellion consisted, and to show that this was their character, Isa. lxv. 2-7. The argument of the apostle is this: viz. the ancient character of the people was that of wickedness; God is represented as stretching out his hands in vain; they rejected

him, and he was sought and found by others. It was *implied*, therefore, that the rebellious Jews would be rejected; and, of course, the apostle was advancing and defending no doctrine which was not found in the writings of the Jews themselves. And thus, by a different course of reasoning, he came to the same conclusion which he had arrived at in the first four chapters of the epistle, that the Gentiles and Jews were on the same level in regard to justification before God.

In the closing part of this chapter the great doctrine is brought forth and defended, that the way of salvation is open for all the world. This, in the time of Paul, was regarded as a novel doctrine. Hence he is at so much pains to illustrate and defend it. And hence, with so much zeal and self-denial, the apostles of the Lord Jesus went and proclaimed it to the nations. This doctrine is not the less important now. And from this discussion we may learn the following truths: (1) The heathen world is *in danger* without the gospel. They are sinful, polluted, wretched. The testimony of all who visit pagan nations accords most strikingly with that of the apostles in their times. Nor is there *any* evidence that the great mass of heathen population has changed for the better. (2) The provisions of the gospel are ample for them—for all. Its power has been tried on many nations; and its mild and happy influence is seen in meliorated laws, customs, habits; in purer institutions; in intelligence and order; and in the various blessings conferred by a pure religion. The same gospel is fitted to produce, on the wildest and most wretched population, the same comforts which are now experienced in the happiest part of our own land. (3) The command of Jesus Christ remains still the same, *to preach the gospel to every creature.* That command has never been repealed or changed. The apostles met the injunction, and performed what they could. It remains for the church to act as they did, to feel as they did, and put forth their efforts as they did, in obeying one of the most plain and

positive laws of Jesus Christ. (4) If the gospel is to be proclaimed everywhere, men must be sent forth into the vast field. Every nation must have an opportunity to say, "How beautiful are the feet of him that preaches the gospel of peace!" Young men, strong and vigorous in the Christian course, must give themselves to this work, and devote their lives in an enterprise which the apostles regarded as honourable to them; and which infinite Wisdom did not regard as unworthy the toils, and tears, and self-denials of the Son of God. (5) The church, in training young men for the ministry, in fitting her sons for these toils, is performing a noble and glorious work, a work which contemplates the triumph of the gospel among all nations. Happy will it be when the church shall feel the full pressure of this great truth, that the gospel MAY BE preached to every son and daughter of Adam; and when every man who enters the ministry shall count it, not self-denial, but a glorious privilege, to be permitted to tell dying pagan men that a Saviour bled for ALL sinners. And happy that day when it can be said with literal truth that their sound has gone out into all the earth; and that as far as the sun in his daily course sheds his beams, so far the Sun of Righteousness sheds also his pure and lovely rays into the abodes of men. And we may learn, also, from this, (6) That God will withdraw his favours from those nations that are disobedient and rebellious. Thus he rejected the ancient Jews; and thus also he will forsake all who abuse his mercies; who become proud, luxurious, effeminate, and wicked. In this respect it becomes the people of this favoured land to remember the God of their fathers; and not to forget, too, that national sin provokes God to withdraw, and that a nation that forgets God must be punished.

CHAPTER XI.

1. *I say then.* This expression is to be regarded as conveying the sense of an objection. Paul, in the previous chapters, had declared the doctrine that all the Jews were to be

CHAPTER XI.

I SAY then, Hath *a* God cast away his people? God forbid.

a 1 Sa.12.22; Ps.77.7,8; 89.31-37.

rejected. To this a Jew might naturally reply, Is it to be believed, that God would cast off his people whom he had once chosen; to whom pertained the adoption, and the promises, and the covenant, and the numerous blessings conferred on a favourite people? It was natural for a Jew to make such objections. And it was important for the apostle to show that *his* doctrine was consistent with all the promises which God had made to his people. The objection, as will be seen by the answer which Paul makes, is formed on the supposition that God had rejected *all his people*, or *cast them off entirely*. This objection he answers by showing, (1) That God had saved *him*, a Jew, and therefore that he could not mean that God had cast off *all* Jews (ver. 1); (2) That now, as in former times of great declension, God *had* reserved a remnant (ver. 2–5); (3) That it accorded with the Scriptures that *a part* should be hardened (ver. 6–10); (4) That the design of the rejection was not *final*, but was to admit the Gentiles to the privileges of Christianity (ver. 11–24); (5) That the Jews should yet return to God, and be reinstated in his favour: so that it could not be objected that God had *finally* and *totally* cast off his people, or that he had violated his promises. At the same time, however, the doctrine which Paul had maintained was true, that God had taken away their *exclusive* and *peculiar* privileges, and had rejected a large part of the nation. ¶ *Cast away.* Rejected, or put off. Has God so renounced them that they *cannot* be any longer his people? ¶ *His people.* Those who have been long in the covenant relation to him; that is, the Jews. ¶ *God forbid.* Literally, *it may not* or *cannot be.* This is an expression strongly denying that this could take place; and means that Paul did not intend to advance such a doctrine, Luke xx. 16; Rom.

For I also am an Israelite, of the seed of Abraham, *of* the tribe of Benjamin.

iii. 4, 6, 31; vi. 2, 15; vii. 7, 13.
¶ *For I am also an Israelite.* To show them that he did not mean to affirm that *all Jews* must of necessity be cast off, he adduces his own case. He was a Jew; and yet he looked for the favour of God, and for eternal life. That favour he hoped now to obtain by being a Christian; and if *he* might obtain it, others might also. "If I should say that *all* Jews must be excluded from the favour of God, then *I* also must be without hope of salvation, for I am a Jew." ¶ *Of the seed of Abraham.* Descended from Abraham. The apostle mentions this to show that he was a Jew in every respect; that he had a title to all the privileges of a Jew, and must be exposed to all their liabilities and dangers. If the seed of Abraham must of necessity be cut off, he must be himself rejected. The Jews valued themselves much on having been descended from so illustrious an ancestor as Abraham (Mat. iii. 9); and Paul shows them that he was entitled to all the privileges of such a descent; comp. Phil. iii. 4, 5. ¶ *Of the tribe of Benjamin.* This tribe was one that was originally located near Jerusalem. The temple was built on the line that divided the tribes of Judah and Benjamin. It is not improbable that it was regarded as a peculiar honour to have belonged to one of those tribes. Paul mentions it here in accordance with their custom; for they regarded it as of great importance to preserve their genealogy, and to be able to state not only that they were *Jews*, but to designate the tribe and family to which they belonged.

2. *God hath not cast away.* This is an explicit denial of the objection. ¶ *Which he foreknew.* The word *foreknew* is expressive not merely of *foreseeing* a thing, but implies in this place a previous purpose or plan; see Note, chap. viii. 29. The meaning of the passage is simply, God has not cast off those whom he had before purposed or designed to be his people.

2 God hath not cast away his people *b* which he foreknew. Wot ye not what the scripture saith of[1] Elias? how he maketh inter-

b ch.8.29.   [1] in.

cession to God against Israel, saying,

3 Lord,*c* they have killed thy prophets, and digged down thine

c 1 Ki.19.10–18.

It is the declaration of a great principle of divine government, that God is not changeable; and that he would not reject those whom he had purposed should be his people. Though the mass of the nation, therefore, should be cast off, yet it would not follow that God had violated any promise or compact; or that he had rejected *any* whom he had foreknown as his true people. God makes no covenant of salvation with those who are in their sins; and if the unbelieving and the wicked, however many external privileges they may have enjoyed, are rejected, it does not follow that he has been unfaithful to *one* whom he had foreknown or designated as an heir of salvation. It follows from this, also, that it is one principle of the divine government that God *will not* reject those who are foreknown or designated as his friends. It is a part of the plan, therefore, that those who are truly renewed shall persevere, and obtain eternal life. ¶ *Wot ye not. Know ye not.* ¶ *What the scripture saith?* The passage here quoted is found in 1 Kings xix. 10–18. ¶ *Of Elias. Of Elijah.* Greek, "*in* Elijah" (εν Ηλιᾳ). This does not mean that it was said *about* Elijah, or *concerning* him; but the reference is to the usual manner of quoting the Scriptures among the Jews. The division into chapters and verses was to them unknown. (See the Introduction to the Notes on Matthew.) Hence the Old Testament was divided into portions designated by *subjects.* Thus Luke xx. 37; Mark xii. 26, "at the bush," means the passage which contains the account of the burning bush (see Notes on those places). Here it means, in that passage or portion of Scripture which gives an account of Elijah. ¶ *He maketh intercession to God against Israel.* The word translated *maketh intercession* (ἐντυγχάνει) means properly to

come to the aid of anyone; to transact the business of anyone; especially, to discharge the office of an advocate, or to plead one's cause in a court of justice. In a sense similar to this it is applied to Christ in his office of making intercession for us in heaven, Heb. vii. 25; Isa. liii. 12. In the English language, the word is constantly used in a good sense, to plead *for* one; never, to plead *against* one; but the Greek word may imply either. It expresses the office of one who manages the business of another; and hence one who manages the business of the state *against* a criminal; and, when followed by the preposition *for,* means to intercede or plead *for* a person; when followed by *against* (κατα), it means to *accuse* or *arraign.* This is its meaning here. He accuses or arraigns the nation of the Jews before God; he charges them with crime; the crime is specified immediately.

3. *Lord, they have killed,* &c. This is taken from 1 Kings xix. 10. The quotation is not literally made, but the sense is preserved. This was a charge which Elijah brought against the whole nation; and the act of killing the prophets he regarded as expressive of the character of the people, or that they were *universally* given to wickedness. The *fact* was true, that they had killed the prophets, &c. (1 Kings xviii. 4, 13); but the *inference* which Elijah seems to have drawn from it, that there were no pious men in the nation, was not well founded. ¶ *And digged down.* Altars, by the law of Moses, were required to be made of earth or unhewn stones, Exod. xx. 24, 25. Hence the expression to *dig* them down means completely to demolish or destroy them. ¶ *Thine altars.* There was one great altar in the front of the tabernacle and the temple, on which the daily sacrifices of the Jews

altars; and I am left alone, and they seek my life.

4 But what saith the answer of God unto him? I have reserved

to myself seven thousand men, who have not bowed the knee to *the image of* Baal.

---

were to be made. But they were not forbidden to make altars also elsewhere, Exod. xx. 25. And hence they are mentioned as existing in other places, 1 Sam. vii. 17; xvi. 2, 3; 1 Kings xviii. 30, 32. These were the altars of which Elijah complained as having been thrown down by the Jews; an act which was regarded as expressive of signal impiety. ¶ *I am left alone.* I am the only prophet which is left alive. We are told that when Jezebel cut off the prophets of the Lord, Obadiah took a hundred of them and hid them in a cave, 1 Kings xviii. 4. But it is not improbable that they had been discovered and put to death by Ahab. The account which Obadiah gave Elijah when he met him (1 Kings xviii. 13) seems to favour such a supposition. ¶ *Seek my life.* That is, Ahab and Jezebel seek to kill me. This they did because he had overcome and slain the prophets of Baal, 1 Kings xix. 1, 2. There could scarcely be conceived a time of greater distress and declension in religion than this. It has not often happened that so many things that were disheartening have occurred to the church at the same period of time. The prophets of God were slain; but one lonely man appeared to have zeal for true religion; the nation was running to idolatry; the civil rulers were criminally wicked, and were the leaders in the universal apostasy; and all the influences of wealth and power were setting in against the true religion to destroy it. It was natural that the solitary man of God should feel disheartened and lonely in this universal guilt; and should realize that *he* had no power to resist this tide of crime and calamities.

4. *The answer of God* (ὁ χρηματισ-μός). This word is used nowhere else in the New Testament. It means *an oracle,* a divine response. It does not indicate the *manner* in which it was done, but implies only that it was an

oracle, or answer made to his complaint by God. Such an answer, at such a time, would be full of comfort, and silence every murmur. The way in which this answer was *in fact* given, was not in a storm, or an earthquake, but in a still, small voice, 1 Kings xix. 11, 12. ¶ *I have reserved.* The Hebrew is, "I have caused *to remain,*" or to be reserved. This shows that it was of God that this was done. Amidst the general corruption and idolatry *he* had restrained a part, though it was a remnant. The honour of having done it he claims for himself, and does not trace it to any goodness or virtue in them. So, in the case of all those who are saved from sin and ruin, the honour belongs not to man, but to God. ¶ *To myself.* For my own service and glory. I have kept them steadfast in my worship, and have not suffered them to become idolaters. ¶ *Seven thousand men. Seven* is often used in the Scriptures to denote an indefinite or round number. Perhaps it may be so here, to intimate that there was a considerable number remaining. This should lead us to hope that, even in the darkest times in the church, there may be many more friends of God than we suppose. Elijah supposed he was alone; and yet at that moment there were thousands who were the true friends of God;—a *small* number, indeed, compared with the multitude of idolaters; but *large* when compared with what was supposed to be remaining by the dejected and disheartened prophet. ¶ *Who have not bowed the knee.* To *bow* or *bend* the knee is an expression denoting worship, Phil. ii. 10; Eph. iii. 14; Isa. xlv. 23. ¶ *To Baal.* The word *Baal* in Hebrew means Lord, or Master. This was the name of an idol of the Phenicians and Canaanites, and was worshipped also by the Assyrians and Babylonians under the name of *Bel* (comp. the Book of *Bel* in the Apocrypha). This god was represented under the image

5 Even[d] so then at this present time also there is a remnant according to the election of grace.

6 And if [e] by grace, then is it no more of works: otherwise grace is no more grace. But if it be of works, then is it no more grace: otherwise work is no more work.

d ch.9.27.   e ch.4.4,5; Ga.5.4; Ep.2.8.

---

of a *bull*, or a *calf;* the one denoting the Sun, the other the Moon. The prevalent worship in the time of Elijah was that of this idol.

5. *At this present time.* In the time when the apostle wrote. Though the mass of the nation was to be rejected, yet it did not follow that *all* were to be excluded from the favour of God. As in the time of Elijah, when all appeared to be dark, and *all* the nation, except one, seemed to have become apostate, yet there was a considerable number of the true friends of God; so in the time of Paul, though the nation had rejected their Messiah, though, as a consequence, *they* were to be rejected as a people, and though they were eminently wicked and corrupt, yet it did not follow that *all* were cast off, or that *any* were excluded on whom God had purposed to bestow salvation. ¶ *A remnant.* That which is *left* or reserved, chap. ix. 27. He refers here, doubtless, to that part of the nation which was truly *pious,* or which had embraced the Messiah. ¶ *According to the election of grace.* By a gracious or merciful *choosing,* or election; and not by any merit of their own. As in the time of Elijah, it was because *God had reserved them unto himself* that any were saved from idolatry, so now it was by the same gracious sovereignty that *any* were saved from the prevalent unbelief. The apostle here does not specify the number, but there can be no doubt that a multitude of Jews had been saved by becoming Christians, though compared with the *nation*—the *multitude* who rejected the Messiah—it was but a remnant.

The apostle thus shows that neither *all* the ancient people of God were cast away, nor that *any* whom *he foreknew* were rejected. And though he had proved that a large part of the Jews were to be rejected, and though infidelity was prevalent, yet still there

were some who had been Jews who were truly pious, and entitled to the favour of God. Nor should they deem this state of things remarkable, for a parallel case was recorded in their own Scriptures. We may learn from this narrative, (1) That it is no unparalleled thing for the love of many to wax cold, and for iniquity to abound. (2) The tendency of this is to produce deep feeling and solicitude among the true friends of God. Thus David says, "Rivers of waters run down mine eyes because they keep not thy law," Ps. cxix. 136; comp. Jer. ix. 1; Luke xix. 41. (3) That in these darkest times we should not be discouraged. There *may be* much more true piety in the world than in our despondency we may suppose. We should take courage in God, and believe that he will not forsake any that are his true friends, or on whom he has purposed to bestow eternal life. (4) It is of God that *all* are not corrupt and lost. It is owing only to the election of grace, to his merciful choosing, that *any* are saved. And as in the darkest times he has reserved a people to himself, so we should believe that he will still meet abounding evil, and save those whom he has chosen from eternal death.

6. *And if grace,* &c. If the fact that any are reserved be by grace, or favour, then it cannot be as a reward of merit. Paul thus takes occasion *incidentally* to combat a favourite notion of the Jews, that we are justified by obedience to the law. He reminds them that in the time of Elijah it was because God had *reserved* them; that the same was the case now; and therefore their doctrine of *merit* could not be true; see chap. iv. 4, 5; Gal. v. 4; Eph. ii. 8, 9. ¶ *Otherwise grace,* &c. If men are justified by their *works,* it could not be a matter of *favour,* but was a *debt.* If it could be that the doctrine

7 What then? Israel *f* hath not obtained that which he seeketh for; but the election hath obtained it, and the rest were blinded[2]

f ch.9.31.   [2] *hardened.*

8 (According as it is written, God hath given them *g* the spirit of [3] slumber, *h* eyes that they should not see, and ears that they should not hear) unto this day.

g Is.29.10.   [3] or, *remorse.*   *h* De.29.4.

of justification by grace could be held, and yet at the same time that the Jewish doctrine of *merit* was true, then it would follow that *grace* had changed its nature, or was a different thing from what the word properly signified. The idea of being saved by *merit* contradicts the very idea of *grace*. If a man *owes* me a *debt*, and pays it, it cannot be said to be done by *favour*, or *by grace*. I have a *claim* on him for it, and there is no *favour* in his paying his just dues. ¶ *But if* it be *of works*, &c. *Works* here mean conformity to the law; and to be saved *by works* would be to be saved *by* such conformity as the *meritorious* cause. Of course there could be no *grace* or *favour* in giving what was *due:* if there was favour, or grace, then *works* would lose their essential characteristic, and cease to be the meritorious cause of procuring the blessings. What is paid as a *debt* is not conferred as a *favour*.

And from this it follows that salvation cannot be *partly* by grace and *partly* by works. It is not because men can advance *any* claims to the favour of God; but from his mere unmerited grace. He that is not willing to obtain eternal life in that way, cannot obtain it at all. The doctrines of *election*, and of salvation by mere grace, cannot be more explicitly stated than they are in this passage.

7. *What then?* What is the proper conclusion from this argument? ¶ *Israel hath not obtained.* That is, the Jews as a people have not obtained that which they sought. They sought the favour of God by their own merit; and as it was impossible to obtain it in that manner, they have, *as a people*, failed of obtaining his favour at all, and will be rejected. ¶ *That which he seeketh for.* To wit, salvation by their own obedience to the

law. ¶ *The election hath.* The *purpose of choosing* on the part of God has obtained, or secured, that which the *seeking* on the part of the Jews could not secure. Or the abstract here may be put for the concrete, and the word "election" may mean the same as *the elect.* The *elect*, the *reserved*, the chosen part of the people, have obtained the favour of God. ¶ *Hath obtained it.* That is, the favour, or mercy, of God. ¶ *The rest.* The great mass of the people who remained in unbelief, and had rejected the Messiah. ¶ *Were blinded.* The word in the original means also *were hardened* ($\epsilon\pi\omega\rho\omega\theta\eta\sigma\alpha\nu$). It comes from a word which signifies properly to become *hard*, as bones do which are broken and are then united; or as the joints sometimes do when they become callous or stiff. It was probably applied also to the formation of a hard substance in the eye, a cataract; and then means the same as to be blinded. Hence, applied to the mind, it means that which is *hard, obdurate, insensible, stupid.* Thus it is applied to the Jews, and means that they were blind and obstinate; see Mark vi. 52, "Their heart was hardened;" ch. viii. 17; John xii. 40. The word does not occur in any other place in the New Testament. This verse affirms simply that "the rest *were* hardened," but it does not affirm anything about the *mode* by which it was done. In regard to "the election," it is affirmed that it was *of God,* ver. 4. Of the remainder, *the fact* of their blindness is simply mentioned, without affirming anything of the cause; see ver. 8.

8. *According as it is written.* That is, they are blinded in accordance with what is written. The *fact* and the *manner* accord with the ancient declaration. This is recorded in Isa. xxix. 10, and in Deut. xxix. 4. The

9 And David saith, *Let their table be made a snare, and a trap,

i Ps.69.22,23.

and a stumbling-block, and a recompense unto them.

---

same sentiment is found also substantially in Isa. vi. 9, 10. The principal place referred to here, however, is doubtless Isa. xxix. 10, "For the Lord hath poured out upon you the spirit of deep sleep, and hath closed your eyes; the prophets and your rulers hath he covered." The quotation is not, however, *literally* made either from the Hebrew or the Septuagint; but *the sense* is preserved. The phrase "according as" means, *upon the same principle,* or in the same manner. ¶ *God hath given.* Expressions like this are common in the Scriptures, where *God* is represented as having an agency in producing the wickedness and stupidity of sinners; see chap. ix. 17, 18; see Note, Mat. xiii. 15; Mark iv. 11, 12; see also 2 Thes. ii. 11. This quotation is not made literally. The Hebrew in Isaiah is, God has *poured upon* them the spirit of slumber. The sense, however, is retained. ¶ *The spirit of slumber.* The *spirit* of slumber is not different from slumber itself. The word *spirit* is often used thus. The word *slumber* here is a literal translation of the Hebrew. The Greek word, however (κατανύξεως), implies also the notion of *compunction,* and hence in the margin it is rendered *remorse.* It means any emotion, or *any* influence whatever, that shall *benumb* the faculties, and make them insensible. Hence it here means simply insensibility. ¶ *Eyes that they should not see,* &c. This expression is not taken literally from any *single* place in the Old Testament; but expresses the general sense of several passages, Isa. vi. 10; Deut. xxix. 4. It denotes a state of mind not different from a spirit of slumber. When we sleep, the eyes are insensible to surrounding objects, and the ear to sounds. Though in themselves the organs may be perfect, yet the mind is so asleep that they were not; and we have eyes which then do not see, and ears which do not hear. Thus with the Jews.

Though they had all the proper faculties for understanding and receiving the gospel, yet they rejected it. They were stupid and insensible to its claims and its truths. ¶ *Unto this day.* Until the day that Paul wrote. The characteristic of the Jews that existed in the time of Isaiah, existed also in the time of Paul. It was a trait of the people; and their insensibility to the demands of the gospel developed nothing new in them.

9, 10. *And David saith,* &c. This quotation is made from Ps. lxix. 22, 23. This psalm is repeatedly quoted as having reference to the events recorded in the New Testament. (See Note on Acts i. 2.) This quotation is introduced *immediately* after one that undoubtedly refers to the Lord Jesus—ver. 21, "They gave me also gall for my meat, and in my thirst they gave me vinegar to drink." The passage here quoted immediately follows as an *imprecation* of vengeance for their sins. "Let their table," &c. The quotation is not made, however, either literally from the Hebrew or from the Septuagint, but the *sense* only is retained. The Hebrew is, "Let their.table before them be for a snare, and for those at peace, let it be for a gin." The Septuagint is, "Let their table before them be for a snare, and for a stumbling-block, and for an offence." The ancient Targum is, "Let their table which they had prepared before me be for a snare, and *their sacrifices* be for an offence." The meaning is this. The word *table* denotes food. In this they expected pleasure and support. David prays that even this, where they expected joy and refreshment, might prove to them the means of punishment and righteous retribution. A *snare* is that by which birds or wild beasts were taken. They are decoyed into it, or walk or fly carelessly into it, and it is sprung suddenly on them. So of the Jews. The petition is, that *while they* were seeking refreshment and joy, and anticipating at their table no danger,

10 Let their eyes be darkened, that they may not see, and bow down their back alway.

it might be made the means of their ruin. The only way in which this could be done would be, that their *temporal* enjoyments would lead them away from God, and produce stupidity and indifference to their spiritual interests. This is often the result of the pleasures of the *table*, or of seeking sensual gratifications. The apostle does not say whether this prayer was right or wrong. The use which he seems to make of it is this, that David's imprecation was to be regarded in *the light of a prophecy;* that what he prayed for would come to pass; and that this *had actually* occurred in the time of the apostle; that their very enjoyments, their national and private privileges, had been the means of alienating them from God; had been a snare to them; and was the cause of their blindness and infidelity. This also is introduced in the psalm as a *punishment* for giving him vinegar to drink; and their treatment of the Messiah was the immediate cause why all this blindness had come upon the Jews. ¶ *A trap.* This properly means anything by which *wild beasts* are taken in hunting. The word *snare* more properly refers to birds. ¶ *And a stumbling-block.* Anything over which one stumbles or falls. Hence anything which occasions us to sin, or to ruin ourselves. ¶ *And a recompense.* The Hebrew word translated "*that which should have been* for *their* welfare," is capable of this meaning, and may denote *their recompense,* or that which is appropriately rendered to them. It means here that their ordinary comforts and enjoyments, instead of promoting their permanent welfare, may be the occasion of their guilt and ruin. This is often the effect of earthly comforts. They *might* lead us to God, and *should* excite our gratitude and praise; but they are often abused to our spiritual slumber and guilt, and made the occasion of our ruin. The rich are thus often most forgetful of God; and the very abundance of their blessings made the means of darkness of mind, ingratitude,

prayerlessness, and ruin. Satisfied with them, they forget the Giver; and while they enjoy many earthly blessings, God sends barrenness into their souls. This was the guilt of Sodom, "pride, and fulness of bread, and abundance of idleness" (Ezek. xvi. 49); and against this Moses solemnly warned the Jews, Deut. vi. 11, 12; viii. 10-12. This same caution might be extended to the people of this land, and especially to those who are rich, and are blessed with all that their hearts have wished. From the use which the apostle makes of this passage in the Psalms, it is clear that he regarded it rather *as a prophetic denunciation* for their sins—a prediction of what *would be* — than as a *prayer.* In his time it had been fulfilled; and the very national privileges of the Jews, on which they so much prided themselves, and which *might* have been so great blessings, were the occasion of their greater sin in rejecting the Messiah, and of their greater condemnation. Thus their table was made a trap, &c.

10. *Let their eyes be darkened.* This is taken literally from the psalm, and was evidently the *main* part of the passage which the apostle had in his eye. This was fulfilled in the insensibility and blindness of the Jews. And the apostle shows them that it was long ago predicted, or *invoked,* as a punishment on them for giving the Messiah vinegar to drink, Ps. lxix. 21, 23. ¶ *And bow down their back alway.* The Hebrew (Ps. lxix. 23) is, "Let their loins *totter* or shake," *i.e.* as one does when he has on him a heavy burden. The apostle has retained this sense. It means, let them be called to bear heavy and oppressive burdens, let them be subjected to toil or servitude, as a reward for their sins. That this had come upon the Jews in the time of Paul is clear; and it is further clear that it came upon them, as it was implied in the psalm, in consequence of their treatment of the Messiah. Much difficulty has been felt in reconciling

11 I say then, Have they stumbled that they should fall?

God forbid: but *rather* [k]through their fall salvation *is come* unto

k Ac.13.46; 28.24-28; ch.10.19.

the petitions in the Psalms for calamities on enemies, with the spirit of the New Testament. Perhaps they cannot all be thus reconciled; and it is not at all improbable that many of those imprecations were wrong. David was not a perfect man; and the Spirit of inspiration is not responsible for his imperfections. Every *doctrine* delivered by the sacred writers is true; every fact recorded is recorded as it was. But it does not follow that all the *men* who wrote, or about whom a narrative was given, were perfect. The reverse is the fact. And it does not militate against the inspiration of the Scriptures that we have a *record* of the failings and imperfections of those men. When they uttered improper sentiments, when they manifested improper feelings, when they performed wicked actions, it is no argument against the inspiration of the Scriptures that they were recorded. All that is done in such a case, and all that inspiration demands, is that they be recorded *as they are*. We wish to see human nature as it is; and one design of making the record of such failings is to show what *man* is, even under the influence of religion; not as a *perfect* being, for that would not be true; but as he actually exists mingled with imperfection. Thus many of the wishes of the ancient saints, imperfect as they were, are *condemned* as sinful by the spirit of the Christian religion. They were never *commended* or *approved*, but they are *recorded* just to show us what was *in fact* the character of man, even partially under the influence of religion. Of this nature, probably, were many of the petitions in the Psalms; and the Spirit of God is no more answerable for the feeling because it is recorded, than he is for the feelings of the Edomites when they said, "Rase it, rase it to the foundation," Ps. cxxxvii. 7. Many of those prayers, however, were imprecations on his enemies as a public man, as the magistrate of the land. As it is *right* and *desirable* that the robber

and the pirate should be detected and punished; as all good men seek it, and it is indispensable for the welfare of the community, where is the impropriety of *praying* that it may be done? Is it not right to pray that the laws may be executed; that justice may be maintained; and that restraint should be imposed on the guilty? Assuredly this may be done with a very different spirit from that of *revenge*. It may be the prayer of the *magistrate* that God will help him in that which he is *appointed* to do, and in what *ought* to be done. Besides, many of these imprecations were regarded as simply *predictions* of what *would be* the effect of sin; or of what God *would* do to the guilty. Such was the case we are now considering, as understood by the apostle. But in a *prediction* there can be nothing wrong.

11. *Have they stumbled that they should fall?* This is to be regarded as an objection, which the apostle proceeds to answer. The meaning is, is it the design of God that the Jews should totally and irrecoverably be cast off? Even admitting that they are now unbelieving, that they have rejected the Messiah, that they have stumbled, is it the purpose of God finally to exclude them from mercy? The expression to *stumble* is introduced because he had just mentioned a *stumbling-stone*. It does not mean to fall down to the ground, or to fall so that a man may not recover himself; but to strike the foot against an obstacle, to be arrested in going, and to be in danger of falling. Hence it means to *err*, to *sin*, to be in danger. To *fall* expresses the state when a man pitches over an obstacle so that he cannot recover himself, but falls to the ground. Hence to err, to sin, or to be cast off irrecoverably. The apostle shows that this last was not the way in which the Jews had fallen, that they were not to be cast off for ever, but that occasion was taken *by* their fall to introduce the Gentiles to the privileges of the gospel, and then

the Gentiles, for to provoke them to jealousy.

12 Now if the fall of them *be* the riches of the world, and the [4] dimin-

 [4] or, *decay;* or, *loss.*

---

they should be restored. ¶ *God forbid.* By no means; see ver. 1. ¶ *But rather through their fall.* By means of their fall. The word *fall* here refers to all their conduct and doom at the coming of the Messiah, and in the breaking up of their establishment as a nation. Their rejection of the Messiah; the destruction of their city and temple; the ceasing of their ceremonial rites; and the rejection and dispersion of their nation by the Romans, all enter into the meaning of the word *fall* here, and were all the occasion of introducing salvation to the Gentiles. ¶ *Salvation.* The Christian religion, with all its saving benefits. It does not mean that all the Gentiles were to *be saved*, but that the way was open; they might have access to God, and obtain his favour through the Messiah. ¶ *The Gentiles.* All the world that were not Jews. The rejection and fall of the Jews contributed to the introduction of the Gentiles in the following manner: (1) It broke down the barrier which had long subsisted between them. (2) It made it consistent and proper, as *they* had rejected the Messiah, to send the knowledge of him to others. (3) It was connected with the destruction of the temple, and the rites of the Mosaic law; and taught *them*, and all others, that the worship of God was not to be confined to any single place. (4) The calamities that came upon the Jewish nation scattered the inhabitants of Judea, and with the Jews also those who had become Christians, and thus the gospel was carried to other lands. (5) These calamities, and the conduct of the Jews, and the close of the Jewish economy, were the means of giving to apostles and other Christians right views of the true design of the Mosaic institutions. If the temple had remained, if the nation had continued to flourish, it would have been long before they would have been effectually detached from those rites. Experience showed, even as it was, that they were slow in learning that the Jewish ceremonies were to cease. Some of the most agitating questions in the early church pertained to this; and if the temple had not been destroyed, the contest would have been much longer and more difficult. ¶ *For to provoke them to jealousy.* According to the prediction of Moses, Deut. xxxii. 21; see Rom. x. 19.

12. *If the fall of them.* If their lapse, or falling. If their *temporal* rejection and being cast off for a time has already accomplished so much. ¶ *Be the riches of the world.* The word *riches* means *wealth, abundance* of property; more than is *necessary* to the supply of our wants. Hence it means also anything that may *promote* our comfort or happiness, as wealth is the *means* of securing our welfare. The gospel is called *riches*, as it is the means of our highest enjoyment, and eternal welfare. It is the means of conferring numberless spiritual blessings on the *Gentile* world; and as this was done by the fall of the Jews, so it could be said that *their* fall was the riches of the world. It was the *occasion* or *means* without which the blessings of the gospel could not be conferred on the world. ¶ *The diminishing of them.* Margin, *decay, loss* (ἥττημα). This word means *diminution, defect, that which is lacked* or *wanting.* Hence also judgment, condemnation. Here it means their degradation; the withdrawing of their special privileges; their rejection. It stands opposed to "their fulness." ¶ *The riches of the Gentiles.* The means of conferring important blessings on the Gentiles. ¶ *How much more their fulness.* The word *fulness* (πλήρωμα) means that which *fills up*, or completes anything. Thus it is applied to that which fills a vessel or cup; also to the piece of cloth which is put in to *fill up* the rent in a garment, Mat. ix. 16; to the fragments which were left when Christ had fed the five thousand, Mark viii. 20; Rom. xiii. 10, "Love is the ful-

ishing of them the riches of the Gentiles, how much more their fulness?

13 For I speak to you Gentiles, inasmuch as *I am the apostle

l Ac.9.15; Ga.1.16; Ep.3.8.

filling of the law," *i.e.* it is the *filling up* of the law, or that which renders the obedience complete; see Gal. v. 14. Here it stands opposed to their *fall*, and their *diminution*, and evidently means their complete restoration to the favour of God; their recovery from unbelief and apostasy. That there *will* be such a recovery, the apostle proceeds to show. The sentiment of the passage then is, If their rejection and punishment, their being cut off from the favour of God —an event apparently so unlikely to promote the spread of true religion—if their being *withdrawn* from all active influence in spreading the true knowledge of God, be yet the occasion of so many blessings to mankind as have attended the spread of the gospel in consequence of it; how much more shall we expect when they shall be restored; when the energy and zeal of the Jewish nation shall *unite* with the efforts of others in spreading the knowledge of the true Messiah. In what way, or when, this shall be, we know not. But it is easy to see that, if the Jewish people should be converted to the Christian faith, they would have facilities for spreading the truth, which the church has never had without them. (1) They are scattered in all nations, and have access to all people. (2) Their conversion, after so long unbelief, would have all the power and influence of *a miracle* performed in view of all nations. It would be seen *why* they had been preserved, and their conversion would be a most striking fulfilment of the prophecies. (3) They are familiar with the languages of the world, and their conversion would *at once* establish many Christian missionaries in *the heart* of all the kingdoms of the world. It would be kindling at once a thousand lights in all the dark parts of the earth. (4) The *Jews* have shown that they are eminently fitted to spread the true religion. It was by *Jews* converted to Christianity that the gospel was first spread. Each of the apostles was

a Jew; and they have lost none of the ardour, enterprise, and zeal that always characterized their nation. Their conversion would be, therefore, to give to the church a host of missionaries prepared for their work, familiar with all customs, languages, and climes, and already in the heart of all kingdoms, and with facilities for their work *in advance,* which others must gain only by the slow toil of many years.

13. *For I speak to you Gentiles.* What I am saying respecting the Jews, I say with reference to you who are Gentiles, to show you in what manner you have been admitted to the privileges of the people of God; to excite your gratitude; to warn you against abusing those mercies, &c. As Paul also was *appointed* to preach to them, he had a right to speak to them with authority. ¶ *I am the apostle of the Gentiles.* The apostle of the Gentiles, not because *other* apostles did not preach to Gentiles, for they all did, except perhaps James, nor because Paul did not himself preach occasionally among the Jews; but because he was especially called to carry the gospel to the Gentiles, and that this was his original commission (Acts ix. 15); because he was principally employed in collecting and organizing churches in heathen lands; and because the charge of the Gentile churches was especially intrusted to him, while that of the Jewish churches was especially intrusted to Peter; see Gal. i. 16; Eph. iii. 8; Gal. ii. 7, 8. As Paul was especially appointed to this office, he claimed special authority to address those who were gathered into the Christian church from heathen lands. ¶ *I magnify mine office.* I honour (δοξάζω) my ministry. I esteem it of great importance; and by thus showing that the gospel is to be preached to the Gentiles, that the barrier between them and the Jews is to be broken down, that the gospel may be preached to all men, I show that the office which *proclaims* this is one of signal honour. A minister may

of the Gentiles, I magnify mine office;

14 If by any means I may provoke to emulation *them which are*

not magnify *himself*, but he may magnify *his office*. He may esteem *himself* as less than the least of all saints, and unworthy to be called a servant of God (Eph. iii. 8), yet he may feel that he is an ambassador of Christ, intrusted with a message of salvation, entitled to the respect due to an ambassador, and to the honour which is appropriate to a messenger of God. To unite these two things constitutes the dignity of the Christian ministry.

14. *If by any means.* If, even by stating unpleasant truths, if by bringing out all the counsel of God, even that which threatens their destruction, I may arrest their attention, and save them. ¶ *I may provoke to emulation.* I may awaken up to zeal, or to an earnest desire to obtain the like blessings. This was in accordance with the prediction of Moses, that the calling in of the Gentiles would excite their attention, and provoke them to deep feeling; Note, chap. x. 19. The apostle expected to do this by calling their attention to the ancient prophecies; by alarming their fears about their own danger; and by showing them the great privileges which *Gentiles* might enjoy under the gospel; thus appealing to them by every principle of benevolence, by all their regard for God and man, to excite them to seek the same blessings. ¶ *My flesh.* My countrymen. My kinsmen. Those belonging to the same family or nation, chap. ix. 3; Gen. xxix. 14; Judg. ix. 2; 2 Sam. v. 1; Isa. lviii. 7. ¶ *And save some of them.* This desire the apostle often expressed; see chap. ix. 2, 3; x. 1, 2. We may see here, (1) That it is the earnest wish of the ministry to save the souls of men. (2) That they should urge every argument and appeal with reference to this. (3) That even the most awful and humbling truths *may* have this tendency. No truth could be more likely to irritate and offend than

my flesh, and might [m]save some of them.

15 For if the casting away of them *be* the reconciling of the

[m] 1 Co.7.16.

that the Jews would be cast off; and yet the apostle used this so faithfully, and yet so tenderly, that he expected and desired it might be the means of saving the souls of his countrymen. Truth often irritates, enrages, and thus excites the attention. Thought or inquiry, *however* it may be excited, may result in conversion. And thus, even restlessness, and vexation, and anger, *may* be the means of leading a sinner to Jesus Christ. It should be no part of a minister's object, however, to *produce* anger. It is a bad emotion; in itself it is evil; and if men can be won to embrace the Saviour *without* anger, it is better. No wise man would excite a storm and tempest that might require infinite power to subdue, when the same object could be gained with comparative peace, and under the mild influence of love. (4) It is right to use all the means in our power, not absolutely wicked, to save men. Paul was full of devices; and much of the success of the ministry will depend on a wise use of plans, that may, by the divine blessing, arrest and save the souls of men.

15. *For if the casting away of them.* If their rejection as the *peculiar* people of God—their exclusion from their national privileges, on account of their unbelief. It is the same as "the *fall* of them," ver. 12. ¶ Be *the reconciling of the world.* The word reconciliation (καταλλαγὴ) denotes commonly a *pacification* of contending parties; a removing the occasion of difference, so as again to be united, 1 Cor. vii. 11, "Let her remain unmarried, or be *reconciled* to her husband." It is commonly applied to the *reconciliation*, or pacification, produced between man and God by the gospel. They are brought to union, to friendship, to peace, by the intervention of the Lord Jesus Christ, Rom. v. 10; 2 Cor. v. 18, 19, "God was in Christ reconciling

world, what *shall* the receiving *of them be,* but life from the dead?

16 For if ⁿ the first-fruit *be*

n Le.23.10; Nu.15.18-21.

holy, the lump *is* also *holy:* and if the root *be* holy, so *are* the branches.

---

the world unto himself." Hence the ministry is called the "ministry of reconciliation," 2 Cor. v. 18. And hence this word is used to express the *atonement,* Rom. v. 11, "By whom we have now received the *atonement*" (*the reconciliation*). In this place it means that many of the Gentiles—the world—had become reconciled to God as the *result* of the casting off of the Jews. By *their* unbelief, the way had been opened to preach the gospel to the Gentiles; it was *the occasion* by which God sent it to the nations of the earth; comp. Acts xiii. 46. ¶ *The receiving* of them. The same as was denoted (ver. 12) by *their fulness.* If the casting them off—an event so little likely, apparently, to produce any good effect—was nevertheless *overruled* so as to produce important benefits in the spread of the gospel, how much more may we expect will be accomplished by their conversion and return—an event *fitted in itself* to produce an important influence on mankind? One would have *supposed* that *their* rejection of the Messiah would have been an important obstacle *in the way* of the gospel. It was overruled, however, to promote its increase. Their *return* will have a *direct* tendency to spread it. How much more, therefore, may we expect to be accomplished by that? ¶ *But life from the dead.* This is an instance of the peculiar, glowing, and vigorous manner of the apostle Paul. His mind catches at the thought of what *may be* produced by the recovery of the Jews, and no ordinary language would convey his idea. He had already exhausted the usual forms of speech by saying that even their rejection had *reconciled* the world, and that it was the *riches* of the Gentiles. To say that their *recovery*—a striking and momentous event; an event so much better fitted to produce important results—would be attended by the conversion of the world, would be insipid and tame. He uses, there-

fore, a most bold and striking figure. The *resurrection of the dead* was an image of the most vast and wonderful event that could take place. This image, therefore, in the apostle's mind, was a striking illustration of the great change and reformation which should take place when the Jews should be restored, and the effect should be felt in the conversion also of the Gentile world. Some have supposed that the apostle here refers to a *literal* resurrection of the dead, as the conversion of the Jews. But there is not the slightest evidence of this. He refers to the recovery of the nations from the *death of sin,* which shall take place when the Jews shall be converted to the Christian faith. The prophet Ezekiel (chap. xxxvii. 1-14) has also used the same image of the resurrection of the dead to denote a great moral change among a people. It is clear here that the apostle fixed his eye on a future conversion of the Jews to the gospel, and expected that their conversion would *precede* the universal conversion of the Gentiles to the Christian faith. There could be no event that would make so immediate and decided an impression on the pagan world as the conversion of the Jews. They are scattered everywhere; they have access to all people; they understand all languages; and their conversion would be like kindling up thousands of lights at once in the darkness of the pagan world.

16. *For if the first-fruit* be *holy.* The word *first-fruit* (ἀπαρχὴ) used here denotes the *firstling* of fruit or grain, which was separated from the mass and presented as an offering to God. The Jews were required to present such a portion of their harvest to God, as an expression of gratitude and of their sense of dependence, Num. xv. 19–21. Till this was done, it was not lawful to partake of the harvest. The offering of this was regarded as rendering the mass *holy,*

17 And if some of ⁰ the branches be broken off, and thou, ᵖ being a wild olive-tree, wert graffed in ⁵ among them, and with them partakest of the root and fatness of the olive-tree;

o Je.11.16.　　p Ep.2.12,13.　　　　5 or, for.

i.e. it was lawful then to partake of it. The first-fruits were regarded as among the best portions of the harvest; and it was their duty to devote to God that which would be the best expression of their thanksgiving. This was the general practice in relation to all that the land produced. The expression here, however, has reference to the small portion of *dough* or *kneaded meal* that was offered to God; and then the mass or *lump* (φύραμα) was left for the use of him who made the offering, Num. xv. 20. ¶ Be *holy.* Be set apart, or consecrated to God, as he commanded. ¶ *The lump.* The *mass.* It refers here properly to the *dough* of which a part had been offered. The same was true also in relation to the harvest, after the *wave sheaf* had been offered; of the flock, after the first male had been offered, &c. ¶ Is *also* holy. It is lawful then for the owner to partake of it. The offering of *a part* has consecrated the whole. By this illustration Paul doubtless means to say that the *Jewish nation,* as a people, were set apart to the service of God, and were so regarded by him. Some have supposed that by the *first-fruit* here the apostle intends to refer to the early converts made to the Christian faith in the first preaching of the gospel. But it is more probable that he refers to the *patriarchs,* the pious men of old, as the *first-fruits* of the Jewish nation; see ver. 28. By *their* piety the nation was, in a manner, sanctified, or set apart to the service of God; implying that yet the great mass of them would be reclaimed and saved. ¶ *If the root be holy.* This figure expresses the same thing as is denoted in the first part of the verse. The *root* of a tree is the source of nutritious juices necessary for its growth, and gives its character to the tree. If that be sound, pure, vigorous, we expect the same of the branches. A root bears a similar relation to the tree that the first-fruit does to the mass of bread. Perhaps there is allusion here to Jer. xi. 16, where the Jewish nation is represented under the image of "a green olive-tree, fair, and of goodly fruit." In this place the reference is doubtless to Abraham and the patriarchs, as the *root* or founders of the Jewish nation. If they were holy, it is to be expected that the distant branches, or descendants, would also be so regarded. The mention of the *root* and *branches* of a tree gives the apostle occasion for an illustration of the relation at that time of the Jews and Gentiles to the church of Christ.

17. *If some of the branches.* The illustration here is taken from the practice of those who ingraft trees. The useless branches, or those which bear poor fruit, are cut off, and a better kind inserted. "If some of the natural descendants of Abraham, the holy root, are cast off because they are unfruitful, *i.e.* because of unbelief and sin." ¶ *And thou.* The word *thou* here is used to denote the *Gentile,* whom Paul was then particularly addressing. ¶ *Being a wild olive-tree.* From this passage it would seem that the *olive-tree* was sometimes cultivated, and that cultivation was necessary in order to render it fruitful. The cultivated olive-tree is "of a moderate height, its trunk knotty, its bark smooth and ash-coloured, its wood is solid and yellowish, the leaves are oblong, and almost like those of the willow, of a green colour, &c. The wild olive is smaller in all its parts" (Calmet). The wild olive was unfruitful, or its fruit very imperfect and useless. The ancient writers explain this word by "unfruitful, barren" (Schleusner). This was used, therefore, as the emblem of unfruitfulness and barrenness, while the cultivated olive produced much fruit. The meaning here is, that the Gentiles had been like the wild olive, unfruitful in holiness; that they had been uncul-

18 Boast *q* not against the branches. But if thou boast, thou bearest not the root, but the root thee.

q 1 Co.10.12.

tivated by the institutions of the true religion, and consequently had grown up in the wildness and sin of nature. The Jews had been like a cultivated olive, long under the training and blessing of God. ¶ *Wert graffed in.* The process of grafting consists in inserting a scion or a young shoot into another tree. To do this, a useless limb is removed; and the ingrafted limb produces fruit according to its new nature or kind, and not according to the tree in which it is inserted. In this way a tree which bears no fruit, or whose branches are decaying, may be recovered, and become valuable. The figure of the apostle is a very vivid and beautiful one. The ancient root or stock, that of Abraham, &c., was good. The branches—the Jews in the time of the apostle—had become decayed and unfruitful, and broken off. The Gentiles had been graffed into this stock, and had restored the decayed vigour of the ancient people of God; and a fruitless church had become vigorous and flourishing. But the apostle soon proceeds to keep the Gentiles from exaltation on account of this. ¶ *Among them.* Among the branches, so as to partake *with* them of the juices of the root. ¶ *Partakest of the root.* The ingrafted limb would derive nourishment from the root as much as though it were a natural branch of the tree. The Gentiles derived now the benefit of Abraham's faith and holy labours, and of the promises made to him and to his seed. ¶ *Fatness of the olive-tree.* The word *fatness* here means *fertility, fruitfulness*—the rich juices of the olive producing fruit; see Judg. ix. 9.

18. *Boast not,* &c. The tendency of men is to triumph over one that is fallen and rejected. The danger of pride and boasting on account of privileges is not less in the church than elsewhere. Paul saw that some of the

19 Thou wilt say then, The branches were broken off, that I might be graffed in.

20 Well; because of unbelief

Gentiles *might* be in danger of exultation over the fallen Jews, and therefore cautions them against it. The ingrafted shoot, deriving all its vigour and fruitfulness from the stock of another tree, ought not to boast against the branches. ¶ *But if thou boast.* If thou art so inconsiderate and wicked, so devoid of humility, and lifted up with pride, as to boast, yet know that there is no occasion for it. If there *were* occasion for boasting, it would rather be in the root or stock which sustains the branches; least of all can it be in those which were graffed in, having been before wholly unfruitful. ¶ *Thou bearest not the root.* The source of all your blessings is in the ancient stock. It is clear from this, that the apostle regarded the church as one; and that the Christian economy was only a prolongation of the ancient dispensation. The tree, even with a part of the branches removed, and others ingrafted, retains its identity, and is never regarded as a different tree.

19. *Thou wilt say then.* Thou who art a Gentile. ¶ *The branches were broken off,* &c. The Jews were rejected in order that the gospel might be preached to the Gentiles. This would seem to follow from what the apostle had said in ver. 11, 12. Perhaps it might be said that there was some ground of exultation from the fact that God had rejected his ancient people for the sake of making a way open to admit the Gentiles to the church. The objection is, that the branches were broken off *in order that* others might be graffed in. To this Paul replies in the next verse, that this was not the *reason* why they were rejected, but their *unbelief* was the cause.

20. *Well.* True. It is true they were broken off; but in order to show that there was no occasion for boasting, he adds that they were not rejected *in order* to admit others, but

they were broken off; and thou standest by faith. Be not high-minded, but fear:

21 For if God spared not the

r Phi.2.12.

because of their unbelief, and that *their* fate should have a salutary impression on those who had no occasion for boasting, but who might be rejected for the same cause. This is an instance of remarkable *tact* and delicacy in an argument, admitting the *main* force of the remark, but giving it a slight change in accordance with the truth, so as to parry its force, and give it a practical bearing on the very point which he wished to enforce. ¶ *Thou standest by faith.* The continuance of these mercies to you depends on your fidelity. If you are faithful, they will be preserved; if, like the Jews, you become unbelieving and unfruitful, like them you will be also rejected. This fact should repress boasting, and excite to anxiety and caution. ¶ *Be not high-minded.* Do not be elated in the conception of your privileges, so as to produce vain self-confidence and boasting. ¶ *But fear.* This *fear* stands opposed to the spirit of boasting and self-confidence, against which he was exhorting them. It does not mean *terror* or *horror*, but it denotes humility, watchfulness, and solicitude to abide in the faith. Do not be haughty and high-minded against the Jew, who has been cast off, but "demean yourself as a humble believer, and one who has need to be continually on his guard, and to fear lest he may fall through unbelief, and be cast off" (Stuart). We may here learn, (1) That there is danger lest those who are raised to eminent privileges should become unduly exalted in their own estimation, and despise others. (2) The tendency of *faith* is to promote humility and a sense of our dependence on God. (3) The system of salvation by faith produces that solicitude, and careful guarding, and watchfulness, which is necessary to preserve us from apostasy and ruin.

21. *For if God*, &c. If God did not refrain from rejecting the Jews

natural branches, *take heed* lest he spare not thee.

22 Behold therefore the goodness and severity of God; on

who became unbelievers, assuredly he will not refrain from rejecting you in the same circumstances. It may be supposed that he will be quite as ready to reject the *ingrafted* branches, as to cast off those which belonged to *the parent stock.* The situation of the Gentiles is not such as to give them any security over the condition of the rejected Jew.

22. *Behold therefore*, &c. Regard, or contemplate, for purposes of your own improvement and benefit, the dealings of God. We should look on *all* his dispensations of judgment or of mercy, and derive lessons from all to promote our own steadfast adherence to the faith of the gospel. ¶ *The goodness.* The benevolence or mercy of God towards you in admitting you to his favour. This calls for gratitude, love, confidence. It demands expressions of thanksgiving. It should be highly prized, in order that it may excite to diligence to secure its continuance. ¶ *The severity of God.* That is, towards the Jews. The word *severity* now suggests sometimes the idea of *harshness*, or even of *cruelty* (Webster). But nothing of this kind is conveyed in the original word here. It properly denotes *cutting off*, ἀποτο-μίαν, from ἀποτέμνω, to cut off; and is commonly applied to the act of the gardener or vine-dresser in trimming trees or vines, and cutting off the decayed or useless branches. Here it refers to the act of God in *cutting off* or rejecting the Jews as useless branches; and conveys no idea of injustice, cruelty, or harshness. It was a just act, and consistent with all the perfections of God. It indicated a purpose to do that which was *right*, though the inflictions might *seem* to be severe, and though they *must* involve them in many heavy calamities. ¶ *On them which fell, severity.* On the Jews, who had been rejected because of their unbelief. ¶ *But towards thee, goodness.* Towards the

them which fell, severity; but towards thee, goodness, ᵍif thou continue in *his* goodness: otherwise ᵗthou also shalt be cut off.

23 And they also, ᵘif they bide not still in unbelief, shall be

s He.3.6,14; 10.23,38.   *t* Jn.15.2.   *u* 2 Co.3.16.

Gentile world, benevolence. The word *goodness* properly denotes *benignity* or *benevolence.* Here it signifies the kindness of God in bestowing these favours on the Gentiles. ¶ *If thou continue in* his *goodness.* The word "his" is not in the original. And the word goodness may denote *integrity, probity, uprightness,* as well as favour, Rom. iii. 12, "There is none that doeth *good.*" The Septuagint often thus uses the word, Ps. xiii. 1, 3, &c. This is probably the meaning here; though it may mean "if thou dost continue in a state of favour;" that is, if your faith and good conduct shall be such as to make it proper for God to continue his kindness towards you. Christians do not *merit* the favour of God by their faith and good works; but their obedience is an indispensable condition on which that favour is to be continued. It is thus that the grace of God is magnified, at the same time that the highest good is done to man himself. ¶ *Otherwise thou also shalt be cut off.* Comp. John xv. 2. The word *thou* refers here to the Gentile churches. In relation to them the favour of God was dependent on their fidelity. If they became disobedient and unbelieving, then the same *principle* which led him to withdraw his mercy from the Jewish people would lead also to their rejection and exclusion. And on this principle God has acted in numberless cases Thus his favour was withdrawn from the seven churches of Asia (Rev. i.–iii.), from Corinth, from Antioch, from Philippi, and even from Rome itself.

23. *And they also.* The Jews. ¶ *If they bide not,* &c. If they do not continue in wilful obstinacy and rejection of the Messiah. As their unbelief was the sole cause of their rejection, so if that be removed, they may

graffed in : for God is able to graff them in again.

24 For if thou wert cut out of the olive-tree which is wild by nature, and wert graffed contrary to nature into a good olive-tree ;

be again restored to the divine favour. ¶ *For God is able,* &c. He has, (1) *Power* to restore them, to bring them back and replace them in his favour. (2) He has not *bound* himself *utterly* to reject them, and for ever to exclude them. In this way the apostle reaches his purpose, which was to show them that God had not cast away his people, or finally rejected the Jewish nation, ver. 1, 2. That God has this power, the apostle proceeds to show in the next verse.

24. *For if thou.* If you who are Gentiles. ¶ *Wert cut out of.* Or, if thou wert of the cutting of the wild olive-tree. ¶ *Which is wild by nature.* Which is uncultivated and unfruitful. That is, if you were introduced into a state of favour with God from a condition which was one of enmity and hostility to him. The argument here is, that it was in itself as difficult a thing to *reclaim* them, and change them from opposition to God to friendship, as it would seem difficult or impossible to reclaim and make fruitful the wild olive-tree. ¶ *And were graffed contrary to nature.* Contrary to your natural habits, thoughts, and practices. There was among the Gentiles no inclination or tendency towards God. This does not mean that they were *physically* depraved, or that their disposition was *literally* like the wild olive; but it is used, for the sake of illustration, to show that their moral character and habits were unlike those of the friends of God. ¶ *How much more,* &c. The meaning of this whole verse may be thus expressed : "If God had mercy on the Gentiles, who were outcasts from his favour, shall he not much rather on those who were so long his people, to whom had been given the promises, and the covenants, and the law, whose ancestors had been so many of them his friends, and among

how much more shall these, which be the natural *branches*, be graffed into their own olive-tree?

25 For I would not, brethren, that ye should be ignorant of this

mystery, lest ye should be wise in your own conceits, that [6]blind ness [v]in part is happened to Israel, until [w]the fulness of the Gentiles be come in.

[6] or, *hardness.　v* ver.7; 2 Co.3.14.　*w* Lu.21.24.

whom the Messiah was born?" In some respects, there are facilities among the Jews for their conversion, which had not existed among the Gentiles. They worship one God; they admit the authority of revelation; they have the Scriptures of the Old Testament; they expect a Messiah; and they have a *habit* of professed reverence for the will of God.

25. *Ignorant of this mystery.* The word *mystery* means properly that which is *concealed*, *hidden*, or *un-known*. And it especially refers, in the New Testament, to the truths or doctrines which God had reserved to himself, or had not before communicated. It does not mean, as with us often, that there was anything *unintelligible* or *inscrutable* in the nature of the doctrine itself, for it was commonly perfectly plain when it was made known. Thus the doctrine, that the division between the Jews and the Gentiles was to be broken down, is called a *mystery*, because it had been, to the times of the apostles, concealed, and was then revealed fully for the first time, Rom. xvi. 25; Col. i. 26, 27; comp. 1 Cor. xv. 51; Mark iv. 11; Eph. i. 9; iii. 3. Thus the doctrine which the apostle was stating was one that until then had been concealed, or had not been made known. It does not mean that there was anything unintelligible or incomprehensible in it, but until then it had not been made known. ¶ *Lest ye should be wise in your own conceits.* Paul communicated the truth in regard to this, lest they should attempt to inquire into it; should speculate about the reason why God had rejected the Jews; and should be elated with the belief that they had, by their own skill and genius, ascertained the cause. Rather than leave them to vain speculations and self-gratulation, he chose to cut short all inquiry, by stating the truth about their present and future

state. ¶ *Blindness.* Or hardness; see ver. 7. ¶ *In part.* Not *totally*, or entirely. They are not absolutely or completely blinded. This is a qualifying expression; but it does not denote *what* part or portion, or for what time it is to continue. It means that the blindness in respect to the whole nation was only partial. Some were then enlightened, and had become Christians, and many more *would* be. ¶ *To Israel.* To the Jews. ¶ *Until the fulness of the Gentiles,* &c. The word *fulness* in relation to the Jews is used in ver. 12. It means, until the abundance or the great multitude of the Gentiles shall be converted. The word is not elsewhere used in respect to the Gentiles; and it is difficult to fix its meaning definitely. It doubtless refers to the future spread of the gospel among the nations; to the time when it may be said that the *great mass*, the abundance of the nations, shall be converted to God. At present they are, as they were in the times of the apostle, idolaters, so that the *mass* of mankind are far from God. But the Scriptures have spoken of a time when the gospel shall spread and prevail among the nations of the earth; and to this the apostle refers. He does not say, however, that the Jews may not be converted until *all* the Gentiles become Christians; for he expressly supposes (ver. 12–15) that the conversion of the Jews will have an important influence in extending the gospel among the Gentiles. Probably the meaning is, that this blindness is to continue until *great numbers* of the Gentiles shall be converted; until the gospel shall be extensively spread; and *then* the conversion of the Jews will be *a part* of the rapid spread of the gospel, and will be among the most efficient and important aids in completing the work. If this is the

26 And so all Israel shall be saved: as it is written, *There shall come out of Sion the Deliv-

x Is.59.20.

case, then Christians may labour still for their conversion. They may *seek* that in connection with the effort to convert the heathen; and they may toil with the expectation that the conversion of the Jews and Gentiles will not be separate, independent, and distinct events; but will be intermingled, and will be perhaps simultaneous. The word *fulness* may denote such a *general* turning to God, without affirming that each individual shall be thus converted to the Christian faith.

26. *And so.* That is, in this manner; or when the great abundance of the Gentiles shall be converted, then all Israel shall be saved. ¶ *All Israel.* All the Jews. It was a maxim among the Jews that "every Israelite should have part in the future age" (Grotius). The apostle applies that maxim to his own purpose; and declares the sense in which it would be true. He does not mean to say that *every* Jew of every age would be saved; for he had proved that a large portion of them would be, in his time, rejected and lost. But the time would come when, *as a people,* they would be recovered; when the *nation* would turn to God; and when it could be said of them that, *as a nation,* they were restored to the divine favour. It is not clear that he means that even then every *individual* would be saved, but the *body* of them, the great *mass* of the nation would be. Nor is it said *when* this would be. This is one of the things which "the Father hath put in his own power," Acts i. 7. He has given us the assurance that it *shall* be done, to encourage us in our efforts to save them; and he has concealed the *time* when it shall be, lest we should relax our efforts, or feel that no exertions were needed to accomplish what *must* take place at a fixed time. ¶ *Shall be saved.* Shall be recovered from their rejection; be restored to the divine favour; become followers of the Mes-

erer, and shall turn away ungodliness from Jacob:

27 For*y* this *is* my covenant

y Je.31.31,&c.; He.10.16.

siah, and thus be saved as all other Christians are. ¶ *As it is written.* Isa. lix. 20. The quotation is not *literally* made, but the *sense* of the passage is preserved. The Hebrew is, "There shall come to Zion a Redeemer, and for those who turn from ungodliness in Jacob." There can be no doubt that Isaiah refers here to the times of the gospel. ¶ *Out of Sion.* Zion was one of the hills of Jerusalem. On this was built the city of David. It came thus to be, in general, the church, or people of God. And when it is said that the Redeemer should come *out of Zion,* it means that he should arise among that people, be descended from themselves, or should not be a foreigner. The LXX., however, render it, "The Redeemer shall come *on account of* Zion." So the Chaldee paraphrase, and the Latin Vulgate. ¶ *And shall turn away,* &c. The Hebrew is, "to those forsaking ungodliness in Jacob." The Septuagint has rendered it in the same manner as the apostle.

27. *For this* is *my covenant,* &c. This expression is found immediately following the other in Isa. lix. 21. But the apostle connects with it a part of *another* promise taken from Jer. xxxi. 33, 34; or rather he *abridges* that promise, and expresses *its substance,* by adding, "when I shall take away their sins." It is clear that he intended to express the *general sense* of the promises, as they were well known to the Jews, and as it was a point concerning which he did not need to argue or reason with them, that God hath made a covenant with them, and intended to restore them if they were cast off, and should then repent and turn to him. The time and manner in which this shall be, is not revealed. It may be remarked, however, that that passage does *not* mean that the Redeemer shall come *personally* and preach to them, or reappear for the purpose of

unto them, when I shall take away their sins.

28 As concerning the gospel, *they are* enemies for your sakes: but as touching the election,

they are beloved for the fathers' sakes.

29 For the gifts and calling of God *are* ᵃ without repentance.

z De.10.15.　　　　a Nu.23.19.

recalling them to himself; nor does it mean that they will be restored to the land of their fathers. Neither of these ideas is contained in the passage. God will doubtless convert the Jews, as he does the Gentiles, by human means, and in connection with the prayers of his people; so that the Gentiles shall yet *repay* the toil and care of the ancient Jews in preserving the Scriptures, and preparing the way for the Messiah; and *both* shall rejoice that they were made helps in spreading the knowledge of the Messiah.

28. *As concerning the gospel.* So far as the gospel is concerned; or, in order to promote its extension and spread through the earth. ¶ They are *enemies.* The word *enemies* here stands opposed to "beloved;" and as in *one* respect, to wit, on account of "election," they were still beloved, *i.e.* beloved *by God*, so in another respect they were his enemies, *i.e.* opposed to him, or cast off from him. The enemies of God denote all who are not his true friends, Col. i. 21; Rom. v. 10; comp. ver. 8. The word here is applied to the Jews because they had rejected the Messiah; had become opposed to God; and were therefore rejected by him. ¶ *For your sakes.* For your advantage. Their rejection has become the occasion by which the gospel has been preached to you; comp. ver. 11, 19, 20. ¶ *As touching the election.* So far as the purpose of election is concerned. That is, the election of their fathers and of the nation to be the peculiar people of God. ¶ They are *beloved.* God still regards them with interest; has purposes of mercy towards them; intends still to do them good. This does not mean that he *approved* of their conduct or character, or that he had for them the same kind of affection which he would have had if they had been obedient.

God does not love a sinful character; but he may have still purposes of mercy, and regard men with deep interest on whom he intends yet to bestow mercy. ¶ *For the fathers' sakes.* Comp. Deut. x. 15. He had chosen their fathers to be his peculiar people. He had made many promises to Abraham respecting his seed, and extended these promises to his remotest posterity. Though salvation is by grace, and not from human merit, yet God has respect to his covenant made with the fathers, and will not forget his promises. It is not on account of any *merit* of the fathers or of ancient saints, but solely because God had made a covenant with them; and this purpose of *election* would be manifest to their children in the latest times. As those contemplated in the covenant made with Abraham, God retained for them feelings of peculiar interest, and designed their recovery to himself. It is clear here that the word *election* does not refer to *external* privileges; for Paul is not teaching the doctrine that they shall be restored to the external privileges of Jews, but that they shall be truly converted to God. Yet this should not be abused by others to lead them to security in sin. No man has any security of happiness, and of the favour of God, but he who complies with the terms of his mercy. His commands are explicit to repent and believe, nor can there be safety except in entire compliance with the terms on which he is willing to bestow eternal life.

29. *For the gifts.* The favours or benefits which God bestows on men. The word χάρισμα properly denotes any benefit which is conferred on another as a mere matter of *favour*, and not of *reward;* see Rom. v. 15, 16; vi. 23. Such are *all* the favours which God bestows on sinners, includ-

30 For as ye ᵇin times past have not ⁷believed God, yet have now obtained mercy through their unbelief:

b Ep.2.2.

31 Even so have these also now not ⁷believed, that through your mercy they also may obtain mercy.

7 or, obeyed.

ing pardon, peace, joy, sanctification, and eternal life. ¶ *And calling of God.* The word *calling* (κλῆσις) here denotes that act of God by which he extends an *invitation* to men to come and partake of his favours, whether it be by a personal revelation as to the patriarchs, or by the promises of the gospel, or by the influences of his Spirit. All such invitations or callings imply a pledge that he will bestow the favour, and will not *repent*, or turn from it. God never draws or invites sinners to himself without being willing to bestow pardon and eternal life. The word *calling* here, therefore, has not respect to external privileges, but to that *choosing* of a sinner, and influencing him to come to God, which is connected with eternal life. ¶ *Without repentance.* This does not refer to *man*, but to *God.* It does not mean that God confers his favours on man without his exercising repentance, but that *God* does not repent, or change, in his purposes of bestowing his gifts on man. What he promises he will fulfil; what he purposes to do, he will not change from or repent of. As he made promises to the fathers, he will not repent of them, and will not depart from them; they shall all be fulfilled; and thus it was certain that the ancient people of God, though many of them had become rebellious, and had been cast off, should not be forgotten and abandoned. This is a *general* proposition respecting God, and one repeatedly made of him in the Scriptures; see Num. xxiii. 19, "God is not a man, that he should lie; neither the son of man, that he should repent: hath he said, and shall he not do it? or hath he spoken, and shall he not make it good?" Ezek. xxiv. 14; 1 Sam. xv. 29; Ps. lxxxix. 35, 36; Tit. i. 2; Heb. vi. 18; Jam. i. 17. It follows from this, (1) That all the promises made to the people of God shall be ful-

filled. (2) That his people need not be discouraged or desponding in times of persecution and trial. (3) That none who become his true friends will be forsaken, or cast off. God does not bestow the gift of repentance and faith, of pardon and peace, on men, for a temporary purpose; nor does he capriciously withdraw them, and leave the soul to ruin. When he renews a soul, it is with reference to his own glory; and to withdraw those favours, and leave such a soul once renewed to go down to hell, would be as much a violation of all the principles of his nature as it would be to all the promises of the Scripture. (4) For God to forsake such a soul, and leave it to ruin, would imply that he *did* repent. It would suppose a *change* of purpose and of feeling. It would be the character of a capricious being, with no settled plan or principles of action; no confidence could be reposed in him, and his government would be unworthy the affections and trust of his intelligent creation.

30. *For as ye.* You who were Gentiles. ¶ *In times past.* Before the gospel was preached. This refers to the former idolatrous and sinful state of the heathen world; comp. Eph. ii. 2; Acts xiv. 16. ¶ *Have not believed God.* Or have not *obeyed* God. This was the character of all the heathen nations. ¶ *Yet have now obtained mercy.* Have been pardoned and admitted to the favour of God. ¶ *Through their unbelief.* By means of the unbelief and rejection of the Jews; see Note on ver. 11.

31. *Even so have these,* &c. That is, the Jews. ¶ *That through your mercy,* &c. The *immediate* effect of the unbelief of the Jews was to confer salvation on the Gentiles, or to open the way for the preaching of the gospel to them. But its *remote* effect would be to secure the preaching of the gospel again to the Jews. Through

32 For ^cGod hath ⁸concluded them all in unbelief, that he might have mercy upon all.

33 O ^d the depth of the riches

c ch.3.9; Ga.3.22.
⁸ or, *shut them all up together.* *d* Ps.107.8,&c.

both of the wisdom and knowledge of God! ^ehow unsearchable *are* his judgments, and his ways past finding out!

e Job 11.7; Ps.92.5.

the *mercy,* that is, the *compassion* or deep feeling of the converted Gentiles, through the deep and tender pity which they would feel for the blinded and degraded Jews, the gospel should be again carried to them, and they should be recalled to the long-lost favour of God. Each party should thus cause salvation to come to the other—the Jews to the Gentiles by their *unbelief;* but the Gentiles, in their turn, to the Jews by their *belief.* We may here learn, (1) That the Jews are to be converted by the instrumentality of the Gentiles. It is not to be by miracle, but by the regular and common way in which God blesses men. (2) That this is to be done by the *mercy,* or *compassion* of the Gentiles; by their taking pity on the lost and wretched condition of the Jewish people. (3) It is to be when the *abundance* of the Gentiles—that is, when great numbers of the Gentiles —shall be called in. It may be asked here whether the time is not approaching for the Gentiles to make efforts to bring the Jews to the knowledge of the Messiah. Hitherto those efforts have been unsuccessful; but it will not always be so; the time is coming when the promises of God in regard to them shall be fulfilled. Christians shall be moved with deep compassion for the degraded and forsaken Jews, and they shall be called into the kingdom of God, and made efficient agents in extending the gospel through the whole world. May the time soon come when they shall feel as they *should,* for the rejected and forsaken children of Abraham, and when their labours for their conversion shall be attended with success.

32. *For God hath concluded,* &c. The word here translated "concluded" (συνέκλεισε), is rendered in the margin "shut them all up together." It is properly used in reference to those who are shut up in prison, or to those in a city who are shut up by a besieging army, 1 Mac. v. 5; vi. 18; xi. 65; xv. 25; Josh. vi. 6; Isa. xlv. 1. It is used in the New Testament of *fish* taken in a net, Luke v. 6, "They *inclosed* a great multitude of fishes;" Gal. iii. 22, "But the Scripture hath *concluded* all under sin, that the promise," &c. In this place the Scripture is declared to have *shut them up* under sin, *i.e.* *declared* them to be sinners; gave no hope of rescue by any works of their own; and thus *kept them* (ver. 23) "*shut up* unto the faith which should afterwards be revealed." All are represented, therefore, as in *prison,* inclosed or confined by God, and to be liberated only in his own way and time. In regard to the *agency* of God in this, we may remark, (1) That the word does not mean that God *compelled* them to disbelieve the gospel. When, in Gal. iii. 22, the Scripture is said to have *included* all under sin, it is not meant that the Scripture *compelled* them not to believe. (2) The word does not imply that the sin and unbelief for which they were shut up were not voluntary. Even when a man is committed to prison, the crime which brought him there is voluntary, and for it he is responsible. (3) The keeper of a prison does no wrong in confining a criminal; or the judge in condemning him; or the executioner in fulfilling the sentence of the law. So of God. What he does is not to *compel* men to remain under unbelief, but to *declare* that they are so; so to encompass them with the proof of it that they shall realize that there is no escape from the evidence of it, and thus to *press* on them the evidence of their need of a Saviour. This he does in relation to all sinners who ever become converted. (4) Yet God permitted this; suffered Jews and Gentiles to fall into

unbelief, and to be concluded under it, because he had a special purpose to answer in leaving man to the power of sin and unbelief. One of those purposes was, doubtless, to manifest the power of his grace and mercy in the plan of redemption. (5) In all this, and in all other sin, man is voluntary. He chooses his course of evil; and God is under no obligation to *compel* him to do otherwise. Being *under* unbelief, God declares the *fact*, and avails himself of it, in the plan of salvation by grace. ¶ *Them all.* Both Jews and Gentiles. ¶ *In unbelief* (εἰς). *Unto* unbelief. He has delivered them over *unto* unbelief, as a man is delivered over into prison. This is the literal meaning of the expression. ¶ *That he might have mercy upon all. Mercy* is favour shown to the undeserving. It could not have been shown to the Jews and the Gentiles unless it was before proved that they were guilty. For this purpose proof was furnished that they were all in unbelief. It was clear, therefore, that if favour was shown to either, it must be on the same ground, that of mere undeserved *mercy.* Thus all men were on a level; and thus all might be admitted to heaven without any invidious distinctions, or any dealings that were not in accordance with mercy and love. "The emphasis in this verse is on the word MERCY. It signifies that God is under obligation to no one, and therefore that all are saved by grace, because all are equally ruined" (Calvin). It does not prove that all men will be saved; but that those who *are* saved shall be alike saved by the mercy of God; and that He intends to confer salvation on Jews and Gentiles on the same terms. This is properly the close of the argument of this epistle. By several independent trains of reasoning, the apostle had come to the same conclusion, that the Jews had no peculiar privileges in regard to religion, that all men were on a level, and that there was no hope of salvation for any but in the mercy of a sovereign God. This conclusion, and the wonderful train of events which had led to this state of things, give rise to

the exclamations and ascriptions or praise with which the chapter closes.

33. *O the depth,* &c. This passage should have been translated, "O the depth of the riches, *and* of the wisdom, and of the knowledge of God." The apostle has *three* subjects of admiration. Our translation, by the word "both" introduced here, confines it to two. The apostle wishes to express his admiration of the riches, *and* the wisdom, and the knowledge of God. So the Syriac, Arabic, &c. Our translation has followed the Latin Vulgate. The word *depth* is applied in the Scriptures to anything vast and incomprehensible. As the *abyss* or the *ocean* is unfathomable, so the word comes to denote that which words cannot express, or that which we cannot comprehend, Ps. xxxvi. 6, "Thy judgments are a great deep;" 1 Cor. ii. 10, "The Spirit searcheth . . . the deep things of God;" Rev. ii. 24, "The *depths* of Satan"—the deep, profound, cunning, and wicked plans of Satan. ¶ *Riches.* See Note, ver. 12. The word denotes the abundant blessings and mercies which had been conferred on sinful men by the gospel. These were vast and wonderful. The pardon of sin; the atonement; the hope of heaven; the peace of the gospel; all bestowed on the sinful, the poor, the wretched, and the dying; all bespeak the great mercy and *rich* grace of God. So every pardoned sinner may still exclaim. The grace of God which pardons him is felt to be indeed wonderful, and past comprehension. It is beyond the power of language to express; and all that the Christian can do, is to follow the example of the apostle, and sit down in profound admiration of the rich grace of God. The expression "the depth of the riches" is a Hebraism, meaning the deep or profound riches. ¶ *The wisdom.* Wisdom is the choice of the best means to accomplish the best ends. The end or design which God had in view was to bestow mercy on all; *i.e.* to save men by *grace,* and not by their own works, ver. 32. He intended to establish a glorious system that should present his *mercy* as the prominent attribute,

standing out in living colours in all the scheme of salvation. This was to be alike shown in relation to Jews and Gentiles. The wonderful wisdom with which this was done is the object of the apostle's profound admiration. This wisdom was seen, (1) In adapting the plan to the condition of man. All were sinners. The apostle in this epistle has fully shown that all had come short of the glory of God. Man had no power to save himself by his own wisdom. The Jews and Gentiles in different ways had sought to justify themselves, and had both failed. God had suffered both to make the experiment in the most favourable circumstances. He had left the world for four thousand years to make the trial, and then introduced the plan of divine wisdom, just so as to meet the manifest wants and woes of men. (2) This was shown in his making the *Jews* the occasion of spreading the system among the Gentiles. They were cast off and rejected; but the God of wisdom had made even this an occasion of spreading his truth. (3) The same wisdom was yet to be seen in his appointing the Gentiles to carry the gospel back to the Jews. Thus they were to be mutual aids until all their interests should be blended, and the entire race should be united in the love of the same gospel, and the service of the same God and Saviour. When, therefore, this profound and wonderful plan is contemplated, and its history traced from the commencement to the end of time, no wonder that the apostle was fixed in admiration at the amazing wisdom of him who devised it, and who has made all events subservient to its establishment and spread among men. ¶ *And knowledge.* That is, foreknowledge, or omniscience. This *knowledge* was manifest, (1) In the profound view of man, and acquaintance with all his wants and woes. (2) In a view of the precise scheme that would be fitted to recover and save. (3) In a view of the time and circumstances in which it would be best to introduce the scheme. (4) In a discernment of the effect of the rejection of the Jews, and of the preaching of the

gospel among the Gentiles. Who but God could see that such effects would follow the rejection of the Jews? Who but he could *know* that the gospel should yet prevail among all the nations? We have only to think of the changes in human affairs; the obstacles to the gospel; the difficulties to be surmounted; and the vast work yet to be done, to be amazed at the knowledge which can adapt such a scheme to men, and which can certainly predict its complete and final spread among all the families of man. ¶ *How unsearchable.* The word *unsearchable* means that which cannot be investigated or fully understood. ¶ *His judgments.* This word in this place evidently means his *arrangement,* his *plan,* or *proceeding.* It sometimes refers to laws; at other times to the decision or determination of God; at others to the inflictions of his justice. In this last sense it is now commonly used. But in the case before us it means his arrangements for conferring the gospel on men; comp. Ps. xxxvi. 7, "His *judgments* are a great deep." ¶ *His ways.* The word rendered *ways* properly denotes a *path* or *road* on which one travels. Hence it comes also to denote the *course* or manner of life in which one moves; or his principles or morals; his doctrine or teaching, &c. Applied to God, it denotes his mode or manner of doing things; the order, &c., of his divine providence; his movements, in his great plans, through the universe, Acts xiii. 10, "Wilt thou not cease to pervert the *right ways* of the Lord?"—to oppose, or to render vain, his plan of guiding and saving man; Heb. iii. 10, "They have not known my ways;" Ps. lxxvii. 19, "Thy way is in the sea, . . . thy footsteps are not known." Here it refers particularly to his *way* or plan of bringing all nations within the reach of his mercy in the gospel. ¶ *Past finding out.* Literally, which cannot be *tracked* or *traced* out. The footsteps cannot be followed. As if his path were in the sea (Ps. lxxvii. 19), and the waves closed immediately, leaving no *track;* it cannot be followed or sought out. It is known that he has passed,

34 Forʸ who hath known the mind of the Lord? or who hath been his counsellor?

f Is.40.13; Je.23.18.

35 Orᵍ who hath first given to him, and it shall be recompensed unto him again?

g Job 41.11.

but there is no way of tracing his goings. This is a beautiful and striking figure. It denotes that God's plans are deep and beyond our comprehension. We can see the proofs that he is everywhere; but *how* it is, we cannot comprehend. We are permitted to see the vast movements around us; but the invisible hand we cannot see, nor trace the footsteps of that mighty God who performs his wonders on the ocean and on the land.

34. *For who hath known*, &c. This verse is a quotation, with a slight change, from Isa. xl. 13, "Who hath directed the Spirit of the Lord, or being his counsellor hath taught him?" It is designed to express the *infinite* wisdom and knowledge of God, by affirming that no being could teach him or counsel him. Earthly monarchs have counsellors of state, whom they may consult in times of perplexity or danger. But God has no such council. He sits alone; nor does he call in any or all of his creatures to advise him. All created beings are not qualified to contribute *anything* to enlighten or to direct him. It is also designed to silence all opposition to his plans, and to hush all murmurings. The apostle had proved that this *was* the plan of God. However mysterious and inscrutable it might appear to the Jew or the Gentile, yet it was his duty to submit to God, and to confide in his wisdom, though he was not able to trace the reason of his doings.

35. *Or who hath*, &c. The sentiment in this verse is found substantially in Job xli. 11, "Who hath prevented me, that I should repay him?" The Hebrew word "prevented" means to *anticipate*, to *go before*; and God asks, "Who has *anticipated* me; who has conferred favours on me before I have on him; who has thus laid me under *obligation* to him?" This is the sense in which the apostle uses the word here. Who has, by his services, laid God under obligation to recompense

or pay him again? It is added in Job, "Whatsoever is under the whole heaven is mine." Thus Paul, contrary to the prevailing doctrine of the Jews, shows that no one could plead his own merits, or advance with a *claim* on God. All the favours of salvation must be bestowed by mercy or grace. God owned them all; and he had a right to bestow them when and where he pleased. The same claim to *all* things is repeatedly made by God, Ex. xix. 5; Deut. x. 14; Ps. xxiv. 1; l. 12. ¶ *Shall be recompensed.* Repaid as a matter of debt. None of God's mercies can be conferred in that way; if they could, man could bring God under obligation, and destroy the freeness and benevolence of his favours.

36. *For of him* (ἐξ αὐτοῦ). Comp. 1 Cor. i. 30; viii. 6. This expression doubtless means that he is the original source and fountain of all blessings. He is the Creator of all, the rich "fountain from which all streams of existence take their rise." The design of this verse is to show that no creature has any *claim* on God. Jews and Gentiles must alike receive salvation on the ground of his *mercy*. So far from having a *claim* on God, the apostle here affirms that *all* things have come from him, and therefore all must be derived to us. Nothing has been produced by chance, or haphazard; nothing by created skill or might. All has been formed by God; and therefore he has a right to dispose of all. ¶ *And through him* (δι αὐτοῦ). That is, by his immediate operating agency. The former expression, "of him," affirmed that he was the *original* source of all things; this declares that all are *by* him, or through him, as their *immediate* cause. It is not merely by his plan or purpose; it is by his agency, by the direct exertion of his power in their creation and bestowment. By his power they are still directed and controlled. Human agency, therefore, could not lay him under any obligation. He does not

36 For[h] of him, and through him, and to him, *are* all things:

to [9] whom *be* glory for ever. Amen.

h 1 Co.8.6; Col.1.16.

[9] *him.*

need the aid of man; and he did not call in that aid in the creation and government of the world. He is the independent Creator and Lord, and on him none can have a claim. ¶ *To him* (εἰς αὐτὸν). This expression denotes the *final cause*, the reason or end for which all things were formed. It is to promote *his* honour and glory. It is to manifest his praise, or to give a proper putting forth of the glorious attributes of God; that the exceeding greatness, and goodness, and grandeur of his character might be evinced. It is not to promote his *happiness*, for he was eternally happy; not to *add* anything to him, for he is infinite; but that he might act *as God*, and have the honour and praise that is due to God. As this was the design of all things, so it followed that the bestowment of his favours must be in accordance with this—in such a way as to promote *his* glory; and not so as to consult the feelings or views of either Jews or Gentiles. ¶ *All things.* The universe; the creation; or still more particularly, the things of which the apostle is discoursing. He does not affirm that he is the author of sin or of sinful thoughts; not that he creates evil, or that evil is designed to promote his glory. The apostle is not discoursing of these, but of his method of bestowing his favours; and he says that *these* are to be conferred in such a way as to promote *his* honour, and to declare the praise of him who is the original source, the creator, and the proprietor of all things. ¶ *To whom* be *glory.* This ascription of praise is the appropriate close of the *argumentative* part of the epistle, as well as appropriate to the train of remarks into which the apostle had fallen. It expresses his hearty *amen* in concurrence with this view; the deep desire of a pious man that all *might* be to God's glory and honour. He had not merely come to it by *reasoning*, but it was the sincere desire of his soul that it *might* be so. The Christian does

not merely *admit* this doctrine; he is not merely *driven* to it by argument, but it finds a hearty response in his bosom. He rejoices in it; and sincerely desires that all may be to the honour of God. Sinners are often *compelled* by argument to *admit* it, but they do not love it. They would rejoice were it otherwise, and be glad if they were permitted rather to seek their own glory than that of the living God. ¶ *Glory.* Praise, honour. ¶ *For ever.* Not merely amid transitory events now, but ever onward to eternity. This will be the case. There never will be a time when the affairs of the universe shall not be conducted with reference to the glory of God. That honour and glory shall shine brighter and brighter, and all worlds shall be perfectly adapted to show his praise, and to evince his greatness, goodness, power, and love for ever and ever. Thus let it be, is the language of every one that truly loves him.

This closes the argumentative part of the epistle. From the close of this chapter we may make the following observations.

1. God is infinitely wise, and just, and good. This is seen in all his plans and doings, and especially in the glorious plan of saving men.

2. It becomes man to be *humble.* He can see but few of the reasons of the doings of an infinite God. He is not qualified to sit in judgment on his plans. He is not fitted to arraign him. There is nothing more absurd than for a man to contend with God, or to find fault with his plans; and yet there is nothing more common. Man speaks, and thinks, and reasons on the great things pertaining to the divine mind and plan, as if he were qualified to counsel the being of infinite wisdom, and to arraign at the bar of his own reason the being of infinite goodness.

3. It is our duty to be *submissive* to God. His plans may often require him to cross the path of our pleasures,

or to remove some of our enjoyments. He tries us by requiring us to put confidence in him where we cannot *see* the reason of his doings, and to *believe* that he is qualified for universal empire. In all such cases it is our duty to submit to his will. He is seeking a grander and nobler object than our private good. He is seeking the welfare of a vast universe; and he best knows in what way that can be promoted.

4. God is the Creator and Proprietor of all things. It would be possible to prove this from his works. But his word unequivocally asserts it. He has formed, and he upholds, and he directs all things for his glory. He who formed all has a right to all. He who is the source of life has the right to direct it, or to withdraw the gift. He on whom all depend has a right to homage and praise.

5. He has formed a universe that is eminently adapted to declare his glory. It evinces infinite power in its creation; and it is fitted to fill the mind with ever-growing wonder and gladness in its contemplation. The sacred writers were filled with rapture when they contemplated it; and all the discoveries of astronomy, and geology, and science in general, in modern times, are fitted to carry forward the wonder, and fill the lips with new expressions of praise. The universe is vast and grand enough to occupy the thoughts for ever. How little do we know of the wonders of his creation, even pertaining to this little world; to our own bodies and souls; to the earth, the ocean, the beast and the reptile, the bird and the insect; how much less of that amazing view of worlds and systems which modern astronomy has opened to our view,—the vast starry frame which the eye can penetrate for millions and millions of miles, and where it finds world piled on world, and system rising above system, in wonderful order and grandeur, and where the utmost power of the telescope can as yet find no bounds.

6. Equally true is this in his moral government. The system is such as to excite our wonder and praise. The creation and control of free and active and mighty minds is as wonderful as the creation and control of matter, even the vast masses of the planetary systems. Creation is filled with minds. God has peopled the worlds with conscious, free, and active intelligences. The wonderful wisdom by which he controls them; the amazing moral power by which he guards and binds them to himself, by which he restrains and awes the rebellious; and the complete subjection by which he will bring all yet at his feet, is as much replete with wonder as the wisdom and skill by which he framed the heavens. To govern *mind* requires more wisdom and skill than to govern matter. To control angels and men evinces more glory than to roll the streams or the ocean, or than to propel and guide the planets. And especially is this true of the plan of salvation. That wondrous scheme is adapted to call forth eternal praise, and to show *for ever* the wisdom and mercy of God. Without *such* a plan, we cannot see how the Divinity could be fully manifested; *with* that, we see God as God, vast, grand, mighty, infinite; but still seeking to do good, and having power to enter any vast mass of iniquity, and to diffuse purity and peace over the face of an alienated and dying world.

7. The salvation of sinners is not to promote their own glory primarily, but that of God. "He is first, and he last; he is midst, and without end," in their salvation. God seeks his own honour, and seeks it by their return and their obedience. But if they *will not* promote his glory in that way, they must be made to promote it in their ruin.

8. It is the duty of men to seek the honour of this infinitely wise and holy God. It commends itself to every man's conscience. God has formed us all; and man *can* have no higher destiny and honour than to be permitted to promote and spread abroad through all the universe the knowledge of a Being whose character is infinitely lovely, whose government is right, and whose presence and favour will diffuse blessings of salvation and eternal peace on all the wide creation that will be obedient to his will.

CHAPTER XII.

I BESEECH you therefore, brethren, by the mercies of God, that

ye ^apresent your bodies a living
sacrifice, holy, acceptable unto God,
which is your reasonable service.

a 1 Co.6.15-20.

CHAPTER XII.

1. *I beseech you.* The apostle,
having finished the *argument* of this
epistle, proceeds now to close it with
a *practical* or *hortatory* application,
showing its bearing on the duties of
life, and the practical influence of
religion. None of the doctrines of the
gospel are designed to be cold and
barren speculations. They bear on
the hearts and lives of men; and the
apostle therefore calls on those to
whom he wrote to dedicate themselves
without reserve unto God. ¶ *Therefore.* As the effect or result of the
argument or doctrine. In other words,
the whole argument of the eleven first
chapters is fitted to show the obligation on us to devote ourselves to God.
From expressions like these, it is clear
that the apostle never supposed that
the tendency of the doctrines of grace
was to lead to licentiousness. Many
have affirmed that such was the tendency of the doctrines of justification
by faith, of election and decrees, and
of the perseverance of the saints. But
it is plain that Paul had no such
apprehensions. After having fully
stated and established those doctrines,
he concludes that we ought *therefore*
to lead holy lives, and on the ground
of them he exhorts men to do it. ¶ *By
the mercies of God.* The word *by*
(διὰ) denotes here the *reason* why they
should do it, or the *ground of appeal.*
So great had been the mercy of God,
that this constituted a *reason why*
they should present their bodies, &c.;
see 1 Cor. i. 10; Rom. xv. 30. The
word *mercies* here denotes favour
shown to the undeserving, or kindness,
compassion, &c. The plural is used
in imitation of the Hebrew word for
mercy, which has no singular. The
word is not often used in the New
Testament; see 2 Cor. i. 3, where
God is called "the Father of mercies;"
Phil. ii. 1; Col. iii. 12; Heb. x. 28.
The particular mercy to which the
apostle here refers, is that shown to
those whom he was addressing He

had proved that all were by nature
under sin; that they had no claim on
God; and that he had showed great
compassion in giving his Son to die
for them in this state, and in pardoning their sins. This was a ground or
reason why *they* should devote themselves to God. ¶ *That ye present.*
The word used here commonly denotes
the action of bringing and presenting
an animal or other sacrifice before an
altar. It implies that the action was
a free and voluntary offering. Religion is free; and the act of devoting
ourselves to God is one of the most
free that we ever perform. ¶ *Your
bodies.* The *bodies* of animals were
offered in sacrifice. The apostle specifies their *bodies* particularly in reference to that fact. Still the entire
animal was devoted; and Paul evidently meant here the same as to say,
present YOURSELVES, your entire person, to the service of God; comp.
1 Cor. vi. 16; Jam. iii. 6. It was not
customary or proper to speak of a
sacrifice as an offering of a soul or
spirit, in the common language of the
Jews; and hence the apostle applied
their customary language of sacrifice
to the offering which Christians were
to make of themselves to God. ¶ *A
living sacrifice.* A *sacrifice* is an
offering made to God as an atonement
for sin; or *any* offering made to him
and his service as an expression of
thanksgiving or homage. It implies
that he who offers it presents it *entirely*,
releases all claim or right to it, and
leaves it to be disposed of for the
honour of God. In the case of an
animal, it was slain, and the blood
offered; in the case of any other offering, as the first-fruits, &c., it was set
apart to the service of God; and he
who offered it released all claim on it,
and submitted it to God, to be disposed
of at his will. This is the offering
which the apostle entreats the Romans
to make: to devote themselves to God,
as if they had no longer any *claim* on

themselves; to be disposed of by him; to suffer and bear all that he might appoint; and to promote *his* honour in any way which *he* might command. This is the nature of true religion. ¶ *Living* (ζῶσαν). The expression probably means that they were to devote the vigorous, active powers of their bodies and souls to the service of God. The Jew offered his victim, slew it, and presented it *dead*. It could not be presented again. In opposition to this, we are to present ourselves with all our living, vital energies. Christianity does not require a service of death or inactivity. It demands vigorous and active powers in the service of God the Saviour. There is something very affecting in the view of such a sacrifice; in regard- ing life, with all its energies, its intel- lectual, and moral, and physical powers, as one long *sacrifice*—one continued offering unto God. An immortal being *presented* to him; presented voluntarily, with all his energies, from day to day, until life shall close, so that it may be said that he has lived and died an offering made freely unto God. This is religion. ¶ *Holy.* This means properly without blemish or defect. No other sacrifice could be made to God. The Jews were ex- pressly forbid to offer that which was lame, or blind, or in any way deformed, Deut. xv. 21; Lev. i. 3, 10; iii. 1; xxii. 20; Deut. xvii. 1; comp. Mal. i. 8. If offered without any of these defects, it was regarded as *holy, i.e.* appropriately set apart, or consecrated to God. In like manner we are to consecrate to God our *best* faculties; the vigour of our minds and talents, and time. Not the feebleness of sick- ness merely; not old age alone; not time which we cannot otherwise em- ploy, but the first vigour and energies of the mind and body; our youth, and health, and strength. Our sacrifice to God is to be not divided, separate; but it is to be entire and complete. Many are expecting to be Christians in sickness; many in old age; thus purposing to offer unto him the blind and the lame. The sacrifice is to be free from sin. It is not to be a divided, and broken, and polluted service. It

is to be with the best affections of our hearts and lives. ¶ *Acceptable unto God.* They are exhorted to offer such a sacrifice as *will be* acceptable to God; that is, such a one as he had just specified, one that was living and holy. No sacrifice should be made which is not acceptable to God. The offerings of the heathen; the pilgrim- ages of the Mahometans; the self- inflicted penalties of the Roman Ca- tholics, uncommanded by God, can- not be acceptable to him. Those services will be acceptable to God, and those only, which he appoints· comp. Col. ii. 20–23. Men are not to *invent* services; or to *make* crosses; or to *seek* persecutions and trials; or to *provoke* opposition. They are to do just what God requires of them, and that will be acceptable to God. And this fact, that what we do is acceptable to God, is the highest recompense we can have. It matters little what *men* think of us, if *God* approves what we do. To please *him* should be our highest aim; the fact that we *do* please him is our highest reward. ¶ *Which is your reasonable service.* The word rendered *service* (λατρείαν) properly denotes *worship*, or the *homage* rendered to God. The word *reasonable* with us means that which is "governed by reason; think- ing, speaking, or acting conformably to the dictates of reason" (Webster); or that which can be shown to be rational or proper. This does not express the meaning of the original. That word (λογικὴν) denotes that which pertains to the mind, and a reasonable service means that which is mental, or pertaining to reason. It stands opposed, not to that which is foolish or unreasonable, but to the *external* service of the Jews, and such as they relied on for salvation. The worship of the Christian is that which pertains to the *mind*, or is spiritual; that of the Jew was *external*. Chrysostom renders this phrase "your spiritual ministry." The Syriac, "That ye present your bodies, &c., *by a rational ministry.*"

We may learn from this verse, (1) That the proper worship of God is the free homage of the mind. It is not

2 And *b*be not conformed to this world: but be ye transformed by the renewing of your mind,

that ye may *c*prove what *is* that good, and acceptable, and perfect will of God.

b 1 Jn.2.15.

c Ep.5.10,17.

---

forced or constrained. The offering of ourselves should be voluntary. No other can be a true offering, and none other can be acceptable. (2) We are to offer our entire selves, all that we have and are, to God. No other offering can be such as he will approve. (3) The character of God is such as should lead us to that. It is a character of mercy; of long-continued and patient forbearance, and it should influence us to devote ourselves to him. (4) It should be done without delay. God is as *worthy* of such service *now* as he ever *will* or *can* be. He has every possible *claim* on our affections and our hearts.

2. *And be not conformed,* &c. The word rendered *conformed* properly means to put on the *form, fashion,* or *appearance* of another. It may refer to *anything* pertaining to the habit, manner, dress, style of living, &c., of others. ¶ *Of this world* (τῷ αἰῶνι τούτῳ). The word which is commonly rendered *world,* when applied to the material universe, is κόσμος, *cosmos.* The word used here properly denotes an *age,* or *generation* of men. It may denote a *particular* generation, or it may be applied to the race. It is sometimes used in each of these senses. Thus here it may mean that Christians should not conform to the maxims, habits, feelings, &c., of a wicked, luxurious, and idolatrous age, but should be conformed solely to the precepts and laws of the gospel; or the same principle may be extended to *every age,* and the direction may be, that Christians should not conform to the prevailing habits, style, and manners of the world, the people who know not God. They are to be governed by the laws of the Bible; to fashion their lives after the example of Christ; and to form themselves by principles different from those which prevail in the world. In the *application* of this rule there is much difficulty. Many may think that *they* are not

conformed to the world, while they can easily perceive that their neighbour is. They indulge in many things which others may think to be conformity to the world, and are opposed to many things which others think innocent. The design of this passage is doubtless to produce a spirit that should not find *pleasure* in the pomp and vanity of the world; and which will regard all vain amusements and gaieties with disgust, and lead the mind to find pleasure in better things. ¶ *Be ye transformed.* The word from which the expression here is derived means *form, habit* (μόρφη). The direction is, "Put on another *form,* change the *form* of the world for that of Christianity." This word would properly refer to the *external appearance,* but the expression which the apostle immediately uses, "renewing of the mind," shows that he did not intend to use it with reference to that only, but to the change of the whole man. The meaning is, do not cherish a spirit devoted to the world, following its vain fashions and pleasures, but cultivate a spirit attached to God, and his kingdom and cause. ¶ *By the renewing.* By the *making new;* the changing into *new* views and feelings. The Christian is often represented as a *new creature,* 2 Cor. v. 17; Gal. vi. 15; Eph. iv. 24; 1 Pet. ii. 2. ¶ *Your mind.* The word translated *mind* properly denotes *intellect,* as distinguished from the will and affections. But here it seems to be used as applicable *to the whole spirit* as distinguished from the *body,* including the understanding, will, and affections. As if he had said, Let not this change appertain to the *body* only, but to the *soul.* Let it not be a mere *external* conformity, but let it have its seat in the spirit. All external changes, if the mind was not changed, would be useless, or would be hypocrisy. Christianity seeks to reign in the *soul;* and having its seat there, the external

3 For I say, through the grace given unto me, to every man that is among you, ^dnot to think

d ch.11.20.

conduct and habits will be regulated accordingly. ¶ *That ye may prove.* The word used here (δοκιμάζω) is commonly applied to *metals*, to the operation of testing, or trying them by the severity of fire, &c. Hence it also means to explore, investigate, ascertain. This is its meaning here. The sense is, that such a *renewed* mind is essential to a successful inquiry after the will of God. Having a *disposition* to obey him, the mind will be prepared to understand his precepts. There will be a *correspondence* between the feelings of the heart and his will; a nice *tact* or taste, which will admit his laws, and see the propriety and beauty of his commands. A renewed heart is the best preparation for studying Christianity; as a man who is *temperate* is the best fitted to understand the arguments for temperance; the man who is chaste, has most clearly and forcibly the arguments for chastity, &c. A heart in love with the fashions and follies of the world is ill-fitted to appreciate the arguments for humility, prayer, &c. "If any man will do his will, he shall know of the doctrine whether it be of God," John vii. 17. The *reason why* the heart is renewed is, that we may do the will of God: the heart that *is* renewed is best fitted to appreciate and understand his will. ¶ *That good,* &c. This part of the verse might be rendered, that ye may investigate the will of God, or ascertain the will of God, that which is good and perfect, and acceptable. The *will of God,* relates to his commands in regard to our conduct, his doctrines in regard to our belief, his providential dealings in relation to our external circumstances. It means what God demands of us, in whatever way it may be made known. They do not err from his ways who seek his guidance, and who, not confiding in their own wisdom, but in God, commit their way to him. "The meek will he guide in judgment, and the meek will he teach his way," Ps. xxv. 9,

of himself more highly than he ought to think; but to think ¹soberly, according as God hath

1 to sobriety.

The word *good* here is not an *adjective* agreeing with "will," but a *noun.* "That ye may find the will of God, that which is good and acceptable." It implies that that thing which is *good is* his will; or that we may find his will by finding that which is good and perfect. That is good which promotes the honour of God and the interests of his universe. ¶ *Perfect.* Free from defect, stain, or injury. That which has all its parts complete, or which is not disproportionate. Applied to religion, it means that which is *consistent,* which is *carried out;* which is evinced in all the circumstances and relations of life. ¶ *Acceptable.* That which will be pleasing to God, or which he will approve. There is scarcely a more difficult text in the Bible than this, or one that is more full of meaning. It involves the main *duty* of religion, to be separated from the world; and expresses the *way* in which that duty may be performed, and in which we may live so as to ascertain and do the will of God. If all Christians would obey this, religion would be everywhere honoured. If all would separate from the vices and follies, the amusements and gaieties of the world, Christ would be glorified. If all were truly renewed in their minds, they would lose their relish for such things, and seeking only to do the will of God, they would not be slow to find it.

3. *For I say.* The word "for" shows that the apostle is about to introduce some additional considerations to enforce what he had just said, or to show how we may evince a mind that is not conformed to the world. ¶ *Through the grace.* Through the *favour,* or in virtue of the favour of the apostolic office. By the *authority* that is conferred on me to declare the will of God as an apostle; see Note, chap. i. 5; see also Gal. i. 6, 15; ii. 9; Eph. iii. 8; 1 Tim. i. 14. ¶ *Not to think,* &c. Not to *over-estimate* himself, or to think more of himself than

he ought to. What is the true standard by which we *ought* to estimate ourselves he immediately adds. This is a caution against *pride;* and an exhortation not to judge of ourselves by our talents, wealth, or office, but to form another standard of judging of ourselves by our Christian character. The Romans would probably be in much danger from this quarter. The prevailing habit of judging among them was according to rank, or wealth, or eloquence, or office. While this habit of judging prevailed in the world around them, there was danger that it might also prevail in the church. And the exhortation was that they should not judge of their own characters by the usual modes among men, but by their Christian attainments. There is no sin to which men are more prone than an inordinate self-valuation and pride. Instead of judging by that which constitutes true excellence of character, they pride themselves on that which is of no intrinsic value; on rank, and titles, and external accomplishments; or on talents, learning, or wealth. The only true standard of character pertains to the principles of action, or to that which constitutes the *moral* nature of the man; and to that the apostle calls the Roman people. ¶ *But to think soberly.* Literally, "to think so as to act soberly or wisely." So to estimate ourselves as to act or demean ourselves wisely, prudently, modestly. Those who over-estimate themselves are proud, haughty, foolish in their deportment. Those who think of themselves as they ought, are modest, sober, prudent. There is no way to maintain a wise and proper conduct so certain, as to form a humble and modest estimate of our own character. ¶ *According as God hath dealt.* As God has *measured* to each one, or apportioned to each one. In this place the *faith* which Christians have, is traced to God as its giver. This *fact,* that God has given it, will be itself one of the most effectual promoters of humility and right feeling. Men commonly regard the objects on which they pride themselves as things of their own creation, or as depending on themselves. But let an object be

regarded as the gift of God, and it ceases to excite *pride,* and the feeling is at once changed into *gratitude.* He, therefore, who regards *God* as the source of all blessings, and he only, will be a humble man. ¶ *The measure of faith.* The word *faith* here is evidently put for *religion,* or Christianity. Faith is a main thing in religion. It constitutes its *first* demand, and the Christian religion, therefore, is characterized by its *faith,* or its *confidence* in God; see Mark xvi. 17; comp. Heb. xi.; Rom. iv. We are not, therefore, to be elated in our view of ourselves; we are not to judge of our own characters by wealth, or talent, or learning, but by our attachment to God, and by the influence of faith on our minds. The meaning is, judge yourselves, or estimate yourselves, by your *piety.* The propriety of this rule is apparent, (1) Because no other standard is a correct one, or one of value. Our talent, learning, rank, or wealth, is a very improper rule by which to estimate ourselves. All may be wholly unconnected with moral worth; and the worst as well as the best men may possess them. (2) God will judge us in the day of judgment by our attachment to Christ and his cause (Mat. xxv.); and that is the true standard by which to estimate ourselves here. (3) Nothing else will secure and promote humility but this. All other things may produce or promote pride, but this will effectually secure humility. The fact that *God* has given all that we have; the fact that the poor and obscure may have as true an elevation of character as ourselves; the consciousness of our own imperfections and shortcomings in the Christian faith; and the certainty that we are soon to be arraigned to try this great question, whether we have evidence that we are the friends of God; will all tend to promote humbleness of mind, and to bring down our usual inordinate self-estimation. If all Christians judged themselves in this way, it would remove at once no small part of the pride of station and of life from the world, and would produce deep attachment for those who are blessed with the faith of the gospel,

dealt to every man *the measure of faith.

4 For as we have ᶠmany members in one body, and all

e Ep.4.7,&c.   f 1 Co.12.4,12.

members have not the same office;

5 So we, *being* many, ᵍare one body in Christ, and every one members one of another.

g Ep.1.23.

though they may be unadorned by any of the wealth or trappings which now promote pride and distinctions among men.

4. *For.* This word here denotes a further *illustration* or proof of what he had just before said. The duty to which he was exhorting the Romans was, not to be unduly exalted or elevated in their own estimation. In order to produce proper humility, he shows them that God has appointed certain orders or grades in the church; that all are useful in their proper place; that we should seek to discharge our duty in our appropriate sphere; and *thus* that due subordination and order would be observed. To show this, he introduces a beautiful comparison drawn from the human body. There are various members in the human frame; all useful and honourable in their proper place; and all designed to promote the order, and beauty, and harmony of the whole. So the church is one body, consisting of many members, and each is fitted to be useful and comely in its proper place. The same comparison he uses with great beauty and force in 1 Cor. xii. 4–31; also Eph. iv. 25; v. 30. In that chapter the comparison is carried out to much greater length, and its influence shown with great force. ¶ *Many members.* Limbs, or parts; feet, hands, eyes, ears, &c., 1 Cor. xii. 14, 15. ¶ *In one body.* Constituting one body; or united in one, and making one person. Essential to the existence, beauty, and happiness of the one body or person. ¶ *The same office.* The same use or design; not all appointed for the same thing; one is to see, another to hear, a third to walk with, &c., 1 Cor. xii. 14–23.

5. *So we,* being *many.* We who are Christians, and who are numerous as individuals. ¶ *Are one body.* Are united together, constituting one society, or one people, mutually dependent, and having the same great

interests at heart, though to be promoted by us according to our peculiar talents and opportunities. As the welfare of the same body is to be promoted in one manner by the feet, in another by the eye, &c.; so the welfare of the body of Christ is to be promoted by discharging our duties in our appropriate sphere, as God has appointed us. ¶ *In Christ.* One body, *joined to* Christ, or connected *with* him as the head, Eph. i. 22, 23, "And gave him to be *head* over all things to the church, which is his *body;*" comp. John xv. 1–7. This does not mean that there is any *physical* or *literal* union, or any destruction of personal identity, or anything particularly mysterious or unintelligible. Christians acknowledge him as their *head,* *i.e.* their lawgiver; their counsellor, guide, and Redeemer. They are bound to him by peculiarly tender ties of affection, gratitude, and friendship; they are united *in him, i.e.* in acknowledging him as their common Lord and Saviour. Any other union than this is impossible; and the sacred writers never intended that expressions like these should be explained *literally.* The union of Christians to Christ is the most tender and interesting of any in this world, but no more mysterious than that which binds friend to friend, children to parents, or husbands to their wives; comp. Eph. v. 23–33.* ¶ *And every one members one of another.* Comp. 1 Cor. xii. 25, 26. That is, we are so united as to be mutually dependent; each one is of service to the other; and the existence and office of the one is necessary to the usefulness of the other. Thus the members of the body may be said to be members one of another; as the feet could not, for example, perform their functions or be

* See Supplementary Note on chap. viii. ver. 17.

6 Having then *h* gifts differing according to the grace that is

h 1 Pe.4.10,11.

of use if it were not for the eye; the ear, the hand, the teeth, &c., would be useless if it were not for the other members, which go to make up the entire person. Thus in the church every individual is not only necessary in his place as an individual, but is needful to the proper symmetry and action of the whole. And we may learn here, (1) That no member of the church of Christ should esteem himself to be of no importance. In his own place he may be of as much consequence as the man of learning, wealth, and talent may be in his. (2) God designed that there should be differences of endowments of nature and of grace in the church; just as it was needful that there should be differences in the members of the human body. (3) No one should despise or lightly esteem another. All are necessary. We can no more spare the foot or the hand than we can the eye; though the latter may be much more curious and striking as a proof of divine skill. We do not despise the hand or the foot any more than we do the eye; and in all we should acknowledge the goodness and wisdom of God. See these thoughts carried out in 1 Cor. xii. 21–25.

6. *Having then gifts.* All the endowments which Christians have are regarded by the apostle as *gifts.* God has conferred them; and this fact, when properly felt, tends much to prevent our thinking of ourselves more highly than we ought to think, ver. 3. For the use of the word rendered *gifts,* see chap. i. 11; v. 15, 16; vi. 23; xi. 29; 1 Cor. vii. 7; xii. 4, 9, 28, &c. It may refer to natural endowments as well as to the favours of grace; though in this place it refers doubtless to the distinctions conferred on Christians in the churches. ¶ *Differing.* It was never designed that all Christians should be equal. God designed that men should have different endowments. The very nature of society supposes this. There never was a state of perfect equality in anything; and it would

given to us, whether prophecy, *let us prophesy* according to the proportion of faith;

be impossible that there should be, and yet preserve society. In this, God exercises a sovereignty, and bestows his favours as he pleases, injuring no one by conferring favours on others; and holding *me* responsible for the right use of what *I* have, and not for what may be conferred on my neighbour. ¶ *According to the grace.* That is, the *favour,* the *mercy* that is bestowed on us. As all that we have is a matter of *grace,* it should keep us from pride; and it should make us willing to occupy our appropriate place in the church. True honour consists not in splendid endowments, or great wealth and office. It consists in rightly discharging the duties which God requires of us in our appropriate sphere. If all men held their talents as the gift of God; if all would find and occupy in society the place for which God designed them, it would prevent no small part of the uneasiness, the restlessness, the ambition, and misery of the world. ¶ *Whether prophecy.* The apostle now proceeds to *specify* the different classes of gifts or endowments which Christians have, and to exhort them to discharge aright the duty which results from the rank or office which they held in the church. The first is *prophecy.* This word properly means to predict *future events,* but it also means to declare the divine will; to interpret the purposes of God; or to make known in any way the truth of God, which is designed to influence men. Its *first* meaning is to *predict* or *foretell* future events; but as those who did this were messengers of God, and as they commonly connected with such *predictions,* instructions and exhortations in regard to the sins, and dangers, and duties of men, the word came to denote *any* who warned, or threatened, or in any way communicated the will of God; and even those who uttered devotional sentiments or praise. The name in the New Testament is commonly connected with *teachers,* Acts xiii. 1, "There were in the church at Antioch certain *prophets*, and teachers, as Barnabas," &c.; xv. 32, "And Judas and Silas, being *prophets* themselves," &c.; xxi. 10, "A certain prophet named Agabus." In 1 Cor. xii. 28, 29, *prophets* are mentioned as a class of teachers immediately *after* apostles, "And God hath set some in the church; first apostles, secondly *prophets*, thirdly teachers," &c. The same class of persons is again mentioned in 1 Cor. xiv. 29–32, 39. In this place they are spoken of as being under the influence of *revelation*, "Let the prophets speak two or three, and let the other judge. If anything be *revealed* to another that sitteth by, let the first hold his peace. And the spirits of the prophets are subject to the prophets;" ver. 39, "Covet to *prophesy*, and forbid not to speak with tongues." In this place endowments are mentioned under the name of *prophecy* evidently in advance even of the power of speaking with tongues. Yet all these were to be subject to the authority of the apostle, 1 Cor. xiv. 37. In Eph. iv. 11, they are mentioned again in the same order, "And he gave some apostles; and some prophets; and some evangelists; and some pastors, and teachers," &c. From these passages the following things seem clear in relation to this class of persons. (1) They were an order of teachers distinct from the apostles, and *next* to them in authority and rank. (2) They were under the influence of revelation, or inspiration in a certain sense. (3) They had power of *controlling* themselves, and of speaking or keeping silence as they chose. They had the power of *using* their prophetic gifts as *we* have the ordinary faculties of our minds; and of course of *abusing* them also. This abuse was apparent also in the case of those who had the power of speaking with tongues, 1 Cor. xiv. 2, 4, 6, 11, &c. (4) They were subject to the apostles. (5) They were *superior* to the other teachers and pastors in the church. (6) The office or the endowment was *temporary*, designed for the settlement and establishment of the church; and then, like the apostolic office, having accomplished its purpose, to be disused,

and to cease. From these remarks, also, will be seen the propriety of *regulating* this office by apostolic authority; or stating, as the apostle does here, the *manner* or *rule* by which this gift was to be exercised. ¶ *According to the proportion.* This word (ἀναλογίαν) is nowhere else used in the New Testament. The word properly applies to mathematics (Schleusner), and means the ratio or proportion which results from comparison of one number or magnitude with another. In a large sense, therefore, as applied to other subjects, it denotes *the measure* of anything. With us it means *analogy*, or the congruity or resemblance discovered between one thing and another, as we say there is an *analogy* or *resemblance* between the truths taught by reason and revelation. (See Butler's *Analogy*.) But this is not its meaning here. It means the *measure*, the *amount* of faith bestowed on them, for he was exhorting them to (ver. 3) "think soberly, according as God hath dealt to every man *the measure of faith*." The word *faith* here means evidently, not the truths of the Bible elsewhere revealed; nor their *confidence* in God; nor their personal piety; but the *extraordinary endowment* bestowed on them by the gifts of prophecy. They were to *confine* themselves strictly to that; they were not to *usurp* the apostolic authority, or to attempt to exercise *their* peculiar office; but they were to *confine* themselves *strictly* to the functions of their office according to the measure of their faith, *i.e.* the extraordinary endowment conferred on them. The word *faith* is thus used often to denote that extraordinary confidence in God which attended the working of miracles, &c., Mat. xvii. 26; xxi. 21; Luke xvii. 6. If this be the fair interpretation of the passage, then it is clear that the interpretation which applies it *to systems of theology*, and which demands that we should interpret the Bible so as to accord with the system, is one that is wholly unwarranted. It is to be referred solely to this class of religious teachers, without reference to any system of doctrine, or to anything which had been revealed to any

7 Or ministry *let us wait* on *our* ministering; or he that teacheth, on teaching;

8 Or he that exhorteth, on exhortation: he that [2]giveth, *let*

2 or, *imparteth.*

---

other class of men; or without affirming that there is any resemblance between one truth and another. All that may be true, but it is not the truth taught in this passage. And it is equally clear that the passage is not to be applied to teachers now, except as an illustration of the *general principle* that even those endowed with great and splendid talents are not to over-estimate them, but to regard them as the gift of God; to exercise them in subordination to his appointment; and to seek to employ them in the manner, the place, and to the purpose that shall be according to his will. *They are to employ them in the purpose for which God gave them;* AND FOR NO OTHER.

7. *Or ministry* (διακονίαν). This word properly means *service* of any kind, Luke x. 40. It is used in religion to denote the *service* which is rendered to Christ as the *Master*. It is applied to *all* classes of ministers in the New Testament, as denoting their being the *servants* of Christ, and it is used particularly to denote that class who from this word were called *deacons, i.e.* those who had the care of the poor, who provided for the sick, and who watched over the *external* matters of the church. In the following places it is used to denote the *ministry*, or *service*, which Paul and the other apostles rendered in their public work: Acts i. 17, 25; vi. 4; xii. 25; xx. 24; xxi. 19; Rom. xi. 13; xv. 31; 2 Cor. v. 18; vi. 3; Eph. iv. 12; 1 Tim. i. 12. In a few places this word is used to denote the office which the *deacons* fulfilled, Acts vi. 1; Acts xi. 29; 1 Cor. xvi. 15; 2 Cor. xi. 8. In this sense the word *deacon* (διάκονος) is most commonly used, as denoting the office which was performed in providing for the poor and administering the alms of the church. It is not easy to say in what sense it is used here. I am inclined to the opinion that he did *not* refer to those who were appropriately called *dea-*

cons, but to those engaged in the office of the *ministry of the word,* whose business it was to preach, and thus to serve the churches. In this sense the word is often used in the New Testament, and the connection seems to demand the same interpretation here. ¶ *On* our *ministering.* Let us be wholly and diligently occupied in this. Let this be our great business, and let us give entire attention to it. Particularly the connection requires us to understand this as directing those who *ministered* not to aspire to the office and honours of those who prophesied. Let them not think of themselves more highly than they ought, but be engaged entirely in their own appropriate work. ¶ *He that teacheth.* This word denotes those who *instruct*, or communicate knowledge. It is clear that it is used to denote a class of persons different, in some respects, from those who *prophesied* and from those who *exhorted*. But in what this difference consisted is not clear. *Teachers* are mentioned in the New Testament in the grade next to the *prophets*, Acts xiii. 1; 1 Cor. xii. 28, 29; Eph. iv. 11. Perhaps the difference between the *prophets*, the *ministers*, the *teachers*, and the *exhorters* was this, that the first spake by inspiration; the second engaged in all the functions of the ministry properly so called, including the administration of the sacraments; the teachers were employed in communicating instruction simply, teaching the *doctrines* of religion, but without assuming the office of ministers; and the fourth *exhorted*, or entreated Christians to lead a holy life, without making it a particular subject to *teach*, and without pretending to administer the ordinances of religion. The fact that *teachers* are so often mentioned in the New Testament, shows that they were a class by themselves. It may be worthy of remark that the churches in New England had, at first, a class of men who were called

him do it [3]with simplicity; [i]he that ruleth, with diligence; he

that showeth mercy, [k]with cheerfulness.

teachers. One was appointed to this office in every church, distinct from the pastor, whose proper business it was to *instruct* the congregation in the *doctrines* of religion. The same thing exists substantially now in most churches, in the appointment of Sunday-school *teachers*, whose main business it is to instruct the children in the doctrines of the Christian religion. It is an office of great importance to the church; and the exhortation of the apostle may be applied to them: that they should be assiduous, constant, diligent in their teaching; that they should confine themselves to their appropriate place; and should feel that their office is of great importance in the church of God, and remember that this is *his* arrangement, designed to promote the edification of his people.

8. *He that exhorteth.* This word properly denotes one who urges to the *practical duties* of religion, in distinction from one who teaches its *doctrines.* One who presents the *warnings* and the *promises* of God to excite men to the discharge of their duty. It is clear that there were persons who were recognized as engaging especially in this duty, and who were known by this appellation, as distinguished from prophets and teachers. How long this was continued there is no means of ascertaining; but it cannot be doubted that it may still be expedient, in many times and places, to have persons designated to this work. In most churches this duty is now blended with the other offices of the ministry. ¶ *He that giveth.* Margin, *"imparteth."* The word denotes the person whose office it was to distribute, and probably designates him who distributed the *alms* of the church, or him who was the *deacon* of the congregation. The *connection* requires that this meaning should be given to the passage; and the word rendered *giveth* may denote one who imparts or distributes that which has been *committed to him for that purpose*, as well

as one who gives out of his private property. As the apostle is speaking here of *offices* in the church, the former is evidently that which is intended. It was deemed an important matter among the early Christians to impart *liberally* of their substance to support the poor, and provide for the needy, Acts ii. 44 – 47; iv. 34 – 37; v. 1 – 11; Gal. ii. 10; Rom. xv. 26; 2 Cor. viii. 8; ix. 2, 12. Hence it became necessary to appoint persons over these contributions, who should be especially charged with the management of them, and who would see that they were properly distributed, Acts vi. 1 – 6. *These* were the persons who were denominated *deacons*, Phil. i. 1; 1 Tim. iii. 8, 12. ¶ *With simplicity.* See Mat. vi. 22, "If thine eye be *single*," &c.; Luke xi. 34. The word *simplicity* (ἁπλότης) is used in a similar sense to denote *singleness*, honesty of aim, purity, integrity, without any mixture of a base, selfish, or sinister end. It requires the bestowment of a favour without seeking any *personal* or selfish ends; without partiality, but actuated only by the desire to bestow them in the best possible manner to promote the object for which they were given, 2 Cor. viii. 2; ix. 11, 13; i. 12; Eph. vi. 5; Col. iii. 22. It is plain that when *property* was intrusted to them, there would be danger that they might be tempted to employ it for selfish and sinister ends, to promote their influence and prosperity; and hence the apostle exhorted them to do it with a *single aim* to the object for which it was given. Well did he know that there was nothing more tempting than the possession of wealth, though given to be appropriated to others. And this exhortation is applicable not only to the deacons of the churches, but to all who in this day of Christian benevolence are intrusted with money to advance the kingdom of the Lord Jesus Christ. ¶ *He that ruleth.* This word properly designates one who is *set over* others, or who *presides* or rules, or one who attends with diligence and care to a thing. In 1 Thes. v. 12, it is used in relation to ministers in general: "And we beseech you, brethren, to know them which labour among you, and *are over you* in the Lord;" 1 Tim. iii. 4, 5, 12, it is applied to the head of a family, or one who diligently and faithfully performs the duty of a father: "One that ruleth well his own house;" 1 Tim. v. 17, it is applied to "*elders*" in the church: "Let the elders that rule well," &c. It is not elsewhere used, except in Tit. iii. 8, 14, in a different sense, where it is translated "*to maintain* good works." The prevailing sense of the word, therefore, is to *rule*, to *preside over*, or to have the management of. But to what class of persons reference is had here, and what was precisely their duty, has been made a matter of controversy, and it is not easy to determine. Whether this refers to a *permanent* office in the church, or to an *occasional* presiding in their assemblies convened for business, &c., is not settled by the use of the word. It has the idea of *ruling*, as in a family, or of *presiding*, as in a deliberative assembly; and either of these ideas would convey all that is implied in the original word; comp. 1 Cor. xii. 28. ¶ *With diligence.* This word properly means *haste* (Mark vi. 25; Luke i. 39); but it also denotes *industry, attention, care;* 2 Cor. vii. 11, "What *carefulness* it wrought in you;" 12, "That our *care* for you in the sight of God," &c.; viii. 7, 8 (Gr.); Heb. vi. 11. It means here that they should be *attentive* to the duties of their vocation, and engage with *ardour* in that which was committed to them to do. ¶ *He that showeth mercy.* It is probable, says Calvin, that this refers to those who had the care of the sick and infirm, the aged and the needy; not so much to *provide* for them by charity, as to attend on them in their affliction, and to take care of them. To the *deacons* was committed the duty of distributing alms, but to others that of *personal* attendance. This can hardly be called an *office*, in the technical sense; and yet it is not improbable

that they were designated to this by the church, and requested to perform it. There were no hospitals and no almshouses. Christians felt it their duty to show personal attention to the infirm and the sick; and so important was their office, that it was deemed worthy of notice in a general direction to the church. ¶ *With cheerfulness.* The direction given to those who distributed alms was to do it *with simplicity*, with an honest aim to meet the purpose for which it was intrusted to them. The direction here varies according to the duty to be performed. It is to be done with cheerfulness, pleasantness, joy; with a kind, benign, and happy temper. The importance of this direction to those in this situation is apparent. Nothing tends so much to enhance the value of personal attendance on the sick and afflicted, as a kind and cheerful temper. If anywhere a mild, amiable, cheerful, and patient disposition is needed, it is near a sick-bed, and when administering to the wants of those who are in affliction. And whenever we may be called to such a service, we should remember that this is indispensable. If moroseness, or impatience, or fretfulness is discovered in us, it will pain those whom we seek to benefit, embitter their feelings, and render our services of comparatively little value. The needy and infirm, the feeble and the aged, have enough to bear without the impatience and harshness of professed friends. It may be added that the example of the Lord Jesus Christ is the brightest which the world has furnished of this temper. Though constantly encompassed by the infirm and the afflicted, yet he was always kind, and gentle, and mild, and has left before us *exactly* what the apostle meant when he said, "he that showeth mercy with cheerfulness." The example of the good Samaritan is also another instance of what is intended by this direction; comp. 2 Cor. ix. 7. This direction is particularly applicable to a physician.

We have here an account of the establishment, the order, and the duties of the different members of the

9 Let[l] love be without dissimulation. Abhor[m] that which is evil; cleave to that which is good.

l 1 Pe.1.22.　　　*m* Ps.34.14.

Christian church. The amount of it all is, that we should discharge with fidelity the duties which belong to us in the sphere of life in which we are placed; and not despise the rank which God has assigned us; not to think of ourselves more highly than we ought; but to act well our part, according to the station where we are placed, and the talents with which we are endowed. If this were done, it would put an end to discontent, ambition, and strife, and would produce the blessings of universal peace and order.

9. *Let love.* The apostle proceeds to specify the duties of Christians in general, that they might secure the beauty and order of the church. The first which he specifies is *love.* This word here evidently refers to *benevolence,* or to good-will toward all mankind. In ver. 10 he specifies the duty of brotherly love; and there can be no doubt that he here refers to the benevolence which we ought to cherish towards all men. A similar distinction is found in 2 Pet. i. 7, "And to brotherly-kindness add *charity,*" *i.e.* benevolence, or good-will, and kind feelings to others. ¶ *Without dissimulation.* Without *hypocrisy.* Let it be sincere and unfeigned. Let it not consist in words or professions only, but let it be manifested in acts of kindness and in deeds of charity, 1 John iii. 18; comp. 1 Pet. i. 22. Genuine benevolence is not that which merely *professes* attachment, but which is evinced by acts of kindness and affection. ¶ *Abhor that which is evil.* The word *abhor* means to hate; to turn from; to avoid. The word *evil* here has reference to *malice,* or *unkindness,* rather than to evil in general. The apostle is exhorting to *love,* or kindness; and *between* the direction to love all men, and the particular direction about brotherly love, he places this general direction to abhor that which is evil; that which is evil in relation *to the subject under*

10 Be [n]kindly affectioned one to another [4]with brotherly love; [o]in honour preferring one another.

n 1 Pe.2.17.　　*4* or, *in the love of the brethren.*
　　　　　　　o 1 Pe.5.5.

discussion, that is, *malice* or *unkindness.* The word *evil* is not unfrequently used in this limited sense to denote some particular or special evil, Mat. v. 37, 39, &c.; comp. Ps. xxxiv. 14; 2 Tim. ii. 19; Ps. xcvii. 10; 1 Thes. v. 22. ¶ *Cleave to that which is good.* The word rendered *cleave to* denotes properly the act of *gluing,* or uniting firmly by glue. It is then used to denote a very firm *adherence* to an object; to be firmly united to it. Here it means that Christians should be *firmly attached* to that which is good, and not *separate* or *part* from it. The *good* here referred to is particularly that which pertains to *benevolence*—to all men, and especially to Christians. It should not be *occasional only,* or irregular; but it should be constant, active, decided.

10. Be *kindly affectioned.* The word here used occurs nowhere else in the New Testament. It properly denotes tender affection, such as that which subsists between parents and children; and it means that Christians should have similar feelings towards each other, as belonging to the same family, and as united in the same principles and interests. The Syriac renders this, "Love your brethren, and love one another;" comp. 1 Pet. ii. 17. ¶ *With brotherly love.* Or in love to the brethren. The word denotes the affection which subsists between *brethren.* The duty is one which is often presented in the New Testament, and which our Saviour intended should be regarded as a badge of discipleship; see Note, John xiii. 34, 35, "By this shall all men know that ye are my disciples, if ye have love one to another;" John xv. 12, 17; Eph. v. 2; 1 Thes. iv. 9; 1 Pet. i. 22; 1 John ii. 7, 8; iii. 11, 23; iv. 20, 21. The apostle Paul in this place manifests his peculiar manner of writing. He does not simply enjoin brotherly love, but he adds that it should be *kindly affectioned.*

11 Not[p] slothful in business; fervent[q] in spirit; [r]serving the Lord.

p Ac.20.34,35.   *q* Col.4.12.   *r* He.12.28.

12 Rejoicing[s] in hope; [t]patient in tribulation; [u]continuing instant in prayer;

s ch.5.2,3.   *t* Ja.1.4.   *u* Lu.18.1.

It should be with the *tenderness* which characterizes the most endearing natural relationship. This he expresses by a word which is made for the occasion (φιλόστοργοι), blending love with natural affection, and suffering it to be manifest in your intercourse with one another. ¶ *In honour.* In *showing* or *manifesting* respect or honour. Not in *seeking* honour, or striving after respect, but in showing it to one another. ¶ *Preferring one another.* The word *preferring* means going before, leading, setting an example. Thus in showing mutual respect and honour, they were to strive to excel; not to see which could *obtain* most honour, but which could *confer* most, or manifest most respect; comp. 1 Pet. i. 5; Eph. v. 21. Thus they were to be studious to show to each other all the respect which was due in the various relations of life; children to show proper respect to parents, parents to children, servants to their masters, &c.; and *all* to strive by mutual kindness to promote the happiness of the Christian community. How different this from the spirit of the world; the spirit which seeks, not to confer honour, but to obtain it; which aims, not to diffuse respect, but to attract all others to give honour to us. If this single direction were to be obeyed in society, it would put an end at once to no small part of the envy, and ambition, and heart-burning, and dissatisfaction of the world. It would produce contentment, harmony, love, and order in the community; and stay the progress of crime, and annihilate the evils of strife, and discord, and malice. And especially, it would give order and beauty to the church. It would humble the ambition of those who, like Diotrephes, love to have the pre-eminence (3 John 9), and make every man willing to occupy the place for which God has designed him, and rejoice that his brethren may be exalted to higher posts of responsibility and honour.

11. *Not slothful.* The word rendered *slothful* refers to those who are slow, idle, destitute of promptness of mind and activity; comp. Mat. xxv. 16. ¶ *In business* (τῇ σπουδῇ). This is the same word which in ver. 8 is rendered *diligence.* It properly denotes *haste, intensity, ardour of mind;* and hence also it denotes *industry, labour.* The direction means that we should be diligently occupied in our proper employment. It does not refer to any *particular* occupation, but is used in a *general sense* to denote *all* the labour which we may have to do; or is a direction to be faithful and industrious in the discharge of all our appropriate duties; comp. Eccl. ix. 10. The tendency of the Christian religion is to promote *industry.* (1) It teaches the value of time. (2) Presents numerous and important things to be done. (3) It inclines men to be conscientious in the improvement of each moment. (4) And it takes away the mind from those pleasures and pursuits which generate and promote indolence. The Lord Jesus was constantly employed in filling up the great duties of his life, and the effect of his religion has been to promote industry wherever it has spread both among nations and individuals. An *idle man* and a *Christian* are names which do not harmonize. Every Christian has enough to do to occupy *all* his time; and he whose life is spent in ease and in doing nothing, should doubt altogether his religion. God has assigned us much to accomplish; and he will hold us answerable for the faithful performance of it; comp. John v. 17; ix. 4; 1 Thes. iv. 11; 2 Thes. iii. 10, 12. All that would be needful to transform the idle, and vicious, and wretched, into sober and useful men, would be to give to them the spirit of the Christian religion; see the example of Paul, Acts xx. 34, 35. ¶ *Fervent.* This word

is usually applied to water, or to metals so *heated* as to bubble, or boil. It hence is used to denote *ardour, intensity,* or, as we express it, a *glow*— meaning intense zeal, Acts xviii. 25. ¶ *In spirit.* In your mind or heart. The expression is used to denote a mind filled with intense ardour in whatever it is engaged. It is supposed that Christians would first find appropriate objects for their labour, and then engage in them with intense ardour and zeal. ¶ *Serving.* Regarding yourselves as the servants of the Lord. This direction is to be understood as connected with the preceding, and as growing out of it. They were to be diligent and fervid, and in *doing so* were to regard themselves as *serving* the Lord, or to do it in obedience to the command of God, and to promote his glory. The propriety of this caution may easily be seen. (1) The tendency of worldly employments is to take off the affections from God. (2) Men are prone to forget God when deeply engaged in their worldly employments. It is proper to recall their attention to him. (3) The right discharge of our duties in the various employments of life is to be regarded as serving God. He has arranged the order of things in this life to promote employment. He has made industry essential to happiness and success; and hence to be industrious from proper motives is to be regarded as acceptable service of God. (4) He has *required* that all such employments should be conducted with reference to his will and to his honour, 1 Cor. x. 31; Eph. vi. 5; Col. iii. 17, 22–24; 1 Pet. iv. 11. The meaning of the whole verse is, that Christians should be *industrious,* should be ardently engaged in some lawful employment, and that they should pursue it with reference to the will of God, in obedience to his commands, and to his glory.

12. *Rejoicing in hope.* That is, in the hope of eternal life and glory which the gospel produces; see Notes on chap. v. 2, 3. ¶ *Patient in tribulation.* In affliction patiently enduring all that may be appointed. Christians may be enabled to do this by the sustaining influence of their *hope* of future glory; of being admitted to that world where there shall be no more death, and where all tears shall be wiped away from their eyes, Rev. xxi. 4; vii. 17; comp. Jam. i. 4. See the influence of *hope* in sustaining us in affliction more fully considered in the Notes on chap. viii. 18–28. ¶ *Continuing instant in prayer.* That is, *be persevering* in prayer; see Col. iv. 2; see Notes, Luke xviii. 1. The meaning of this direction is, that in order to discharge aright the duties of the Christian life, and especially to maintain a joyful hope, and to be sustained in the midst of afflictions, it is necessary to cherish a spirit of prayer, and to live near to God. How *often* a Christian should pray, the Scriptures do not inform us. Of David we are told that he prayed seven times a day (Ps. cxix. 164); of Daniel, that he was accustomed to pray three times a day (Dan. vi. 10); of our Saviour we have repeated instances of his praying mentioned; and the same of the apostles. The following rules, perhaps, may guide us in this. (1) Every Christian should have some *time* allotted for this service, and some *place* where he may be alone with God. (2) It is not easy, perhaps not possible, to maintain a life of piety without *regular* habits of secret devotion. (3) *The morning,* when we have experienced God's protecting care, when the mind is fresh, and the thoughts are as yet clear and unoccupied with the world, when we go forth to the duties, trials, and temptations of the day; and *the evening,* when we have again experienced his goodness, and are about to commit ourselves to his protecting care, and when we need his pardoning mercy for the errors and follies of the day, seem to be times which commend themselves to all as appropriate seasons for private devotion. (4) Every person will also find other times when private prayer will be needful, and when he will be inclined to it. In affliction, in perplexity, in moments of despondency, in danger, and want, and disappointment, and in the loss of friends, we shall feel the propriety of drawing near to God, and of pouring out the heart before

13 Distributing[v] to the necessity of saints; [w]given to hospitality.

14 Bless[x] them which persecute you: bless, and curse not.

v Ps.41.1; He.13.16. *w* He.13.2; 1 Pe.4.9. *x* Mat.5.44.

him. (5) Besides this, every Christian is probably conscious of times when he feels *peculiarly inclined* to pray; *he feels just like praying;* he has a spirit of supplication; and nothing *but* prayer will meet the instinctive desires of his bosom. We are often conscious of an earnest desire to see and converse with an absent friend, to have communion with those we love; and we value such fellowship as among the happiest moments of life. So with the Christian. He may have an earnest desire to have communion with God; his heart pants for it, and he cannot resist the propensity to seek him, and pour out his desires before him. Compare the feelings expressed by David in Ps. xlii. 1, 2, "As the hart panteth after the water-brooks, so panteth my soul after thee, O God. My soul thirsteth for God, for the living God; when shall I come and appear before God?" comp. Ps. lxiii. 1. Such seasons should be improved; they are the "spring-times" of our piety; and we should expand every sail, that we may be "filled with all the fulness of God." They are happy, blessed moments of our life; and *then* devotion is sweetest and most pure; and then the soul knows what it is to have *fellowship* with the Father and with his Son Jesus Christ, 1 John i. 3. (6) In addition to all this, Christians may be in the habit of praying to God without the formality of retirement. God looks upon the heart; and the *heart* may pour forth its secret desires to Him even when in business, when conversing with a friend, when walking, when alone, and when in society. Thus the Christian may live a life of prayer; and it shall be one of the characteristics of his life that *he prays!* By this he shall be known; and in this he shall learn the way to possess peace in religion.

"In every joy that crowns my days,
  In every pain I bear,
My heart shall find delight in praise
  Or seek relief in prayer.

"When gladness wings my favour'd hour,
  Thy love my thoughts shall fill;
Resign'd when storms of sorrow lower,
  My soul shall meet thy will.

"My lifted eye, without a tear,
  The gathering storm shall see;
My steadfast heart shall know no fear,
  That heart shall rest on thee."

13. *Distributing.* The word used here denotes having things in *common* (κοινωνοῦντες). It means that they should be *communicative*, or should regard their property as so far *common* as to supply the wants of others. In the earliest times of the church, Christians had all things in common (Notes, Acts ii. 44), and felt themselves bound to meet all the wants of their brethren. One of the most striking effects of Christianity was to loosen their grasp on *property*, and dispose them to impart liberally to those who had need. The direction here does not mean that they should *literally* have all things *in common;* that is, to go back to a state of *savage barbarity;* but that they should be liberal, should *partake* of their good things with those who were needy; comp. Gal. vi. 6; Rom. xv. 27; Phil. iv. 15; 1 Tim. vi. 18. ¶ *To the necessity.* To the *wants.* That is, distribute to them such things as they *need* —food, raiment, &c. This command, of course, has reference to the *poor.* ¶ *Of saints.* Of Christians, or the friends of God. They are called *saints* as being holy (ἅγιοι), or consecrated to God. This duty of rendering aid to *Christians* especially, does not interfere with the general love of mankind. The law of the New Testament is (Gal. vi. 10), "As we have opportunity, let us do good to all men, especially to them who are of the household of faith." The Christian is indeed to love all mankind, and to do them good as far as may be in his power, Mat. v. 43, 44; Tit. iii. 8; 1 Tim. vi. 18; Heb. xiii. 16. But he is to show *particular* interest in the welfare of his brethren, and to see that the poor members of the church

are provided for; for, (1) They are our brethren; they are of the same family; they are attached to the same Lord; and to do good to them is to evince love to Christ, Mat. xxv. 40; Mark ix. 41. (2) They are left especially to the care of the church; and if the church neglects them, we may be sure the world will also, Mat. xxvi. 11. Christians, especially in the time of the apostles, had reason to expect little compassion from the men of the world. They were persecuted and oppressed; they would be embarrassed in their business, perhaps thrown out of occupation by the opposition of their enemies; and it was therefore peculiarly incumbent on their brethren to aid them. To a certain extent it is always true, that the world is reluctant to aid the friends of God; and hence the poor followers of Christ are in a peculiar manner thrown on the benefactions of the church. (3) It is not improbable that there might be a peculiar reason at that time for enjoining this on the attention of the Romans. It was a time of persecution, and perhaps of extensive distress. In the days of Claudius (about A.D. 50), there was a famine in Judea which produced great distress, and many of the poor and oppressed might flee to the capital for aid. We know, from other parts of the New Testament, that at that time the apostle was deeply interested in procuring aid for the poor brethren in Judea, Rom. xv. 25, 26; comp. Acts xix. 21; 2 Cor. viii. 1-7; ix. 2-4. But the same reasons for aiding the *poor* followers of Christ will exist substantially in every age; and one of the most precious *privileges* conferred on men is to be permitted to assist those who are the friends of God, Ps. xli. 1-3; Pr. xiv. 21. ¶ *Given to hospitality.* This expression means that they should *readily* and *cheerfully* entertain strangers. This is a duty which is frequently enjoined in the Scriptures, Heb. xiii. 2, "Be not forgetful to entertain strangers, for thereby many have entertained angels unawares;" 1 Pet. iv. 9, "Use hospitality one to another without grudging." Paul makes this especially the duty of a

Christian bishop, 1 Tim. iii. 2, "A bishop then must . . . be given to hospitality;" Tit. i. 8. Hospitality is especially enjoined by the Saviour, and its exercise commanded, Mat. x. 40, 42, "He that receiveth you receiveth me," &c. The *want* of hospitality is one of the charges which the Judge of mankind will allege against the wicked, and on which he will condemn them, Mat. xxv. 43, "I was a stranger, and ye took me not in." It is especially commended to us by the example of Abraham (Gen. xviii. 1-8), and of Lot (Gen. xix. 1, 2), who thus received angels unawares. It was one of the virtues on which *Job* particularly commended himself, and which he had not failed to practise, Job xxxi. 16, 17, "If I have withheld the poor from their desire, or have caused the eyes of the widow to fail; or *have eaten my morsel myself alone, and the fatherless hath not eaten thereof,*" &c. In the time of our Saviour it was evidently practised in the most open and frank manner, Luke x. 7, "And in the same house remain, eating and drinking such things as they give." A remarkable instance is also mentioned in Luke xi. 5. This virtue is no less common in Eastern nations at present than it was in the time of Christ. It is *eminently* the virtue of oriental nations, of their ardent and open temperament. It springs up naturally in countries thinly settled, where the sight of a stranger would be therefore peculiarly pleasant; in countries, too, where the occupation was chiefly to attend flocks, and where there was much leisure for conversation; and where the population was too sparse, and the travellers too infrequent, to justify *innkeeping* as *a business.* From all these causes, it has happened that there are, properly speaking, no *inns* or *taverns* in the regions around Palestine. It was customary, indeed, to erect places for lodging and shelter at suitable distances, or by the side of springs or watering places, for travellers to lodge in. But they are built at the public expense, and are unfurnished. Each traveller carries his own bed and clothes and cooking utensils, and such places are merely designed as a *shelter* for caravans (see Robinson's Calmet, art. "Caravanserai"). It is still so; and hence it becomes, in their view, a virtue of high order to entertain, at their own tables, and in their families, such *strangers* as may be travelling. Niebuhr says, that "the hospitality of the Arabs has always been the subject of praise; and I believe that those of the present day exercise this virtue no less than the ancients did. There are, in the villages of Tehama, houses which are public, where travellers may lodge and be entertained some days *gratis*, if they will be content with the fare; and they are much frequented. When the Arabs are at table, they invite those who happen to come to eat with them, whether they be Christians or Mahometans, gentle or simple."— "The primitive Christians," says Calmet, "considered one principal part of their duty to consist in showing hospitality to strangers. They were in fact so ready in discharging this duty, that the very heathen admired them for it. They were hospitable to all strangers, but especially to those who were of the household of faith. Believers scarcely ever travelled without letters of communion, which testified the purity of their faith, and procured for them a favourable reception wherever the name of Jesus Christ was known" (Calmet, *Dict.*). Calmet is also of opinion that the two minor epistles of John may be such letters of recommendation and communion; comp. 2 John 10. It may be added, that it would be particularly expected of Christians that they should show hospitality to the ministers of religion. They were commonly poor; they received no fixed salary; they travelled from place to place; and they would be dependent for support on the kindness of those who loved the Lord Jesus Christ. This was particularly intended by our Saviour's instructions on the subject, Mat. x. 11–13, 40–42. The duty of *hospitality* is still binding on Christians and all men. The law of Christ is not repealed. The customs of society are indeed changed; and one evidence of advancement in commerce and in security, is furnished in the fact that *inns* are now provided and patronized for the traveller in all Christian lands. Still this does not lessen the obligations to show hospitality. It is demanded by the very genius of the Christian religion; it evinces proper love towards mankind; it shows that there is a feeling of *brotherhood* and kindness towards others, when such hospitality is shown.

It unites society, creates new bonds of interest and affection, to show kindness to the stranger and to the poor. To what *extent* this is to be done, is one of those questions which are to be left to every man's conscience and views of duty. No *rule* can be given on the subject. Many men have not the means to be extensively hospitable; and many are not placed in situations that require it. No rules *could* be given that should be applicable to *all* cases; and hence the Bible has left the *general* direction, has furnished examples where it was exercised, has recommended it to mankind, and then has left every man to act on the rule, as he will answer it to God; see Mat. xxv. 34–46.

14. *Bless them*, &c. See Note, Mat. v. 44; comp. Luke vi. 28. ¶ *Bless, and curse not.* Bless only; or continue to bless, however long or aggravated may be the injury. Do not be provoked to anger, or to cursing, by any injury, persecution, or reviling. This is one of the most severe and difficult duties of the Christian religion; and it is a duty which nothing else *but* religion will enable men to perform. To *curse* denotes properly to *devote to destruction.* Where there is power to do it, it implies the destruction of the object. Thus the fig-tree that was cursed by the Saviour soon withered away, Mark xi. 21. Thus those whom *God* curses will be certainly destroyed, Mat. xxv. 41. Where there is not *power* to do it, *to curse* implies the invoking of the aid of God to devote to destruction. Hence it means to imprecate; to implore a curse from God to rest on others; to pray that God would destroy them. In a larger sense still, it means to abuse by reproachful words; to calumniate; or

15 Rejoice[y] with them that do rejoice, and weep with them that weep.

16 Be[z] of the same mind one

toward another. Mind[a] not high things, but [5]condescend to men of low estate. Be[b] not wise in your own conceits.

y 1 Co.12.26.   z 1 Pe.3.8.

a Je.45.5.   5 or, *be contented with mean things.*
              b Is.5.21.

to express one's self in a violent, profane, and outrageous manner. In this passage it seems to have especial reference to this.

15. *Rejoice with them*, &c. This command grows out of the doctrine stated in ver. 4, 5, that the church is *one;* that it has one interest; and therefore that there should be common sympathy in its joys and sorrows. Or, enter into the welfare of your fellow-Christians, and show your attachment to them by rejoicing that *they* are made happy; comp. 1 Cor. xii. 26, "And whether . . . one member be honoured, all the members rejoice with it." In this way happiness diffuses and multiplies itself. It becomes expanded over the face of the whole society; and the *union* of the Christian body tends to enlarge the sphere of happiness and to prolong the joy conferred by religion. God has bound the family of man together by these sympathies, and it is one of the happiest of all devices to perpetuate and extend human enjoyments. ¶ *Weep*, &c. See Note on John xi. 35. At the grave of Lazarus our Saviour evinced this in a most tender and affecting manner. The design of this direction is to produce mutual kindness and affection, and to divide our sorrows by the sympathies of friends. Nothing is so well fitted to do this as the sympathy of those we love. All who are afflicted know how much it diminishes their sorrow to see others sympathizing with them, and especially those who evince in their sympathies the Christian spirit. How sad would be a suffering world if there were none who regarded our griefs with interest or with tears! if every sufferer were left to bear his sorrows unpitied and alone! and if all the ties of human sympathy were rudely cut at once, and men were left to suffer in solitude and unbefriended! It may be added that it is the special duty of Christians to sympathize in each

other's griefs, (1) Because their Saviour set them the example; (2) Because they belong to the same family; (3) Because they are subject to similar trials and afflictions; and, (4) Because they cannot expect the sympathy of a cold and unfeeling world.

16. *Be of the same mind*, &c. This passage has been variously interpreted. "Enter into each other's circumstances in order to see how you would yourself feel" (Chrysostom). "Be agreed in your opinions and views" (Stuart). "Be united or agreed with each other" (Flatt). Comp. Phil. ii. 2; 2 Cor. xiii. 11. A literal translation of the Greek will give somewhat a different sense, but one evidently correct. "Think of, *i.e.* regard, or seek after the same thing for each other; *i.e.* what you regard or seek for *yourself*, seek also for your brethren. Do not have divided interests; do not be pursuing different ends and aims; do not indulge counter plans and purposes; and do not seek honours, offices, for yourself which you do not seek for your brethren, so that you may still regard yourselves as brethren on a level, and aim at the same object." The Syriac has well rendered the passage: "And what you think concerning yourselves, the same also think concerning your brethren; neither think with an elevated or ambitious mind, but accommodate yourselves to those who are of humbler condition;" comp. 1 Pet. iii. 8. ¶ *Mind not high things.* Greek, Not thinking of high things. That is, not seeking them, or aspiring after them. The connection shows that the apostle had in view those things which pertained to worldly offices and honours; wealth, and state, and grandeur. They were not to seek them for themselves; nor were they to court the society or the honours of the men in an elevated rank in life. Christians were commonly of the poorer ranks, and they were to seek their companions and joys

17 Recompense^c to no man evil for evil. Provide^d things

c Mat.5.39; 1 Pe.3.9.

honest in the sight of all men.

d 2 Co.8.21.

there, and not to aspire to the society of the great and the rich; comp. Jer. xlv. 5, "And seekest thou great things for thyself? Seek them not;" Luke xii. 15. ¶ *Condescend* (συναπαγομενοι). Literally, "*being led away by,* or *being conducted by.*" It does not properly mean to *condescend,* but denotes a *yielding,* or being guided and led in the thoughts, feelings, plans, by humble objects. Margin, "be *contented with mean things.*" ¶ *To men of low estate.* In the Greek the word here is an adjective (ταπεινοις), and may refer either to *men* or to *things,* either in the masculine or neuter gender. The sentiment is not materially changed whichever interpretation is adopted. It means that Christians should seek the objects of interest and companionship, not among the great, the rich, and the noble, but among the humble and the obscure. They should do it because their Master did it before them; because his friends are most commonly found among those in humble life; because Christianity prompts to benevolence rather than to a fondness for pride and display; and because of the influence on the mind produced by an attempt to imitate the great, to seek the society of the rich, and to mingle with the scenes of gaiety, folly, and ambition. ¶ *Be not wise,* &c. Comp. Isa. v. 21, "Woe unto them that are wise in their own eyes, and prudent in their own sight." See Note, chap. xi. 25. The meaning is, do not trust in the conceit of your own superior skill and understanding, and refuse to hearken to the counsel of others. ¶ *In your own conceits.* Greek, *among yourselves.* Syriac, "in your own opinion." The direction here accords with that just given, and means that they should not be elated with pride above their brethren; or be headstrong and self-confident. The tendency of religion is to produce a low estimate of our own importance and attainments.

17. *Recompense.* Render, give, or return; see Note, Mat. v. 39. This is probably one of the most difficult precepts of Christianity; but the law of Christ on the subject is unyielding. It is a solemn demand made on all his followers, and it *must* be obeyed. ¶ *Provide.* The word rendered *provide* means properly to *think* or *meditate beforehand.* Make it a matter of *previous thought,* of *settled plan,* of *design.* This direction would make it a matter of *principle* and fixed purpose to do that which is right; and not to leave it to the fluctuations of feeling, or to the influence of excitement. The same direction is given in 2 Cor. viii. 21. ¶ *Things honest.* Literally, things *beautiful,* or *comely.* The expression here does not refer to *property,* or to *provision* made for a family, &c. The connection requires us to understand it respecting *conduct,* and especially our conduct towards those who injure us. It requires us to evince a spirit and to manifest a deportment in such cases, that shall be *lovely* and *comely* in the view of others; such as all men will approve and admire. And the apostle wisely cautions us to *provide* for this, *i.e.* to think of it beforehand, to make it a matter of fixed principle and purpose, so that we shall not be overtaken and excited by passion. If left to the time when the offence shall be given, we may be excited and off our guard, and may therefore evince an improper temper. All persons who have ever been provoked by injury (and who has not been?) will see the profound wisdom of this caution to *discipline* and *guard* the temper by previous purpose, that we may not evince an improper spirit. ¶ *In the sight of all men.* Such as all must approve; such that no man can blame; and, therefore, such as shall do no discredit to religion. This expression is taken from Prov. iii. 4. The passage shows that men may be expected to approve a mild, kind, and patient temper in the reception of injuries; and facts show that this is the case. The Christian spirit is one that the world *must* approve, however little it is disposed to act on it.

18 If it be possible, as much as lieth in you, *e*live peaceably with all men.

e Ps.34.14; He.12.14.

19 Dearly beloved, *f*avenge not yourselves; but *rather* give place unto wrath; for it is written,

f Le.19.18.

---

18. *If it be possible.* If it can be done. This expression implies that it could not always be done. Still it should be an object of desire; and we should endeavour to obtain it. ¶ *As much as lieth in you.* This implies two things: (1) We are to do our utmost endeavours to preserve peace, and to appease the anger and malice of others. (2) We are not to *begin* or to *originate* a quarrel. So far as *we* are concerned, we are to seek peace. But then it does not always depend on us. Others may oppose and persecute us; they will hate religion, and may slander, revile, and otherwise injure us; or they may commence an assault on our persons or property. For *their* assaults we are not answerable; but we *are* answerable for our conduct towards them; and on no occasion are we to commence a warfare with them. It may not be *possible* to prevent their injuring and opposing us; but it is possible not to begin a contention with them; and *when they* have commenced a strife, to seek peace, and to evince a Christian spirit. This command doubtless extends to everything connected with strife; and means that we are not to *provoke* them to controversy, or to prolong it when it is commenced; see Ps. xxxiv. 14; Mat. v. 9, 39, 40, 41; Heb. xii. 14. If all Christians would follow this command, if they would never *provoke* to controversy, if they would injure no man by slander or by unfair dealing, if they would compel none to prosecute them in law by want of punctuality in payment of debts or honesty in business, if they would do nothing to irritate, or to prolong a controversy when it is commenced, it would put an end to no small part of the strife that exists in the world.

19. *Dearly beloved.* This expression of tenderness was peculiarly appropriate in an exhortation to peace. It reminded them of the affection and friendship which ought to subsist among them as brethren. ¶ *Avenge*

not yourselves. To *avenge* is to take satisfaction for an injury by inflicting punishment on the offender. To take such satisfaction for injuries done to society, is lawful and proper for a magistrate, chap. xiii. 4. And to take satisfaction for injuries done by sin to the universe, is the province of God. But the apostle here is addressing private individual Christians. And the command is, to avoid a spirit and purpose of revenge. But this command is not to be so understood that we may not seek for *justice* in a regular and proper way before civil tribunals. If our character is assaulted, if we are robbed and plundered, if we are oppressed contrary to the law of the land, religion does not require us to submit to such oppression and injury without seeking our rights in an orderly and regular manner. If it did, it would be to give a premium to iniquity, to countenance wickedness, and require a man, by becoming a Christian, to abandon his rights. Besides, the magistrate is appointed for the praise of those who do well, and to punish evil-doers, 1 Pet. ii. 14. Further, our Lord Jesus did not surrender his rights (John xviii. 23); and Paul demanded that he himself should be treated according to the rights and privileges of a Roman citizen, Acts xvi. 37. The command here *not to avenge ourselves* means, that we are not to take it out of the hands of God, or the hands of the law, and to inflict it ourselves. It is well known that where there are no laws, the business of vengeance is pursued by individuals in a barbarous and unrelenting manner. In a state of savage society, vengeance is *immediately* taken, if possible, or it is pursued for years, and the offended man is never satisfied until he has imbrued his hands in the blood of the offender. Such was eminently the case among the Indians of this country (America). But Christianity seeks the ascendency of the

Vengeance*g* is mine; I will repay, saith the Lord.

g De.32.35.

laws; and in cases which do not admit or require the interference of the laws, in private assaults and quarrels, it demands that we bear injury with patience, and commit our cause unto God; see Lev. xix. 18. ¶ *But* rather *give place unto wrath.* This expression has been interpreted in a great variety of ways. Its obvious design is to induce us not to attempt to avenge ourselves, but to leave it with God. To *give place,* then, is to leave it for God to come in and execute wrath or vengeance on the enemy. Do not execute wrath; leave it to God; commit all to him; leave yourself and your enemy in his hands, assured that he will vindicate you and punish him. ¶ *For it is written.* Deut. xxxii. 35. ¶ *Vengeance* is *mine.* That is, it belongs to me to inflict revenge. This expression implies that it is *improper* for men to interfere with that which properly belongs to God. When we are angry, and attempt to avenge ourselves, we should remember, therefore, that we are infringing on the prerogatives of the Almighty. ¶ *I will repay,* &c. This is said in substance, though not in so many words, in Deut. xxxii. 35, 36. Its design is to assure us that those who deserve to be punished, shall be; and that, therefore, the business of revenge may be safely left in the hands of God. Though *we* should not do it, yet if it ought to be done, it will be done. This assurance will sustain us, not in the *desire* that our enemy shall be punished, but in the belief that *God* will take the matter into his own hands; that he can administer it better than we can; and that if our enemy *ought* to be punished, he will be. *We,* therefore, should leave it all with God. That God will vindicate his people, is clearly and abundantly proved in 2 Thes. i. 6–10; Rev. vi. 9–11; Deut. xxxii. 40–43.

20. *Therefore, if thine enemy hunger,* &c. This verse is taken almost literally from Prov. xxv. 21, 22. Hunger and thirst here are put for want in general. If thine enemy is

20 Therefore, *h*if thine enemy hunger, feed him; if he thirst, give

h Pr.25.21,22; Mat.5.44.

needy in any way, do him good, and supply his wants. This is, in spirit, the same as the command of the Lord Jesus (Mat. v. 44), "Do good to them that hate you," &c. ¶ *In so doing.* It does not mean that we are to do this *for the sake* of heaping coals of fire on him, but that this *will be* the result. ¶ *Thou shalt heap,* &c. Coals of fire are doubtless emblematical of *pain.* But the idea here is not that in doing so we shall call down divine vengeance on the man; but the apostle is speaking of the natural effect or result of showing him kindness. Burning coals heaped on a man's head would be expressive of intense agony. So the apostle says that the *effect* of doing good to an enemy would be to produce pain. But the pain will result from shame, remorse of conscience, a conviction of the evil of his conduct, and an apprehension of divine displeasure that may lead to repentance. To do this, is not only perfectly right, but it is desirable. If a man can be brought to reflection and true repentance, it should be done. In regard to this passage we may remark, (1) That the way to promote *peace* is to do good even to enemies. (2) The way to bring a man to repentance is to do him good. On this principle God is acting continually. He does good to all, even to the rebellious; and he designs that his goodness should lead men to repentance, Rom. ii. 4. Men will resist wrath, anger, and power; but *goodness* they cannot resist; it finds its way to the heart; and the conscience does its work, and the sinner is overwhelmed at the remembrance of his crimes. (3) If men would act on the principles of the gospel, the world would soon be at peace. No man would suffer himself many times to be overwhelmed in this way with coals of fire. It is not human nature, bad as it is; and if Christians would meet all unkindness with kindness, all malice with benevolence, and all wrong with right, peace would soon pervade the

him drink: for in so doing thou shalt heap coals of fire on his head.

21 Be [i] not overcome of evil, but overcome evil with good.

i Pr.16.32.

community, and even opposition to the gospel might soon die away.

21. *Be not overcome of evil.* Be not *vanquished* or *subdued* by injury received from others. Do not suffer your temper to be excited; your Christian principles to be abandoned; your mild, amiable, kind, and benevolent temper to be ruffled by any opposition or injury which you may experience. Maintain your Christian principles amidst all opposition, and thus show the power of the gospel. They are overcome by evil who suffer their temper to be excited, who become enraged and revengeful, and who engage in contention with those who injure them, Prov. xvi. 22. ¶ *But overcome evil with good.* That is, subdue or vanquish evil by doing good to others. Show them the loveliness of a better spirit; the power of kindness and benevolence; the value of an amiable, Christian deportment. So doing, you may disarm them of their rage, and be the means of bringing them to better minds.

This is the noble and grand sentiment of the Christian religion. Nothing like this is to be found in the heathen classics; and nothing like it ever existed among pagan nations. Christianity alone has brought forth this lovely and mighty principle; and one design of it is to advance the welfare of man by promoting peace, harmony, and love. The idea of *overcoming evil with good* never occurred to men until the gospel was preached. It never has been acted on except under the influences of the gospel. On this principle God shows kindness; on this principle the Saviour came, and bled, and died; and on this principle all Christians should act in treating their enemies, and in bringing a world to the knowledge of the Lord Jesus. If Christians will show benevolence, if they will send forth proofs of love to the ends of the

CHAPTER XIII.

LET every soul be [a] subject unto the higher powers. For [b] there is no power but of

a 1 Pe.2.13.   b Da.2.21.

earth, the evils of the world will be overcome. Nor can the nations be converted until Christians act on this great and most important principle of their religion, *on the largest scale possible,* TO "OVERCOME EVIL WITH GOOD."

CHAPTER XIII.

1. *Let every soul.* Every person. In the seven first verses of this chapter, the apostle discusses the subject of the duty which Christians owe to civil government—a subject which is extremely important, and at the same time exceedingly difficult. There is no doubt that he had express reference to the peculiar situation of the Christians at Rome; but the subject was of so much importance that he gives it a *general* bearing, and states the great principles on which all Christians are to act. The circumstances which made this discussion proper and important were the following: (1) The Christian religion was designed to extend throughout the world. Yet it contemplated the rearing of a kingdom amid other kingdoms, an empire amid other empires. Christians professed supreme allegiance to the Lord Jesus Christ; he was their lawgiver, their sovereign, their judge. It became, therefore, a question of great importance and difficulty, *what kind* of allegiance they were to render to earthly magistrates. (2) The kingdoms of the world were then *pagan* kingdoms. The laws were made by pagans, and were adapted to the prevalence of heathenism. Those kingdoms had been generally founded in conquest, and blood, and oppression. Many of the monarchs were blood-stained warriors, were unprincipled men; and were polluted in their private, and oppressive in their public character. Whether Christians were to acknowledge the laws of such kingdoms and

of such men was a serious question, and one which could not but occur very early. It would occur also very soon in circumstances that would be very affecting and trying. Soon the hands of these magistrates were to be raised against Christians in the fiery scenes of persecution; and the duty and extent of submission to them became a matter of very serious inquiry. (3) Many of the early Christian churches were composed of Jewish converts. Yet the Jews had long been under Roman oppression, and had borne the foreign yoke with great uneasiness. The whole heathen magistracy they regarded as founded in a system of idolatry; as opposed to God and his kingdom; and as abomination in his sight. With these feelings they had become Christians; and it was natural that their former sentiments should exert an influence on them after their conversion. How far they should submit, if at all, to heathen magistrates, was a question of deep interest; and there was danger that the *Jewish* converts might prove to be disorderly and rebellious citizens of the empire. (4) Nor was the case much different with the *Gentile* converts. They would naturally look with abhorrence on the system of idolatry which they had just forsaken. They would regard all as opposed to God. They would denounce the *religion* of the pagans as abomination; and as that religion was interwoven with the civil institutions, there was danger also that they might denounce the government altogether, and be regarded as opposed to the laws of the land. (5) There *were* cases where it was right to *resist* the laws. This the Christian religion clearly taught; and in cases like these, it was indispensable for Christians to take a stand. When the laws interfered with the rights of conscience, when they commanded the worship of idols, or any moral wrong, then it was their duty to refuse submission. Yet in what cases this was to be done, where the line was to be drawn, was a question of deep importance, and one which was not easily settled. It is quite probable, however, that the main danger was, that the early Christians would err in *refusing* submission, even when it was proper, rather than in undue conformity to idolatrous rites and ceremonies. (6) In the *changes* which were to occur in human governments, it would be an inquiry of deep interest, what part Christians should take, and what submission they should yield to the various laws which might spring up among the nations. The *principles* on which Christians should act are settled in this chapter. ¶ *Be subject.* Submit. The word denotes that kind of submission which soldiers render to their officers. It implies *subordination;* a willingness to occupy our proper place, to yield to the authority of those over us. The word used here does not designate the *extent* of the submission, but merely enjoins it in general. The general principle will be seen to be, that we are to obey in all things which are not contrary to the law of God. ¶ *The higher powers.* The magistracy; the supreme government. It undoubtedly here refers to the Roman magistracy, and has relation not so much to the *rulers* as to the supreme *authority* which was established as the constitution of government; comp. Mat. x. 1; xxviii. 18. ¶ *For.* The apostle gives a *reason* why Christians should be subject; and that reason is, that magistrates have received their appointment from God. As Christians, therefore, are to be subject to God, so they are to honour *God* by honouring the arrangement which he has instituted for the government of mankind. Doubtless, he here intends also to repress the vain curiosity and agitation with which men are prone to inquire into the *titles* of their rulers; to guard them from the agitation and conflicts of party, and of contentions to establish a favourite on the throne. It might be that those in power had not a proper title to their office; that they had secured it, not according to justice, but by oppression; but into that question Christians were not to enter. The government was established, and they were not to seek to overturn it. ¶ *No power.* No office; no magistracy; no civil rule. ¶ *But of*

God: the powers that be are [1]ordained of God.

2 Whosoever therefore resisteth

[1] or, *ordered.*

the power, resisteth the ordinance of God: and they that resist shall receive to themselves damnation.

God. By God's permission, or appointment; by the arrangements of his providence, by which those in office had obtained their power. God often claims and asserts that *He* sets up one, and puts down another, Ps. lxxv. 7; Dan. ii. 21; iv. 17, 25, 34, 35. ¶ *The powers that be.* That is, all the civil magistracies that exist; those who have the *rule* over nations, by whatever means they may have obtained it. This is equally true at all times, that the powers that exist, exist by the permission and providence of God. ¶ *Are ordained of God.* This word *ordained* denotes the *ordering* or *arrangement* which subsists in a *military* company, or army. God sets them *in order*, assigns them their location, changes and directs them as he pleases. This does not mean that he *originates* or causes the evil dispositions of rulers, but that he *directs* and *controls* their appointment. By this we are not to infer, (1) That he approves their conduct; nor, (2) That what they do is always right; nor, (3) That it is our duty *always* to submit to them. Their requirements *may be* opposed to the law of God, and then we are to obey God rather than man, Acts iv. 19; v. 29. But it is meant that the power is intrusted to them by God; and that he has the authority to remove them when he pleases. If they abuse their power, however, they do it at their peril; and *when* so abused, the obligation to obey them cëases. That this is the case, is apparent further from the nature of the *question* which would be likely to arise among the early Christians. It *could not be* and *never was* a question, whether they should obey a magistrate when he commanded a thing that was plainly contrary to the law of God. But the question was, whether they should obey a heathen magistrate *at all.* This question the apostle answers in the affirmative, because *God* had made government necessary, and because it was arranged and ordered by

his providence. Probably also the apostle had another object in view. At the time in which he wrote this epistle, the Roman empire was agitated with civil dissensions. One emperor followed another in rapid succession. The throne was often seized, not by right, but by crime. Different claimants would rise, and their claims would excite controversy. The object of the apostle was to prevent Christians from entering into those disputes, and from taking an active part in a political controversy. Besides, the throne had been *usurped* by the reigning emperors, and there was a prevalent disposition to rebel against a tyrannical government. Claudius had been put to death by poison; Caligula in a violent manner; Nero was a tyrant; and amidst these agitations, and crimes, and revolutions, the apostle wished to guard Christians from taking an active part in political affairs.

2. *Whosoever therefore resisteth,* &c. That is, they who rise up against *government itself;* who seek anarchy and confusion; and who oppose the regular execution of the laws. It is implied, however, that those laws shall not be such as to violate the rights of conscience, or oppose the laws of God. ¶ *Resisteth the ordinance of God.* What God has ordained, or appointed. This means clearly that we are to regard *government* as instituted by God, and as agreeable to his will. *When* established, we are not to be agitated about the *titles* of the rulers; not to enter into angry contentions, or to refuse to submit to them, because we are apprehensive of a defect in their *title,* or because they may have obtained it by oppression. If the government is established, and if its decisions are not a manifest violation of the laws of God, we are to submit to them. ¶ *Shall receive to themselves damnation.* The word *damnation* we apply now exclusively to the punish-

3 For rulers are not a terror to good works, but to the evil. Wilt thou then not be afraid of the power? ^cdo that which is good, and thou shalt have praise of the same:

c 1 Pe.2.14.

ment of hell; to future torments. But this is not necessarily the meaning of the word which is here used (κρίμα). It often simply denotes *punishment*, Rom. iii. 8; 1 Cor. xi. 29; Gal. v. 10. In this place the word implies *guilt* or *criminality* in resisting the ordinance of God, and affirms that the man that does it shall be punished. Whether the apostle means that he shall be punished by *God*, or by the *magistrate*, is not quite clear. Probably the *latter*, however, is intended; comp. ver. 4. It is also true that such resistance shall be attended with the displeasure of God, and be punished by him.

3. *For rulers.* The apostle here speaks of rulers *in general.* It may not be *universally* true that they are not a terror to good works, for many of them have *persecuted* the good; but it is generally true that they who are virtuous have nothing to fear from the laws. It is *universally* true that the design of their appointment by God was, not to injure and oppress the good, but to detect and punish the evil. Magistrates, *as such*, are not a terror to good works. ¶ *Are not a terror*, &c. Are not appointed to *punish the good.* Their appointment is not to inspire terror in those who are virtuous and peaceable citizens; comp. 1 Tim. i. 9. ¶ *But to the evil.* Appointed to detect and punish evildoers, and therefore an object of terror to them. The design of the apostle here is evidently to reconcile Christians to submission to the government, from its *utility.* It is appointed to protect the good against the evil; to restrain oppression, injustice, and fraud; to bring offenders to justice, and thus promote the peace and harmony of the community. As it is designed to promote order and happi-

4 For he is the minister of God to thee for good. But if thou do that which is evil, be afraid: for he beareth not the sword in vain: for he is the minister of God, a revenger of God to exe-

ness, it should be submitted to; and so long as *this* object is pursued, government should receive the countenance and support of Christians. But if it departs from this principle, and becomes the protector of the evil and the oppressor of the good, the case is reversed, and the obligation to its support must cease. ¶ *Wilt thou not*, &c. If you do evil by resisting the laws, and in any other manner, will you not fear the power of the government? Fear is *one* of the means by which men are restrained from crime in a community. On many minds it operates with much more power than any other motive. And it is one which a magistrate must make use of to restrain men from evil. ¶ *Do that which is good.* Be a virtuous and peaceable citizen; abstain from crime, and yield obedience to all the just laws of the land. ¶ *And thou shalt have praise of the same.* Comp. 1 Pet. ii. 14, 15. You shall be unmolested and uninjured, and shall receive the commendation of being peaceable and upright citizens. The prospect of that protection, and even of that reputation, is not an unworthy motive to yield obedience to the laws. Every Christian should desire the reputation of being a man seeking the welfare of his country, and the just execution of the laws.

4. *The minister of God.* The *servant* of God; he is appointed by God to do his will, and to execute his purposes. ¶ *To thee.* For your benefit. ¶ *For good.* That is, to protect you in your rights; to vindicate your name, person, or property; and to guard your liberty, and secure to you the results of your industry. The magistrate is not appointed directly to *reward* men, but they *practically* furnish a reward by protecting and defending them, and securing to them the interests of justice. ¶ *If thou do*

cute wrath upon him that doeth evil.

5 Wherefore *ᵃye* must needs be

d Ec.8.2.

subject, not only for wrath, but also for conscience' sake.

6 For, for this cause pay ye

---

that, &c. That is, if any citizen should do evil. ¶ *Be afraid.* Fear the just vengeance of the laws. ¶ *For he beareth not the sword in vain.* The *sword* is an instrument of punishment, as well as an emblem of war. Princes were accustomed to wear a sword as an emblem of their authority; and the *sword* was often used for the purpose of *beheading,* or otherwise punishing the guilty. The meaning of the apostle is, that he does not wear this badge of authority as an unmeaning show, but that it will be used to execute the laws. As this is the design of the power intrusted to him, and as he will *exercise* his authority, men should be influenced *by fear* to keep the law, even if there were no better motive. ¶ *A revenger,* &c. In chap. xii. 19, vengeance is said to belong to God. Yet he *executes* his vengeance by means of subordinate agents. It belongs to him to take vengeance by direct judgments, by the plague, famine, sickness, or earthquakes; by the appointment of magistrates; or by letting loose the passions of men to prey upon each other. When a magistrate inflicts punishment on the guilty, it is to be regarded as the act of God taking vengeance *by him;* and on this principle only is it right for a judge to condemn a man to death. It is not because one man has by nature any right over the life of another, or because *society* has any right collectively which it has not as individuals; but because *God* gave life, and because he has chosen to take it away, when crime is committed, by the appointment of magistrates, and not by coming forth himself visibly to execute the laws. Where *human* laws fail, however, he often takes vengeance into his own hands, and by the plague, or some signal judgments, sweeps the guilty into eternity. ¶ *To* execute *wrath.* For an explanation of the word *wrath,* see Notes on chap. i. 18.

It denotes here *punishment,* or the just execution of the laws. It may be remarked that this verse is an *incidental* proof of the propriety of capital punishment. The *sword* was undoubtedly an instrument for this purpose, and the apostle mentions its use without any remark of *disapprobation.* He enjoins subjection to those who *wear the sword,* that is, to those who execute the laws *by that;* and evidently intends to speak of the magistrate *with the sword,* or in inflicting capital punishment, as having received the appointment of God. The tendency of society now is *not* to too sanguinary laws. It is rather to forget that God has doomed the murderer to death; and though humanity should be consulted in the execution of the laws, yet there is no humanity in suffering the murderer to live to infest society, and endanger many lives in the place of his own, which was forfeited to justice. Far better that one murderer should die, than that he should be suffered to live to imbrue his hands, perhaps, in the blood of many who are innocent. But the authority of God has settled this question (Gen. ix. 5, 6), and it is neither right nor safe for a community to disregard his solemn decisions; see Blackstone's *Commentaries,* vol. iv. p. 8, [9.]

5. *Wherefore* (διο). The *reasons* why we should be subject, which the apostle had given, were two, (1) That government was appointed by God. (2) That violation of the laws would necessarily expose to punishment. ¶ Ye *must needs be.* It is *necessary* (ἀνάγκη) to be. This is a word stronger than that which implies mere *fitness* or propriety. It means that it is a matter of high obligation or *necessity* to be subject to the civil ruler. ¶ *Not only for wrath.* Not only on account of the *fear of punishment,* or the fact that wrath will be executed on evil-doers. ¶ *For conscience' sake.* As a matter of conscience, or of *duty*

tribute also: for they are God's ministers, attending continually upon this very thing.

7 Render[e] therefore to all their

e Mat. 22. 21.

dues; tribute to whom tribute *is due;* custom to whom custom; fear to whom fear; honour to whom honour.

---

to God, because *he* has appointed it, and made it necessary and proper. A good citizen yields obedience because it is the will of God; and a Christian makes it a part of his religion to maintain and obey the just laws of the land; see Mat. xxii. 21; comp. Eccl. viii. 2, "I counsel thee to keep the king's commandment, and *that in regard of the oath of God."*

6. *For this cause.* Because they are appointed by God; for the sake of conscience, and in order to secure the execution of the laws. As they are appointed by God, the tribute which is needful for their support becomes an act of homage to God, an act performed in obedience to his will, and acceptable to him. ¶ *Tribute also.* Not only be subject (ver. 5), but pay what may be necessary to support the government. *Tribute* properly denotes the *tax,* or annual compensation, which was paid by one province or nation to a superior, as the price of protection, or as an acknowledgment of subjection. The Romans made all conquered provinces pay this *tribute;* and it would become a question whether it was *right* to acknowledge this claim, and submit to it. Especially would this question be agitated by the Jews and by Jewish Christians. But on the principle which the apostle had laid down (ver. 1, 2), it was right to do it, and was demanded by the very purposes of government. In a larger sense the word *tribute* means any tax paid on land or personal estate for the support of the government. ¶ *For they are God's ministers.* His servants; or they are appointed by him. As the government is *his* appointment, we should contribute to its support as a matter of conscience, because we thus do honour to the arrangement of God. It may be observed here, also, that the fact that civil rulers are the ministers of God, invests their character with great sacredness, and should impress

upon *them* the duty of seeking to do his will, as well as on others the duty of submitting to them. ¶ *Attending continually.* As they attend to this, and devote their time and talents to it, it is proper that they should receive a suitable support. It becomes then a duty for the people to contribute cheerfully to the necessary expenses of the government. If those taxes should be unjust and oppressive, yet, like other evils, they are to be submitted to, until a remedy can be found in a proper way.

7. *Render therefore,* &c. This injunction is often repeated in the Bible; see Notes on Mat. xxii. 21; see also Mat. xvii. 25–27; 1 Pet. ii. 13–17; Prov. xxiv. 21. It is one of the most lovely and obvious of the duties of religion. Christianity is not designed to break in upon the proper order of society, but rather to establish and confirm that order. It does not rudely assail existing institutions; but it comes to put them on a proper footing, to diffuse a mild and pure influence over all, and to secure *such* an influence in all the relations of life as shall tend best to promote the happiness of man and the welfare of the community. ¶ Is due. To whom it properly belongs by the law of the land, and according to the ordinance of God. It is represented here as a matter of *debt,* as something which is *due* to the ruler; a fair *compensation* to him for the service which he renders us by devoting his time and talents to advance *our* interests, and the welfare of the community. As taxes are a *debt,* a matter of strict and just obligation, they should be paid as conscientiously and as cheerfully as any other just debts, however contracted. ¶ *Custom* (τέλος). The word rendered *tribute* means, as has been remarked, the tax which is paid by a *tributary* prince or dependent people; also the tax imposed on land or real estate. The word here translated *custom* means properly the

revenue which is collected on *merchandise*, either imported or exported. ¶ *Fear*. See ver. 4. We should stand in awe of those who wear the sword, and who are appointed to execute the laws of the land. As the execution of their office is fitted to excite *fear*, we should render to them that reverence which is appropriate to the execution of their office. It means a solicitous anxiety lest we do anything to offend them. ¶ *Honour*. The difference between this and *fear* is, that this rather denotes *reverence*, *veneration*, *respect* for their names, offices, rank, &c. The former is the *fear* which arises from the dread of punishment. Religion gives to men all their just titles, recognizes their rank and office, and seeks to promote due subordination in a community. It was no part of the work of our Saviour, or of his apostles, to quarrel with the mere *titles* of men, or to withhold from them the customary tribute of respect and homage; comp. Acts xxiv. 3; xxvi. 25; Luke i. 3; 1 Pet. ii. 17. In this verse there is summed up the duty which is owed to magistrates. It consists in rendering to them proper honour; contributing cheerfully and conscientiously to the necessary expenses of the government; and in yielding obedience to the laws. These are made a part of the duty which we owe to God, and should be considered as enjoined by our religion.

On the subject discussed in these seven verses, the following *principles* seem to be settled by the authority of the Bible, and are now understood: (1) That government is essential; and its necessity is recognized by God, and it is arranged by his providence. God has never been the patron of anarchy and disorder. (2) Civil rulers are dependent on God. He has the entire control over them, and can set them up or put them down when he pleases. (3) The authority of God is superior to that of civil rulers. They have no right to make enactments which interfere with *his* authority. (4) It is not the business of civil rulers to regulate or control religion. That is a distinct department, with which they have no concern, except to pro-

tect it. (5) The rights of all men are to be preserved. Men are to be allowed to worship God according to the dictates of their own conscience, and to be protected in those rights, provided they do not violate the peace and order of the community. (6) Civil rulers have no right to persecute Christians, or to attempt to secure conformity to their views by force. The conscience cannot be compelled; and in the affairs of religion man must be free.

In view of this subject we may remark, (1) That the doctrines respecting the rights of civil rulers, and the line which is to be drawn between their powers and the rights of conscience, have been slow to be understood. The struggle has been long; and a thousand persecutions have shown the anxiety of the magistrate to rule the conscience, and to control religion. In pagan countries it has been conceded that the civil ruler had a right to control the *religion* of the people: church and state there have been one. The same thing was attempted under Christianity. The magistrate still claimed this right, and attempted to enforce it. Christianity resisted the claim, and asserted the independent and original rights of conscience. A conflict ensued, of course, and the magistrate resorted to persecutions, to *subdue* by force the claims of the new religion and the rights of conscience. Hence the ten fiery and bloody persecutions of the primitive church. The blood of the early Christians flowed like water; thousands and tens of thousands went to the stake, until Christianity triumphed, and the right of religion to a free exercise was acknowledged throughout the empire. (2) It is matter of devout thanksgiving that the subject is now settled, and the principle is now understood. In our own land (America) there exists the happy and bright illustration of the true principle on this great subject. The rights of conscience are regarded, and the laws peacefully obeyed. The civil ruler understands his province; and Christians yield a cheerful and cordial obedience to the laws. The church and state move on in their

8 Owe no man anything, but to love one another: for *f*he that loveth another hath fulfilled the law.

f Ja.2.8.

9 For this, *g* Thou shalt not commit adultery, Thou shalt not kill, Thou shalt not steal, Thou shalt not bear false witness,

g Ex.20.13,&c.

own spheres, united only in the purpose to make men happy and good; and divided only as they relate to different departments, and contemplate, the one, the rights of civil society, the other, the interests of eternity. Here, every man worships God according to his own views of duty; and at the same time, here is rendered the most cordial and peaceful obedience to the laws of the land. Thanks should be rendered without ceasing to the God of our fathers for the wondrous train of events by which this contest has been conducted to its issue; and for the clear and full understanding which we now have of the different departments pertaining to the church and the state.

8. *Owe no man any thing.* Be not *in debt* to anyone. In the previous verse the apostle had been discoursing of the duty which we owe to magistrates. He had particularly enjoined on Christians to pay to *them* their just dues. From this command to discharge fully this obligation, the transition was natural to the subject of debts *in general*, and to an injunction not to be indebted to *anyone*. This law is enjoined in this place, (1) Because it is a part of our duty as good citizens; and, (2) Because it is a part of that law which teaches us to love our neighbour, and to *do no injury to him*, ver. 10. The interpretation of this command is to be taken with this limitation, that we are not to be indebted to him so as to *injure* him, or to work *ill* to him.

This rule, together with the other rules of Christianity, would propose a remedy for all the evils of bad debts in the following manner. (1) It would teach men to be *industrious*, and this would commonly prevent the *necessity* of contracting debts. (2) It would make them *frugal, economical*, and *humble*, in their views and manner of life. (3) It would teach them to bring up their families in habits of industry. The Bible often enjoins that; see Note, chap. xii. 11; comp. Phil. iv. 8; Prov. xxiv. 30–34; 1 Thes. iv. 11; 2 Thes. iii. 10; Eph. iv. 25. (4) Religion would produce sober, chastened views of the end of life, of the great design of living; and would take off the affections from the splendour, gaiety, and extravagances which lead often to the contraction of debts, 1 Thes. v. 6, 8; 1 Pet. i. 13; iv. 7; Tit. ii. 12; 1 Pet. iii. 3, 5; 1 Tim. ii. 9. (5) Religion would put a period to the *vices* and unlawful desires which now prompt men to contract debts. (6) It would make them *honest* in paying them. It would make them conscientious, prompt, friends of truth, and disposed to keep their promises.

¶ *But to love one another.* Love is a debt which *can* never be discharged. We should feel that we *owe* this to all men, and though by acts of kindness we may be constantly discharging it, yet we should feel that it can *never* be fully met while there is opportunity to do good. ¶ *For he that loveth*, &c. In what way this is done is stated in ver. 10. The law in relation to our neighbour is there said to be simply that we do no *ill* to him. Love to him would prompt to no injury. It would seek to do him good, and would thus fulfil all the purposes of justice and truth which we owe to him. In order to illustrate this, the apostle, in the next verse, runs over the laws of the ten commandments in relation to our neighbour, and shows that all those laws proceed on the principle that we are to *love* him, and that love would prompt to them all.

9. *For this. This* which follows is the sum of the laws. *This* is to regulate us in our conduct towards our neighbour. The word *this* here stands opposed to "*that*" in ver. 11. *This* law of love would prompt us to seek

Thou shalt not covet ; and if *there be* any other commandment, it is briefly comprehended in this saying, namely, [h] Thou shalt love thy neighbour as thyself.

10 Love worketh no ill to his neighbour : therefore love *is* the fulfilling of the law.

h Le.19.18; Mat.22.39,40.

---

our neighbour's good; *that* fact, that our salvation is near, would prompt us to be active and faithful in the discharge of all the duties we owe to him. ¶ *Thou shalt not commit adultery.* All the commands which follow are designed as an illustration of the duty of loving our neighbour; see these commands considered in the Notes on Mat. xix. 18, 19. The apostle has not enumerated *all* the commands of the second table. He has shown generally what they required. The command to honour our parents he has omitted. The reason might have been that it was not so immediately to his purpose when discoursing of love to a *neighbour* —a word which does not immediately suggest the idea of near relatives. The expression, "Thou shalt not bear false witness," is rejected by the best critics as of doubtful authority, but it does not materially affect the spirit of the passage. It is wanting in many MSS. and in the Syriac version. ¶ *If* there be *any other commandment.* The law respecting parents; or if there be any duty which does not seem to be *specified* by these laws, it is implied in the command to love our neighbour as ourselves. ¶ *It is briefly comprehended.* Greek, it may be reduced to *this head;* or it is summed up in this. ¶ *In this saying.* This word, or command. ¶ *Thou shalt love,* &c. This is found in Lev. xix. 18. See it considered in the Notes on Mat. xix. 19. If this command were fulfilled, it would prevent all fraud, injustice, oppression, falsehood, adultery, murder, theft, and covetousness. It is the same as our Saviour's golden rule. And if every man would do to others as he would wish them to do to him, all the design of the law would be at once fulfilled.

10. *Love worketh no ill,* &c. Love would seek to do him good; of course it would prevent all dishonesty and crime towards others. It would prompt to justice, truth, and benevolence. If this law were engraven on every man's heart, and practised in his life, what a change would it immediately produce in society ! If all men would at once *abandon* that which is fitted to *work ill* to others, what an influence would it have on the business and commercial affairs of men ! How many plans of fraud and dishonesty would it at once arrest ! How many schemes would it crush ! It would silence the voice of the slanderer ; it would stay the plans of the seducer and the adulterer; it would put an end to cheating, and fraud, and all schemes of dishonest gain. The gambler desires the property of his neighbour without any compensation, and thus works *ill* to him. The dealer in *lotteries* desires property for which he has never toiled, and which must be obtained at the expense and loss of others. And there are many *employments* all whose tendency is to work *ill* to a neighbour. This is pre-eminently true of the traffic in *ardent spirits.* It cannot do him good, and the almost uniform result is to deprive him of his property, health, reputation, peace, and domestic comfort. He that sells his neighbour liquid fire, knowing what *must* be the result of it, is not pursuing a business which works no *ill* to him; and love to that neighbour would prompt him to abandon the traffic; see Hab. ii. 15, "Woe unto him that giveth his neighbour drink, that puttest thy bottle to him, and makest him drunken also, that thou mayest look on their nakedness." ¶ *Therefore,* &c. *Because* love does no harm to another, it is *therefore* the fulfilling of the law—implying that all that the law requires is to *love* others. ¶ *Is the fulfilling.* Is the *completion,* or meets the requirements of the law. The law of God on this *head,* or in regard to our duty to our neighbour, requires us to do justice towards him, to observe truth, &c. *All* this will be

11 And that, knowing the time, that now *it is* high time

i 1 Th.5.5–8.

to awake out of sleep; for now *is* our salvation nearer than when we believed.

---

met by *love;* and if men truly *loved* others, all the demands of the law would be satisfied. ¶ *Of the law.* Of the law of Moses, but particularly the ten commandments.

11. *And that.* The word "that," in this place, is connected in signification with the word "this" in ver. 9. The meaning may be thus expressed: All the requirements of the law towards our neighbour may be met by two things: one is (ver. 9, 10), by love; the other is (ver. 11–14), by remembering that we are near to eternity; keeping a deep sense of *this* truth before the mind. *This* will prompt to a life of honesty, truth, and peace, and contentment, ver. 13. The doctrine in these verses (11–14), therefore, is, *that a deep conviction of the nearness of eternity will prompt to an upright life in the intercourse of man with man.* ¶ *Knowing the time.* Taking a proper *estimate* of the time. Taking just views of the shortness and the value of time; of the design for which it was given, and of the fact that it is, in regard to us, rapidly coming to a close. And still further considering, that the time in which you live is the time of the gospel, a period of light and truth, when you are particularly called on to lead holy lives, and thus to do justly to all. The *previous* time had been a period of ignorance and darkness, when oppression, and falsehood, and sin abounded. This, the time of the *gospel,* when God had *made known* to men his will that they should be pure. ¶ *High time.* Greek, "*the hour.*" ¶ *To awake,* &c. This is a beautiful figure. The dawn of day, the approaching light of the morning, is the time to arouse from slumber. In the darkness of night, men sleep. So says the apostle. The world has been sunk in the *night* of heathenism and sin. At that time it was to be expected that they would sleep the sleep of spiritual death. But now the morning light of the gospel dawns. The Sun of righteousness has arisen. It is

time, therefore, for men to cast off the deeds of darkness, and rise to life, and purity, and action; comp. Acts xvii. 30, 31. The same idea is beautifully presented in 1 Thes. v. 5–8. The meaning is, "Hitherto we have walked in darkness and in sin. Now we walk in the light of the gospel. We know our duty. We are sure that the God of light is around us, and is a witness of all we do. We are going soon to meet him, and it becomes us to rouse, and to do those deeds, and those only, which will bear the bright shining of the light of truth, and the scrutiny of him who is 'light, and in whom is no darkness at all,'" 1 John i. 5. ¶ *Sleep.* Inactivity; insensibility to the doctrines and duties of religion. Men, by nature, are active only in deeds of wickedness. In regard to religion they are insensible, and the slumbers of night are on their eyelids. Sleep is "the kinsman of death," and it is the emblem of the insensibility and stupidity of sinners. The deeper the ignorance and sin, the greater is this insensibility to spiritual things, and to the duties which we owe to God and man. ¶ *For now* is *our salvation.* The word *salvation* has been here variously interpreted. Some suppose that by it the apostle refers to the personal reign of Christ on the earth (Tholuck, and the Germans generally). Others suppose it refers to deliverance from *persecutions.* Others, to increased *light* and knowledge of the gospel, so that they could more clearly discern their duty than when they became believers (Rosenmüller). It probably, however, has its usual meaning here, denoting that deliverance from sin and danger which awaits Christians in heaven; and is thus equivalent to the expression, "You are advancing nearer to heaven. You are hastening to the world of glory. Daily we are approaching the kingdom of light; and, in prospect of that state, we ought to lay aside every sin, and live more and more in preparation for a world of

12 The night is far spent, the day is at hand: *let us therefore cast off the works of darkness, and let us *put on the armour of light.

k Ep.5.11.   l Ep.6.13,&c.

13 Let *m* us walk ²honestly, as in the day; *n*not in rioting and drunkenness, *o*not in chambering

m Phi.4.8; 1 Pe.2.12.   2 or, *decently*.
n 1 Pe.4.3.   o 1 Co.6.9,10.

---

light and glory." ¶ *Than when we believed.* Than when we *began* to believe. Every day brings us nearer to a world of perfect light.

12. *The night.* The word *night*, in the New Testament, is used to denote *night* literally (Mat. ii. 14, &c.); the starry heavens (Rev. viii. 12); and then it denotes a state of *ignorance* and *crime*, and is synonymous with the word darkness, as such deeds are committed commonly in the night, 1 Thes. v. 5. In this place it seems to denote our present imperfect and obscure condition in this world, as contrasted with the pure light of heaven. The *night*, the time of comparative obscurity and sin in which we live even under the gospel, is far gone in relation to us, and the pure splendours of heaven are at hand. ¶ *Is far spent.* Literally, "is cut off." It is becoming *short;* it is hastening to a close. ¶ *The day.* The full splendours and glory of redemption in heaven. Heaven is often thus represented as a place of pure and splendid day, Rev. xxi. 23, 25; xxii. 5. The times of the *gospel* are represented as times of *light* (Isa. lx. 1, 2, 19, 20, &c.); but the reference here seems to be rather to the still brighter glory and splendour of heaven, as the place of pure, unclouded, and eternal day. ¶ *Is at hand.* Is near; or is drawing near. This is true respecting all Christians. The day is near, or the time when they shall be admitted to heaven is not remote. This is the uniform representation of the New Testament, Heb. x. 25; 1 Pet. iv. 7; Jam. v. 8; Rev. xii. 20; 1 Thes. v. 2–6; Phil. iv. 5. That the apostle did not mean, however, that the end of the world was near, or that the day of judgment would come soon, is clear from his own explanations; see 1 Thes. v. 2–6; comp. 2 Thes. ii. ¶ *Let us therefore.* As we are about to enter on the glories of that eternal day, we

should be pure and holy. The *expectation* of it will teach us to *seek* purity; and a pure life alone will fit us to enter there, Heb. xii. 14. ¶ *Cast off.* Lay aside, or put away. ¶ *The works of darkness.* Dark, wicked deeds, such as are specified in the next verse. They are called *works of darkness*, because darkness in the Scriptures is an emblem of crime, as well as of ignorance, and because such deeds are commonly committed in the night, 1 Thes. v. 7, "They that be drunken, are drunken *in the night;*" comp. John iii. 20; Eph. v. 11–13. ¶ *Let us put on.* Let us clothe ourselves with. ¶ *The armour of light.* The word *armour* (ὅπλα) properly means *arms*, or instruments of war, including the helmet, sword, shield, &c., Eph. vi. 11–17. It is used in the New Testament to denote the *aids* which the Christian has, or the *means of defence* in his warfare, where he is represented as a soldier contending with his foes, and includes truth, righteousness, faith, hope, &c., as the instruments by which he is to gain his victories. In 2 Cor. vi. 7, it is called "the armour of righteousness on the right hand and on the left." It is called armour of *light*, because it is not to accomplish any deeds of darkness or of crime; it is appropriate to one who is pure, and who is seeking a pure and noble object. Christians are represented as the *children of light*, 1 Thes. v. 5; Note, Luke xvi. 8. By the armour of light, therefore, the apostle means those graces which stand opposed to the deeds of darkness (ver. 13); those graces of faith, hope, humility, &c., which shall be appropriate to those who are the children of the day, and which shall be their defence in their struggles with their spiritual foes. See the description in full in Eph. vii. 11–17.

13. *Let us walk.* To *walk* is an expression denoting *to live;* let us *live*, or *conduct*, &c. ¶ *Honestly.* The

and wantonness, not in strife and envying.

14 But[p] put ye on the Lord Jesus

p Ga.3.27.

Christ, and [q]make not provision for the flesh, to *fulfil* the lusts *thereof.*

q Ga.5.16.

word here used means rather in a *decent* or *becoming* manner; in a manner *appropriate* to those who are the children of light. ¶ *As in the day.* As if all our actions were seen and known. Men by day, or in open light, live decently; their foul and wicked deeds are done in the night. The apostle exhorts Christians to live as if all their conduct were seen, and they had nothing which they wished to conceal. ¶ *In rioting.* Revelling; denoting the licentious conduct, the noisy and obstreperous mirth, the scenes of disorder and sensuality, which attend luxurious living. ¶ *Drunkenness.* Rioting and drunkenness constitute the *first* class of sins from which he would keep them. It is scarcely necessary to add that these were common crimes among the heathen. ¶ *In chambering.* "Lewd, immodest behaviour" (Webster). The Greek word includes illicit indulgences of all kinds, adultery, &c. The words chambering and wantonness constitute the *second* class of crimes from which the apostle exhorts Christians to abstain. That these were common crimes among the heathen, it is not necessary to say; see Notes to Rom. i.; also Eph. v. 12. It is not possible, nor would it be proper, to describe the scenes of licentious indulgence of which all pagans are guilty. As Christians were to be a peculiar people, therefore,[i] the apostle enjoins on them purity and holiness of life. ¶ *Not in strife.* Strife and envying are the *third* class of sins from which the apostle exhorts them. The word *strife* means *contention, disputes, litigations.* The exhortation is, that they should live in peace. ¶ *Envying.* Greek, zeal. It denotes any intense, vehement, *fervid* passion. It is not improperly rendered here by envying. These vices are properly introduced in connection with the others. They usually accompany each other. Quarrels and contentions come out of scenes of drunkenness and de-

bauchery. But for such scenes, there would be little contention, and the world would be comparatively at peace. 14. *But put yet on.* Comp. Gal. iii. 17. The word rendered "put ye on" is the same used in ver. 12, and is commonly employed in reference to *clothing* or *apparel.* The phrase *to put on* a person, which seems a harsh expression in our language, was one not unfrequently used by Greek writers, and means to imbibe his principles, to imitate his example, to copy his spirit, to become like him. Thus in Dionysius Halicarnassus the expression occurs, "having *put on* or clothed themselves with Tarquin;" *i.e.* they imitated the example and morals of Tarquin. So Lucian says, "having *put on* Pythagoras;" having received him as a teacher and guide. So the Greek writers speak of putting on Plato, Socrates, &c., meaning to take them as instructors, to follow them as disciples. (See Schleusner.) Thus to put on the Lord Jesus means to take him as a pattern and guide, to imitate his example, to obey his precepts, to become like him, &c. In *all* respects the Lord Jesus was unlike what had been specified in the previous verse. He was temperate, chaste, pure, peaceable, and meek; and to *put him on* was to imitate him in these respects, Heb. iv. 15; vii. 26; 1 Pet. ii. 22; Isa. liii. 9; 1 John iii. 5. ¶ *And make not provision.* The word *provision* here is that which is used to denote *provident care,* or preparation for future wants. It means that we should not make it an object to gratify our lusts, or study to do this by laying up anything beforehand with reference to this design. ¶ *For the flesh.* The word *flesh* is used here evidently to denote the corrupt propensities of the body, or those which he had specified in ver. 13. ¶ *To* fulfil *the lusts* thereof. With reference to its corrupt desires. The gratification of the flesh was the main object among the

CHAPTER XIV.

H IM that is weak in the faith receive ye, *but* [1] not to doubt-ful disputations.

1 *or, not to judge* his *doubtful thoughts.*

Romans. Living in luxury and licentiousness, they made it their great object of study to multiply and prolong the means of licentious indulgence. In respect to this, Christians were to be a separate people, and to show that they were influenced by a higher and purer desire than this grovelling propensity to minister to sensual gratification. It is right, it is a Christian duty, to labour to make provision for all the *real* wants of life. But the real wants are few; and with a heart disposed to be pure and temperate, the necessary wants of life are easily satisfied; and the mind may be devoted to higher and purer purposes.

CHAPTER XIV.

The fourteenth chapter is designed to settle some difficult and delicate questions that could not but arise between the Jews and Gentiles respecting food and the observance of particular days, rites, &c. The *occasions* of these questions were these: The converts to Christianity were from both Jews and Gentiles. There were many Jews in Rome; and it is probable that no small part of the church was composed of them. The New Testament everywhere shows that they were disposed to bind the Gentile converts to their own customs, and to insist on the observance of the peculiar laws of Moses; see Acts xv. 1, 2, &c.; Gal. ii. 3, 4. The *subjects* on which questions of this kind would be agitated were, circumcision, days of fasting, the distinction of meats, &c. A part of these only are discussed in this chapter. The views of the apostle in regard to *circumcision* had been stated in chap. iii. and iv. In *this* chapter he notices the disputes which would be likely to arise on the following subjects: (1) The use of *meat*, evidently referring to the question whether it was lawful to eat the meat that was offered in sacrifice to idols, ver. 2. (2) The distinctions and observances of the days of Jewish

2 For one believeth that he may eat all things: another, who is weak, eateth herbs.

3 Let not him that eateth de-

fastings, &c., ver. 5, 6. (3) The laws observed by the Jews in relation to animals as *clean* or *unclean*, ver. 14. It is probable that these are mere *specimens* adduced by the apostle to settle *principles* of conduct in regard to the Gentiles, and to show to each party how they ought to act in *all* such questions.

The apostle's design here is to allay all these contentions by producing peace, kindness, charity. This he does by the following considerations, viz. (1) That we have no right to *judge* another man in this case, for he is the servant of God, ver. 3, 4. (2) That whatever course is taken in these questions, it is done conscientiously, and with a desire to glorify God. In such a case there should be kindness and charity, ver. 6, &c. (3) That we must stand at the judgment-seat of Christ, and give an account *there;* and that *we*, therefore, should not usurp the office of judging, ver. 10–13. (4) That there is really nothing unclean of itself, ver. 14. (5) That religion consisted in more important matters than *such* questions, ver. 17, 18. (6) That we should follow after the things of peace, &c., ver. 19–23. The principles of this chapter are applicable to all *similar* cases of difference of opinion about rites and ceremonies, and unessential doctrines of religion; and we shall see that, if they were honestly applied, they would settle no small part of the controversies in the religious world.

1. *Him that is weak.* The design here is to induce Christians to receive to their fellowship those who had scruples about the propriety of certain things, or that might have peculiar prejudices and feelings as the result of education or former habits of belief. The apostle, therefore, begins by admitting that such an one may be *weak, i.e.* not fully established, or not with so clear and enlarged views about Christian liberty as others might have. ¶ *In the faith.* In believing. This

does not refer to *saving faith* in Christ, for he might have that; but to belief in regard *to the things which the apostle specifies*, or which would come into controversy. Young converts have often a peculiar delicacy or sensitiveness about the lawfulness of many things in relation to which older Christians may be more fully established. To produce peace, there must be kindness, tenderness, and faithful teaching; not denunciation, or harshness, on one side or the other. ¶ *Receive ye.* Admit to your society or fellowship; receive him kindly, not meet with a cold and harsh repulse; comp. chap. xv. 7. ¶ *Not to doubtful disputations.* The plain meaning of this is, "Do not admit him to your society for the purpose of debating the matter in an angry and harsh manner; of repelling him by denunciation; and thus, *by the natural reaction of such a course*, confirming him in his doubts." Or, "do not deal with him in such a manner as shall have a tendency to increase his scruples about meats, days, &c." (Stuart). The *leading* idea here — which all Christians should remember—is, that a harsh and angry denunciation of a man in relation to things not morally wrong, but where he may have honest scruples, will only tend to confirm him more and more in his doubts. To denounce and abuse him will be to confirm him. To receive him affectionately, to admit him to fellowship with us, to talk freely and kindly with him, to do him good, will have a far greater tendency to overcome his scruples. In questions which now occur about modes of *dress*, about *measures* and means of promoting revivals, and about rites and ceremonies, this is by far the wisest course, if we wish to overcome the scruples of a brother, and to induce him to think as we do.—Greek, "unto doubts or fluctuations of opinions or reasonings." Various senses have been given to the words, but the above probably expresses the true meaning.

2. *For one believeth.* This was the case with the Gentiles in general, who had none of the scruples of the Jew about the propriety of eating certain kinds of meat. Many of the converts who had been Jews might also have had the same view as the apostle Paul evidently had, while the great mass of Jewish converts might have cherished these scruples. ¶ *May eat all things.* That is, he will not be restrained by any scruples about the lawfulness of certain meats, &c. ¶ *Another who is weak.* There is reference here, doubtless, to the Jewish convert. The apostle admits that he was *weak*, *i.e.* not fully established in the views of Christian liberty. The question with the Jew doubtless was, whether it was lawful to eat the meat which was offered in sacrifice to idols. In those sacrifices a part only of the animal was offered, and the remainder was eaten by the worshippers, or offered for sale in the market like other meat. It became an inquiry whether it was lawful to eat this meat; and the question in the mind of a Jew would arise from the express command of his law, Ex. xxxiv. 15. This question the apostle discussed and settled in 1 Cor. x. 20–32, which see. In that place the general principle is laid down, that it was lawful to partake of that meat as a man would of any other, *unless it was expressly pointed out to him as having been sacrificed to idols, and unless his partaking of it would be considered as countenancing the idolaters in their worship*, ver. 28. But with this principle many Jewish converts might not have been acquainted; or what is quite as probable, they might not have been disposed to admit its propriety. ¶ *Eateth herbs.* Herbs or *vegetables* only; does not partake of meat at all, for *fear* of eating that, inadvertently, which had been offered to idols. The Romans abounded in sacrifices to idols; and it would not be easy to be certain that meat which was offered in the market, or on the table of a friend, had *not* been offered in this manner. To avoid the possibility of partaking of it, even *ignorantly*, they chose to eat no meat at all. The scruples of the Jews on the subject might have arisen in part from the fact that sins of *ignorance* among them subjected them to certain penalties, Lev. iv. 2, 3, &c.; v. 15; Num. xv. 24, 27–29. Josephus says (*Life*, § 3) that in his time there were certain

spise him that eateth not; and let not him which eateth not judge him that eateth: for God hath received him.

4 Who[a] art thou that judgest another man's servant? to his own master he standeth or fall-

a Ja.4.12.

priests of his acquaintance who "supported themselves with figs and nuts." These priests had been sent to Rome to be tried on some charge before Cæsar; and it is probable that they abstained from meat because it might have been offered to idols. It is expressly declared of Daniel when in Babylon, that he lived on pulse and water, that he might not "defile himself with the portion of the king's meat, nor with the wine which he drank," Dan. i. 8–16.

3. *Let not him that eateth.* That is, he who has no scruples about eating *meat*, &c., who is not restrained by the law of the Jews respecting the clean and unclean, or by the fact that meat *may* have been offered to idols. ¶ *Despise him.* Hold him in contempt, as being unnecessarily scrupulous, &c. The word *despise* here is happily chosen. The Gentiles would be very likely to *despise* the Jew as being restrained by foolish scruples and mere distinctions in matters of no importance. ¶ *Him that eateth not.* Him that is restrained by scruples of conscience, and that will eat only *vegetables,* ver. 2. The reference here is doubtless to the *Jew.* ¶ *Judge him.* To *judge* here has the force of *condemn.* This word also is very happily chosen. The Jew would not be so likely to *despise* the Gentile for what he did as to *judge* or condemn him. He would deem it too serious a matter for contempt. He would regard it as a violation of the law of God, and would be likely to assume the right of *judging* his brother, and pronouncing him guilty. The apostle here has happily met the whole case in all disputes about rites, and dress, and scruples in religious matters that are not essential. One party commonly *despises* the other as being needlessly and foolishly scrupulous; and the other makes it a matter of *conscience,* too serious for ridicule and contempt, and a matter to neglect which is, in

their view, deserving of condemnation. The true direction to be given in such a case is, *to the one party,* not to treat the scruples of the other with derision and contempt, but with tenderness and indulgence. Let him have his way in it. If he can be *reasoned* out of it, it is well; but to attempt to *laugh* him out of it is unkind, and will tend only to confirm him in his views. And *to the other party,* it should be said they have no *right* to judge or condemn another. If I cannot see that the Bible requires a particular cut to my coat, or makes it my duty to observe a particular festival, he has no right to judge me harshly, or to suppose that I am to be rejected and condemned for it. He has a right to *his* opinion; and, while I do not *despise* him, he has no right to *judge* me. This is the foundation of true charity; and if this simple rule had been followed, how much strife, and even bloodshed, would it have spared in the church! Most of the contentions among Christians have been on subjects of this nature. Agreeing substantially in the *doctrines* of the Bible, they have been split up into sects on subjects just about as important as those which the apostle discusses in this chapter. ¶ *For God hath received him.* This is the same word that is translated "receive" in ver. 1. It means here that God hath received him kindly; or has acknowledged him as his own friend; or he is a true Christian. These scruples, on the one side or the other, are not inconsistent with true piety; and as *God* has acknowledged him as *his,* notwithstanding his opinions on these subjects, so *we* also ought to recognize him as a Christian brother. Other denominations, though they may differ from us on some subjects, may give evidence that they are recognized by God as his; and where there is this evidence, we should neither despise nor judge them.

4. *Who art thou,* &c. That is, who

eth. Yea, he shall be holden up: for *b* God is able to make him stand.

5 One *c* man esteemeth one day

b Is.40.29.   *c* Col.2.16.

above another: another esteemeth every day *alike*. Let every man be fully ² persuaded in his own mind.

² or, *assured*.

---

gave you this right to sit in judgment on others? comp. Luke xii. 14. There is reference here particularly to the *Jew*, who, on account of his ancient privileges, and because he had the law of God, would assume the prerogative of *judging* in the case, and insist on conformity to his own views; see Acts xv. The doctrine of this epistle is uniformly, that the Jew had no such privilege, but that in regard to salvation he was on the same level with the Gentile. ¶ *That judgest*, &c. Comp. Jam. iv. 12. This is a principle of common sense and common propriety. It is not ours to sit in judgment on the servant of another man. He has the control over him; and if *he* chooses to forbid his doing anything, or to allow him to do anything, it pertains to *his* affairs not ours. To attempt to control him, is to intermeddle improperly, and to become a " busybody in other men's matters," 1 Pet. iv. 15. Thus Christians are the servants of God; they are answerable to him; and *we* have no right to usurp *his* place, and to act as if we were "lords over his heritage," 1 Pet. v. 3. ¶ *To his own master*. The servant is responsible to his master only. So it is with the Christian in regard to God. ¶ *He standeth or falleth*. He shall be approved or condemned. If his conduct is such as pleases his master, he shall be approved; if not, he will be condemned. ¶ *Yea, he shall be holden up*. This is spoken of the Christian only. In relation to the servant, he might stand or fall; he might be approved or condemned. The master had no power to keep him in a way of obedience, except by the hope of reward, or the fear of punishment. But it was not so in regard to the Christian. The Jew who was disposed to *condemn* the Gentile might say, that he admitted the general principle which the apostle had stated about the servant; that it was just what he was saying, that

he might *fall*, and be condemned. But no, says the apostle, this does not follow in relation to the Christian. He shall not fall. God has power to make him stand; to hold him; to keep him from error, and from condemnation, and *he shall be holden up*. He shall not be suffered to fall into condemnation, for it is the *purpose* of God to keep him; comp. Ps. i. 5. This is one of the incidental but striking evidences that the apostle believed that all Christians should be kept by the power of God through faith unto salvation. ¶ *Is able*. See John x. 29. Though a master cannot exert such an influence over a servant as to *secure* his obedience, yet *God* has this power over his people, and will preserve them in a path of obedience.

5. *One man esteemeth*. Gr., *judgeth* (κρίνει). The word is here properly translated *esteemeth;* comp. Acts xiii. 46; xvi. 15. The word originally has the idea of *separating*, and then *discerning*, in the act of judging. The expression means that one would set a higher value on one day than on another, or would regard it as more sacred than others. This was the case with the *Jews* uniformly, who regarded the days of their festivals, and fasts, and Sabbaths as peculiarly sacred, and who would retain, to no inconsiderable degree, their former views, even after they became converted to Christianity. ¶ *Another esteemeth*. That is, the *Gentile* Christian. Not having been brought up amidst the Jewish customs, and not having imbibed their opinions and prejudices, they would not regard these days as having any special sacredness. The appointment of those days had a special reference *to the Jews*. They were designed to keep them as a separate people, and to prepare the nation for the *reality*, of which their rites were but the shadow. When the Messiah came, the passover,

the feast of tabernacles, and the other peculiar festivals of the Jews, of course vanished, and it is perfectly clear that the apostles never intended to inculcate their observance on the Gentile converts. See this subject discussed in the second chapter of the Epistle to the Galatians. ¶ *Every day alike.* The word "alike" is not in the original, and it may convey an idea which the apostle did not design. The passage means that he regards *every day* as consecrated to the Lord, ver. 6. The question has been agitated whether the apostle intends in this to include the Christian Sabbath. Does he mean to say that it is a matter of *indifference* whether this day be observed, or whether it be devoted to ordinary business or amusements? This is a very important question in regard to the Lord's day. That the apostle did *not* mean to say that it was a matter of indifference whether it should be kept as holy, or devoted to business or amusement, is plain from the following considerations. (1) The discussion had reference only to the peculiar customs of the *Jews*, to the rites and practices which *they* would attempt to impose on the Gentiles, and not to any questions which might arise among Christians *as Christians*. The inquiry pertained to *meats*, and festival observances among the Jews, and to their scruples about partaking of the food offered to idols, &c.; and there is no more propriety in supposing that the subject of the Lord's day is introduced here than that he advances principles respecting *baptism* and *the Lord's supper.* (2) The *Lord's day* was doubtless observed by *all* Christians, whether converted from Jews or Gentiles; see 1 Cor. xvi. 2; Acts xx. 7; Rev. i. 10; comp. Notes on John xx. 26. The propriety of observing *that day* does not appear to have been a matter of controversy. The only inquiry was, whether it was proper to *add* to that the observance of the Jewish Sabbaths, and days of festivals and fasts. (3) It is expressly said that those who did not regard the day regarded it as not to God, or to honour God, ver. 6. They did it as a matter of respect to him and his institutions, to promote his glory, and to advance his kingdom. Was this ever done by those who disregard the Christian Sabbath? Is their design ever to promote his honour, and to advance in the knowledge of him, by *neglecting* his holy day? Who knows not that the Christian Sabbath has *never* been neglected or profaned by any design to glorify the Lord Jesus, or to promote his kingdom? It is for purposes of business, gain, war, amusement, dissipation, visiting, crime. Let the heart be filled with a sincere desire to *honour the Lord Jesus,* and the Christian Sabbath will be reverenced, and devoted to the purposes of piety. And if any man is disposed to plead *this passage* as an excuse for violating the Sabbath, and devoting it to pleasure or gain, let him quote it *just as it is, i.e.* let *him neglect the Sabbath from a conscientious desire to honour Jesus Christ.* Unless *this* is his motive, the passage cannot avail him. But this motive never yet influenced a Sabbath-breaker. ¶ *Let every man,* &c. That is, subjects of this kind are not to be pressed as matters of conscience. Every man is to examine them for himself, and act accordingly. This direction pertains to the subject under discussion, and not to any other. It does not refer to subjects that were *morally* wrong, but to ceremonial observances. If the *Jew* esteemed it wrong to eat meat, he was to abstain from it; if the Gentile esteemed it right, he was to act accordingly. The word "*be fully persuaded*" denotes the highest conviction, not a matter of opinion or prejudice, but a matter on which the mind is made up by examination; see Rom. iv. 21; 2 Tim. iv. 5. This is the general principle on which Christians are called to act in relation to festival days and fasts in the church. If some Christians deem them to be for edification, and suppose that their piety will be promoted by observing the days which commemorate the birth, and death, and temptations of the Lord Jesus, they are not to be reproached or opposed in their celebration. Nor are they to attempt to im-

6 He that ³regardeth the day, regardeth *it* unto the Lord; and he that regardeth not the day, to the Lord he doth not regard *it*. He that eateth, eateth to the Lord; for

³ or, *observeth.*

he giveth God thanks: and he that eateth not, to the Lord he eateth not; and giveth God thanks.

7 For *d* none of us liveth to himself, and no man dieth to himself.

d 1 Pe.4.2.

---

pose them on others as a matter of conscience, or to reproach others because they do not observe them. 6. *He that regardeth.* Greek, *thinketh of;* or pays attention to; that is, he that *observes* it as a festival, or as holy time. ¶ *The day.* Any of the days under discussion; the days that the Jews kept as religious occasions. ¶ *Regardeth* it *unto the Lord.* Regards it as *holy,* or as set apart to the service of God. He believes that he is *required* by God to keep it, *i.e.* that the laws of Moses in regard to such days are binding on him. ¶ *He that regardeth not the day.* Or who does not observe such distinctions of days as are demanded in the laws of Moses. ¶ *To the Lord,* &c. That is, he does not believe that God *requires* such an observance. ¶ *He that eateth.* The Gentile Christian, who freely eats all kinds of meat, ver. 2. ¶ *Eateth to the Lord.* Because he believes that God does not forbid it; and because he desires, in doing it, to glorify God, 1 Cor. x. 31. *To eat to the Lord,* in this case, is to do it believing that such is his will. In all other cases, it is to do it feeling that we receive our food from him; rendering thanks for his goodness, and desirous of being strengthened that we may do his commands. ¶ *He giveth God thanks.* This is an incidental proof that it is our duty to give God thanks at our meals for our food. It shows that it was the *practice* of the early Christians, and has the commendation of the apostle. It was also uniformly done by the Jews, and by the Lord Jesus, Mat. xiv. 19; xxvi. 26; Mark vi. 41; xiv. 22; Luke ix. 16; xxiv. 30. ¶ *To the Lord he eateth not.* He abstains from eating because he believes that God requires him to do it, and with a desire to obey and honour him. ¶ *And giveth God thanks.*

That is, the Jew thanked God for the law, and for the favour he had bestowed on him in giving him more light than he had the Gentiles. For this privilege they valued themselves highly, and this feeling, no doubt, the converted Jews would continue to retain, deeming themselves as specially favoured in having a *peculiar* acquaintance with the law of God. 7. *For none of us,* &c. Whether by nature Jews or Gentiles. In the great principles of religion we are now united. Where there was evidence of a sincere desire to do the will of God there should be charitable feeling, though there was difference of opinion and judgment in many smaller matters. The meaning of the expression is, that no Christian lives to gratify his own inclinations or appetites. He makes it his great aim to do the will of God; to subordinate all his desires to his law and gospel; and though, therefore, one should eat flesh, and should feel at liberty to devote to common employments time that another deemed sacred, yet it should not be uncharitably set down as a desire to indulge his sensual appetites, or to become rich. Another motive *may be* supposed, and where there is not positive *proof* to the contrary, *should be* supposed; see the beautiful illustration of this in 1 Cor. xiii. 4–8. To live *to ourselves* is to make it the great object to become rich or honoured, or to indulge in the ease comfort, and pleasures of life. These are the aim of all men but Christians; and in nothing else do Christians more differ from the world than in this; see 1 Pet. iv. 1, 2; 2 Cor. v. 15; 1 Cor. vi. 19, 20; Mat. x. 38; xvi. 24; Mark viii. 34; x. 21; Luke ix. 23. On no point does it become Christians more to examine themselves than on this. To *live to ourselves* is an evidence that we are

8 For whether we live, we live unto the Lord: and whether we die, we die unto the Lord; whether we live therefore, or die, we are the Lord's.

9 For*e* to this end Christ both

e Phi.2.9-11.

strangers to piety. And if it be the great motive of our lives to live at ease (Amos vi. 1)—to gratify the flesh, to gain property, or to be distinguished in places of fashion and amusement—it is evidence that we know nothing of the power of that gospel which teaches us *to deny ourselves, and take up our cross daily.* ¶ *No man.* No one—the same Greek word (οὐδεὶς) which is used in the former part of the verse. The word is used only in reference to *Christians* here, and makes no affirmation about other men. ¶ *Dieth to himself.* See ver. 8. This expression is used to denote the *universality* or the *totality* with which Christians belong to God. Everything is done and suffered with reference to his will. In our conduct, in our property, in our trials, in our death, we are *his;* to be disposed of as he shall please. In the grave, and in the future world, we shall be equally his. As this is the great principle on which *all* Christians live and act, we should be kind and tender towards them, though in some respects they differ from us.

8. *For whether we live.* As long as we live. ¶ *We live unto the Lord.* We live to do his will, and to promote his glory. This is the grand purpose of the life of the Christian. Other men live to gratify themselves; the Christian to do those things which the Lord requires. By *the Lord* here the apostle evidently intends the Lord Jesus, as it is evident from ver. 9; and the truth taught here is, that it is the leading and grand purpose of the Christian to do honour to the Saviour. It is this which constitutes his peculiar character, and which distinguishes him from other men. ¶ *Whether we die.* In the dying state, or in the state of the dead; in the future world. We are *nowhere* our own. In all conditions we are *his,* and bound to do his will. The connection of this declaration with the argument is this:—Since we belong to another in every state, and are bound to do his will, we have no right to assume the prerogative of sitting in judgment on another. We are subjects, and are bound to do the will of Christ. All other Christians are subjects in like manner, and are answerable, not to us, but directly to the Lord Jesus, and should have the same liberty of conscience that we have. The passage proves also that the soul does not cease to be conscious at death. We are still the Lord's; his even when the body is in the grave; and his in all the future world; see ver. 9.

9. *For to this end.* For this purpose or design. The apostle does not say that this was the *only* design of his death, but that it was a main purpose, or an object which he had distinctly in view. This declaration is introduced in order to confirm what he had said in the previous verse, that in all circumstances we are the Lord's. This he shows by the fact that Jesus died *in order* that we *might* be his. ¶ *And rose.* This expression is rejected by most modern critics. It is wanting in many manuscripts, and has been probably introduced in the text from the margin. ¶ *And revived.* There is also a variation in the Greek in this place, but not so great as to change the sense materially. It refers to his *resurrection,* and means that he was *restored to life* in order that he might exercise dominion over the dead and the living. ¶ *That he might be Lord.* Greek, that he might *rule over.* The Greek word used here implies the idea of his being *proprietor* or *owner* as well as *ruler.* It means, that he might exercise entire dominion over all, as the sovereign Lawgiver and Lord. ¶ *Both of the dead.* That is, of those who *are* deceased, or who have gone to another state of existence. This passage proves that those who die are not annihilated; that they do not cease to be conscious; and that they still are under the dominion of the Mediator.

died, and rose, and revived, that he might be Lord both of the dead and living.

Though their bodies moulder in the grave, yet the spirit lives, and is under his control. And though the body dies and returns to its native dust, yet the Lord Jesus is still its Sovereign, and shall raise it up again.

"God our Redeemer lives,
And often from the skies
Looks down and watches all our dust,
Till he shall bid it rise."

It gives an additional sacredness to the grave when we reflect that the tomb is under the watchful care of the Redeemer. Safe in his hands, the body may sink to its native dust with the assurance that in his own time he will again call it forth, with renovated and immortal powers, to be for ever subject to his will. With this view we can leave our friends with confidence in his hands when they die, and yield our own bodies cheerfully to the dust when he shall call our spirits hence. But it is not only over the *body* that his dominion is established. This passage proves that the departed souls of the saints are still subject to him; comp. Mat. xxii. 32; Mark xii. 27. He not only has *dominion* over those spirits, but he is their protector and Lord. They are safe under his universal dominion. And it does much to alleviate the pains of separation from pious, beloved friends, to reflect that they depart still to love and serve the same Saviour in perfect purity, and unvexed by infirmity and sin. Why should we wish to recall them from his perfect love in the heavens to the poor and imperfect service which they would render if in the land of the living? ¶ *And living.* To the redeemed, while they remain in this life. He died to *purchase* them to himself, that they might become his obedient subjects; and they are bound to yield obedience by all the sacredness and value of the price which he paid, even his own precious blood; comp. 1 Cor. vi. 20, "For ye are bought with a price; therefore glorify God in your body, and in your spirit, which are God's;" vii. 23; Rev. xiv.

10 But why dost thou judge thy brother? or why dost thou set at nought thy brother? for

4 (Greek, *bought*); 1 Pet. ii. 9 (Greek, *purchased*). If it be asked how this *dominion over the dead and the living* is connected with the death and resurrection of the Lord Jesus, we may reply, (1) That it is secured over Christians from the fact that they are *purchased* or *ransomed* by his precious blood; and that they are bound by this sacred consideration to live to him. This obligation every Christian feels (1 Pet. i. 18), and its force is continually resting on him. It was by the love of Christ that he was ever brought to love God at all; and his deepest and tenderest obligations to live to him arise from this source, 2 Cor. v. 14, 15. (2) Jesus, by his death and resurrection, established a dominion over the grave. He destroyed him that had the power of death (Heb. ii. 14), and triumphed over him, Col. ii. 15. Satan is a humbled foe; and his sceptre over the grave is wrested from his hands. When Jesus rose, in spite of all the power of Satan and of men, he burst the bands of death, and made an invasion on the dominions of the dead, and showed that he had power to control all. (3) This dominion of the Lord Jesus is felt by the spirits on high. They are subject to him *because* he redeemed them, Rev. v. 9. (4) It is often revealed in the Scriptures that *dominion* was to be given to the Lord Jesus as the reward of his sufferings and death; see Note to John xvii. 2, 4, 5; v. 26–29; Phil. ii. 5–11; Eph. i. 20, 21; Heb. ii. 9, 10; xii. 2. The *extent* of his dominion as mediator is affirmed, in this place, only to be over the dead and the living; that is, over the human race. Other passages of the Scripture, however, seem to imply that it extends over all worlds.

10. *But why*, &c. Since we are all subjects and servants alike, and must all stand at the same tribunal, what right have we to sit in judgment on others? ¶ *Thou judge.* Thou who

we shall all stand before the judgment-seat of Christ.

11 For it is written, *f As* I live,

f Is. 45. 23.

saith the Lord, every knee shall bow to me, and every tongue shall confess to God.

12 So then every one of us

---

art a *Jewish* convert, why dost thou attempt to arraign the *Gentile* disciple, as if he had violated a law of God? comp. ver. 3. ¶ *Thy brother.* God has recognized him as his friend (ver. 3), and he should be regarded by thee as *a brother* in the same family. ¶ *Or why dost thou set at nought.* Despise, ver. 3. Why dost thou, who art a *Gentile* convert, despise the *Jewish* disciple as being unnecessarily scrupulous and superstitious? ¶ *Thy brother.* The Jewish convert is now a brother; and all the contempt which you Gentiles once cherished for the Jew should cease, from the fact that *he* is now *a Christian.* Nothing will do so much, on the one hand, to prevent a censorious disposition, and on the other, to prevent contempt for those who are in a different rank in life, as to remember that they are *Christians,* bought with the same blood, and going to the same heaven as ourselves. ¶ *We must all stand,* &c. That is, we must all be tried alike at the same tribunal; we must answer for our conduct, not to our fellow-men, but to Christ; and it does not become us to sit in judgment on each other.

11. *For it is written.* This passage is recorded in Isa. xlv. 23. It is not quoted literally, but the sense is preserved. In Isaiah there can be no doubt that it refers to Jehovah. The speaker expressly calls himself Jehovah, the name which is appropriate to God alone, and which is never applied to a creature, ver. 18, 21, 24, 25. In the place before us, the words are applied by Paul expressly to Christ; comp. ver. 10. This mode of quotation is a strong incidental proof that the apostle regarded the Lord Jesus as divine. On no other principle could he have made these quotations. ¶ *As I live.* The Hebrew is, "I have sworn by myself." One expression is equivalent to the other. An *oath* of God is often expressed by the phrase "as I live," Num. xiv. 21; Isa. xlix. 18;

Ezek. v. 11; xiv. 16, &c. ¶ *Saith the Lord.* These words are not in the Hebrew text, but are added by the apostle to show that the passage quoted was spoken by the Lord, the Messiah; comp. Isa. xlv. 18, 22. ¶ *Every knee shall bow to me.* To *bow the knee* is an act expressing homage, submission, or adoration. It means that every person shall acknowledge him as God, and admit his right to universal dominion. The passage in Isaiah refers particularly to the homage which *his own people* should render to him; or rather it means that all who are saved shall acknowledge *him* as their God and Saviour. The original reference was not to *all men,* but only to those who should be saved, Isa. xlv. 17, 21, 22, 24. In this sense the apostle uses it; not as denoting that *all men* should confess to God, but that all *Christians,* whether Jewish or Gentile converts, should alike give account to Him. *They* should all bow before their common God, and acknowledge *his* dominion over them. The passage originally did not refer particularly to the day of judgment, but expressed the truth that all believers should acknowledge his dominion. It is as applicable, however, to the judgment, as to any other act of homage which his people will render. ¶ *Every tongue shall confess to God.* In the Hebrew, "Every tongue shall swear." Not swear *by God,* but to *him;* that is, pay to him our vows, or *answer to him on oath* for our conduct; and this is the same as *confessing* to him, or acknowledging him as our Judge.

12. *So then.* Wherefore; or according to the doctrine of the Old Testament. ¶ *Every one of us.* That is, every Christian; for the connection requires us to understand the argument only of Christians. At the same time it is a truth abundantly revealed elsewhere, that *all men* shall give account of their conduct to God, 2 Cor. v. 10; Mat. xxv.; Eccl. xii. 14. ¶ *Give*

shall give account of himself to
God.

13 Let us not therefore judge
one another any more: but judge

this rather, that no man put a
stumbling-block or an occasion to
fall in *his* brother's way.

14 I know, and am persuaded

---

account of himself. That is, of his
character and conduct; his words and
actions; his plans and purposes. In
the fearful arraignment of that day
every work and purpose shall be
brought forth, and tried by the unerring standard of justice. As we shall
be called to so fearful an account with
God, we should not be engaged in condemning our brethren, but should examine whether we are prepared to give
up our account with joy, and not with
grief. ¶ *To God.* The judgment will
be conducted by the Lord Jesus, Mat.
xxv. 31–46; Acts xvii. 31. All judgment is committed to the Son, John
v. 22, 27. Still we may be said to
give account to God, (1) Because He
appointed the Messiah to be the Judge
(Acts xvii. 31); and, (2) Because the
Judge himself is divine. The Lord
Jesus being God as well as man, the
account will be rendered directly to
the Creator as well as the Redeemer
of the world. In this passage there are
two incidental proofs of the divinity
of the Lord Jesus Christ. *First,* the
fact that the apostle applies to him
language which in the prophecy is
expressly spoken by *Jehovah;* and,
secondly, the fact that Jesus is
declared to be the Judge of all. No
being that is not *omniscient* can be
qualified to judge the secrets of all
men. None who has not *seen* human
purposes at all times, and in all places;
who has not been a witness of the conduct by day and by night; who has
not been present with all the race at
all times, and who in the great day
cannot discern the true character of
the soul, can be qualified to conduct
the general judgment. Yet none can
possess these qualifications but God.
The Lord Jesus, "the judge of quick
and dead" (2 Tim. iv. 1), is therefore
divine.

13. *Let us not therefore judge,* &c.
Since we are to give account of ourselves at the same tribunal, since we
must be there on the same *level,* let us

not suppose that we have a right here
to sit in judgment on our fellow-Christians. ¶ *But judge this rather.* If disposed to *judge,* let us be employed in
a better kind of judging; let us come
to a determination not to injure the
cause of Christ. This is an instance
of the happy *turn* which the apostle
would give to a discussion. Some men
have an irresistible propensity to sit
in judgment, to pronounce opinions.
Let them make good use of that. It
will be well to exercise it on that
which can do no injury, and which
may turn to good account. Instead of
forming a judgment about *others,* let
the man form a determination about
his own conduct. ¶ *That no man,* &c.
A *stumbling-block* literally means anything laid in a man's path, over which
he may fall. In the Scriptures, however, the word is used commonly in a
figurative sense to denote anything
which shall cause him to *sin,* as sin is
often represented by *falling;* see Note,
Mat. v. 29. And the passage means
that we should resolve to act so as not
by any means to be the occasion of
leading our brethren into sin, either
by our example or by a severe and
harsh judgment, provoking them to
anger, or exciting jealousies, and envy-
ings, and suspicions. No better rule
than this could be given to promote
peace. If every Christian, instead of
judging his brethren severely, would
resolve that *he* would so live as to
promote peace, and so as not to lead
others into sin, it would tend more,
perhaps, than any other thing to advance the harmony and purity of the
church of Christ.

14. *I know.* This is an admission
made to the *Gentile* convert, who believed that it was lawful to partake of
food of every kind. This the apostle
concedes, and says he is fully apprised
of this. But though he knew this, yet
he goes on to say (ver. 15), that it
would be well to regard the conscientious scruples of others on the subject.

by the Lord Jesus, that *there is* nothing [4]unclean of itself: but to him that esteemeth anything to be [4]unclean, to him *it is* unclean.

[4] *common.*

It may be remarked here, that the apostle Paul had formerly quite as many scruples as any of his brethren had then. But his views had been changed. ¶ *And am persuaded.* Am convinced. ¶ *By the Lord Jesus.* This does not mean by any *personal* instruction received from the Lord Jesus, but by all the knowledge which he had received by inspiration of the nature of the Christian religion. The *gospel* of Jesus had taught him that the rites of the Mosaic economy had been abolished, and among those rites were the rules respecting clean and unclean beasts, &c. ¶ *There is nothing unclean.* Gr., *common.* This word was used by the Jews to denote that which was *unclean*, because, in their apprehension, whatever was partaken by the multitude, or all men, must be impure. Hence the words *common* and *impure* are often used as expressing the same thing. It denotes that which was forbidden by the laws of Moses. ¶ *To him that esteemeth*, &c. He makes it a matter of conscience. He regards certain meats as forbidden by God; and while he so regards them, it would be wrong for him to partake of them. Man may be in error, but it would not be proper for him to act in violation of what he *supposes* God requires.

15. *But if thy brother*, &c. This address is to the *Gentile* convert. In the previous verse, Paul admitted that the prejudice of the Jew was not well-founded. But admitting that, still the question was, *how* he should be treated while he had that prejudice. The apostle here shows the Gentile that *he* ought not so to act as unnecessarily to wound his feelings, or to grieve him. ¶ *Be grieved.* Be pained, as a conscientious man always is, when he sees another, and especially a Christian brother, do anything which *he* esteems to be wrong. The *pain* would be real, though the *opinion* from which it arose might not

15 But if thy brother be grieved with *thy* meat, now walkest thou not [5]charitably. Destroy[g] not him with thy meat, for whom Christ died.

[5] *according to charity.* [g] 1 Co.8.11.

be well founded. ¶ *With* thy *meat.* Greek, on account of meat, or food; that is, because *you* eat that which he regards as unclean. ¶ *Now walkest.* To *walk*, in the sacred Scriptures, often denotes to act, or to do a thing, Mark vii. 5; Acts xxi. 21; Rom. vi. 4; viii. 1, 4. Here it means that *if* the Gentile convert persevered in the use of such food, notwithstanding the conscientious scruples of the Jew, he violated the law of love. ¶ *Charitably.* Greek, according to charity, or love; that is, he would violate that law which required him to sacrifice his own comfort to promote the happiness of his brother, 1 Cor. xiii. 5; x. 24, 28, 29; Phil. ii. 4, 21. ¶ *Destroy not him.* The word *destroy* here refers, doubtless, to the ruin of the soul in hell. It properly denotes ruin or destruction, and is applied to the *ruin* or *corruption* of various things, in the New Testament. To *life* (Mat. x. 39); to a reward, in the sense of *losing* it (Mark x. 41; Luke xv. 4); to food (John vi. 27); to the Israelites, represented as *lost* or wandering (Mat. x. 6); to *wisdom* that is rendered vain (1 Cor. i. 9); to *bottles*, rendered useless (Mat. ix. 17), &c. But it is also frequently applied to destruction in hell, to the everlasting ruin of the soul, Mat. x. 28, "Who is able to destroy both soul and body in *hell;*" Mat. xviii. 14; John iii. 15; Rom. ii. 12. That *this* is its meaning here is apparent from the parallel place in 1 Cor. viii. 11, "And through thy knowledge shall thy weak brother *perish.*" If it be asked how the eating of meat by the Gentile convert could be connected with the perdition of the Jew, I reply, that the apostle supposes that in this way an occasion of stumbling would be afforded to him, and he would come into condemnation. He might be led by example to partake against his own conscience, or he might be excited to anger, disgust,

16 Let not then your good be evil spoken of:

17 For[h] the kingdom of God is

not meat and drink; but [i]righteousness, and [k]peace, and [l]joy in the Holy Ghost.

h Mat.6.33.

i Phi.3.9.　k Jn.16.33; ch.5.1; Phi.4.7.　l ch.15.13.

and apostasy from the Christian faith. Though the apostle believed that all who were true Christians would be saved (Rom. viii. 30-39), yet he believed that it would be brought about by the use of means, and that nothing should be done that would tend to hinder or endanger their salvation, Heb. vi. 4-9; ii. 1. God does not bring his people to heaven without the use of *means adapted to the end*, and one of those means is that employed here to warn professing Christians against such conduct as might jeopard the salvation of their brethren. ¶ *For whom Christ died.* The apostle speaks here of the possibility of endangering the salvation of those for whom Christ died, just as he does respecting the salvation of those who are in fact Christians. By those for whom Christ died, he undoubtedly refers here to *true Christians*, for the whole discussion relates to them, and them only; comp. ver. 3, 4, 7, 8. This passage should not be brought, therefore, to prove that Christ died for all men, or for any who shall finally perish. Such a doctrine is undoubtedly true— [in this sense, that there is in the death of Christ a *sufficiency for all*, and that the *offer* is *to* all] (comp. 2 Cor. v. 14, 15; 1 John ii. 2; 2 Pet. ii. 1), but it is not the truth which is taught here. The design is to show the criminality of a course that would tend to the ruin of a brother. For these weak brethren, Christ laid down his precious life. He loved them; and shall we, to gratify our appetites, pursue a course which will tend to defeat the work of Christ, and ruin the souls redeemed by his blood?

16. *Let not then your good*, &c. That which you esteem to be right, and which may be right in itself. You are not bound by the ceremonial law. You are free from the yoke of bondage. This freedom you esteem to be *a good* —a favour—a high privilege. And so it is; but you should not make such

a use of it as to do injury to others. ¶ *Be evil spoken of.* Greek, be blasphemed. Do not so use your Christian liberty as to give occasion for railing and unkind remarks from your brethren, so as to produce contention and strife, and thus to give rise to evil reports among the wicked about the tendency of the Christian religion, as if it were adapted only to promote controversy. How much strife would have been avoided if all Christians had regarded this plain rule! In relation to dress, and rites, and ceremonies in the church, we may be conscious that we are right; but an obstinate adherence to them may only give rise to contention and angry discussions, and to evil reports among men of the tendency of religion. In such a case we should yield our private, unimportant personal indulgence to the good of the cause of religion and of peace.

17. *For the kingdom of God.* For an explanation of this phrase, see Note, Mat. iii. 2. Here it means that the *peculiarities* of the kingdom of God, or of the church of Christ on earth, do not consist in observing the distinctions between meats and drinks. It was true that by these things the Jews had been particularly characterized, but the Christian church was to be distinguished in a different manner. ¶ *Is not.* Does not consist in, or is not distinguished by. ¶ *Meat and drink.* In observing distinctions between different kinds of food, or making such observances a matter of conscience, as the Jews did. Moses did not prescribe any particular drink or prohibit any, but the Nazarites abstained from wine and all kinds of strong liquors; and it is not improbable that the Jews had invented some distinctions on this subject which they judged to be of importance. Hence it is said in Col. ii. 16, "Let no man judge you in meat or *in drink;*" comp. 1 Cor. viii. 8; iv. 20. ¶ *But righteousness.* This word

18 For he that in these things serveth Christ, *is* acceptable to God, and approved of men.

19 Let *m* us therefore follow after the things which make for peace,

m Ps.34.14; He.12.14.

here means *virtue, integrity,* a faithful discharge of all the duties which we owe to God or to our fellow-men. It means that the Christian must so live as to be appropriately denominated a righteous man, and not a man whose whole attention is absorbed by the mere ceremonies and outward forms of religion. To produce this, we are told, was the main design, and the principal teaching of the gospel, Tit. ii. 12; comp. Rom. viii. 13; 1 Pet. ii. 11. Thus it is said (1 John ii. 29), "Every one that doeth righteousness is born of God;" iii. 10, "Whosoever doeth not righteousness is not of God;" comp. 1 John iii. 7; 1 Cor. xv. 34; 2 Cor. iii. 9; vi. 7, 14; Eph. v. 9; vi. 14; 1 Tim. vi. 11; 1 Pet. ii. 24; Eph. iv. 24. He that is a righteous man, whose characteristic it is to lead a holy life, is a Christian. If his great aim is to do the will of God, and if he seeks to discharge with fidelity all his duties to God and man, he is renewed. On that righteousness he will not *depend* for salvation (Phil. iii. 8, 9), but he will regard this character and this disposition as evidence that he is a Christian, and that the Lord Jesus is made unto him "wisdom, and righteousness, and sanctification, and redemption," 1 Cor. i. 30. ¶ *And peace.* This word, in this place, does not refer to the internal *peace* and happiness which the Christian has in his own mind (comp. Notes on chap. v. 1); but to peace or concord in opposition to *contention* among brethren. The tendency and design of the kingdom of God is to produce concord and love, and to put an end to alienation and strife. Even though, therefore, there might be ground for the opinions which some cherished in regard to rites, yet it was of more importance to maintain peace than obstinately to press those matters at the expense of strife and contention. That the tendency of the gospel is to promote peace, and to induce men to lay aside

all causes of contention and bitter strife, is apparent from the following passages of the New Testament: 1 Cor. vii. 15; xiv. 33; Gal. v. 22; Eph. iv. 3; 1 Thes. v. 13; 2 Tim. ii. 22; Jam. iii. 18; Mat. v. 9; Eph. iv. 31, 32; Col. iii. 8; John xiii. 34, 35; xvii. 21-23. This is the second evidence of piety on which Christians should examine their hearts—a disposition to promote the peace of Jerusalem, Ps. cxxii. 6; xxxvii. 11. A contentious, quarrelsome spirit; a disposition to magnify trifles; to make the shibboleth of party an occasion of alienation, and heart-burning, and discord; to sow dissensions on account of unimportant points of doctrine or of discipline, is full proof that there is no attachment to Him who is the Prince of peace. Such a disposition does infinite dishonour to the cause of religion, and perhaps has done more to retard its progress than all other causes put together. Contentions commonly arise from some small matter in doctrine, in dress, in ceremonies; and often the smaller the matter the more fierce the controversy, till the spirit of religion disappears, and desolation comes over the face of Zion.

"The Spirit, like a peaceful dove,
Flies from the realms of noise and strife."

¶ *And joy.* This refers, doubtless, to the *personal* happiness produced in the mind by the influence of the gospel; see Notes, chap. v. 1-5. ¶ *In the Holy Ghost.* Produced *by* the Holy Ghost, chap. v. 5; comp. Gal. v. 22, 23.

18. *In these things.* In righteousness, peace, and joy. ¶ *Serveth Christ.* Or obeys Christ, who has commanded them. He receives Christ as his *master* or *teacher* and does *his* will in regard to them. To do these things is to do honour to Christ, and to show the excellency of his religion. ¶ *Is acceptable to God.* Whether he be converted from the Jews or the Gentiles. ¶ *And approved of men.* That is, men will *approve* of such conduct; they will esteem it to be right, and to

and *n*things wherewith one may edify another.

n 1 Co.14.12.

20 For meat destroy not the work of God. All *o* things in-

o Tit.1.15.

be in accordance with the spirit of Christianity. He does not say that the wicked world will *love* such a life, but it will commend itself to them as such a life as men *ought* to lead.

19. *Let us therefore follow*, &c. The object of this verse is to persuade the church at Rome to lay aside their causes of contention, and to live in harmony. This exhortation is founded on the considerations which the apostle had presented, and may be regarded as the conclusion to which the argument had conducted him. ¶ *The things which make for peace.* The high purposes and objects of the Christian religion, and not those smaller matters which produce strife. If men aim at the great objects proposed by the Christian religion, they will live in peace. If they seek to promote their private ends, to follow their own passions and prejudices, they will be involved in strife and contention. There *are* great common objects before *all* Christians in which they can unite, and in the pursuit of which they will cultivate a spirit of peace. Let them all strive for holiness; let them seek to spread the gospel; let them engage in circulating the Bible, or in doing good in any way to others, and their smaller matters of difference will sink into comparative unimportance, and they will unite in one grand purpose of saving the world. Christians have more things in which they *agree* than in which they differ. The points in which they are agreed are of infinite importance; the points on which they differ are commonly some minor matters, in which they may "agree to differ," and still cherish love for all who bear the image of Christ. ¶ *And things wherewith*, &c. That is, those things by which we may render *aid* to our brethren; the doctrines, exhortations, counsels, and other helps which may benefit them in their Christian life. ¶ *May edify.* The word *edify* means properly to *build*, as a house; then to *rebuild* or *reconstruct;* then to adorn or ornament; then to do any-

thing that will confer favour or advantage, or which will further an object. Applied to the church, it means to do anything by teaching, counsel, advice, &c., which will tend to promote its great object; to aid Christians, to enable them to surmount difficulties, to remove their ignorance, &c., Acts ix. 31; 1 Cor. viii. 1; xiv. 4. In these expressions the idea of a *building* is retained, reared on a firm, tried corner-stone, the Lord Jesus Christ, Eph. ii. 20; Isa. xxviii. 16. Compare Rom. ix. 33. Christians are thus regarded, according to Paul's noble idea (Eph. ii. 20–22), as one great temple erected for the glory of God, having no separate interest, but as united for one object, and therefore bound to do all that is possible, that each other may be fitted to their appropriate place, and perform their appropriate function in perfecting and adorning this temple of God.

20. *For meat.* By your obstinate, pertinacious attachment to your own opinions about the distinctions of meat and drinks, do not pursue such a course as to lead a brother into sin, and ruin his soul. Here is a new argument presented why Christians should pursue a course of charity—that the opposite would tend to the ruin of the brother's soul. ¶ *Destroy not.* The word here is that which properly is applied to pulling down an edifice; and the apostle continues the figure which he used in the previous verse. Do not pull down or destroy the *temple* which God is rearing. ¶ *The work of God.* The work of God is that which God *does*, and here especially refers to his work in rearing *his church.* The *Christian* is regarded peculiarly as the work of God, as God renews his heart and makes him what he is. Hence he is called God's "building" (1 Cor. iii. 9), and his "workmanship, created in Christ Jesus unto good works" (Eph. ii. 10), and is denominated "a new creature," 2 Cor. v. 17. The meaning is, "Do not so conduct yourself, in regard to

deed *are* pure; *p* but *it is* evil for that man who eateth with offence.

p 1 Co.8.10-13.

21 *It is* good neither to eat flesh, nor to drink wine, nor *any thing* whereby thy brother stumbleth, or is offended, or is made weak.

---

the distinction of meats into clean and unclean, as to cause your brother to sin, and to impair or ruin the work of religion which God is carrying on in his soul." The expression does not refer to *man* as being the work of God, but to the *piety* of the Christian; to that which God, by his Spirit, is producing in the heart of the believer. ¶ *All things indeed* are *pure.* Comp. ver. 14. This is a concession to those whom he was exhorting to peace. All things under the Christian dispensation are lawful to be eaten. The distinctions of the Levitical law are not binding on Christians. ¶ *But* it is *evil.* Though pure in itself, yet it may become an occasion of sin, if another is grieved by it. It is evil to the man who pursues a course that will give offence to a brother; that will pain him, or tend to drive him off from the church, or lead him any way into sin. ¶ *With offence.* So as to offend a brother; such as *he* esteems to be sin, and by which he will be grieved.

21. It is *good.* It is right; or it is better. This verse is an explanation or enlarged specification of the meaning of the former. ¶ *To eat flesh.* That is, such flesh as the *Jewish* convert regarded as unclean, ver. 2. ¶ *Nor to drink wine.* Wine was a common drink among the Jews, and usually esteemed lawful. But the Nazarites were not allowed to drink it (Num. vi. 3), and the Rechabites (Jer. xxxv.) drank no wine, and it is possible that some of the early converts regarded it as unlawful for Christians to drink it. Wine was, moreover, used in libations in heathen worship, and perhaps the Jewish converts might be scrupulous about its use from this cause. The caution here shows us what should be done *now* in regard to the use of wine. It may not be possible to prove that wine is absolutely unlawful, but still many friends of *temperance* regard it as such, and are grieved at its use. They esteem the

habit of using it as tending to intemperance, and as encouraging those who cannot afford expensive liquors. Besides, the wines which are now used are different from those which were common among the ancients. That was the pure juice of the grape. That which is now in common use is mingled with alcohol, and with other intoxicating ingredients. Little or none of the wine which comes to this country is pure. And in this state of the case, does not the command of the apostle here require the friends of temperance to abstain even from the use of wine? ¶ *Nor* any thing. Any article of food or drink, or any course of conduct. So valuable is peace, and so desirable is it not to offend a brother, that we should rather deny ourselves to any extent, than to be the occasion of offences and scandals in the church. ¶ *Stumbleth.* For the difference between this word and the word *offended,* see Note, Rom. xi. 11. It means here that by eating, a Jewish convert might be led to eat also, contrary to his own conviction of what was right, and thus be led into sin. ¶ *Or is made weak.* That is, shaken, or rendered less stable in his opinion or conduct. By being led to imitate the Gentile convert, he would become less firm and established; he would violate his own conscience; his course would be attended with regrets and with doubts about its propriety, and thus he would be made *weak.* In this verse we have an eminent instance of the charity of the apostle, and of his spirit of concession and kindness. If this were regarded by all Christians, it would save no small amount of strife, and heart-burnings, and contention. Let a man begin to act on the principle that peace is to be promoted, that other Christians are not to be offended, and what a change would it at once produce in the churches, and what an influence would it exert over the life!

22 Hast thou faith? have *it* to thyself before God. Happy *q* *is* he that condemneth not himself in that thing which he alloweth.

q 1 Jn.3.21.

23 And he that *6*doubteth is damned if he eat, because *he* *eateth* not of faith : for *r*whatsoever is not of faith is sin.

6 or, discerneth and putteth a difference between meats.　　*r* He.11.6.

---

22. *Hast thou faith?* The word *faith* here refers only to the subject under discussion—to the subject of meats, drinks, &c. Do you believe that it is right to eat all kinds of food, &c.? The apostle had admitted that this was the true doctrine ; but he maintains that it should be so held as not to give offence. ¶ *Have* it *to thyself.* Do not obtrude your faith or opinion on others. Be satisfied with cherishing the opinion, and acting on it in private, without bringing it forward to produce disturbance in the church. ¶ *Before God.* Where God only is the witness. God sees your sincerity, and will approve your opinion. That opinion cherish and act on, yet so as not to give offence, and to produce disturbance in the church. God sees your sincerity ; he sees that you are right ; and you will not offend him. Your brethren do *not* see that you are right, and *they* will be offended. ¶ *Happy* is *he,* &c. This state of mind, the apostle says, is one that is attended with peace and happiness ; and this is a *further* reason why they should indulge their opinion in private, without obtruding it on others. They were conscious of doing right, and that consciousness was attended with peace. This fact he states in the form of a universal proposition, as applicable not only to *this* case, but to *all* cases ; comp. 1 John iii. 21. ¶ *Condemneth not himself.* Whose conscience does not reprove him. ¶ *In that which he alloweth.* Which he *approves,* or which he *does.* Who has a clear conscience in his opinions and conduct. Many men indulge in practices which their consciences condemn, many in practices of which they are in doubt. But the way to be happy is to have a *clear conscience* in what we do ; or in other words, if we have *doubts* about a course of conduct, it is not safe to indulge in that course,

but it should be at once abandoned. Many men are engaged in *business* about which they have many doubts ; many Christians are in doubt about certain courses of life. But they can have *no doubt* about the propriety of abstaining from them. They who are engaged in the slave-trade ; or they who are engaged in the manufacture or sale of ardent spirits ; or they who frequent the theatre or the ball-room, or who run the round of fashionable amusements, if professing Christians, MUST often be troubled with *many* doubts about the propriety of their manner of life. But they can have no doubt about the propriety of an *opposite* course. Perhaps a single inquiry would settle all debate in regard to these things : *Did anyone ever become a slave-dealer, or a dealer in ardent spirits, or go to the theatre, or engage in scenes of splendid amusements, with any belief that he was imitating the Lord Jesus Christ, or with any desire to honour him or his religion?* But one answer would be given to this question ; and in view of it, how striking is the remark of Paul, "Happy is he that condemneth not himself in that which he alloweth !"

23. *He that doubteth.* He that is not fully satisfied in his mind ; who does not do it with a clear conscience. The margin has it rendered correctly, "He that discerneth and putteth a difference between meats." He that conscientiously believes, as the Jew did, that the Levitical law respecting the difference between meats was binding on Christians. ¶ *Is damned.* We apply this word almost exclusively to the future punishment of the wicked in hell. But it is of importance to remember, in reading the Bible, that this is not of necessity its meaning. It means properly *to condemn ;* and here it means only that the person who should thus violate the dictates of his conscience would incur guilt, and

CHAPTER XV.

WE then that are strong ought
to *a*bear the infirmities of
a ch.14.1; Ga.6.2.

would be blameworthy in doing it.
But it does not affirm that he would
inevitably sink to hell. The same
construction is to be put on the expression in 1 Cor. xi. 29, " He that
eateth and drinketh unworthily, eateth
and drinketh damnation to himself."
¶ *For whatsoever, &c. Whatever is
not done with a full conviction that it
is right, is sinful; whatever is done
when a man doubts whether it is right,
is sin.* This is evidently the fair
interpretation of this place. Such
the connection requires. It does not
affirm that all or any of the actions of
impenitent and unbelieving men are
sinful, which is true, but not the truth
taught here; nor does it affirm that
all acts which are not performed by
those who have faith in the Lord
Jesus, are sinful; but the discussion
pertains to Christians; and the whole
scope of the passage requires us to
understand the apostle as simply saying that a man should not do a thing
doubting its correctness; that he
should have a strong conviction that
what he does is right; and that if he
has *not* this conviction, it is sinful.
The rule is of universal application.
In all cases, if a man does a thing
which he does not *believe* to be right,
it is a sin, and his conscience will
condemn him for it. It may be proper, however, to observe that the converse of this is not always true, that
if a man believes a thing to be right,
that therefore it is not sin. For
many of the persecutors were conscientious (John xvi. 2; Acts xxvi. 9);
and the murderers of the Son of God
did it ignorantly (Acts iii. 17; 1 Cor.
ii. 8); and yet were adjudged as guilty
of enormous crimes; comp. Luke xi.
50, 51; Acts ii. 23, 37.

In this chapter we have a remarkably fine discussion of the nature of
Christian charity. Differences of
opinion will arise, and men will be
divided into various sects; but if the
rules which are laid down in this
chapter were followed, the conten-

the weak, and not to please ourselves.
2 Let*b* every one of us please
b 1 Co.9.19; Phi.2.4,5.

tions, and altercations, and strifes
among Christians would cease. Had
these rules been applied to the controversies about rites, and forms, and
festivals that have arisen, peace might
have been preserved. Amid all such
differences, the great question is,
whether there is true love to the Lord
Jesus. If there is, the apostle teaches
us that we have no right to judge a
brother, or despise him, or contend
harshly with him. Our object should
be to promote peace, to aid him in
his efforts to become holy, and to
seek to build him up in holy faith.

CHAPTER XV.

It may be of importance to state
that, between the last verse of the
preceding chapter and the first verse
of this, the Arabic version, some
MSS., and many of the Greek fathers,
as Chrysostom, Theodoret, Theophy-
lact, &c., have introduced ver. 25-27
of chap. xvi. of this epistle. Why
this was done, has been a matter of
controversy. The discussion, however, is of no practical importance,
and most critics concur in the opinion
that the present arrangement of the
Greek text is genuine.

1. *We then that are strong.* The
apostle resumes the subject of the
preceding chapter; and continues the
exhortation to brotherly love and
mutual kindness and forbearance. By
the *strong* here he means the strong
in faith in respect to the matters
under discussion; those whose minds
were free from doubts and perplexi-
ties. His own mind was free from
doubt, and there were many others,
particularly of the Gentile converts,
that had the same views. But many
also, particularly of the *Jewish* converts, had many doubts and scruples.
¶ *Ought to bear.* This word *bear*
properly means *to lift up, to bear
away, to remove.* But here it is used
in a larger sense—*to bear with, to be
indulgent to, to endure patiently, not
to contend with,* Gal. vi. 2; Rev. ii.

his neighbour for *his* good to edification.

3 For[c] even Christ pleased not

c Jn.6.38.

himself; but, as it is written, [d]The reproaches of them that reproached thee fell on me.

d Ps.69.9.

2, "Thou canst not bear them that are evil." ¶ *And not to please ourselves.* Not to make it our main object to gratify our own wills. We should be willing to deny ourselves, if by it we may promote the happiness of others. This refers particularly to *opinions* about meats and drinks; but it may be applied to Christian conduct generally, as denoting that we are not to make our own happiness or gratification the standard of our conduct, but are to seek the welfare of others; see the example of Paul, 1 Cor. ix. 19, 22; see also Phil. ii. 4; 1 Cor. xiii. 5, "Love seeketh not her own;" x. 24, " Let no man seek his own, but every man another's wealth;" also Mat. xvi. 24.

2. *Please* his *neighbour.* That is, all other persons, but especially the friends of the Redeemer The word *neighbour* here has special reference to the members of the church. It is often used, however, in a much larger sense; see Luke x. 36. ¶ *For* his *good.* Not seek to secure for him indulgence in those things which would be injurious to him, but in all those things whereby his welfare would be promoted. ¶ *To edification.* See Note, chap. xiv. 19.

3. *For even Christ.* The apostle proceeds, in his usual manner, to illustrate what he had said by the example of the Saviour. To a Christian, the example of the Lord Jesus will furnish the most ready, certain, and happy illustration of the nature and extent of his duty. ¶ *Pleased not himself.* This is not to be understood as if the Lord Jesus did not voluntarily and cheerfully engage in his great work. He was not *compelled* to come and suffer. Nor is it to be understood as if he did not *approve* the work, or see its propriety and fitness. If he had not, he would never have engaged in its sacrifices and self-denials. But the meaning may be expressed in the following

particulars: (1) He came to do the will or desire of God in *undertaking* the work of salvation. It was the will of God; it was agreeable to the divine purposes; and the Mediator did not consult his own happiness and honour in heaven, but cheerfully came to *do the will* of God, Ps. xl. 7, 8; comp. Heb. x. 4-10; Phil. ii. 6; John xvii. 5. (2) Christ, when on earth, made it his great object to do the will of God, to finish the work which God had given him to do, and not to seek his own comfort and enjoyment. This he expressly affirms, John vi. 38; v. 30. (3) He was willing for this to endure whatever trials and pains the will of God might demand, not seeking to avoid them or to shrink from them. See particularly his prayer in the garden, Luke xxii. 42. (4) In his life, he did not seek personal comfort, wealth, or friends, or honours. He denied himself to promote the welfare of others; he was poor that they might be rich; he was in lonely places that he might seek out the needy and provide for them. Nay, he did not seek to preserve his own life when the appointed time came to die, but gave himself up for all. (5) There may be another idea which the apostle had here. He bore with patience the ignorance, blindness, erroneous views, and ambitious projects of his disciples. He evinced kindness to them when in error; and was not harsh, censorious, or unkind, when they were filled with vain projects of ambition, or perverted his words, or were dull of apprehension. So, says the apostle, *we* ought to do in relation to our brethren. ¶ *But as it is written.* Ps. lxix. 9. This psalm, and the former part of this verse, is referred to the Messiah; comp. ver. 21, with Mat. xxvii. 34, 48. ¶ *The reproaches.* The calumnies, censures, harsh, opprobrious speeches. ¶ *Of them that reproached thee.* Of the wicked, who vilified and abused the

4 For^e whatsoever things were written aforetime were written for our learning, that we through

e 1 Co.10.11; 2 Ti.3.16,17.

patience and comfort of the scriptures might have hope.

5 Now the God of patience and

---

law and government of God. ¶ *Fell on me.* In other words, Christ was willing to suffer reproach and contempt in order to do good to others. He endured calumny and contempt all his life, from those who by their lips and lives calumniated God, or reproached their Maker. We may learn here, (1) That the contempt of Jesus Christ is contempt of him who appointed him. (2) We may see the kindness of the Lord Jesus in being willing thus to *throw himself* between the sinner and God; to *intercept*, as it were, our sins, and to bear the effects of them in his own person. He stood between *us* and God; and both the reproaches, and the divine displeasure due to them, *met* on his sacred person, and produced the sorrows of the atonement—his bitter agony in the garden and on the cross. Jesus thus showed his love of God in being willing to bear the reproaches aimed at him; and his love to *men* in being willing to endure the sufferings necessary to atone for these very sins. (3) If Jesus thus bore reproaches, *we* should be willing also to endure them. We suffer in the cause where he has gone before us, and where he has set us the example; and as *he* was abused and vilified, we should be willing to be so also.

4. *For whatsoever things,* &c. This is a *general* observation which struck the mind of the apostle, from the particular case which he had just specified. He had just made use of a striking passage in the Psalms to his purpose. The thought seems suddenly to have occurred to him that *all* the Old Testament was admirably adapted to express Christian duties and doctrine, and he therefore turned aside from his direct argument to express this sentiment. It should be read as a parenthesis. ¶ *Were written aforetime.* That is, in ancient times; in the Old Testament. ¶ *For our learning.* For our *teaching* or

instruction. Not that this was the *only* purpose of the writings of the Old Testament, to instruct Christians; but that all the Old Testament might be useful *now* in illustrating and enforcing the doctrines and duties of piety towards God and man. ¶ *Through patience.* This does not mean, as our translation might seem to suppose, patience *of the Scriptures,* but it means that by patiently enduring sufferings, in connection with the consolation which the Scriptures furnish, we might have hope. The *tendency* of patience, the apostle tell us (Rom. v. 4), is to produce *hope;* see Notes on this place. ¶ *And comfort of the scriptures.* By means of the consolation which the writings of the Old Testament furnish. The word rendered *comfort* means also *exhortation* or *admonition.* If this is its meaning here, it refers to the admonitions which the Scriptures suggest, instructions which they impart, and the exhortations to patience in trials. If it means *comfort,* then the reference is to the examples of the saints in affliction; to their recorded expressions of confidence in God in their trials, as of Job, Daniel, David, &c. Which is the precise meaning of the word here, it is not easy to determine. ¶ *Might have hope.* Note, chap. v. 4. We may learn here, (1) That afflictions may prove to be a great blessing. (2) That their proper tendency is to produce *hope.* (3) That the way to find support in afflictions is to go to the Bible. By the example of the ancient saints, by the expression of their confidence in God, by their patience, *we* may learn to suffer, and may not only be *instructed,* but may find *comfort* in all our trials; see the example of Paul himself in 2 Cor. i. 2–11.

5. *Now the God of patience.* The God who is *himself* long-suffering, who bears patiently with the errors and faults of his children, and who can *give* patience, may he give you of his

consolation grant you to be *like-minded one toward another, ¹ac-cording to Christ Jesus;

6 That ye may *g*with one mind *and* one mouth glorify God, even

f 1 Co.1.10. ¹ or, *after the example of.* *g* Ac.4.24,32.

the Father of our Lord Jesus Christ.

7 Wherefore receive ye one another, *h*as Christ also received us, to the glory of God.

h Ep.1.6.

Spirit, that you may bear patiently the infirmities and errors of each other. The example of God here, who bears long with his children, and is not angry soon at their offences, is a strong argument why Christians should bear with each other. If God bears long and patiently with *our* infirmities *we* ought to bear with each other. ¶ *And consolation.* Who gives or imparts consolation. ¶ *To be like-minded,* &c. Gr., to think the same thing; that is, to be united, to keep from divisions and strifes. ¶ *According to Christ Jesus.* According to the example and spirit of Christ; his was a spirit of peace. Or, according to what his religion requires. The name of Christ is sometimes thus put for his religion, 2 Cor. xi. 4; Eph. iv. 20. If all Christians would imitate the example of Christ, and follow his instructions, there would be no contentions among them. He earnestly sought in his parting prayer their unity and peace, John xvii. 21-23.

6. *That ye may with one mind.* The word here used is translated "with one accord," Acts i. 14; ii. 1; iv. 24. It means unitedly; with one purpose; without contentions, and strifes, and jars. ¶ *And one mouth.* This refers, doubtless, to their prayers and praises. That they might join without contention and unkind feeling in the worship of God. Divisions, strife, and contention in the church prevent union in worship. Though the *body* may be there, and the church *professedly* engaged in public worship, yet it is a *divided* service; and the prayers of strife and contention are not heard, Isa. lviii. 4. ¶ *Glorify God.* Praise or honour God. This would be done by their union, peace, and harmony; thus showing the tendency of the gospel to overcome the sources of strife and contention among men,

and to bring them to peace. ¶ *Even the Father,* &c. This is an addition designed to produce love. (1) He is *a Father;* we, then, his children, should regard him as pleased with the union and peace of his family. (2) He is the Father of OUR LORD; our *common* Lord; our Lord who has commanded us to be united, and to love one another. By the desire of honouring *such* a Father, we should lay aside contentions, and be united in the bands of love.

7. *Wherefore.* In view of all the considerations tending to produce unity and love, which have been presented. He refers to the various arguments in this and the preceding chapter. ¶ *Receive ye one another.* Acknowledge one another as Christians, and treat one another as such, though you may differ in opinion about many smaller matters; see chap. xiv. 3. ¶ *As Christ also received us.* That is, received us as his friends and followers; see chap. xiv. 3. ¶ *To the glory of God.* In order to promote his glory. He has redeemed us, and renewed us, in order to promote the honour of God; comp. Eph. i. 6. As Christ has received us in order to promote the glory of God, so ought we to treat each other in a similar manner for a similar purpose. The exhortation in this verse is to those who had been divided on various points pertaining to rites and ceremonies; to those who had been converted from among *Gentiles* and *Jews;* and the apostle here says that Christ had received *both.* In order to enforce this, and especially to show the *Jewish* converts that they ought to receive and acknowledge their *Gentile* brethren, he proceeds to show, in the following verses, that Christ had reference to *both* in his work. He shows this in reference to the *Jews* (ver. 8), and to

8 Now I say that Jesus Christ was a minister of the circumcision for the truth of God, *to confirm the promises *made* unto the fathers.

9 And that the Gentiles might glorify God for *his* mercy; as it is written, *For this cause I will

i Ac.3.25,26.   *k* Ps.18.49.

confess to thee among the Gentiles, and sing unto thy name.

10 And again he saith, *Rejoice, ye Gentiles, with his people.

11 And again, *Praise the Lord, all ye Gentiles; and laud him, all ye people.

l De.32.43.   *m* Ps 117.1.

---

the *Gentiles*, ver. 9–12. Thus he draws all his arguments from the work of Christ.

8. *Now I say.* I affirm, or maintain. I, a *Jew*, admit that his work had reference to the Jews; I affirm also that it had reference to the Gentiles. ¶ *That Jesus Christ.* That *the Messiah.* The force of the apostle's reasoning would often be more striking if we would retain the word *Messiah*, and not regard the word *Christ* as a mere surname. It is the name of his *office;* and to *a Jew* the name *Messiah* would convey much more than the idea of a mere proper name. ¶ *Was a minister of the circumcision.* Exercised his office—the office of the Messiah—among the Jews, or with respect *to* the Jews, for the purposes which he immediately specifies. He was born a Jew; was circumcised; came *to* that nation; and died in their midst, without having gone himself to any other people. ¶ *For the truth of God.* To confirm or establish the truth of the promises of God. He remained among them in the exercise of his ministry, to show that God was *true*, who had said that the Messiah should come to them. ¶ *To confirm the promises*, &c. To *establish*, or to show that the promises were true; see Note, Acts iii. 25, 26. The *promises* referred to here, are those particularly which related to the coming of the Messiah. By thus admitting that the Messiah was the minister of the circumcision, the apostle conceded all that the Jew could ask, that he was to be peculiarly *their* Messiah; see Note, Luke xxiv. 47.

9. *And that the Gentiles*, &c. The benefits of the gospel were not to be confined to *the Jews;* and as God

designed that those benefits should be extended to the *Gentiles*, so the Jewish converts ought to be willing to admit them and treat them as brethren. That God *did* design this, the apostle proceeds to show. ¶ *Might glorify God.* Might *praise*, or give thanks to God. This implies that the favour shown to them was a *great* favour. ¶ *For his mercy.* Greek, on account of the mercy shown to them. ¶ *As it is written.* Ps. xviii. 49. The expression there is one of David's. He says that he will praise God for his mercies *among* the heathen, or when surrounded *by* the heathen; or that he would confess and acknowledge the mercies of God to him, as we should say, *to all the world.* The apostle, however, uses it in this sense, that the *Gentiles* would *participate* with the Jew in offering praise to God, or that they would be united. This does not appear to have been the original design of David in the psalm, but the *words* express the idea of the apostle. ¶ *And sing*, &c. Celebrate thy praise. This supposes that *benefits* would be conferred on them, for which they would celebrate his goodness.

10. *And again*, &c. Deut. xxxii. 43. In this place the *nations* or Gentiles are called on to rejoice with the Jews, for the interposition of God in their behalf. The design of the quotation is to show that the Old Testament speaks of the Gentiles as called on to celebrate the praises of God; of course, the apostle infers that they are to be introduced to the same privileges as his people.

11. *And again.* Ps. cxvii. 1. The object in this quotation is the same as before. The apostle accumulates quotations to show that it was the

12 And again Esaias saith,
There[n] shall be a [o]root of Jesse,
and he that shall rise to reign
over the Gentiles; in him shall
the Gentiles trust.
13 Now the God of hope fill

n Is.11.1,10.　　o Re.5.5; 22.16.

common language of the Old Testament, and that he was not depending
on a single expression for the truth of
his doctrine. ¶ *All ye Gentiles.* In
the psalm, "all ye *nations;*" but the
original is the same. ¶ *And laud
him. Praise* him. The psalm is
directly in point. It is a call on *all*
nations to praise God—the very point
in the discussion of the apostle.
12. *Esaias saith.* Isaiah, chap. xi.
1, 10. ¶ *There shall be a root.* A
descendant, or one that should proceed from him when he was dead.
When a tree dies, and falls, there may
remain a *root* which shall retain life,
and which shall send up a sprout of a
similar kind. So Job says (chap. xiv.
7), "For there is hope of a tree, if it
be cut down, that it will sprout again,
and that the tender branch thereof
will not cease." So in relation to
Jesse. Though *he* should fall, like an
aged tree, yet his name and family
should not be extinct. There should
be a descendant who should rise, and
reign over the Gentiles. The Lord
Jesus is thus called also the "root
and the offspring of David," Rev.
xxii. 16; v. 5. ¶ *Of Jesse.* The
father of David, 1 Sam. xvii. 58.
The Messiah was thus descended from
Jesse. ¶ *He that shall rise.* That is,
as a sprout springs up from a decayed
or fallen tree. Jesus thus *rose* from
the family of David, that had fallen
into poverty and humble life in the
time of Mary. ¶ *To reign over the
Gentiles.* This is quoted from the
LXX. of Isa. xi. 10. The Hebrew is,
"Which shall stand up for an ensign
of the people;" that is, a standard to
which they shall flock. Either the
Septuagint or the Hebrew would
express the idea of the apostle. The
substantial sense is retained, though
it is not literally quoted. The idea
of his *reigning* over the Gentiles is

you with [p]all joy and peace in
believing, that ye may abound in
hope, through the power of the
Holy Ghost.
14 And I myself also [q]am persuaded of you, my brethren, that

p ch.14.17.　　q He.6.9; 2 Pe.1.12.

one that is fully expressed in the
second Psalm. ¶ *In him,* &c. Hebrew, "To it shall the Gentiles seek."
The sense, however, is the same. The
design of this quotation is the same
as the preceding, to show that it was
predicted in the Old Testament that
the Gentiles should be made partakers
of the privileges of the gospel. The
argument of the apostle is, that if
this was designed, then converts to
Christianity from among the *Jews*
should lay aside their prejudices, and
receive them as their brethren, entitled
to the same privileges of the gospel
as themselves. The *fact* that the
Gentiles would be admitted to these
privileges, the apostle had more fully
discussed in chap. x. xi.
13. *Now the God of hope.* The God
who *inspires* or *produces* the Christian hope. ¶ *All joy and peace.*
Chap. xiv. 17. If they were filled
with this, there would be no strife and
contention. ¶ *In believing.* The
effect of believing is to produce this
joy and peace. ¶ *That ye may
abound,* &c. That your hope may be
steadfast and strong. ¶ *Through the
power,* &c. By means of the powerful operation of the Holy Spirit. It
is by his power alone that the Christian has the hope of eternal life; see
Eph. i. 13, 14; Rom. viii. 24.
14. *And I myself also.* The apostle
here proceeds to show them why
he had written this epistle, and to
state his confidence in them. He had
exhorted them to peace; he had opposed some of their strongest prejudices; and in order to secure their
obedience to his injunctions, he now
shows them the deep interest which
he had in their welfare, though he had
never seen them. ¶ *Am persuaded.*
He had never seen them (chap. i. 10–
13), but he had full confidence in
them. This confidence he had ex-

ye also are full of goodness, filled with ʳall knowledge, able also to admonish one another.

15 Nevertheless, brethren, I have

r 1 Co.8.1,7,10.

written the more boldly unto you in some sort, as putting you in mind, ˢbecause of the grace that is given to me of God.

s Ep.3.7,8.

pressed more fully in the first chapter. ¶ *Of you.* Concerning you. I have full confidence in you. ¶ *My brethren.* An address of affection; showing that he was not disposed to assume undue authority, or to lord it over their faith. ¶ *Are full of goodness.* Filled with *kindness* or *benevolence.* That is, they were *disposed* to obey any just commands; and that consequently any errors in their opinions and conduct had not been the effect of obstinacy or perverseness. There was indeed danger in the city of Rome of pride and haughtiness; and among the Gentile converts there might have been some reluctance to receive instruction from a foreign Jew. But the apostle was persuaded that all this was overcome by the mild and humbling spirit of religion, and that they were disposed to obey any just commands. He made this observation, therefore, to conciliate respect to his authority as an apostle. ¶ *Filled with all knowledge.* That is, instructed in the doctrines and duties of the Christian religion. This was true; but there might be still some comparatively unimportant and non-essential points on which they might not be entirely clear. On these the apostle had written; and written, not professedly to communicate *new* ideas, but to *remind* them of the great principles on which they were before instructed, ver. 15. ¶ *Able also, &c.* That is, you are so fully instructed in Christian principles, as to be able to give advice and counsel, if it is needed. From this verse we may learn, (1) That when it is our duty to give instruction, admonition, or advice, it should be in a kind, conciliating manner; not with harshness, or with the severity of authority. Even *an apostle* did not assume harshness or severity in his instructions. (2) There is no impropriety in speaking of the good qualities of Christians in

their presence; or even of *commending* and *praising* them when they deserve it. The apostle Paul was as far as possible from always dwelling on the faults of Christians. When it was necessary to reprove them, he did it, but did it with tenderness and tears. When he *could* commend, he preferred it; and never hesitated to give them credit to the utmost extent to which it could be rendered. He did not *flatter*, but he told the truth; he did not commend to excite pride and vanity, but to encourage, and to prompt to still more active efforts. The minister who always censures and condemns, whose ministry is made up of complaints and lamentations, who never speaks of Christians but in a strain of fault-finding, is unlike the example of the Saviour and of Paul, and may expect little success in his work; comp. Rom. i. 8; xvi. 19; 1 Cor. i. 5; 2 Cor. viii. 7; ix. 2; Phil. i. 3–7; Heb. vi. 9; 2 Pet. i. 12.

15. *Nevertheless.* Notwithstanding my full persuasion of your knowledge and your purpose to do right. Perhaps he refers also to the fact that he was a stranger to them. ¶ *The more boldly.* More boldly than might have been expected from a stranger. The reason why he showed this boldness in declaring his sentiments, he immediately states—that he had been specially called to the office of instructing the Gentiles. ¶ *In some sort* (ἀπὸ μέρους). In part. Some have supposed that he referred to a *party* at Rome—the Gentile party (Whitby). Some refer it to different *parts* of his epistle—on some subjects (Stuart). Probably the expression is designed to qualify the phrase *more boldly.* The phrase, says Grotius, *diminishes* that of which it is spoken, as 1 Cor. xiii. 9, 12; 2 Cor. i. 14; ii. 5; and means the same as "somewhat more freely;" that is, I have been induced to write the more freely,

16 That I should be the minister of Jesus Christ to the Gen-

---

partly because I am appointed to this very office. I write somewhat more freely to a church among the Gentiles than I even should to one among the Jews, *because* I am appointed to this very office. ¶ *As putting you in mind.* Greek, calling to your *remembrance*, or *reminding* you; comp. 2 Pet. i. 12, 13. This was a delicate way of communicating instruction. The apostles presumed that all Christians were acquainted with the great doctrines of religion; but they did not command, enjoin, or assume a spirit of dictation. How happy would it be if all teachers would imitate the example of the *apostles* in this, and be as modest and humble *as they were.* ¶ *Because of the grace,* &c. Because God has conferred the *favour* on me of appointing me to this office; see Note, chap. i. 5.

16. *The minister* (λειτουργὸν). This is not the word which is commonly translated *minister* (διάκονος). This word is properly appropriated to those who minister in public offices or the affairs of the state. In the New Testament it is applied mainly to the Levitical priesthood, who ministered and served at the altar, Heb. xi. 11. It is, however, applied to the ministers of the New Testament, as discharging *substantially* the same offices towards the church which were discharged by the Levitical priesthood; *i.e.* as engaged in promoting the welfare of the church, occupied in holy things, &c., Acts xiii. 2, "As they *ministered* to the Lord and fasted," &c. It is used in a larger sense still in Rom. xv. 27; 2 Cor. ix. 12. ¶ *To the Gentiles.* Comp. chap. i. 5; Acts ix. 15. ¶ *Ministering* (ἱερουργοῦντα). Performing the office of a priest in respect to the gospel of God. The office of a *priest* was to offer sacrifice. Paul here retains the *language*, though without affirming or implying that the ministers of the New Testament were literally *priests* to offer sacrifice. The word used here occurs nowhere else in the New Testament. Its mean-

---

tiles, ministering the gospel of God, *t* that the ²offering up of the Gen-

t Is.66.20.   ² or, *sacrificing.*

ing here is to be determined from the connection. The question is, What is the *sacrifice* of which he ·speaks? It is the *offering up*—the sacrifice of the Gentiles. The Jewish sacrifices were abolished. The Messiah had fulfilled the design of their appointment, and they were to be done away. (See the Epistle to the Hebrews.) There was to be no further *literal* sacrifice. But now the *offerings* of the Gentiles were to be as acceptable as had been the offerings of the Jews. God made no distinction; and in speaking of these offerings, Paul used *figurative* language drawn from the Jewish rites. But assuredly he did not mean that the offerings of the Gentiles were *literal* sacrifices to expiate sins; nor did he mean that there was to be an order of men who were to be called *priests* under the New Testament. If this passage *did* prove that, it would prove that it should be confined to the *apostles,* for it is of them only that he uses it. The meaning is this: "Acting in the Christian church substantially as the priests did among the Jews; that is, endeavouring to secure the acceptableness of the offerings which the Gentiles make to God." ¶ *That the offering up.* The word here rendered *offering up* (προσφορὰ) commonly means *a sacrifice* or an *expiatory* offering, and is applied to Jewish sacrifices, Acts xxi. 26; xxiv. 17. It is also applied to the sacrifice which was made by our Lord Jesus Christ when he offered himself on the cross for the sins of men, Eph. v. 2; Heb. x. 10. It does not always mean *bloody* sacrifices, but is used to denote *any* offering to God, Heb. x. 5, 8, 14, 18. Hence it is used in this large sense to denote the *offering* which the Gentiles who were converted to Christianity made of themselves; their *devoting* or dedicating themselves to God. The *language* is derived from the customs of the Jews, and the apostle represents himself *figuratively* as a *priest* presenting this

tiles might be acceptable, *u*being sanctified by the Holy Ghost.

17 I *v* have therefore whereof I may glory through Jesus Christ in *w*those things which pertain to God.

18 For I will not dare to speak

u Ac.20.32.   *v* 2 Co.12.1,&c.   *w* He.5.1.

offering to God. ¶ *Might be acceptable.* Or, approved by God. This was in accordance with the prediction in Isa. lxvi. 20, "They shall bring all your brethren for an offering unto the Lord out of all nations," &c. This does not mean that it was by any *merit* of the apostle that this offering was to be rendered acceptable; but that he was appointed to prepare the way; so that *their* offering, as well as that of the Jews, might come up before God. ¶ *Being sanctified.* That is, *the offering* being sanctified, or made holy. The sacrifice was *prepared,* or made fit *to be* an offering, among the Jews, by salt, oil, or frankincense, according to the nature of the sacrifice, Lev. vi. 14, &c. In allusion to this, the apostle says that the offering of the Gentiles was rendered holy, or fit to be offered, by the converting and purifying influences of the Holy Spirit. They were prepared, not by salt and frankincense, but by the cleansing influences of God's Spirit. The same idea, substantially, is expressed by the apostle Peter in Acts x. 46; xi. 17.

17. *I have therefore,* &c. I have cause of glorying. I have cause of rejoicing that God has made me a minister to the Gentiles, and that he has given me such success among them. The ground of this he states in ver. 18–22. ¶ *Glory.* Of boasting (καύχη-σιν, the word usually rendered *boasting*), Jam. iv. 16; Rom. iii. 27; 2 Cor. vii. 14; viii. 24; ix. 3, 4; x. 15; xi. 10, 17. It means also *praise, thanksgiving* and *joy,* 1 Cor. xv. 31; 2 Cor. i. 12; vii. 4; viii. 24; 1 Thes. ii. 19. This is its meaning here, that the apostle had great cause of *rejoicing* or *praise* that he had been so highly honoured in the appointment *to* this office, and in his success *in* it.

of any of those things which Christ hath not wrought by me, *x*to make the Gentiles obedient, by word and deed.

19 Through *y* mighty signs and wonders, by the power of the Spirit of God; so that from Jeru-

x Ga.2.8.   *y* Ac.19.11.

¶ *Through Jesus Christ.* By the assistance of Jesus Christ; ascribing his success among the Gentiles to the *aid* which Jesus Christ had rendered him. ¶ *In those things which pertain to God.* Comp. Heb. v. 1. The things of religion; the things which God has commanded, and which pertain to his honour and glory. They were not things which pertained to *Paul,* but to *God:* not wrought *by* Paul, but *by* Jesus Christ; yet he might rejoice that he had been the means of diffusing so far those blessings. The success of a minister is not for *his own* praises, but for the honour of God; not by *his* skill or power, but by the aid of Jesus Christ; yet he may rejoice that *through* him such blessings are conferred on men.

18. *For I will not dare to speak.* I should be restrained; I should be afraid to speak, if the thing were not as I have stated. I should be afraid to set up a claim beyond that which is strictly in accordance with the truth. ¶ *Which Christ hath not wrought by me.* I confine myself *strictly* to what I have done. I do not arrogate to myself what Christ had done by others. I do not exaggerate my own success, or claim what others have accomplished. ¶ *To make the Gentiles obedient.* To bring them to obey God in the gospel. ¶ *By word and deed.* By *preaching,* and by all other means; by miracle, by example, &c. The *deeds,* that is, the *lives,* of Christian ministers are often as efficacious in bringing men to Christ as their public ministry.

19. *Through mighty signs and wonders.* By stupendous and striking miracles; see Note, Acts ii. 43. Paul here refers, doubtless, to the miracles which he had himself wrought; see Acts xix. 11, 12, "And God wrought special miracles by the hands of Paul,"

salem, and round about unto Illyricum, ²I have fully preached the gospel of Christ.

20 Yea, so have I strived to

z ch.1.14-16.

&c. ¶ *By the power of the Spirit of God.* This may either be connected with *signs and wonders,* and then it will mean that those miracles were performed by the power of the Holy Spirit; or it may constitute a new subject, and refer to the gift of prophecy, the power of speaking other languages. Which is its true meaning cannot, perhaps, be ascertained. The interpretations *agree* in this, that he traced his success in *all* things to the aid of the Holy Spirit. ¶ *So that from Jerusalem.* Jerusalem, as a *centre* of his work; the centre of all religious operations and preaching under the gospel. This was not the place where *Paul* began to preach (Gal. i. 17, 18), but it was the place where the *gospel* was first preached, and the apostles began to reckon their success from that as a point; comp. Note, Luke xxiv. 49. ¶ *And round about* (καὶ κύκλῳ). In a circle. That is, taking Jerusalem as a centre, he had fully preached round that centre until you come to Illyricum. ¶ *Unto Illyricum.* Illyricum was a province lying to the north-west of Macedonia, bounded north by a part of Italy and Germany, east by Macedonia, south by the Adriatic, west by Istria. It comprehended the modern Croatia and Dalmatia. So that, taking Jerusalem as a centre, Paul preached not only in Damascus and Arabia, but in Syria, in Asia Minor, in all Greece, in the Grecian Islands, and in Thessaly and Macedonia. This comprehended no small part of the then known world; *all* of which had heard the gospel by the labours of one indefatigable man. There is nowhere in the *Acts* express mention of Paul's going *into* Illyricum; nor does the expression imply that he preached the gospel *within* it, but only *unto* its borders. It may have been, however, that when in Macedonia, he crossed over into that country; and this is rendered somewhat probable from the fact that *Titus*

preach the gospel, ᵃnot where Christ was named, lest I should build upon another man's foundation:

21 But, as it is written, ᵇTo

a 2 Co.10.13-16.   *b* Is.52.15.

is mentioned as having gone into *Dalmatia* (2 Tim. iv. 10), which was a part of Illyricum. ¶ *I have fully preached.* The word here used means properly *to fill up* (πεπληρωκέναι), to *complete,* and here is used in the sense of *diffusing abroad,* or of *filling up* all that region with the gospel; comp. 2 Tim. iv. 17. It means that he had faithfully diffused the knowledge of the gospel in all that immense country.

20. *Yea, so have I strived.* The word used here (φιλοτιμούμενον) means properly *to be ambitious, to be studious of honour;* and then to *desire* earnestly. In that sense it is used here. He earnestly desired; he made it a point for which he struggled, to penetrate into regions which had not heard the gospel. ¶ *Not where Christ was named.* Where the gospel had not been before preached. ¶ *Lest I should build,* &c. That is, he desired to found churches himself; he regarded himself as particularly called to this. Others might be called to edify the church, but he regarded it as *his* office to make known the name of the Saviour where it was not before known. This work was particularly adapted to the ardour, zeal, energy, and bravery of such a man as Paul. Every man has his proper gift; and there are some particularly fitted to *found* and establish churches; others to edify and comfort them; comp. 2 Cor. x. 13-16. The apostle chose the higher honour, involving most danger and responsibility; but still *any* office in building up the church is honourable.

21. *But as it is written.* Isa. lii. 15. This is not literally quoted, but the sense is retained. The design of quoting it is to justify the principle on which the apostle acted. It was revealed that the gospel should be preached to the Gentiles; and he regarded it as a high honour to be the instrument of carrying this prediction into effect.

whom he was not spoken of, they shall see: and they that have not heard shall understand.

22 For which cause also I have been [3] much [c] hindered from coming to you;

23 But now having no more place in these parts, and having a great desire these many years to come unto you;

3 or, many ways; or, oftentimes.   c 1 Th.2.18.

24 Whensoever I take my journey into Spain, I will come to you: for I trust to see you in my journey, and [d] to be brought on my way thitherward by you, if first I be somewhat filled [4] with your company.

25 But now [e] I go unto Jerusalem, to minister unto the saints.

26 For it hath pleased them of

d Ac.15.3; 3 Jn.6.   4 with you.   e Ac.19.21.

22. *For which cause.* I have been so entirely occupied in this leading purpose of my life that I have not been able to come to you. ¶ *Much hindered.* Many ways; not many times. I had so frequent and urgent demands on my time elsewhere, that I could not come to you. ¶ *From coming to you.* Where the gospel *has been* preached. I have desired to come, but have been unable to leave the vast region where I might preach the gospel to those who had never heard it.

23. *But now,* &c. Having no further opportunity in these regions to preach to those who have never heard the gospel. ¶ *In these parts.* In the regions before specified. He had gone over them, had established churches, had left them in the care of elders (Acts xx. 17), and was now prepared to penetrate into some new region, and lay the foundation of other churches. ¶ *And having a great desire,* &c. See chap. i. 9–13.

24. *Whensoever I take my journey into Spain.* Ancient Spain comprehended the modern kingdoms of Spain and Portugal, or the whole of the Spanish peninsula. It was then subject to the Romans. It is remarkable, even here, that the apostle does not say that his principal object was to visit the church at Rome, much as he desired that, but only to *take it in his way* in the fulfilment of his higher purpose to preach the gospel in regions where Christ was not named. Whether he ever fulfilled his purpose of visiting *Spain* is a matter of doubt. Some of the fathers, Theodoret (on Phil. i. 25; 2 Tim. iv. 17) among others, say that, after he was released from his

captivity when he was brought before Nero, he passed two years in Spain. If he was imprisoned a *second* time at Rome, such a visit is not improbable as having taken place *between* the two imprisonments. But there is no certain evidence of this. Paul probably projected *many* journeys which were never accomplished. ¶ *To be brought on my way,* &c. To be assisted by you in regard to this journey; or to be accompanied by you. This was the custom of the churches, Acts xv. 3; xvii. 14, 15; xx. 38; xxi. 5; 1 Cor. xvi. 6, 11; 3 John 6. ¶ *If first,* &c. If on my journey before I go into Spain. ¶ *Somewhat.* Greek, *in part.* As though he could not be *fully* satisfied with their company, or could not hope to enjoy their society as fully and as long as he could desire. This is a very tender and delicate expression. ¶ *Filled.* This is a strong expression, meaning to be *satisfied,* to enjoy. To be *filled* with a thing is to have great satisfaction and joy in it. ¶ *With your* company. Greek, *with you;* meaning, in your society. The expression *to be filled* with one, in the sense of being *gratified,* is sometimes used in the classic writers. See Clarke on this verse.

25. *But now I go,* &c. I am about to go now. The mention of this intended journey to Jerusalem is introduced in several other places, and is so mentioned that Dr. Paley has derived from it a very strong argument for the genuineness of this epistle.[*] This intended journey is mentioned in Acts xix. 21, "Paul purposed in the spirit, when he had passed through Macedonia and Achaia, *to go to Jerusalem,*

* Paley's *Horæ Paulinæ,* chap. ii. no. 1.

Macedonia^f and Achaia to make a
certain contribution for the poor
saints which are at Jerusalem.

27 It hath pleased them, verily;
and their debtors they are. For if

f 2 Co.8.1; 9.2,12.

the Gentiles have been made partakers of their spiritual things,
^gtheir duty is also to minister unto
them in carnal things.

28 When, therefore, I have per-

g 1 Co.9.11.

---

*saying, After I have been there, I must
also see Rome;"* see also Acts xx. 2,
3. That he *went* to Jerusalem according to his purpose is recorded in
his defence before Felix (Acts xxiv.
17), " Now after many years, I came
to bring alms to my nation, and offerings." ¶ *To minister to the saints.*
To supply their necessities by bearing
the contribution which the churches
have made for them.

26. *For it hath pleased them of Macedonia.* That is, they have done it
cheerfully and *voluntarily.* See their
liberality and cheerfulness commended
by the apostle in 2 Cor. viii. 1–6; ix.
2. Paul had been at much pains to
obtain this collection, but still they
did it freely; see 2 Cor. ix. 4–7. It
was with reference to *this* collection
that he directed them to lay by for this
purpose as God had prospered them on
the first day of the week, 1 Cor. xvi.
1. ¶ *Of Macedonia.* That is, the
Christians in Macedonia—those who
had been Gentiles, and who had been
converted to the Christian religion,
ver. 27. Macedonia was a country
of Greece, bounded north by Thrace,
south by Thessaly, west by Epirus,
and east by the Ægean Sea. It was
an extensive region, and was the kingdom of Philip, and his son Alexander
the Great. Its capital was Philippi,
at which place Paul planted a church.
A church was also established at
Thessalonica, another city of that
country, Acts xvi. 9, &c.; comp. xviii.
5; xix. 21; 2 Cor. vii. 5; 1 Thes. i.
1, 7, 8; iv. 10. ¶ *And Achaia.*
Achaia in the largest sense comprehended *all* ancient Greece. Achaia
Proper, however, was a province of
Greece embracing the western part
of the Peloponnesus, of which Corinth
was the capital; see Note, Acts xviii.
12. This place is mentioned as having been concerned in this collection
in 2 Cor. ix. 2. ¶ *The poor saints,*

&c. The Christians who were in
Judea were exposed to peculiar trials.
They were condemned by the sanhe-
drim, opposed by the rulers, and persecuted by the people; see Acts viii.
1, &c.; xii. 1, &c. Paul sought not
only to relieve them by this contribution, but also to promote fellow-feeling
between them and the Gentile Christians. And *this* circumstance would
tend much to enforce what he had been
urging in chap. xiv. xv. on the duty of
kind feeling between the Jewish and
Gentile converts to Christianity.
Nothing tends so much to wear off
prejudice, and to prevent unkind feeling in regard to others, as to set about
some purpose *to do them* good, or to
unite *with* them in doing good.

27. *Their debtors.* The reason he
immediately states; comp. Rom. i.
14. ¶ *Of their spiritual things.* Have
received the gospel by the instrumentality of those who had been Jews;
and were admitted now to the same
privileges with them. ¶ *Carnal things.*
Things pertaining to the flesh; that
is, to this life. On this ground the
apostle puts the obligation to support
the ministers of the gospel, 1 Cor.
ix. 11. It becomes a matter of *debt,*
where the hearer of the gospel *receives,*
in spiritual blessings, far more than
he confers by supporting the ministry.
Every man who contributes his due
proportion to support the gospel may
receive far more, in return, in his own
peace, edification, and in the order
and happiness of his family, than his
money could purchase in any other
way. The *gain* is on his side, and the
money is not lost. The minister is
not a beggar; and that which is necessary to his support is not almsgiving.
He has an equitable claim—as much
as a physician, or a lawyer, or a teacher
of youth has—on the necessaries and
comforts of life.

28. *Have sealed to them.* That is,

formed this, and have sealed to them *this fruit, I will come by you into Spain.

29 And I am sure that, *when I come unto you, I shall come in the fulness of the blessing of the gospel of Christ.

h Phi.4.17.   *i* ch.1.11,12.

---

have *secured it* to them. To seal an instrument of writing, a contract, deed, &c., is to *authenticate it*, to make it *sure*. In this sense it is used here. Paul was going himself to see that it was placed *securely* in their hands. ¶ *This fruit.* This result of the liberality of the Gentile churches—the fruit which their benevolence had produced. ¶ *I will come*, &c. This was Paul's full purpose; but it is not clear that he ever accomplished it; Note, ver. 24. ¶ *By you.* Taking Rome in my way.

29. *I am sure.* Greek, I know—expressing the fullest confidence, a confidence that was greatly confirmed by the success of his labours elsewhere. ¶ *In the fulness of the blessing*, &c. This is a Hebrew mode of expression, where one noun performs the purpose of an adjective, and means *with a full or abundant blessing.* This confidence he expressed in other language in chap. i. 11, 12; see Notes. ¶ *Of the gospel of Christ.* Which the gospel of Christ is fitted to impart. Thus every minister of the gospel should wish to go. This should be his ever-burning desire in preaching. Paul went to Rome; but he went in bonds, Acts xxvii. xxviii. But though he went in this manner, he was permitted there to preach the gospel for at least two years; nor can we doubt that his ministry was attended with the anticipated success, Acts xxviii. 30, 31. God may disappoint us in regard to the *mode* in which we purpose to do good; but if we really desire it, he will enable us to do it in *his own way.* It *may* be better to preach the gospel *in bonds* than at liberty; it *is* better to do it even in a prison, than not at all. Bunyan wrote the *Pilgrim's Progress* to amuse his heavy hours during a twelve years' cruel imprisonment. If he had

30 Now I beseech you, brethren, for the Lord Jesus Christ's sake, and for *the love of the Spirit, *that ye strive together with me in *your* prayers to God for me;

31 That*m* I may be delivered from them that *do not believe in

k Phi.2.1.   *l* Col.4.12.   *m* 2 Th.3.2.
5 or, *are disobedient.*

---

been at liberty, he probably would not have written it at all. The great desire of his heart was accomplished, but a *prison* was the place in which to do it. Paul preached, but preached in chains.

30. *For the Lord Jesus Christ's sake.* Greek, by or through (διὰ) our Lord Jesus Christ. It means, probably, out of love and regard to him; in order to promote his honour and glory, and to extend his kingdom among men. Paul desired to be delivered from the hands of the Jews, that he might promote the honour of Jesus Christ among the Gentiles. ¶ *And for the love of the Spirit* (διὰ). By the mutual love and sympathy which the Spirit of God produces in the minds of all who are the friends of God. I beseech you now to manifest that love by praying earnestly for me. ¶ *That ye strive together with me.* That you unite with me in earnest prayer. The word *strive* denotes intense *agony* or effort, such as was used by the wrestlers in the Greek games; and then the *agony*, or strong effort which a man makes in prayer, who is earnestly desirous to be heard. The use of the word here denotes Paul's earnest desire that they should make an *intense* effort in their prayers that he might be delivered. Christians, though at a distance from each other, may unite their prayers for a common object. Christians everywhere *should* wrestle in prayer for the ministers of the gospel, that they may be kept from temptations; and especially for those who are engaged, as the apostle was, in arduous efforts among the heathen, that they may be kept from the many dangers to which they are exposed in their journeyings in pagan lands.

31. *That I may be*, &c. The unbelieving Jews in Judea had been op-

Judea; and that my service which *I have* for Jerusalem may be accepted of the saints;

32 That I may come unto you

with joy by the will of God, and may with you be refreshed.

33 Now the *n*God of peace *be* with you all. Amen.

n 1 Co.14.33; He.13.20.

posed to Paul's conversion. They could not forget that he had borne letters of commission from them to persecute the Christians at Damascus. They regarded him as an apostate. They had heard of his success among the Gentiles; and they had been informed that he "taught all the Jews among the Gentiles to forsake the laws of Moses," Acts xxi. 21. Hence the apostle could not but be aware that, in returning to Judea, he exposed himself to peculiar dangers. His fears, as the result showed, were well founded. They evinced all the opposition to him which he had ever anticipated, Acts xxi. ¶ *And that my service.* My ministry; or the act of service which I am going to perform for them—referring to the contribution which he was bearing for the poor saints at Jerusalem. ¶ *For Jerusalem.* For the poor Christians in Jerusalem. ¶ *May be accepted of the saints.* That the poor Christians there may be willing to receive it. The grounds of *doubt* and *hesitation* whether they would be willing to receive this, seem to have been two : (1) Many, even among Christians, might have had their minds filled with prejudice against the apostle, from the reports constantly in circulation among the Jews, that he was opposing and denouncing the customs of Moses. Hence, in order to satisfy them, when he went up to Jerusalem, he actually performed a *vow*, in accordance with the law of Moses, to show that he did not intend to treat his laws with contempt, Acts xxi. 22, 23, 26, 27. (2) Many of the converts from Judaism might be indisposed to receive an offering made by *Gentiles.* They might have retained many of their former feelings—that the Gentiles were polluted, and that they ought to have no fellowship with them. Early opinions and prejudices wear off by slow degrees. Christians retain former notions long after their conversion;

and often many years are required to teach them enlarged views of Christian charity. It is not wonderful that the Christians in Judea should have been slow to learn all the ennobling lessons of Christian benevolence, surrounded as they were by the institutions of the Jewish religion, and having been themselves educated in the strictest regard for those institutions.

32. *That I may come to you.* That I may not be impeded in my intended journey by opposition in Judea. ¶ *With joy.* Joy to myself in being permitted to come; and producing joy to you by my presence. ¶ *By the will of God.* If God will; if God permit. After all his desires, and all their prayers, it still depended on the will of God; and to that the apostle was desirous to submit. This should be the end of our most ardent desires, and this the object of all our prayers, that the will of God should be done; comp. Jam. iv. 14, 15. Paul *did* go by the will of God; but he went in bonds. ¶ *And be refreshed.* Greek, may find *rest* or *solace* with you.

33. *Now the God of peace.* God, the author or promoter of peace and union. In ver. 13 he is called the God of hope. Here the apostle desires that the God who gives peace would impart to them union of sentiment and feeling, particularly between the Jewish and Gentile Christians—the great object for which he laboured in his journey to Judea, and which he had been endeavouring to promote throughout this epistle; see 1 Cor. xiv. 33; Heb. xiii. 20.

This is the close of the doctrinal and hortatory parts of this epistle. The remainder is made up chiefly of salutations. In the verses concluding this chapter, Paul expressed his earnest desire to visit Rome. He besought his brethren to pray that he might be delivered from the unbelievers among the Jews. His main desire was

CHAPTER XVI.

I COMMEND unto you Phebe our sister, which is a servant of the church which is at Cenchrea;

2 That ye *receive her in the Lord, as becometh saints, and that ye assist her in whatsoever busi-

a Phi.2.29.

granted. He was permitted to visit Rome; yet the very thing from which he sought to be delivered, the very opposition of the Jews, made it necessary for him to appeal to Cæsar, and this was the means of his accomplishing his desire. (See the closing chapters of the Acts of the Apostles.) God thus often grants our *main* desire; he hears our prayer; but he may make use of that from which we pray to be delivered as the *means* of fulfilling our own requests. The Christian prays that he may be sanctified; yet at the same time he may pray to be delivered from affliction. God will hear his *main* desire, to be made holy; will convert that which he fears into a blessing, and make it the means of accomplishing the great end. It is right to express our *desires—all* our desires—to God; but it should be with a willingness that he should choose his own means to accomplish the object of our wishes. Provided the *God of peace* is with us, all is well.

CHAPTER XVI.

The epistle concludes with various salutations. The *names* which occur in this chapter are chiefly *Greek;* and the persons designated had been probably inhabitants of Greece, but had removed to Rome for purposes of commerce, &c. Possibly some of them had been converted under the ministry of the apostle himself during his preaching in Corinth and other parts of Greece. It is remarkable that the name of *Peter* does not occur in this catalogue; which is conclusive evidence, contrary to the Papists, that Peter was not then known by Paul to be in Rome.

1. *I commend.* It was common then, as now, to bear letters of introduction to strangers, commending the person thus introduced to the favourable regards and attentions of those to whom the letters were addressed, 2 Cor. iii. 1; Acts xviii. 27. This epistle,

with the apostle's commendation, was designed thus to introduce its bearer to the Roman Christians. The mention of Phebe in this manner leaves it beyond a doubt that she was either the bearer of this epistle, or accompanied those who bore it to Rome. The epistle was therefore written, probably, at Corinth. (See Introduction.) ¶ *Our sister.* A member of the Christian church. ¶ *Which is a servant.* Greek, "who is a *deaconess.*" It is clear from the New Testament that there was an order of women in the church known as *deaconesses.* Reference is made to a class of females whose duty it was to *teach* other females, and to take the general superintendence of that part of the church, in various places in the New Testament; and their existence is expressly affirmed in early ecclesiastical history. They appear to have been commonly aged and experienced widows, sustaining a fair reputation, and fitted to guide and instruct those who were young and inexperienced; comp. 1 Tim. v. 3, 9–11; Tit. ii. 4. The *Apostolical Constitutions,* book iii., say, "Ordain a deaconess who is faithful and holy, for the ministries toward the women." Pliny, in his celebrated letter to Trajan, says, when speaking of the efforts which he made to obtain information respecting the opinions and practices of Christians, "I deemed it necessary to put two maidservants who are called *ministræ* [that is *deaconesses*] to the torture, in order to ascertain what is the truth." The reasons of their appointment among the Gentiles were these: (1) The females were usually separate from the men. They were kept secluded, for the most part, and not permitted to mingle in society with men, as is the custom now. (2) It became necessary, therefore, to appoint aged and experienced females to instruct the young, to visit the sick, to provide for them, and to perform for them the

ness she hath need of you: for she hath been a succourer of many, and of myself also.

3 Greet *b* Priscilla and Aquila, my helpers in Christ Jesus:

4 Who have for my life laid

b Ac.18.2,&c.

services which male deacons performed for the whole church. It is evident, however, that they were confined to these offices, and that they were never regarded as an order of ministers, or suffered *to preach* to congregations, 1 Tim. ii. 12; 1 Cor. xiv. 34. ¶ *Of the church,* &c. This is the only mention which occurs of a church at that place. It was probably collected by the labours of Paul. ¶ *At Cenchrea.* This was the *seaport* of Corinth. Corinth was situated on the middle of the isthmus, and had *two* harbours, or ports: *Cenchrea* on the east, about eight or nine miles from the city; and *Lechœum* on the west. Cenchrea opened into the Ægean Sea, and was the principal port. It was on this *isthmus,* between these two ports, that the *Isthmian* games were celebrated, to which the apostle refers so often in his epistles.

2. *That ye receive her,* &c. That you acknowledge her as being in the Lord, or as being a servant of the Lord; that is, as a Christian; comp. chap. xiv. 3; Phil. ii. 29. ¶ *As becometh saints.* As it is proper that Christians should treat their brethren. ¶ *She hath been a succourer of many.* The word used here (προστάτις), means properly *a patron, a help,* and was applied by the Greeks to one who *presided* over an assembly; to one who became *a patron* of others; who aided or defended them in their cause; and especially to one who undertook to manage the cause of *strangers* and foreigners before the courts. It was, therefore, an honourable appellation. Applied to Phebe, it means probably that she had shown great kindness in various ways to the apostle, and to other Christians—probably by receiving them into her house; by administering to the sick, &c. Such persons have a claim on the respect and Christian attentions of others.

3. *Greet Priscilla and Aquila.* Salute; implying the apostle's kind remembrance of them, and his wishes

for their welfare. ¶ *Priscilla.* Priscilla was the wife of Aquila. They are mentioned in Acts xviii. 2, 26; 1 Cor. xvi. 19. Paul at first found them at Corinth. Aquila was a Jew, born in Pontus, who had resided at Rome, and who had left Rome, and come to Corinth, when Claudius expelled the Jews from Rome; see Notes, Acts xviii. 2. It is probable that they were converted under the preaching of Paul. Paul lived with them, and they had the advantage of his private instruction, Acts xviii. 3; comp. 26. At the death of Claudius, or whenever the decree for the expulsion of the Jews was repealed, it is probable that they returned to Rome. ¶ *My helpers.* My fellow-workers. They had aided him in his work. A particular instance is mentioned in Acts xviii. 26. They are mentioned as having been with Paul when he wrote the First Epistle to the Corinthians, 1 Cor. xvi. 19. ¶ *In Christ Jesus.* In the Christian cause.

4. *Who have for my life.* In order to save my life. ¶ *Laid down their own necks.* To *lay down the neck* is to lay the head on a block to be cut off with the axe; or to bow down the head as when the neck was exposed to be cut off by the sword of the executioner. The meaning is, that they had hazarded their lives, had exposed themselves to imminent danger, to save the life of Paul. On what occasion this was done is not known, as it is not elsewhere referred to in the New Testament. As Paul, however, lived with them (Acts xviii. 3), and as he was often persecuted by the Jews, it is probable that he refers to some such period when he was persecuted, when Aquila and Priscilla took him into their house at the imminent hazard of their lives. ¶ *All the churches of the Gentiles.* All the churches that had been founded by the apostles. They *felt* their deep obligation to them for having saved the life of him who had been their

down their own necks; unto whom not only I give thanks, but also all the churches of the Gentiles.

5 Likewise *greet* ᶜthe church that is in their house. Salute my well-beloved Epenetus, who is the first-fruits of Achaia unto Christ.

6 Greet Mary, who bestowed much labour on us.

ᶜ 1 Co.16.19.

7 Salute Andronicus and Junia, my kinsmen and my fellow-prisoners, who are of note among the apostles; who also were ᵈin Christ before me.

8 Greet Amplias, my beloved in the Lord.

9 Salute Urbane, our helper in Christ; and Stachys my beloved.

ᵈ Ga.1.22.

founder, and who was their spiritual father.

5. *The church that is in their house.* Aquila and Priscilla are mentioned (Acts xviii. 26) as having received *Apollos* into their family, to instruct him more perfectly. The church in their house is also mentioned, 1 Cor. xvi. 19. This may mean either the church that was accustomed to assemble for worship at their hospitable mansion; or it may mean their own family with their guests, regarded as a *church.* In those times Christians had no houses erected for public worship, and were therefore compelled to meet in their private dwellings. ¶ *Salute.* The same word before translated "*greet.*" ¶ *Who is the first-fruits.* One who first embraced Christianity under my preaching in Achaia. The *first-fruits* were a small part of the harvest, which was first gathered and offered to the Lord, Ex. xxii. 29; xxiii. 16; Lev. ii. 12; Deut. xviii. 4. In allusion to this, Paul calls Epenetus the first-fruits of the great spiritual harvest which had been gathered in Achaia. ¶ *Achaia.* See Note, chap. xv. 26. This name and those which follow are chiefly *Greek;* but we know little of the persons mentioned, except what is here recorded.

6. *Who bestowed much labour on us.* Who laboured much for us. Nothing more is known of her but this honourable mention of her name. It is probable that these persons were formerly residents in Greece, and that the apostle had there become acquainted with them, but that they had now removed to Rome.

7. *My kinsmen.* In Rom. ix. 3, the

apostle calls *all* the Jews *his kinsmen,* and it has been doubted whether he means anything more here than that they were *fellow Jews.* But as many others who were Jews are mentioned here without this appellation, and as he especially designates these persons, and Herodian (ver. 11), it seems probable that they were remote relatives of the apostle. ¶ *My fellow-prisoners.* Paul was often in prison; and it is probable that on some of those occasions they had been confined with him; comp. 2 Cor. xi. 23, "In prisons more frequent." ¶ *Who are of note.* The word translated *of note* (ἐπίσημοι), denotes properly those who are *marked,* designated, or distinguished in any way, used either in a good or bad sense; comp. Mat. xxvii. 16. Here it is used in a good sense. ¶ *Among the apostles.* This does not mean that they *were* apostles, as has been sometimes supposed. For, (1) There is no account of their having been appointed as such. (2) The expression is not one which would have been used if they *had* been. It would have been "who were distinguished *apostles;*" comp. Rom. i. 1; 1 Cor. i. 1; 2 Cor. i. 1; Phil. i. 1. (3) It by no means implies that they were apostles. All that the expression fairly implies is, that they were known to the other apostles; that they were regarded by them as worthy of their affection and confidence; that they had been known by them, as Paul immediately adds, before *he* was himself converted. They had been converted *before* he was, and were distinguished in Jerusalem among the early Christians, and honoured with the friendship of the other apostles. (4) The design of the office

10 Salute Apelles, approved in Christ. Salute them which are of Aristobulus's [1]*household.*

11 Salute Herodian my kinsman. Greet them that be of the [1]*household* of Narcissus, which are in the Lord.

12 Salute Tryphena and Tryphosa, who labour in the Lord. Salute the beloved Persis, which laboured much in the Lord.

13 Salute Rufus, [e]chosen in the Lord; and his mother and mine.

14 Salute Asyncritus, Phlegon, Hermas, Patrobas, Hermes, and the brethren which are with them.

15 Salute Philologus, and Julia, Nereus, and his sister, and Olympas, and all the saints which are with them.

16 Salute one another with an holy kiss. The churches of Christ salute you.

17 Now I beseech you, brethren, mark them which cause [g]divisions

1 or, friends.   e Ep.1.4; 2 Jn.1.

f 1 Co.16.20; 1 Pe.5.14.   g 1 Ti.6.3-5.

of *apostles* was to bear *witness* to the life, death, resurrection, doctrines, and miracles of Christ; comp. Mat. x.; Acts i. 21, 22; xxii. 15. As there is no evidence that they had been *witnesses* of these things, or appointed to it, it is improbable that they were set apart to the apostolic office. (5) The word *apostles* is used sometimes to designate *messengers* of churches; or those who were *sent* from one church to another on some important business, and *if* this expression meant that they *were* apostles, it could only be in some such sense as having obtained deserved credit and eminence in that business; see Phil. ii. 25; 2 Cor. viii. 23. ¶ *Who were in Christ,* &c. Who were *converted* before I was. The meaning is clear. The expression, *in Christ,* means to be united to him, to be interested in his religion, to be Christians.

10. *Approved in Christ.* An approved or tried Christian; approved and beloved by Christ.

12. *Tryphena and Tryphosa.* These names, with the participle rendered "who labour," are in the feminine gender, and these were probably two holy women who performed the office of deaconesses, or who ministered to the sick, and who, with Persis, thus by example, and perhaps by instruction, laboured to promote the spread of Christianity. Pious females then, as now, were able to do much in their proper sphere to extend the truths and blessings of the gospel.

13. *Chosen in the Lord. Elect* in the Lord; that is, a chosen follower

of Christ. ¶ *And his mother and mine.* "His mother in a literal sense, and mine in a figurative one." An instance of the delicacy and tenderness of Paul; of his love for this disciple and his mother, as if he were of the same family. Religion binds the hearts of all who embrace it tenderly together. It makes them feel that they are one great family, united by tender ties, and joined by peculiar attachments. See what the Lord Jesus declared in Mat. xii. 47–50, and his tender address to John when he was on the cross, John xix. 26, 27.

16. *Salute one another.* Greet one another in an affectionate manner; that is, treat each other with kindness and love, and evince all proper marks of affection. ¶ *With an holy kiss.* This mode of salutation has been practised at all times; and particularly in Eastern nations. It was even practised by *men;* see Note, Luke xxii. 47, 48. The use of the word *holy* here serves to denote that Paul intended it as an expression of *Christian* affection, and to guard against all improper familiarity and scandal. It was common, according to Justin Martyr (*Apology*), for the early Christians to practise it in their religious assemblies. ¶ *The churches of Christ.* That is, the churches in the vicinity of the place where the apostle wrote this epistle; probably the churches particularly in Achaia.

17. *Now I beseech you.* One great object of this epistle had been to

and offences contrary to the doctrine which ye have learned; [h]and avoid them.

h Mat.18.17; 1 Co.5.11; 2 Th.3.6,14.

promote *peace* between the Jewish and Gentile converts. So much did this subject press upon the mind of the apostle, that he seems unwilling to leave it. He returns to it again and again; and even after the epistle is apparently concluded, he returns to it, to give them a new charge on the subject. ¶ *Mark them.* Observe attentively, cautiously, and faithfully (Phil. iii. 17); be on your guard against them. Ascertain *who are* the real causes of the divisions that spring up, and avoid them. ¶ *Which cause.* Who make. Probably he refers here to *Jewish* teachers, or those who insisted strenuously on the observance of the rites of Moses, and who set up a claim for greater purity and orthodoxy than those possessed who received the Gentile converts as Christian brethren. The Jews were perpetually thus recalling the Christian converts to the law of Moses; insisting on the observance of those rites; troubling the churches, and producing dissensions and strifes, Gal. iii. 1; v. 1–8; Acts xv. 1, 24. ¶ *Divisions.* Dissensions; parties; factions, 1 Cor. iii. 3; Gal. v. 20. The very *attempt* to form such parties was evil, no matter what the pretence. They who attempt to form parties in the churches are commonly actuated by some evil or ambitious design. ¶ *And offences.* Scandals; or that give occasion for others to fall into sin. These two things are different. The first means parties; the other denotes such a course of life as would lead others into sin. The *Jew* would form parties, on the pretence of superior holiness; the Gentiles, or some bold Gentile convert, might deride the scrupulous feelings of the Jew, and might thus lead him into *sin* in regard to what his conscience really forbade; see chap. xiv. 15. These persons on both sides were to be avoided, and they were to refuse to follow them, and to cultivate the spirit of unity and peace. ¶ *Contrary to the doctrine.*

18 For they that are such serve not our Lord Jesus Christ, [i]but their own belly; and by [k]good

i Phi.3.19. k Col.2.4; 2 Pe.2.3.

To the *teaching* which you have received in this epistle and elsewhere; the teaching that these divisions should cease; that the Jewish ceremonies are not binding; that all should lay aside their causes of former difference, and be united in one family; see chap. xiv. xv. ¶ *And avoid them.* Give them no countenance or approbation. Do not follow them; comp. 1 Tim. vi. 3, 4, 5; 2 John 10; Gal. i. 8, 9. That is, avoid them *as teachers;* do not follow them. It does not mean that they were to be treated harshly; but that they were to be avoided in their *instructions.* They were to disregard all that they could say tending to produce alienation and strife; and resolve to cultivate the spirit of peace and union. This would be an admirable rule if always followed. Let men make *peace* their prime object; resolve to love all who *are* Christians, and it will be an infallible gauge by which to measure the arguments of those who seek to promote alienations and contentions.

18. *Serve not.* Obey not. Though they are professedly, yet they are not his real friends and followers. ¶ *But their own belly.* Their own *lusts;* their own private interests; they do this to obtain support. The authors of parties and divisions, in church and state, have this usually in view. It is for the indulgence of some earthly appetite; to obtain office or property; or to gratify the love of dominion. ¶ *And by good words.* Mild, fair, plausible speeches; with an appearance of great sincerity, and regard for the truth; comp. Col. ii. 4; 2 Pet. iii. 3. Men who cause divisions commonly make great pretensions to peculiar love of truth and orthodoxy; and put on the appearance of great sincerity, sanctity, and humility. ¶ *And fair speeches.* Greek εὐλογίας, eulogy, praise, flattery. This is another very common art. *Flattery* is one of the most powerful means of

words and fair speeches deceive the hearts of the simple.

19 For your obedience ^{l}is come abroad unto all *men.* I am glad therefore on your behalf: but yet I would have you ^{m}wise unto that which is good, and ^{2}simple concerning evil.

l ch.1.8.   *m* Mat.10.16. ^{2} or, *harmless.*

20 And the ^{n}God of peace shall ^{3}bruise^o Satan under your feet ^{p}shortly. The ^{q}grace of our Lord Jesus Christ *be* with you. Amen.

21 Timotheus my work-fellow, and Lucius, and Jason, and Sosipater, my kinsmen, salute you.

n ch.15.33. ^{3} or, *tread.*   *o* Ge.3.15.
p Re.12.10.   *q* 1 Co.16.23,&c.; Re.22.21.

forming parties in the church; and *a little special attention,* or promise of an office, or commendation for talents or acquirements, will secure *many* to the purposes of party whom no regard for truth or orthodoxy could influence a moment. ¶ *Deceive the hearts of the simple.* The minds of the unsuspecting, or those who are without guile (τῶν ἀκάκων). The apostle means to designate those who are simple-hearted, without any disposition to deceive others themselves, and of course without any suspicions of the *designs* of others. He has thus drawn the art of making parties with the hand of a master. First, there are smooth, plausible pretences, as of great love for truth. Then, an artful mingling of attentions and flatteries; and all this practised on the minds of the unsuspecting, drawing their *hearts* and *affections* towards themselves. Happy would it have been if the art had been confined to his own times.

19. *For your obedience,* &c. Chap. i. 8. Your mild, obedient disposition to learn, and to obey the precepts of the teachers of religion. ¶ *I am glad,* &c. I rejoice that you evince such a disposition. But he immediately adds, that *this* was just the temper to be imposed upon, and cautions them against that danger. ¶ *Wise unto that which is good.* Evince understanding of that which is adapted to promote good and worthy ends. ¶ *Simple concerning evil.* Greek, *harmless.* Not disposed to do wrong; having no plan and yielding to none of the allurements of evil. You have shown your wisdom in *obeying* the gospel. I would have you still evince wisdom towards *every good* design; but to be unacquainted with *any* plan of evil. Do not yield to those plans, or follow

those who would lead you into them.

20. *And the God of peace.* The God who promotes peace, chap. xv. 33. ¶ *Will bruise.* The *language* here refers to the prediction in Gen. iii. 15. It here means *to subdue, to gain the victory over.* It denotes Paul's confidence that they *would* gain the victory, and would be able to overcome all the arts of those who were endeavouring to sow discord and contention among them. ¶ *Satan.* The word *Satan* is Hebrew, meaning originally *an accuser, a calumniator,* and then *an enemy.* It is given to the prince of evil spirits from his enmity to God and men. He is here regarded as the *author* of all attempts to promote discord in the church, by whomsoever those attempts were made. Hence they who attempt to produce divisions are called "his ministers," 2 Cor. xi. 15. God would disappoint their malignant purposes, and promote the prevalence of peace. ¶ *The grace.* The favour, the mercy, &c. The Lord Jesus is the Prince of peace (Isa. ix. 6; comp. Luke ii. 14; John xiv. 27), and this expression is *a prayer* to him, or an earnest wish expressed, that the design of his coming might be accomplished in promoting the prevalence of order and peace; comp. 1 Cor. xvi. 23; Rev. xxii. 21.

21. *Timotheus.* Timothy; to whom the epistles which bear his name were written. He was long the companion of Paul in his labours, Acts xvi. 1; 1 Cor. xvi. 10; 2 Cor. i. 1, 19; Phil. ii. 29; 1 Thes. iii. 2; 1 Tim. i. 2; Heb. xiii. 23. ¶ *And Lucius.* He is mentioned in Acts xiii. 1, as a prophet and teacher, a native of Cyrene. Nothing more is known of him. ¶ *My kinsmen.* Ver. 7.

22 I Tertius, who wrote *this* epistle, salute you in the Lord.

23 Gaius*ʳ* mine host, and of the whole church, saluteth you. Erastus*ˢ* the chamberlain of the city saluteth you, and Quartus a brother.

r 1 Co.1.14; 3 Jn.1.   *s* Ac.19.22.

24 The*ᵗ* grace of our Lord Jesus Christ *be* with you all. Amen.

25 Now*ᵘ* to him that is of power to establish you according to my gospel and the preaching of Jesus Christ, (according to *ᵛ*the revelation of the mystery, which

t ver.20. *u* Ep.3.20; Jude 24. *v* Ep.1.9; Col.1.26,27.

---

22. *I Tertius.* Of Tertius nothing more is known than is mentioned here. ¶ *Who wrote* this. It is evident that Paul employed an amanuensis to write this epistle, and perhaps he commonly did it. Tertius, who thus wrote it, joins with the apostle in affectionate salutations to the brethren at Rome. To the epistle, Paul signed his own name, and added a salutation in his own handwriting. Col. iv. 18, "The salutation by the hand of me Paul;" and in 2 Thes. iii. 17, he says that this was done in every epistle; 1 Cor. xvi. 21. ¶ *In the Lord.* As Christian brethren.

23. *Gaius mine host.* Who has received me into his house, and shown me hospitality. The word *host* means one who entertains another at his own house without reward. ¶ *And of the whole church.* Who has opened his house to entertain *all* Christians; or to show hospitality to them all. He was baptized by Paul himself at Corinth (1 Cor. i. 14); and was so highly esteemed by the church that John wrote an epistle to him, 3 John 1. He was probably a wealthy citizen of Corinth, who freely opened his house to entertain Christians, and for the purpose of religious worship. ¶ *Erastus.* Erastus is mentioned (Acts xix. 22) as having been sent by Paul with Timothy into Macedonia. He is also mentioned (2 Tim. iv. 20) as having resided at Corinth. ¶ *The chamberlain.* A *chamberlain* is properly an officer who has charge of a chamber, or of chambers. In England, the lord chamberlain is the sixth officer of the crown, and has charge of the king's lodgings, and wardrobe, &c. He has also an important rank on days of public solemnities, as the coronation day, &c. The word used here is com-

monly in the New Testament translated *steward*. It properly means one who has charge of domestic affairs, to provide for a family, to pay the servants, &c. In this place it means one who presided over the pecuniary affairs of the *city*, and should have been translated *the treasurer; the city treasurer*—an office of trust and of some importance, showing that *all* who were converted at Corinth were not of the lowest rank. This is implied in 1 Cor. i. 26, "Not *many* wise men, not *many* mighty, not *many* noble, are called," implying that there were *some* such. ¶ *Quartus a brother.* A fellow-Christian.

25. *Now to him.* This and the two following verses are found in many manuscripts at the close of chapter xiv. Its proper place, however, is here; and the apostle thus concludes the whole epistle with an ascription of praise. ¶ *To him*, &c. To God; be glory, ver. 20. ¶ *Is of power.* Greek, is able; who has power, Eph. iii. 20; Jude 24, "Now unto him that is able to keep you from falling," &c. God only can keep Christians in the path of salvation; and it was well to bring that truth prominently into view at the close of the epistle. ¶ *To establish you.* To strengthen and confirm you. ¶ *According to my gospel.* According to the gospel which I preach; the doctrines which I have been defending in this epistle. It is called *his* gospel, not because he was the author of it, or because others did not preach it also, but because he had been *particularly* defending it in this epistle. The doctrines which he had advanced were just those which were fitted to strengthen and confirm them,—the doctrine of justification, of election, of perseverance, and of the protection and favour of God to both Jews and

was kept secret since the world began,

26 But now is made manifest, and by the scriptures of the prophets, according to the commandment of the everlast-

ing God, *w* made known to all nations for the obedience of faith;)

27 To *x* God only wise, *be* glory, through Jesus Christ, for ever. Amen.

w Mat.28.19.   *x* 1 Ti.1.17; Jude 25.

Gentiles. These were the doctrines which he had defended; and it might easily be shown that *these* are the doctrines that give stability to the Christian faith, hope, and love. ¶ *And the preaching of Jesus Christ.* Not his *personal* preaching; but according to that preaching of which Christ is the author and the subject; and particularly, as the following clause shows, to the doctrines by which the partition between the Jews and the Gentiles was broken down, and by which they were admitted to the same privileges and hopes. ¶ *According to the revelation.* According to the communication of that which has been so long concealed, but which is now made manifest. The word *revelation* refers to the *publication* of the plan by the gospel. ¶ *Of the mystery.* The word *mystery* means properly that which *is hidden* or *concealed*, and is thus applied to any doctrine which was not before known. It does not mean necessarily that which is *unintelligible;* but that which had not been before revealed; see Note to Mat. xiii. 11. The word here seems to refer to the principal doctrines of the gospel; its main truths, which had been concealed, especially from the entire Gentile world, but which were now made known. ¶ *Which was kept secret.* Which were kept in *silence* (Greek, σεσιγημένον), were not divulged or proclaimed. ¶ *Since the world began.* In all past times. This refers particularly to the Gentiles. The Jews had some obscure intimations of these truths, but they were now made known to all the world. The phrase "since the world began" is in Greek, "in eternal times;" that is, in *all* past times; or, as we should say, they have been *always* concealed.

26. *But now is made manifest.* Is revealed, or made known; that which

was so long concealed is now divulged, *i.e.* God's plan of saving men is now made known to all nations. ¶ *And by the scriptures*, &c. By the *writings* of the prophets. The prophetic writings contained the doctrines, obscurely indeed, but so as to be an important means of disseminating and confirming the truth that the Gentiles should be made acquainted with the gospel. To those writings the apostle had repeatedly appealed in his defence of the proposition that the gospel was to be preached to the Gentile world, chap. x. xi. xv. The prophetic writings, moreover, were extensively scattered among the Gentile nations, and thus were readily appealed to in defence of this position. Their writings being thus translated, and read, were an important means of propagating the truths of the Christian religion. ¶ *According to the commandment*, &c. By his command through Jesus Christ; made known in the gospel of his Son. ¶ *The everlasting God.* God who is *eternal*, and therefore unchanged. He who has indeed *concealed* this truth, but who has always *intended* that it should be revealed. ¶ *To all nations.* Mat. xxviii. 19; comp. Col. i. 23. ¶ *For the obedience of faith.* To produce obedience to the requirements of the gospel; see Note, chap. i. 5.

27. *To God only wise.* The apostle here resumes the doxology which had been interrupted by the parenthesis. The attribute of *wisdom* is here brought into view, because it had been particularly displayed in this plan which was now revealed. It evinced, in an eminent degree, the *wisdom* of God. That wisdom was evinced in devising the plan; in adapting it to the renewing of the heart; the justification of the sinner; his preservation, guidance, and sanc-

Written to the Romans from Corinthus, *and sent* by Phebe, servant of the church at Cenchrea.

---

tification; and in the manner in which the divine attributes had all been seen to harmonize. All this the apostle had illustrated in the previous parts of the epistle; and now, full of the convictions of this wisdom, he desires that all the praise and honour should be to God. The *tendency* of the plan is to promote his glory. The *obligation* on all who are benefited by it is to give him praise. ¶ Be *glory.* Praise; honour. ¶ *Through Jesus Christ.* By means of the work which Jesus Christ has performed; through him now as mediator and intercessor in the heavens.

The subscription, "Written to the Romans," &c., is evidently added by some other hand, but by whom is unknown. Paul assuredly would not write this to inform the Romans that it was sent by Phebe, whom he had just commended to their kindness. It has been shown, moreover, that no reliance is to be placed on any of the subscriptions to the epistles. Some of them are known to be false. By whom they were added is unknown. In this case, however, the fact which it states is correct, that it was written from Corinth, and sent by Phebe.

APPENDIX.

ROME.

Ancient Rome was situated nearly on the site of the modern city, in Latium, on several hills (whence the poetical appellation of the *seven-hilled city*), on both sides of the river Tiber, not far from the Mediterranean Sea; but the principal part of the city lay upon the eastern side of the river. Here is situated the Pincian Mount, and nearer the river the Campus Martius (the site of most of the modern city), the Capitoline Hill, the Roman Forum, and Mount Aventine. The Quirinal, Palatine, and Cœlian Hills form a second range, eastward of the preceding, extending from north to south; the Viminal and Esquiline, a third. On the western side of the Tiber are the Vatican Mount and Janiculum.

Different epochs are assigned for the foundation of Rome, but the date generally adopted is 753 years before Christ. The history of Rome is divided into three periods, in the first of which Rome was a kingdom, in the second a republic, and in the third an empire.

Our design here is simply to present such a view of the monuments of Rome as may serve to make our illustrations more intelligible and interesting, and give the reader some idea of the imperial city in the days of Paul, and of the changes that have passed over it since his martyred body was interred by friendly hands near the Via Ostiensis. Wherever it is practicable, our description shall be inwoven with the personal history of the apostle, in so far as the more reliable traditions may enable us to trace it.

The following contrasted condition of Ancient and Modern Rome is abridged from an able article in the *Bibliotheca Sacra* for 1854:—" Through what vicissitudes has the city of the Cæsars passed! Of the Regal period (244 years), nought but the old Tullian wall, the Italian prison overhanging the Forum, now the 'Mammertine,'[1] and the Cloaca Maxima show remains. Of the Republican period

(461 years), some bridges, military ways, as the Appian, along which the apostle travelled, and aqueducts, are traceable. Of the Imperial (507 years), more meets the delighted eye of the antiquarian. The Pantheon (A.D. 27), the Colosseum (A.D. 80), the columns of Trajan and Antoninus, the arches of Titus, Septimius Severus, and Constantine, the mausoleum of Hadrian (*Castel di St. Angelo*), and other structures, show something of their former grandeur. But yet how changed! Let the visitor, as he enters Rome, take his stand upon the tower of the Capitol, and turn his face to the north-west, towards the high dome of St. Peter's. Modern Rome lies mostly before him, covering the sloping sides of the Quirinal and Pincian Hills, the ancient Campus Martius, and the Vatican Hill, with the sides of the Janiculum west of the Tiber. The seven hills of ancient Rome, except the Capitoline, on which he stands, are mainly behind him, strewed with ruins of towers and walls, temples and theatres, circuses and baths, palaces and senate-houses, triumphal arches and columns. Let him first survey the Capitoline Hill. He cannot identify the spot on which the Asylum, 'the place of refuge,' stood, nor that of the Capitolium of Tarquinius, the strong citadel of Rome, whose gates were of brass, and whose gilded dome shone from afar. The Capitol now standing, with its museum and palaces, though built from the designs of Michael Angelo, only mocks the man who would see the great sanctuary and citadel of Rome; where the senate had, during kings, consuls, and emperors, held their deliberations in times of danger; where Cicero thundered against Catiline, and whither Pompey, Cæsar, and other generals were led along the Via Sacra, and up from the Forum in proud triumph.

" Let him now turn his back upon St. Peter's and the Vatican, and face the Colosseum. Ancient Rome lies before him. He looks down on the Forum instituted by Romulus, decorated and enlarged by subsequent rulers; a place for the assemblies of the people, and the administration of justice, sur-

---

[1] The scene, according to Baronius, of the imprisonment both of Peter and of Paul.

rounded by the Capitol, temples, porticos, and palaces; having within the tribunal of justice, the statue of Marsyas, and the Rostra, adorned with trophies from the seas and statues of distinguished men, from which the Roman orators addressed the people. But he looks in vain for such a forum as this. The very pavement on which the bustling millions of old Rome here trod lies buried with twenty feet of rubbish from falling columns, pillars, and arches, which have been crumbling for centuries. He next looks over the Forum, at the Palatine Hill, but he sees nothing of Augustus' imperial palace, set with rows of oak, and fronting the Via Sacra; nothing of the rich library, or of the marble temple of the Palatine Apollo, or even of the 'golden house' of Nero, vast in its extent, reaching the Esquiline, and richly adorned with gold and silver, and precious stones, and statues, and paintings, and other costly ornaments; nay, on the spot where at an earlier date could have been seen the elegant mansions of the Gracchi, of Crassus, Hortensius, and Cicero, the visitor can see little but the Farnese gardens, or other miserable places, to mock the genius of the past. He need look no farther to feel that the Rome he is now looking at is not ROME. The 'Lux orbis Terrarum,' the 'Arx omnium Gentium,' the 'Queen city of the world,' is no longer found upon her seven hills."[1]

Of existing remains, which the visitor of Rome, standing on the Capitol, and looking southward, may see lying before him, some of the most important are the column of Phocas; the three pillars of the Comitium, models of the Corinthian order of architecture; the ruins of the palace of the Cæsars on Mount Palatine; and the Arch of Titus, erected to commemorate the conquest of Jerusalem, and with that view representing the triumphal procession of the conqueror, the captive Jews, and the spoils of the Holy Place. The Capitol is now surmounted by a square of palaces built by Paul III., from designs by Michael Angelo. Further, towards the south and east, is the Colosseum, the glory of Rome, and the wonder of the world. These two monuments of ancient Rome, the Colosseum and the Palace of the Cæsars, though not existing till several years after the death of Paul, may yet be taken as fair specimens of the architecture of the city in his time. The palace particularly must have been modelled on that which Paul had often visited, and within which he had gathered fruits of his ministry.

Shortly after the burning of Rome, Nero built his magnificent golden house or palace, to which allusion has already been made. This structure was burned to the ground, and again rebuilt in the reign of Commodus, and the ruins which are now seen are those of this latter building. As already noticed, it may be taken as a fair approximation to the palace of Paul's time, and the eye of the Christian, therefore, rests with the deepest interest on "its mouldering vestiges of imperial splendour, matted together and overgrown with the cypress and the vine." There were saints in Cæsar's household (Phil. iv. 22). Under the shadow of the palace and the throne Paul won his converts.

The Colosseum was a gigantic building erected by Vespasian, and has been regarded by many as a greater wonder than the Pyramids of Egypt. It was built in one year, by the compulsory labour of 12,000 Jews and Christians. The traveller, it is said, after having viewed the Colosseum by daylight, should return to gaze again by the light of the moon, to have a just idea of its solemn and stupendous grandeur. "It was a building of an elliptic figure, 564 feet in length, and 467 in breadth, founded on fourscore arches, and rising, with four successive orders of architecture, to the height of 140 feet. The outside of the edifice was incrusted with marble, and decorated with statues. The slopes of the vast concave, which formed the inside, were filled and surrounded with sixty or eighty rows of seats, of marble likewise, covered with cushions, and capable of seating with ease above fourscore thousand spectators. Sixty-four vomitories or doors poured forth the immense multitude. An ample canopy protected from the sun and rain. The air was continually refreshed by the playing of fountains, profusely impregnated with the grateful scent of aromatics. In the centre of the edifice the arena or stage was strewed with the finest sand, and successively assumed the most different forms. At one moment it seemed to rise out of the earth like the garden of the Hesperides, and was afterwards broken into the rocks and caverns of Thrace. The subterranean pipes con-

[1] Prof. Spear, in *Bibliotheca Sacra*, July, 1854, pp. 559-561.

veyed an inexhaustible supply of water, and what had just before appeared a level plain, might be suddenly converted into a wide lake, covered with armed vessels, and replenished with the monsters of the deep."[1] The Colosseum and the circus were the scenes of gladiatorial combats, which were witnessed not only by the populace, but by the most refined classes, and by the gentler sex. Bartlett says in his own happiest manner: "Few, we should think, can stand within this area, once slippery with human gore, and repeople the mouldering seats of the amphitheatre, tier above tier to the very sky, not only with the populace, but with all that was great and beautiful in ancient Rome; with the most refined patrician, and even with woman, gazing with one feeling of eager delight, not only on the skill, but on the very blood of their victims, without a shudder. But 'Time, the beautifier,' has thrown over the scene a solemn charm; feeding 'like dull fire upon a hoary brand,' on the stupendous ruin; in which now, worn with the rents and weather-stains of ages, the huge broken vaults and buttresses are all overgrown by a wild garland of ivy, and bird-haunted foliage—it has half obliterated the dark page of history, and withdraws the mind from its past purpose to its present beauty."[2]

Leaving the Capitol and the stupendous monuments of the power and greatness of ancient Rome, we request the reader to accompany us north-west to where the Yellow Tiber takes a strong bend under the base of the Janiculum. The region on the opposite side, to which there was access by many bridges, was the abode of the Jews, the ancient "Ghetto." The feet of Paul must often have traversed these bridges. With this part of the city he must have grown familiar, as we may suppose him almost daily to have passed and repassed between his Gentile converts in the palace, and his Jewish countrymen on the other side of the river. Farther to the north still, is the Vatican and church of St. Peter's, where, in despite of Paul, Popery has established a power in many respects greater and more terrible than that whose representatives dwelt on Mount Palatine. In this quarter, by the riverside, stands the castle of St. Angelo, as it is now called, built by the Emperor Hadrian about A.D. 130 as his own

mausoleum. Here were deposited his remains, as well as those of succeeding emperors, down to the time of Septimius Severus. It was early diverted from its original purpose and turned into a fortress, and was long a stronghold of the papal power. It is a massive circular tower 987 feet in circumference, standing on a square basement, each side of which is 247 feet long. It derives its present name from a bronze statue of the Archangel Michael on the summit. The splendid bridge of St. Angelo was built by Hadrian as a means of communication with his mausoleum, and was originally called the Ælian Bridge, from one of the emperor's names.

Let us now turn for a moment to the closing scenes of our apostle's life. A graphic and picturesque pen[3] has thus reproduced Paul's first walk amid the glories of Rome. "Entering within the city by the Porta Capena, Julius and his prisoners moved on with the Aventine on their left, close round the base of the Cœlian, and through the hollow ground which lay between this hill and the Palatine; thence over the low ridge called Velia, where afterwards was built the arch of Titus, and then descending by the *Sacra Via* into that space which was the centre of imperial power and magnificence—the Forum of Rome. All around were the stately buildings which were raised in the closing years of the republic, and by the earlier emperors. In front was the Capitoline Hill. Close on the left, covering that hill (the Palatine) whose name is associated in every modern European language with the notion of imperial splendour, were the vast ranges of the palace, the house of Cæsar. And here (unless indeed it was in the great Prætorian camp, outside the city wall), Julius gave up his prisoner to Burrus the Prætorian præfect."

Our apostle is now, after a considerable interval, in the presence of Nero. The knowledge we have of the manner in which cases of appeal to the emperor were conducted in those times, enables us, with probable accuracy, to depict the scene. "Nero, after the example of Augustus, heard these causes in the imperial palace. Here, at one end of a splendid hall, lined with the precious marbles of Egypt and of Libya, we must imagine the Cæsar seated in the midst of his assessors. These counsellors, twenty in number, were men of the highest rank.

---

[1] *Antiquities of Rome.*
[2] *Footsteps of our Lord and his Apostles*, p. 235.

[3] Howson's.

Among them were the two consuls, and selected representatives of each of the other great magistracies of Rome. The remainder consisted of senators chosen by lot." Over this bench of distinguished judges presided the blood-stained adulterer Nero, who already, at the early age of twenty-five, had murdered mother, and wife, and brother. Contrary, however, to what might have been expected at such a tribunal, Paul was on this occasion set at liberty, through what influence is unknown. Possibly the emperor disdained to intermeddle in questions which might appear to him in no way to affect the wellbeing of the state. On his liberation, Paul is supposed to have visited many of the scenes of his former labours in Asia and Greece, to have visited Spain, and probably Crete and Dalmatia. Arrested at Nicopolis in mid-winter of A.D. 68, he was hurried to Rome, and executed there in the summer of the same year.[1] The fact of a second imprisonment has, however, been much disputed. But the weight of evidence is in its favour, and it is now very generally admitted.[2] The testimony of the early church is decisive on the point.

On occasion of our apostle's second trial, the forms would be somewhat different from those observed on his first trial. It was now an ordinary criminal case, and not a case of appeal to the emperor, and would, therefore, according to the custom of the times, come on before the præfect of the city. The scene, in all likelihood, was in one of the great basilicas of the Forum. "From specimens which still exist, as well as from the descriptions of Vetruvius, we have an accurate knowledge of the character of those halls of justice. They were rectangular buildings, consisting of a central nave and two aisles, separated from the nave by rows of columns. At the end of the nave was the tribune, in the centre of which was placed the magistrate's curule chair of ivory, elevated on a platform called the tribunal. Here also sat the assessors of the præfect. On the sides were seats for distinguished persons, in front, the prisoner, accusers, and advocates. The public was admitted into the remainder of the nave and aisles; and, at any trial of importance, a vast multitude of spectators was usu-

ally present." In such a scene we may imagine Paul. Fearlessly he defended himself. No advocate or friend appeared for him. At his first answer no man stood by him. For a time he was remanded to prison.[3] He seems, however, to have had no hope of deliverance from the very first.[4] The great fire, which Nero himself was suspected to have kindled, and in which so large a part of Rome was consumed, had taken place in the interval, between Paul's first and second imprisonment (A.D. 64). The emperor blamed the Christians. The result was a fierce persecution. In these circumstances, so conspicuous a Christian as Paul, became a mark for the rage of the heathen. He understood the circumstances, and prepared himself at once to die. He was again dragged before the tribunal, and condemned. His beloved Timotheus was far away; and although, in obedience to the command of Paul, he may have hastened to Rome, it is doubtful if he arrived in time for the closing scene. His Roman citizenship secured for the apostle the privilege of decapitation. The scene of his execution was the Ostian Road (Via Ostiensis). "As he issued forth from the gate, his eyes must have rested for a moment on that sepulchral pyramid which stood beside the road, and still stands unshattered amid the wreck of so many centuries upon the same spot. The Mausoleum of Caius Cestius rises conspicuously amongst humbler graves, and marks the site where Papal Rome suffers her Protestant sojourners to bury their dead. It is the only surviving monument of the martyrdom of Paul, a monument unconsciously erected by a pagan to the memory of a martyr." A small troop of soldiers conduct the prisoner—Paul the aged—through the busy crowd that thronged the road between the metropolis and its harbour. Arrived at the place of execution, the headsman's sword[5] terminated the earthly career of the apostle. His remains were laid by friends in the Catacombs,[6] which furnished to the Christian community in these times a refuge for the living, and a grave for the dead. Other accounts place the grave of the apostle on or near the spot where he died.[7]

---

1 The dates of Lardner and others are slightly different; the date of Paul's death being A.D. 66.
2 See an able article in Kitto's *Bib. Cyclopedia*—Timothy, Epistles to; also Horne's *Introduction*.

3 2 Tim. iv. 17, 21.   4 2 Tim. iv. 6-8.
5 So Clement, contemporary with Paul; Caius, the Roman presbyter, A.D. 200; and Jerome.
6 Eusebius.   7 Jerome.